MORAL PHILOSOPHY *for* MODERN LIFE

Anthony Falikowski, Ph.D.

Prentice Hall Allyn and Bacon Canada
Scarborough, Ontario

Dedicated with love to the greatest moral teachers in my life.

Thank you Michelle for teaching me about human feelings and matters of fairness;
Thank you Heather for giving me instruction on loyalty and gratitude;
Thank you Michael for your lessons on acceptance and optimism; and finally,
Thank you Pamela for showing me what selfless love and unswerving commitment to right action are all about.

Your teachings have confirmed to me the wisdom of the ages, the sayings of the sages.

Canadian Cataloguing in Publication Data

Falikowski, Anthony, 1953-
Moral philosophy for modern life

Includes bibliographical references and index.
ISBN 0-13-598046-1

1. Ethics. I. Title.

BJ1012.F344 1998 170 C97-930686-8

Prentice-Hall, Inc., Upper Saddle River, New Jersey
Prentice-Hall International (UK) Limited, London
Prentice-Hall of Australia, Pty. Limited, Sydney
Prentice-Hall Hispanoamericana, S.A., Mexico City
Prentice-Hall of India Private Limited, New Delhi
Prentice-Hall of Japan, Inc., Tokyo
Simon & Schuster Southeast Asia Private Limited, Singapore
Editora Prentice-Hall do Brasil, Ltda., Rio de Janeiro

ISBN 0-13-598046-1

Vice-President, Editorial Director: Laura Pearson
Acquisitions Editor: Cliff Newman
Developmental Editor: Carol Whynot
Production Editor: Marjan Farahbaksh
Copy Editor: Marie Graham
Production Coordinator: Leora Conway
Photo Research: Marijke Leupen
Cover and Interior Design: Julia Hall
Cover Image: Terrence Jon Dyke/Archives Inc.
Page Layout: Heidi Palfrey

1 2 3 4 5 RRD 01 00 99 98 97

Printed and bound in the United States of America

Page 466 constitutes an extension of the copyright page. Every reasonable effort has been made to obtain permissions for all articles and data used in this edition. If errors or omissions have occurred, they will be corrected in future editions provided written notification has been received by the publisher.

TABLE OF CONTENTS

NOTE TO THE INSTRUCTOR

Moral Philosophy for Modern Life is designed as an introductory level textbook for postsecondary students. It can be used in moral philosophy, liberal arts, humanities, social science, general education, critical reasoning, and generic skills courses, as well as in any vocational program of study containing an ethics component.

Moral Philosophy for Modern Life offers beginners a comprehensive and integrated "outcomes-based" approach to the study of ethics. Adopting a learning-centered orientation, the book shifts attention away from what the instructor will cover and places it on what the students will know and be able to do as a result of their philosophical study. With this subtle, but significant pedagogical shift, instructors using this text will feel more confident at course end that the stated exit competencies have been achieved by students. Students, on the other hand, will be able to use the pedagogical aids included in the text to make their education in ethics more self-directed. This book suits a student-centered paradigm of education, wherein instructors become more like mentors, coaches, or learning directors and less like experts or moral authorities on controversial ethical matters.

Broad in its overall scope, *Moral Philosophy for Modern Life* consists of three components: theories, skills, and applications. Before starting the theory component, the "Preview and Introduction" of the book underscores the practicality of rational ethics by pointing to its therapeutic value and relevance for establishing an objective basis for moral criticism and social reform. Also, in the Preview and Introduction, students are invited to complete something newly developed that I call the Moral Preference Indicator (MPI)—an informal instrument to be used to help them identify their preferred ethical orientations to life. Students are asked to complete the MPI again after finishing the moral theory portion of the book to discover if their ethical perspectives have changed as a result of critical thought and reflection.

In Part One, three of the historically most important approaches to morality are covered under the headings of Character Ethics, Utilitarian Ethics and Deontological Ethics. The works of Plato, Aristotle, Jeremy Bentham, John Stuart Mill, Immanuel Kant and John Rawls are used as a theoretical springboard for moral application and analysis. Reviewing these philosophers and their moral perspectives will serve students well as they embark on the difficult task of grappling with matters of personal morality and decision making on controversial social issues. Further studies in ethical theory are encouraged by other suggested readings and source references. Although the several classical moral positions offered in this book provide students with a good start, it is, clearly, not an end point. A full treatment of all or even most moral positions, however, would not be useful here, given the more practical, introductory focus of the book. As the proverbial saying goes, the longest journey must begin with the first step.

In Part Two, students begin to develop those reasoning skills necessary for rational debate in matters of morality. For instance, they learn how to distinguish between factual statements and value judgments, how to understand processes of inductive and deductive logic, how to construct logical/practical syllogisms, how to test for the soundness of arguments, and how to identify instances of fallacious and invalid reasoning. With all of this "how to" learning behind them, students will be prepared for critical analysis and objective evaluation of the issues debated later in the book. The development of critical reasoning abilities will also enable students to construct a rational foundation for moral thinking and action.

Part Three deals with contemporary moral issues. Outstanding readings selected for their relevance, interest value, and readability are gathered together under the headings of Business Ethics, Legal and Societal Ethics, Biomedical Ethics, Sexual Ethics and Global Ethics. Included with each reading are pedagogical aids designed to help students understand and analyze its contents. Critical analysis of the readings will offer students practice when it comes to applying ethical principles to real world problems.

SPECIAL FEATURES OF MORAL PHILOSOPHY FOR MODERN LIFE

Comprehensive and Integrated Approach

As mentioned, this text takes a comprehensive and integrated approach to moral philosophy. Theories, reasoning skills, and applications are combined to help students learn how to approach ethical decision making in a rational and informed fashion. Unlike "social issues" books that omit theories or "theories" books that leave out applications, and unlike some "logic" and "critical reasoning" texts that neglect moral theories and/or applications altogether, *Moral Philosophy for Modern Life* integrates all these components in a way that promotes students' moral understanding and furthers their abilities to deal with the moral complexities of everyday modern life.

Readability

Experience has taught me that in order to teach philosophy effectively, one must operate according to the K.I.S.S. principle—"Keep it simple, Sylvia!" Philosophical ethics is difficult enough for students without confusing them with the use of unnecessarily convoluted language and incomprehensible vocabulary. Every effort has been made to make the writing style of *Moral Philosophy for Modern Life* accessible to students. All too often people tell me that their first philosophy course was their last. When I ask why, they usually say that they could not understand the books and articles they were expected to read. The ideas seemed interesting enough; they just could not get past the awkward language and technical vocabulary. This text is written *not* to discourage students, but to encourage them with interesting ideas presented in an accessible and understandable way. A glossary and list of key terms help students identify and understand those concepts having particular importance (see my Message to Students).

Built-in Student Study Guide

To help achieve learning-centered educational outcomes, *Moral Philosophy for Modern Life* incorporates a built-in student study guide. The learning aids that are included help foster mastery of theoretical content, proficiency in critical thinking, as well as the ability to deal with different moral problems using appropriate rational strategies. The inclusion of a built-in study guide means that students need not buy an extra workbook at additional cost.

The guide included in this book is intended as an optional aid, not as a required tool. Certain instructors may wish to integrate some, or all, of the elements of the guide into their lesson plans to complement their teaching. Others may wish to have students use the guide for self-directed study outside the classroom. Many aspects of the guide are suitable for tutorial sessions. Regardless of how it is used, the guide offers many individual and group learning opportunities. Instructors and students can use their own goals and preferences to determine how they will employ the guide.

The built-in study guide used in Parts One and Two of this book is based on the SQ3R method of learning. SQ3R stands for survey, question, read, recite, and review. Chapters are designed so that students can

a. *Survey* the content to be covered,
b. Use Philosophical Focus *Questions* to direct their attention,
c. *Read* the material presented, and
d. *Recite* and *Review* what was covered for self-testing.

As part of the built-in guide, you will find

- Chapter overviews
- Numbered learning outcomes
- Philosophical focus questions
- Boldfacing
- A glossary
- A list of key terms
- Chapter end progress checks
- Summaries of major points

Details on how to use the various components of the SQ3R method of self-directed learning are included in my "Message to Students."

In Part Three of this book, a number of other learning aids, in addition to those comprising the SQ3R methodology, are used. Readings taken from various books and journals are accompanied by synopses, content quizzes, discussion questions and a generic argument analysis worksheet. Information on how to use these teaching-learning aids can be found at the beginning of Part Three (see pages 212–13).

Moral Preference Indicator (MPI)

Moral Philosophy for Modern Life contains a moral preference self-diagnostic. By completing the "Moral Preference Indicator" (MPI) found in the "Preview and Introduction," students are helped to identify their normative or value-related preferences for ethical decision making and action. Students using the MPI will discover whether they prefer a moral perspective based on utilitarian, deontological or character-based virtue considerations. By completing the MPI a second time, after coverage of ethical theories in Part One, students can then determine whether or not they have changed their moral viewpoints following careful theoretical study and analysis.

Self-Diagnostic: How Rational Is My Thinking?

Part Two of the book starts with a reasoning level self-assessment. By completing this informal diagnostic and developmental tool, students get some preliminary indication of how good their current logical thinking skills are. This tool deals with inductive logic, deductive logic, and frequently made logical mistakes stemming from fallacious reasoning. After finishing Part Two, students can return to the reasoning self-diagnostic to discover what progress has been made in their development as rational thinkers.

Biographical Briefs

Sometimes it is easier to appreciate the writings of the philosophers by knowing something about the philosophers themselves. For this reason, "Biographical Briefs" are provided to put names and faces on the various moral theories discussed. These briefs will also help to place moral theories into a personal, historical context.

Back to the Source

Moral Philosophy for Modern Life is written, in part, to decipher difficult and complex moral theories for beginning students in philosophy. Without some initial guidance, interpretation, and summary, the original works of the philosophers would be simply too imposing for many undergraduate students. Yet, to complete an introductory ethics course without having read any of the philosophers' actual works would seem inappropriate. For this reason, short excerpts are taken from the original sources and presented in a feature called "Back to the Source." These sourceworks are highly aligned to the material in the chapter in which they are found. They will benefit students by giving them a philosophical sampling of the real thing.

Philosophers at Work

This book encourages students not only to learn about moral philosophy but also to *do* a lot of moral philosophizing themselves. Philosophy is best understood not as a body of knowledge, but as an activity or method of thinking. With this in mind, students are given opportunities in the text to apply theories, test arguments, analyze ideas, and interpret social issues from an ethical perspective. In this feature, students will be encouraged to engage in personal reflections and group discussions in class or in tutorial. They will also be helped to develop intellectual attitudes conducive to rational living.

Mindwork Meditations

Students using this text are encouraged to keep a personal journal. To facilitate making journal entries, they are provided with opportunities in the book for "Mindwork Meditations." Such meditations do not require a stilling or emptying of the mind, as in eastern mysticism, but rather thought and mental activity relating to some problem, question or issue. Keeping a journal can be a wonderful way for students to record their thoughts, feelings, and reflections during their philosophical quest in your course. They can volunteer to read their journal entries in class, submit them for evaluation, or simply keep them for a personal record of their philosophical development as rational thinkers. How the journal is used is up to you and the members of your class.

Philosophical Focus Questions

Philosophical Focus Questions are included in the book as part of its built-in Student Study Guide. These questions serve to direct students' attention to chapter content, which is essential to mastering designated learning outcomes. The focus questions can also serve as a basis of discussion and debate in classroom or tutorial sessions.

Practical Applications

Part Three of this book consists of articles relating to personal and contemporary sociomoral issues. The articles included have been selected for their clarity and relevance to modern life. Students should find them interesting and thought provoking and a good means by which to practice their moral reasoning skills—skills that will serve them well on their journeys into the moral domain of life.

Source References and Related Readings

For anyone wishing to pursue their interests in any topic covered in *Moral Philosophy for Modern Life*, source references and related readings are provided. These will assist students and instructors alike to find more information on topics that interest them.

Appendix 1: So What Is the Answer?

The answers to chapter-end "Progress Checks" and "Content Quizzes" are found in Appendix 1. They help to verify student understanding of course content.

Appendix 2: How to Write a Moral Position Paper

Probably the hardest task facing philosophical beginners is having to write their first thesis defense. Having opinions is one thing; rationally defending one's point of view with reasoned arguments is quite another. In Appendix 2, students are taken through a process of reasoning that shows them how to take contrasting viewpoints and objections into account, while defending their own moral positions in a formal, written format.

Appendix 3: Philosopher's Tool Kit

This tool kit includes information about philosophical bibliographies, computer software, professional directories, journals, ethical resources on the internet, mailing lists, and other services. This tool kit is a veritable grab-bag of goodies for the philosophical enthusiast. It will be useful for research purposes and for further ethical explorations.

SUPPLEMENTS

Test Item File

A test file is available in both printed and computerized forms. The file contains 1280 items—broken down by chapter—in multiple choice, true and false, short answer and essay formats. Questions are identified by level of difficulty; the answers to all questions are page referenced to the text.

Prentice Hall Allyn and Bacon Custom Test

The Prentice Hall Allyn and Bacon Custom Test is a test generator designed to allow the creation of personalized exams. It is available in DOS, Windows and Macintosh formats.

Inspirational Quotations

Included in *Moral Philosophy for Modern Life* are thought-provoking quotations designed to inspire, uplift, and sometimes to disturb and challenge. I hope you enjoy them as much as I enjoyed selecting them for your interest and personal reflection. Speaking of quotations, here is one from an unknown philosopher writing in the latter part of the twentieth century. I think it captures the spirit and rationale behind the writing of this book.

Theory without application feels empty.
Application without theory is blind.
Reason is their devoted matchmaker,
Laboring in the temple of the mind.

A.F.

MESSAGE TO STUDENTS

My name is Tony Falikowski. I am the author of *Moral Philosophy for Modern Life* and I would like to welcome you to the interesting and stimulating world of ethical inquiry. In this text, we will embark on a journey that will take us through some difficult and, oftentimes, uphill terrain. Energy and effort will be required to reach our ultimate destination of moral enlightenment, but, once on our way, the fruits of rational inquiry will quench our thirst for truth and understanding. I cannot guarantee that we will arrive at our final destination by term's end, but I can assure you the journey has the potential to be life transforming. This course in applied ethics could change your worldview forever—I mean this seriously! The timing could not be better—you are here and ready; your philosophy teacher has appeared. Let us join minds and accompany your course instructor as we set off together on a journey—one that will lead to your personal ethical illumination.

To help you find your way through the theoretical forests and over the cracks and faultlines in logic, a built-in student study guide has been included as a convenient navigation device. This guide will enable you to master the various moral theories discussed, to practice logical-analytical reasoning skills and to apply both theories and skills to real world ethical problems. The study guide will assist you in your self-directed efforts to learn moral philosophy and to appreciate its relevance to everyday modern life.

The study guide in Parts One and Two of this text is based on the *SQ3R Method of Learning*. SQ3R is an acronym standing for *Survey, Question, Read, Recite and Review*. Part Three of this text, "Applying Ethics in the Real World," has its own set of distinct learning aids. Each reading is accompanied by a synopsis, a content quiz, a number of discussion questions, and a generic argument analysis worksheet. Information on how these learning aids are to be used can be found by referring to the introductory remarks to Part Three (see pages 212–13). For now, let me take you through the SQ3R process used in Part One and Two of this text. If you follow this system, it will help you master the content and skills targeted in the intended learning outcomes included in each chapter. In plain terms: you are more likely to pass the course and to do well! Let me take you through the SQ3R process.

(1) SURVEY THE CONTENT TO BE COVERED

Chapters one to nine begin with overviews that provide a preview of what is to be covered. By simply glancing at the headings, you can survey (S) the material you will be expected to master.

Look Over the Learning Outcomes

To make the overview and survey process easier, learning outcomes have been stated explicitly. By perusing them at the outset, you can discover what you will be expected to know or to do. To promote the mastery of content and skills, outcomes are numbered and placed near the text where they are addressed. After completing a chapter, you should review the list of learning outcomes to ensure that you have assimilated the information and have developed the skills marked for mastery. If not, you can go back and address the appropriate sections of the chapter.

(2) DIRECT YOUR READING ATTENTION BY USING "PHILOSOPHICAL FOCUS QUESTIONS"

Each chapter in Parts One and Two contains Philosophical Focus Questions. These questions make up the "Q" portion of the SQ3R methodology. You should examine the questions before actually reading the main text of the chapter. As suggested by the heading itself, the questions serve to focus your attention while you read so that you will know what to look for and what is important. Your instructor may use these questions for classroom discussion. Concentrate on the answers to the focus questions while you read. This will help you prepare for discussions, whether they take place in regular classes or in tutorial sessions.

(3) READ THE CHAPTER

Once you have an idea of what is in the chapter and what to look for, go ahead and read. I caution you to be patient. Reading philosophy is not like reading the newspaper or comic strips. Do not be surprised if you find yourself reading the same paragraph or page over several times before you understand the meaning. You are being introduced to a new way of thinking and it has a technical vocabulary all its own. You are also being asked to think and to communicate with a precision and clarity never so demanded in your academic career until now. Try not to get discouraged. Like the saying goes, "Anything worthwhile takes time."

Highlighted Key Terms

Given the inherent difficulty of philosophy, you should not be left to guess what is important. Just in case the Philosophical Focus Questions have not been a sufficient guide, key terms and concepts have been **boldfaced** to make clear what is especially significant and worth remembering. A list of boldfaced key terms is found just before the progress checks of each chapter in Parts One and Two.

Glossary

Because it would be unwieldy to include definitions of all the key terms contained in the main body of this text, I have included a glossary of the "most important" ones. These definitions, along with the other boldfaced terms and the focus questions, should enable you to pick out and to understand what is essential for mastery of the chapter.

(4) RECITE AND REVIEW

Progress Checks

After reading the chapter, you should start the recitation and review process by doing the Progress Check. Your mastery of the content is reflected in your ability to correctly answer questions contained in the check. Your responses to each of the progress checks can be verified by referring to Appendix 1: So What is the Answer?

Summary of Major Points

Chapter summaries found in Parts One and Two also comprise the recitation and review component of the SQ3R methodology. You may examine them before and/or after doing the progress checks to consolidate learning and to make sure that outcomes have been achieved. Reviewing the summaries is something you should do at test time to maximize your chances for success.

On that note, let me wish you well. You are at the edge of the moral domain. From past explorations inside, I can tell you that it is a fine kingdom. I hope you will like it there!

ACKNOWLEDGMENTS

In writing this book, I spent a great deal of time trying to make it useful and accessible for the students who would use it. The more I tried, the more I appreciated the efforts of my graduate and undergraduate philosophy teachers at university. I now realize how much their knowledge and professional expertise helped me and, indirectly, made *Moral Philosophy for Modern Life* possible. Acknowledging this fact, I wish to express a long-belated thank you to professors Dwight Boyd, John Eisenberg, Christopher Olsen, Wayne Sumner, and Kenneth Schmitz (now retired), all at the University of Toronto. Their stimulating and challenging courses, in addition to their expert guidance and support, inspired me to embark on the professional path that I did. I hope that students enjoy my philosophy classes as much as I did theirs. Thanks guys!

On the subject of students, I wish to thank the thousands I have taught for helping me to develop the skill of expressing difficult thought in relatively plain and simple language. Student questions and perplexities, brought to my attention in class, have served to reinforce my belief that "*If you would help those who suffer, you must speak their language.*"

Of course, thanks are in order to all of those at Prentice Hall who contributed to the realization of this book. I wish to acknowledge the efforts of Rebecca Bersagel and Cliff Newman, acquisitions editors at PH, who continue to place their confidence in my project proposals. I would also like to thank Marie Graham, the copy editor for this text. She helped to make editorial decision making fun over the phone. Carol Whynot deserves honorable mention too. Carol's professionalism and her efficient management of practical matters kept the development of this project moving along smoothly. Marjan Farahbaksh served as the production editor on this book and so deserves credit for its completion as well.

I should not forget the reviewers who offered their valuable comments on preliminary drafts of this book. They are Marilyn Burstein, Art Institute of Pittsburgh; John Black, Malaspina University-College; Samantha Brennan, University of Western Ontario; and Jack Ornstein, Concordia University. I know this book is better because of their insightful remarks and helpful suggestions. Please do not hold them responsible for any deficiencies that may remain.

Finally, I wish to express my heartfelt appreciation to my family for their patience and understanding. Writing a book takes time—time away from them. Thank you Pamela, Michael, Heather, and Michelle for not complaining and letting dad "do his thing." Although my mind was sometimes preoccupied with writing, I can assure you that you were always a present reality in my heart. I love you all!

ABOUT THE AUTHOR

Dr. Anthony Falikowski is an internationally published author and a full-time professor at Sheridan College in Oakville, Ontario. A graduate of the University of Toronto, he has spent more than fifteen years offering courses in philosophy, psychology, and human relations. A certified Reality Therapist, Enneagram Teacher, and Personality Type Analyst, Tony conducts organizational as well as behavioral training and development workshops as a part-time consultant. His next major research project is to develop a "Higher Reality Therapy" based on the therapeutic applications of philosophical wisdom. At Sheridan, Tony has been nominated for the President's Award of Teaching Excellence. He has also been listed in "Who's Who in the Humanities" by the Chicago Biographical Center and in "Profiles in Business and Management: An International Directory of Scholars and Their Research," published by the Harvard Business School in Boston, Massachusetts. In addition to *Moral Philosophy for Modern Life*, other books written by Tony are: *The Philosophy of Human Nature*; *Moral Philosophy: Theories, Skills, and Applications*; and *Mastering Human Relations*. With his eclectic academic and professional background, Tony has fashioned an approach to ethical study that is refreshingly innovative and motivating for students.

Tony is happily married and lives with his wife, three children, and pet cat Mittens in the town of Oakville, just steps from the shores of Lake Ontario. For fun, he likes to jog, play pick-up hockey, go on family hikes, and listen to rock music at high volumes as a way of staying in touch with his primitive self. He worries constantly that this is the only "self" there really is!

PREVIEW AND INTRODUCTION: THE PRACTICAL VALUE OF PHILOSOPHICAL ETHICS

Vain is the word of a philosopher which does not heal any suffering of man. For just as there is no profit in medicine if it does not expel the diseases of the body, so there is no profit in philosophy either if it does not expel the suffering of the mind.

Epicurus

A number of years ago, a theater arts student taking my moral philosophy course as a general education elective raised his hand in class. He was obviously very agitated and upset. We had been discussing the ethics of abortion that day when he suddenly blurted out: "C'mon Tony, you've been studying this ethics stuff for years. You're the expert. Let's stop all of this arguing. It's driving me crazy. Just tell me, will you, is abortion right or wrong?"

As I think back to the painful experience of my theater arts student, I cannot help but become a little disturbed myself by the mental torment he was suffering. He was, apparently, experiencing considerable anxiety in his efforts to make the correct moral value judgment on the controversial issue of abortion. He knew that abortion was a serious matter and that it was important for him to take the right moral position on it; yet, he was uncertain about how to decide for himself. He wanted me to decide for him.

Philosophy does not give, it can only awaken.

Karl Jaspers

If a man is truly wise, he does not bid you enter his house of wisdom, but rather, leads you to the threshold of your own mind.

Anonymous

Wisdom out of suffering.
Greek Saying

It is by invisible hands that we are tortured most.
Friedrich Nietzsche

Like my theater arts student, many others in society experience mental anguish when making important ethical decisions. Values must be championed, people must be confronted, principles must be defended, and sometimes difficult or unpleasant actions must be carried out. When there is much uncertainty or diversity of opinion, psychological tension can result. Moral doubt can be a significant source of stress in everyday life.

All humanity is sick. I come therefore to you as a physician who has diagnosed this universal disease and is prepared to cure it.
The Buddha

Nowadays everyone in the world is deluded about right and wrong, and confused about benefit and harm. Because so many people share this sickness, no one perceives that it is a sickness.
Lao Zi

In desperate efforts to cope with this moral suffering of the mind, some individuals like my tormented student look to experts and gurus for answers. By placing faith in the judgment of others, people try to relieve themselves of the burden of having to decide for themselves. By granting moral authority to an ethics professor, a cult leader, a politician or military officer, some attempt to escape from the personal responsibility of making moral decisions as independent agents. If any wrong-doing or bad judgment arises as a result of the escape attempts, then the moral authorities are to blame, not the would-be moral escape artists.

It is possible that, in some cases, deferring to moral authority is little more than a veiled attempt to get off the moral hook of life. Perhaps the most obvious example of this is found in the war crimes trials that followed World War II. At that time, a number of senior German officers pleaded innocent to war crimes charges on the grounds that they were just obeying orders from the *Fuhrer*. In their minds, they were not responsible. World opinion seems to suggest otherwise.

Another psychological strategy to relieve morally induced mental stress is to quit thinking and simply to conclude that all values are a matter of personal preference. Once this stance is adopted, there is no real need to agonize over moral matters whatsoever. After all, on this account, no one person has the right to make a value judgment on the actions or character of another. As the saying goes, “different strokes for different folks.” People just have different feelings and opinions about what is morally acceptable in any situation or given set of circumstances.

If a man begins with certainties, he shall end in doubts. But if he is content to begin with doubts, he shall end in certainties.

Francis Bacon

Standing in the middle of the road is very dangerous; you get knocked down by the traffic from both sides.

Margaret Thatcher

Too often we enjoy the comfort of opinion without the discomfort of thought.

John F. Kennedy

Man is not only often much more immoral than he believes, but also much more moral than he thinks.

Sigmund Freud

Although this relativistic position is one that some might wish to defend and though it offers some psychological solace, it is fraught with difficulties. If, for example, everybody is right and nobody is wrong, because rightness and wrongness are relative to the person, culture or generation and so on, then opposite and conflicting positions could both be right at the same time—a proposition that does not make very much logical sense. Furthermore, if there is no objective way to decide matters of right and wrong or good and bad, then there would be no ethical basis for criticizing social policies or for improving society. Things like slavery, child abuse or discrimination against women would have to be accepted on the grounds that, morally speaking, it is all a matter of personal opinion and how people feel at the time.

If we are not to abandon morality in our lives and the possibility of social progress, if we do not wish to wash our hands of moral responsibility or to escape from it by becoming mindless followers and sheep, we must look for adequate ways to make moral decisions for ourselves.

The hottest places in hell are reserved for those who, in time of great moral crisis, maintain their neutrality.

Dante

Fortunately, for us, a great many thinkers have grappled for centuries with the problems of ethical decision making. We need not bow down and worship these thinkers; nor do we have to accept all of what they say to us unconditionally. This would be mindless following again. As thoughtful and mature adults, what we can do is to consider intelligently the insights the thinkers have to offer and to evaluate their moral philosophies from a rational, objective perspective. We can decide which ideas have worth, which ones need alteration, and which ones must be rejected altogether. We can do all this if we choose to be free and independent thinkers ourselves, and if we assume at the outset that, when it comes to moral matters, debate is meaningful and that there are better and worse decisions to be made.

May God grant us the wisdom to know right,
The will to choose it,
And the strength to make it endure.
King Arthur in "First Knight," the movie

Your medicine is in you and you do not observe it. Your ailment is from yourself, and you do not register it.
Hazrat Ali

Let our purpose be ideal and our action be practical.
Sir Wilfred Laurier

ORGANIZATION OF BOOK

In Part One of *Moral Philosophy for Modern Life* we will examine three major moral perspectives that have developed over the centuries. They are historically important insofar as they have very much influenced our common-sense thinking about morality today. They include the character ethics of Plato and Aristotle, the utilitarian ethics of Jeremy Bentham and John Stuart Mill, and the deontological (pronounced dee-on-toe-logical) duty and rights-based ethics of Immanual Kant and John Rawls.

Of course, in any introductory text on applied ethics, not all moral perspectives can be covered. Space and time considerations make a complete and comprehensive treatment of all theories impractical. I have thus chosen to omit for our immediate purposes nonrational, nonwestern, and religious ethical perspectives. By doing so, I am not suggesting that existentialist ethics, oriental philosophy or Christian morality, for example, have less worth or justifiability compared with those western, rational perspectives I have selected for treatment. Whether or not all of morality is rational, for instance, is a debatable point. So too is the notion whether or not morality can make sense without the existence of a supreme being.

The theoretical questions just raised, though interesting and philosophically important, are beyond the scope of this more practical and applied introductory text. The ethical perspectives I have chosen for consideration simply suit us best for getting started with the business of having to make moral decisions in the real world. In my efforts to respect religious diversity and the pluralistic values of North American society, I have opted for a rational approach to practical ethics. Although people's religious and ethnic backgrounds differ in a multicultural society like ours, reason is the one common element that binds us together as moral persons. After you have completed this introductory course in applied ethics, I invite you to revisit ethical theory by looking at those moral perspectives not covered here. Think about what differences, if any, they would make on your practical day-to-day moral decision making.

Hagar

Once we have completed our coverage of the moral theories in Part One, we will move on in Part Two to the treatment of moral reasoning skills necessary for effective ethical decision making. First, you will learn about the differences between scientific and philosophical approaches to the study of morality. You will learn about the different kinds of moral claims that people make and how those claims can be supported. You will be introduced to the differences between opinions and reasoned arguments. You will come to appreciate and understand why only the latter have philosophical worth. In learning to construct reasoned arguments, you will also be introduced to inductive and deductive logic. Not only will you be given a chance to practice these thinking procedures but also you will learn how to test rationally the values and principles on which moral arguments are based. Also, in Part Two, you will be given information to provide you with a "logical self-defense" against irrationality and dishonest attempts to persuade. You will learn how to identify informal logical fallacies, or what I call "sleazy logic," to protect yourself from the threat of nonsense, attack, and diversionary tactics designed to manipulate.

In Part Three, we will use our newly acquired theoretical knowledge and reasoning skills to discuss selected ethical issues that dominate modern life. We will take our theories and skills and apply them to some of the most important and relevant issues of the day. This application will underscore the practical importance of ethics. You will come to appreciate how philosophical ethics can, in fact, have lasting therapeutic value. By offering direction and providing a method for moral decision making, a study of applied ethics can relieve some of the suffering of the mind—at least where moral uncertainty is concerned.

Let no one be slow to seek wisdom when he is young, nor weary in the search thereof when he is grown old. For no age is too early or too late for the health of the soul. And to say that the reason for studying philosophy has not yet come, or that it is past and gone, is like saying the season for happiness is not yet or that it is no more.

Epicurus

you must emerge from the conflict if you are to bring peace to other minds.

A Course in Miracles

Before we move on to Part One and Plato to discover what practical wisdom he has to share with us, let us turn to the Moral Preference Indicator (MPI) which follows. By completing the MPI you will begin to identify some of your underlying beliefs and assumptions in regard to morality. After studying the philosophers, you may wish to complete the MPI again to determine if there has been a shift in your moral perspective or if your moral position has been strengthened.

MORAL PREFERENCE INDICATOR (MPI)

Aim

The purpose of the MPI is to help you identify your moral preferences in regard to the three major moral perspectives to be discussed in this book. Discovering your preferences and learning about other possible preferences will help you to understand better the nature of moral disagreement and some of the reasons why people do not always see eye to eye.

Once you have covered ethical theories in Part One of *Moral Philosophy for Modern Life*, you should complete the MPI again to discover if there has been a shift in your moral position. After you learn more about the various perspectives, you may wish to change your moral point of view.

Directions

Below are statements clustered in groups of three (a, b, and c). Your task is to read each grouping and to circle the letter next to the statement you agree with most. If you like all three statements, pick the one for which you have even the slightest preference. Only pick one. If you dislike all three statements, pick the statement you dislike least. Make sure you respond to all 15 groupings. (After coverage of theories in Part One, you will be given a second opportunity to complete the MPI to compare your scores between pre- and post-theoretical study.)

When it comes to morality, I believe

1. a. the ends justify the means
   b. the ends do not justify the means
   c. the end of morality is living the ethically good life
2. a. virtue is its own reward
   b. the right thing to do is to promote good consequences
   c. the right thing to do is to do your duty
3. a. some actions are right or wrong in themselves
   b. the rightness or wrongness of an action depends on its results
   c. correct actions promote inner harmony
4. a. wrong-doing is essentially a product of ignorance
   b. wrong-doing is essentially a violation of duty
   c. wrong-doing is a failure to promote the common good

5. a. we are morally obligated to fulfill our potentialities as persons
   b. morality is a way of achieving human happiness
   c. morality is about following rational principles
6. a. if an action is morally unacceptable, then it is unacceptable for everyone
   b. whether or not an action is morally acceptable depends on circumstances and people's wants
   c. an action is morally acceptable if it promotes the development of our higher faculties
7. The fundamental moral question is:
   a. what is the good at which human behavior aims?
   b. how can we reduce suffering and promote human welfare?
   c. what are my obligations?
8. The basis of morality is:
   a. character
   b. utility (i.e., benefit, pleasure)
   c. duty
9. The ultimate end of morality is:
   a. the greatest happiness for the greatest number
   b. justice
   c. developing an appropriate lifestyle based on wisdom and moderation
10. Acting morally involves
    a. doing what nature requires
    b. the principle of respect for persons
    c. a preliminary calculation of any action's pros and cons
11. Which option below captures best the central issues of morality?
    a. pain and pleasure
    b. freedom and responsibility
    c. lifestyle and states of character
12. Morality is
    a. absolute
    b. dependent upon people and circumstances
    c. determined by our rational natures
13. The best thing to do is
    a. develop your potential as a human being
    b. promote happiness
    c. honor your obligations

14. Moral principles are
    a. universal and unconditional
    b. specific and conditional
    c. self-referring, but applicable to others too
15. A proper system of morality
    a. helps people to achieve their goals
    b. maintains fairness, equality, and freedom
    c. helps people to develop proper habits of conduct

Scoring Instructions

For each question you have circled either a, b, or c. If, for example, you circled "a" for number one, now circle "u" below, next to Question 1. If you circled "b" for number 2, now circle "u," next to Question 2, and so on. When you are finished, add the total number of u's, d's and c's you have circled. You can then plot your scores on the circular graph, Figure PI.1 "The Sphere of Rational Ethics," and shade in as indicated by your scores. The shaded graph will provide a circular profile of your moral preferences.

Scoring Sheet

Answers

Answer	a	b	c
Question			
1	u	d	c
2	c	u	d
3	d	u	c
4	c	d	u
5	c	u	d
6	d	u	c
7	c	u	d
8	c	u	d
9	u	d	c
10	c	d	u
11	u	d	c
12	d	u	c
13	c	u	d
14	d	u	c
15	u	d	c

Total Number

u's = _____ (Utilitarian Ethics)
d's = _____ (Deontological Ethics)
c's = _____ (Character Ethics)

Plot your scores on "The Sphere of Rational Ethics"

Figure PI.1 THE SPHERE OF RATIONAL ETHICS

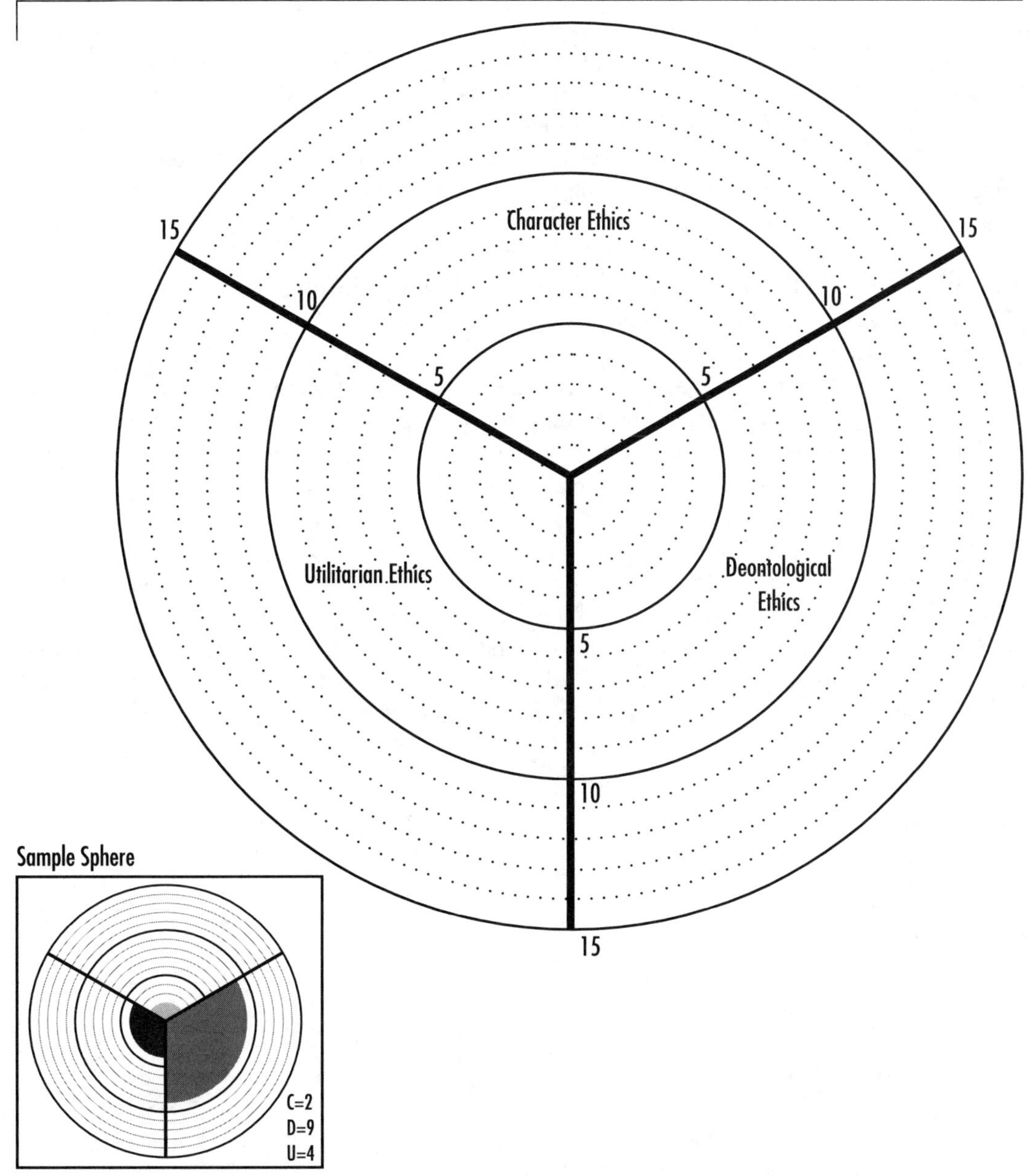

Explanation of Results

The statements contained in the MPI reflect three major rational ethical positions that have been identified in the history of moral philosophy. Any single statement in the indicator makes an assertion, claim or assumption consistent with a particular moral point of view, either utilitarian, deontological or character-based. By graphing your results and reading the descriptions of moral viewpoints below, you can now begin to identify your moral preferences in regard to ethical decision making. (Note that nonrational, oriental, and religious ethical perspectives are not reflected by the MPI.)

Utilitarian Ethics: (u is your highest score.) As a utilitarian, I do not believe that actions (e.g., abortion) are right or wrong in themselves. I think that circumstances must be taken into account and that the costs and benefits of alternative courses of action must be weighed before deciding what is the morally correct thing to do. At bottom, morality is about maximizing happiness and relieving human misery and pain; thus, an action is good or bad depending on the consequences for human welfare.

Deontological Ethics: (d is your highest score.) As a deontologist or duty-based ethicist, I believe that rational principles can be used to determine the morality of actions. Morality is not about making sure people are happy; it is about doing your duty. Rightness reigns over goodness. Doing the right thing for the right reason is more important than maximizing pleasure, benefit or utility. Actions are based on rules or maxims. If a rule is morally acceptable, then it applies to everyone consistently, fairly, and unconditionally. People's rights cannot be bargained away or compromised through some kind of calculation of consequences.

Character Ethics: (c is your highest score.) As a character ethicist, I see morality largely in regard to self-realization. Morality is about developing appropriate virtues, attitudes, lifestyles, and states of mind. The ethically good life requires us to fulfill our function as human beings, to harmonize our "souls" or internal workings, and to seek moral knowledge through rational contemplation. Morality raises eternal questions like, "How should I live?" "What is the good life?" and "What kind of person should I strive to become?"

1

PART ONE

UNDERSTANDING ETHICAL THEORIES

Character Ethics

In our initial coverage of moral theories, we will be turning to what can be called the virtue or "character ethics" of Plato and Aristotle. Both philosophers offer immeasurable practical wisdom to help us develop as moral persons. Plato explains how people's lives can be poisoned by such things as greed and vanity and how, as a result, people can develop corrupt characters. According to Plato, a life based on insatiable desires or on self-glorifying pursuits can never be truly satisfying for such a life creates a psychological imbalance that leaves the human soul disquieted and disturbed.

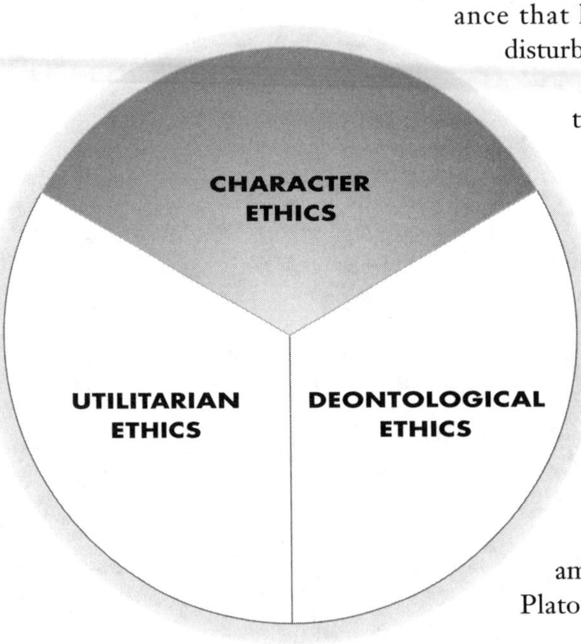

CHARACTER ETHICS

UTILITARIAN ETHICS

DEONTOLOGICAL ETHICS

Aristotle reminds us of the differences between types of goals. Some, he says, are instrumental—a means to further ends. Others are intrinsically valuable—they are ends in themselves. "Happiness" is deemed to be the ultimate end of life, something not only intrinsically valuable but also sufficient unto itself. With these distinctions in mind, Aristotle points out how in life we often confuse the various types of ends and how, as a result, we choose to live misguided lifestyles not befitting rational beings.

In what follows, you will be given ample opportunity to reflect on the ideas of Plato and Aristotle, to apply them to your own understanding of people's behavior, and to engage in a self-evaluation of your own personal ethics and lifestyle as they have developed to date. In the end, you should gain considerable moral insight into yourself and others. A solid foundation will be constructed for a reevaluation of your personal values.

Character is fate.

Heraclitus

The unexamined life is not worth living.

Socrates

1 CHAPTER ONE

PLATO: CORRUPT CHARACTERS AND PHILOSOPHER KINGS

Overview

Biographical Brief: "Plato"
Plato's Teleology
Plato's Vision of the Soul
Moral Balance and Plato's Functional Explanation of Morality
"Back to the Source" Feature from Plato's *The Republic*
Platonic Character Type Index (PCTI)
Plato's Character Types
- Philosopher Kings/Rulers
- Timarchic Character
- Oligarchic Character
- Democratic Character
- Tyrannical Character

Key Terms
Progress Check 1.1
Summary of Major Points
Source References and Related Readings

Learning Outcomes:

After successfully completing this chapter, you will be able to:

1.1 place Plato into historical perspective;
1.2 state two fundamental moral questions posed by Plato;
1.3 explain Plato's doctrine of teleology;
1.4 describe the soul and its internal workings;
1.5 form an initial hypothesis about your Platonic character type;
1.6 outline the psychological make-up of the Philosopher King/Ruler;
1.7 describe the features and flaws of Plato's corrupt character types.

PHILOSOPHICAL FOCUS QUESTIONS

1. What is meant by saying that Plato offers us a "functional explanation of morality"?
2. What role does the soul play in Plato's functional explanation?
3. What happens when the soul is not functioning properly?
4. What is the ideal character like, according to Plato?
5. What are corrupt characters like? How are their motivations different? Is there anything to which they all fall prey?

1.1

CORBIS–BEHMANN

Plato (427–347 B.C.)

BIOGRAPHICAL BRIEF*

Plato lived from 427 to 347 B.C. He was born into a wealthy family that was both aristocratic and politically influential. His importance to intellectual history was underscored by Alfred North Whitehead, who once stated that all of western philosophy is but a series of footnotes on the work of Plato.

When Plato was 40, he founded the "Academy," an independent institution of learning which continued to exist for almost nine hundred years until the Roman Emperor Justinian closed it in A.D. 529. The Academy was a quiet retreat where teachers and students could meet to pursue knowledge . . . . Students throughout Greece enrolled to partake in the adventure of learning and to experience personal growth toward wisdom. The Academy can be regarded as the precursor of today's modern university.

Plato himself studied under Socrates, once described by the Oracle at Delphi as the wisest man in Athens. Fifteen years after the tragic trial and death of Socrates, Plato began to write "dialogues" in which Socrates was the principal speaker. The dialogues explored moral, political, logical, religious, and cosmological topics. Though Socrates never actually recorded his ideas, we derive from the dialogues a profile of Socrates' personality and a statement of his doctrines which likely bear a very close resemblance to his actual philosophy and the historical figure himself. When reading Plato it is sometimes difficult, therefore, to determine what is attributable to Plato and what comes from Socrates. Some argue that the early works of Plato are more reflective of Socratic thinking, while the later works begin to reflect Plato's own philosophical investigations. Plato's most famous work is . . . *The Republic*. Other works by Plato include *The Apology*, *Crito*, *Phaedo*, and *Symposium*.

**From Falikowski,* Moral Philosophy, *p.6.*

even in the outwardly most respectable of us there is a terribly bestial and immoral type of desire, which manifests itself particularly in dreams. Do you think I'm talking sense, and do you agree?

Plato (circa 400 B.C.)

1.2

As we enter the world of ethical theory, let us take what guidance we can from the immortal wisdom of Plato. In his writings, Plato addressed perennial questions like "What constitutes the good life?" and "What sort of individual should I strive to become?" To answer such questions, Plato paid particular attention to the soul. He believed that, like the body, the soul could enjoy health or could suffer from dysfunction. If the soul is to become and to remain healthy, then, for Plato, there must be established a certain harmonious balance of psychic elements within the self. Physical, emotional, and intellectual components of the personality must be coordinated to work smoothly. A smoothly functioning psyche constitutes a healthy, well-ordered soul and an imbalanced psyche constitutes a disordered one. The insight that we gain from this thinking is that if one wishes to live a life of virtue, then certain inner adjustments may be required. Morality is, in large part, an "inside job." To understand precisely what is meant by this suggestion, it is necessary to consider Plato's notion of **teleology** and how it fits into his concept of the **soul**.

1.3 PLATO'S TELEOLOGY

Plato adheres to the doctrine of teleology. According to this doctrine, everything in the universe has a proper function to perform within a harmonious hierarchy of purposes. The development of anything thus follows from the fulfillment of the purpose for which it was designed. For us to evaluate something as good or bad, we must examine and appraise it in light of its proper function. Does it perform well what it was designed to do? Take a pen, for example. A pen performs well if it writes smoothly and without blotting. This is what a pen is designed to do. Given the function of a pen, we should not expect it to perform well as an eating utensil or a weapon of self-defense. It would be inappropriate to describe a pen as bad simply because eating with it is too difficult or defending oneself with it is not very effective. Our evaluation of a pen's good or bad performance depends on its designated purpose.

As with humans, we too have a function. In view of Plato's teleological explanation of morality, we live the morally good life insofar as we perform our distinctively human function well. Being less efficient than a robot on a factory assembly line, for instance, does not make us bad or morally deficient. We are not designed by nature to be mindless machines. What we are designed to do and how we are supposed to function, according to Plato, can be best understood by turning to his explanation of the structure and workings of the human soul.

1.4

PLATO'S VISION OF THE SOUL

Plato conceptualizes human nature in terms of a three-part division of the soul. When reading about the soul, try not to invest it with any religious significance. Understand it as a metaphor to explain the main motives or impulses to action. For Plato, the soul is the principle of life and movement. Since the bodily self is inanimate, it must be moved by something and, for Plato, that something is the soul. While Plato's discussion of the soul is not intended as a scientific analysis of the mind, seeing the soul metaphorically as something akin to psyche, self or personality structure is helpful for analytical purposes.

Happiness resides not in possessions and not in gold,
The feeling of happiness dwells in the soul.
Democritus 420 B.C.

The soul, as conceptualized by Plato, is made up of **reason**, **spirit**, and **appetite**. Each part of the soul aims at different things. Take appetite first. Appetite, or "**desire**" as it is sometimes called, seeks to satisfy our biological instinctive urges. It looks after the physical side of our lives. There is an element in all of us that functions to achieve physical pleasure, release from pain, and material want satisfaction. We all wish to eat, drink, sleep, act upon our sexual urges, minimize pain, experience pleasure, acquire a certain number of possessions, and live comfortably. When we diet, date, shop, and workout, for example, we are being driven by appetite—the physical side of our selves.

Spirit is the second structural element of the human soul. It is the drive toward action. Sometimes referred to as "**passion**," it includes our self-assertive tendencies. It targets glory, honor, reputation and the establishment of a good name. Spirit also provides the impetus or force behind all ambitious pursuits, competitive struggles, moral indignation and outrage, human enterprise and pugnacity. As the emotional element of the psyche, spirit manifests itself in our need to love and be loved. It is present when we wish to make an impression, to be accepted and admired by others or when we work hard to be liked.

You like me, you really like me!
Sally Field, A "spirited" Academy Award acceptance speech

Reason is the third element of the soul. It is the part we might refer to as the intellect. Reason can be described as the faculty that calculates, measures, and decides. It seeks knowledge and understanding. It affords us insight and allows us to anticipate the future with foresight. By means of reason we are able to think and to make up our minds before we act. We can weigh options, compare alternatives, suppress dangerous urges, and make reasonable choices. Whenever you are curious, trying to make sense of things, or whenever you display an inquiring mind in your search for meaning, reason is that which moves you.

1.5 MORAL BALANCE AND PLATO'S FUNCTIONAL EXPLANATION OF MORALITY

Having outlined the parts of the soul, let us go back to Plato's **functional explanation of morality**. Remember that, for Plato, anything is good to the extent that it performs its function well. So the question now becomes: How is the human soul supposed to work?

In answer to this, Plato suggests that the soul that is functioning properly is doing so in a kind of harmonious **moral balance**. When the faculty of reason governs both appetite and spirit, that is, our physical desires, as well as our passions and emotions, then an orderly and well-balanced moral character results. In other words, people who are living the morally good life, or are living life as it ideally ought to be lived, maintain a rational, biological, and emotional equilibrium with reason in control.

> ***The outward work will never be puny if the inward work is great.***
>
> *Meister Eckhart*

Control of inner harmony by reason is not easy to achieve. We all experience turmoil and psychological conflict. It is as if there are warring factions within the mind that cause tension and upheaval. This internal conflict is not abnormal or psychopathological—it is part of the human condition. Inner struggle is part of life.

> ***For the flesh lusteth against the Spirit, and the Spirit against the flesh: and these are contrary the one to the other: so that ye cannot do the things that ye would.***
>
> *St. Paul's Letter to the Galatians, 5:17*

> ***You are not at peace because you are not fulfilling your function.***
>
> *A Course in Miracles*

To help us better appreciate this struggle, Plato describes it metaphorically using the example of a charioteer in control of two horses. The charioteer symbolizes the faculty of reason; the horses represent appetite and spirit. One horse (appetite) "needs no touch of the whip, but is guided by word and admonition only." The other horse (spirit) is unruly, "the mate of insolence and pride . . . hardly yielding to whip and spur." While the charioteer (reason) has a clear vision of the destination and the good horse is on track, the bad horse "plunges and runs away, giving all manner of trouble to his companion and charioteer" (Plato, quoted in Stumpf, 1993, p. 63).

Zeal without knowledge is a runaway horse.

Proverb

In the scenario presented to us by Plato, we have two horses moving in different directions while a charioteer watches his commands go unheeded. The charioteer's job is to guide and control the horses. What is clear is that the chariot cannot go anywhere unless the charioteer can work together with the two horses and bring them under control. So too with life. Just as both horses are necessary to achieve the charioteer's goal, appetite and spirit are indispensable to reason. Reason identifies the goal; it harnesses the power of appetite and spirit and then proceeds toward its identified destination. Appetite and spirit cannot be disposed of. They are essential to the well-ordered functioning of the human soul.

PHILOSOPHERS AT WORK

Think about the last time you let your appetites, feelings or passions "run wild." What were the immediate consequences and longer term results? Do you agree with Plato that reason should rule our lives? Why or why not?

When reason is in control and the soul is functioning in a harmonious balance, we can say that it is functioning as it should. For Plato, fulfillment of our function as human beings is equivalent to the attainment of **moral virtue**. When we are unhappy or when we have lost our sense of well-being, disharmony of the soul is the problem. If the "wild horses" of passion and desire are running rampant in our lives, then we fall into a disorder manifesting itself in ignorance. We begin to confuse **appearance** with **reality**. We mistake apparent goods for real goods. We pursue things we think will make us happy when, in fact, they will not. We make wrong choices and do wrong things out of false knowledge. As poor misguided souls, we fall prey to moral evil and corruption. Only by allowing reason to regain control of our lives can we enjoy peace of mind, inner harmony, and lasting happiness. Reason can offer us true knowledge of what is ultimately good, and only reason can properly guide us in what we should do with our lives. Only reason can yield knowledge necessary for moral virtue; ignorance can produce only evil and misdirection.

Study, therefore, to withdraw the love of your soul from all things that are visible, and to turn it to things that are invisible.

Thomas à Kempis

BACK TO THE SOURCE*

Plato would say that when a character is morally balanced, i.e., when each part is performing its specific function, then we find "justice" in the individual. The term "justice" is used because throughout The Republic *Plato draws parallels between society and the individual. As in a just society, which is well-ordered and not governed by people corrupted by greed (appetite) or vain ambition (spirit), but is directed by wisdom and virtue (reason), so too are just individuals not enslaved by insatiable desires and unbridled passions. Such things are governed and limited in their expression by reason. In* The Republic, *we read the following:*

'Well, it's been a rough passage, but we have pretty well reached agreement that there are the same three elements in the personality of the individual as there are in the state.'

'True.'

'Must it not follow, then, that the individual is wise in the same way and with the same part of himself as the state?'

'That is so.'

'And that the individual is brave with the same part and in the same way as the state, and that there is the same correspondence in all the other constituents of excellence?'

'That must follow.'

'And so, my dear Glaucon,' I went on, 'we shall also say that the individual man is just in the same way that the state is just.'

'That must inevitably follow too.'

'And I suppose we have not forgotten that the state was just when the three elements within it each minded their own business.'

'No, I don't think we've forgotten that.'

'Then we must remember that each of us will be just and perform his proper function only if each part of him is performing its proper function.'

'Yes, we must certainly remember that.'

'So, the reason ought to rule, having the wisdom and foresight to act for the whole, and the spirit ought to obey and support it.'

'Certainly.'

'And this concord between them is effected, as we said, by a combination of intellectual and physical training, which tunes up the reason by a training in rational argument and higher studies, and tones down and soothes the element of "spirit" by harmony and rhythm.'

'Certainly.'

'When these two elements have been so brought up, and trained and educated to their proper function, they must be put in charge of appetite, which forms the greater part of each man's make-up and is naturally insatiable. They must prevent it taking its fill of the so-called physical pleasures, for otherwise it will get too large and strong to mind its own business and will try to subject and control the other elements, which it has no right to do, and so wreck the life of all of them.'

**From Plato,* The Republic, *trans. Desmond Lee, pp. 218–222. Reprinted by permission of Frederick Warne & Co. Footnotes not reproduced.*

'True.'

'At the same time,' I went on, 'won't these two elements be the best defense that mind and body have against external enemies? One of them will do the thinking, the other will fight under the orders of its superior and provide the courage to carry its decisions into effect.'

'Yes, I agree.'

'And we call an individual brave because of this part of him, I think, when he has a spirit which holds fast to the orders of reason about what he ought or ought not to fear, in spite of pleasure and pain?'

'That is quite right.'

'And we call him wise in virtue of that small part of him which is in control and issues the orders, knowing as it does what is best for each of the three elements and for the whole made up of them.'

'Yes, I agree.'

'Then don't we call him self-disciplined when all these three elements are in friendly and harmonious agreement, when reason and its subordinates are all agreed that reason should rule and there is no civil war among them?'

'That is exactly what we mean by self-control or discipline in a city or in an individual.'

'And a man will be just by following the principle we have stated so often.'

'That must be so.'

'Well, then,' I said, 'is our picture in any way indistinct? Does it look as if justice in the individual were different from what we found it to be in the state?'

'I can't see any difference,' he answered.

'If there are still any doubts in our minds,' I said, 'a few commonplace examples should finally convince us.'

'What sort of examples?'

'Well, suppose for instance we were asked whether our state or a man of corresponding nature and training would embezzle money deposited with him. Do you think we should reckon him more likely to do it than other people?'

'He would be the last person to do such a thing.'

'And wouldn't it be out of the question for him to commit sacrilege or theft, or to betray his friends or his country?'

'Out of the question.'

'And he would never break a solemn promise or any other agreement.'

'Certainly not.'

'And he would be the last man to commit adultery, dishonor his parents, or be irreligious.'

'The last man,' he agreed.

'And is not the reason for all this that each element within him is performing its proper function, whether it is giving or obeying orders?'

'Yes, that is the reason.'

'Are you now convinced, then, that justice is what produces men and states of this character?'

'Yes, I am quite convinced,' he said.

'So our dream has come true, and, as we guessed, we have been lucky enough, with god's help, to run across a basic pattern of justice at the very beginning of the foundation of our state.'

'Yes, we have.'

'In fact, my dear Glaucon, the provision that the man naturally fitted to be a shoemaker, or carpenter, or anything else, should stick to his own trade has turned out to be a kind of adumbration of justice—hence its usefulness.'

'So it seems.'

'Justice, therefore, we may say, is a principle of this kind; its real concern is not with external actions, but with a man's inward self, his true concern and interest. The just man will not allow the three elements which make up his inward self to trespass on each other's functions or interfere with each other, but, by keeping all three in tune, like the notes of a scale (high, middle, and low, and any others there be), will in the truest sense set his house to rights, attain self-mastery and order, and live on good terms with himself. When he has bound these elements into a disciplined and harmonious whole, and so become fully one instead of many, he will be ready for action of any kind, whether it concerns his personal or financial welfare, whether it is political or private; and he will reckon and call any of these actions just and honorable if it contributes to and helps to maintain this disposition of mind, and will call the knowledge which controls such action wisdom. Similarly, he will call unjust any action destructive of this disposition, and the opinions which control such action ignorance.'

'That is all absolutely true, Socrates.'

'Good,' I said. 'So we shan't be very far wrong if we claim to have discovered what the just man and the just state are, and in what their justice consists.'

'No, we shan't.'

'Shall we make the claim, then?'

'Yes.'

'So much for that,' I said. 'And next, I suppose, we ought to consider injustice.'

'Obviously.'

'It must be some kind of civil war between these same three elements, when they interfere with each other and trespass on each other's functions, or when one of them rebels against the rest to get control when it has no business to do so, because its natural role is to be a slave to the rightfully controlling element. This sort of situation, when the elements of the mind are confused and displaced, is what constitutes injustice, indiscipline, cowardice, ignorance and, in short, wickedness of all kinds.'

'Yes, that's so.'

'And if we know what injustice and justice are, it's clear enough, isn't it, what acting unjustly and doing wrong are or, again, what acting justly is?'

'How do you mean?'

'Well,' I said, 'there is an exact analogy between these states of mind and bodily health and sickness.'

'How?'

'Healthy activities produce health, and unhealthy activities produce sickness.'

'True.'

'Well, then, don't just actions produce justice, and unjust actions injustice?'

'They must.'

'And health is produced by establishing a natural relation of control and subordination among the constituents of the body, disease by establishing an unnatural relation.'

'True.'

'So justice is produced by establishing in the mind a similar natural relation of control and subordination among its constituents, and injustice by establishing an unnatural one.'

'Certainly.'

'It seems, then, that excellence is a kind of mental health or beauty or fitness, and defect a kind of illness or deformity or weakness.'

'That is so.'

'And each is in turn the result of one's practice, good or bad.'

'They must be.'

1.5

PLATONIC CHARACTER TYPE INDEX (PCTI)

The PCTI is an informal self-analytical tool that can help you begin identifying which part of your psyche or "soul" is dominant in your life at this time. Knowledge of this fact can help you to understand better the internal workings of your "Platonic character type." Such information can also suggest paths for future character development and healthy personality maintenance. Your results are not intended to be scientifically valid, but rather suggestive. (I am not sure the soul lends itself very well to empirical, scientific investigation!) The accuracy of the results ultimately will be determined by your own rational self-analysis or, should I say, "philosophical psychoanalysis."

Instructions

Next to each phrase below, indicate how reflective of you the item, action or activity is. Unless absolutely necessary, try to avoid 3 as your answer. Answering 3 too often will not likely reveal any character preferences.

1 = not reflective of me at all
2 = hardly reflective of me
3 = moderately reflective of me
4 = very reflective of me
5 = exactly reflective of me

How accurate would it be to say that you

_____ 1. seek truth

_____ 2. wish to become famous

_____ 3. want to make large sums of money

_____ 4. enjoy being carefree

_____ 5. experience pleasure through artificial or chemical means

_____ 6. trust thinking more than sensory perception

_____ 7. are competitive

_____ 8. wish strongly to live a materially comfortable lifestyle

_____ 9. avoid restrictions and restraints

_____ 10. look out for number one

_____ 11. pursue knowledge (as opposed to data or information)

_____ 12. have difficulty dealing with subordinates (those lower in rank)

_____ 13. do not waste time on activities that have little financial payoff

_____ 14. treat all wants as equal

_____ 15. do what you want regardless of the consequences for other people

_____ 16. control your physical urges and biological appetites

_____ 17. want to be liked by others

_____ 18. value being economical

_____ 19. live in the moment and for the moment

_____ 20. deceive people to get what you want

_____ 21. do what is right, putting aside personal feelings and wants

_____ 22. value achievement (fame) over money

_____ 23. avoid financial disaster

_____ 24. enjoy equally all the pleasures of life

_____ 25. fall prey to manias or compulsions

_____ 26. like intellectual thought

_____ 27. try to look successful to others

_____ 28. seize opportunities to better yourself economically

_____ 29. take life a day at a time

_____ 30. tell people whatever is necessary to get what you want

_____ 31. display temperance (moderation)

_____ 32. assume an attitude of superiority

_____ 33. work hard to ensure the basic necessities of life

_____ 34. do what feels good

_____ 35. take by force, if necessary

_____ 36. regulate personal habits

_____ 37. enjoy exhibitions of courage and strength

_____ 38. live consistently with the principle: Money first, then morality

_____ 39. frequently change your mind about what you want

_____ 40. display addictive behavior

Scoring

Next to each of the question numbers below, fill in your response. Add the total scores for each column and then plot them on your PCTI. See the example for help on how to do this.

PK	Tim	O	D	T
1	2	3	4	5
6	7	8	9	10
11	12	13	14	15
16	17	18	19	20
21	22	23	24	25
26	27	28	29	30
31	32	33	34	35
36	37	38	39	40
_____	_____	_____	_____	_____

	Totals
PK = Philosopher King/Ruler	_____
Tim = Timarchic Character	_____
O = Oligarchic Character	_____
D = Democratic Character	_____
T = Tyrannical Character	_____

Figure 1.1 PLATONIC CHARACTER TYPE BAR GRAPH INDEX

Example:

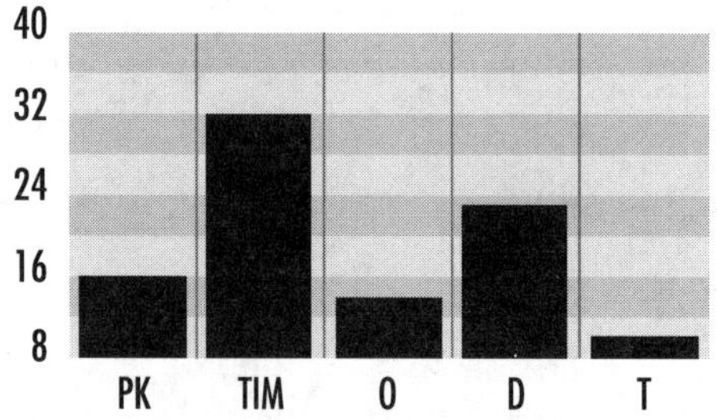

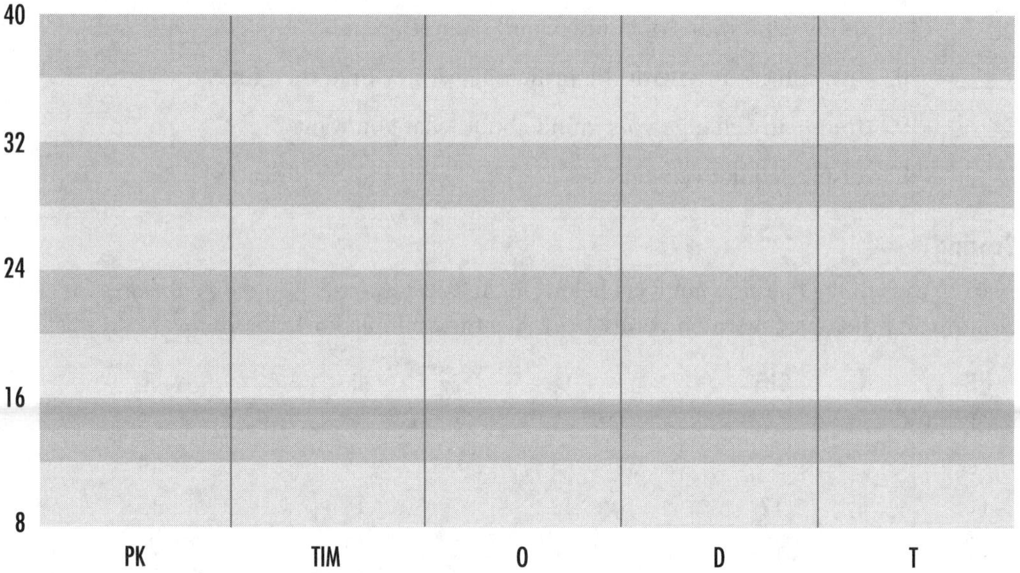

Interpretation

To learn what your results mean, refer to the abbreviated descriptions in Figure 1.2. More information on each character type is found in the main text (pp. 28 to 34). Note that you probably have a mixture of different character elements making up your personality. It is unlikely that anyone is purely one type. Nonetheless, the character type with the highest score may be most reflective of what you are like as a individual right now. Your responsibility is to decide for yourself. After reading the descriptions of the character types, you may be favorably impressed or you may feel the need to change as a result. The moral decision is yours!

Figure 1.2 ABBREVIATED DESCRIPTIONS OF PLATONIC CHARACTER TYPES

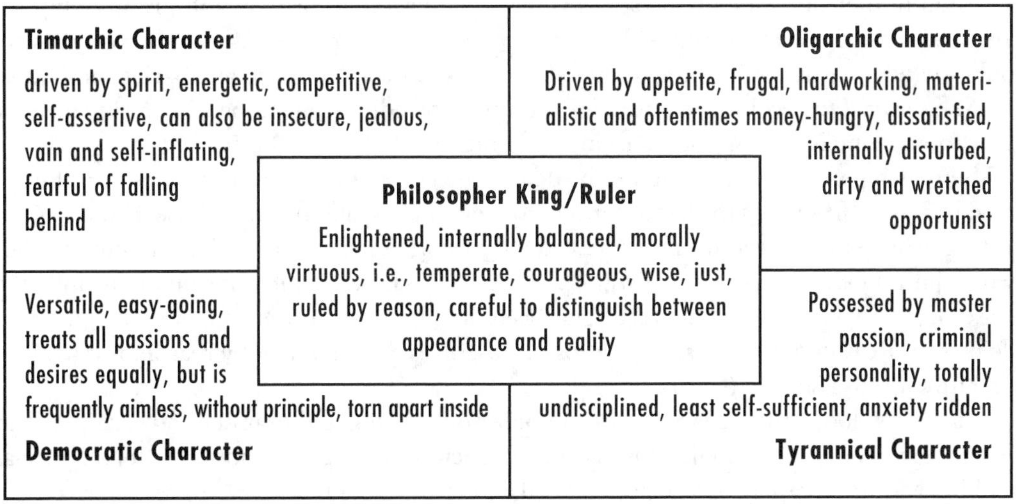

Timarchic Character
driven by spirit, energetic, competitive, self-assertive, can also be insecure, jealous, vain and self-inflating, fearful of falling behind

Oligarchic Character
Driven by appetite, frugal, hardworking, materialistic and oftentimes money-hungry, dissatisfied, internally disturbed, dirty and wretched opportunist

Philosopher King/Ruler
Enlightened, internally balanced, morally virtuous, i.e., temperate, courageous, wise, just, ruled by reason, careful to distinguish between appearance and reality

Versatile, easy-going, treats all passions and desires equally, but is frequently aimless, without principle, torn apart inside
Democratic Character

Possessed by master passion, criminal personality, totally undisciplined, least self-sufficient, anxiety ridden
Tyrannical Character

PLATO'S CHARACTER TYPES

Know thyself.

Socrates

In *The Republic*, differently functioning "souls" are described using the notion of **Plato's character types**. The ideal character is exemplified by the philosopher king or ruler. Corrupt, or should I say, imperfect types are called the timarchic, oligarchic, democratic and tyrannical characters. You will note that all of these types have political sounding labels. The reason for this, according to Plato, is that in each kind of societal structure there is a corresponding individual who is admired within it, so that in an oligarchy, for instance, the values and attributes of the oligarchic character are praised. Likewise in a timarchic society, the qualities you find in the timarchic person would be cherished. Understand that not every individual in a particular society necessarily displays the corresponding character type. Oligarchs can be found in democracies. Virtuous people can be found in tyrannies and so on. The point is that individuals give rise to societies that, in turn, praise the qualities possessed by those individuals.

An interesting parallel between individuals and societies can also be seen by looking at the **class system** proposed by Plato for the **just society**—the system that functions in harmonious balance. In the ideal or just society, there would emerge three classes of people corresponding to the three parts of the soul. Each class would serve different, but complementary, roles. First, there would be those whose lives would be driven primarily by the appetites. These would be the **craftsmen, artisans,** and **traders**. In modern terms, we might see these people as the workers, consumers, and business class. Second, there would be the **auxiliaries** (a subdivision of guardians), motivated in their lives mostly by spirit. They would serve to protect and preserve internal order under the guidance of rulers. Examples of people fitting into this class in today's world would include the police, militia, and civil servants. Third, from the auxiliaries, individuals would be selected to become the most highly trained and educated members of an elite guardian class proper, namely the philosopher kings (or rulers).

Membership in any class would not be determined by birth or inheritance; rather, children would be moved from class to class according to merit and capability. Only those who passed the most rigorous tests and who would be best suited to work for the good of the community would become philosopher rulers. In the just society, the lower classes would not gain undue influence or else an internal anarchy would result, just as it does in the soul when appetite or spirit overrule reason. Reason must rule as must those whose lives are governed by reason, not by greed (appetite) or self-assertion (spirit).

Let us now look at the character of the philosopher king and examine in more detail the corrupt character types located at lower levels of society. Though the notion that an elite class should govern society may not be popular today, Plato argued that:

> the human race will not be free of evils until either the stock of those who rightly and truly follow philosophy acquire political authority, or the class who have power in the cities be led by some dispensation of providence to become real philosophers.

In short, rulers must become philosophers or philosophers must become rulers if we are to establish the ideal society. Just as reason must rule the soul, so too must philosophers rule the social order if the just society is ever to become a reality.

PHILOSOPHERS AT WORK

What do you think about having a class system in society? Is our society presently governed by philosopher kings/rulers? What has been the result? Should the leaders in our society come from an intellectually and morally elite ruling class? Why or why not? If you object to a class system, is your honest objection to rule by an elite based on a hidden fear that you may not qualify to govern? *Comment.* If commitment to justice and truth does not make the philosopher king fit to rule, then what makes anyone a good social leader?

1.6
Philosopher Kings/Rulers

According to Plato, the just society is a form of **aristocracy**. In an aristocracy, **philosopher kings** who belong to the **guardian class** become the rulers. (Note no gender discrimination is intended by the use of the label "kings"—qualified women also would be selected to serve as rulers in Plato's aristocracy.)

Philosopher kings (or rulers) are morally virtuous individuals. They are **temperate**. No physical appetites or material desires enslave these individuals. Virtuous souls regulate their appetites by reason. Philosophers also display the virtue of **courage**, a passion that supports reason in its judgments and decisions to act. Plato says, "He is deemed courageous whose spirit retains in pleasure and in pain the commands of reason about what he ought or ought not to fear . . . ."

The morally virtuous person is also **wise**. The individual knows what is best for each part of the soul. A wise person "has in him that little part which rules, and which proclaims these commands [of reason]; that part too being supposed to have a knowledge of what is for the interest of each of the three parts of the whole. . . ." In addition, philosopher rulers are **just**. With respect to character, remember that just means balanced and **functioning harmoniously**. In the just character of the philosopher king, reason, emotion, and physical nature work well together, with reason in charge, of course. It is the faculty of reason that prevents inner rebellion and disorder of the soul. It establishes an internal constitution based on peaceful coexistence.

Besides being truly virtuous, another distinguishing characteristic about philosopher kings is that they have special knowledge. By an elaborate process of education, philosopher kings learn how to distinguish between appearance and reality. They learn how to acquaint themselves intellectually with the eternal and immutable **realm of forms**. The "forms," so-called, can be known only by reason and, according to Plato, are more real than the transitory things that we see, hear, taste, touch, and feel. Sensory experience can yield only imperfect approximations of the ideal forms. For example, it is rational acquaintance with the form "justice" that allows us to describe any act as fair or unfair, just or unjust. Even though we have never seen complete fairness or universal justice in the world, we still know what it is. Reason offers us perfect knowledge in an imperfect world. It shows us what the eyes have not seen.

The seen is the changing,
The unseen is the unchanging.
Plato

Those who fall prey to imperfect or **false knowledge** offered by the senses, and those who become morally side-tracked by the physical appetites or emotions, end up living disordered lives of ignorance and unhappiness. Philosopher rulers make no such mistake. They are not lured away from truth and moral goodness by misleading appearances, by the "drone's honey" or the "power monger's prestige and influence." Philosopher kings appreciate how such things can only end in moral bankruptcy and disillusionment. Philosopher kings are enlightened souls who are not entrapped by fantasies and temptations but are guided on the right path by the light of true moral goodness.

Now, before you bow down in humble worship of your philosophy teacher, understand that "being a philosopher king" today has nothing to do with occupation, but it has everything to do with character and disposition. A philosophy teacher may teach all the right things, but for selfish and vainglorious motives to which he or she will not admit. Joe or Jill Average, on the other hand, may display many, or all, of the philosopher king's virtues without ever teaching the subject itself. Be aware, then, that anybody, even the student sitting beside you in class, could be a "closet philosopher." Maybe it is time for you to come out of the "king's closet" yourself and to continue your character training as one of society's future guardians? Will you accept the call?

1.7
Timarchic Character

looking out for number one
Author

The dominant part of the soul that drives the **timarchic character** is spirit. People with timarchic characters are distinguished, in large part, by their energy, competitiveness, and the urge to dominate. For example, do you know anyone whose life seems to be based on "oneupmanship"? Can whatever story you have to tell be "bettered" by your timarchic friend? Is whatever you have done always been unfavorably compared or belittled by your timarchic friend's (alleged) superior performance? In short, does it seem that being with this person (maybe you) is like being engulfed in a continual struggle, an athletic contest or a battle of wills? If so, then you can appreciate what this character type brings to the table of life.

Timarchic characters are self-assertive individuals. They like to be "out there" making impressions on people or at least trying to do so. No matter how favorable the impression made or how successful the person is, they still retain a nagging insecurity. Reputations must be maintained, people must continue to be impressed; nobody else must be allowed to dominate, control or look better. Life at the top of the ladder of success is very precarious. Once at the top, there is only one way to go—down—down in the estimation of others and, hence, down in one's own estimation. The pride and ambition characterizing timarchic persons can thus create only a very thin veneer of confidence. Below the surface, these people fear that they will fall behind, be defeated, humiliated or embarrassed, that approval from others will be withdrawn at any time. These fears will manifest themselves in jealousy as timarchic persons begrudge the successes of others.

There is perhaps nothing worse than reaching the top of the ladder and discovering that you're on the wrong wall.
Joseph Campbell

A life based on single-minded ambition, for instance, investing years of life in aiming at winning an olympic gold medal in the shot-put event, may leave a person wasted and may result in financial ruin. Finishing twelfth, out of the medals and out of the record books, with no fame, no endorsements and possibly no perceived future could also leave the person embittered and insecure. Failed efforts at vainglorious pursuits are not always pretty to witness. With or without success, the timarchic character is destined to a life of underlying fears, jealousies, and insecurities. Ignorant of the fact that vanity and self-inflation cannot ultimately lead to a tranquil and balanced soul, timarchic characters will never achieve a true and lasting happiness. At best, they will achieve only a cheap and transitory semblance of it.

to gain insight into the depths of our reality . . . requires a very calm and quiet mind. It is impossible to see into the depths of a pool when it is turbulent.

S.N Goenka

1.7 Oligarchic Character

and the higher the prestige of wealth and the wealthy, the lower that of goodness and good men will be.

Plato

In a society where wealth dominates and the wealthy are in control (arguably, our own), the qualities of the **oligarchic character** are revered. In the oligarch, we discover a character transformation from the ambitious, competitive type of person to the money-loving businessperson. Suggesting that our own society is a form of oligarchy is probably an accurate assessment. After all, is it not true many people in North American society judge the worth of an individual by what that person owns? "How much are they worth?" we ask. Is it not a widespread belief that "you are a somebody, so called, because you own many expensive things"—that having a lot of cash makes you a V.I.P. (a very important person)? When people say they want to "better" themselves, is it not the case that they usually mean acquire more wealth and material possessions?

Of course, not everybody in contemporary society displays an oligarchic character. Those who do are simply the ones who are recognized and rewarded. They are the ones on the cover of *Fortune* magazine or featured in the *Financial Post* or *Wall Street Journal*. Wherever they are found, the oligarchs' main objective in life is to make money. In the oligarchic character, appetite rules and dominates the rest of the soul by a desire for riches. When reason is called upon, it is called upon only in the service of making more money. Spirit, by contrast, is "forbidden to admire or value anything but wealth and the wealthy, or to compete for anything but the acquisition of wealth and whatever leads to it."

The oligarch is frugal, economical, and hardworking. As little as possible is wasted on nonessentials. Hard effort is spent on trying to satisfy only necessary wants. Unnecessary wants and desires, which do not function to accumulate greater wealth, are regarded as pointless and, therefore, repressed.

The character imperfections of the oligarch are, perhaps, most plainly evident in the huckster, pedlar or hawker on late-night television infomercials. Plato says the oligarch possesses a squalid (dirty and wretched) character "always on the make and putting something by" others. The person who can "sell snow to an Eskimo," get you to buy more than what you wanted, or persuade you to purchase what you really do not need, is the one who becomes rich, famous, and admired.

In the oligarch, there is a dramatic movement from ambition to avarice. For the oligarch, there is no advantage to having a good name and a moral reputation if there are no financial rewards. Because money and profit are the basic driving forces behind the oligarchic character, the person will be dishonest when able. The only deterrent is fear of punishment; there is certainly no moral conviction or taming of desire by reason.

Grub first, then ethics.
Anonymous Oligarch

Plato described oligarchs as having dual personalities. They usually manage to maintain a certain degree of respectability as, on the whole, better desires master the worse. It is as if good and bad desires engage in a battle for dominance within the psyche. The unfortunate result is that oligarchic individuals are never really at peace within themselves. When the worse desires are subdued, the oligarch manages "a certain degree of respectability, but comes nowhere near the real goodness of an integrated and balanced character."

Finally, though some degree of social respectability can be achieved by oligarchs, they will likely make little significant contribution to public life, where money and profit may have to be sacrificed. An oligarch might ask, "Why be a politician, for example, when there is so little financial reward?" Do you know that the lowest paid hockey player in the National Hockey League has a greater "market value" and earns more money than the prime minister of Canada, the leader of thirty million people. Oligarchs would probably say, "Rightly so." When it comes to the worth of a man or woman, oligarchs would most likely let the market decide. Given the thinking of oligarchs, their achievements and ambitions in public life are not likely to amount to much, but, then again, they are also not likely to sustain large financial losses in pursuing vain ambitions of power or political glory.

The Good Life is getting everything you want,
provided that everything you want is good.
Author

1.7
Democratic Character

In contrast to the oligarchic character who distinguishes between necessary and unnecessary desires, the **democratic character** does not. All desires and appetites are treated equally. Democrats are charming but aimless individuals, spending as much money, time, and effort on necessary desires as on unnecessary ones. For the democratic personality, no pleasure is underprivileged, each gets its fair share of encouragement. This type of character lives from day to day, indulging in any momentary pleasure that presents itself. The pleasures are varied. Plato says:

> One day it's wine, women and song, the next water to drink and a strict diet; one day it's hard physical training, the next indolence and careless ease, and then a period of philosophic study. Often he takes to politics and keeps jumping to his feet and saying or doing whatever comes into his head. Sometimes all his ambitions and efforts are military, sometimes they are all directed to success in business. There's no order or restraint in his life, and he reckons his way of living is pleasant, free and happy, and sticks to it through thick and thin. (Plato, 1976, p. 381)

People displaying a democratic character are versatile because they lack principles. The problem is that if people do not live a rational, principled life, then diverse and incompatible pleasures, appetites, and passions can pull them in different directions at the same time. Their personalities are, consequently, not integrated and functioning harmoniously. Individuals with a democratic character are torn apart inside. As Plato says, there is no order or restraint. Rather, there is disorder and lack of control. Persons obsessively pursuing different and sometimes conflicting pleasures cannot avoid becoming disorganized and fragmented. Their lives exhibit a definite lack of rational coherence and direction. Democrats are like children in a candy store. They are excited but torn apart inside because they want everything in the store at the same time—and this is impossible.

These are my principles. If you don't like them, I have others.
Groucho Marx

Plato speculates about how the democratic character is formed. He believes that children raised in a strict oligarchic household, where unnecessary pleasures have been denied, eventually are lured by those people outside the family who do enjoy them. A basic diet, for instance, becomes insufficient or unsatisfactory. A desire grows for luxurious and exotic food. Simple tastes are replaced by sophisticated and extravagant ones. Unnecessary desires, immediate pleasures, and extravagant tastes eventually transform the oligarchic person into a democratic character. Plato writes:

> When a young man, brought up in the narrow economical way we have described, gets a taste of the drones' honey and gets into brutal and dangerous company, where he can be provided with every variety and refinement of pleasure, . . . the result [is] that his internal oligarchy starts turning into a democracy. (Plato, *ibid.*, p. 378)

1.7
Tyrannical Character

an excessive desire for liberty at the expense of everything else is what undermines democracy and leads to the demand for tyranny.
Plato

According to Plato, the **tyrannical character** is the worst, being the most unhappy and undesirable. The tyrant personifies the criminal personality. People with a tyrannical character suffer from a kind of mania. As maniacs, they possess one **master passion** that controls all other idle desires. This master passion becomes so powerful that it runs wild, causing madness in the individual. The object of this passion may be sex, alcohol or other drugs. In the tyrannical personality's pursuit of pure pleasure, no shame or guilt is experienced. All discipline is swept away and usurped by madness. Tyrannical people are thus the least self-sufficient of all individuals. Their satisfaction depends entirely on external things and objects of maniacal desire. The tyrant is full of anxiety and constantly trying to fulfill his or her unrelenting appetite for more. Tyrants will do anything and everything to satisfy themselves, even if they must perform terrible deeds and become hated in the process. Tyrants' lives are lawless and disgusting. Though all of us have aggressive, bestial, and erotic urges—evidenced especially in dreams—most of us are able to control them; the tyrant, however, cannot.

If and when tyrants have spent all of their money indulging their master passion, they will start borrowing to satisfy it. When they are no longer able to borrow, they may proceed to rob, commit fraud or engage in acts of violence. Tyrannical characters become thieves, pickpockets, kidnappers, church robbers, and murderers to satisfy their manias. From this fact alone, it should be clear why tyrants are the most morally corrupt of all character types.

PHILOSOPHERS AT WORK

Pick out a well-known personality or a notorious individual from contemporary society, or history, if you prefer. The person could be an actor, sports celebrity, villain, businessperson, literary figure or fictional character from any book, movie or television show. Examine and appraise that person's actions, intentions, and motivations. What Platonic character type does that individual display? Give support for your answer.

MINDWORK MEDITATION

Now that you know more about philosopher kings and corrupt character types, reexamine your results and the Platonic Character Type Index (p. 23). Do you think the results are accurate for you? What changes, if any, will you have to make to more closely approximate the philosopher king? What appetites and/or passions will you have to better control to achieve psychological equilibrium or inner peace?

Key Terms

teleology
soul
reason
spirit
appetite
desire
passion
functional explanation of morality
moral balance
moral virtue
appearance
reality
Plato's character types
class system
just society
craftsmen
artisans
traders
auxiliaries
aristocracy
philosopher kings
guardian class
temperate
courage
wise
just
functioning harmoniously
realm of forms
false knowledge
timarchic character
oligarchic character
democratic character
tyrannical character
master passion

Progress Check 1.1

Instructions: Fill in the blanks with the appropriate responses listed below.

The Republic
soul
reason
oligarchic
forms
teleology
timarchic
auxiliaries
tyrannical
self-assertion
guardian
Academy
ignorance
harmonious balance
physical

1. In Athens, Plato founded the _____, a place of higher learning where questions of philosophy were discussed.
2. Plato's most famous writing is a book called _____.
3. If the human soul is to function properly, it must maintain a(n) _____ of psychic elements.
4. According to Plato's doctrine of _____, everything in nature has a proper function to perform.
5. Plato conceptualizes human nature as of a three-part division of the _____.
6. The appetite element of human nature looks after our _____ wants, needs, and desires.
7. Spirit or passion is that element of human nature aimed at _____, reputation, and honor.
8. _____is that which allows us to calculate, measure, and predict events.
9. For Plato, the cause of moral wrong-doing and evil is _____.
10. Philosopher kings/rulers belong to the _____ class of Plato's just society.
11. The most wretched of all character types is the _____ character.
12. The money-hungry person is captured in Plato's description of the _____ character.
13. Competitive and self-willed individuals possess a(n) _____ character.
14. In the class-based utopian society proposed by Plato, _____ would serve to protect and maintain order under the directorship of the philosopher kings.
15. Philosopher kings/rulers have special knowledge. They have a rational acquaintance with the realm of _____.

Summary of Major Points

1. What are the two basic moral questions raised by Plato?
   What constitutes the good life?
   What sort of individual should one strive to become?
2. What is meant by teleology?
   A doctrine stating that the development of anything follows from the purpose for which it was designed.
   According to this notion, something is good to the extent that it performs its function well.

3. **What is Plato's vision of the soul?**
   Three parts: appetite, spirit, and reason.
   Each part aims at different things—
   e.g., appetite: physical wants and needs;
   spirit: drive toward action and self-assertion;
   reason: the ruling faculty of the soul; it aims at knowledge, wisdom, and understanding.

4. **What is the difference between a healthy and an unhealthy soul?**
   A healthy soul is balanced with reason in control.
   An unhealthy soul is imbalanced and disordered with appetite or spirit overcoming the rule of reason.

5. **What is ignorance? What are the results of ignorance?**
   It is expressed by an imbalanced soul operating in disharmony.
   It leads to the pursuit of apparent goods, not real ones.
   It gives rise to evil and moral corruption.
   It is a confusion between appearance and reality.

6. **What is Plato's just society like?**
   It is based on a class system.
   Its classes include: workers, auxiliaries, and guardians.
   The just society functions harmoniously with guardians in charge.
   Its workers are driven by appetites.
   Its auxiliaries are motivated by spirit.
   Its guardian class is ruled by reason.

7. **What are Plato's character types? What are they like?**
   Philosopher king/ruler: governed by reason; member of the guardian class; harmonious personality; virtuous, i.e., temperate, courageous, wise, and just; possesses knowledge of the realm of forms.
   Timarchic character: spirit dominated; competitive; insecure; self-willed.
   Oligarchic character: driven by appetite; disillusioned by goals of timarchic character; replaces ambition with avarice; replaces pride with greed; squalid character; lacks moral convictions and inner peace.
   Democratic character: treats all appetites and desires equally; charming but aimless; versatile but lacking in principles; extravagant tastes; lacks order and restraint.
   Tyrannical character: worst type; most unhappy; possessed by a master passion or mania; has no guilt or shame; least self-sufficient of all types; no control over aggressive, bestial urges; quite capable of fraud, deceit, and all types of illegal behavior.

Source References and Related Readings

Albert, Ethel, Theodore Denise, and Sheldon P. Peterfreund. *Great Traditions in Ethics*, 5th edition. Belmont Ca.: Wadsworth, 1984.

Bloom, Allan. *The Republic of Plato*, 2nd edition. New York: Basic Books, 1968.

Falikowski, Anthony. *Moral Philosophy: Theories, Skills, and Applications*. Englewood Cliffs, N.J.: Prentice Hall, 1990.

Plato. *The Republic*, 2nd edition. Translated by Desmond Lee. Middlesex, England: Penguin Books, 1976.

Stumpf, Samuel Enoch. *Socrates to Sartre: A History of Philosophy*, 5th edition. Toronto: McGraw-Hill Inc., 1993.

Wolff, Robert Paul. *About Philosophy*, 6th edition. Upper Saddle River, N.J.: Prentice Hall, 1996.

CHAPTER TWO

2 ARISTOTLE: VIRTUE AND VICE, THE GOOD LIFE IS NICE

Overview

Biographical Brief "Aristotle"
Aristotle's Teleology
Happiness or "*Eudaimonia*" and the Ends of Human Life
- Types of Ends
- Happiness as the Ultimate End
- Features of the Ultimate End
- The Good Life as a Fulfillment of our Distinctive Function

Alternative Lifestyles
- The Lifestyle of Pleasure and Appetite Gratification
- The Statesman's Lifestyle
- The Contemplative Lifestyle as the Highest Form of Human Functioning
- Virtue and the Virtuous Lifestyle
  - Kinds of Virtue: Intellectual and Moral
  - Doctrine of the Mean

Back to the Source Feature from Aristotle's *Nichomachean Ethics*
Key Terms
Progress Check 2.1
Summary of Major Points
Source References and Related Readings

Learning Outcomes:

After successfully completing this chapter, you will be able to:

2.1 provide historical background information on Aristotle;
2.2 explain Aristotle's teleology using the concept of "entelechy";
2.3 describe the various ends of humanity;
2.4 explain why happiness or eudaimonia is the ultimate end;

2.5 appreciate better how the good life is tied to successful living;
2.6 identify our uniquely human function as living organisms;
2.7 compare and contrast alternative lifestyles;
2.8 give Aristotle's reasoning behind the claim that the contemplative lifestyle is the highest form of human functioning;
2.9 describe the role of virtue in our pursuit of happiness;
2.10 define and understand Aristotle's Doctrine of the Mean;
2.11 outline the conditions for truly virtuous behavior.

PHILOSOPHICAL FOCUS QUESTIONS

1. In what sense is Aristotle's philosophy a self-realization ethic?
2. How does Aristotle's teleology differ from that of Plato?
3. What kinds of ends in life do people pursue?
4. What is the ultimate good in human life?
5. How is it that people "miss the mark" in their lives and fail to find happiness?
6. What lifestyle is most befitting of human beings? Why?
7. In what sense does the virtuous lifestyle lead to a secondary form of happiness?
8. What is meant by Aristotle's Doctrine of the Mean?

2.1

LIBRARY OF CONGRESS

Aristotle (384-322 B.C.)

BIOGRAPHICAL BRIEF*

Aristotle was born in Stagira in 384 B.C. He was the son of a physician who lived and worked at the royal court of Amyntas II, king of Macedonia. At the age of 17 Aristotle went to Athens to enroll at the Academy. For 20 years he worked and studied under Plato, for whom he had respect as a philosopher and good feelings as a friend. Upon the death of Plato, Aristotle left Athens and spent a number of years in Asia Minor, where he married Pythias, the niece of a local king. Aristotle eventually returned to Macedonia, in order to become tutor to the heir of the throne, namely Alexander, who later became known as Alexander the Great. After an 8-year stay in Macedonia, he left again for Athens in 335–334 B.C. In Athens, Aristotle established a new school called the Lyceum. It was patterned after Plato's Academy insofar as community life,

**From Falikowski,* Moral Philosophy, *p. 17.*

friendliness, intent on learning, and dialogue were emphasized. Many of Aristotle's dialogues with students were conducted while strolling down a garden path (peripatos). In view of this, followers of Aristotle have come to be know as "peripatetics." In 323 B.C. Aristotle felt compelled to leave Athens again. Alexander the Great died suddenly while returning from one of his Asian conquests. The Athenians, who were under the yoke of Alexander, regarded his death as an opportunity to rid themselves of Macedonian control. Knowing his Macedonian ties and fearing the prospect of having to stand trial for impiety like Socrates, Aristotle fled Athens. He died in exile one year later in 322 B.C.Aristotle's wife died somewhat earlier. Aristotle's son, Nichomachus, after whom *Nichomachean Ethics* is named, was born as a product of a domestic union with Herpyllis.

Aristotle wrote on subjects as varied as logic, ethics, aesthetics, metaphysics, biology, physics, psychology, and politics. He had a profound influence on medieval Hebrew, Arabic, and Christian philosophers, most notably Saint Thomas Aquinas and his later scholastic followers who helped to formulate the official moral theology of the Catholic Church. Works by Aristotle include: *Categories, Prior and Posterior Analytics, Physics, On the Heavens, On the Soul, Metaphysics, Nichomachean Ethics, Politics, Rhetoric,* and *Eudemian Ethics.*

2.2
ARISTOTLE'S TELEOLOGY

Aristotle begins ***Nichomachean Ethics*** with the following words: "Every craft and every investigation, and likewise every action and decision, seems to aim at some good." He points out, for example, that health is the end of medicine, a ship is the end of shipbuilding, victory is the end of military leadership, and wealth is the end of household management or home economics. This focus on the ends of human activity is what makes Aristotle a **teleologist**. For him, all human action has a purpose or an end to achieve.

Like his mentor Plato, Aristotle incorporates within his teleological framework a functional explanation of morality—in this case, a kind of **self-realization ethic**. In his efforts to understand what constitutes the ultimate good or end of life, Aristotle examines human activity in terms of its function. He says:

> perhaps we shall find the best good if we first find the function of a human being. For just as the good, i.e. [doing] well, for a flautist, a sculptor, and every craftsman, and, in general, for whatever has a function and [characteristic] action, seems to depend on its function, the same seems to be true for a human being, if a human being has some function. (Aristotle, 1985, pp. 15-16)

If on this functional account, a good flautist, say, is one that plays well, then a good life is one that is well-lived and good persons are those who perform their distinctively human function well or with excellence. To better appreciate how the good life is tied to function, let us consider briefly Aristotle's notion of "**entelechy**" (pronounced en-tel-e-key). Aristotle maintained that every living thing in nature possesses an "inner urge" to become its unique self. An acorn has the inner urge to become an oak tree; a newborn child has something within itself to become an adult and so on. If each and every thing has an end within itself to achieve, i.e., its entelechy, then things do not just happen randomly, but develop according to their natural design or designated purpose.

Now, whereas an acorn cannot become a willow tree, due to its own entelechy, humans can by contrast, as more complex and self-willed organisms, fail to actualize their inner potentialities and, consequently, fail to express their entelechy. In ways soon to be illustrated, we, as humans, can fail ourselves at our own self-realization by missing the mark and following paths that take us away from our essential or "true selves." We can "mis-function," so to speak, and become less than what we were meant to become by natural design. By examining Aristotle's notions of happiness and the ends of human life, we can discover how and why we often fall short of living the good life and actualizing our potentialities.

2.3 HAPPINESS OR "*EUDAIMONIA*" AND THE ENDS OF HUMAN LIFE

Although Plato and Aristotle are both teleologists who offer us a functional explanation of morality, their similarities abruptly end when it comes to their efforts to locate the source of true goodness in life. Plato maintained that knowledge of the good had to be discovered apart from the concrete world of everyday experience. One had to go beyond the tangible world, where things are imperfect and transitory, to a world of unchanging and immutable forms. Knowledge of goodness required, for Plato, a rational acquaintance with a supernatural realm. By contrast, Aristotle worked from experience and common sense beliefs to identify the ultimate good of humankind.

though we love both the truth and our friends [namely Plato], piety requires us to honor the truth first.

Aristotle

Grounding his reasoning, then, on people's experience and beliefs, as well as on common sense and human observation, Aristotle concluded that, no matter who you are or where you live, **happiness** is the ultimate end of life. As he points out, people from all walks of life believe that it is happiness toward which all of human behavior is ultimately aimed. To understand more precisely what is meant by happiness and in what sense it is ultimate, let us examine Aristotle's distinctions among the various types of ends that people pursue.

Types of Ends

In the *Nichomachean Ethics*, Aristotle discusses a hierarchy of goods corresponding to a **hierarchy of ends**. Ends can be **instrumental**, **intrinsic**, or **ultimate**. When we pursue a good corresponding to an instrumental end, we want to achieve that end because we think it will lead to something else further down the road. For instance, your goal next summer may be to get a job picking tomatoes. This would be, with little doubt, not an end in itself, but a means to a further end, say, earning a paycheque. While earning a paycheque is a pretty good end, the paycheque itself is a means to a further end, perhaps the purchase of a new car. You may be dreaming about buying a flashy automobile so that you can impress your friends; yet, on closer inspection, even this turns out to be only a means. One could ask why it is that you want to impress your friends. Whatever answer you give to this question points to a still more distant end. Instrumental ends are never for themselves, but for the sake of something else.

Intrinsic ends are different from instrumental ends. Acts performed for their intrinsic worth are performed for their own sake. They are valued in themselves, not because of what they produce or what they lead to. Wars, for example, do not have intrinsic value; they are fought to achieve such things as liberty and justice. Even victory in war is not an end in itself, according to Aristotle, for it is simply a means to create the conditions by which people, as human beings, can fulfill their purpose. But to ask why someone wants liberty or justice would be somewhat bewildering because it is generally accepted that such things have intrinsic value, that they are good in themselves.

Recognizing that there are many "goods" relating to different kinds of ends, Aristotle discusses what captures the highest good or ultimate end of life. For him, it is "happiness" or, as the Greeks call it, "*eudaimonia.*"

Happiness lies in the absorption in some vocation which satisfies the soul.
Sir William Osler

Being "happy", unlike say being intelligent, is not a matter of having some power or disposition; it is a matter of exercising one's powers and realizing one's dispositions.
Jonathan Barnes

All the things I really like to do are either immoral, illegal or fattening.
Alexander Woolcott

2.4
Happiness as the Ultimate End

Viewing happiness or ***eudaimonia*** as the ultimate end of human conduct means that no matter whether we want a job picking tomatoes, an automobile, victory in war or peace in the land, the reason is really that we want to be happy when all is said and done. Jobs, automobiles, and other things are instrumental goods pointing to something beyond themselves. They are not final and, hence, do not represent ultimate goodness.

Aristotle is careful to distinguish happiness as the ultimate good from other things like physical pleasure and amusement. For Aristotle, happiness is serious business that takes us beyond mere fun and the satisfaction of bodily urges. Although such things, no doubt, are pleasurable and have their rightful place in human experience, they cannot serve as the ultimate basis for living the good life. Even something as noble sounding as moral virtue cannot, for Aristotle, capture ultimate goodness. Many would agree that moral virtue has intrinsic value—"virtue is its own reward"—however, it is possible that we could live a virtuous life in misery and pain, seriously undermining anything that could be described as a happy or good life. Courageous and just people can suffer illness and misfortune that makes their lives something far less than happy. Thus, while moral virtue is an intrinsic end, it is, nonetheless, incomplete.

Because moral virtue is not self-sufficient, it too cannot serve as the ultimate basis of the good life. Make no mistake about the fact that morality is a good for Aristotle; the point is that moral activity represents a **secondary form of happiness**, subordinate to something still higher. Going back to amusement and sensuality for a moment, though they are surely pleasurable, they are not as enduring and secure as other forms of higher pleasure which lie beyond them. This is why they are subordinate as well in the hierarchy of human goods.

Features of the Ultimate End

Aristotle argues that the **ultimate end of life** must fulfill three conditions. First, the ultimate end must be **self-sufficient**, in a way that moral virtue alone is not. It must make life desirable and lack nothing. Second, this end must be **final**. It must be desirable in itself. In this sense, the ultimate good is intrinsically, not instrumentally, valuable. Third, this end must be **attainable**. A goal that cannot be achieved in principle may lead to such things as frustration and despair. For Aristotle, the only end that is final, self-sufficient, and attainable is happiness. If in the end, however, happiness is not about fun, pleasure, sensuality or amusement, then the question still remains, "What is it?"

we regard something as self-sufficient when all by itself it makes a life choiceworthy and lacking nothing; and that is what we think happiness does.

Aristotle

2.5

In his introductory remarks to Aristotle's *Nichomachean Ethics*, Jonathan Barnes elaborates upon *eudaimonia*, the Greek term for happiness, to help us understand what Aristotle meant by it. Barnes uses *eudaimonia* to point out, for example, that Aristotle is not a **hedonist**. Happiness (or *eudaimonia*) is not about the pursuit of pleasure, something many of us equate it with. Although happiness contributes to an enjoyable life, it is not about having a constant succession of pleasurable experiences. The Greek concept of *eudaimonia*, Barnes tells us, should be understood as "well-living" and "well-acting." Happiness is a normative or value-related concept, not an emotional or psychological one. Happiness is not a feeling, but a mode of living. To express it otherwise, it is not a **state**, but an **activity**. Barnes goes on to suggest that, "The notion of *eudaimonia* is closely tied, in a way in which the English common sense notion of happiness is not, to **success**: the *eudaimon* is the man who makes a success of his life and actions, who realizes his aims and ambitions as a man, who fulfils himself" (Thomson, 1974, p. 34). Barnes does not wish to reduce Aristotle's concept of happiness to success, but his reading of Aristotle does lead him to the conclusion that in the *Nichomachean Ethics* we are not directly being told how to be morally good people or even how to be humanly happy. Barnes maintains that Aristotle is, in fact, trying to explain to us how to live successful human lives and how to fulfill ourselves as human beings. If this is so, then the *Nichomachean Ethics* is more about character development than about moral behavior.

PHILOSOPHERS AT WORK

Using Aristotelian insights, explore the relationship between achievement and success. Are the two notions roughly equivalent? Why or why not? Is it possible to achieve and to fail in life at the same time? Explain.

2.6
The Good Life as a Fulfillment of our Distinctive Function

Aristotle's search for our **distinctive function** as human beings begins with a comparison between plants and people. He finds that plants and humans share life in common; that is, they are both living organisms, they both grow, develop, and take in nourishment in the process. Aristotle thus concludes that mere existence based on nutrition (eating, drinking) and growth is not peculiar to human beings. We share these aspects of life with plants.

Aristotle next compares us with animals. Humans share with animals a sensory capacity to experience the world. In this respect, sense perception or sensuality make us no different than a horse, an ox or any other animal for that matter. A life committed to sensation and physical appetite gratification is, therefore, not befitting of humans; it is the life of cattle and sheep. (As an aside, it is interesting how Aristotle's thinking here still exists in popular culture centuries after it was introduced. People who overindulge their physical or sexual appetites are often unkindly referred to today as "pigs"—of course, no offense is intended to that species of animal. Others, whose lives are largely devoted to doing nothing but lazing around all day, are said to be "vegging-out" or living like "couch-potatoes"—again, no offense is intended to the humble Idaho or lowly spud from Prince Edward Island. On a more serious note, we even sometimes consider terminating the lives of so-called "vegetables"—people on life support systems who manage to survive, but show virtually no human response. Some say such a life is not worth living. In some people's minds, being human involves activity beyond mere existence.)

In Aristotle's account, the fulfillment of our distinctively human function involves the exercise of our **rational capacities**. He says, "Now we take the human function to be a certain kind of life, and take this life to be the soul's activity and actions that express reason." Shortly, we will look at why the rational lifestyle is most befitting of humans, but before we do, let us examine some **alternative lifestyles** that fall short of the human ideal of the good life. Once we know what the good life is not, we will be better able to appreciate what it is.

When asked how much money it takes to make someone happy,
the rich billionaire replied "Just a little more."
Author

Pleasure is the bait of sin.
Plato

2.7
ALTERNATIVE LIFESTYLES

The Lifestyle of Pleasure and Appetite Gratification

Many individuals believe that happiness and the good life are found in the **lifestyle of pleasure and appetite gratification**. The accumulation of large sums of money, for instance, allows people to satisfy their desires. Yet, money has only instrumental worth. Coins and bank notes have no intrinsic value. They are simply used to acquire other things beyond themselves. Money is merely a means.

Money can't buy happiness.
Perennial Wisdom

For Aristotle, happiness is also not about pleasure; remember, he is not a hedonist. For him, to see life primarily or exclusively as the pursuit of pleasure would be to advocate for people an existence suitable for pigs and cattle. Besides, pleasure must be a lesser good because it too is an instrumental end. We pursue pleasure because we believe it will make us happy. If we did not think this, then we would not bother chasing it in our lives. Pleasure is again the means or a way to become happy—or so many think. Paradoxically, pursuit of pleasure is what often makes us miserable. As the Buddhist reminds us, desire or "craving" is the source of human suffering. Even if we manage to satisfy our cravings, we run the risk of oversatisfaction leading to such things as obesity and addiction. Like the young child who plays with scissors that could cause injury, we sometimes crave lower pleasures that, in the end, could hurt us.

The Statesman's Lifestyle

Some people recognize the "vulgarity" of a life devoted to the endless pursuit of pleasure, so they pursue what, in their minds, is a higher or more noble good. They choose to live **the statesman's lifestyle** of action where honor is paramount. As with the pursuit of pleasure, Aristotle rejects this lifestyle as humanity's highest good. Such a life depends too much on the fickle opinions of others. We may work for a long time to gain their approval, an approval that can be withdrawn at any time. Even if virtue, not honor, is regarded as the end of political life, problems still exist. Virtuous people can suffer terrible evils and misfortunes. Their life's circumstances may prevent them from acting and expressing their virtues publically. Lack of resources, for instance, may stop them from doing what they want to do or what they believe ought to be done. Furthermore, as with pleasure, the goods of the statesman are subordinate goods because they remain instrumentally valuable. People seek honor because they believe that it will make them happy. If honor did not make them happy and if, say, misery were its result, then honor would cease to be sought as an end. Happiness is *not* sought for the sake of honor; honor is sought for the sake of happiness. Honor is, therefore, something lower in the hierarchy of human goods.

2.7
2.8

The love of study, a passion which derives fresh vigor from enjoyment, supplies each day and hour with a perpetual source of independent and rational pleasure.
Gibbon (1737–1794)

Mental pleasures never cloy [stop up]; unlike those of the body, they are increased by repetition, approved by reflection, and strengthened by enjoyment.
Nathaniel Cotton

The Contemplative Lifestyle as the Highest Form of Human Functioning

As previously discussed, Aristotle maintains that it is in the exercise of our rational capacities that we distinguish ourselves from plant life and animal existence. It is reason that makes us unique and it is in rational activity that we express our true selves or entelechy. In view of this, Aristotle defines **the good life** in rational terms. He says, "the best and most pleasant life is the life of the intellect, since the intellect is in the fullest sense the man [human being]. So this life will also be the happiest."

In Book 1 of *Nichomachean Ethics*, Aristotle expresses the nature of happiness in the following terms: "an activity of the soul in accordance with virtue." It is interesting to note that, "Being 'happy', unlike, say, being intelligent, is not a matter of having some power or disposition; it is a matter of exercising one's powers and realizing one's dispositions" (Thomson, *ibid.*, p. 35). Happiness is not an emotional state or psychological condition, but an activity, a doing of the mind.

The world is a comedy to those who think, a tragedy to those who feel.
Proverb

Do not be confused by Aristotle's use of the term "**soul**" in the quotation above. For Aristotle, having a soul simply means to be alive or animate in ways that inanimate (souless) objects like rocks are not. Activities of the soul are those things that living creatures can do by nature's design. Growth and sensation are aspects of the soul shared with plants and animals. The highest part of the soul involves the activity of reasoning. Now, if the good thing is that which performs its function well, then for Aristotle, the teleologist, the good person is one who reasons well, like a virtuoso, we might say. To reason "in accordance with virtue" is not to display some kind of saintliness. To reason in accordance with virtue means that one reasons in an excellent way, i.e., that one performs the rational function well.

Aristotle reasons that **the contemplative lifestyle** is humanity's highest good because, first, it is most self-sufficient. A lifestyle based on pleasure and enjoyment or political honor, for example, requires many externals and accessories. By contrast, people can practice contemplation alone, without much else, or at least less than the other two lifestyles require. Second, contemplation is intrinsically choiceworthy. "Nothing is gained from it except the act of contemplation, whereas from [other] practical activities we expect to gain something more or less over and above the action." Third, contemplation provides the purest pleasure with the greatest permanence and enduring qualities. The contemplative lifestyle also provides great leisure and as much freedom from fatigue as is humanly possible. Pursuing politics and pleasure gives little time for rest. Aristotle even goes so far as to suggest that the contemplative life transcends mere mortal existence and becomes something god-like. When we engage in rational activity, he says, we express that within us which is **divine**.

To act is human, to reason is divine.
Author

You will never rest until you know your function and fulfill it, for only in this can your will and your Father's be wholly joined. To have Him is to be like Him, and He has given Himself to you. You who have God must be as God, for His function became yours with His gift. Invite this knowledge back into your mind, and let nothing that obscures it enter.
A Course in Miracles

As an eminently common-sense philosopher, Aristotle recognizes the obstacles and difficulties that can easily prevent the attainment of happiness. A good life can be marred, for example, by a bad or an untimely death. Aristotle also argues that happiness must be seen in the context of a complete life. People cannot be said to have lived happy lives by virtue of some momentary state or life event. Unlike pleasure or ecstasy, happiness cannot be short-lived.

PHILOSOPHERS AT WORK

People often say that winning the lottery would make them happy or that buying new clothes or a new car would make them happy or that having sex with an attractive partner would make them happy. How would Aristotle reply? What do you think would make you happy? If Aristotle were alive today, how would he respond to you? How would you respond to him?

Although riches cannot guarantee happiness (witness all the unhappy millionaires), Aristotle recognizes how, practically speaking, they can help out a lot. It is easier to be happy if you are rich than if you are penniless and living out on the streets. Sure, having a good mental attitude and positive outlook on life are important to happiness, but so too is physical health. Aristotle would say that you cannot be happy in the fullest sense if, for example, you are chronically ill, unattractive or if you are mentally deficient. Put simply, things can get in the way of anyone's personal happiness. A certain amount of luck is required.

Life is difficult, then you die.

Existentialist saying

Another way to look at the good life is to see it as some kind of **balancing process**. "The highest and fullest happiness, according to Aristotle, comes from a life of reason and contemplation—not a life of inactivity or imbalance, but a rationally ordered life in which intellectual, physical and social needs are all met under the governance of reason and moderation" (Soccio, 1995, p. 194). Think of the workaholic striving to become rich and successful. That person may gain in wealth, but miss much in life. He or she may seldom slow down enough to appreciate life's blessings or hardly ever stop to smell the roses. Also, the person trying to find happiness in public life will usually be insecure and less self-sufficient than most. Famous people may easily fall out of favor. They may need security guards and advisors or a whole entourage of people for personal support. People in public life lack an independence or self-sufficiency that is provided by the contemplative life.

PHILOSOPHERS AT WORK

Many advertisers present us with images of "the good life" in their product commercials. What are some of those images? Viewing these commercials from an Aristotelian perspective, what could be said about them? Do you think the advertisers can deliver on their promises? Discuss.

2.7
2.9

Virtue and the Virtuous Lifestyle

As intimated earlier, the life of unbroken contemplation is something god-like or divine for Aristotle. As something less than gods, however, most of us can aspire to live that kind of life for only brief periods at a time. In fact, many of us cannot hope realistically to live it at all because of our life circumstances, temperaments, and character dispositions. All people for some of the time, and many people for all of the time, therefore, must be contented with the performance of the second best of human activities. Although a divinely gifted few are capable of constant rational contemplation of knowledge and the truth, happiness for most of us "mere mortals" will consist in the practice of **virtue** and living an upright life (Thomson, 1974, p. 39). This being the case, let us examine Aristotle's understanding of virtue and the virtuous lifestyle so we can place happiness within reach of ordinary individuals. Although we should not discourage efforts to achieve ultimate happiness found only through rational contemplation, we should recognize our personal and practical limitations and work toward "secondary happiness" as necessary.

Journey toward the ultimate good, for if you fall short of your destination, you will still find yourself on the road to happiness.

Author

Kinds of Virtue: Intellectual and Moral: For Aristotle, there are two kinds of virtue: **intellectual** and **moral**. Intellectual virtue involves things like wisdom and understanding and is acquired chiefly through instruction. Moral virtue, by contrast, includes things like temperance and patience and results as a product of **habit**. When we speak of individuals as morally good persons, we are referring not to their intellectual activities but to their feelings and actions—the elements of moral virtue.

Using Aristotle's self-realization ethic, we can say that we are constituted by nature to have the potential for moral virtue, but that its actualization or development can occur only through practice. People become generous by giving, brave by doing brave acts or just by performing just acts. Unlike animals, we are not preprogramed by genetics or instinct to behave in this way or that. We, as humans, have choices to make about how we will conduct ourselves in the world.

So it is a matter of no little importance what sort of habits we form from the earliest age—it makes a vast difference, or rather all the difference in the world.

Aristotle

2.10

Doctrine of the Mean: If we are to develop states of character that will enable us to fulfill our proper function as rational beings or at least to find secondary happiness in the moral life, then we must try to live our lives in moderation or according to what Aristotle calls the **Doctrine of the Mean**. Many people today loosely refer to it as the Principle of the Golden Mean. Virtue, for Aristotle, is a "purposive disposition, lying in a mean that is relative to us and determined by a rational principle, and by that which a prudent man would use to determine it. It is a mean between two kinds of vice, one of excess and the other of deficiency . . ." (Aristotle, 1985, Book 2, pp. 101–102). Right conduct, then, is incompatible with excess or deficiency. You can eat too much (gluttony) or too little (anorexia); you can work too much (workaholism) or too little (sloth) and so on. To live morally, we must find a mid-point or happy balance between two extremes. Put simply, the morally virtuous life must be lived in **moderation**.

To suggest that the morally virtuous life must be lived in moderation does not mean that we can calculate what is too much or too little. For example, for a tiny person, a double-cheeseburger may be an excessive amount of food, but may not be enough food for a professional football player. Nutritional needs vary according to physical size and stature and considerations of moderation must take this into account. When deciding what constitutes moderation, we must determine the "golden mean" from our individual perspectives. In many cases, greater tolerance or sensitivity can move the moral mean from one point to another. Although this fact may seem to undermine precision when determining the right or virtuous course of action in any particular situation, Aristotle suggests that we should not demand more precision from an inquiry than the inquiry permits. The study of moral virtue, or at least the practice of moral virtue, is not an exact science.

2.11

The performance of a virtuous act is no guarantee that one is actually virtuous. A soldier may run into battle because the commanding officer may be more frightening than the enemy. Such an act would not be indicative of courage, though running into battle is something the courageous person would do. Likewise, an individual may avoid stealing because of fear of punishment, not because of any virtuous trait. For Aristotle, the virtuous person must enjoy being virtuous. The virtuous individual chooses to be virtuous and does not regret it. Virtue becomes its own reward. Charitable behavior is thus displayed cheerfully and joyfully, not with bitterness and reluctance. In the context of physical pleasure, Aristotle writes:

> He who abstains from the pleasures of the body and rejoices in the abstinence is temperate, while he who is vexed at having to abstain is profligate; and again, he who faces danger with pleasure, or, at any rate, without pain, is courageous, but he to whom this is painful is a coward. For moral virtue or excellence is closely concerned with pleasure and pain. It is pleasure that moves us to do what is base, and pain that moves us to refrain from what is noble. And therefore, as Plato says, man needs to be so trained from his youth up as to find pleasure and pain in the right objects. This is what sound education means. (Aristole, *ibid.*, p. 37)

To enjoy the things we ought, and to hate the things we ought, has the greatest bearing on excellence of character.

Aristotle

Temperate acts must be performed gladly or without pain and regret if they are to be considered virtuous, and they must also fulfill certain other conditions. First, individuals must know what they are doing. Second, they must consciously and deliberately choose to perform virtuous acts. Third, they must perform them for their own sake. And finally, the action performed must not be an isolated incident, but rather a manifestation of an enduring state of character. One donation does not a charitable person make. Nor is giving only to enhance one's reputation or to reduce one's taxable income a virtue, according to Aristotle. The act of giving must be performed for itself.

I'll scratch your back, if you'll scratch mine.

Expression of false virtue

Virtue does not apply to all activities, and a proper mean does not exist for some types of behavior. Although one may drink or eat in moderation, one cannot murder, steal or commit adultery in moderation; nor can one establish a virtuous level of hatred, envy or spite. These attitudes and behaviors are bad in themselves. Since these things are always wrong, it is absurd to look for moderation or excess where they are concerned.

In his *Nichomachean Ethics*, Aristotle provides a list of virtues capturing the means between various vices of excess and deficiency. You can read the "Back to the Source" feature to discover what they are. For now, you may wish to note that courage, for instance, is the mean between rashness and foolhardiness and modesty is the mean between shyness and shamelessness. These are common and easily appreciated virtues.

Now that you know the characteristics of virtue and what some of them are, you can proceed on your destination of the good life.

Books are like maps, but there is also the necessity of traveling.

Gurdjieff

BACK TO THE SOURCE*

A provisional definition of virtue

So virtue is a purposive disposition, lying in a mean that is relative to us and determined by a rational principle, and by that which a prudent man would use to determine it.[1] It is a mean between two kinds of vice, one of excess and the other of deficiency; and also for this reason, that whereas these vices fall short of or exceed the right measure in both feelings and actions, virtue discovers the mean and chooses it. Thus from the point of view of its essence and the definition of its real nature, virtue is a mean; but in respect of what is right and best, it is an extreme.

But the rule of choosing the mean cannot be applied to some actions and feelings, which are essentially evil

But not every action or feeling admits of a mean; because some have names that directly connote depravity, such as malice, shamelessness and envy, and among actions adultery, theft and murder. All these, and more like them, are so called[2] as being evil in themselves; it is not the excess or deficiency of them that is evil. In their case, then, it is impossible to act rightly; one is always wrong. Nor does acting rightly or wrongly in such cases depend upon circumstances—whether a man commits adultery with the right woman or at the right time or in the right way, because to do anything of that kind is simply wrong. One might as well claim that there is a mean and excess and deficiency even in unjust or cowardly or intemperate actions. On that basis there must be a mean of excess, a mean of deficiency, an excess of excess and a deficiency of deficiency. But just as in temperance and courage there can be no mean or excess or deficiency, because the mean is in a sense an extreme, so there can be no mean or excess or deficiency in the vices that we mentioned; however done, they are wrong. For in general neither excess nor deficiency admits of a mean, nor does a mean admit of excess and deficiency.

The doctrine of the mean applied to particular virtues

vii. But a generalization of this kind is not enough; we must apply it to particular cases. When we are discussing actions, although general statements have a wider application, particular statements are closer to the truth. This is because actions are concerned with particular facts, and theories must be brought into harmony with these. Let us, then, take these instances from the diagram.[3]

In the field of Fear and Confidence[4] the mean is Courage; and of those who go to extremes the man who exceeds in fearlessness has no name to describe him (there are many nameless cases), the one who exceeds in confidence is called Rash, and the one who shows an excess of fear and a deficiency of confidence is called Cowardly. In the field of Pleasures and Pains—not in all, especially not in all pains—the mean is Temperance,[5] the excess

---

**Aristotle,* Nichomachean Ethics, *trans. Terence Irwin. Footnotes have been renumbered.*

Licentiousness; cases of defective response to pleasures scarcely occur, and therefore people of this sort too have no name to describe them, but let us class them as Insensible. In the field of Giving and Receiving Money the mean is Liberality, the excess and deficiency are Prodigality and Illiberality; but these show excess and deficiency in contrary ways to one another: the prodigal man goes too far in spending and not far enough in getting, while the illiberal man goes too far in getting money and not far enough in spending it. This present account is in outline and summary, which is all that we need at this stage; we shall give a more accurate analysis later.[6]

Table 2.1 TABLE OF VIRTUES AND VICES

SPHERE OF ACTION OR FEELING	EXCESS	MEAN	DEFICIENCY
Fear and Confidence	Rashness *thrasutēs*	Courage *andreia*	Cowardice *deilia*
Pleasure and Pain	Licentiousness *akolasia*	Temperance *sōphrosunē*	Insensibility *anaisthēsia*
Getting and Spending (minor)	Prodigality *asōtia*	Liberality *eleutheriotēs*	Illiberality *aneleutheria*
Getting and Spending (major)	Vulgarity *apeirokalia, banausia*	Magnificence *megaloprepeia*	Pettiness *mikroprepeia*
Honor and Dishonor (major)	Vanity *chaunotēs*	Magnanimity *megalophsūchia*	Pusillanimity *mikropsūchia*
Honor and Dishonor (minor)	Ambition *philotīmmia*	Proper ambition	Unambitiousness *aphilotīmia*
Anger	Irascibility *orgilotēs*	Patience *prāotēs*	Lack of spirit *aorgēsia*
Self-expression	Boastfulness *alazoneia*	Truthfulness *alētheia*	Understatement *eirōneia*
Conversation	Buffoonery *bōmolochia*	Wittiness *eutrapelia*	Boorishness *agroikia*
Social Conduct	Obsequiousness *areskeia* Flattery *kolakeia*	Friendliness *philia*(?)	Cantankerousness *duskolia (duseris)*
Shame	Shyness *katalplēxis*	Modesty *aidōs*	Shamelessness *anaischuntia*
Indignation	Envy *phthonos*	Righteous indignation *nemesis*	Malicious enjoyment *epichairekakia*

But there are other dispositions too that are concerned with money. There is a mean called Magnificence (because the magnificent is not the same as the liberal man: the one deals in large and the other in small outlays); the excess is Tastelessness and Vulgarity, the deficiency Pettiness. These are different from the extremes between which liberality lies; how they differ will be discussed later.[7] In the field of Public Honor and Dishonor the mean is Magnanimity, the excess is called a sort of Vanity, and the deficiency Pusillanimity. And just as liberality differs, as we said,[8] from magnificence in being concerned with small outlays, so there is a state related to Magnanimity in the same way, being concerned with small honors, while magnanimity is concerned with great ones; because it is possible to aspire to <small> honors in the right way, or to a greater or less degree than is right. The man who goes too far in his aspirations is called Ambitious, the one who falls short, Unambitious; the one who is a mean between them has no name. This is true also of the corresponding dispositions, except that the ambitious man's is called Ambitiousness. This is why the extremes lay claim to the intermediate territory. We ourselves sometimes call the intermediate man ambitious and sometimes unambitious; that is, we sometimes commend the ambitious and sometimes the unambitious. Why it is that we do this will be explained in our later remarks.[9] Meanwhile let us continue our discussion of the remaining virtues and vices, following the method already laid down.

In the field of Anger, too, there is excess, deficiency and the mean. They do not really possess names, but we may call the intermediate man Patient and the mean Patience; and of the extremes the one who exceeds can be Irascible and his vice Irascibility, while the one who is deficient can be Spiritless and the deficiency Lack of Spirit.

There are also three other means which, though different, somewhat resemble each other. They are all concerned with what we do and say in social intercourse, but they differ in this respect, that one is concerned with truthfulness in such intercourse, the other two with pleasantness—one with pleasantness in entertainment, the other with pleasantness in every department of life. We must therefore say something about these too, in order that we may better discern that in all things the mean is to be commended, while the extremes are neither commendable nor right, but reprehensible. Most of these too have no names; but, as in the other cases, we must try to coin names for them in the interest of clarity and to make it easy to follow the argument.

Well, then, as regards Truth the intermediate man may be called Truthful and the mean Truthfulness; pretension that goes too far may be Boastfulness and the man who is disposed to it a Boaster, while that which is deficient[10] may be called Irony and its exponent Ironical. As for Pleasantness in Social Entertainment, the intermediate man is Witty, and the disposition Wit; the excess is Buffoonery and the indulger in it a Buffoon; the man who is deficient is a kind of Boor and his disposition Boorishness. In the rest of the sphere of the Pleasant—life in general—the person who is pleasant in the right way is Friendly and the mean is Friendliness; the person who goes too far, if he has no motive, is Obsequious; if his motive is self-interest, he is a Flatterer. The man who is deficient and is unpleasant in all circumstances is Cantankerous and Ill-tempered.

There are mean states also in the sphere of feelings and emotions. Modesty is not a virtue, but the modest man too is praised. Here too one person is called intermediate and another excessive—like the Shy man who is overawed at anything. The man who feels too little shame or none at all is Shameless, and the intermediate man is Modest. Righteous Indignation is a mean between Envy and Spite, and they are all concerned with feelings of pain or pleasure at the experiences of our neighbors. The man who feels righteous indignation is distressed at instances of undeserved good fortune, but the envious man goes further and is distressed at *any* good fortune, while the spiteful man is so far from feeling distress[11] that he actually rejoices.

However, we shall have occasion to continue this discussion elsewhere.[12] After that we shall treat of Justice, distinguishing its two kinds—because the word is used in more senses than one—and explain in what way each of them is a mean.[13] [We shall also treat similarly of the rational virtues.][14]

The mean is often nearer to one extreme than to the other, or seems nearer because of our natural tendencies

viii. Thus there are three dispositions, two of them vicious (one by way of excess, the other of deficiency), and one good, the mean. They are all in some way opposed to one another: the extremes are contrary both to the mean and to each other, and the mean to the extremes. For just as the equal is greater compared with the less, and less compared with the greater, so the mean states (in both feelings and actions) are excessive compared with the deficient and deficient compared with the excessive. A brave man appears rash compared with a coward, and cowardly compared with a rash man; similarly a temperate man appears licentious compared with an insensible one and insensible compared with a licentious one, and a liberal man prodigal compared with an illiberal one and illiberal compared with a prodigal one. This is the reason why each extreme type tries to push the mean nearer to the other: the coward calls the brave man rash, the rash man calls him a coward; and similarly in all other cases. But while all these dispositions are opposed to one another in this way, the greatest degree of contrariety is that which is found between the two extremes. For they are separated by a greater interval from one another than from the mean, just as the great is further from the small, and the small from the great, than either is from the equal. Again, some extremes seem to bear a resemblance to a mean; e.g. rashness seems like courage, and prodigality like liberality; but between the extremes there is always the maximum dissimilarity. Now contraries are by definition as far distant as possible from one another;[15] hence the further apart things are, the more contrary they will be. In some cases it is the deficiency, in others the excess, that is more opposed to the mean; for instance, the more direct opposite of courage is not the excess, rashness, but the deficiency, cowardice; and that of temperance is not the deficiency, insensibility, but the excess, licentiousness. This result is due to two causes. One lies in the nature of the thing itself. When one extreme has a closer affinity and resemblance to the mean, we tend to oppose to the mean not that extreme but the other. For instance, since rashness is held to be nearer to courage and more like it than cowardice is, it is cowardice that we tend to oppose to courage, because the extremes that are further from the mean are thought to be more opposed to it. This is one cause, the one that lies in the *thing*. The other lies in ourselves. It is the things towards which we have the stronger natural inclination that seem to us more opposed to the mean. For example, we are naturally more inclined towards pleasures, and this makes us more prone towards licentiousness than towards temperance; so we describe as more contrary to the mean those things towards which we have the stronger tendency. This is why licentiousness, the excess, is more contrary to temperance.[16]

Summing up of the foregoing discussion, together with three practical rules for good conduct

ix. We have now said enough to show that moral virtue is a mean, and in what sense it is so: that it is a mean between two vices, one of excess and the other of deficiency, and that it is such because it aims at hitting the mean point in feelings and actions. For this reason it is a difficult business to be good; because in any given case it is difficult to find the mid-point[17]—for instance, not everyone can find the center of a circle; only the man who knows how. So too it is easy to get angry—anyone can do that—or to give and spend money; but to feel or act towards the right person to the right extent at the right time for the right reason in the right way—that is not easy, and it is not everyone that can do it. Hence to do these things well is a rare, laudable and fine achievement.

For this reason anyone who is aiming at the mean should (1) keep away from that extreme which is more contrary to the mean, just as Calypso advises:

> Far from this surf and surge keep thou thy ship.[18]

For one of the extremes is always more erroneous than the other; and since it is extremely difficult to hit the mean, we must take the next best course, as they say, and choose the lesser of the evils; and this will be most readily done in the way that we are suggesting. (2) We must notice the errors into which we ourselves are liable to fall (because we all have different natural tendencies—we shall find out what ours are from the pleasure and pain that they give us), and we must drag ourselves in the contrary direction; for we shall arrive at the mean by pressing well away from our failing—just like somebody straightening a warped piece of wood. (3) In every situation one must guard especially against pleasure and pleasant things, because we are not impartial judges of pleasure. So we should adopt the same attitude towards it as the Trojan elders did towards Helen, and constantly repeat their pronouncement;[19] because if in this way we relieve ourselves of the attraction, we shall be less likely to go wrong.

Notes

1. It is purposive as being a deliberately cultivated and exercised state of the appetitive faculty; and the mean is determined not merely by a general principle but by the application of it to particular circumstances by a man of good character and intelligence; cf. ch. ix. below.
2. Or 'are censured.'
3. Or 'table'; see p. 194, where the Greek names of the several virtues and vices are shown.

4. These should be regarded (for the understanding of A.'s general theory) as forming a single continuum with extremes Rashness and Cowardice; the reference to Fearlessness may be ignored.
5. Generally 'self-control' is a better rendering.
6. 1115a4–1138b14.
7. 1122a20–b18.
8. Just above.
9. 1125b11–25.
10. By understating the truth; in fact 'understatement' is often a better equivalent than 'irony.'
11. At their *bad* fortune, because the Greek word means literally 'rejoicing at misfortune.'
12. In Book V.
13. 1115a4ff.
14. The words in square brackets were almost certainly added by another hand; A. never calls the intellectual virtues 'rational,' nor did he regard them as mean states. The intellectual virtues are discussed in Book VI.
15. Cf. *Metaphysics* 1018a25ff.
16. sc. 'than insensibility is' (1109a3f.).
17. Or 'mean.'
18. In our text of Homer these words are spoken not by Calypso (the nymph who detained Odysseus on her island) but by Odysseus himself quoting the enchantress Circe's advice to steer closer to Scylla (the lesser evil) than to Charybdis (*Odyssey* xii. 219f.).
19. As a sort of charm or spell. The elders paid tribute to her beauty, but said that she ought to be sent back to Greece, for fear of the consequences for Troy if she remained (*Illiad* iii. 156–60).

MINDWORK MEDITATION

It might be interesting and insightful for you to reflect on your current lifestyle and selection of goals in your life. Are you currently living a moral life, a contemplative life, a life of pleasure and enjoyment or a lifestyle consistent with the values of the statesperson? What would you say and why? Furthermore, how would you describe your chosen ends in life? What is it that you want, desire or crave? Are these ends instrumental or intrinsically valuable? Would Aristotle say you are on the right track to happiness or living a successful life? Why?

Key Terms

Nichomachean Ethics
teleologist
self-realization ethic
entelechy
happiness
hierarchy of ends
instrumental
intrinsic
ultimate
eudaimonia
secondary form of happiness
ultimate end of life
self-sufficient
final
attainable
hedonist
state
activity
success
distinctive function
rational capacities
alternative lifestyles
the lifestyle of pleasure and appetite gratification
the statesman's lifestyle
the good life
soul
the contemplative lifestyle
divine
balancing process
virtue
intellectual
moral
habit
Doctrine of the Mean
moderation

Progress Check 2.1

Instructions: Fill in the blanks with the appropriate responses listed below.

moderation
teleologist
entelechy
successful
self-sufficient
Alexander the Great
intrinsic
insecure
complete
divine
luck
habit
deficiency
sake
self-realization
means
hedonist
rational
cattle
contemplative
secondary
eudaimonia
Plato
intellectual
modesty

1. Aristotle was mentor to _____.
2. Aristotle was a student of _____.
3. The assumption that everything in nature aims at some end or good makes Aristotle a _____.
4. Aristotle's concept of morality and moral development is a kind of _____ ethic.
5. The inner urge for something to actualize its potentialities is the definition of _____.
6. The Greek word for happiness is _____.
7. The ends of human life can be either _____, instrumental or ultimate.
8. Instrumental ends correspond to goods that are a _____ to further ends.
9. *Eudaimonia* implies _____ living.
10. Moral virtue is not the ultimate end of life, but, nonetheless, it can lead to _____ happiness.
11. The ultimate end of life must be final, attainable, and _____.
12. Aristotle's pursuit of happiness does not make him a _____. The pursuit of pleasure is not the ultimate end of the good life.
13. The distinctive function of any human being involves a _____ activity.
14. Living solely for the sake of pleasure puts human life on the same level as _____.
15. A life of statesmanship is _____ because it depends on the whims of the fickle masses.
16. Happiness is not a one-time event; it must be understood in the context of a _____ life. It is only at the end of life that one can say whether or not one has lived a good life.
17. The _____ lifestyle is the highest form of human existence.
18. Rational activity is something humans engage in that is most god-like or _____.
19. An otherwise good life can be marred by an untimely death or by a bad _____.
20. There are two types of virtue, moral and _____.
21. Moral virtue involves the development of _____. For example, we become just by performing just acts.
22. Aristotle's Doctrine of the (Golden) Mean would have us live our lives somewhere between excess and _____.
23. Moral virtue involves a lifestyle of _____.
24. Virtuous acts must be performed knowingly and gladly and for their own _____, if they are to be considered truly virtuous.
25. The virtue of _____ is the mean between shyness and shamelessness.

Summary of Major Points

1. What makes Aristotle a teleologist?
   His focus on the ends of human activity.
   His functional explanation of morality, i.e., his self-realization ethic.
   His incorporation of the concept of "entelechy" into his theory of human development.

2. **What is the end of human life?**
   Happiness or "*eudaimonia.*"
   The ultimate end is final, self-sufficient, and intrinsically valuable.
   It involves successful living, the good life taken as a whole.
   It is not hedonism.
   The fulfillment of our distinctively human function, i.e., a rational activity of the soul in accordance with virtue.
3. **How are humans distinctive? What do they share with other life forms?**
   The same as plants in regard to nutrition and growth.
   The same as animals in regard to sensory capacities.
   They are different because the higher part of the soul involves rational activity.
   Humans have the capacity to be happy and to live the good life, unlike plants and lower level organisms.
4. **What lifestyles are discussed by Aristotle?**
   The lifestyle of pleasure and appetite gratification.
   The statesman's lifestyle.
   The contemplative lifestyle.
   The virtuous lifestyle.
5. **Which lifestyle is most befitting of humans? Why?**
   The contemplative lifestyle is ideal.
   It incorporates activities of the rational soul.
   It is most god-like or divine.
   It is the highest form of human existence.
6. **Which lifestyle is within reach of most of us? By what is it characterized?**
   The virtuous lifestyle is a more realistic aspiration for most of us compared with the contemplative lifestyle.
   Virtue offers us secondary happiness.
   The virtuous lifestyle represents a lifestyle of moderation.
   The virtuous lifestyle underscores the idea that happiness is a normative or value-related notion, not a psychological state.
7. **What is meant by the "Doctrine of the Mean"?**
   According to this doctrine, right conduct is incompatible with excess or deficiency.
   To live morally or virtuously, we must find a happy balance between the two extremes.
   The mean between excess and deficiency is determined in relation to particular individuals.
   Think of it as living in moderation.
8. **What are some virtues?**
   Courage: the mean between cowardice and rashness.
   Modesty: the mean between shyness and shamelessness.
   Truthfulness: the mean between boastfulness and understatement.
   Wittiness: the mean between buffoonery and boorishness.

Source References and Related Readings

Aristotle. *Nichomachean Ethics.* Translated by Terence Irwin. Indianapolis, Ind.: Hackett Publishing Co., 1985.

Barnes, Jonathan. *The Cambridge Companion to Aristotle.* New York: Cambridge University Press, 1995.

Copleston, Frederick. *A History of Philosophy: Volume 1, Greece and Rome.* New York: Image Books, 1993.

Falikowski, Anthony. *Moral Philosophy: Theories, Skills, and Applications.* Englewood Cliffs, N.J.: Prentice Hall, 1990.

Ross, W.D. *Aristotle.* New York: Methuen, 1923.

Soccio, Douglas. *Archetypes of Wisdom,* 2nd edition. Toronto: Wadsworth Publishing Co., 1995.

Sommers, Christina Hoff. *Vice and Virtue in Everyday Life.* Orlando: Harcourt, Brace Jovanovich, 1985.

Thomson, J.A.K. (Trans.). *The Ethics of Aristotle, The Nichomachean Ethics.* Toronto: Penguin Books, 1976. Introduction by Jonathan Barnes.

Utilitarian Ethics

From the Greek humanism of Plato and Aristotle, we now move on to the utilitarian ethics of Jeremy Bentham and John Stuart Mill. Utilitarianism is a school of moral thought that has significantly influenced modern British and North American society. A major difference you will notice in this treatment of morality is the decidedly socio-political emphasis. In our coverage of Plato and Aristotle, we focused on those elements of their philosophies most pertinent to individual morality. Specifically, we looked at the nature and workings of the human soul. We learned, for example, how, for Plato, the soul is comprised of three elements and how these three should function in harmonious balance. We also saw how, for Aristotle, the good life entails an activity of rational contemplation, a process that reflects the highest form of human functioning. For both Plato and Aristotle, the development of virtue is deemed essential to character development and the cultivation of an ideal lifestyle.

As we turn now to utilitarianism, we will change our focus from matters of soul, virtue, and character development to considerations of society, law, and political legislation. Morality is not a purely personal affair devoted exclusively to self-realization and keeping the "inner peace." Morality is also about the common good and the preservation of public order. Laws and legislators, people and policy makers, do not live in a moral vacuum. Embedded in our social relationships, as well as in the operations of our socio-political institutions, are moral values and principles (e.g., fairness and honesty). Establishing a solid basis of moral criticism is important, for doing this gives us the tools to progress and develop toward a more just society. Let us turn now to the philosophy of Jeremy Bentham for guidance on our continuing quest for moral truth and understanding.

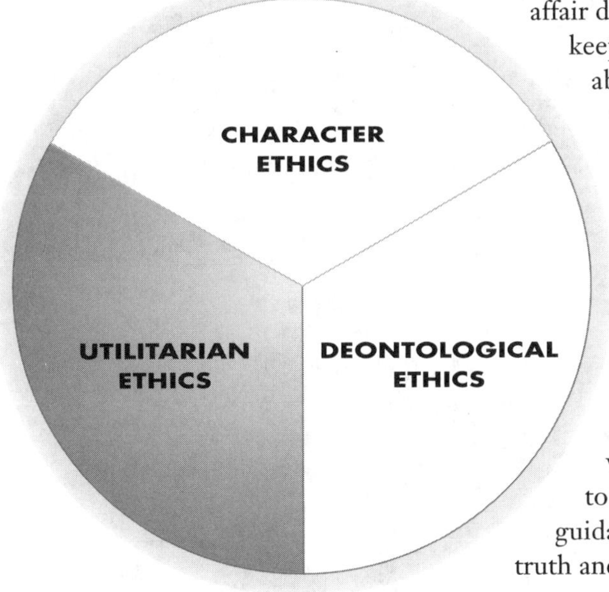

CHAPTER THREE

3 JEREMY BENTHAM: PAIN AND PLEASURE ARE THE MEASURE

Overview

Learning Outcomes:

After successfully completing this chapter, you will be able to:

3.1 define and understand the principle of utility;
3.2 distinguish between psychological and ethical egoism;
3.3 explain why Bentham chooses happiness or utility as the basis of morality;
3.4 list the sanctions identified by Bentham;
3.5 appreciate how sanctions serve as causal and determining forces in human behavior;
3.6 give the limits of legal jurisdiction as defined by Bentham;
3.7 know when it is not profitable to punish from a utilitarian perspective;

3.8 punish mischief and misbehavior with utilitarian considerations in mind;
3.9 perform a "hedonic calculation" illustrating how to put the principle of utility into real life practice.

PHILOSOPHICAL FOCUS QUESTIONS

1. In general terms, how is Bentham's utilitarian treatment of morality different from Plato and Aristotle's Greek humanism?
2. According to Bentham, what is the primary motivating force in human life?
3. From a utilitarian perspective, what is the right/wrong thing to do?
4. What prevents people from doing anything and everything they want?
5. What is the proper business of law? What is beyond the scope of the law?
6. What is the right way to punish wrong behavior?
7. When should punishments be avoided?
8. What is a hedonic calculus? What are its elements? How do you do one?

CORBIS–BEHMANN

Jeremy Bentham
(1748–1832)

BIOGRAPHICAL BRIEF*

Jeremy Bentham was born in London in 1748. As a child, he was intellectually precocious. By the age of 4 Bentham was already studying Latin grammar and, at the age of 12, he enrolled at Queen's College, Oxford. In 1763 Bentham earned a Bachelor of Arts degree and thereupon began legal studies at Lincoln's Inn. In that same year, he returned to Oxford for what turned out to be one of the most decisive experiences of his intellectual life. Bentham attended a number of lectures on law given by Sir William Blackstone. Blackstone presented his legal theory based on "natural rights". Regarding this theory as little more than rhetorical nonsense, Bentham began setting the stage for the development of his own utilitarian conception of law, justice, and society. Bentham earned his Master of Arts degree in 1766 and then proceeded to London. Having never really developed a fondness for the legal profession, he decided against becoming a practicing lawyer. Instead, he embarked on a literary career, the basic object of which was to bring order and moral defensibility into what he perceived as the deplorable state of the law and the social realities it made possible in his day. Jeremy Bentham can thus be regarded as a social reformer. He undertook the task of trying to modernize

**From Falikowski,* Moral Philosophy, *p. 47.*

British political and social institutions. There is little doubt that it was due at least in part to his influence that an historical landmark was established, the Reform Bill of 1832, which transformed the nature of British politics. The control of Britain's parliament was taken away from the landed aristocracy and placed into the hands of the urban bourgeoisie.

On a personal note, Jeremy Bentham was the godfather of John Stuart Mill, son of James Mill, a friend and colleague. John Stuart Mill later became the godfather of Bertrand Russell, a famous English philosopher who led the fight for nuclear disarmament in the 1960s. Starting with Bentham, an interesting philosophical lineage begins to evolve that has had political activism as an essential element.

Nature has placed mankind under the governance of two sovereign masters, pain and pleasure. It is for them alone to point out what we ought to do, as well as to determine what we shall do.

Jeremy Bentham

3.1 THE PRINCIPLE OF UTILITY

In the world of moral philosophy, when the subject of **utilitarianism** (pronounced "you-til-i-tare-ian-ism") is raised, the name **Jeremy Bentham** is one of the first to come to mind. For many, his name is virtually synonymous with this ethical theory. It should be noted, however, that Bentham was not the sole inventor of this idea. Elements of utilitarianism are found in the writings of such people as Thomas Hobbes and John Locke. Bentham's significant contribution to utilitarianism is his connection of its basic principles and assumptions to the problems of his time. He sought to provide nineteenth-century English society with philosophical foundations for moral thought and practical social reform. Bentham believed that ethical questions could be answered in a **spirit of scientific objectivity**. He rejected such things as tradition, aristocratic privilege, and religious faith as legitimate bases for moral evaluation. He believed that such things too easily serve the interests of the dominant and ruling classes and that they lead to the continued mistreatment of the poor and disenfranchised. Rather than appeal to religious, political or cultural authorities, Bentham chose to adopt a much more common-sense, empirical approach to the improvement of society. He argued that people's actions and those of governments could, and should, be evaluated according to their practical consequences or how much good they produce. For Bentham, no action is necessarily right or wrong in itself. The ethical value of anything is determined by its real-life results. Utilitarianism is, therefore, a form of **consequentialism**. It is the effect of an action that establishes its moral worth.

what has an aptness to produce pleasure in us is what we call good and what is apt to produce pain in us we call evil.

John Locke

In his most famous work, *An Introduction to the Principles of Morals and Legislation* (1789), Bentham outlines his objective basis for morality. He calls it the **principle of utility**. Bentham writes:

> By the principle of utility is meant that principle which approves of every action whatsoever, according to the tendency which it appears to have to augment or diminish the happiness of the party whose interest is in question: or, what is the same thing in other words, to promote or to oppose that happiness. I say of every action whatsoever; and therefore not only of every action of a private individual, but of every measure of government. (Bentham, 1939, p. 792)

The term "utility" is one you might not use in everyday conversation. Think of it as the same thing as **benefit**, **advantage**, **pleasure**, **happiness**, and **goodness**. Whatever prevents mischief, pain, evil, suffering or unhappiness also has utility or utilitarian value for Bentham.

PHILOSOPHERS AT WORK

Try to come up with examples of things or actions having utilitarian value. What has disutility or the effect of producing negative consequences? Do you agree with Bentham that "utility," not religion, political authority or tradition should act as the moral foundation for society? Why or why not?

3.2
3.3

THE PROBLEM OF PLEASURE

Simple pleasures are the last refuge of the complex.
Oscar Wilde

The pursuit of pleasure
Is the most pleasant pleasure.
Montaigne

Speed provides the one genuinely modern pleasure.
Aldous Huxley

The pleasure of all things increases by the same danger that should deter it.
Seneca

The man is richest whose pleasures are the cheapest.
Thoreau

Bentham's utilitarianism is based on **psychological egoism**. He says it is human nature for us to seek pleasure and to avoid pain. To quote Bentham: "Nature has placed mankind under the governance of two sovereign masters, pain and pleasure. It is for them alone to point out what we ought to do, as well as to determine what we shall do" (Bentham, *ibid*., p. 791). This, in itself, is not problematic. If this were all Bentham were saying, then we would be making nothing other than a psychological claim about human behavior which we could try to verify empirically or scientifically. To assert that humans are motivated by a self-interested pursuit of pleasure would simply make Bentham a psychological egoist. Bentham, however, goes further and becomes an ethical egoist as well. He argues that because it *is* in our nature to seek pleasure, that is what we morally *ought* to do. For him, pleasure becomes a value that we ought to pursue and a standard against which to judge all actions and activities. In making a connection between "moral or ethical oughts" and "pleasure," Bentham is suggesting that right and wrong or good and bad cannot be properly understood in any other way. The right or good thing to do is to seek pleasure, for it is only pleasure and the avoidance of pain that give actions any real value. Conversely, the wrong or bad thing to do is to reduce or minimize the amount of pleasure experienced. It is also wrong to promote pain, misery, and suffering.

The Is-Ought Fallacy

Bentham's leap from psychological egoism to **ethical egoism** might make good intuitive sense to you. From a purely logical perspective, however, it falls prey to what, in logic, is called the **"is-ought fallacy."** When this fallacy (i.e., form of faulty logic) is committed, the reasoner tries unjustifiably to derive a moral "ought" from an "is" of experience. To illustrate, just because it *is* true that people lie, kill, cheat, and steal, we cannot conclude solely on that basis that they *should* or *ought* to do so, for obvious reasons. In fact, even if we suggested that people are inherently evil by nature (the biological equivalent to original sin), we probably still would not accept evil behavior on the grounds that we are so constituted by nature. More likely, we could say that the right thing to do is to suppress our (natural) aggressive, bestial, and dishonest inclinations. The "is" is that in fact which "ought" to be repressed or somehow extinguished. As we can see, then, arguing from what is true to what ought to be is clearly a problematic and debatable step.

Bentham did not deal at length with the is-ought problem inherent in his utilitarianism. What he did do is to suggest that all other moral theories were either vague and inconsistent or else reducible to pleasure and the principle of utility in the end. Furthermore, providing no substantial defense or justification of the principle of utility as the basis of morality, he simply concluded that "that which is used to prove everything else, cannot itself be proved: a chain of proofs must have their commencement somewhere. To give such proof is as impossible as it is needless."

PHILOSOPHERS AT WORK

Do you think Bentham's acceptance of pleasure (utility) as a standard of morality is justified? Why or why not? Would it be wise to accept an "unnatural" morality, one that requires us to work against our natural urges and inclinations? What would Bentham say? Discuss.

3.4
THE THEORY OF SANCTIONS

The art of life is the art of avoiding pain.
Thomas Jefferson

The Business of government is to promote the happiness of society by punishing and rewarding.
Jeremy Bentham

If, as Bentham claims, psychological egoism is what motivates people to behave as they do, then what is preventing them from doing anything they want at any time they want, even if this entails violating others? For Bentham, the answer is found in the notion of **sanctions**. Think of a sanction as a source of pleasure and pain that acts to give binding force to any law or rule of conduct. Sanctions can also be seen as rewards and punishments or as causal and determining factors influencing our behavior. According to Bentham, we, as individuals, respond egoistically to sanctions trying to maximize our pleasure and minimize our pain. We generally avoid behaving in ways that lead to pain and other negative sanctions; we generally prefer acting in ways that lead to pleasure, happiness, and personal benefit or satisfaction. Sanctions govern what we do, perhaps more than we sometimes realize.

3.5

Sanctions come in a variety of types. **Physical sanctions** are not administered by any human or divine source. They are what bind us to the laws of nature. For example, you cannot jump off the CN Tower in Toronto or off a mountain peak in Washington State without suffering the consequences. Because we recognize the physical sanctions associated with certain kinds of dangerous acts like these, virtually all of us refrain from them.

Moral Sanctions arise in our informal relationships with others. If you have ever experienced "peer group pressure," you can probably appreciate the power, influence, and control that public opinion can have. To spare ourselves mental pain or embarrassment and loneliness, we often go along with the crowd and conform to the expectations of others. Other people actually contribute to the governance of our behavior in ways in which we are not always consciously aware. For instance, if your friends start avoiding you because you constantly lie to them, you may be dissuaded from continuing the practice. The pain or underlying fear of ostracism is often enough to prompt a change in behavior.

In addition to physical and moral sanctions, our behavior can also be regulated by **religious sanctions**, if we believe in a rewarding and punishing supreme being, as in the Judeo-Christian tradition. People may do what is right according to their religion, church or holy book in hope of entering the gates of heaven or because they fear the hell-fire of eternal damnation. Religious sanctions affecting the afterlife can impact on behavior in the here and now.

Finally, Bentham writes of **political sanctions**. These sanctions are issued formally by judges and magistrates on behalf of the state. Punishments issuing from the state (province, county, municipality, federal court, and so on) include things like fines, penalties, and jail-terms. Fear of such things is what deters people from breaking the law and violating the rights of other citizens. On a positive note, things like peace and good order, which result from abiding by the law, are what people find rewarding. Such things create the conditions most conducive to our pursuit of pleasure.

In response to sanctions, Bentham was most interested in the political type. As a reformer, he wished to change the laws of English society in such a fashion that the general welfare would be promoted by each individual pursuing his or her own advantage. Political sanctions, that is, the rewards and punishments issued by a carefully crafted legal system, would promote the greatest happiness for the greatest number. Thus, for Bentham, laws should serve utilitarian ideals. Laws are not necessarily right or wrong in themselves, but they are acceptable only to the extent that they further human happiness.

LAW AND PUNISHMENT

But all punishment is mischief: all punishment in itself is evil. Upon the principle of utility, if it ought at all to be admitted, it ought to be admitted in as far as it promises to exclude some greater evil.

Jeremy Bentham

As a social reformer, Bentham made significant use of the principle of utility in the context of law and punishment. In his mind, the law should be concerned with increasing the total happiness of the community by discouraging specifically those acts producing evil consequences. Such acts are, by definition, criminal and offensive. They inflict pain or somehow decrease the pleasure of specific individuals, groups or the community at large. It is the job of government, then, to promote the happiness of people by punishing those who commit offensive acts that, by the principle of utility, have been clearly established as evil.

3.6
The Scope of Legal Jurisdiction

The kinds of acts that should or should not be under the law's jurisdiction became a matter of reclassification for Bentham. He believed that the English laws of his day unjustifiably controlled many areas of individual or private morality that had no significant effect on public affairs or on the general happiness. He argued that matters of **private ethics**, involving such things as duties to oneself, sexual conduct, and prudence, were beyond the proper scope of the law. He also felt that acts of beneficence or kindness toward others, though nice and conducive to people's happiness, were also not appropriate for legislation. Such positive acts should not be legally required. We cannot properly be compelled by law to be generous, altruistic or self-sacrificing for the benefit of others.

Some examples of English laws that failed the test of utility in Bentham's day include the following: imprisoning people for failing to pay their debts, requiring membership in the Anglican church for certain political offices, specifying capital punishment for such crimes as picking pockets, and punishing people for drunkenness and fornication. (Runkle, 1982, p. 33)

The state has no business in the bedrooms of the nation.
Pierre Elliot Trudeau

PHILOSOPHERS AT WORK

Are there any laws today that in your opinion, or in the opinion of others, are unjustifiable because they violate personal rights. If so, which ones? Discuss possible objections to these laws from a utilitarian perspective. (*Hint*: At least two debatable laws deal with automobiles and their operation.)

Though interested in the use of punishment as a way of discouraging evil conduct, Bentham was not a **retributivist**. He was not in favor of meting out punishment for its own sake or as a way of "getting even" with wrong-doers. According to Bentham, punishment itself constitutes an evil because it inflicts suffering and pain. Thus punishing violations of proper social conduct could be justified only if the pain inflicted prevented or excluded some other greater pain. You can see it as a necessary evil of sorts. Certainly, though, from a utilitarian perspective, retribution for retribution's own sake must be rejected in principle. Inflicting pain for the purpose of "getting back at" is intrinsically wrong. No useful purpose is served by making an individual suffer because his or her act caused a victim pain.

3.7 When Not to Punish

Bentham provides us with several utilitarian guidelines for the administration of **punishment**. Punishment should not be administered where it is **groundless**. If a wrong-doing has, in fact, not been committed, then punishment should not be forthcoming. Also, if the wrongdoer can compensate the victim and if the compensation is assured, then punishment should not be inflicted.

Punishment must be avoided where it is **inefficacious**. If punishment does not work to prevent mischief or wrongful acts, then it should be avoided. For example, retroactive legislation (i.e., making yesterday's acceptable act wrong starting today) and resulting sanctions (i.e., punishing yesterday's legal act today) are ineffective and unjustifiable. Such legislation may, indeed, have disutility and breed disrespect for legislators. Punishing the insane or very young children is also wrong since neither group has a true sense of responsibility.

Punishments should also not be administered where they would prove to be **unprofitable** or too expensive. If the punishment to be inflicted creates greater mischief (i.e., pain or suffering) than the act that it was intended to extinguish or to deter others from performing, then it should be avoided. Finally, punishment should be avoided where **needless**. Where mischief can be avoided without punishment, then punishment should not be given. If an explanation and condemnation of a particular wrong-doing is enough to dissuade another from committing it again, then punishment is not in order.

3.8

How to Punish

After explaining when not to punish, Bentham goes on in the *Principles of Morals and Legislation* to provide us with guidelines on how to punish when we must. These guidelines are, of course, based on utilitarian principles. To start, when punishments are inflicted, they must outweigh the profit of the offense that is committed. If parking in downtown Calgary or Los Angeles, for example, costs $15.00 daily and if parking fines are only $10.00, then the pain of the punishment does not outweigh the profit derived from the offense. In this case, you could actually save money by breaking the law. To reduce the likelihood of parking violations, the fine would have to be increased well beyond $15.00 so that payment of a parking fine would "hurt" and, therefore, act as a deterrence.

In situations where two different offenses are involved, the punishment for the more serious offense must be sufficient to induce the individual to prefer the lesser offense. If small crimes and large crimes are given the same punishments, and if there is more to gain in committing the larger crime, then we promote greater mischief rather than less, or less serious, mischief.

When punishing, we should also take care that each of the offenders receives the same punishment for the same offense. If two people commit the same crime, for instance, manslaughter, in morally equivalent circumstances, and if we place one person on probation for three months and place the other person in jail for ten years, then the workings of the legal system would likely be called into question on grounds of unfairness, inconsistency or, perhaps, discrimination.

From a utilitarian perspective, the punishment should never exceed the bare minimum required to make it effective. Many would argue that cutting off a person's hand for the crime of theft is excessive and unwarranted. Such severe punishment may work, but if less punishment can work too, then that is the preferred option. Punishment should not encourage sadistic pleasure or blood vengeance; remember, it is a necessary evil that is sometimes required to root out other, greater evils. As a utilitarian, one should never cause more pain than absolutely necessary.

If there is little chance for an offender to be caught in the act of wrong-doing, then the punishment should be greater. If there is little risk and little punishment associated with the mischief involved, then the likelihood that wrong-doing will occur is increased again. For Bentham, punishment should be increased in proportion to the declining likelihood that one will get caught.

For more details regarding sanctions and the proper administration of punishment, turn to the "Back to the Source" feature.

BACK TO THE SOURCE*

Chapter XIII
Cases Unmeet for Punishment

I. General view of cases unmeet for punishment.

i. The general object which all laws have, or ought to have, in common, is to augment the total happiness of the community; and therefore, in the first place, to exclude, as far as may

**From Bentham,* An Introduction to the Principles of Morals and Legislation. *Footnotes have been renumbered.*

be, everything that tends to subtract from that happiness: in other words, to exclude mischief.

ii. But all punishment is mischief: all punishment in itself is evil. Upon the principle of utility, if it ought at all to be admitted, it ought only to be admitted in as far as it promises to exclude some greater evil.

iii. It is plain, therefore, that in the following cases punishment ought not to be inflicted.

1. Where it is *groundless*: where there is no mischief for it to prevent; the act not being mischievous upon the whole.
2. Where it must be *inefficacious*: where it cannot act so as to prevent the mischief.
3. Where it is *unprofitable*, or too *expensive*: where the mischief it would produce would be greater than what it prevented.
4. Where it is *needless*: where the mischief may be prevented, or cease of itself, without it: that is, at a cheaper rate. . . .

Chapter XIV
Of the Proportion Between Punishments and Offenses

i. We have seen that the general object of all laws is to prevent mischief; that is to say, when it is worth while; but that, where there are no other means of doing this than punishment, there are four cases in which it is *not* worth while.

ii. When it *is* worth while, there are four subordinate designs or objects, which, in the course of his endeavors to compass, as far as may be, that one general object, a legislator, whose views are governed by the principle of utility, comes naturally to propose to himself.

iii. 1. His first, most extensive, and most eligible object, is to prevent, in as far as it is possible, and worth while, all sorts of offenses whatsoever: in other words, so to manage, that no offense whatsoever may be committed.

iv. 2. But if a man must needs commit an offense of some kind or other, the next object is to induce him to commit an offense *less* mischievous, *rather* than one *more* mischievous: in other words, to choose always the *least* mischievous, of two offenses that will either of them suit his purpose.

v. 3. When a man has resolved upon a particular offense, the next object is to dispose him to do *no more* mischief that is *necessary* to his purpose: in other words, to do as little mischief as is consistent with the benefit he has in view.

vi. 4. The last object is, whatever the mischief be, which it is proposed to prevent, to prevent it at as *cheap* a rate as possible.

vii. Subservient to these four objects, or purposes, must be the rules or canons by which the proportion of punishments[1] to offenses is to be governed.

viii. Rule 1. 1. The first object, it has been seen, is to prevent, in as far as it is worth while, all sorts of offenses: therefore,

The value of the punishment must not be less in any case than what is sufficient to outweigh that of the profit of the offense.

If it be, the offense (unless some other considerations, independent of the punishment, should intervene and operate efficaciously in the character of tutelary motives) will be sure to be committed notwithstanding: the whole lot of punishment will be thrown away: it will be altogether *inefficacious*.

ix. The above rule has been often objected to, on account of its seeming harshness: but this can only have happened for want of its being properly understood. The strength of the temptation, *ceteris paribus*, is as the profit of the offense: the quantum of the punishment must rise with the profit of the offense: *ceteris paribus*, it must therefore rise with the strength of the temptation. This there is no disputing. True it is, that the stronger the temptation, the less conclusive is the indication which the act of delinquency affords of the depravity of the offender's disposition. So far then as the absence of any aggravation, arising from extraordinary depravity or disposition, may operate, or at the utmost, so far as the presence of a ground of extenuation, resulting from the innocence or beneficence of the offender's disposition, can operate, the strength of the temptation may operate in abatement of the demand for punishment. But it can never operate so far as to indicate the propriety of making the punishment ineffectual, which it is sure to be when brought below the level of the apparent profit of the offense.

The partial benevolence which should prevail for the reduction of it below this level, would counteract as well those purposes which such a motive would actually have in view, as those more extensive purposes which benevolence ought to have in view: it would be cruelty not only to the public, but to the very persons in whose behalf it pleads: in its effects, I mean, however opposite in its intention. Cruelty to the public, that is cruelty to the innocent, by suffering them, for want of an adequate protection, to lie exposed to the mischief of the offense: cruelty even to the offender himself, by punishing him to no purpose, and without the chance of compassing that beneficial end, by which alone the introduction of the evil of punishment is to be justified.

x. Rule 2. But whether a given offense shall be prevented in a given degree by a given quantity of punishment, is never anything better than a chance; for the purchasing of which, whatever punishment is employed, is so much expended in advance. However, for the sake of giving it the better chance of outweighing the profit of the offense,

The greater the mischief of the offense, the greater is the expense, which it may be worth while to be at, in the way of punishment.

xi. Rule 3. The next object is, to induce a man to choose always the least mischievous of two offenses; therefore

Where two offenses come in competition, the punishment for the greater offense must be sufficient to induce a man to prefer the less.

xii. Rule 4. When a man has resolved upon a particular offense, the next object is, to induce him to do no more mischief than what is necessary for his purpose: therefore

The punishment should be adjusted in such manner to each particular offense, that for every part of the mischief there may be a motive to restrain the offender from giving birth to it.

xiii. Rule 5. The last object is, whatever mischief is guarded against, to guard against it at as cheap a rate as possible: therefore

The punishment ought in no case to be more than what is necessary to bring it into conformity with the rules here given.

xiv. Rule 6. It is further to be observed, that owing to the different manners and degrees in which persons under different circumstances are affected by the same exciting cause, a punishment which is the same in name will not always either really produce, or even so much as appear to others to produce, in two different persons the same degree of pain: therefore

That the quantity actually inflicted on each individual offender may correspond to the quantity intended for similar offenders in general, the several circumstances influencing sensibility ought always to be taken into account.

xv. Of the above rules of proportion, the four first, we may perceive, serve to mark out the limits on the side of diminution; the limits *below* which a punishment ought not to be diminished: the fifth, the limits on the side of increase; the limits *above* which it ought not to be *increased*. The five first are calculated to serve as guides to the legislator: the sixth is calculated, in some measure, indeed, for the same purpose; but principally for guiding the judge in his endeavors to conform, on both sides, to the intentions of the legislator. . . .[2]

Notes

1. The same rules (it is to be observed) may be applied, with little variation, to rewards as well as punishment: in short, to motives in general, which, according as they are of the pleasurable or painful kind, are of the nature of *reward* or *punishment*: and, according as the act they are applied to produce is of the positive or negative kind, are styled impelling or restraining.
2. Chap. XV examines the properties which punishment must have if it is to be successful in its function, and Chap. XVI gives a classification of offenses.—Editor.

3.9
THE HEDONIC CALCULUS

Quantity of pleasure being equal, pushpin is as good as poetry.

Jeremy Bentham

There is no such thing as pure pleasure; some anxiety always goes with it.

Ovid

To help individuals, as well as lawmakers and legislators, decide what ought to be done in any given set of circumstances, Bentham developed what has come to be known as the **hedonic**

calculus. As the term itself suggests, the hedonic calculus is the calculation of pleasure or hedonistic consequences. Remember that Bentham wanted to conduct moral inquiry in a spirit of scientific objectivity. By using the hedonic calculus to determine the pleasures and pains produced by any action or policy, he thought we could decide empirically on what is the right or good thing to do. The hedonic calculus might be more understandable if you see it as a kind of "cost-benefit" analysis. In moral and ethical decision making, Bentham recommends that the bottom line should be the maximization of pleasure and the minimization or elimination of pain. Actions producing the greatest happiness for the individual or those concerned are the actions we morally ought to perform.

The hedonic calculus gives us seven criteria by which to measure the pleasure and pain produced by any particular action. They are:

1. ***Intensity:*** Ask how strong the pleasure or emotional satisfaction is.
2. ***Duration:*** Ask how long the pleasure will last. Will it be short-lived or long-lasting?
3. ***Certainty:*** Ask how likely or unlikely it is that pleasure will actually result. What is the probability of the result?
4. ***Propinquity:*** Ask how soon the pleasure will occur. How near are the consequences?
5. ***Fecundity:*** Ask how likely it is that the action will produce more pleasure in the future. Will the good/pain produced create more good/pain down the road?
6. ***Purity:*** Ask if there will be any pain accompanying the action (some pleasurable acts are accompanied by painful elements). Is there some bad you have to take with the good?
7. ***Extent:*** Ask how many other people will be affected by the considered action.

When making a moral or ethical decision, what Bentham suggests you do is attach numerical values to each of the elements listed above. You can use any scale you like. For our purposes, let us use a scale ranging from -100 to +100. Negative values indicate pain, positive values indicate pleasure. Thus, -100 means high pain, -50 means moderate pain, and -10 means low pain. Similarly, +100 stands for high pleasure, +50 stands for moderate pleasure, and +10 stands for low pleasure. Once the scale is determined, what you then do is perform a pain-pleasure calculation of alternative courses of action. (There is an actual sequence of calculation discussed by Bentham in the *Principles of Morals and Legislation*, see Chapter VI.)

Suppose you have to decide between doing "A" and "not-doing A"; which should you choose from a utilitarian perspective? First, look at "A" in regard to its intensity, duration, and other elements of the hedonic calculus. How much pleasure and how much pain is produced? On balance, is there more pleasure or more pain? Now, consider "not-doing A." Again, calculate the quantities of pain and pleasure using the criteria of the hedonic calculus. Once the calculations are done for each alternative action—"doing A" versus "not doing A"—they should then be compared. The alternative action producing the most pleasure is the morally preferable one. If both alternatives produce a net balance of pain, then the alternative producing the least pain is to be preferred.

Intense, long, certain, speedy, fruitful, pure—
Such marks in pleasure and in pains endure.
Such pleasures seek, if private be thy end;
If it be public, wide let them extend.
Such pains avoid, whichever by they view;
If pains must come, let them extend to few.
Jeremy Bentham

I should add here that if the implications of the considered action go beyond the individual to include others, then Bentham recommends that we repeat the hedonic calculus taking their interests into account. What is the net balance of pleasure and pain for others if alternative "A" is performed? What are the hedonic consequences for them if "A" is not performed? Take note that Bentham was interested not only in maximizing the happiness of the individual but also in maximizing the happiness of the broader community. Thus, if our actions impact on others, then they must be accounted for in our hedonic calculation.

At this point, I might add that Bentham was not unrealistic. For him "It is not to be expected that this [hedonic calculation] process should be strictly pursued previously to every moral judgment, or to every legislative or judicial operation." (Bentham, *ibid.*, p. 804) To do a formal hedonic calculation every time we were about to act would be highly impractical. Yet, according to Bentham, each of us goes through some semblance of this process on a common-sense, intuitive level—only we may do it so quickly that we are virtually unconscious that we have done it. We may not wittingly go through all of the criteria outlined by Bentham, but, in general terms, we probably go through some kind of weighing and balancing process or else we consider the pros and cons before we act.

The hedonic calculus can be made more understandable by working out an actual example. Let us say that you are back in high school and that you are thinking about going on to college or university in a distant city. The school you have in mind has the best program in your chosen field and, for years, you have longed to attend it. The problem is that you have become involved in a serious relationship with someone who prefers that you stay in your hometown and find employment at the local manufacturing plant. You two have discussed the possibility of marriage, though no firm commitments have been made either way. Your dilemma involves choosing between (a) staying at home to work and continuing to develop your personal relationship with your special someone, and (b) going away to school and pursuing your career and academic dreams. What is the best thing to do? Let us find out using the hedonic calculus. Note that a complete calculation would entail not only a consideration of your interests but also a consideration of the interests of the other party involved. For brevity's sake, we will do a partial calculation based only on your interests. The values given to each part of the decision would likely vary in real life from person to person. I will take the liberty here of reading your mind and feeling your emotions.

An Hedonic Calculation

Alternative A—Stay at Home and Work in the Local Plant

1. *Intensity*: If I choose to stay at home, I will probably experience intense feelings of disappointment. I may also become regretful and may possibly resent how another person has frustrated the pursuit of my personal dream. Some of the resentment and anger I feel will be diminished by the loving feelings I have for my boyfriend/girlfriend and by the love I feel for my family.

   (-50)

2. *Duration*: Any acute feelings of anger and resentment are likely to subside in a relatively short period of time. Nagging doubts, however, may remain for years, causing unpleasantness and insecurity. Time may heal, but the emotional scars may remain quite visible.

   (-25)

3. *Certainty*: Who knows, what people want often changes. I might change my mind about working at the plant. It is possible that I will learn to like it there, though I really believe I will not.

   (-10)

4. *Propinquity*: The frustration and disappointment will result fairly soon. It is now July and classes start in September. The mental pain is not that far down the road.

   (-50)

5. *Fecundity*: If I stay at home, I can save myself a lot of money. Mom and dad will not accept rent from me so I will be able to save almost everything I earn. I also will not have to pay ridiculously high tuition fees that I cannot afford. I will be able to invest the money I earn in the stock market. I do not think I could ever recoup what I would lose in wages, residence, and tuition by going to college or university.

   (+100)

6. *Purity*: Sure, there will be financial gains if I stay at home, but considerable pain will be experienced due to possible missed opportunities. There will be things I never learn and people I never meet because I opt for the financially preferable course of action.

   (-25)

7. *Extent*: Other people will be affected by my decision. Mom and dad do not value formal education, so they would prefer that I stay home. My boyfriend/girlfriend also prefers that I stay home. I get the feeling that people in the neighborhood would also like me to stay. They say they would miss me if I went away.

   (+100)

Utilitarian Value of Alternative A

	Utility	*Disutility*
Intensity		-50
Duration		-25
Certainty		-10
Propinquity		-50
Fecundity	+100	
Purity		-25
Extent	+100	
	+200	-160

Alternative A would produce +40 net units of pleasure.

Alternative B—Go Away to School

1. *Intensity:* If I choose to go away to school, the excitement will be wonderful. I will be enthused, energized, and optimistic about going to a new place, meeting new people, and learning new things.

   (+75)

2. *Duration:* I know my positive feelings will tend to subside in time. Reality hits during exams. I am likely to miss my family and my special loved one. I know I can sometimes easily become bored. Nonetheless, I think the experience will be great and I will like it.

   (+25)

3. *Certainty:* Well, if I go, I am pretty certain of having fun and enjoying myself. I have been accepted both at the school and at the residence, so I know that there are no practical obstacles about going. I guess it is possible my roommate and I will be incompatible, but I will hope for the best.

   (+75)

4. *Propinquity:* The good times at school start soon. We are just weeks away from "homecoming," pub-crawls, intermural sports—you name it. If I choose to go to school, I will not have to wait long to enjoy myself.

   (+75)

5. *Fecundity:* I know that by going to school, I am going to cultivate my mind and possibly open up new horizons I never dreamt of before. I do not know of anyone who has ever been hurt by knowledge and understanding. On the downside, I do stand to lose a lot of money over the next four years. Getting a job at the plant would have paid well and I could have invested my earnings. No doubt about it, I will lose in the immediate future, but I hope to make it up over my lifetime.

   (+25)

6. *Purity:* I know that going off to school is not all fun and games, at least if I want to pass. Studying is hard and so are exams. You cannot party when you are doing an "all-nighter" memorizing Plato. Furthermore, I am likely to encounter professors and courses I do not really like. I guess school has its good and bad sides, just like everything else.

   (+10)

7. *Extent:* I know the people around me will be sorry to see me go. They will be saddened and possibly lonely. I hope my boyfriend/girlfriend does not take my decision personally. I do not mean to hurt, but I cannot help but think that hurt feelings will be created anyway.

   (-50)

Utilitarian Value of Alternative B

	Utility	*Disutility*
Intensity	+75	
Duration	+25	
Certainty	+75	
Propinquity	+75	
Fecundity	+25	
Purity	+10	
Extent		-50
	+285	-50

Alternative B would produce +235 units of pleasure.

Comparing Alternatives

	A	**B**
	Staying at Home	*Going to School*
Intensity	-50	+75
Duration	-25	+25
Certainty	-10	+75
Propinquity	-50	+75
Fecundity	+100	+25
Purity	-25	+10
Extent	+100	-50
	+40 units	+235 units

Findings: Alternative B produces greater pleasure than Alternative A.
Conclusion: Alternative B is the right thing to do.

PHILOSOPHERS AT WORK

This exercise can be done individually or in small groups. Your task will be to perform a hedonic calculation for the following situation. Imagine that you are on the student council and that you are away on a convention. At the convention, you meet another student delegate from the United States. After a few drinks and some pleasant conversation, you are propositioned and invited to that person's hotel room for an "overnight stay." You hesitate because you are engaged to be married. What should you do? Decide using Bentham's hedonic calculus.

Overtime Discussion: What problems, if any, did you discover doing your hedonic calculation? Assuming you are the student in the situation above, would you want your fiancé/fiancée to be a utilitarian? Why or why not?

MINDWORK MEDITATION

As moral philosophers, both Bentham and Aristotle are interested in promoting people's happiness. Do you think happiness is best achieved through hedonic calculations (Bentham) or by the cultivation of character (Aristotle)? Which philosopher do you think is on the better track? Why? Reflect upon these questions and record your thoughts.

Key Terms

utilitarianism
Jeremy Bentham
spirit of scientific objectivity
consequentialism
principle of utility
benefit
advantage
pleasure
happiness
goodness
psychological egoism
ethical egoism
is-ought fallacy
sanctions
physical sanctions
moral sanctions
religious sanctions
political sanctions
private ethics
retributivist
punishment
groundless
inefficacious
unprofitable
needless
hedonic calculus
intensity
duration
certainty
propinquity
fecundity
purity
extent

Progress Check 3.1

Instructions: Fill in the blanks with the appropriate responses listed below.

spirit of scientific objectivity	fecundity
principle of utility	utility
ethical egoist	political
sanction	private ethics
Jeremy Bentham	retroactive legislation
retributivist	nature
inefficacious	hedonic calculus
psychological egoist	is-ought
intensity	consequences
intrinsically	extent

1. _____ leads us to seek pleasure and to avoid pain.
2. _____ is a utilitarian philosopher.
3. Morality is not a purely subjective matter; it can be approached in a(n) _____.
4. For Jeremy Bentham, the morality of any particular action can be determined by an evaluation of its _____.
5. Bentham argues that the basis or foundation of morality should be the _____.
6. Equivalent terms for _____ are benefit, advantage, goodness, pleasure and happiness.
7. To claim that humans are naturally motivated to seek pleasure makes one a(n) _____.
8. To argue that one ought to pursue pleasure is to make one a(n) _____.
9. To argue that one should do something simply because that is the way things are is to commit the _____ fallacy.
10. A source of pain and pleasure that gives binding force to laws and rules of conduct is called a(n) _____.
11. Judges and magistrates administer _____ sanctions in their efforts to govern and to maintain order within society.
12. Jeremy Bentham is not a(n) _____; he believes that punishment in itself is evil and should be used only when necessary to exclude some greater evil.
13. _____ is/are beyond the proper scope of the law.
14. Punishments that do not work are _____.
15. Illegalizing and punishing acts that were legal when performed entails _____, something Bentham considered to be wrong.
16. For Bentham, moral decision making involves a kind of cost-benefit analysis, or what can be termed a(n) _____.
17. When we ask how strong the pleasure or emotional satisfaction is that is produced by any act, we are referring to the act's _____.

18. Whether or not an action's immediate consequences will lead to future benefits relates to the action's _____.
19. When we ask how many people are likely to be affected by an action, we refer to the _____ of its consequences.
20. According to utilitarianism, actions are not _____ right or wrong; consequences determine their moral value.

Summary of Major Points

1. **How did Jeremy Bentham approach the study of morality?**
   He approached it in a spirit of scientific objectivity.
   He rejected tradition, aristocratic privilege, and religion as legitimate bases for moral systems of thought.
   He used English laws and legislation.
2. **What is meant by the principle of utility?**
   According to this principle, good actions are those that increase happiness; bad actions are those that cause pain, suffering, misery or a decrease in happiness.
   Utility can be equated with benefit, advantage, pleasure, happiness, and goodness.
   Disutility is equivalent to liability, disadvantage, pain, unhappiness, and evil.
3. **How are psychological and ethical egoism different?**
   Psychological egoism is a psychological theory about human motivation; it states that people seek pleasure by nature.
   Ethical egoism is a moral theory; it states that the right thing to do is to pursue pleasure; that is what we ought to do.
4. **What is meant by the "is-ought" fallacy?**
   This is a logical mistake whereby one tries to derive a moral "ought" from an "is" of experience.
   What is should not necessarily or always be.
5. **What is a sanction? What are some examples?**
   A sanction is a source of pain and pleasure giving binding force to any law or rule of conduct.
   Sanctions can also be rewards and punishments serving as causal, determining factors in our behavior.
   Examples of sanctions are: physical, moral, religious, political.
6. **How does Bentham view punishment?**
   He is not in favor of retribution.
   He would use punishment only as a necessary evil to prevent a greater evil.
7. **When should one not punish?**
   When it is groundless, inefficacious (not effective), unprofitable, and needless.
8. **What considerations should be taken into account when punishing?**
   Punishment must outweigh the profit of the offense.
   Greater offenses should be given greater punishments.

Punishment for the same crime should be meted out fairly and consistently.
Punishment should not exceed the bare minimum to be effective.
Crimes with little risk of getting caught should be given stricter punishments.

9. **What is the hedonic calculus?**
   A process of calculation used to determine which action will produce the greatest utility. It is comprised of seven criteria: intensity, duration, certainty, propinquity, purity, fecundity, and extent.

Source References and Related Readings

Ayer, A.J. "The Principle of Utility" in *Philosophical Essays*. Edited by A.J. Ayer. New York: St. Martin's Press, 1955.

Bentham, Jeremy. "An Introduction to the Principles of Morals and Legislation" in *The English Philosophers from Bacon to Mill*. Edited by E.A. Burtt. New York: The Modern Library, 1939.

Falikowski, Anthony. *Moral Philosophy: Theories, Skills, and Applications*. Englewood Cliffs, N.J.: Prentice-Hall, 1990.

Narveson, Jan. *Morality and Utility*. Baltimore: Johns Hopkins University Press, 1967.

Runkle, Gerald. *Ethics: An Examination of Contemporary Moral Problems*. New York: Holt, Rinehart and Winston, 1982.

Smart, J.J. *Outline of a Utilitarian System of Ethics*. London: Cambridge University Press, 1961.

Soccio, Douglas. *Archetypes of Wisdom: An Introduction to Philosophy*, 2nd edition. Belmont, Ca.: Wadsworth Publishing Co., 1995.

Stumpf, Samuel Enoch. *Philosophy: History and Problems*. New York: McGraw-Hill Inc., 1994.

White, Thomas. *Discovering Philosophy*. Upper Saddle River, N.J.: Prentice Hall, 1996.

CHAPTER FOUR

4

JOHN STUART MILL: THE HIGH ROAD TO HAPPINESS

Overview

Biographical Brief: "John Stuart Mill"
Mill's Acceptance and Defense of Utilitarianism
Pleasure: It is the Quality that Matters
Higher versus Lower Pleasures
Higher Pleasures can be Risky Business
Breaks from Bentham
Egoistic versus Altruistic Utilitarianism
Mill's Rejection of the Hedonic Calculus
Reducing Human Misery
Democracy and the Proper Limits of Governmental Authority
Back to the Source Feature from Mill's *On Liberty*
Key Terms
Progress Check 4.1
Summary of Major Points
Source References and Related Readings

Learning Outcomes

After successfully completing this chapter, you will be able to:

4.1 present John Stuart Mill's position on the principle of utility;
4.2 explain Mill's qualitative distinction between higher and lower pleasures and why the former are better than the latter;
4.3 discuss the risks of pursuing higher pleasures;
4.4 outline the basic differences between Mill and Bentham regarding their utilitarian philosophies;

4.5 give the reasons why Mill rejects Bentham's hedonic calculus;
4.6 offer the utilitarian position on human misery and its reduction;
4.7 state Mill's position on the proper limits of governmental authority over the individual.

PHILOSOPHICAL FOCUS QUESTIONS

1. What was it about utilitarianism that some people found offensive and that made it necessary for Mill to present a defense against its critics?
2. Is it appropriate to distinguish between types of pleasures, saying that some pleasures are better than others? Would some people be reluctant to make such a distinction? Why?
3. What role does human dignity have to play in Mill's utilitarian ethics?
4. What are some risks that are associated with pursuing higher pleasures?
5. How is Mill less of an ethical egoist than Bentham?
6. Why is there a problem in doing hedonic calculations?
7. What can be said about human misery and suffering from a utilitarian point of view?

LIBRARY OF CONGRESS

John Stuart Mill
(1806–1873)

BIOGRAPHICAL BRIEF*

John Stuart Mill was born in London, England, in 1806. He was the eldest child of Harriet and James Mill, a Scotsman who was an accomplished author, friend, and colleague of Jeremy Bentham. James Mill was an intensely intellectual man. This is evidenced by the fact that he conducted an educational experiment with his son John. The young Mill was put through a rigorous program of home education by his father. At the age of three, John Stuart was learning Greek, and by age eight he was reading Plato and other Greek authors in the original. Along with Latin and arithmetic, extensive reading was part of Mill's rigorous curriculum. Each morning, John Stuart was expected to give a recitation of the previous day's reading to his father.

The young Mill did not become an academic by profession. His research and writing were done in conjunction with his duties as a civil servant in the East India Company. Mill imposed upon himself an onerous regimen in his position, one which eventually led to his psychological collapse at age 20. The depression associated with his "nervous breakdown" lasted several months. Mill gradually recovered from his gloomy state by allowing emotion and sentiment to grow within him. His father's unfeeling disposition had apparently impacted negatively on John Stuart's affective development and psychological health. He once wrote that

**From Falikowski,* Moral Philosophy, *p. 57.*

he was never allowed to be a boy and to experience normal childhood friendships and playfulness. Fortunately for Mill, his one-sided, highly intellectualized personality became more balanced. His feelings for humanity were cultivated by reading Wordsworth's poetry and by developing a loving friendship with Harriet Taylor, who later became his wife.

J. S. Mill was convinced that his wife was a talented thinker who, unfortunately, was not appreciated because of the discrimination against women at that time. Acutely sensitive to the matter of discrimination, Mill addressed it in a work entitled *The Subjection of Women*. J. S. Mill's objections to sexism make him a predecessor of contemporary feminism. On this note, it should be pointed out that he was elected to Parliament in 1865. As part of his political struggle he fought for the exploited Negroes of Jamaica; and he tried to increase the power and influence of the working class in England, hoping to bring it into the country's political and economic mainstream. He also worked for the redistribution of lands in Ireland. J. S. Mill can be described as a political thinker, social reformer, activist, and moral philosopher. Selected works include: *Utilitarianism*, *On Liberty*, *A System of Logic*, *The Principles of Political Economy*, and *Considerations on Representative Government*.

4.1 MILL'S ACCEPTANCE AND DEFENSE OF UTILITARIANISM

As a young man, J.S. Mill was influenced by Jeremy Bentham, primarily through his father, James Mill, who had been not only a friend to Bentham but also a collaborator who assisted him in shaping his political ideas. The young Mill was particularly impressed by Bentham's **principle of utility**. Recall that Bentham used this principle as an alternative to trying to derive concepts of morality and lawmaking from notions like "right reason" and "natural law." Mill wrote: "the principle of utility, understood as Bentham understood it . . . gave unity to my conceptions of things. I now had opinions, a creed, a doctrine, a philosophy; in one among the best senses of the word, a religion; the inculcation and diffusion of which could be made the principle outward purpose of life" (Stumpf, 1994, p. 372).

Convictions are more dangerous enemies of truth than lies.

Friedrich Nietzsche

MINDWORK MEDITATION

Are there any values, beliefs or principles that give unity and purpose to your life right now? If so, which ones? How do these things operate in practical terms when it comes to action and personal decision making? If you do not have a fundamental life principle or concrete value system by which to direct your life, then ask the question, "Why not?" Is having some kind of life-directing principle necessary? What has life been like so far without one? How will you know when you find the principle or value system that you should base your life on? How would you expect your life to change?

In his classic essay, *Utilitarianism*, Mill set out to defend the principle of utility against its critics. In the process, he arrived at a version of **utilitarianism** that differed significantly from Bentham's. For instance, whereas Bentham regarded all pleasures as equal in value and different only in amount, Mill made a distinction between higher and lower quality pleasures, suggesting that the former were better than the latter. He also rejected Bentham's hedonic calculus and opted for a less egoistic form of hedonism than the one advanced by Bentham. Let us take a few moments to look more closely at Mill's utilitarian revisions.

PHILOSOPHERS AT WORK

John Stuart Mill based his adult life on the principle of utility and committed himself to it. Are there any alternative principles, creeds, values to which other people have devoted their lives? What are they and who became their devotees? (*Help*: Think of some heroic or saintly individuals and the goals toward which they have worked.)

4.2 PLEASURE: IT IS THE QUALITY THAT MATTERS

In the *Principles of Morals and Legislation*, Bentham limited his discussion of pleasure solely to quantity. He argued that pleasures differ only in amount, saying things like, "pushpin [a child's game] is as good as poetry." For Bentham, the only criterion for goodness is the amount of pleasure that an act can produce.

Bentham's contention that all pleasures are equal contains considerable intuitive appeal. In North American society, for instance, where we value democracy and tolerance for diversity, the notion that some pleasures could be deemed better than others or that some pleasurable pursuits could be considered wrong, inferior or misguided compared with others may seem offensive or appear somewhat elitist. Liberal-minded thinkers would likely be reluctant to say, "My pleasures are better than yours" or "These pleasures are better than those." Notwithstanding such a disinclination to make value judgments on the worth of particular pleasures, Mill does so and he does so in defense of utilitarianism.

Mill recognizes that there is a danger in seeing moral life exclusively in regard to the pursuit of pleasure. If pleasure is not properly understood, some people may view a utilitarian lifestyle as something vulgar and more befitting of swine than of humans. Indeed, the pursuit of pleasure, understood in its basest terms, would be regarded by religionists, at least, as sinful. Self-denial in regard to pleasure is often considered virtuous or saintly. Denying oneself something pleasurable is a ritual performed by many Christians during Lent. To put pleasure into proper perspective and to defend its pursuit against its critics, Mill made a distinction between the **quantity** and **quality** of pleasure.

HIGHER VERSUS LOWER PLEASURES

For Mill, more important than the amount is the type of pleasure experienced. Mill believed that pleasures could be categorized as either **higher** or **lower** and that the higher ones were better. He argued that human beings possess psychological faculties that are elevated above the level of animal appetites. At the lower grade of existence, Mill placed **bodily pleasures** and those of physical sensation. At the higher grade of existence, Mill placed the pleasures of the **intellect**, those relating to our **feelings** and **imagination** and those relating to our **moral sentiments** and sensitivities. Rather than degrade life, the pursuit of such higher pleasures can ennoble and dignify it. With proper upbringing and education, people can cultivate their minds and learn to take pleasure in the objects of nature, the achievements of arts, the imaginative language of poetry, the incidents of history, and the ways of humankind—past, present and future. With all this in view, there is no need to see pleasure as a base and abject pursuit. It can offer a sense of **human dignity** and worth to ordinary people's lives. According to Mill, people who object to pleasure as the ultimate aim of life probably interpret it too narrowly as something base.

> ***Human beings have faculties more elevated than the animal appetites and, when once made conscious of them, do not regard anything as happiness which does not include their gratification.***
>
> *J.S. Mill*

According to Mill, once people are made aware of the differences between higher and lower pleasures, they do not, and will not, accept any definition of happiness that does not include the development of their nobler and distinctively human faculties. He writes:

> Now it is an unquestionable fact that those who are equally acquainted with and equally capable of appreciating and enjoying both [kinds of pleasure] do give a most marked preference to the manner of existence which employs their higher faculties. Few human creatures would consent to be changed into any of the lower animals for a promise of the fullest allowance of a beast's pleasures; no intelligent human being would consent to be a fool, no instructed person would be an ignoramus, no person of feeling and conscience would be selfish and base, even though they should be persuaded that the fool, the dunce, or the rascal is better satisfied with his lot than they are with theirs. (Mill, 1957, pp. 12–13)

From the quotation above, we see how Mill concludes that higher pleasures are better. They should be preferred because they are, in fact, favored by anyone familiar with both types of pleasure. Besides this, mental pleasures are thought to be superior to bodily pleasures because they offer greater **permanency**, **safety**, and **uncostliness**. There is nothing in higher pleasures themselves that make them superior; their superiority is located in their circumstantial advantages. Let us take the drinking of alcohol to illustrate the point. The experience of going out on an alcoholic binge may be intensely pleasurable for any given individual. Stress is relieved, inhibitions disappear, and all sensations are heightened. (Sound like last weekend?) The pleasure derived from an alcoholic binge, however, is short-lived; overconsumption of alcohol is likely to harm one's liver and impair, or otherwise negatively affect, one's brain. With current costs and levels of taxation in this country, going out "drinking" is also very likely to require a significant outlay of money. Once the numbing bodily pleasure that is derived from alcohol has disappeared, you may, like so many others, experience negative aftereffects, such as a hangover and an empty wallet. While intoxicated, you may have said and done things that you now regret. The pleasure was not only short-lived but also probably cost you a lot and even placed your personal safety at risk. Let us say you were feeling "so good" that you did not worry about driving home drunk. Once sober, you cannot believe what a stupid thing you did.

It's better to be a human being dissatisfied, than a pig satisfied; better to be Socrates dissatisfied than a fool satisfied.

J.S. Mill

In contrast to the physical pleasure obtained from drinking intoxicating alcohol, consider the more refined pleasure of listening to beautiful music or appreciating nature or art. Such things present no danger and they are typically inexpensive. Watching a sunset or listening to the sounds of a babbling brook costs nothing; listening to the radio will cost you a few cents on your hydro bill. The aftereffects of higher pleasures are also preferable. Rather than feel emptiness, regret or disgust, one is more likely to feel ennobled and spiritually uplifted as a result of cultivating one's mind and the **higher faculties**. The higher pleasures of the mind appeal to our sense of human dignity, not to our base appetites which we share with animals.

PHILOSOPHERS AT WORK

Mill's emphasis on the higher pleasures and the higher faculties of humankind is reminiscent of another philosopher we have studied in this text. Who is that philosopher and what does he have in common with Mill?

4.3
HIGHER PLEASURES CAN BE RISKY BUSINESS

As suggested, higher pleasures are probably safer than most physical pleasures or those associated with appetite gratification. This is not to say, however, that pursuit of higher pleasure is totally without risk. Mill writes:

> A being of higher faculties requires more to make him happy, is capable of probably more acute suffering, and certainly accessible to it at more points, than one of an inferior type; but in spite of these liabilities, he can never really wish to sink into what he feels to be a lower grade of existence. (Mill, *ibid.*, p. 13)

The **inferior type** of individual is more likely to find contentment in the lower pleasures of life than the **superior type**, who perceives most sources of happiness in the world as imperfect.

Nonetheless, the superior type can learn to bear these worldly imperfections and be satisfied with the exercise of his or her higher faculties. Mill believes that it is the **sense of dignity**, abundant in the higher type, that makes objects of lower pleasure undesirable or at least less desirable than those things that are humanly elevating. Equating the inferior type's lifestyle with animal level existence, Mill writes: "It is better to be a human being dissatisfied than a pig satisfied; better to be Socrates dissatisfied than a fool satisfied" (Mill, *ibid.*).

In addition to the possibility of experiencing greater frustration in pursuit of higher pleasures, superior type individuals face another risk. They may occasionally (or frequently) succumb to temptations and opt for pleasures of a lower sort. This fact poses no obstacles for Mill. People may be perfectly aware, for instance, that sensual indulgence (e.g., sexual appetite satisfaction with a prostitute) could injure their health (e.g., with A.I.D.S.), that health is a greater good compared with such indulgence, and yet, still opt to do that which is, potentially, very injurious. Apart from improper development and moral weakness, or what Mill calls **infirmity of character**, the problem is that once people have devoted themselves to lower pleasures (more easily obtained), they may become incapable of enjoying the higher type. In this regard, Mill says:

> Capacity for the nobler feelings is in most natures a very tender plant, easily killed, not only by hostile influences, but by more want of sustenance; and in the majority of young persons it speedily dies away if the occupations to which their position in life has devoted them, and the society into which it has thrown them, are not favorable to keeping that higher capacity in exercise. Men lose their high aspirations as they lose their intellectual tastes, because they have not time or opportunity for indulging them; and they addict themselves to inferior pleasures, not because they deliberately prefer them, but because they are either the only ones to which they have access or the only ones which they are any longer capable of enjoying. (Mill, *ibid.*, pp. 14–15)

PHILOSOPHERS AT WORK

Think about all the sources of pleasure and amusement in today's popular culture. Do they nourish and cultivate our higher natures or feed our lower and base instincts? Explain and illustrate. When it comes to encouraging proper character development, is there anything that we, as a society, need to do? If so, what and why? If not, why not?

4.4 BREAKS FROM BENTHAM

By making a distinction between higher and lower pleasures, Mill's defense of utilitarianism represents a significant departure from Bentham's original position. Clearly, for Mill, not all pleasures are equal; pushpin, Packman or pinball for that matter are all not as good as poetry. The standard of goodness in behavior, therefore, no longer involves the simple maximization of pleasure, rather it involves the fulfillment of our distinctively human faculties. As one writer puts it, "if it is better to be Socrates dissatisfied than a pig satisfied, morality is proportionate to the happiness we find in being truly human and not in the pleasure we experience" (Stumpf, 1994, p. 376).

Given these remarks, it becomes a debatable point whether or not Mill actually abandoned utilitarianism for something else he called by the same name. This is something to think about. Nonetheless, support for the notion that Mill remains a full-fledged utilitarian can be mustered by pointing out that he has not abandoned pleasure as the ultimate standard of morality, only that he has opted for a higher standard not recognized by Bentham.

EGOISTIC VERSUS ALTRUISTIC UTILITARIANISM

the happiness which forms the utilitarian standard of what is right in conduct is not the agent's own happiness, but that of all concerned.

J.S. Mill

Earlier, in our examination of Jeremy Bentham, we learned how he was both a psychological and ethical hedonist. Not only did Bentham believe that we are designed by nature to seek pleasure and to avoid pain but also that, morally speaking, that is what we ought to do. As a psychological and ethical hedonist, Bentham was in favor of **enlightened self-interest**. He maintained that communities and societies are nothing more than collections of individuals, so that by furthering individual interests, what we do, in effect, is promote the common good and benefit the larger community or society of which the individual is a part. Bentham held that individuals would respond to legal and political sanctions egoistically (i.e., in terms of their own self-interest) and that if proper laws and legislation were put in place, we could construct a social system best suited for individuals to promote their personal welfare and to advance their self-interested pursuits. Hedonic calculations were, therefore, supposed to be performed from the vantage point of the individual(s) whose interests were most directly affected in any given situation or set of circumstances.

With John Stuart Mill, we find a significant movement away from the egoistic utilitarianism of Bentham. Although, like Bentham, Mill is in favor of promoting "the greatest happiness for the greatest number," his approach to accomplishing this end is different. First, when it comes to deciding what one ought to do, the person making the decision can assume no special or preferred status. Mill writes: "the happiness which forms the utilitarian standard of what is right in conduct is not the agent's own happiness but that of all concerned. As between his own happiness and that of others, utilitarianism requires him to be as strictly impartial as a disinterested and benevolent spectator" (Stumpf, 1983, p. 348).

In the golden rule of Jesus of Nazareth, we read the complete spirit of the ethics of utility. "To do as you would be done by" and "to love your neighbor as yourself," constitute the ideal perfection of utilitarian morality.

J.S. Mill

In my opinion, John Stuart Mill is a closet-Aristotelian.

Author

If one's own personal interests have no special or preferred place in utilitarian decision making, then the right thing to do may not always be what benefits the person most. Doing the right thing may sometimes require **personal sacrifice** or **altruism**—namely, putting others' interests before one's own, doing things for their sake. Of course, as a utilitarian, Mill is opposed to self-sacrifice where it does not increase the sum total of happiness or the greatest happiness for the greatest number. Simply to deny oneself is to cause frustration, pain or suffering—things that have only **disutility**. There is no virtue in the reduction of pleasure when it is unnecessary. In the ideal scenario "laws and social arrangements should place the happiness or . . . the interest of every individual as nearly as possible in harmony with the interest of the whole." If there is an identity of interests between the individual and the community, then self-sacrifice will usually be unnecessary because in doing things that benefit others, one in turn benefits oneself. If proper social engineering and character education occur, the impulse or inclination to promote the general good will become an habitual motive of action. In view of this, Mill defends utilitarianism against those critics who regard it as little more than a base or convenient morality of self-interest. As we see, Mill's **altruistic utilitarianism** contains feelings for humanity and a disinterested and impartial pursuit of the good. His suggestion that we seek the greatest happiness is not always, or necessarily, my (or your) greatest happiness, but the greatest happiness of the greatest number.

4.4
4.5

MILL'S REJECTION OF THE HEDONIC CALCULUS

Another of Mill's significant departures from Bentham is on the issue of calculating pleasures. Bentham believed that by means of the **hedonic calculus** one could quantify pleasures and determine, in a spirit of scientific objectivity, what action or policy would be likely to result in the best consequences or greatest utility. Mill, on the other hand, does not believe that pleasure and pain can be calculated in Bentham's sense. He asks:

> What means are there of determining which is the acutest of two pains, or the intensest of two pleasurable sensations, except the general suffrage [opinion or vote] of those who are familiar with both? Neither pains nor pleasures are homogeneous, and pain is always heterogeneous with pleasure. What is there to decide whether a particular pleasure is worth purchasing at the cost of a particular pain, except the feelings and judgment of the experienced? (Stumpf, 1983, p. 348)

Above, we see that Mill regards pains and pleasures as **incommensurable**. One cannot compare pain and pleasure because they are essentially different in kind. In the same section of *Utilitarianism* from which the quotation above was taken, Mill asserts that it is only those who have knowledge of both higher and lower pleasures that should have the final say when decisions between the two must be made. When these "experienced" people conflict among themselves, then majority opinion should rule. Whether it be the majority or the experienced knowledgeable individual who decides, however, it is only a "preference" for one pleasure over another that can be expressed. Apart from this, there is no other impartial tribunal where some kind of objective calculation can be performed.

It is a kind of spiritual snobbery that makes people think they can be happy without money.
Albert Camus

4.6 REDUCING HUMAN MISERY

John Stuart Mill recognizes that from some moral perspectives it could be argued that human beings have no "right" to be happy and, therefore, are not necessarily entitled to happiness. In fact, historically, many religious people have felt that happiness is God's eternal reward in heaven for living a morally good life on earth. By displaying the virtues of faith, hope, and charity, many people believe they can earn the right to be eternally happy at God's right-hand (or should I say left-hand?) side. Despite the objection to our entitlement to be happy, Mill continues his defense of utilitarianism by asserting that we have at least a moral duty to prevent or to reduce unhappiness. Whenever possible, we should make efforts to eliminate or to mitigate pain and suffering. Doing this is, of course, part of the utilitarian prescription for life. Even people who claim no entitlements to happiness would likely be in favor of reducing human suffering in the world. On this note, Mill believes that many of the world's evils, which cause unhappiness, can be eradicated. Poverty is one example. Mill contends that this social ailment can be cured by the wisdom of society and the good sense of individuals. Disease, another evil, can certainly be reduced by proper physical and moral education. Mill states that:

> All the grand sources, in short, of human suffering are in a great degree, many of them almost entirely, conquerable by human care and effort; and though their removal is grievously slow—though a long succession of generations will perish in the breach before the conquest is completed, and this world becomes all that, if will and knowledge were not wanting, it might easily be made—yet every mind sufficiently intelligent and generous to bear a part, however small and inconspicuous, in the endeavor will draw a noble enjoyment from the contest itself, which he would not for any bribe in the form of selfish indulgence consent to be without. (Mill, *ibid.*, p. 20)

Speaking of entitlements to happiness, what have you done for me lately?
Author

PHILOSOPHERS AT WORK

Do you honestly believe that you have the "right" to be happy? When you are not happy, is it because someone is violating your rights or treating you inappropriately? Are others doing you wrong? Furthermore, do you have a duty to make others happy? If so, in what ways? If not, then why must others cater to your happiness? Discuss this with classmates.

Let us say, hypothetically, that we could ensure people's health and that we could redistribute the wealth in the land so that everybody had more than enough to survive. Would they necessarily be happy then? The answer is probably no. Although people may not suffer great physical pains or mental anguish resulting from maltreatment or some kind of economic or political injustice, happiness may, nonetheless, elude them. Mill has a psychological explanation for this. He maintains that for people who are "fortunate in their outward lot [and who] do not find in life sufficient enjoyment to make it valuable to them the cause generally is caring for nobody but themselves" (Mill, *ibid.*, p. 18). Apart from **selfishness**, "the principle cause which makes life unsatisfactory is want of **mental cultivation**" (Mill, *ibid.*). The uncultivated mind is surrounded by many possible sources of pleasure, yet it discovers few lasting ones. It is continuously bored and searching for something else. The cultivated mind, by contrast, finds endless pleasure in all that surrounds it—in natural beauty, the cultural and artistic achievements of society, the drama of history, the workings and development of human civilization, and the prospects for the future of humanity.

Want something long enough and you don't.
Proverb

If you think about it for a moment, Mill is probably right to suggest that there is enough that is interesting and enjoyable in life to make everyone happy, at least in principle. For example, as someone who lives in Oakville, Ontario, Canada, I am often overwhelmed to think that I live in the best country in the world (a recent conclusion by the United Nations for the fourth time in a decade); that I live in one of the safest and most prosperous communities in that best country; that I am surrounded by all forms of entertainment and amusement; that science and technology bring the stars and continents to my doorstep (or at least to my television set and computer terminal); that, arguably, I enjoy one of the best educational and health-care systems on the planet; that so much knowledge and opportunity is available to me; that I can enjoy peace in the land and live harmoniously with friends and family, and so on and so on. What kind of mind must it take to be bored and dissatisfied with all of this? For Mill, it would have to be an uncultivated mind that lacks appreciation and yearns only for the lower pleasures of self-indulgence. It is only the uncultivated mind that has not developed a sincere interest in the public good and can take no pleasure in the satisfaction of others. It is the uncultivated mind that does not, or is unable to, enjoy the improvement of the human condition. By contrast, the cultivated mind can find happiness in working for the common good, appreciating the abundance of life, satisfying curiosity, and pursuing higher intellectual interests. For Mill, happiness is not about living for oneself in a selfish, egoistic fashion, and it would be misinterpreting him to say that his utilitarian philosophy suggests this. Mill's utilitarianism is designed to lead to a reduction of suffering and misery in the world and to an increase in human happiness.

The next time you point the finger of blame at someone or something, calling that person or activity boring, remember that there are three fingers pointing back at you.
Author

When the people lack a proper sense of awe, then some awful visitation will descend upon them.
Lao Tzu

4.7

DEMOCRACY AND THE PROPER LIMITS OF GOVERNMENTAL AUTHORITY

Whatever crushes individuality is despotism, by whatever name it may be called.
J.S. Mill

Considerations of self-development and the greatest happiness principle led Mill to reflect on the proper relationships that should exist between the individual and the government. In his work entitled *On Liberty*, Mill addressed the issue of **social liberty**. In it he asked about the nature and limits of the power that can be legitimately exercised by society over the individual. Though Mill was in favor of **democracy** as the best form of government to further individual growth and development, as well as the common good, he was, nonetheless, aware of its inherent dangers and he cautioned against abuses of governmental control. For example, in a democracy, things typically get done by majority rule. This allows for the possibility that the majority may choose to oppress the minority. A type of coercion may also arise involving the tyranny of public opinion. Society may impose, by means other than laws and civil penalties, its own ideas and practices as rules of acceptable conduct on everyone, including dissenters.

PHILOSOPHERS AT WORK

Part One: Are there any identifiable minorities in history or in contemporary North American society that, arguably, have suffered at the hands of the majority? Name those minorities and describe the nature of the oppression or injustice perpetrated against them.
Part Two: Are there any state, provincial or federal laws that in your estimation, or in the estimation of others, violate individual rights by regulating what should be considered a matter of personal choice or private conduct? What are some of those controversial laws? (*Hint*: Think automobiles, pounds and ounces, provincial street signs.)

Aware of the potential problems inherent in democracy, Mill claims: "There is a limit to the legitimate interference of collective opinion with individual independence: and to find that limit, and maintain it against encroachment, is as indispensable to a good condition of human affairs, as protection against political despotism" (Mill, 1975, p. 6). Put simply, Mill believed that an acceptable form of democratic government should include certain safeguards. These safeguards should be designed to defend against the forces that would hinder individuals from realizing themselves and their goals in a free and open fashion. Let us turn now to the "Back to the Source" feature to read exactly what Mill does argue on the proper limits of government.

BACK TO THE SOURCE*

The object of this Essay is to assert one very simple principle, as entitled to govern absolutely the dealings of society with the individual in the way of compulsion and control, whether the means used be physical force in the form of legal penalties, or the moral coercion of public opinion. That principle is, that the sole end for which mankind are warranted, individually or collectively, in interfering with the liberty of action of any of their number, is self-protection. That the only purpose for which power can be rightfully exercised over any member of a civilized community, against his will, is to prevent harm to others. His own good, either physical or moral, is not a sufficient warrant. He cannot rightfully be compelled to do or forebear because it will be better for him to do so, because it will make him happier, because, in the opinions of others, to do so would be wise, or even right. These are good reasons for remonstrating with him, or reasoning with him, or persuading him, or entreating him, but not for compelling him, or visiting him with any evil in case he do otherwise. To justify that, the conduct from which it is desired to deter him must be calculated to produce evil to some one else. The only part of the conduct of any one, for which he is amenable to society, is that which concerns others. In the part which merely concerns himself, his independence is, of right, absolute. Over himself, over his own body and mind, the individual is sovereign.

It is, perhaps hardly necessary to say that this doctrine is meant to apply only to human beings in the maturity of their faculties. We are not speaking of children, or of young persons below the age which the law may fix as that of manhood or womanhood. Those who are still in a state to require being taken care of by others, must be protected against their own actions as well as against external injury. For the same reason, we may leave out of consideration those backward states of society in which the race itself may be considered as in its nonage. The early difficulties in the way of spontaneous progress are so great, that there is seldom any choice of means for overcoming them; and a ruler full of the spirit of improvement is warranted in the use of any expedients that will attain an end, perhaps otherwise unattainable. Despotism is a legitimate mode of government in dealing with barbarians, provided the end be their improvement, and the means justified by actually effecting that end. Liberty, as a principle, has no application to any state of things anterior to the time when mankind have become capable of being improved by free and equal discussion. Until then, there is nothing for them but implicit obedience to an Akbar or a Charlemagne, if they are so fortunate as to find one. But as soon as mankind have attained the capacity of being guided to their own improvement by conviction or persuasion (a period long since reached in all nations with whom we need here concern ourselves), compulsion, either in the direct form or in that of pains and penalties for non-compliance, is no longer admissible as a means to their own good, and justifiable only for the security of others.

**From Mill,* On Liberty. *Footnotes have been renumbered.*

It is proper to state that I forego any advantage which could be derived to my argument from the idea of abstract right, as a thing independent of utility. I regard utility as the ultimate appeal on all ethical questions; but it must be utility in the largest sense, grounded on the permanent interests of man as a progressive being. Those interests, I contend, authorize the subjection of individual spontaneity to external control, only in respect to those actions of each, which concern the interest of other people. If any one does an act hurtful to others, there is a *prima facie* case for punishing him, by law, or, where legal penalties are not safely applicable, by general disapprobation. There are also many positive acts for the benefit of others, which he may rightfully be compelled to perform; such as to give evidence in a court of justice; to bear his fair share in the common defense, or in any other joint work necessary to the interest of the society of which he enjoys the protection; and to perform certain acts of individual beneficence, such as saving a fellow-creature's life, or interposing to protect the defenseless against ill-usage, things which whenever it is obviously a man's duty to do, he may rightfully be made responsible to society for not doing. A person may cause evil to others not only by his actions but by his inaction, and in either case he is justly accountable to them for the injury. The latter case, it is true, requires a much more cautious exercise of compulsion than the former. To make any one answerable for doing evil to others is the rule; to make him answerable for not preventing evil is, comparatively speaking, the exception. Yet there are many cases clear enough and grave enough to justify that exception. In all things which regard the external relations of the individual, he is *de jure* amenable to those whose interests are concerned, and, if need be, to society as their protector. There are often good reasons for not holding him to the responsibility; but these reasons must arise from the special expediencies of the case: either because it is a kind of case in which he is on the whole likely to act better, when left to his own discretion, than when controlled in any way in which society have it in their power to control him; or because the attempt to exercise control would produce other evils, greater than those which it would prevent. When such reasons as these preclude the enforcement of responsibility, the conscience of the agent himself should step into the vacant judgment seat, and protect those interests of others which have no external protection; judging himself all the more rigidly, because the case does not admit of his being made accountable to the judgment of his fellow-creatures.

But there is a sphere of action in which society, as distinguished from the individual, has, if any, only an indirect interest; comprehending all that portion of a person's life and conduct which affects only himself, or if it also affects others, only with their free, voluntary, and undeceived consent and participation. When I say only himself, I mean directly, and in the first instance; for whatever affects himself, may affect others *through* himself; and the objection which may be grounded on this contingency, will receive consideration in the sequel. This, then, is the appropriate region of human liberty. It comprises, first, the inward domain of consciousness; demanding liberty of conscience in the most comprehensive sense; liberty of thought and feeling; absolute freedom of opinion and sentiment on all subjects, practical or speculative, scientific, moral, or theological. The liberty of expressing and publishing opinions may seem to fall under a different principle, since it belongs to that part of the conduct of an individual which concerns other people; but, being almost of as much importance as the liberty of thought itself, and resting in great part on the same reasons, is practically inseparable from it. Secondly, the principle requires liberty of tastes and pursuits; of framing the plan of our life to suit our own character; of doing as we like, subject to such consequences as may follow: without impediment from our fellow-creatures, so long as what we do does not harm them, even though they should think our conduct foolish, perverse, or wrong. Thirdly, from this liberty of each individual, follows the liberty, within the same limits, of combination among individuals; freedom to unite, for any purpose not involving harm to others: the persons combining being supposed to be of full age, and not forced or deceived.

No society in which these liberties are not, on the whole, respected, is free, whatever may be its form of government; and none is completely free in which they do not exist absolute and unqualified. The only freedom which deserves the name, is that of pursuing our own good in our own way, so long as we do not attempt to deprive others of theirs, or impede their efforts to obtain it. Each is the proper guardian of his own health, whether bodily, or mental and spiritual. Mankind are greater gainers by suffering each other to live as seems good for themselves, than by compelling each to live as seems good for the rest.

Though this doctrine is anything but new, and, to some persons, may have the air of a truism, there is no doctrine which stands more directly opposed to the general tendency of existing opinion and practice. Society has expended fully as much effort in the attempt (according to its lights) to compel people to conform to its notions of personal [and] of social excellence. The ancient commonwealths thought themselves entitled to practice, and the ancient philosophers countenanced, the regulation of every part of private conduct by public authority, on the ground that the State had a deep interest in the whole bodily and mental discipline of every one of its citizens; a mode of thinking which may have been admissible in small republics surrounded by powerful enemies, in constant peril of being subverted by foreign attack or internal commotion, and to which even a short interval of relaxed energy and self-command might so easily be fatal that they could not afford to wait for the salutary permanent effects of freedom. In the modern world, the greater size of political communities, and, above all, the separation between spiritual and temporal authority (which placed the direction of men's consciences in other hands than those which controlled their worldly affairs), prevented so great an interference by law in the details of private life; but the engines of moral repression have been wielded more strenuously against divergence from the reigning opinion in self-regarding, than even in social matters; religion, the most powerful of the elements which have entered into the formation of moral feeling, having almost always been governed either by the ambition of a hierarchy, seeking control over every department of human conduct, or by the spirit of Puritanism. And some of those modern reformers who have placed themselves in strongest opposition to the religions of the past, have been noway behind either churches or sects in their assertion of the right of spiritual domination: M. Comte, in particular, whose social systems, as unfolded in his *Système de Politique Positive*, aims at establishing (though by moral more than by legal appliances) a despotism of society over the individual, surpassing anything contemplated in the political ideal of the most rigid disciplinarian among the ancient philosophers.

Apart from the peculiar tenets of individual thinkers, there is also in the world at large an increasing inclination to stretch unduly the powers of society over the individual, both by the force of opinion and even by that of legislation; and as the tendency of all the changes taking place in the world is to strengthen society, and diminish the power of the individual, this encroachment is not one of the evils which tend spontaneously to disappear, but, on the contrary, to grow more and more formidable. The disposition of mankind, whether as rulers or as fellow-citizens, to impose their own opinions and inclinations as a rule of conduct on others, is so energetically supported by some of the best and by some of the worst feelings incident to human nature, that it is hardly ever kept under restraint by anything but want of power: and as the power is not declining, but growing, unless a strong barrier of moral conviction can be raised against the mischief, we must expect, in the present circumstances of the world, to see it increase.

It will be convenient for the argument, if, instead of at once entering upon the general thesis, we confine ourselves in the first instance to a single branch of it, on which the principle here stated is, if not fully, yet to a certain point, recognized by the current opinions. This one branch is the Liberty of Thought: from which it is impossible to separate the cognate liberty of speaking and of writing. Although these liberties, to some considerable amount, form part of the political morality of all countries which profess religious toleration and free institutions, the grounds, both philosophical and practical, on which they rest, are perhaps not so familiar to the general mind, nor so thoroughly appreciated by many even of the leaders of opinion, as might have been expected. Those grounds, when rightly understood, are of much wider application than to only one division of the subject, and a thorough consideration of this part of the question will be found the best introduction to the remainder. Those to whom nothing which I am about to say will be new, may therefore, I hope, excuse me, if on a subject which for now three centuries has been so often discussed, I venture on one discussion more.

Key Terms

principle of utility
utilitarianism
quantity
quality
higher
lower
bodily pleasures
intellect
feelings
imagination
moral sentiments
human dignity
permanency
inferior type
superior type
sense of dignity
infirmity of character
enlightened self-interest
personal sacrifice
altruism
disutility
altruistic utilitarianism
hedonic calculus
incommensurable
selfishness
mental cultivation

safety
uncostliness
higher faculties
social liberty
democracy

Progress Check 4.1

Instructions: Fill in the blanks with the appropriate responses listed below.

intellect
inferior type
disutility
entitlements
quality
sense of dignity
egoistic
democracy
principle of utility
incommensurable
infirmity of character
mental cultivation
selfishness

1. Mill's acceptance of utilitarianism became a defense of the _____.
2. Whereas all pleasures were equal for Bentham, J.S. Mill distinguished between two types in regard to their _____.
3. Higher pleasures are those that are satisfying to the _____ and to our moral sentiments.
4. The higher pleasures contribute to our _____.
5. For Mill, those people who pursue lower pleasures are, by definition, _____ individuals.
6. Regardless of who you are, it is likely that you will sometimes fall prey to your lower appetites because of a(n) _____.
7. Jeremy Bentham's utilitarianism is more _____ than Mill's, whose ethics may require self-sacrifice and acting for the benefit of others.
8. Self-sacrifice, in itself, is not a virtue; in fact, it has _____ and should be avoided except in cases where it is necessary to promote the greatest happiness for the greatest number.
9. The hedonic calculus should be rejected, according to Mill, because pains and pleasures are _____.
10. Historically speaking, many people have opposed the pursuit of pleasure, denying that humans have any _____ to happiness.
11. People who appear to have everything that is necessary to be happy but who still do not find sufficient enjoyment in life probably suffer from _____ and lack of _____.
12. According to Mill, the best form of government is _____.

Summary of Major Points

1. What was Bentham's influence on Mill?
   Mill accepted Bentham's principle of utility as the standard of morality.
   In its defense, Mill articulated his own version of utilitarian ethics.

2. **How are pleasures distinguished?**
   Pleasures are distinguished in terms of quality.
   Some pleasures are higher, or better, and others are lower and inferior.
   Lower pleasures are bodily and physical.
   Higher pleasures relate to the intellect, imagination, moral sentiments, and dignity of persons.
   Higher pleasures tend to possess greater permanency, safety, and uncostliness; they are also ennobling, satisfying and enduring.
3. **How are higher pleasures risky?**
   Pursuit of higher pleasures may cause sensitive, superior-type individuals to suffer more acutely.
   Higher pleasures require stronger character and are more difficult to attain.
4. **What are the basic philosophical differences between Mill and Bentham?**
   Bentham sees pleasure only in terms of quantity; Mill makes a distinction between quantity and quality.
   Mill's utilitarianism is more altruistic and less egoistic than Bentham's.
   Mill rejects Bentham's hedonic calculus.
5. **What are Mill's views on human misery?**
   People have a duty to minimize suffering.
   Much of misery is humanly caused and, therefore, humanly correctable.
   Lack of personal enjoyment in life results from selfishness and want of mental cultivation.
6. **How does Mill conceptualize the relationship between government and the individual?**
   Democracy is the best form of government to allow individual self-expression and self-fulfillment.
   The government should maximize individual liberties within limits.
   Constraining limits can and should be placed on individuals' actions that would harm other people.

Source References and Related Readings

Anschutz, R.P. *The Philosophy of J.S. Mill*. New York: Oxford, 1953.

Borchard, R. *John Stuart Mill: The Man*. London: Penguin, 1957.

Copleston, Frederick. *A History of Philosophy*. Vol. VIII. New York: Doubleday, 1994.

Falikowski, Anthony. *Moral Philosophy: Theories, Skills, and Applications*. Upper Saddle River, N.J.: Prentice Hall, 1990.

Mill, J.S. *Utilitarianism*. Edited by Oscar Piest. Indianapolis, Ind.: The Bobbs-Merrill Co. Inc., 1957.

———. *On Liberty*. Edited by David Spitz. New York: W.W. Norton & Co., 1975.

Stumpf, Samuel. *Philosophy*, 3rd edition. New York: McGraw-Hill, 1983.

———. *Philosophy: History and Problems*, 5th edition. New York: McGraw-Hill, Inc., 1994, Chapter 19, pp. 372–79.

Deontological Ethics

In this last section of Part One, we move on to deontological ethics, the third and final ethical perspective to be discussed in the book. Historically speaking, different variations of this type of ethical theory have emerged, but most philosophers using this descriptive label today would probably associate it with a "rule or duty-based morality" or one that emphasizes right action (rightness) over good consequences (goodness). From this perspective, morally acceptable behavior is a matter of adhering to rationally consistent principles or following acceptable rules of conduct, not promoting utility or people's happiness nor harmonizing the soul or developing character, though doing what is right would, no doubt, often be conducive to the achievement of such things. In any case, acting "on principle" or "for the sake of duty" rather than for the benefit of oneself, say, or for "the greatest happiness of the greatest number" captures the spirit of the deontological position, certainly for Immanuel Kant, our first deontologist discussed in Chapter Five.

In Chapter Six, we will take a brief look at the moral theory of John Rawls, someone who has extended and given contemporary expression to many of Kant's insights and, more generally, to the philosophical social contract tradition. Like Kant, Rawls has eliminated, as much as possible, contaminating empirical variables from moral decision making and has tried to set up fair and impartial procedures of social conflict resolution. He has endeavored to remove subjective and other biasing factors that often impact on moral action and deliberation. As one who, like Kant, emphasizes right action over utility maximization, Rawls has attempted to abstract from the content of moral experience (social conflict in particular) those general ethical principles that can serve as the moral foundations for society and our sociopolitical institutions. On the basis of his rational abstractions and investigations, he concludes that the principle of "justice as fairness" is to be preferred over other alternatives like utility or intuition. He uses this principle to illustrate how rights and duties are correlative and how as rational, autonomous agents, we are all bound by the same moral rules as the members of a just society. With this in mind, let us proceed to discover what, if anything, the ethics of Rawls and Kant have to offer us in the development of our personal moral viewpoints.

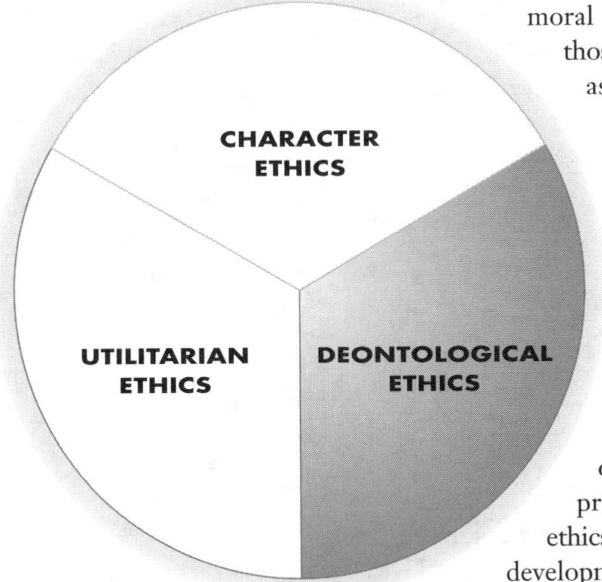

5 CHAPTER FIVE

IMMANUEL KANT: FOR THE SAKE OF DUTY

Overview

Biographical Brief: "Immanuel Kant"
The Rational Basis of Morality
The Concept of the Good Will
The Notion of Duty
- In Accordance with Duty, But not for Duty's Sake
- In Accordance with Duty, But out of Inclination
- In Accordance with Duty, for the Sake of Duty

Moral Duties to Oneself and to Others
Back to the Source Feature from Kant's *Lectures on Ethics*
Maxims and Moral Behavior
Kantian Formalism and the Categorical Imperative
Hypothetical versus Categorical Imperatives
Autonomy versus Heteronomy of the Will
Key Terms
Progress Check 5.1
Summary of Major Points
Source References and Related Readings

Learning Outcomes

After successfully completing this chapter, you will be able to:

5.1 provide the Kantian basis of morality and contrast it with the foundations provided by other philosophers discussed previously in this text;
5.2 explain why morality must be *a priori*;
5.3 give reasons why "the good will" is the only thing good in itself;
5.4 define moral duty and distinguish it from prudence and inclination;

5.5 understand the differences among actions that are moral, nonmoral, and immoral;
5.6 appreciate how morality entails universal duties to oneself and to others;
5.7 give two definitions of the categorical imperative;
5.8 explain what is meant by Kantian formalism;
5.9 distinguish between hypothetical and categorical imperatives;
5.10 comment on the importance of personal autonomy in morality.

PHILOSOPHICAL FOCUS QUESTIONS

1. What has served as the philosophical foundation for morality in the past? What does Kant use as his foundation?
2. What is wrong with basing morality on people's actual behavior?
3. In what does Immanuel Kant find true moral goodness?
4. What role does "duty" play in Kantian ethics?
5. What are maxims? How are they tied in with morality?
6. How is Kantian formalism to be understood? What are the formal criteria of distinctively moral maxims?
7. What, for Kant, is the ultimate principle of morality? What are two of its formulations?
8. How are hypothetical imperatives different from categorical ones?
9. Why is autonomy of the will important for morality?

P.H. Inc. College Archives

Immanuel Kant
(1724–1804)

BIOGRAPHICAL BRIEF*

Immanuel Kant was born in 1724 in the East Prussian town of Königsberg. Belonging to the lower middle class, his parents were deeply religious. Although throughout his life, Kant always maintained an honest respect for religion and a deep moral sense, he eventually abandoned the puritanical pietism that had been a dominating influence in his family. Immanuel Kant's life could hardly be described as eventful and is now famous for its routine. He arose the same time each day and had a fixed hour for all of his daily activities. It has been said that people could set their clocks by Kant's afternoon walks at half past three. Each day he would put on his grey coat and with bamboo cane in hand would walk down Lime Tree

From Falikowski, Moral Philosophy, *p. 27.*

Avenue, now called "Philosopher's Walk" in honor of Kant. Kant never married and in contrast to many of his contemporaries who were filled with the spirit of travel, Kant never ventured more than 40 miles in any direction of Königsberg. This lack of physical travel apparently did not affect the wandering intellectual genius of Kant, however. For more than a dozen years, he lectured as a *privatdozent* at the University of Königsberg in subjects as varied as mathematics, logic, geography, history, and philosophy. He also worked as a family tutor before being appointed professor of philosophy at the University of Königsberg in 1770. Kant is considered by many philosophers today as the greatest thinker since Plato and Aristotle. His influence is evident insofar as his ethical investigations still serve as the basis for much of the debate found in contemporary moral philosophy and applied ethics. His important works include: *Foundations of the Metaphysics of Morals*, *The Metaphysical Principles of Virtue*, *Lectures on Ethics*, and *The Critique of Pure Reason*.

THE RATIONAL BASIS OF MORALITY

Two things fill the mind with ever new and increasing admiration and awe . . . the starry heavens above and the moral law within.

Immanuel Kant

5.1

So far in our treatment of ethical theories, we have learned how thinkers throughout the ages have sought the philosophical foundations of morality in different places and in different things. Recall, for example, how Bentham argued that the morality of particular actions could be established by reference to their consequences. For him, an action was good to the extent that it produced pleasure, bad to the extent that it caused pain. As a utilitarian, John Stuart Mill also saw the value of pleasure, distinguishing, in his case, between higher and lower types. Although he diverged from Bentham on this point, Mill, nonetheless, continued to consider his revised notion of utility as the ultimate criterion for determining the morality of actions. As **consequentialists**, what Mill and Bentham both would agree on is that the moral worth of particular actions can be evaluated by their results.

As for Plato, remember how he too sought the basis of morality in his philosophical investigations. He eventually located moral goodness in a transcendent realm of forms—something timeless and spaceless, not visible or tangible, but knowable only through intellectual acquaintance. By contrast, his Greek friend Aristotle attempted to ground morality in human nature, common experience, and in humanity's pursuit of happiness and the good life. As we see, then, philosophers have struggled for centuries in their quest to find the basis of morality. On our continuing explorations into the moral domain, let us seek to uncover the philosophical footings supporting Kantian **deontological ethics**. It will be interesting to see what he bases morality on!

To start, you should note that Kant is not an **ethical relativist**, meaning that he does not regard morality as a matter of personal opinion or subjective preference; nor does he think that morality is completely dependent on cultural, historical or societal factors. Although it is undeniably true that people are different and often choose to differ with one another on moral matters, that fact alone does not, for him, make everybody right and nobody wrong. It is also certainly true that cultural practices vary throughout the world and that different values are held in higher or lower esteem depending on the society, group or nation involved. Moreover, it cannot be denied that social values undergo changes and transformations over time—compare today's attitudes toward sexuality, for example, with those of the 1950s or Queen Victoria's era.

5.2

In recognition of human diversity and that what people actually do, say, experience, believe, think, feel and value vary, Kant concludes that no **moral certainty** can be found there. If morality is to make any sense, and if it is to be considered valid and binding for all, then moral certainty must be found somewhere apart from the transitory and diverse world of everyday experience. For Kant, it is to be found in the **structure of reason** itself. The ultimate basis of morality must, for him, be **purely rational** or ***a priori***, not in any way derived from experience or dependent upon it. For example, rational moralists would, no doubt, condemn the torturing of innocent children regardless of whether or not anybody actually engages in this practice and whether or not any society condones it. The moral judgment in this instance is not derived from experience or observation of people's behavior. Such knowledge is *a priori* and independent of what people actually do. For Kant, it is up to the human sciences (e.g., anthropology, psychology, and sociology) to inform us about human behavior and the differences among people; it is philosophy's task to use reason to help us determine what is right and wrong. In support of Kant, one could argue that despite the apparent diversity easily observable among people throughout the world, the faculty of reason is one common or universal element shared by all individuals and by all of humanity more generally. Explaining why reason must be the basis of morality, Kant writes:

> Is it not of the utmost necessity to construct a pure moral philosophy which is completely freed from everything which may be only empirical and thus belong to anthropology? That there must be such a philosophy is self-evident from the common idea of duty and moral laws. Everyone must admit that a law, if it is to hold morally, i.e., as a ground of obligation, must imply absolute necessity; he must admit that the command, "Thou shalt not lie" does not apply to men only, as if other rational beings had no need to observe it. The same is true for all other moral laws properly so called. He must concede that the ground of obligation here must not be sought in the nature of man or in the circumstances in which he is placed, but sought *a priori* solely in the concepts of pure reason, and that every other precept which rests on principles of mere existence, even a precept which is in certain respects universal, so far as it leans in the least on empirical grounds (perhaps only in regard to the motive involved), be called a practical rule but never a moral law. (Kant, 1959, p. 5)

PHILOSOPHERS AT WORK

In efforts to appreciate moral diversity, try to identify any norms, values, and beliefs that conflict with one another. Such things could be personal, social, political, religious, and so on. Once you have identified these different and conflicting values, think about the idea that not one of them is better or worse than any of the others. Do you agree? Would you necessarily be biased, chauvinistic or discriminatory if you suggested that some values, beliefs or norms were better than others? Does being tolerant of moral diversity mean that you are obligated to accept everyone's values no matter what? If you would be willing to criticize any value or norm as unacceptable, what would be the basis of your moral disagreement? Discuss.

Overtime Discussion: Is there something that makes people reluctant to criticize the values, behaviors or lifestyle choices of others? If so, what? Do we have any social responsibility to ensure that people make the right choices in their lives? Explain.

5.3 THE CONCEPT OF THE GOOD WILL

The good will is not good because of what it effects or accomplishes or because of its adequacy to achieve some proposed end; it is good only because of its willing, i.e., it is good of itself.

Immanuel Kant

In the "First Section" of the *Foundations of the Metaphysics of Morals*, Kant picks up on the idea that moral goodness is not something external or psychological. He recognizes that **talents of the mind** (e.g., intelligence, judgment, and wit), **qualities of temperament** (e.g., courage, resoluteness, and perseverance) and **gifts of fortune** (e.g., power, riches, honor, and contentment, which contribute to happiness) may in many respects be good and desirable. He also underscores, however, the fact that all such things are not **unconditionally good**. Power, for instance, could lead to pride and arrogance if not corrected by reason and good will. The cool courage of a villain is not morally praiseworthy in itself and the actions following from such a virtue are more likely to cause harm than to lead to ethically acceptable behavior. **The good will** is, according to Kant, good even if it is prevented from achieving its purpose. The goodness of the good will is to be established solely by virtue of its willing. The motive to do the right thing for the right reason is enough to make the good will good. Kant says, "The good will is not good because of what it effects or accomplishes or because of its adequacy to achieve some proposed end; it is good only because of its willing, i.e., it is good of itself" (Kant, *ibid*., p. 10). In view of this, people who are motivated and make efforts to do the right thing, but fail in their attempts, can still be seen to be acting morally. By contrast, people who somehow manage to achieve their ends or, say, enjoy uninterrupted happiness in life, but without the influence of good will motivating their behavior, are not, in Kant's opinion, even worthy to be happy. Right things can be done for the wrong reasons. "Good" things like pleasure or happiness can result from moral injustices—a fact which calls into question the value of such things. This is why only a good will is unconditionally good.

It is better to deserve honors and not have them than to have them and not deserve them.
Mark Twain

It's better to be worthy of happiness, but fail in its attainment than to attain happiness, but fail to be worthy of it.
Author

When exercising good will what you do is to bring forward all the means in your power to do your **duty** (i.e., the right thing). Individuals are morally good or behave in a morally good fashion when they are motivated by the desire to do one's duty, simply for the sake of duty alone. The morally virtuous person is not concerned with maximizing people's happiness or cultivating moderation in one's lifestyle, but with doing what is required by **practical reason** (i.e., reason in its applications to morality). The moral quality of an act is, therefore, established by the rational principle to which the good will consciously assents.

5.4
THE NOTION OF DUTY

Oh Duty, why hast thou not the visage of a sweetie or a cutie?
Ogden Nash

Duty is the necessity of an action executed from respect for [moral] law.
Immanuel Kant

Still in the "First Section" of the *Foundations of the Metaphysics of Morals*, Kant gives us some insight into what he means by "duty," a basic building block of his ethical thinking. For Kant "Duty is the necessity of an action executed from respect for [moral] law" (Kant, *ibid.*, p. 16). He goes on to say "An action performed from duty does not have its moral worth in the purpose which is to be achieved through it but in the **maxim** [i.e., rule of conduct] by which it is determined" (Kant, *ibid.*). We will examine the formal characteristics of moral maxims, but first let us look at a couple of distinctions made by Kant.

Prudence consists in the power to recognize the nature of disadvantages and to take the less disagreeable as good.
Machiavelli

In Accordance with Duty, But not for Duty's Sake

Kant observes that some actions accord with duty, but are not performed for the sake of duty. In other words, people can act consistently with what duty requires, but still not act for the sake of duty or in recognition of the moral law. For example, maybe you have stopped yourself from stealing in the past, not because of any rational choice to do your ethical duty, but because you feared going to jail. If so, then doing the right thing out of fear or self-interest did not give your action any moral quality. Actions like this, performed in accordance with duty but not for duty's sake, do not belong to the moral domain. It is not that they are immoral; they are just not relevant to morality, having no moral status. For Kant, this example of stealing would be an instance of **prudence**, not morality. Doing what is in your self-interest because of self-interest alone is nonmoral behavior. In *Foundations of the Metaphysics of Morals*, Kant offers his own illustration to support the point that not all actions in accordance with moral duty possess moral worth. He uses a business example.

> it is in fact in accordance with duty that a dealer should not overcharge an inexperienced customer, and wherever there is much business the prudent merchant does not do so, having a fixed price for everyone, so that a child may buy of him as cheaply as any other. Thus, the customer is honestly served. But this is far from sufficient to justify the belief that the merchant has behaved in this way from duty and principle or honesty. His own advantage required this behavior; but it cannot be assumed that over and above that he had a direct inclination to the purchaser and that, out of love, as it were, he gave none an advantage in price over another. Therefore, the action was done neither from duty nor from direct inclination, but only for a selfish purpose. (Kant, *ibid.*, pp. 13–14)

the purposes we may have for our actions and their effects as ends and incentives of the will cannot give the actions any unconditional and moral worth.

Immanuel Kant

5.5

In the example above the merchant did the "right" thing out of prudence, not morality. Again, it is not that the reason was wrong; it simply was not moral. It is worth noting, then, that actions can be **moral** (belonging to morality), **nonmoral** (not belonging to the moral domain) and **immoral** (wrong, bad or unjustifiable). To argue, as Kant does, that the merchant has acted prudentially (out of his own advantage) is not to condemn him, nor is it to praise him morally.

5.4

In Accordance with Duty, But out of Inclination

To further clarify the nature of (moral) duty, Kant also distinguishes between actions performed out of **inclination** and those performed out of a recognition of duty. He argues that only the latter is genuinely moral. Suppose, for example, that you are the kind of person who is generally predisposed by temperament to act kindly or benevolently toward others. You simply like being nice to people. In fact, being nice to others is "what comes naturally" to you. If this were so, Kant would say that, as nice as you are, there is still no moral worth to your actions. It is not that you are morally corrupt or that you are doing anything wrong; it is just that the naturally inclined actions you perform have no moral worth. If this seems counter-intuitive, it will help to look at another example of action by inclination. Suppose a husband and wife are completely in love with one another and they both have no inclination to cheat on each other (i.e., each person is inclined to be faithful); should we praise the marital fidelity? From a Kantian perspective, the principle of fidelity is good (because it conforms to the moral law), but the husband or wife who is faithful in this case is not acting in a morally praiseworthy fashion. There was no action performed for the sake of duty. Had the person's inclinations been different (i.e., had the husband or wife been tempted), he or she might have cheated. Doing what you feel like doing without thought or recognition of ethical duty gives your action no moral worth. The "**motive**" behind the action determines its moral status. Distinguishing between inclination and duty, using kindness as an example, Kant writes:

> To be kind where one can is duty, and there are, moreover, many persons so sympathetically constituted that without any motive of vanity or selfishness they find an inner satisfaction in spreading joy, and rejoice in the contentment of others which they have made possible. But I say that, however dutiful and amiable it may be, that kind of action has no true moral worth. (Kant, *ibid.*, p. 14)

In Accordance with Duty, for the Sake of Duty

Well, if morality is not about natural inclination or prudence, then we are left needing further clarification. For Kant, a morally acceptable action must not only accord with duty (i.e., be consistent with it) but it must also be performed by the agent for the sake of duty. The individual must recognize what should be done and do it for that reason alone. "Duty for duty's sake" is another way of putting it. Even if doing the morally right thing is not something we are inclined to do at the moment or if, say, the right action does not appear to produce the best consequences, duty may dictate that we do it nonetheless. To illustrate the moral priority of duty over inclination, Kant asks us to imagine a person whose life has been entirely clouded by sorrow. This person is miserable and all sympathetic feelings toward others have been extinguished. The person still possesses the means to help others and to improve their situations, but his deadened sensibility leaves him untouched by their unfortunate plight. Now, as Kant suggests, if this individual, who is wallowing in self-pity and has no desire or inclination to help others, tears himself away from his own preoccupations to assist another distressed person because of a recognition of duty, then his action assumes moral worth. The individual does what should be done, not out of natural inclination, but for the sake of duty. You could say, then, that a test of moral character is to discover whether one is strong enough to follow duty in spite of one's strong inclination not to do so.

PHILOSOPHERS AT WORK

Immanuel Kant seems to make a lot of "distinctions" in his philosophical ethics. Are these distinctions just nit-picking or are they important? Do they add to clarity or confusion? Also, would you agree that all moral action must be based on duty? Why or why not? How would Kant respond to Jeremy Bentham and his utilitarianism?

5.6
MORAL DUTIES TO ONESELF AND TO OTHERS

Suicide is not an abomination because God has forbidden it; it is forbidden by God because it is abominable.

Kant

In *Lectures on Ethics*, Kant points out that moral duties include not only those obligations we have toward others but also those we have toward ourselves. In other words, Kant allows for both personal and social dimensions of morality. This is not to suggest that personal morality is private and subjective or that duties to oneself are somehow conditional and not applicable to others. For Kant, there are duties that we all have toward ourselves and duties that we all have toward other people. Although it goes almost without saying that morality involves relations and duties to others, Kant contends that individual morality should not be an afterthought or be considered an appendix to ethical inquiry. Too often moral discussion is restricted to social matters and interpersonal conflict. Kant insists, however, that "our duties towards ourselves are of primary importance and should have pride of place" (Kant, 1963, pp. 117–18). Arguing that we can expect nothing from a person who dishonors his own person, he maintains that "a prior condition of our **duties to others** is our **duty to ourselves**; we can fulfill the former only insofar as we first fulfill the latter" (Kant, *ibid.*, p. 118). To illustrate and support his point, Kant asks us to consider drunkards. Such people may do no harm to others and, provided their physical constitutions are strong, they may not even harm themselves. Nonetheless, Kant claims that drunkards become, for us, objects of moral contempt. Such individuals degrade themselves and damage their personal dignity. They lose their inner worth as moral subjects. Kant writes:

> Only if our worth as human beings is intact can we perform our other duties; for it is the foundation stone of all other duties. A man who has destroyed and cast away his personality, has no intrinsic worth, and can no longer perform any manner of duty. (Kant, *ibid.*, p. 121)

In *Lectures on Ethics*, Kant enumerates and explains a number of self-regarding and other-regarding duties. In regard to the former, we have duties of proper self-respect, self-mastery, duties concerning the body and duties concerning how we occupy ourselves in work and in play. In regard to the latter, we have duties to show respect for persons and to honor their inherent worth and dignity. Let us now read what Kant says about "duties to oneself" and "duties to others" by turning to our "Back to the Source" feature.

BACK TO THE SOURCE*

Duties to Oneself

By way of introduction it is to be noted that there is no question in moral philosophy which has received more defective treatment than that of the individual's duty towards himself. No one has framed a proper concept of self-regarding duty. It has been regarded as a detail and considered by way of an afterthought, as an appendix to moral philosophy, on the view that man should give a thought to himself only after he has completely fulfilled his duty towards others. All moral philosophers err in this respect. Gellert[1] hardly even deserves mention here; it does not even occur to him to touch upon the question; he is constantly harping on benevolence and charity, the poet's hobbyhorses. Just as an innkeeper gives a thought to his own hunger when his customers have finished eating, so a man gives a thought to himself at the long last for fear that he might forget himself altogether! Hutcheson, too, although his thought is more philosophic, does not pass this test. The reason for all this is the want of a pure concept, which should form the basis of a self-regarding duty. It was taken for granted that a man's duty towards himself consisted, as Wolff in his turn defined it, in promoting his own happiness. In that case everything would depend on how an individual determined his own happiness; for our self-regarding duties would consist in the universal rule to satisfy all our inclinations in order to further our happiness. This would, however, militate seriously against doing our duty towards others. In fact, the principle of self-regarding duties is a very different one, which has no connexion with our well-being or earthly happiness. Far from ranking lowest in the scale of precedence, our duties towards ourselves are of primary importance and should have pride of place; for (deferring for the moment the definition of what constitutes this duty) it is obvious that nothing can be expected from a man who dishonors his own person. He who transgresses against himself loses his manliness and becomes incapable of doing his duty towards his fellows. A man who performed his duty to others badly, who lacked generosity, kindness and sympathy, but who nevertheless did his duty to himself by leading a proper life, might yet possess a certain inner worth; but he who has transgressed his duty towards himself, can have no inner worth whatever. Thus a man who fails in his duty to himself loses worth absolutely; while a man who fails in his duty to others loses worth only relatively. It follows that the prior condition of our duty to others is our duty to ourselves; we can fulfill the former only in so far as we first fulfill the latter. Let us illustrate our meaning by a few examples of failure in one's duty to oneself. A drunkard does no harm to another, and if he has a strong constitution he does no harm to himself, yet he is an object of contempt. We are not indifferent to cringing servility; man should not cringe and fawn; by so doing he degrades his person and loses his manhood. If a man for gain or profit submits to all indignities and makes himself the plaything of another, he casts away the worth of his manhood. Again, a lie is more a violation of one's duty to oneself than of one's duty to others. A liar, even though by his lies he does no harm to any one, yet becomes an object of contempt, he throws away his personality; his behavior is vile, he has

From Kant, Lectures on Ethics, *trans. Louis Infield.*

transgressed his duty towards himself. We can carry the argument further and say that to accept favors and benefits is also a breach of one's duty to oneself. If I accept favors, I contract debts which I can never repay, for I can never get on equal terms with him who has conferred the favors upon me; he has stolen a march upon me, and if I do him a favor I am only returning a *quid pro quo*; I shall always owe him a debt of gratitude, and who will accept such a debt? For to be indebted is to be subject to an unending constraint. I must for ever be courteous and flattering towards my benefactor, and if I fail to be so he will very soon make me conscious of my failure; I may even be forced to using subterfuge so as to avoid meeting him. But he who pays promptly for everything is under no constraint; he is free to act as he please; none will hinder him. Again, the faint-hearted who complain about their luck and sigh and weep about their misfortunes are despicable in our eyes; instead of sympathizing with them we do our best to keep away from them. But if a man shows a steadfast courage in his misfortune, and though greatly suffering, does not cringe and complain but puts a bold face upon things, to such a one our sympathy goes out. Moreover, if a man gives up his freedom and barters it away for money, he violates his manhood. Life itself ought not to be rated so highly as to warrant our being prepared, in order only not to lose it, to live otherwise than as a man should, i.e. not a life of ease, but so that we do not degrade our manhood. We must also be worthy of our manhood; whatsoever makes us unworthy of it makes us unfit for anything, and we cease to be men. Moreover, if a man offer his body for profit for the sport of others—if, for instance, he agrees in return for a few pints of beer to be knocked about—he throws himself away, and the perpetrators who pay him for it are acting as vilely as he. Neither can we without destroying our person abandon ourselves to others in order to satisfy their desires, even though it be done to save parents and friends from death; still less can this be done for money. If done in order to satisfy one's own desires, it is very immodest and immoral, but yet not so unnatural; but if it be done for money, or for some other reason, a person allows himself to be treated as a thing, and so throws away the worth of his manhood. It is the same with the vices of the flesh (*crimina carnis*), which for that reason are not spoken of. They do no damage to anyone, but dishonor and degrade a man's own person; they are an offense against the dignity of manhood in one's own person. The most serious offense against the duty one owes to oneself is suicide. But why should suicide be so abominable? It is no answer to say "because God forbids it." Suicide is not an abomination because God has forbidden it; it is forbidden by God because it is abominable. If it were the other way about, suicide would not be abominable if it were not forbidden; and I should not know why God had forbidden it, if it were not abominable in itself. The ground, therefore, for regarding suicide and other transgressions as abominable and punishable must not be found in the divine will, but in their inherent heinousness. Suicide is an abomination because it implies the abuse of man's freedom of action: he uses his freedom to destroy himself. His freedom should be employed to enable him to live as a man. He is free to dispose as he pleases of things appertaining to his person, but not of his person; he may not use his freedom against himself. For a man to recognize what his duty is towards himself in this respect is far from easy: because although man has indeed a natural horror of suicide, yet we can argue and quibble ourselves into believing that, in order to rid himself of trouble and misery, a man may destroy himself. The argument makes a strong appeal; and in terms of the rule of prudence suicide may often be the surest and best course; none the less suicide is in itself revolting. The rule of morality, which takes precedence of all rules of reflective prudence, command apodeictically and categorically that we must observe our duties to ourselves; and in committing suicide and reducing himself to a carcass, man uses his powers and his liberty against himself. Man is free to dispose of his condition but not of his person; he himself is an end and not a means; all else in the world is of value only as a means, but man is a person and not a thing and therefore not a means. It is absurd that a reasonable being, an end for the sake of which all else is means, should use himself as a means. It is true that a person can serve as a means for others (e.g. by his work), but only in a way whereby he does not cease to be a person and an end. Whoever acts in such a way that he cannot be an end, uses himself as a means and treats his person as a thing. Man is not free to dispose of his person as a means; and in what follows we shall have more to say on this score.

The duties we owe to ourselves do not depend on the relation of the action to the ends of happiness. If they did, they would depend on our inclinations and so be governed by rules of prudence. Such rules are not moral, since they indicate only the necessity of the means for the satisfaction of inclinations, and cannot therefore bind us. The basis of such obligation is not to be found in the advantages we reap from doing our duty towards ourselves, but in the worth of manhood. This principle does not allow us an unlimited freedom in respect of our own persons. It insists that we must reverence humanity in our own person, because apart from this man becomes an object of contempt, worthless in the eyes of his fellows and worthless in himself. Such faultiness is absolute. Our duties towards ourselves constitute the supreme condition and the principle of all morality; for moral worth is the worth of the person as such; our capacities have a value only in regard to the circumstances in which we find ourselves. Socrates lived in a state of wretchedness; his circumstances were worthless; but though his circumstances were so ill-conditioned, yet he himself was of the highest value. Even though we sacrifice all life's amenities we can make up for their loss and sustain approval by maintaining the worth of our humanity. We may have lost everything else, and yet still retain our inherent worth. Only if our worth as human beings is intact can we perform our other duties; for it is the foundation stone of all other duties. A man who has destroyed and cast away his personality, has no intrinsic worth, and can no longer perform any manner of duty.

• • •

Duties Towards Others

[Duties towards other men] are divisible into two main groups:

1. Duties of good-will, or benevolence.
2. Duties of indebtedness or justice.

Actions falling under the first group are benevolent; those falling under the second are righteous and compulsory.

The duties falling under the first heading do not imply any definite obligation upon us to love other human beings and to do them good. The man who loves his neighbor wishes him well, but of his own impulse; he does so willingly and from a voluntary disposition, not because he is bound to. Love is good-will from inclination; but there can also be good-will on principle. It follows that the pleasure we find in doing good to others may be either direct or indirect. The direct pleasure comes from doing good from obligation, when we enjoy the consciousness of having done our duty. Doing good from love springs from the heart; doing good from obligation springs rather from principles of the understanding. Thus a man may act kindly towards his wife from love, but if his inclination has evaporated he ought to do so from obligation.

But can a moralist say that we have a duty to love others? Love is good-will from inclination. Now whatever depends upon my inclination and not upon my will, cannot be laid upon me as a duty. I certainly cannot love at will, but only when I have an impulse to love. Duty is always a compulsion, which may be either self-imposed or else imposed upon us by others. If then we are under an obligation to be mindful of the welfare of others, on what is this obligation founded? On principles. For let us consider the world and ourselves. The world is an arena on which nature has provided everything necessary for our temporal welfare, and we are nature's guests. We all have an equal right to the good things which nature has provided. These good things have not, however, been shared out by God. He has left men to do the sharing. Every one of us, therefore, in enjoying the good things of life must have regard to the happiness of others; they have an equal right and ought not to be deprived of it. Since God's providence is universal, I may not be indifferent to the happiness of others. If, for instance, I were to find in the forest a table spread with all manner of dishes, I ought not to conclude that it is all for me; I may eat, but I should also remember to leave some for others to enjoy. I ought not even to consume in its entirety any particular dish in case some one else might fancy it also. Recognizing, therefore, that Providence is universal, I am placed under an obligation to restrict my own consumption and to bear in mind that nature's preparations are made for all of us. This is the source of the obligation to benevolence.

But let us consider the man who is benevolent from love, who loves his neighbor from inclination. Such a man stands in need of people to whom he can show his kindness, and is not content until he finds human beings towards whom he can be charitable. A kindly heart gets more pleasure and satisfaction from doing good to others than from its own enjoyment of the good things of life; the inclination to do good is a necessity to it, which must be satisfied. It is not this kindliness of heart and temper which the moralist should seek to cultivate, but good-will from principles. For the former is grounded in inclination and a natural necessity, giving rise to unregulated conduct. Such a man will be charitable, by inclination, to all and sundry; and then, if someone takes advantage of his kind heart, in sheer disgust he will decide from then onwards to give up doing good to others. He has no principle by which to calculate his behavior. Therefore the moralist must establish principles, and commend and inculcate benevolence from obligation. When all the obligations, religious as well as natural, have been expounded, we may go on to inculcate the inclination, though never forgetting that it must be subordinated to principles. On these conditions only may we proceed to expound the motives to acts of benevolence from inclination.

Let us now consider the second group of duties towards others, namely the duties of indebtedness and justice. Here there is no question of inclination, only of the rights of others. It is not their needs that count in this connexion, but their rights; it is not a question of whether my neighbor is needy, wretchedly poor or the reverse; if his right is concerned, it must be satisfied. This group of duties is grounded in the general rule of right.

The chief of these duties is respect for the rights of others. It is our duty to regard them as sacred and to respect and maintain them as such. There is nothing more sacred in the wide world than the rights of others. They are inviolable. Woe unto him who trespasses upon the right of another and tramples it underfoot! His right should be his security; it should be stronger than any shield or fortress. We have a holy ruler and the most sacred of his gifts to us is the rights of man.

Let us take a man who is guided only by justice and not by charity. He may close his heart to all appeal; he may be utterly indifferent to the misery and misfortune around him; but so long as he conscientiously does his duty in giving to every one what is his due, so long as he respects the rights of other men as the most sacred trust given to us by the ruler of the world, his conduct is righteous; let him give to another no trifle in excess of his due, and yet be equally punctilious to keep no jot nor tittle back, and his conduct is righteous. If all of us behaved in this way, if none of us ever did any act of love and charity, but only kept inviolate the rights of every man, there would be no misery in the world except sickness and misfortune and other such sufferings as do not spring from the violation of rights. The most frequent and fertile source of human misery is not misfortune, but the injustice of man.

Notes

1. C.F. Gellert, *Moralische Vorlesungen*, 1770, 2 vols.

MAXIMS AND MORAL BEHAVIOR

According to Kant, anytime you act voluntarily, you operate under some kind of maxim, rule or directive. For instance, if, in situation A, you choose to do B, then you are acting on the maxim "In situation A, do B." This kind of thinking is what has led some people to describe humans as "rule-governed" animals. Unlike lower-level organisms, which are mostly reactive to external stimuli or responsive to instinctual impulses and other determining factors, we, as humans, can act freely and rationally on the basis of self-generated rules or laws of conduct. If this seems a bit vague, imagine yourself lying to your course instructor about the reasons why you missed an ethics term test. You might say that you were ill when, in fact, you slept in because you were up until very late the night before partying with friends. In this case, the personal maxim or rule of conduct underlying your behavior could be expressed something like this: "When in trouble, lie your way out of it" or "If caught doing something wrong, then lie" or "Lie in order to get what you want."

To say maxims underlie our behaviors does not mean to suggest that we always abide by them. For example, on most occasions when you are caught doing something wrong, you might "fess up"; however, at other times, you might lie like the student in the illustration above. You should also note that people are not always or usually aware of the maxims that they use to govern their behavior. Implicit maxims are most likely to come to people's attention and to be made explicit when they are asked to justify their behaviors to others or when conscience forces them to justify their actions to themselves. Aware of them or not, maxims are imbedded in our actions and in the way we behave.

5.7
5.8

KANTIAN FORMALISM AND THE CATEGORICAL IMPERATIVE

In efforts to determine which maxims of behavior are distinctively moral and morally acceptable and which are not, Kant formulated **the categorical imperative**. This moral imperative can be expressed in a number of different ways, but the best-known formulation is the following: "Act only according to that maxim by which you can at the same time will that it should become a universal law." According to this formulation, a moral maxim is one that can, without contradiction, be willed to be a rule of conduct for everyone. The categorical imperative implies that the essence of morality lies in acting on the basis of an **impersonal principle** that is **valid for every person** including oneself. As morality has a **rational foundation** for Kant, he believes that one must be able to **universalize** maxims of conduct in a **logically consistent** fashion if those maxims are to be **binding** on all rational beings. Maxims that cannot be universalized consistently are not moral or morally prescriptive. For example, the maxim "Never help others, but always be helped by them" could not be accepted as a valid moral rule of conduct because of its logical implications. It does not make sense even to talk about accepting help from others if the maxim were universalized and acted upon, because nobody would ever try to help others and, thus, there would be no help to be accepted. From this illustration, we see how the categorical imperative's formal requirement of universal consistency allows us to evaluate the moral acceptability of particular maxims and rules of conduct. The categorical imperative can serve as a test of morality or an ultimate standard for moral evaluation.

A second formulation of the categorical imperative draws attention to its social implications. It states: "Act so that you treat humanity, whether in your own person or in that of another, always as an end and never as a means only" (Kant, *ibid*., p. 47). According to this statement of the categorical imperative, we should show respect for all human beings **unconditionally** and avoid exploiting anyone. When we exploit others and disrespect them in this way, we treat them merely as objects or means to our own ends. We fail to see others as beings whose existence has absolute worth in itself. In Kant's view, the dignity and worth of any human being are not conditional on any empirical factors. Just as you would not wish to be used against your will and exploited by others so they could attain their ends, so too is it wrong for you to use people against their will and to exploit them or treat them only as objects or merely as a means to gain your own ends.

Are you "dis'en" me?
Author

In matters of principle stand like a rock; in matters of taste swim with the current.
Thomas Jefferson

Implicit in what was said above is the formal requirement of **reversibility**. The concept holds that a maxim or rule of conduct is morally unacceptable if the individual acting on it would not wish to be the person most disadvantaged or most adversely affected by its application. If one approves of a maxim, one must approve of it both from the perspective of the one who benefits and from the one most negatively affected. An act must be acceptable **objectively** regardless of whether the individual is at the giving or the receiving end of an action. If, for instance, a person chooses to approve of stealing in his or her own case, then that person must be willing to become victimized by theft if the corresponding maxim is to be deemed acceptable. Presumably, nobody wishes to be robbed and, therefore, no rational moral thinker would accept such a maxim.

The formal criteria of universality, consistency, and reversibility point to the idea that moral maxims must also be **impartial**; that is, the rightness or wrongness of actions and the moral adequacy of their underlying maxims have nothing to do with *who* happens to be in a favored or disadvantaged position regarding the actions. Certain acts are right or wrong in themselves regardless of whose interests are served and regardless of the favorable or unfavorable consequences to oneself, or anyone else for that matter. The categorical imperative is an abstract principle that requires that empirical content particulars be removed, as much as possible, from the ethical appraisal and justification process. Because morality must have a purely rational *a priori* basis, particulars of content referring to specific persons, places, times, interests, desires, inclinations, and so forth, must be removed when the moral acceptability of maxims is being determined. Recall that, for Kant, morality cannot have an empirical or anthropological basis, for this would not provide him with the solid and secure ethical foundation that he seeks. Only reason can provide the **certainty** and **necessity** required for a universal, binding morality.

Another formal (i.e., content free) element contained in the categorical imperative is the notion of **prescriptivity**. One cannot simply opt out of morality if one chooses. Moral requirements are unconditionally binding on all rational beings. One cannot justifiably or consistently argue that morality applies to everyone else "but me" or that everyone else should always tell the truth "but me," and so on. Ethically speaking, you cannot make yourself the exception to the rule. To do so is to use two standards of morality, one for others and one for yourself. If this practice of making personal exceptions were universalized, then nobody would be required to adhere to the moral law and any objective morality would become impossible. You cannot, therefore, be freed of moral obligation simply because you do not feel like living up to the moral law or because making an exception in your case is likely to further your own interests or promote greater happiness within yourself. Distinctively moral maxims and ethical principles of conduct apply to everyone unconditionally, whether people like them or not.

MINDWORK MEDITATION

So far, on your travels into the moral domain, you have come across a number of different cornerstones that could serve as the basis of a personal and social morality. What do you think of Kant's cornerstone, the categorical imperative? Does it provide you with a solid and stable foundation upon which to build your moral life? Why or why not? Do you have another cornerstone in mind? If so, which one? Why is your foundational cornerstone preferable to Kant's?

5.9 HYPOTHETICAL VERSUS CATEGORICAL IMPERATIVES

In everyday language, we often use words like "should," "have to," "ought," and "must," but it is not clearly the case that we always mean to suggest moral obligations are associated with them. Saying to someone "You ought to . . ." may be intended simply as a bit of personal advice, not as a universal ethical prescription. Saying to yourself, "I must . . ." or "I have to . . ." or "I should . . ." may involve some trivial action that does not call forth any moral considerations. Recognizing this, Kant, in *The Foundations of the Metaphysics of Morals*, made a distinction between **categorical and hypothetical imperatives**. He wrote:

> All imperatives command either hypothetically or categorically . . . . If the action [commanded by an imperative] is good only as a means to something else, the imperative is hypothetical; but if it is thought of as good in itself, and hence as necessary in a will which of itself conforms to reason as the principle of this will, the imperative is categorical. (Kant, 1959, p. 31)

Prudence is the knowledge of things to be sought, and those to be shunned.

Cicero

As we have previously learned about categorical imperatives, they imply universal necessity and prescriptivity. They are purely rational and *a priori*. Hypothetical imperatives, by contrast, are **conditional** and **particular** (specific) and, therefore, lack the formal properties of distinctively moral commands. They cannot be universalized and prescribed unconditionally. On the subject of hypothetical imperatives, Kant speaks of **technical imperatives** or **rules of skill** that require us to do certain things *if* we want to achieve specific ends. For instance, if you wish to properly install an interlocking brick patio that will not shift with changing weather conditions, you must prepare the base with appropriate amounts of gravel and sand. Of course, you do not have to do this if you prefer to build a wooden deck or to lay sod.

Kant also draws our attention to **prudential imperatives**, another type of conditional command. Here is an example: "If you wish to make a favorable impression on people, then you should do certain things (e.g., laugh at their humorless jokes)." Again, you have no "moral duty" to make favorable impressions, so you have no ethical obligations to do those things that will accomplish that end. It could be that you are highly introverted, prefer to be alone, and do not care what others think of you. Given, then, that prudential and technical imperatives command us only under certain conditions, they are hypothetical, not moral and categorical.

5.10
AUTONOMY VERSUS HETERONOMY OF THE WILL

Liberty consists in the power of doing that which is permitted by the law.
Cicero

Who then is free?
The wise man who can command himself.
Horace

None are more hopelessly enslaved than those who falsely believe they are free.
Goethe

No man is free who cannot command himself.
Pythagoras

In closing this discussion of Kantian ethics, a brief mention should be made of the role played by **autonomy** in morality, for without personal autonomy, morality becomes an impossibility. When people act morally, they act freely or willfully out of respect or reverence for the moral law. They willingly obey the moral law for the sake of the moral law alone. To go back to a point made earlier, moral agents do their duty for duty's sake, not because of external incentive or coercion. When outside determining forces are not present, then we can speak of **autonomy of the will**. **Heteronomy of the will**, by contrast, is evident when the will obeys laws, rules or injunctions from any other source besides reason. Obeying the law because you fear incarceration or doing your duty only under threat of physical force does not reflect autonomous moral action. Rather, it is more like "covering your butt" to use a colloquial expression. Somehow, I do not think this is what the venerable Kant intended to include in his conception of a universal morality!

Finally, when as autonomous and rational moral agents, we base our actions on universally valid laws that we have laid down for ourselves, we participate in something Kant calls the **realm of ends**—a kind of ideal moral universe in which we respect the intrinsic worth and dignity of all persons. In this kingdom, we never treat people solely as means to our ends, but as ends in themselves. Of course, to some extent, we all use one another. For instance, you may use your neighbor's teenager as a babysitter for your child or your neighbors may use your son or daughter as help to cut their grass. This is not what Kant is talking about. In many practical ways, we all use one another in cooperative social living. It is when we violate others, abuse or mistreat them or use them "merely" as a means to achieve our own ends that we dishonor their dignity as persons.

Key Terms

consequentialists
deontological ethics
ethical relativist
moral certainty
structure of reason
purely rational
a priori
talents of the mind
qualities of temperament
gifts of fortune
unconditionally good
the good will
duty
practical reason
maxim
prudence
moral
nonmoral
immoral
inclination
motive
duties to others
duties to ourselves
the categorical imperative
impersonal principle
valid for every person
rational foundation
universalize
logically consistent
binding
unconditionally
reversibility
objectively
impartial
certainty
necessity
prescriptivity
categorical and hypothetical imperatives
conditional
particular
technical imperatives
rules of skill
prudential imperatives
autonomy
autonomy of the will
heteronomy of the will
realm of ends

Progress Check 5.1

Instructions: Fill in the blanks with the appropriate responses listed below.

moral certainty
good will
duty
immoral
duties to oneself
formalist
objects
categorical imperative
prescriptive
autonomy of the will
conditionally
nonmoral
motive
structure of reason
maxim
deontological
prudential
inclination
impartial
hypothetical

1. Whereas utilitarian morality emphasizes consequences, _____ ethics stresses duty.
2. Immanuel Kant does not believe that any _____ can be found in the diversity of human experience.
3. For Kant, the basis of morality cannot be empirical; it must be found in the _____ itself.
4. The only thing good in itself is the _____.
5. Talents of the mind, qualities of temperament, and gifts of fortune are all only _____ good.
6. _____ is the necessity of an action executed from respect for [moral] law.
7. Actions performed to promote self-interest are not moral, but _____.
8. Actions that are ethically neutral and outside the moral domain are _____.
9. Actions that violate the dignity of others are _____.
10. If you thoughtlessly do the right thing simply because you feel like doing it, then your action is not moral, but is based on _____.
11. The _____ behind any action determines its moral status.
12. Morality involves _____ as well as duties to others.
13. Implicit in any conscious, voluntary action is a _____ or rule of conduct.
14. The _____ is the ultimate principle of morality that enables us to determine which maxims of behavior are moral and/or morally acceptable.
15. Kant tries to remove empirical content from his moral theorizing; this is because he is a _____.
16. The second formulation of the categorical imperative prescribes that we never treat people merely as _____, but always as ends in themselves.
17. Moral maxims are _____; their rightness has nothing to do with particular individuals or who happens to be in a favored or disadvantaged position regarding the actions that follow from them.
18. Moral maxims are universal and unconditional; they are binding or _____ for everybody.
19. Conditional imperatives are _____, not categorical.
20. Moral actions must be freely performed and display _____.

Summary of Major Points

1. On what have philosophers (including Kant) tried to base morality?
   They have based morality on consequences, results, utility, the transcendent realm of forms, human nature, common experience, happiness, the good life, and the structure of reason.
2. What is the only thing having intrinsic value?
   The good will is good in itself.
   Talents of the mind, qualities of temperament, and gifts of fortune are all conditionally good.

3. **What makes the good will good?**
   The motive to do the right thing for the right reason (duty).
   The intention to act on a consistent, universally prescriptive principle.
4. **What is duty?**
   "Duty is the necessity of an action executed from respect for [moral] law." (Kant)
   Actions performed from duty have their worth in the maxims or rules of conduct by which they are determined.
5. **What is important to keep in mind about duty?**
   Not all actions in accordance with duty are performed for duty's sake (nonmoral).
   Some actions in accordance with duty are performed out of inclination and are therefore nonmoral.
   Only actions performed in accordance with duty and for the sake of duty are distinctively moral.
6. **What kinds of moral duties are there?**
   There are duties to oneself: proper self-respect, self-mastery, occupation, and treatment of the body.
   There are duties to others: respect for persons, honor their dignity.
7. **What is a maxim? What can be said of maxims?**
   A maxim is rule or directive or principle of conduct implicit in any voluntary action.
   We are not always consciously aware of them.
   We do not always act consistently with them.
   We use them to justify our behavior to others as well as to ourselves.
8. **What is the categorical imperative? What are two of its formulations?**
   The categorical imperative is, for Kant, the supreme principle of morality from which all other moral maxims are derived and by which they can be evaluated.
   First formulation: Act only according to that maxim by which you can at the same time will that it should become a universal law.
   Second formulation: Act so that you treat humanity, whether in your own person or in that of another, always as an end and never only as a means.
9. **What formal criteria (i.e., content-free standards) characterize the categorical imperative and the morally acceptable maxims that follow from it?**
   The criteria are: impersonality, universality, logical consistency, bindingness/prescriptivity, unconditionality, reversibility, objectivity, impartiality, and certainty.
10. **Besides categorical imperatives that are universal and necessary, what other types are there?**
    There are conditional or hypothetical imperatives containing an "if-then" logical form, e.g., technical imperatives or rules of skill and prudential imperatives.
11. **What is meant by autonomy/heteronomy of the will?**
    Moral acts are autonomous, not heteronomous; such acts are performed freely out of respect or reverence for the moral law, i.e., for the sake of duty. Heteronomous acts are not moral; they are either coerced or instrumental to some further end and are not performed for duty's sake.

Source References and Related Readings

Copleston, Frederick. *A History of Philosophy*. Vol. 6. *Modern Philosophy*, Part II, Kant. Garden City, N.Y.: Image Books, 1960.

Falikowski, Anthony. *Moral Philosophy: Theories, Skills, and Applications*. Englewood Cliffs, N.J.: Prentice Hall, 1990.

Hospers, John. *Human Conduct: Problems of Ethics*. New York: Harcourt Brace Jovanovich, 1972.

Kant, Immanuel. *Foundations of the Metaphysics of Morals*. Translated by Lewis White Beck. The Library of Liberal Arts. Indianapolis, Ind.: The Bobbs-Merrill Co. Inc., 1959.

———. *Lectures on Ethics*. Translated by Louis Infield. Indianapolis, Ind.: Hackett Publishing Co., 1963.

———. *The Metaphysical Principles of Virtue*. Translated by James Ellington. The Library of Liberal Arts. Indianapolis, Ind.: The Bobbs-Merrill Co. Inc., 1964.

Kemp, John. *The Philosophy of Kant*. London: Oxford University Press, 1968.

Korner, S. *Kant*. Harmondsworth, Middlesex: Penguin Books, Ltd., 1955.

Ross, William D. *Kant's Ethical Theory*. New York: Oxford University Press, 1954.

Singer, Marcus T. "The Categorical Imperative" in *Moral Philosophy: An Introduction*. Edited by Jack Glickman. New York: St. Martin's Press, 1976.

CHAPTER SIX

JOHN RAWLS: JUSTICE AS FAIRNESS IS FAIRLY JUST

Overview

Learning Outcomes

After successfully completing this chapter, you will be able to:

6.1 explain what is meant by Rawls' social contractarianism;
6.2 define what Rawls means by society;
6.3 see how "the original position" can be used to arrive at principles of justice;
6.4 define justice as fairness in regard to two principles (i.e., the principle of equal liberty and the difference principle);
6.5 distinguish between Rawls' social contractarianism and utilitarianism;
6.6 identify and explain the "maximin" solution to the problem of social justice.

PHILOSOPHICAL FOCUS QUESTIONS

1. In what ways are social practices and institutions subject to moral and ethical evaluation?
2. How does Rawls conceptualize society? How else could it be conceived? What could be the moral basis of any alternative?
3. Is there anything unrealistic about what Rawls calls "the original position." If so, what? Are there good and sufficient reasons for abandoning this concept?
4. How do Rawlsian and utilitarian conceptions of justice differ?
5. What concept of justice emerges out of the original position?
6. Does Rawls assign different weights to moral concepts such as "goodness" and "rightness"? Explain.
7. Can you provide any contemporary social applications of the equal-liberty principle and the difference principle?
8. What is meant by Rawls' "maximin" solution to the problem of social justice?

HARVARD UNIVERSITY

John Rawls
(1921–)

BIOGRAPHICAL BRIEF*

John Rawls was born in Baltimore in 1921. He studied at Cornell University and at Princeton, where he earned his doctorate in 1950. His social contract theory of society serves to illustrate how classical philosophy continues to exert an influence on contemporary thought. Rawls openly admits his debt to contractarian philosophers like Locke and Rousseau. He also states that his theory is highly Kantian in nature and, as such, is not entirely original. Rawls' important contribution to ethical and sociopolitical philosophy comes from the fact that he has taken Kantian and social contractarian ideas to a higher level of abstraction; he has synthesized and organized these ideas by means of a simplifying framework that allows them to be more fully appreciated. Rawls' updated version of Kantian and social contractarian ethics constitutes, for him, the most appropriate moral basis for a democratic society. He argues that it is better than utilitarian alternatives. The late Lawrence Kohlberg, another Harvard professor and psychological researcher, has argued that the highest stage of moral development in the individual, as evidenced by the most adequate ethical-reasoning abilities, is reflected in the principles of justice articulated by Rawls and extracted from his theoretical device known as "the original position." John Rawls' most important work is entitled *A Theory of Justice*. In it, we find an explanation of his socioethical position and a defense of his views on the moral life of individuals within society.

**From Falikowski,* Moral Philosophy, *p. 78.*

6.1
JUSTICE AND THE SOCIAL CONTRACT TRADITION

The principles of right, and so of justice, put limits on which satisfactions have value; they impose restrictions on what are reasonable conceptions of one's good.
John Rawls

Liberty consists in the power of doing that which is permitted by the law.
Cicero

The philosopher, John Rawls, has developed a theory of justice designed to be a more viable, satisfactory alternative to those concepts of justice provided by other ethical perspectives such as utilitarianism. In his classic work, *A Theory of Justice*, Rawls underscores the idea that sociopolitical institutions are the proper targets of moral evaluation. His theory is constructed to offer us a workable method for solving problems related to social morality. Influenced by Kantian thinking and belonging to the social contract tradition of Locke and Rousseau, Rawls presents the view that the ultimate basis of society rests on a set of **tacit agreements** among its members. From his vantage point, a major theoretical problem related to this idea is that of defining the basic principles entailed in these agreements, which a well-ordered society must espouse if it is to be based on a solid moral foundation.

Justice is the first virtue of social institutions, as truth is of systems of thought. A theory, however elegant and economical must be rejected or revised if it is untrue; likewise laws and institutions no matter how efficient and well-arranged must be reformed or abolished if they are unjust.
John Rawls

Justice is truth in action.
Disraeli

For Rawls, the tacit agreements upon which people would naturally base society involve principles of **justice**. Underscoring the importance of justice, he writes: "Justice is the first virtue of social institutions, as truth is of systems of thought. A theory however elegant and economical must be rejected or revised if it is untrue; likewise laws and institutions no matter how efficient and well-arranged must be reformed or abolished if they are unjust" (Rawls, 1971, p. 3). In the Rawlsian account, every individual possesses an **inviolability** founded on justice, and nothing, not even the welfare of society as a whole, can override it. In a just and moral society the liberties of equal citizenship are established and the **rights**, which are secured by the individual, cannot be made subject to political bargaining. Whether or not we ascribe fundamental rights to persons cannot properly be determined by some kind of calculation of social interests. Rawls claims that the only occasion when a particular injustice is tolerable is when it is required to circumvent an even greater injustice (Rawls, *ibid.*, p. 4).

6.2 THE RAWLSIAN SOCIETY

To better understand how Rawls' notion of justice would operate in practical terms, it is helpful to get a clearer picture of how he conceptualizes **society**. Rawls sees society as a self-sufficient association of individuals. In their interpersonal relationships, people acknowledge that certain rules of conduct are binding on them and, in most instances, are willing to abide by those rules. These binding rules of society constitute a system of cooperation designed to further the good and improve the welfare of those who participate. Society, then, is a type of cooperative venture for purposes of mutual advantage. Within society, we find an **identity of interests**. People generally want the same kinds of things and share the same basic needs. This identity of interests helps to create a system of social cooperation, one that allows for a better life for every individual than would be possible for any single person to enjoy if left to live solely by his or her own efforts (Rawls, *ibid.*, p. 4).

Rawls recognizes, of course, that even within a cooperative system **conflicts of interest** will inevitably arise. Persons will tend to disagree, for instance, about how the greater benefits secured by their collaborative efforts should be distributed. In pursuit of their life goals, persons typically perceive things differently and generally prefer a larger share of benefits to a smaller one. Obviously, not everyone can have a larger share; nor is it always feasible to give everyone access to the same resources. In view of this fact, Rawls believes that:

> [a] set of principles is required for choosing among the various social arrangements which determine this division of advantages and for underwriting an agreement on the proper distributive shares. These principles are the principles of social justice: they provide a way of assigning rights and duties in the basic institutions of society and they define the appropriate distribution of the benefits and burdens of social cooperation. (Rawls, *ibid*, p. 4)

The sentiment of justice is so natural, so universally acquired by all mankind that it seems to be independent of all law, all party, all religion.

Voltaire

As you will see, Rawls' conception of social justice (the basis of a well-ordered society) enables one to become the **ideal observer** in the resolution of any social conflict. His notion of justice is intended to serve as a **common point of view** from which the conflicting claims of opposing parties can be **fairly adjudicated**. A shared understanding of justice allows for individuals with disparate aims and purposes to establish the bonds of **civic friendship** (Rawls, *ibid.*, p. 5). This shared understanding can be regarded as constituting the basic charter of a well-ordered human association. In such an association (society), each person accepts, and knows that other persons accept, the same fundamental principles of justice. When speaking of persons, Rawls also intends to include groups, institutions, and collective agencies. In this vein, we often make reference to companies as "corporate citizens." They too must, in their activities and in their policies, abide by the principles of justice if a well-ordered society is to be maintained.

Abstract liberty, like other mere abstractions, is not to be found.

Burke

6.3 THE ORIGINAL POSITION AND THE "VEIL OF IGNORANCE"

To arrive at the specific principles of social justice, Rawls uses a theoretical device called **the original position**. The original position is a purely **hypothetical situation**: it has never actually existed in reality. It is not an historical event or empirical set of circumstances. In the original position, persons are placed behind a **veil of ignorance**. They are ignorant of their place, class position or social status within society. They do not know how lucky or unlucky they have been in the distribution of natural assets, abilities, intelligence, strength, and so on. They are unaware as well of their peculiar psychological interests and inclinations. They do not know what definition they and others have given to the good life. What is specified about the parties in the original position is that they are **rational**, **free** and **equal members** and that they all wish to maximize their own definitions of the good life, whatever those definitions may entail. Furthermore, Rawls stipulates that in the original position people are **mutually disinterested**. This is not to suggest that the parties are egoists (only concerned with their own worth, prestige, power) but that the parties are generally concerned with furthering their own interests and not with furthering someone else's goals (Rawls, *ibid*., p. 13). In this situation of mutual disinterest, where social cooperation is designed to further individual goals and maximize personal benefits, it is inevitable that parties will come into **conflict** over the distribution of social advantages. It is assumed that people will want a larger, not a smaller, share of the benefits that derive from their efforts toward social cooperation.

Equal rights for all, special privileges for none.

Thomas Jefferson

So far is it from being true that men are naturally equal, that no two people can be half an hour together but one shall acquire an evident superiority over the other.

Johnson (1709-1784)

Assuming that the conflicts among the opposing parties are to be settled peacefully, not through violence and war, Rawls works out his theory by determining which rational principles of conflict resolution would likely be chosen by individuals in the original position, when placed behind the veil of ignorance. Ignorance of one's particular fortune and set of personal interests would ensure that nobody is advantaged or disadvantaged in the initial selection of principles by the outcome of natural chance or by the **contingencies** of social circumstances. In other words, the principles that would be freely chosen and mutually agreed upon by rational and equal parties would be **fair** or **just** from everyone's perspective. As Rawls puts it, "Since all are similarly situated and no one is able to design principles to favor his particular condition, the principles of justice are the result of a fair agreement or bargain" (Rawls, *ibid.*, p. 12). The principles agreed to in the original position define what Rawls calls **justice as fairness**. Before we look more closely at the notion of justice as fairness, it might be fun and interesting to repeat Rawls' thought experiment involving hypothetical negotiations in the original position. Because our repeat performance is not exactly original, let us call our situation "The Similar Position." Turn to the Philosophers at Work feature that follows to see what I mean.

PHILOSOPHERS AT WORK

The Similar Position: Suppose that you and your classmates have been shipwrecked and that you now find yourselves on a deserted island somewhere in uncharted waters. It is unlikely that you will be rescued soon, if ever. You are worried about the possibility that tensions and conflicts could flare up into episodes of physical violence in the future, so you all decide to establish some ground rules and principles that must be obeyed if everybody is going to live together peacefully. In small groups of four to six people, establish the constitutional principles of your newly formed island society. Note that at this point nobody knows who they are or anything about themselves. The violent storm that led to the shipwreck has left everyone in shock and suffering from temporary amnesia. Nonetheless, everyone is still able to think and to reason clearly. You simply know nothing about your past or what your status or position was back home. Under these circumstances, what principles of social organization emerge from "the similar position"?

Part One: In forming your constitution, what assumptions will you make? What, if anything, will people be entitled to? Will you have any duties and responsibilities? If so, which ones? Will anything be forbidden? Why?

Part Two: Now that you have established your constitution, compare it with Rawls' notion of justice as fairness defined by the difference principle and the principle of equal liberty (pp. 134 to 136). Do your group's decisions serve to support or question Rawls' claims about what rational thinkers would produce in an initial situation behind a veil of ignorance?

Above all other things is justice.
Success is a good thing; wealth is good also;
honor is better, but justice excels them all.
David Dudley Field

The concept of justice as fairness, which emerges out of the original position, serves to regulate criticism and reform of all social institutions. With mutually agreed upon principles of justice, people can prepare a constitution and set up a legislature to enact laws that are consistent with these principles. Of course, Rawls realizes that people cannot literally contract from the hypothetical original position, since, at birth, they already find themselves with some particular status and psychological endowment, in some particular society, and given some particular life prospects. Nonetheless, Rawls believes that to the extent a society satisfies the principle of justice as fairness, it conforms to the principles that free and equal individuals would accept for their mutual advantage under circumstances that are fair. Choosing these principles, people can decide *in advance* how they will regulate their claims against one another and what rights, duties, and freedoms will form the constitutional foundation of their society. Before elaborating upon the two specific principles to be included in his notion of justice as fairness, Rawls first explains why he rejects the utilitarian conception of justice. Refusing to accept "utility" as a standard of justice, Rawls writes:

> Offhand it hardly seems likely that persons who view themselves as equals, entitled to press their claims upon one another, would agree to a principle which may require lesser life prospects for some simply for the sake of a greater sum of advantages enjoyed by others . . . . [A] rational man would not accept a basic structure merely because it maximized the algebraic sum of advantages irrespective of its permanent effects on his own rights and interests. Thus it seems that the principle of utility is incompatible with the conception of social cooperation among equals for mutual advantage. (Rawls, *ibid.*, p. 14)

It is untrue that equality is a law of nature. Nature has no equality. Its sovereign law is subordination and dependence.

Vauvenargues (1715–1747)

Democracy is the worst system devised by the wit of man, except for all the others.

Winston Churchill

Democracy arose from men's thinking that if they are equal in any respect, they are equal absolutely.

Aristotle

All social values—liberty and opportunity, income and wealth, and the bases of self-respect—are to be distributed equally unless an unequal distribution of any, or all, of these values is to everyone's advantage . . . . Injustice, then, is simply inequalities that are not to the benefit of all.

John Rawls

Turn now to the "Back to the Source" feature taken from Rawls' *A Theory of Justice*.

BACK TO THE SOURCE*

4. The Original Position and Justification

I have said that the original position is the appropriate initial status quo which insures that the fundamental agreements reached in it are fair. This fact yields the name "justice as fairness." It is clear, then, that I want to say that one conception of justice is more reasonable than another, or justifiable with respect to it, if rational persons in the initial situation would choose its principles over those of the other for the role of justice. Conceptions of justice are to be ranked by their acceptability to persons so circumstanced. Understood in this way the question of justification is settled by working out a problem of deliberation: we have to ascertain which principles it would be rational to adopt given the contractual situation. This connects the theory or justice with the theory of rational choice.

If this view of the problem of justification is to succeed, we must, of course, describe in some detail the nature of this choice problem. A problem of rational decision has a definite answer only if we know the beliefs and interests of the parties, their relations with respect to one another, the alternatives between which they are to choose, the procedure whereby they make up their minds, and so on. As the circumstances are presented in different ways, correspondingly different principles are accepted. The concept of the original position, as I shall refer to it, is that of the most philosophically favored interpretation of this initial choice situation for the purposes of a theory of justice.

But how are we to decide what is the most favored interpretation? I assume, for one thing, that there is a broad measure of agreement that principles of justice should be chosen under certain conditions. To justify a particular description of the initial situation one shows that it incorporates these commonly shared presumptions. One argues from widely accepted but weak premises to more specific conclusions. Each of the presumptions should by itself be natural and plausible; some of them may seem innocuous or even trivial. The aim of the contract approach is to establish that taken together they impose significant bounds on acceptable principles of justice. The ideal outcome would be that these conditions determine a unique set of principles; but I shall be satisfied if they suffice to rank the main traditional conceptions of social justice.

One should not be misled, then, by the somewhat unusual conditions which characterize the original position. The idea here is simply to make vivid to ourselves the restrictions that it seems reasonable to impose on arguments for principles of justice, and therefore on these principles themselves. Thus it seems reasonable and generally acceptable that no one should be advantaged or disadvantaged by natural fortune or social circumstances in the choice of principles. It also seems widely agreed that it should be impossible to tailor principles to the circumstances of one's own case. We should insure further than particular inclinations and aspirations, and persons' conceptions of their good do not affect the principles

---

adopted. The aim is to rule out those principles that it would be rational to propose for acceptance, however little the chance of success, only if one knew certain things that are irrelevant from the standpoint of justice. For example, if a man knew that he was wealthy, he might find it rational to advance the principle that various taxes for welfare measures be counted unjust; if he knew that he was poor, he would most likely propose the contrary principle. To represent the desired restrictions one imagines a situation in which everyone is deprived of this sort of information. One excludes the knowledge of those contingencies which sets men at odds and allows them to be guided by their prejudices. In this manner the veil of ignorance is arrived at in a natural way. This concept should cause no difficulty if we keep in mind the constraints on arguments that it is meant to express. At any time we can enter the original position, so to speak, simply by following a certain procedure, namely, by arguing for principles of justice in accordance with these restrictions.

It seems reasonable to suppose that the parties in the original position are equal. That is, all have the same rights in the procedure for choosing principles; each can make proposals, submit reasons for their acceptance, and so on. Obviously the purpose of these conditions is to represent equality between human beings as moral persons, as creatures having a conception of their good and capable of a sense of justice. The basis of equality is taken to be similarity in these two respects. Systems of ends are not ranked in value; and each man is presumed to have the requisite ability to understand and to act upon whatever principles are adopted. Together with the veil of ignorance, these conditions define the principles of justice as those which rational persons concerned to advance their interests would consent to as equals when none are known to be advantaged or disadvantaged by social and natural contingencies.

There is, however, another side to justifying a particular description of the original position. This is to see if the principles which would be chosen match our considered convictions of justice or extend them in an acceptable way. We can note whether applying these principles would lead us to make the same judgments about the basic structure of society which we now make intuitively and in which we have the greatest confidence; or whether, in cases where our present judgments are in doubt and given with hesitation, these principles offer a resolution which we can affirm on reflection. There are questions which we feel sure must be answered in a certain way. For example, we are confident that religious intolerance and racial discrimination are unjust. We think that we have examined these things with care and have reached what we believe is an impartial judgment not likely to be distorted by an excessive attention to our own interests. These convictions are provisional fixed points which we presume any conception of justice must fit. But we have much less assurance as to what is the correct distribution of wealth and authority. Here we may be looking for a way to remove our doubts. We can check an interpretation of the initial situation, then, by the capacity of its principles to accommodate our firmest convictions and to provide guidance where guidance is needed.

In searching for the most favored description of this situation we work from both ends. We begin by describing it so that it represents generally shared and preferably weak conditions. We then see if these conditions are strong enough to yield a significant set of principles. If not, we look for further premises equally reasonable. But if so, and these principles match our considered convictions of justice, then so far well and good. But presumably there will be discrepancies. In this case we have a choice. We can either modify the account of the initial situation or we can revise our existing judgments, for even the judgments we take provisionally as fixed points are liable to revision. By going back and forth, sometimes altering the conditions of the contractual circumstances, at others withdrawing our judgments and conforming them to principle, I assume that eventually we shall find a description of the initial situation that both expresses reasonable conditions and yields principles which match our considered judgments duly pruned and adjusted. This state of affairs I refer to as reflective equilibrium.[1] It is an equilibrium because at last our principles and judgments coincide; and it is reflective since we know to what principles our judgments conform and the premises of their derivation. At the moment everything is in order. But this equilibrium is not necessarily stable. It is liable to be upset by further examination of the conditions which should be imposed on the contractual situation and by particular cases which may lead us to revise our judgments. Yet for the time being we have done what we can to render coherent and to justify our convictions of social justice. We have reached a conception of the original position.

I shall not, of course, actually work through this process. Still, we may think of the interpretation of the original position that I shall present as the result of such a hypothetical course of reflection. It represents the attempt to accommodate within one scheme both reasonable philosophical conditions on principles as well as our considered judgments of justice. In arriving at the favored interpretation of the initial situation there is no point at which an appeal is made to self-evidence in the traditional sense either of general conceptions or particular convictions. I do not claim for the principles of justice proposed that they are necessary truths or derivable from such truths. A conception of justice cannot be deduced from self-evident premises or conditions on principles; instead, its justification is a matter of the mutual support of many considerations, of everything fitting together into one coherent view.

A final comment. We shall want to say that certain principles of justice are justified because they would be agreed to in an initial situation of equality. I have emphasized that this original position is purely hypothetical. It is natural to ask why, if this agreement is never actually entered into, we should take any interest in these principles, moral or otherwise. The answer is that the conditions embodied in the description of the original position are ones that we do in fact accept. Or if we do not, then perhaps we can be persuaded to do so by philosophical reflection. Each aspect of the contractual situation can be given supporting grounds. Thus what we shall do is to collect together into one conception a number of conditions on principles that we are ready upon due consideration to recognize as reasonable. These constraints express what we are prepared to regard as limits on fair terms of social cooperation. One way to look at the idea of the original position, therefore, is to see it as an expository devise which sums up the meaning of these conditions and helps us to extract their consequences. On the other hand, this conception is also an intuitive notion that suggests its own elaboration, so that led on by it we are drawn to define more clearly the standpoint from which we can best interpret moral relationships. We need a conception that enables us to envision our objective from afar; the intuitive notion of the original position is to do this for us.[2]

Notes

1. The process of mutual adjustment of principles and considered judgments is not peculiar to moral philosophy. See Nelson Goodman, *Fact, Fiction, and Forecast* (Cambridge, Mass., Harvard University Press, 1955), pp. 65-68, for parallel remarks concerning the justification of the principles of deductive and inductive inference.
2. Henri Poincaré remarks: Il nous faut une faculté qui nous fasse voir le but de loin, et, cette faculté, c'est l'intuition." *La Valeur de la Science* (Paris, Flammarion, 1909), p. 27.

6.4
6.5

THE PRINCIPLE OF EQUAL LIBERTY

Having rejected the principle of utility, Rawls contends that persons in the original position would likely choose two fundamental principles. The first is the **principle of equal liberty**. It states that "each person is to have an equal right to the most extensive basic liberty compatible with a similar liberty for others" (Rawls, *ibid.*, p. 60). Note that such a principle would be accepted without a knowledge of anyone's particular ends and without knowledge of what is to anyone's advantage. The implicit agreement, therefore, would be to have everyone's pursuits and interests fall within the boundaries of what the principles of justice require. People would be expected to refrain from choosing ends that would violate the liberties of others and were liberties that they would expect for themselves. The advantage of some could not be purchased justifiably at the expense of others' freedoms—certainly not in a situation of equality and cooperation for mutual advantage. Furthermore, whereas utilitarians such as Bentham do not distinguish among pleasures and see all pleasures as equally valuable and worth pursuing, Rawls maintains that "the principles of right, and so of justice, put limits on which satisfactions have value; they impose restrictions on what are reasonable conceptions of one's good" (Rawls, *ibid.*, p. 31). From the Rawlsian, **deontological**, social contract perspective, the concept of **rightness** overrides and is prior to the concept of **goodness**. The freedom or liberty to pursue specific ends must be limited by considerations of justice. In this vein, Rawls says:

> A just social system defines the scope within which individuals must develop their aims, and it provides a framework of rights and opportunities and the means of satisfaction within and by the use of which these ends may be equitably pursued. The priority of justice is accounted for, in part, by holding that the interests requiring the violation of justice have no value. Having no merit in the first place, they cannot override its claims. (Rawls, *ibid.*, p. 31)

The basic liberties of all citizens required by the first principle include (1) political liberty, that is, the right to vote and run for public office; (2) freedom of speech and assembly; (3) freedom of thought and liberty of conscience; (4) personal freedom; (5) freedom to hold property;

and finally (6) freedom from arbitrary arrest and seizure. The liberties listed here represent the basic rights of every person within society and, ideally, none of them is to be violated. These basic rights define the proper boundaries within which social practices must fall if they are to be considered acceptable, right or just.

The statement of the first principle clearly tells us that people are to be regarded as free and equal. Systems of rules defining practices of various social institutions must, therefore, be administered equitably. There should be a spirit of **impartiality** and **disinterestedness** characterizing the distribution of advantages. No individual should arbitrarily receive preferred treatment. For example, if a firm offers a position of employment and draws up job specifications, the equal liberty principle requires that all applicants be judged by the established criteria. If it were the case that someone without the specified and required credentials were offered the position, the principle would not be upheld because an exception was made, presumably on the basis of irrelevant considerations (e.g., ethnic background). In addition, the principle would not be equitably or fairly administered if particular individuals were excluded on criteria not related to the job (e.g., gender or race). We can see, then, how considerations of rightness and justice can become involved even in social hiring practices, a point that underscores Rawls' claim that social institutions are proper objects of moral evaluation.

6.4
THE DIFFERENCE PRINCIPLE

The difference principle is the second principle falling under Rawls' conception of justice as fairness. It states: "Social and economic inequalities, for example inequalities of wealth and authority, are just only if they result in compensating benefits for everyone, and in particular for the least advantaged members of society" (Rawls, *ibid.*, pp. 14–15). The difference principle should not be misunderstood here as equivalent to the utilitarian greatest happiness principle which seeks to promote the greatest happiness for the greatest number. The difference principle does not permit inequalities in institutional practices on the grounds that the hardships or burdens of some are offset by the greater good of the majority. In Rawls' view, "it is not just that some should have less in order that others may prosper" (Rawls, *ibid.*, p. 15). Rawls does not suggest by this that everyone must be treated precisely the same. He believes that citizens of a country do not object to people having different positions within society (e.g., prime minister, president or judge), each with its own special rights and duties. What they object to is the pattern of honors and rewards set up by a practice (for example, the privileges and salaries of government officials). They may also object to the distribution of power and wealth that comes about by the different ways in which people avail themselves of the opportunities allowed by a particular practice (e.g., the concentration of wealth that may develop in a free market environment and allow for large entrepreneurial and speculative rewards). To justify inequalities, there must be reason to believe that the practice involving the inequality, or resulting in it, will ultimately work for the advantage of *every* person engaging in it—not just the majority. Individuals thus must find their conditions and prospects under a situation of inequality preferable to those under a situation without inequality. In short, every person must gain from the inequality, if that inequality is to be permissible.

For the difference principle, which allows for differences of treatment, to be made acceptable, an important condition must be met. It is necessary that the offices to which special benefits are attached be open to all who meet the necessary requirements. Such offices must be won in a fair competition wherein contestants are judged on their merits. The fact that an excluded individual nevertheless benefits from the efforts put forward by those allowed to compete does not legitimize this unjust treatment, according to Rawls. There are intrinsic goods involved in the skillful and devoted exercise of various offices and practices. If a person is prevented from functioning in those particular offices or practices, then that person is deprived of one of the most important ways in which individuals realize their **human potential**. The person is robbed of his or her humanity, so to speak.

The suggestion that societal positions should be won by fair competition does not mean that absolutely everyone has a right to compete and to be seriously considered for every job. Remember, the difference principle allows for the possibility of inequality if it works to the advantage of every individual and, especially, to the advantage of the least well off. Suppose, for instance, that an airline establishes a minimum level of corrected vision for all of its pilots. Now, such a regulation does, in fact, work against those who cannot reach the minimum. Some people will, in effect, be excluded from consideration for the pilot's job. Nonetheless, this vision requirement should not be regarded as unjust. A pilot with limited vision is a danger to the airline's passengers, as well as to himself or herself. Everyone, including the candidate pilot, benefits by the application of the vision requirement, albeit through a form of "unequal" treatment. (See Barry, 1973, pp. 52–53, for a similar example.) The difference principle may also be at work in some governmental economic policies. One frequently hears how unjust it is that huge corporations are given tax breaks, whereas the average taxpayer is "unduly" saddled with an ever increasing share of the tax burden. It could be argued, however, that by this apparent unequal treatment, corporations will have more available capital to invest in new business ventures; in turn, this will create new or better jobs and certainly benefit those worst off in society, namely, the unemployed. Were the tax burden proportionately equal, perhaps no new job opportunities would be created and the unemployed would remain that way, thus worse, rather than better, off.

6.6

THE MAXIMIN SOLUTION TO THE PROBLEM OF SOCIAL JUSTICE

In closing, it is worth noting that Rawls' combination of the two principles arising out of the original position is called the **maximin solution** to the problem of social justice (Rawls, 1971, p. 152). When the equal liberty principle and the difference principle are combined under the maximin solution, the general rule is to rank alternatives by their worst possible outcomes: thus, we adopt "the alternative the worst outcome of which is superior to the worst outcomes of the others" (Rawls, *ibid.*, pp. 152–153). This guideline helps **maximize** the lot, or welfare, of those

minimally advantaged—a fundamental goal of the Rawlsian just society. The maximin rule focuses our attention on the worst that can happen under each alternative course of action, and it instructs us to make a decision in light of that. Rawls' notion of justice, then, is a **reciprocity** concept. Rightness is not ultimately determined by consequences. Rather, the reciprocity element inherent in Rawls' theory of justice "requires that a practice be such that all members who fall under it could and would accept it and be bound by it" (Rawls, *ibid.*, p. 153). No person has authority over another. Each is willing to accept the worst position as it might be assigned by one's enemy or opponent in a situation of conflict. This makes the element of reciprocity essential to justice as fairness.

PHILOSOPHERS AT WORK

In Rawls' attempt to extract from the original position the principles upon which a just society would be based, we find disembodied rational agents who fit together as a self-sufficient association of individuals. Although all are considered equal and are respectful of each others' rights, cooperation occurs primarily for the purposes of furthering individual self-interests. Standards of justice as fairness are laid down and are used as a way of resolving disputes among societal members. In view of this:

1. Is there any danger in extrapolating from the hypothetical original position to real life, having conceptualized people in society as purely rational agents? Why or why not?
2. Should we consider all people self-interested and self-sufficient? How else could we see them?
3. Do people cooperate with one another only, or primarily, for purposes of furthering their personal interests and for achieving their life goals? Explain.
4. Are there any societies or communities you know of that base their social relations on something other than justice? If so, which ones? How do they function? What is the basis of social cooperation there (i.e., why do people work together)?
5. Finally, what evaluative comments could you make about Rawls' social contractarianism? Do you "buy" his theory?

MINDWORK MEDITATION

John Rawls has made much of the principle of justice as fairness in his sociopolitical moral philosophy. How important is fairness or justice to you personally? Do you think being fair, or just, as a moral person is more important than maximizing goodness or doing what feels right? Why? What are your other thoughts on Rawls?

Key Terms

tacit agreements
justice
inviolability
rights
society
identity of interests
conflicts of interest
ideal observer
common point of view
fairly adjudicated
civic friendship
the original position
hypothetical situation
veil of ignorance
rational
free
equal members
mutually disinterested
conflict
contingencies
fair
just
justice as fairness
principle of equal liberty
deontological
rightness
goodness
impartiality
disinterestedness
the difference principle
human potential
maximin solution
maximize
minimally advantaged
reciprocity

Progress Check 6.1

Instructions: Fill in the blanks with the appropriate responses listed below.

justice
ideal observer
social contract theory
society
original position
principle of equal liberty
maximin principle
reciprocity
identity of interests
inviolate
utilitarianism
veil of ignorance
mutually disinterested
deontological ethics
difference principle

1. John Rawls' theory of justice is intended as a more satisfactory alternative to _____.
2. _____ views morality and matters of justice as a set of tacit agreements among society's members.
3. In the same way that truth is the first virtue of systems of thought, _____ is the first virtue of social institutions.
4. People's basic rights cannot be negotiated or bargained away because they are _____.
5. A(n) _____ is a self-sufficient association of individuals who cooperate for purposes of mutual advantage.

6. Although people are different and often go in different directions in their lives, they, nonetheless, still share a(n) _____ having the same basic needs and wanting generally the same kinds of things.
7. From the position of the _____, conflicts can be fairly and objectively resolved without bias or favoritism.
8. The _____ is a hypothetical situation used by Rawls to draw out the principles of justice as fairness.
9. Persons placed behind a(n) _____ are unaware of any specifics pertaining to themselves (e.g., gender, class, and ability).
10. Persons in the original position are _____, concerned with furthering their own goals, not sacrificing for another's.
11. The _____ states that all people are to be granted the same freedoms. One cannot grant less freedom to others than one would grant to oneself.
12. According to _____, the concept of rightness takes precedence over goodness.
13. The idea that social inequalities in treatment are fair or just only if everyone benefits and only if everyone would be better is captured by the _____.
14. The _____ requires us to compare alternatives before making moral choices. The action whose worst outcome for all is better than the worst outcome of all the other alternatives is the right choice.
15. The concept of _____ requires that we be willing to accept the consequences of a principle that we wish to apply to others.

Summary of Major Points

1. How does Rawls conceptualize society?
   It is a self-sufficient association of individuals.
   It is bound by general rules of conduct.
   It is a system of cooperation designed to promote the welfare of all.
   It is a cooperative venture for purposes of mutual advantage.
2. What is the original position?
   It is a hypothetical situation used by Rawls to derive the first principles upon which a just society would be based.
   It is a situation wherein people are placed behind a "veil of ignorance."
   It is a position in which people are unaware of their status and personal characteristics.
   People in this position are assumed to be rational, free, equal, and mutually disinterested.
3. What is "justice as fairness"? How can it be used?
   It results from the establishment of principles in the original position.
   It can be used to criticize and to reform social institutions.

It can be used for legislative purposes.
It is what free and equal individuals would contract to accept for their mutual advantage under fair circumstances.

4. **What is meant by the "equal liberty principle"?**
Each person is to have an equal right to the most extensive basic liberty compatible with a similar liberty for others.
It guarantees all citizens political liberty, the right to vote and run for public office, freedom of speech and assembly, freedom of thought and liberty of conscience, personal freedom, the right to own property, and freedom from arbitrary arrest and seizure.

5. **How should one understand the difference principle?**
Social and economic inequalities are just only if they result in compensating benefits for everyone—especially for the least advantaged in society.
It differs from the greatest happiness principle.
Applying this principle means that offices having special rights and privileges must be won in fair competition.

6. **What does the maximin solution advise?**
The alternative one should adopt is the alternative having the worst outcome which is superior to the worst outcome of the other alternatives.
It requires one to maximize the lot or welfare of those minimally advantaged in society.
It suggests that all decisions fall acceptably under the equal liberty principle and the difference principle, taken together.

Source References and Related Readings

Barry, B.M. *The Liberal Theory of Justice*. Oxford: Clarendon Press, 1973.
Blocker, H.G. and E.H. Smith, eds. *John Rawls' Theory of Social Justice: An Introduction*. Athens: Ohio University Press, 1980.
Daniels, N., ed. *Reading Rawls*. New York: Basic Books, 1975.
Falikowski, Anthony. *Moral Philosophy: Theories, Skills, and Applications*. Englewood Cliffs, N.J.: Prentice Hall, 1990.
Rawls, John. *A Theory of Justice*. Cambridge, Mass.: Harvard University Press, 1971.
———. "Justice as Fairness." *The Journal of Philosophy*. Vol. 54, Oct. 1957, pp. 653–62.
Wolff, R.P. *Understanding Rawls*. Princeton, N.J.: Princeton University Press, 1976.

POSTSTUDY MORAL PREFERENCE INDICATOR

Instructions and Answer Sheet

Having completed your introductory study of ethical theories, you are now invited to complete the **Moral Preference Indicator** (MPI) a second time (turn to pages 6-10). Your poststudy answers to each of the 15 questions of the MPI can be recorded below. Once you are finished, score your answers as before. You can also display your results graphically, comparing before and after study preferences. Shade in the graphic spheres as appropriate.

Scoring Sheet

Answers

Answer	a	b	c
Question			
1	u	d	c
2	c	u	d
3	d	u	c
4	c	d	u
5	c	u	d
6	d	u	c
7	c	u	d
8	c	u	d
9	u	d	c
10	c	d	u
11	u	d	c
12	d	u	c
13	c	u	d
14	d	u	c
15	u	d	c

Total Number

u's = _____ (Utilitarian Ethics)
d's = _____ (Deontological Ethics)
c's = _____ (Character Ethics)

Plot your scores on "The Ethical Spheres for Comparative Analysis" (Figure PI.1 on page 142).

Figure PI.1 ETHICAL SPHERES FOR COMPARATIVE ANALYSIS

Character Ethics

15 10 5 5 10 15

5 10 15

Utilitarian Ethics

Deontological Ethics

Pre-Theoretical Study

Character Ethics

15 10 5 5 10 15

5 10 15

Utilitarian Ethics

Deontological Ethics

Post-Theoretical Study

MINDWORK MEDITATION

Have your poststudy moral preferences changed at all, and, if so, in what respects? How do you explain your changed preferences or the fact that your preferences remained more or less stable? Are you now more character-based, utilitarian or deontological in your moral thinking? Refer to page 10 of the original MPI for summaries of what each perspective involves.

2

PART TWO

DEVELOPING ETHICAL REASONING SKILLS

In Part One of *Moral Philosophy for Modern Life*, you looked at three fundamentally different moral perspectives. You learned how morality has much to do with things like character, virtue, happiness, utility, fairness, justice, and rationality. Although there is still more to explore in the field of ethical theory (e.g., feminist ethics, religious ethics, existentialism, and so on), you have been introduced to three of the most influential systems of ethical thought in western civilization—not a bad starting point for beginning your ethical journey.

In Part Two of your moral odyssey, we will be traveling into that area of the philosophical kingdom that contains fields of logic and reasoning. Plan to learn about the nature and benefits of argument, how philosophical method differs from science, what attitudes need to be cultivated for proper philosophical discussion, how to test arguments for their validity and soundness, and, finally, what constitutes fallacious reasoning (or what I call "sleazy logic"). You will also be provided with some helpful "Do's and Don'ts" for proper philosophical argumentation. Once you successfully complete Part Two, you will have mastered a few important basics of moral reasoning. Given that you have already acquired a fundamental understanding of the philosophers that we have studied, you will be well prepared in Part Three to start applying your theoretical knowledge and rational thinking skills to contemporary ethical problems. But before we jump the gun, let us direct our attention to matters of reasoning and logic. To see how good your current reasoning skills are, complete and score the self-diagnostic entitled "How Rational is My Thinking?" After completing Part Two, you may wish to complete the self-diagnostic again to gauge the improvement in your ethical thinking skills.

SELF-DIAGNOSTIC: HOW RATIONAL IS MY THINKING?

If people are to engage in productive moral discussions and debates, they must learn to think clearly and to reason correctly according to the norms of accepted logic. In this informal self-diagnostic, you will be given an opportunity to reflect on just how good or how bad your current command of logic is.

Since material in Part Two of *Moral Philosophy for Modern Life* is designed to help you improve your ethical thinking skills, you are invited to repeat the self-diagnostic after finishing this section of the book. If you master the reasoning skills in Part Two, then your scores on this self-diagnostic should improve.

Part A: Deductive Logic

Deductive logic is a process of reasoning that contains two premises and a conclusion strung together as an argument. If a conclusion follows logically from preceding premises and if those premises are true, then the argument is sound and valid in form.

Instructions: Fill in the missing statements for each of the examples below.

1. All Greeks are mortal.

   _____.

   Therefore, Socrates is mortal.

2. _____.
   An oak is a tree.
   Therefore, an oak has leaves.
3. All Canadians have the right to vote.
   Jean-Guy is a Canadian.
   _____.
4. If interest rates decline, then stock prices rise.
   _____.
   So, stock prices will rise.
5. If you do something wrong, your parents will get mad.
   Your parents are not mad.
   _____.
6. If p, then q.
   If q, then r.
   Therefore, if p _____.
7. Either p or q.
   _____.
   Therefore, p.
8. All A are B.
   _____.
   Therefore, some C are B.
9. Cheaters should be punished.
   _____.
   Mary should be punished.
10. Major Premise: p is q.
    Minor Premise: r is p.
    Conclusion: _____.

Part B: Inductive Logic

Each example following contains a conclusion based on either good or bad inductive reasoning. As you will learn shortly, inductive reasoning is a logical thought process leading to probable conclusions. It is based on such things as sensory experience and scientific evidence. The aim here is to see how well you are able to think inductively. Do not be too concerned about the technical term itself, for you have been using inductive logic for years, whether you have known it or not. We just want to see how well you have learned to reason using this method of thinking.

Instructions: Next to each example place the letter G or B. G equals good reasoning; B equals bad reasoning.

1. The Montreal Canadiens have a tradition of winning in professional hockey. They won the Stanley Cup last year for the umpteenth time. I guess they will win again this year.
2. I met Bill yesterday. I learned he is an environmentalist. He must also be a vegetarian. I have met two environmentalists before and both of them refused to eat meat.
3. The sun rose today in the east. It rose yesterday in the east as well. In fact, the sun has been rising in the east for millions of years. It will probably rise in the east tomorrow.
4. All North American cars are "lemons." I know, I have owned cars made by each of the three large manufacturers and each car has constantly broken down and been unreliable for me.
5. Most people in this country favor capital punishment. Yesterday, I went to a prison guard rally at Kingston penitentiary and I asked 100 guards their views on the subject. Ninety-seven were in favor of it.

Part C: Fallacious Reasoning

Fallacious reasoning is what I call "sleazy logic." It is often used to persuade people. Fallacious reasoning either diverts attention from the real issues at hand or else it serves to intimidate. This form of illegitimate thinking distorts reality and often makes inappropriate emotional or psychological appeals. Which examples below reflect acceptable reasoning and which reflect unacceptable fallacious reasoning?

Instructions: Place the letter A next to examples of acceptable reasoning and the letter U next to examples of fallacious reasoning.

1. We should not accept Professor Knowitall's argument that drinking coffee causes cancer. He is just a greedy and vain researcher trying to make a name for himself.
2. Do not believe anything Mr. DeNile says. I know his relatives and they are all liars.
3. If Michael Jordan says that a brand of basketball is the best, it must be so.
4. You ought to be opposed to legalized gambling in the country. Once you permit it, prostitution will necessarily follow. After that will come organized crime. In the end, legalized gambling will make our cities less safe than before.
5. Listen, I hate cheating as much as you do; but when everybody else cheats, you have to cheat too in order to survive.

Answer Key

Part A

1. Socrates is a Greek.
2. All trees have leaves.
3. Therefore, Jean-Guy has the right to vote.
4. Interest rates have declined.
5. Therefore, you did not do anything wrong.
6. Then r.
7. Not q.
8. Some C are A.
9. Mary is a cheater.
10. r is q.

Part B

1. B, the past cannot guarantee the future.
2. B, a conclusion based on a small sample.
3. G, a high probability.
4. B, a generalization based on a small sample and personal experience, not on a larger objective sampling.
5. B, a faulty generalization from an unrepresentative sample.

Part C

1. U, *ad hominem* argument
2. U, guilt by association
3. U, appeal to authority
4. U, slippery slope argument
5. U, two wrongs fallacy

Your Score _____/20 (Add the number of correct answers you obtained. Place this number over 20.)

Interpretation

This self-diagnostic covers three areas of reasoning: deductive logic (Part A), inductive logic (Part B), and fallacious reasoning (Part C). You can begin to reflect on your current ability to think rationally and to identify cases of irrational logic by examining your combined score out of 20. Did you get a high score in one or two parts, but a low score on a third? If so, perhaps you are weak in that area of logical reasoning.

Recommendation

After completing Part Two of *Moral Philosophy for Modern Life*, do this self-diagnostic again. Try to improve your score. The second time be sure to provide explanations for your answers. Mastery of material in Part Two of this book should enable you to get a higher score and to appreciate differences between good and bad reasoning.

CHAPTER SEVEN

7 OPINIONS, ARGUMENTS AND ATTITUDE ADJUSTMENTS

Overview

Learning Outcomes

After successfully completing this chapter, you will be able to:

7.1 compare and contrast philosophy with scientific study;
7.2 explain the differences between normative and metaethical approaches to the study of ethics;
7.3 distinguish between factual statements and value judgments;
7.4 separate moral from nonmoral values;
7.5 identify the differences between opinions and arguments;
7.6 list the benefits of argument;
7.7 describe the attitude adjustments necessary for productive argument.

PHILOSOPHICAL FOCUS QUESTIONS

1. How do science and philosophy differ in their approaches to the study of morality? What are their various tools and methods?
2. What is the difference between normative and metaethical inquiry?
3. In what respects do factual claims differ from value judgments?
4. Are all values moral? Why or why not?
5. Do opinions have any value? If so, how? In what ways is opinionating different from arguing?
6. Why do some people find arguments unpleasant? What do we need to do to make arguments more productive?
7. What are some of the benefits of argument?

7.1
APPROACHES TO THE STUDY OF MORALITY

By now you probably have noticed that (moral) philosophy is something quite different from other traditional fields of study. While it may sound a bit psychological or sociological at times, there is something about the methods and processes of philosophical analysis that makes ethical inquiry different from both the behavioral and social sciences. This is not to suggest that philosophy and science do not sometimes overlap; they do. In building their arguments, philosophers frequently make claims about what is true or factually the case (a matter of science, observation or empirical investigation). Often underlying the work of scientists, on the other hand, are theoretical assumptions having philosophical implications (e.g., all human behavior is determined and freedom is, therefore, an illusion). In fact, as an undergraduate student in psychology, I was led to this realization many years ago. At that time, I was studying the nature and development of moral reasoning in children and adolescents. I was interested in moral development and hoped eventually to get involved in moral and values education. What I discovered was that the psychological researchers I was studying often made philosophical claims and based their scientific studies on ethical assumptions that were often far from clear and self-evident. These assumptions required satisfactory rational justification, something which was, unfortunately, all too often lacking. The deeper I got into studying moral/values development (a psychological matter), the less interested I became in applied scientific study, and the more interested I became in the ethical assumptions underlying the scientific research and investigation I was involved in. The rest, as we say, is history and I now find myself addressing you on the subject of philosophical ethics and not the psychology of moral development. Let us proceed, then, to examine more closely the contrasts between science and philosophy so that we can appreciate, as ethicists, what we are and are not doing.

Scientific Approach

Sciences such as psychology, sociology, and anthropology make morality an object of **empirical study**. To say that morality is studied empirically means that methods of **observation** and **controlled experiment** are used. Scientific researchers attempt to **measure** and **describe** what is **true**, or at least highly **probable**, about moral conduct and experience. A scientist could ask, for example, how likely is it that one will steal if one can get away with it. A feminist researcher could inquire into the possibility that there are gender differences in how people think about moral issues. Whatever empirical questions are asked, it is presumed that answers can be found, in principle, according to the ideal of **scientific objectivity**. Scientists are not in the business of making value judgments about the moral phenomena that they study. Instead, scientists are interested in providing **correlational findings**, **causal** and/or **functional explanations** (e.g., How morality works in personality or functions in society). Given the methods and goals of scientists, we find psychologists, for instance, interested in looking at the relationship between cognitive development and moral reasoning abilities. Sociologists may be intrigued by the functional role of morality in group organization. Anthropologists, by contrast, might be curious about the origins and development of morality in socio-cultural evolution. Whatever their scientific slant, empirical researchers are primarily concerned with the how, why, when, and where questions of morality. If possible, methods of **statistical analysis** are used to **verify** findings or to support claims made about moral experience. In some instances, **predictions** about future moral events might also be offered. Remember, though, that although scientists study the phenomena of morality, they do not wish to be **moralistic**. Their investigations are ideally designed to be **value-neutral**. They do not wish to prescribe what ought to be done; nor do they wish to judge what values are good or bad. Scientists try to express their conclusions as **nonnormative** (non-nor-ma-tive) statements.

> ***You see things; and you say, "Why?" But I dream things that never were and I say, "Why not?"***
>
> *George Bernard Shaw*

7.2

Philosophical Approach

The philosophical approach to the study of morality may be either **normative** or **metaethical**. Normative philosophical inquiry involves going beyond empirical investigation. In contrast to scientific researchers who make empirical claims about what is factually true or is likely the case, philosophers sometimes make **normative** statements about how humans **should** behave or what **ought** to be the case. Normative inquiry frequently leads philosophers to **prescribe** a course of action and to make **evaluative** judgments about what is **right** or **wrong**, **good** or **bad**, **praiseworthy** or **blameworthy**. Thus, while empirical, scientific investigation (or everyday experience) may yield evidence that human beings often act in their own self-interest, the moral philosopher engaged in normative inquiry would ask whether humans should or should not act in this fashion.

The "fact" that they do does not necessarily mean that morally speaking they "should." Think back to the chapter on Bentham where the point was made that most philosophers question the idea that one can derive a moral, normative "ought" from an empirical "is" of experience. Just because it is true that some people kill, steal, cheat, and rape does not mean one can justifiably conclude on that basis that they should or that it is alright to do so. Ethical philosophers engaged in normative inquiry are, thus, not interested in verifying empirical findings (the job of science), but, rather, they are concerned with justifying evaluative judgments about what ought or ought not to be the case, what is good or bad, right or wrong, praiseworthy or blameworthy.

On the subject of "oughts," some normative moral inquiry attempts to establish what ought or ought not to be done in specific moral situations or in particular moral controversies like abortion or capital punishment. Saying, for example, that convicted murderers should be executed or that all abortions are wrong is to make normative statements having ethical relevance. In recent years, many philosophers have descended from the "ivory towers" of academe to debate such matters in the streets of life. It is not uncommon to find ethical philosophers engaged in bioethical debates, business matters or governmental policy decisions. They may take sides, for instance, on the moral and ethical status of reproductive technologies, on the rights of the business community to earn profits or on government legislation regarding the treatment of minority peoples.

Traditionally, however, normative inquiry has tended to be more general in nature. As we learned in Part One, philosophers have articulated over the ages a number of different normative theories that promote diverse ethical principles, values, and considerations. Theories, such as utilitarianism or deontology, can be regarded as blueprints for life. They give direction and guidance in moral action and decision making. By appealing to the general ethical principles contained in these and other normative theories, we can determine what ought or ought not to be done in any specific situation. Some normative theories, like utilitarianism, stress the effects or results of actions when it comes to their moral correctness, while deontological theories, like Kant's, focus more on rational, formal considerations.

Still another way of dealing with morality is from a metaethical (me-ta-eth-i-cal) point of view. A metaethical perspective is the most general and abstract of all. The street-fighting philosopher preoccupied with real-life normative issues might ask whether or not the country's laws on abortion are right; the metaethicist would be more likely to ask what is meant by the term "right" itself. Does "right" mean consistent with the will of the majority? Does "right" mean that which an individual likes? Or, does "right" mean in accordance with divine will? In asking such questions, philosophical metaethicists are not involved in science, but neither are they involved in normative inquiry. They are not out to justify particular moral value judgments about what is right or wrong, and so on; nor are they doing experiments and basing conclusions on surveys and sensory observations. Rather than prescribing, evaluating, and experimenting, metaethicists tend to focus more on the usage of language. They analyze moral terms, examine meanings, and look for **conceptual relationships**. In their work, they often ask for theoretical clarifications and **elucidations** of moral concepts. They try to achieve clarity in thinking by removing vagueness, ambiguity and inconsistency. This is important because there is not much point having a discussion or a debate on any moral issue if we are logically incoherent or if we are using the same words in different ways (i.e., equivocating). Precision in language and meaning is very important to the metaethicist.

Apart from the conceptual and analytical concerns, metaethicists are also interested in investigating and evaluating the **ultimate foundations** of particular ethical systems of thought. For instance, they may study the rationales or justifications provided by any one system's advocacy for a particular fundamental principle like justice. Metaethical inquiry is, thus, theoretically one step removed from normative deliberation. In contrast to the utilitarian philosopher who may wish to prescribe a particular course of action on the basis that it will likely maximize pleasure or happiness, the metaethicist questions why pleasure or happiness should serve as the ultimate ethical foundation of action and decision making in the first place. At this point, you can better appreciate the differences between scientific and philosophical approaches to morality by referring to Table 7.1.

Table 7.1 SOME KEY TERMS ASSOCIATED WITH APPROACHES TO THE STUDY OF MORALITY

SCIENTIFIC APPROACH	PHILOSOPHICAL APPROACH
empirical	rational
factual	normative or nonnormative (metaethical)
what is	what ought/ought not to be
descriptive	prescriptive
verification	justification
empirical support	reasoned argument
correlational/causal	conceptual/analytical
functional	critical
controlled studies	thought experiments (e.g., Rawls' original position)

7.3 THE FACT-VALUE DISTINCTION

Just the facts, ma'am, just the facts.

A reporter's cliche

Implicit in our comparison of scientific and philosophical approaches to morality is the notion that different kinds of claims and statements can be made about it. Some (i.e., factual statements) are more appropriate to empirical scientific inquiry, while others (i.e., value judgments) seem to belong to rational philosophical inquiry. As you will come to appreciate more, sorting out the kinds of statements one can make about moral issues is important, especially if you are going to master the techniques of proper ethical argumentation. If what you are arguing about can be settled by empirical considerations, then you should appeal to scientific findings, surveys, experience or sensory observation. If what you are debating concerns value judgments, then you should appeal to reason to justify your claims. Having said this, let us take a brief look at the distinction between **factual statements** and **value judgments**. Understanding and appreciating this **fact-value distinction** will help to promote productive dialogue on moral matters. It will also help you to avoid some unnecessary conflict and confusion in the future.

Factual Statements

A factual statement is a statement that is true or false in principle. Note that I said true *or* false. Ironically, perhaps, a factual statement can sometimes be false. For instance, "There is green cheese on the moon" is a factual statement, but one that likely is untrue. The claim tells us about what supposedly is the case. Whether or not the statement is actually true or false depends on what we find there. If, after traveling to the moon and performing an exhaustive search, we found no green cheese, then we could conclude with a fair degree of certainty that the statement was false. If, in tunnelling into the moon's surface, we found some green cheese, however, then the factual statement would be true. The point about factual statements is that sensory experience and observation can serve to determine their truth or falsity. Scientific method can also be used to test whether or not something actually is the case. Whenever you make a claim about the way things are, therefore, you are making a factual statement.

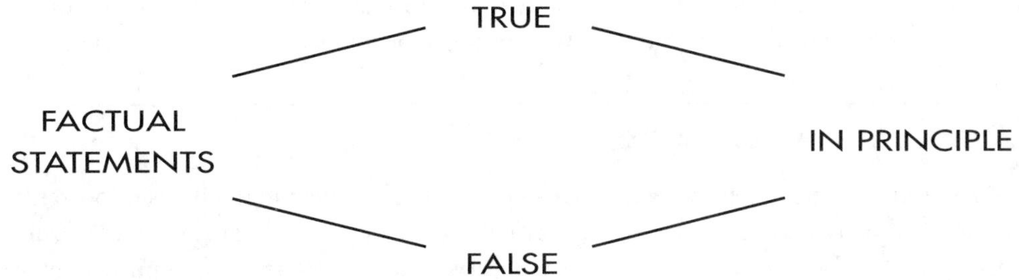

If you were making an assertion about the way things were, not about the way things are, you could refer to newspapers, magazines, past statistics, historical documents, and so on to determine the accuracy or truth of your claim. If, on the other hand, you were making a claim about how things will be in the future, you could always wait until later to see how things turn out. You could also do some kind of statistical, scientific or empirical study to prove your point or to support your prediction about what you claim will be the case. Whether your factual claim deals with past, current or future events, the point is that empirical methods can be used to verify them as true or false or more or less probable.

Value Judgments

Value judgments are very different from factual claims. First of all, they are normative. They make a statement about what should or should not be done or what is good or bad, right or wrong, praiseworthy or blameworthy or better or worse. Examples of value judgments include the following: "Liberal democracy is better than communism," "Hip-hop music is good; country music is bad," "You should not spit on the street," "Divorce is wrong," "Those who give to charity are good," and "People who pay income tax are suckers."

A feature of normative statements or value judgments, if you prefer, is that they cannot be "proven" or "verified" in the same way that empirical, factual statements can. For instance, you cannot look under a microscope or perform an experiment to see whether one form of music is better or worse than another. Whether or not people should spit in public places cannot be decided by observing what they actually do. If most people do not spit, perhaps they should. If they do spit, maybe they should not. You cannot decide by statistics or by personal observation. Telling me what people do, in fact, does not tell me whether or not what they are doing is right.

When dealing with value judgments, we cannot scientifically prove them, as stated, but, rather, we can try to **justify** them by appeals to reason. Value judgments are more or less justifiable, more or less adequate from a rational point of view. We can judge particular actions, events, policies, people, and so on against our accepted ideals, principles, and normative standards. Whether or not the standards that we use to base our value judgments on are acceptable is a matter of rational consideration. If our principles and standards are unjustifiable, the value judgments following from them will be suspect, if not completely unacceptable. If they are vague, then we will not know for sure if they apply in a given case. If our standards are inconsistent or incoherent, then our value judgments likely will not make any sense. I suppose we could therefore say that the acceptability of a particular value judgment hinges on the justifiability of the normative principle or standard on which it is based and on the proper application of that principle or standard in any given instance.

PHILOSOPHERS AT WORK

The ability to distinguish between factual statements and value judgments is important to productive ethical debate. As you have learned, factual statements are those that can be proven true or false in principle by sensory observation or some type of empirical investigation. Value judgments, by contrast, tell us what is good or bad, right or wrong, praiseworthy or blameworthy or obligatory or prohibited. See if you can identify the factual statements and value judgments in the list below.

Instructions: Mark F next to the factual statements and V next to the value judgments.

_____ 1. Applied Ethics is a good course.

_____ 2. Many people cheat on their income tax.

_____ 3. The Pope says premarital sex is wrong.

_____ 4. Firstborn individuals tend to earn more money than later born children.

_____ 5. We should lower immigration quotas.

_____ 6. Student welfare should be eliminated.

_____ 7. Hitler was an evil man.

_____ 8. Abortions are on the increase.

_____ 9. It is wrong to use people for selfish purposes.

_____ 10. There is a law against drinking and driving.

Answer Key
1. v; 2. f; 3. f; 4. f; 5. v; 6. v; 7. v; 8. f; 9. v; 10. f

7.4

Moral and Nonmoral Value Judgments: Value judgments come in two basic varieties: **moral** and **nonmoral**. Many, if not most, philosophers would agree that nonmoral values are based on our **desires**, **tastes**, and **personal preferences** (see Runkle, 1981, pp. 366–67). Things that promote our health, wealth, security, psychological or emotional development, status, power, personal relationships, understanding, pleasures of food, drink, sex, amusement, excitement and enjoyment of beauty in nature and art are all "good," but in a nonmoral **prudential** sense. They are good for our individual welfare and personal want satisfaction.

We may also have the desire to help others. When we do things to benefit others (e.g., give investment tips) or to promote their development, status, power, and so on, we act **benevolently**. We serve to satisfy their wants or desires in life and so we do "good" in the process. Of course, acting on the basis of prudential values or benevolent considerations may be quite consistent with morality and the moral demands placed upon us. Doing what is good for you or for others can be the morally right thing to do. For example, giving investment advice based on accurate information and conservative projections displays moral integrity and truthfulness. By contrast, providing advice based on distorted projections and inaccurate information may be economically "good" for you—the investment broker wishing to make a big commission—but, for many philosophers (certainly of the deontological persuasion), it would not be good in any moral sense. For many ethical thinkers, moral duties override personal wants and desires. Value-based actions that violate rights or fail to fulfill our necessary duties are wrong. So while nonmoral values based on our desires and wants may lead to moral actions, or to ones consistent with our moral duties, they may also lead to nonmoral and ethically questionable behaviors.

The second category of values is based on morality. You might wish to think of these values as "ultimate" or "absolute" or at least as more important than trivial values dealing with such things as personal tastes in music or food. Whether or not "M&Ms" are better than "Smarties," for instance, involves a subjective value judgment of relatively little importance when compared to the (moral) value judgment involved in deciding whether or not to have an abortion or to lie to a friend. According to some contemporary ethicists, distinctively moral values are those that affect human interests in important ways. Other thinkers whom we have previously studied consider moral values as inextricably bound up with things like virtue (Aristotle), rights and justice (Rawls), and unconditional duties (Kant). For utilitarians like Bentham and Mill, utility or happiness becomes the ultimate standard for deciding on the morality of actions. For our purposes here, let us think of moral values as those based on the kinds of considerations just listed. Furthermore, let us consider moral values as **mandatory**. They require us to perform certain actions and to refrain from others. Nonmoral values, on the other hand, can be considered as **optional**. They depend on our wants, desires, tastes, and preferences and are, therefore, subjective and conditional.

PHILOSOPHERS AT WORK

Below is a list of value judgments. Some clearly belong to morality (i.e., are moral); others relate to prudential and other nonmoral considerations. Next to each statement, indicate whether the statement is moral (M) or nonmoral (NM).

_____ 1. Chocolate bars are better than popsicles.

_____ 2. You should not lie to people just to get your own way.

_____ 3. What you ought to do is to invest in mutual funds for your retirement.

_____ 4. You should not say things like that if you want to keep your friends.

_____ 5. Religious schools should not receive public tax support or funding from the government.

_____ 6. Gay couples should be entitled to all of the social benefits available to heterosexual couples.

_____ 7. It is wrong to tax interest income because this reduces consumer confidence.

_____ 8. Single mothers should not be entitled to student welfare.

_____ 9. Rap music is awful.

_____ 10. It is bad to smoke.

Answer Key
1. nm; 2. m; 3. nm; 4. nm; 5. m; 6. m; 7. nm; 8. m; 9. nm; 10. nm

7.5
OPINIONS VERSUS ARGUMENTS

The recipe for perpetual ignorance is: Be satisfied with your opinions and content with your knowledge.

Elbert Hubbard

The distinction between moral and nonmoral value judgments leads us into a consideration of the differences between **opinions** and **arguments**. When someone makes a value judgment like "Basketball is a better sport than hockey," it is often accompanied by the reply "Well, that's just your opinion." Saying that eating shrimp is better than eating smelts is also likely to be considered a matter of opinion. As the saying goes, there is simply no accounting for taste. In fact, it would seem rather silly or out of place to try to justify our tastes or our preferences and desires, for that matter. Such things are personal and subjective. We often like what we like or want what we want for no reason in particular. As we have already learned, value judgments stemming from our likes and wants are nonmoral (i.e., not related to morality) and, therefore, not binding on others. Let us now look more closely at the differences between opinions and arguments so we can avoid getting caught up in disagreements over matters of opinion for which there are no objective resolutions.

We cling to our own point of view as though everything depended upon it. Yet our opinions have no permanence; like autumn and winter, they gradually pass away.

Chuang Tzu

Personal Opinions

There are different kinds of opinions, some more acceptable than others. Judges and lawyers, for instance, may issue opinions on the legality of particular public policies (e.g., hiring quotas). Medical doctors may offer their considered opinions on the advisability of surgery or the best therapeutic procedures for a patient. Such professional opinions are usually based on extensive research, expert knowledge, and careful thought. Although these opinions do not always turn out to be right, it is often reasonable to accept them.

By contrast to expert legal and medical opinion, we hear daily expressions of personal opinion in which we tend to place far less confidence, probably because we perceive these opinions as thoughtless, emotionally charged, biased or bigoted and discriminatory. In one respect, everyday thoughtless opinions are cheap. We can afford to have them on any topic, even if we know little, or nothing, about the topic itself. Personal opinions are especially abundant when the subject is a controversial moral one (Johnson and Blair, 1983, pp. 1–2).

A characteristic about everyday personal opinions is that they are usually not accompanied by reasons. No **grounds** are given for adopting them. No rational process of thought supports them or leads to them. Frequently, personal opinions are simply blurted out in a spontaneous, knee-jerk fashion. They may be intended, either consciously or unconsciously, to fill space in idle conversation, express emotions or elicit reactions from others. (Do you hate silence in conversations or ever say things just to "bug" someone?) Getting under people's skin or disturbing them is something newspaper editorialists, as well as radio and T.V. talk show hosts, do all the time. By their opinionating, they may also try to make people think about, or reconsider, their viewpoints on some contemporary social issue.

To the extent that personally stated opinions initiate discussion and cause us to stop and think, they are worthwhile. In many cases, they serve as the first step to genuine philosophical argument and debate. They can act as a springboard for further ethical analysis and deliberation.

The problem, however, is that all too often discussions begin and end with statements of unreasoned opinion. Emotions are vented and viewpoints are stridently expressed, but little progress is made into further insight, understanding or clarification of the issues involved. Unfortunately, many people take great pleasure in forcing their opinions upon others, winning shouting matches, name calling, and making others look foolish or stupid (witness the Geraldo, Montel Williams, Jerry Springer, and Phil Donahue shows). The truth is that screaming and oneupmanship do not take us very far down the road of sober thought and rational moral understanding.

We find comfort among those who agree with us, growth among those who don't.
Frank Clarke

On this planet, anything we think may be held against us . . . .
Mr. Spock, "Once Upon a Planet," Star Trek

From personal experience, I have noticed, especially at social gatherings, that people often try to avoid disagreements on controversial social and ethical issues. I suspect they fear that a fight may ensue and spoil everyone's fun. Because unpleasantness is usually associated with disagreement and because strongly expressed opinions may hurt other people's feelings, many individuals avoid arguments like the plague. Shortly, we will look at the formal structure of arguments and how to test them for validity and soundness. Because "arguments" have been given such a "bad rep" in the nonphilosophical community, I think it is worthwhile to pause and take a look at their benefits and required attitude adjustments.

Reasoned Arguments

Someone once said that there are two unavoidable things in life: death and taxes. I would like to offer a third necessity, namely, **disagreement**. If you think about it, it is virtually impossible to avoid disagreements. Whether friends are discussing sports, entertainment, culture, religion, politics, art, education, business, morality, or anything else for that matter, you almost always find differences of opinion.

Because many people have come to associate disagreements with mindless opinionating and unpleasant emotions, they often try to avoid controversial topics and prefer to keep things "light" by having superficial conversations. Instead of discussing the war-torn Middle East, for example, they might prefer to discuss the weather. Rather than talk about the role of women in the church, they discuss plans for the holiday. The point is, if you say nothing important or controversial everybody will get along just fine. When things get too serious, presumably nobody will have fun. If you wish to believe this notion personally, try to be in favor of everybody and everything at the same time—stand for nothing important; agree with all points of view (even if they conflict), and never discuss anything significant. I suggest that, if you adopt this defensive strategy, your interpersonal communications will tend to be less rewarding and meaningful than they otherwise could be—or do you disagree? This idea brings me to the benefits of argument.

My idea of an agreeable person is a person who agrees with me.
Benjamin Disraeli

The unexamined life is not worth living.
Socrates

7.6
Benefits of Argument

If we cannot avoid disagreements, and if opinionating simply tends to hurt feelings and confuse the issues, then we had better get better at arguing in legitimate ways. Engaged in properly, (philosophical) argument can open our minds. It can shake us from our ignorance and blind prejudice. Without argument, people are free to rest on a bed of unexamined beliefs. Lies may be taken for truths. Gross injustices may be accepted as normal, traditional or what nature intended. For instance, before some thoughtful and ethically sensitive people began to question and to seriously disagree with the values of the day, women and Blacks were regarded as inferior and were unfairly denied their basic rights. In part, because of the philosophical challenges raised in protest, they are now considered equal and, in principle, share the same basic entitlements as the rest of us. We see clearly in this case how argument, disagreement, and social criticism can serve a positive social purpose. Such things can expose prejudice and rectify injustices. In short, argument has social value.

Argument also has advantages for personal growth. When challenged by argument, we are not allowed the luxury of mindless response. Saying things or doing things without thinking becomes more difficult in light of disagreement. This should not discourage us. By engaging in productive dialogue with those who disagree with us, we may, in the end, strengthen our viewpoints, modify them to make them more acceptable or discard them when they are no longer useful or supportable. In fact, when people choose to argue and disagree with us, we might wish to see this act as a kind of compliment. If our views were regarded as totally insignificant or if we were not taken seriously by others, nobody would waste time on us. When someone chooses to debate with us, we can assume that the other individual has at least heard us and is willing to take notice of what we have said.

Another practical value of argument is that it can promote professional development. For instance, years ago I asked a colleague to critically review a chapter I had written for a college textbook. After promising he would, the colleague never followed through with his promise. In retrospect, I am less disappointed about the broken promise than I am about the chapter turning out to be weaker than it otherwise would have been if I had rewritten it in response to my colleague's expert critique. I was planning to use his criticism and opposing arguments of interpretation to refine my work. I was looking forward to some productive dialogue that never took place. One could argue that where there is little disagreement, there is little development of thought.

> ***A great many people think they are thinking when they are merely rearranging their prejudices.***
>
> *William James*

7.7

ATTITUDE ADJUSTMENTS FOR ARGUMENT

If people are going to argue in personally and socially constructive ways, certain **attitude adjustments** will be required. For example, we should welcome properly conducted arguments, not avoid them. This does not mean that we should get into serious arguments with everyone we meet; this would be highly impractical and time consuming. On the other hand, opportunities for meaningful discussion should not be missed. Rather than get defensive or belligerent about conflicting viewpoints, we should see them as opportunities for personal growth and social improvement and understanding. If these viewpoints are presented in an honest and sincere fashion, then they pose legitimate challenges we can use for ethical insight and developmental purposes. If our critic's disagreements are ill-founded, we can bring this to light. If they are justified, then we are given the opportunity to modify our views or to abandon our positions entirely. It is an admirable philosophical virtue to be able to change your thinking under the weight of contrary evidence or in response to legitimate criticism.

As well as opening up to argument, we should try to develop an attitude of **rational disinterestedness** (Falikowski, 1990, p. 105). In other words, we should try to remain as objective and impartial as possible. This attitude requires that we stop trying to impose our viewpoints on others. Properly conducted argument is not about winning and losing. It is not a matter of looking good at someone else's expense or "one-upping" another person. The problem is that many people view argument as a competition where there are winners and losers. Because losing an argument can be embarrassing or a threat to self-esteem, some people will say or do almost anything rather than lose. For instance, in the middle of a heated argument have your ever invented facts or statistics to support your argument? Be honest, now! Have you ever said things you do not really believe or cannot support as a way of winning or not losing face? If you have, then you can appreciate how psychological and emotional factors can affect ethical reasoning processes. If you, or the person you are arguing with, are busy making things up, then no wonder arguments are often seen as useless and unpleasant and something to avoid. Before we can engage in useful and productive arguments, we have to get our "psychological acts" in order.

An important recommendation I can make comes from the example of Plato's teacher, Socrates. Centuries ago, Socrates was declared to be the wisest man in Athens by the Oracle at Delphi. Aware of his ignorance, Socrates set out to disprove the Oracle by finding someone wiser. After searching long and hard, he concluded that everyone he encountered was ignorant, just like him. If he possessed greater wisdom, that greater wisdom must have come from his awareness of his ignorance. Others were unaware of their ignorance. They pretended to know what they did not. In light of this historical example, you may wish to reduce your pretensions to knowledge. If you have no ignorance to hide, because you freely and openly admit what you do not know, then you greatly reduce the need to communicate defensively. If you reduce your defensiveness, you can then engage in more fruitful dialogue and enjoy more satisfying communications. Rather than trying to defeat others in communication or debate, you should endeavor to display **Socratic humility**, to listen carefully for understanding and to respond intelligently and thoughtfully to what others have to say. Constructive attitudes toward disagreement and argument can provide enormous benefits. In the next chapter, we will learn how to put arguments together to make our disagreements as productive and useful as possible.

MINDWORK MEDITATION

Think of the last time you had an "argument" with someone. What was the argument about? While arguing, did you adopt an attitude of Socratic humility? Were you objective and impartial in listening and responding to the points made? Were you willing to change your mind in view of counterarguments or did you have your mind made up at the outset? What about your partner in the argument; how would he or she answer the questions just posed? Finally, was your argument useful and constructive or harmful and a waste of energy? What will you have to do next time if you are going to have a proper philosophical debate?

Key Terms

empirical study
observation
controlled experiment
measure
describe
true
probable
scientific objectivity
correlational findings
causal/functional explanations
statistical analysis
verify
predictions
moralistic
value-neutral
nonnormative
normative
praiseworthy/blameworthy
conceptual relationships
elucidations
ultimate foundation
factual statements
value judgments
fact-value distinction
justify
moral/nonmoral values
desires
tastes
personal preferences
prudential
benevolently
mandatory
optional
opinions (personal/professional)

metaethical
should
ought
prescribe
evaluative
right/wrong
good/bad
arguments
grounds
disagreement
attitude adjustments
rational disinterestedness
Socratic humility

Progress Check 7.1

Instructions: Fill in the blanks with the appropriate responses listed below.

prescribe
ultimate foundations
nonmoral
opinions
social value
rational disinterestedness
attitude adjustments
normative claims
factual claims
mandatory
beliefs
metaethical
arguments
prudential
justify
empirical study

1. Science makes morality an object of _____.
2. Rather than _____ what morally ought to be done, scientists wish to remain value-neutral and limit themselves to description and functional explanation.
3. Philosophical ethics can be normative or _____.
4. Scientists "verify" their claims; philosophers _____ theirs.
5. Metaethicists study the _____ of ethical systems.
6. _____ can be verified; _____ are justified.
7. Value judgments can be moral or _____.
8. Values relating to our status, wealth, and pleasure are _____.
9. Obligations stemming from nonmoral values are optional; moral values are _____, prescriptive for all.
10. _____ are groundless. They seem to lead nowhere and appear to be based on little more than personal preference, taste or subjective feeling.
11. _____ are comprised of a series of related statements leading to a conclusion.
12. Without argument, people might rest on a bed of unexamined _____.
13. Philosophical argument has both personal benefit and _____.
14. If people are going to argue in constructive and productive ways, certain _____ may be necessary.
15. If you choose to remain fair, impartial, and objective, you will develop the attitude of _____.

Summary of Major Points

1. **How are philosophy and science different in their approaches to the study of morality?**
   Philosophy is rational, prescriptive, evaluative, normative, concerned with justification and the foundations of ethical systems (metaethics).
   Science is empirical, factual, descriptive, correlational/causal, concerned with functional explanations and verifying claims.
2. **What is meant by the fact-value distinction?**
   Factual claims assert what "is" (what was or what will be the case in fact).
   Factual claims are true or false in principle.
   Factual claims are empirically verifiable.
   By contrast, value judgments are normative.
   Value judgments state what is right/wrong, better/worse, good/bad, praiseworthy/blameworthy and what is obligatory/prohibited.
   Value judgments are justified, not verified.
3. **Are all values moral?**
   No, there are both moral and nonmoral values (i.e., values that do not belong to the realm of morality).
   Nonmoral values may be prudential (related to self-interest) or benevolent (promoting the interests of others).
   Moral values pertain to things like virtue, rights, and duties.
   Obligations arising from moral values are mandatory; those from nonmoral values are optional.
4. **How do opinions and arguments differ?**
   Opinions are subjective expressions of feelings or tastes without any basis in carefully reasoned thought.
   Opinions have no rational grounds and seem to go nowhere.
   Arguments are based on principles and axioms or values.
   Arguments contain a process of thought wherein conclusions are derived from preceding premises.
5. **How are arguments beneficial?**
   They can open our minds and shake us from ignorance and blind prejudice.
   They can contribute to social progress.
   They can promote personal growth and professional development.
6. **What attitude adjustments are beneficial for productive argument?**
   We should welcome arguments, not avoid them.
   We should reduce and try to eliminate personal defensiveness and aggressiveness when arguing.
   We should be willing to change our minds if counterevidence and counterarguments are good.
   We should develop the attitude of Socratic humility.

Source References and Related Readings

Falikowski, Anthony. *Moral Philosophy: Theories, Skills, and Applications.* Upper Saddle River, N.J.: Prentice Hall, 1990.

Johnson, R.H. and J.A. Blair. *Logical Self-Defense*, 2nd edition. Toronto: McGraw-Hill Ryerson, 1983.

Rosenberg, Jay F. *The Practice of Philosophy—A Handbook for Beginners*, 2nd edition. Upper Saddle River, N.J.: Prentice Hall, 1984.

Runkle, Gerald. *Good Thinking—An Introduction to Logic.* New York: Holt, Rinehart and Winston, 1981.

Russon, Lilly-Marlene and Martin Curd. *Principles of Reasoning.* New York: St. Martin's Press, 1989.

Woodhouse, Mark B. *A Preface to Philosophy*, 5th edition. Belmont, Cal.: Wadsworth, 1994.

CHAPTER EIGHT

8 LOGIC AND LEGITIMATE ARGUMENT

Overview

- Deductive Logic
  - Deductive Arguments
    - Form versus Content
  - *Modus Ponens*
  - *Modus Tollens*
  - Syllogisms
    - Hypothetical Syllogisms
    - Disjunctive Syllogisms
    - Syllogisms of Class Membership
    - Practical Syllogisms
- Inductive Logic
  - Argument from Past Experience
  - Argument by Analogy
  - Argument by Inductive Generalization
- Key Terms
- Progress Check 8.1
- Summary of Major Points
- Source References and Related Readings

Learning Outcomes

After successfully completing this chapter, you will be able to:

8.1 appreciate the difference between the logical form of an argument and the content that gives it substance;

8.2 symbolically state some basic forms of deductive logic;

8.3 identify forms of invalid deductive reasoning;

8.4 define and give examples of inductive logic;

8.5 compare and contrast inductive and deductive reasoning.

PHILOSOPHICAL FOCUS QUESTIONS

1. From a purely philosophical perspective, what is an argument? What is it not?
2. Does the validity of an argument depend on the content or subject being debated? Explain.
3. What are some forms of valid deductive reasoning?
4. What are some forms of invalid deductive logic?
5. Can you give some examples of logical syllogisms? What type is most often used in ethical debate? How is this type different from other types?
6. How does inductive logic differ from deductive logic?
7. What are some forms of inductive reasoning?

DEDUCTIVE LOGIC

In much the same way that we have building codes to ensure that a house is built well, there is also a "thinking code," that is guidelines and rules for what makes an argument pass "philosophical inspection." We find this code in that part of philosophy called logic.

Thomas White

So far we have looked at some of the benefits of argument and have examined the attitude adjustments that are advisable if proper ethical debate is to occur. What we have not done is to look at arguments themselves, something we will do now.

From a purely philosophical perspective, an **argument** is not an interpersonal event or a confrontation of egos; rather, it is a series of related statements that lead to a conclusion. By concentrating on the forms of argument, their validity and soundness, and not on the person or persons with whom we disagree, we can divest ourselves of the unpleasant feelings and contaminating psychological influences that often interfere with rational debate. We can proceed to examine ethical and philosophical positions impartially and objectively. Let us begin by looking at the structure of **deductive arguments**.

Deductive Arguments

If this book was designed to be a course in logic, then it would be appropriate to examine the many subtleties and intricate forms of deductive reasoning. Since, as philosophical beginners, we are looking at logical thinking as a means to improve our ethical decision-making skills and our abilities to evaluate moral arguments, we will limit our discussion here to a few of the more common and basic forms of **deductive logic**. We will also discuss some invalid forms of reasoning before we move on to a treatment of inductive reasoning, another type of thinking that is important to master for critical, analytical purposes.

8.1

Form versus Content: Before we get to the various types of deductive argument, it is helpful to distinguish between their **form** and **content**. Moral arguments are typically about something; that is, they have a subject. It may be a practice (e.g., artificial insemination), an event (e.g., a bombing in the Middle East) or an act (e.g., civil disobedience) that provides the "stuff" or content of the argument. Regardless of the issue under debate, if the arguments involved are to be considered valid, they must display an acceptable **logical form.** In other words, a formal structure can be abstracted from any content-related argument. The more common forms have been given standardized names, some of which have strange sounding Latin origins like the first one we will examine: *Modus Ponens.*

8.1
8.2

Modus Ponens (MP)

Many arguments that you will hear expressed in conversation and debate contain the ***Modus Ponens (MP)*** form. Arguments of this form have been determined to be valid and so this logical form can be used to test arguments for their validity. Of course, the *MP* argument is not the *only* valid form of reasoning and therefore an argument not displaying the *MP* form is not necessarily invalid. As you will see, there is more than one type of **valid reasoning**. Below are two *MP* arguments containing different content, but identical forms.

> Whenever the economy goes into a recession, church attendance increases. Since we are currently in an economic recession, we can conclude that church attendance has increased or will do so shortly.
>
> If a person has an xx genotype, that person is a female. Pat has an xx genotype, so we can conclude Pat is female.

If we abstract from the content of these two very different arguments, we can see that they still share the same formal structure expressed below. (Note: There is nothing significant about the selection of the letters "p" and "q"; the letters could have been "x," "y" or "b.")

If p, then q	or	$p \rightarrow q$
p	(alternative	$\underline{p}$
So, q	notation)	$\therefore q$

Example One:

Whenever the economy goes into a recession (p), then church attendance increases (q).
Since we are currently in an economic recession (p).
(So, q) We can conclude that church attendance has increased.

Example Two:

If a person has an xx genotype (p), the person is a female (q).
Pat has an xx genotype (p).
(So, q) Therefore, Pat is a female.

8.3

When using the *MP* form of argument, you should be careful not to make any mistakes. In this logical form, the proper thing to do is to **affirm the antecedent**. In the opening statement "If p, then q," "p" becomes the **antecedent** and "q" the **consequent**. If you affirm the consequent, an invalid faulty form of argument results. Formally, affirming the consequent looks like this:

If p, then q	(or)	$p \rightarrow q$
q		q
So, p		$\therefore p$

If we provide some content to the formal expression above, we can easily see how affirming the consequent is an invalid form of reasoning. Stewart and Blocker (1987, p. 61) provide us with the following example:

> If it rains (p) the streets will be wet (q), and the streets are wet (q). So it must have rained (p).

In the example above, it may be true that the streets are wet. It may also be true that if it rains, the streets will get wet. It may even be further true that the streets are wet because it has rained in this particular instance. Yet, it *is not necessarily true* that it must always rain for the streets to be wet. It could be that a water main has burst or that someone has hosed down the road because of an oil spill. These possibilities point to the fact that a false conclusion can be reached from true premises if the proper and valid form of argumentation is not followed. When testing arguments for their validity, one thing you can do is to construct an obviously invalid counterexample, as in the preceding case, that possesses the same form as the argument you are evaluating. If you can show that false conclusions (or ones that do not follow necessarily) arise when the consequent is affirmed, then you can demonstrate how this form of reasoning is invalid. See a counterexample to our example about rain and wet streets.

If I bought a new BMW (p), I would be broke (q).
I am broke (q).
So, I must have bought a new BMW (p).

As you can well imagine, it is possible to be broke without buying a BMW. Maybe a business deal fell through or a business bankruptcy has caused you to lose money. In short, affirming the consequent in *MP* reasoning is invalid logic. It does not lead to a necessary conclusion.

Modus Tollens (MT)

Modus Tollens (MT) is a second form of valid logic. In an *MT* argument, an inference results by **denying the consequent**. Formally, *MT* is expressed in the following fashion:

If p, then q	(or)	$p \rightarrow q$
not q		$-q$
So, not p		$\therefore -p$

We can return to our earlier example about rain and wet streets to put some content in this valid *MT* form of reasoning.

If it rains (p), the streets get wet (q).
The streets did not get wet (not q).
So, it has not rained (not p).

8.3
The invalid form of *MT* reasoning would involve **denying the antecedent**.

If p, then q	(or)	$p \rightarrow q$
not p		$-p$
So, not q		$\therefore -q$

The unacceptability of denying the antecedent is illustrated by the example below:

If it rains (p), there are clouds (q).
It is not raining (not p).
So, there are no clouds (not q).

Again, we see in the argument above that a false conclusion follows from two preceding premises that are true. Experience teaches us that there can be clouds in the sky without any rain falling. Of course, it is possible that it is not raining and that there is no cloud cover. Nonetheless, our counterexample underscores the fact that clouds could fill the sky even if rain did not fall. Once a counterexample like this one demonstrates how false conclusions can follow from arguments possessing a particular logical form, an argument of that form must be rejected as invalid.

Syllogisms

With the study of logical forms Aristotle made that decisive step that led to the science of logic.

Hans Reichenbach

An extremely important form of deductive argument often used in moral and ethical debate is the **syllogism**. The syllogism actually comes in many forms, but we will limit ourselves to hypothetical and disjunctive syllogisms, as well as to those involving class membership and practical value reasoning.

Watch your P's and Q's.

Some logical advice

8.2

Hypothetical Syllogisms: Hypothetical syllogisms are comprised of a series of "if-then" statements following a string. This string contains two premises and a conclusion. It is because this type of syllogism contains "conditional" premises that it is referred to as hypothetical. An example of a hypothetical syllogism is the following:

> If you obtain a pass on this test (p), you will successfully complete your last course (q). On top of that, if you successfully complete your last course (q), you will earn your diploma (r). So, if you pass the test (p), you will earn your diploma (r).

Expressed formally,

If p, then q
If q, then r
Therefore, if p then r

(or)

$$\begin{array}{r} p \rightarrow q \\ q \rightarrow r \\ \hline \therefore p \rightarrow r \end{array}$$

8.3

The invalid form of a hypothetical syllogism is:

If p, then q
If p, then r
Therefore, if q then r

To appreciate why the form above is invalid, see the example below.

If you study (p), you will pass the final exam (q).
If you study (p), you will graduate (r).
Therefore, if you pass the final exam (q), you will graduate (r).

The invalid form of the hypothetical syllogism above indicates that your passing the final exam guarantees your graduation just because you have studied; surely this does not follow. It is possible to study, pass the final exam and still fail the course and, thus, fail to graduate. (See Woodhouse, 1994, p. 63.)

8.2

Disjunctive Syllogisms: Like the hypothetical syllogism, the **disjunctive syllogism** is made up of three statements. Unlike the former, which deals with a logical chain of consequences, this one involves an either/or choice. This choice may be expressed symbolically by "v." To express either p or q, one could write "p v q." An example of a disjunctive syllogism is the following:

> Either Mary has made the right decision (p) or she has made the wrong decision (q). Since she has not made the wrong decision (not q), she has therefore made the right one (p).

Expressed formally,

Either p or q	(or)	$p \vee q$
not q		$-q$
Therefore, p		$\therefore p$

If Mary had made the wrong decision, then the disjunctive syllogism would be altered so:

Either p or q	(or)	$p \vee q$
not p		$-p$
Therefore, q		$\therefore q$

8.3

The invalid form of the disjunctive syllogism (called **affirming the inclusive disjunct**) is expressed below.

Either p or q	(or)	Either p or q
p		q
Therefore, not q		Therefore, not p

To see why affirming the inclusive disjunct is invalid, consider the following example.

> Either Fred gets paid a lot (p) or he inherited lots of money (q).
> Fred gets paid a lot (p).
> Therefore, he did not inherit lots of money (q).

In this invalid form of reasoning, one starts by stating that either p or q is so, meaning that only one and not the other can be true. In fact, both disjuncts could be true at the same time. Maybe Fred does get paid well and perhaps he has inherited lots of money as well. P does not preclude q or vice versa. The "or" here is "inclusive," which allows both disjuncts in the first premise to be true. If the disjuncts were "exclusive," i.e., if both p and q could not be true at the same time, then "If p, not q" or "If q, not p." Here is an example of a disjunctive syllogism which is exclusive.

> It cannot be that mother is both alive (p) and dead (q).
> Because she is alive (p),
> She cannot be dead (q).

Expressed formally:

> It cannot be both p and q
> p
> So, not q

8.2
8.3

Table 8.1 SOME VALID AND INVALID FORMS OF DEDUCTIVE LOGIC

VALID LOGICAL FORMS			
Modus Ponens	***Modus Tollens***	**Hypothetical Syllogism**	**Disjunctive Syllogism**
If p, then q	If p, then q	If p, then q	Either p or q
p	not q	If q, then r	Not q
So, q	So, not p	So, if p, then r	So, p
			(or)
			Either p or q
			Not p
			So, q
INVALID LOGICAL FORMS			
Affirming the Consequent	**Denying the Antecedent**	**Hypothetical Fallacy**	**Affirming the (Inclusive) Disjunct**
If p, then q	If p, then q	If p, then q	Either p or q
q	Not p	If p, then r	p
So, p	So, not q	If q, then r	So, not q
			(or)
			Either p or q
			q
			So, not p

Logic is the beginning of wisdom, not the end.

Spock, "Startrek VI, The Undiscovered Country"

PHILOSOPHERS AT WORK

For each of the reasoning examples below, indicate whether the logic is valid (V) or invalid (I). Below each example, give the logical form contained in it.

_____ 1. If Fred lost his wallet, then he lost his student identification. If he lost his student identification, then he will not be allowed to join any varsity teams. Therefore, if Fred lost his wallet, then he will not be allowed to join any varsity teams.

Logical Form: _____

_____

_____

_____ 2. Either I am going to school or I am going to earn a lot of money. I am going to school. Therefore, I am not going to earn a lot of money.

Logical Form: _____

_____

_____

_____ 3. If we go to war, I will be very upset. I am very upset. So, we went to war.

Logical Form: _____

_____

_____

_____ 4. If you lie to people, then they will not trust you. People do trust you. So you have not lied.

Logical Form: _____

_____

_____

Answer Key

1. Valid hypothetical syllogism

Form: If p, then q

If q, then r

Therefore, if p then r

2. Invalid—affirming the inclusive disjunct; one can both go to school *and* earn lots of money

   Form: Either p or q

   p

   Therefore, not q

3. Invalid—affirming the consequent; you can become upset for reasons other than going to war

   Form: If p, then q

   q

   So, p

4. Valid—*Modus Tollens* form

   Form: If p, then q

   not q

   So, not p

8.2

Syllogisms of Class Membership: There are also *syllogisms of class membership* that consist in drawing inferences from class membership. See below.

Major Premise:	All A are B.	A is B
Minor Premise:	All C are A.	C is A
Conclusion:	Therefore all C are B.	∴ C is B

Adding some content to this formal structure, we come up with the following example:

Major Premise:	All men (A) are mortal (B).
Minor Premise:	Socrates (C) is a man (A).
Conclusion:	Therefore, Socrates (C) is mortal (B).

Another variation of a class membership syllogism is provided below.

All A are B.
Some C are A.
Therefore, some C are B.

All bankers (A) are conservative (B).
Some people (C) are bankers (A).
Therefore, some people (C) are conservative (B).

8.3
An invalid form of class syllogism can be expressed in the following symbolic fashion:

All A is B.
All C is B.
Therefore, all C is A.

Adding some content to the invalid logical form above, we can easily see that the conclusion does not follow from true preceding premises.

All cats (A) are animals (B).
All dogs (C) are animals (B).
Therefore, all dogs (C) are cats (A).

8.2
Practical Syllogisms: What I am calling a **practical syllogism** is basically the same in form as a syllogism of class membership. Again, it contains three statements having a conclusion derived from two preceding premises. The difference is that in the case of a practical syllogism, the first statement or **major premise** is a normative assertion or some kind of **value judgment**. Hence, the major premise of a practical syllogism is not empirically true or false or analytically true, that is, true by definition. The major premise of a practical syllogism, called the **value premise**, cannot be proven true by sensory observation or scientific study. Rather, it can be justified only by rational processes of thought. Since normative assertions involving principles of right conduct, standards of goodness, and so on, cannot be based on what "is" the case, for what is may frequently be unjustified, evil or immoral, the ultimate basis of justification for the value premise is reason, not experience. Using reason, we can test the adequacy of the value premises that serve as the starting points of our arguments.

The equivalent of the **minor premise** in the class syllogism is the practical syllogism's **factual premise**. As the term implies, the factual premise makes some type of empirical claim about the world. The factual premise is either true or false in principle. Although we may be unable at present to prove the truth or falsity of a particular factual premise, given our limited knowledge, experience or technology, it must be possible to do so in principle.

Finally, the **conclusion** of a practical syllogism is also expressed as a value judgment. It typically makes a statement about what is better or worse, obligatory or prohibited, good or bad, right or wrong and praiseworthy or blameworthy. Below are two examples of practical syllogisms.

Example One:

Value Premise: All acts that threaten the safety of individuals (S) are wrong (P).
Factual Premise: Illegal toxic waste dumping (Q) is an act that threatens the safety of individuals (S).
Conclusion: Illegal toxic waste dumping (Q) is wrong (P).

Formally expressed:	All S is P.	(or)	S is P
	Q is S.		Q is S
	Therefore, Q is P.		∴ Q is P

Example Two:

Value Premise:	Anyone who kills to earn a living (S) is evil (P).
Factual Premise:	Bonnie and Clyde (Q) kill to earn a living (S).
Conclusion:	Bonnie and Clyde (Q) are evil (P).

A necessity for one thing to happen because another has happened does not exist. There is only logical necessity.

Ludwig Wittgenstein

In the next chapter, we will return to practical syllogisms and learn how to rationally test their value premises for **adequacy**. We will also examine more closely the relationships among validity, truth, and soundness when they involve moral discussion and debate. Before we do so, however, let us take a brief look at inductive logic, another form of reasoning often used in support of factual claims embedded within larger practical syllogisms.

PHILOSOPHERS AT WORK

Below you will find incomplete syllogisms. Fill in the missing statements and indicate next to each syllogism whether it is practical (P), i.e., value-related, or value-neutral (VN).

_____ 1. Deceiving the public is wrong.

_____.

Advertisers are wrong.

_____ 2. All Russian communists live by the principles of Lenin and Marx.

Vladimir is a Russian communist.

_____.

_____ 3. All acts of violence are inherently evil.

Stabbing someone to death is an act of violence.

_____.

_____ 4. _____

Ralf is a bachelor.

Ralf is an unmarried man.

_____ 5. Triangles are three-sided figures.

_____.

That is a three-sided figure.

Answer Key

1. P, Advertisers deceive the public.
2. VN, Therefore, Vladimir lives by the principles of Lenin and Marx.
3. P, Therefore, stabbing someone to death is inherently evil.
4. VN, All bachelors are unmarried men.
5. VN, That is a triangle.

8.4
INDUCTIVE LOGIC

Probabilities direct the conduct of the wise man.
Cicero

A reasonable probability is the only certainty.
E.W. Howe

Argument from Past Experience

As one form of **inductive logic, arguments from past experience**, like other forms of inductive logic, can lead only to **probable conclusions**. Inductive conclusions are, therefore, weaker or stronger by degree and need not be accepted or rejected in an all-or-nothing fashion. Thus, in contrast to forms of deductive logic, examples of inductive logic are never said to be valid or invalid. To see why, let us take the following illustration. Suppose, for instance, that we are informed that Wendy has lied on her job application, on her income tax return, and to her husband. We might then conclude that she has lied about information provided on her medical history required to purchase a life insurance policy. Because she has lied before in other instances, we conclude she has lied this time as well. In other words, we use past experience to support our current conclusion. Since our inductive conclusion is based on the facts of experience, however, and because these facts are never complete and because new facts may have the effect of weakening, changing or contradicting today's assumptions, we can never be absolutely sure about our conclusion (Barry, 1983, p. 334). Perhaps Wendy has experienced some kind of religious or moral conversion that has led to a complete character transformation. Maybe Wendy was a liar since her youth, but is now an honest and responsible citizen. Many empirical variables could weaken the soundness of the inductive inference made in this case.

There is nothing in which an untrained mind shows itself more hopelessly incapable, than in drawing the proper conclusions from its own experience.

J.S. Mill

Argument by Analogy

A second form of inductive reasoning involves **argument by analogy**. "Analogical arguments proceed from the similarities of two or more things in certain respects to their similarity in some additional respect" (Woodhouse, 1994, p. 61). Analogical arguments have the following form.

> Items A, B and C have characteristics X and Y.
> A and B have characteristic Z.
> Therefore, C probably has characteristic Z also.

This analogical form of inductive reasoning is the type used to argue for the probable existence of life on other planets. If significant similarities can be found between earth and other celestial bodies, and if earth supports life, then one might wish to argue by analogy that those other celestial bodies also support life. Notice again, there is no certainty or deductive necessity about this conclusion; there is only a lesser or greater probability.

Argument by Inductive Generalization

A third form of inductive reasoning is **argument by inductive generalization**. When we make an inductive generalization, we make a statement about all, some, or none of a class based on our empirical examination of only a part of that class. It is important not to confuse inductive generalizations with generalized descriptions. Suppose, for instance, that we surveyed an introductory ethics class on its views about abortion and we found that 88 percent of class members were in favor of allowing it unconditionally. In stating this, one would be presenting only a generalized description of what is the case for that group. If we were to conclude, however, that 88 percent of all postsecondary students in North America were in favor of allowing abortions, then we would be making an inductive generalization.

As you can appreciate in the example above, inductive generalizations can easily be prone to error unless certain precautions are taken. For example, when making inductive generalizations, it is important to work from **large samples**. Basing a conclusion about tens of thousands of students in North America on a limited sample of one class is no guarantee that the findings are truly **representative** of the whole group about which a conclusion is being made.

It is important to note that large samples alone do not guarantee that generalizations based on them will be representative, as desired. If the larger sample we need were drawn exclusively from Catholic colleges, say, then the results might tend to be more reflective of the specific religious view held by a special subgroup of students and not representative of the entire post-secondary student population of North America, taken as a whole. The views of students at Catholic colleges might not represent those of the majority attending secular institutions. In addition to being large, then, samples must also be **fair**. All members within a class (in this case, postsecondary students in North America) must have an equal chance of being selected for survey or study. Otherwise, inductive generalizations are likely to be **skewed**. Arguments by inductive generalization based on biased or skewed samples are less acceptable than those based on fair and large ones that are more representative of the group under discussion.

8.5

In closing this section on argument, refer to Table 8.2 for a comparison between inductive and deductive logical thinking.

Table 8.2 COMPARING INDUCTIVE AND DEDUCTIVE ARGUMENTS

EXAMPLE OF DEDUCTIVE ARGUMENT	EXAMPLE OF INDUCTIVE ARGUMENT
All birds have wings. Every swan is a bird.	Every swan that has ever been observed has wings.
Therefore, every swan has wings.	Therefore, every swan has wings.
If the form of the argument is valid and the premises are true, then the conclusion must be true also.	If the premises are true, then the conclusion is likely, though not necessarily, true.
Deductive arguments are either valid or invalid.	Inductive arguments are better or worse.

MINDWORK MEDITATION

Take a moment and try to remember the last time you had an important argument or a dispute with someone. What was the subject, topic or event that you were arguing over? On the left side of a piece of paper list in point form some of the things you said and then on the right side of the page list what the other person said. Try to extract from the list the major assumptions and conclusions expressed by both of you. Knowing what you now know about reasoning, try to reconstruct the "content" of your debate into "formal" arguments containing premises and conclusions. Were all the arguments expressed reflective of valid syllogisms or other acceptable forms of inductive and deductive logic? Were some of the arguments invalid and unacceptable? Illustrate and explain.

Key Terms

argument
deductive argument
deductive logic
form
content
logical form
Modus Ponens
valid reasoning
affirm the antecedent
antecedent
consequent
Modus Tollens
denying the consequent
denying the antecedent
syllogism
hypothetical syllogisms
disjunctive syllogism
affirming the inclusive disjunct
syllogisms of class membership
practical syllogism
major premise
value judgment
value premise
minor premise
factual premise
conclusion
adequacy
inductive logic
argument from past experience
probable conclusions
argument by analogy
argument by inductive generalization
large samples
representative
fair
skewed

Progress Check 8.1

Instructions: Fill in the blanks with the appropriate responses listed below.

Modus Ponens
denies
judgment
inductive generalization
worse
hypothetical
form
affirms
invalid
value
interpersonal
consequent
probable
disjunct
analogical

1. In philosophy, an argument is not a(n) _____ event or "fight" between individuals.
2. Ethical arguments have both _____ and content. They deal with a subject matter and display some sort of structure explicitly or implicitly.
3. If p, then q

   p

   So, q

   The logical structure above is termed _____.
4. In *Modus Tollens* reasoning, an inference results by denying the _____.
5. In *Modus Ponens* reasoning, an invalid argument results when one _____ the consequent.

6. In an invalid form of *Modus Tollens* reasoning, one _____ the antecedent.
7. If a false conclusion results from two preceding premises that are true, then the argument is _____.
8. If p, then q
   If q, then r
   Therefore, if p then r

   This is a(n) _____ syllogism.
9. Affirming the inclusive _____ is an invalid form of the disjunctive syllogism.
10. The major premise of a practical syllogism is called the _____ premise.
11. The conclusion of a practical syllogism is a value _____.
12. Inductive reasoning can lead only to _____ conclusions.
13. When we make a(n) _____, we make a statement about all, some or none of a class based on our empirical examination of only a part of that class.
14. Inductive logic is not valid or invalid, but rather is better or _____.
15. A(n) _____ argument proceeds from the similarities of two or more things in certain respects to their similarity in some additional respect.

Summary of Major Points

1. What is an argument?
   It is a series of related statements leading to a conclusion.
   It is not an interpersonal event or a confrontation of egos.
   Arguments can be deductive or inductive.
2. What are some of the general characteristics of deductive arguments?
   They come in various forms (e.g., *Modus Ponens*, practical syllogisms).
   They lead to necessary conclusions which are derived from preceding premises.
   They are either valid or invalid.
3. What is the form-content distinction about in logic?
   Underlying the content of any deductive argument is some kind of formal structure which is either valid or invalid.
   Unrelated arguments from different fields can possess the same logical form.
4. What are some forms of deductive argument?
   Some forms are *Modus Ponens*, *Modus Tollens*, hypothetical syllogisms, disjunctive syllogisms, syllogisms of class membership and practical syllogisms.
5. What is inductive logic?
   It is a process of reasoning leading to probable, not necessary, conclusions.
   Inductive logic is better or worse, not valid or invalid.
6. What are some forms of inductive logic?
   Some forms are argument from experience, argument by analogy, and argument by inductive generalization.

Source References and Related Readings

Barry, Vincent. *Philosophy: A Text with Readings*, 2nd edition. Belmont, Cal.: Wadsworth Publishing Co., 1983.

Cohen, Elliot D. *Making Value Judgements: Principles of Sound Reasoning*. Malabar, Fla.: Krieger Publishing Co. Inc., 1985.

Runkle, Gerald. *Good Thinking: An Introduction to Logic*, 2nd edition. New York: Holt, Rinehart and Winston, 1981.

Russow, Lilly-Marlene and Martin Curd. *Principles of Reasoning*. New York: St. Martin's Press, 1989.

Stewart, David and H. Gene Blocker. *Fundamentals of Philosophy*, 2nd edition. New York: MacMillan Publishing Co., 1987.

Woodhouse, Mark B. *A Preface to Philosophy*, 5th edition. Belmont. Cal.: Wadsworth Publishing Co., 1994.

CHAPTER NINE

9

FAULTY AND FALLACIOUS REASONING

Learning Outcomes

After successfully completing this chapter, you will be able to:

9.1 evaluate arguments more effectively;
9.2 distinguish among the concepts of validity, truth, and soundness;
9.3 critically analyze and appraise each part of a practical syllogism;
9.4 test the value premises upon which practical syllogisms are based;
9.5 explain the general nature of logical fallacies;
9.6 identify and explain the reasoning procedures involved in various examples of fallacious reasoning;
9.7 list some do's and don'ts for rational debates.

PHILOSOPHICAL FOCUS QUESTIONS

1. Is a valid argument necessarily sound? Explain why or why not.
2. How is the practical syllogism particularly relevant for ethics and ethical inquiry?
3. At what levels can the practical syllogism be evaluated?
4. What tests can be used to establish the adequacy of value premises contained within particular practical syllogisms?
5. What is a logical fallacy? What are some examples?
6. What should you do and not do when having a rational debate?

9.1 HOW TO EVALUATE ARGUMENTS

Men stumble over the truth from time to time, but most pick themselves up and hurry off as if nothing happened.
Winston Churchill

Logic is neither an art nor a science, but a dodge.
Strendal

Before we move on to Part Three, "Applying Ethics in the Real World," we will consider in Chapter Nine some of the ways and means of determining whether the arguments we will soon face on various topics are good ones. To some extent, we have done this already. For example, in our coverage of inductive logic, we learned how generalizations must be based on fair and representative samples. In regard to inductive arguments by analogy, we should keep in mind that the strength of relationship should be examined as well as the nature and number of characteristics that relate one case with another. As for deductive logic, our treatment of it revealed that in

Modus Ponens arguments it is wrong to affirm the consequent, while denying the antecedent is unacceptable in *Modus Tollens* reasoning. We found as well that it is incorrect to affirm the inclusive disjunct in a disjunctive syllogism wherein the antecedent and consequent can both be true. About hypothetical syllogisms, we learned to keep our p's and q's in order.

From our initial studies in logic, we have also come to appreciate the special importance of practical syllogisms to ethical inquiry and debate. Practical syllogisms are based on value premises that lead to particular ethical conclusions. Shortly, we will look at how to analyze and break down each part of the practical syllogism for purposes of evaluation and critique. After that, we will look at some "sleazy" reasoning techniques, known as "logical fallacies," that irrational thinkers often use in their efforts to win debates and persuade people to accept their points of view, whether they be justified or not. Before examining the "sleaze" and analyzing the practical syllogism for evaluative purposes, let us first clarify some important terminology to prevent confusion later on.

There is no greater lie than a truth misunderstood.
William James

9.2

VALIDITY, TRUTH, AND SOUNDNESS

In everyday conversations you often hear people say things like "That's a valid point," or "That's a valid statement" or perhaps "Your criticism is valid." In strict logical terms, however, "points," "statements," and "criticisms" are not valid, arguments are. Factual statements may be true or false or more or less likely; criticisms may be justified or unjustified, and good points may be based on accurate observations. But when it comes to logic, **validity** refers to the form of the argument within which a particular point or statement becomes a relevant part.

Validity should be clearly distinguished from another logical notion, namely, **soundness**. The concept of soundness also refers to arguments, but not narrowly and exclusively to their logical form. A sound argument is one that is valid in form, contains true (or acceptable) premises, and leads to a necessary conclusion. An **unsound** argument, by contrast, can be valid in form, but, because its premises are untrue or unacceptable, the conclusion is false or one that must be rejected. In formal argument, then, **truth** refers to the **veracity** of the individual statements contained within the syllogism itself; validity refers to an argument's form or structure, and soundness involves a combination of truth and formal validity. Having said this, remember that necessary conclusions are found only in deductive logic, not in inductive logic. Thus, soundness is a concept appropriately applied to the former and not the latter type of reasoning. Inductive logic is better or worse by degree.

It is interesting and, perhaps, ironic to note that valid arguments may sometimes have to be rejected on rational grounds. To appreciate why, look at the example that follows.

Major Premise:	All birds (A) are black (B).	All A is B
Minor Premise:	Prince Philip (C) is a bird (A).	C is A
Conclusion:	Prince Philip (C) is black (B).	C is B

What you have here is a valid syllogism of class membership. The logical form of the argument is found to the right. What is obvious about this valid syllogism is that the conclusion is obviously false. Prince Philip is not black. You should note as well that the minor premise makes a factual claim that is likewise false: Prince Philip is not a bird. Even further, we could dispute the major premise in this argument, because we know that some birds are blue and others are red, so even if Prince Philip were a bird, the conclusion would still not be necessarily true. He could be a cardinal or a blue-jay. This example serves to underscore the point that when valid arguments containing unacceptable premises lead to false conclusions, then those arguments are unsound and must be rejected. By contrast, when arguments are valid in form, and when they possess premises that lead to necessary conclusions, they are sound and certainly more acceptable.

9.1
9.3

EVALUATING PRACTICAL SYLLOGISMS

Now that we know the differences between sound and merely valid arguments and the role that truthful claims play in their construction, let us see how we should go about evaluating those **practical syllogisms** that support moral value judgments and particular ethical viewpoints. When analyzing an ethical argument, for example, in an article or book, the first thing to do is to extract the major claims, premises, and conclusions presented by the author. Next, assemble them into coherent syllogisms in ways that are consistent with, or reflective of, the author's thinking. We do not wish to misrepresent or distort what was intended. Once the practical syllogisms (implicitly or explicitly) contained in the article or book are extracted, paraphrased and/or reassembled as necessary, the evaluation can begin.

The first thing to do is ask whether for any one syllogism the stated conclusion follows from the preceding **premises** (both factual and value). Can we derive the conclusion or infer it from the factual statements and value judgments made before? If not, then there is a flaw in the formal structure of the argument. See the flawed argument below. Notice how the conclusion does not follow.

Value Premise:	All that encourages violence (A) is evil (B).	All A is B
Factual Premise:	Heavy metal music (C) encourages violence (A).	C is A
Conclusion:	My son (D) should not buy Metallica CDs (E).	D is E

In the practical syllogism above, we see that the conclusion, which, in itself, may or may not be justifiable, does not follow logically from the preceding premises. The conclusion that would make the argument valid is: "Heavy metal music is evil (C is B)." The conclusion, as it is stated above, introduces two new elements (D and E) that give the argument an invalid form. Invalid arguments need not be accepted, regardless of how desirable their conclusions might be.

After you have examined the conclusion of any syllogism to see whether it follows from preceding premises, the second thing to do is to direct your attention to the **factual premise** contained in the argument. Is the factual claim empirically verifiable? Can it be supported by observation, experiment or common everyday experience? Are there studies or surveys that lend it weight? In short, is the factual premise more or less likely to be true? In our music example, we could look for any psychological and/or sociological studies dealing more generally with the effects of heavy metal music on individual conduct or social behavior. We could ask whether it is true, in fact, that such music does encourage violence. Are the studies conclusive or inconclusive? Does the weight of the evidence suggest that it does or does not encourage violence? Are there recent studies that contradict earlier ones? Have faulty uses of inductive reasoning (e.g., unfounded generalizations) led to the factual claim embedded in the larger argument? Obviously, when evaluating the truth of factual claims, we enter the realm of possibility and likelihood. We do not always know absolutely whether or not a particular factual claim is necessarily true. As we learned before, inductive logic, often used to support factual claims, can provide only probability, not absolute certainty. We should not be discouraged by this insight, however. It should help us, in fact, to develop an attitude of Socratic humility when it comes to ethical argument. If we are often dealing with probabilities and likelihoods when we defend our moral positions, then it is unwise to be rigid and dogmatic. Our "facts" may be wrong or, at least, questionable. They may be inconclusive or incomplete. Tomorrow's facts might contradict today's. With this in mind, we can more easily suspend judgment and reason with greater caution and care.

The third thing to do to evaluate practical syllogisms is to appraise the acceptability of the value premises upon which the arguments are based. If the **value premise** from which a moral value **conclusion** is derived is unacceptable, then so too is the argument, regardless of its formal validity. Remember, valid arguments containing untrue or unacceptable premises are unsound. In the next section, we will look at four rational tests that can be used to evaluate the value premises upon which deductive syllogistic arguments are built.

9.4
TESTING VALUE PREMISES

The pendulum of the mind oscillates between sense and nonsense, not between right and wrong.

Carl Jung

Role-Exchange Test

One way of determining the acceptability of a value premise is by using the **role-exchange test** (Coombs, Daniels and Wright, 1978). This test requires us to ask ourselves whether we would be willing to exchange places with the person or persons most disadvantaged by the application of a particular moral rule or principle in a given set of circumstances. If we are not prepared to be the ones most disadvantaged by the application of the rule or principle in question, then it is probably unjustified or inadequate in some fashion. Let us suppose that a number of school trustees argued about whether Vladimir Gorky and Fred Runningbear should be allowed to enroll at an exclusive private boarding school. Further, let us assume that the only reason given for not enrolling them is that these students are not white, Anglo-Saxon, and Protestant (W.A.S.P.). If such were the case, the argument would go something like this.

Value Premise:	Students who are not W.A.S.P. should not attend this private school.
Factual Premise:	Vladimir and Fred are not W.A.S.P.
Conclusion:	Vladimir and Fred should not attend this private school.

Applying the role-exchange test requires us to ask whether we would like to exchange places with Vladimir and Fred and still accept the principle supporting the conclusion. Presumably, neither we nor the school trustees would like our options reduced or our freedoms restricted simply because of our racial, ethnic or religious background. The trustees would, no doubt, dislike being discriminated against, just as we would. But, if the trustees could not accept being treated unfairly if the proposed principle were applied to them, then the principle, acting as the value premise of their argument, would fail the role-exchange test. It would have to be rejected on rational ethical grounds.

9.4

New Cases Test

If a moral rule or ethical principle is deemed acceptable and used as a value premise to justify a value judgment or normative conclusion in one particular set of circumstances, then it should be equally applicable to other similar sets of circumstances. If it is not, then there is likely something wrong with the rule or principle itself. For example, let us conclude that "Maria's actions were wrong" or that "Maria did the wrong thing," and let us also say that we base our moral conclusion on the premise that "People should never lie." To test this principle, let us examine it in the case where it applies to Maria, but also in other **new case tests**. What we are asking really is whether or not it is so that "people should never lie."

Case Number One: When asked about its whereabouts, Maria tells her dad that she does not know where his wallet is when, in fact, she has stolen it and used the money inside it to buy an article of clothing. Question: Does the principle about lying hold up in case number one? Well, in this case, Maria is lying only to satisfy her personal wants. She is lying to promote her own selfish interests. Intuitively, most of us, I suspect, would regard Maria's actions as wrong. Lying to get what you want is probably unjustified regardless of who's involved. To the extent this is true, our principle about lying holds up.

Case Number Two: Suppose, however, that we are in Nazi Germany and Maria is hiding political refugees from Hitler's SS officers. The SS come to her door and ask her questions concerning the whereabouts of those refugees. If she tells the truth, those refugees die. If she lies, then Maria saves their lives. In this second case, many moral thinkers would argue that lying is quite acceptable. Most would probably argue that Maria would do nothing morally wrong if she lied. Yet, if this is true, our principle, "People should never lie" has been weakened by a new case where it does not apply.

Case Number Three: Imagine a Canadian spy has been captured during wartime. The spy is interrogated and asked if she has any information regarding a number of military secrets, which, if made known, would lead to widespread death and destruction. The spy actually does have the information the enemy wants. If she tells the truth, widespread death and destruction will result; if she lies, the lives of many allies will be saved and destruction will be minimized. Again, in this case, most moral thinkers would likely excuse any lies told by our spy. Some might even go further and say that our spy "should" lie or is "obligated" to lie by virtue of her special role, if nothing else. There might even be some people who would describe the spy as a traitor if she did not lie. In other words, lying in this case could arguably be morally required. But, if this is so, then we have another case wherein our principle about lying does not apply. It appears, then, to be quite debatable that "People should never lie." Perhaps lying is generally wrong except in cases where life and national security are concerned. Thus, the principle, as stated, might have to be modified to make it more acceptable. The more new cases we can find where it does not apply, the weaker the principle becomes. There may be so many exceptions to the rule that the rule in its current statement is no longer useful for moral guidance and direction.

9.4 Consistency and Universalizability Test

In order for value premises, stated as ethical principles, to be justifiable, they must be **logically consistent** and **universalizable**. Inconsistent principles are those that are **self-contradictory**. Because they are irrational, they cannot serve as a solid basis for the justification of particular moral conclusions. The following principle is inconsistent: "People should make promises with the intention of breaking them." Some might claim that politicians actually live by this principle in their efforts to get elected. To the extent that they do, they are guilty of an inconsistency. The concept of promise keeping necessarily entails the intention of keeping one's word. Making a promise with no intention of keeping it is self-contradictory. Promises intended to be broken are not promises at all, but are deceptions or lies.

Apart from failing the **consistency test**, the principle about promise making and breaking fails the closely related **universalizability test** as well. If everyone made promises with the intention of breaking them, the whole idea of promise making would become self-defeating. Promises would become unbelievable. When applying the universalizability test, we ask "What if everyone acted according to this principle?" or "Could I will that everyone should live by this principle?" If one cannot will that a particular value premise be acted upon or accepted by all or if it is inconsistent and self-defeating, the value premise is inadequate and unjustified.

9.4 Higher-Order Principle Test

Another way to test value premises is to apply the **higher-order principle test**. What we do in this case is take the value premise of one syllogism and see if there is a broader general principle in a higher-order syllogism that can be used to support the value premise itself. If the starting point

Figure 9.1 HIGHER-ORDER PRINCIPLE TEST

Higher-order argument supporting particular conclusion in syllogism I

Syllogism III
Value Premise
Factual Premise
Conclusion

Syllogism II
Value Premise
Factual Premise
Conclusion

becomes

Syllogism I
Value Premise
Factual Premise
Conclusion

becomes

Value premises become gradually more general in each supporting syllogism

Particular Conclusion

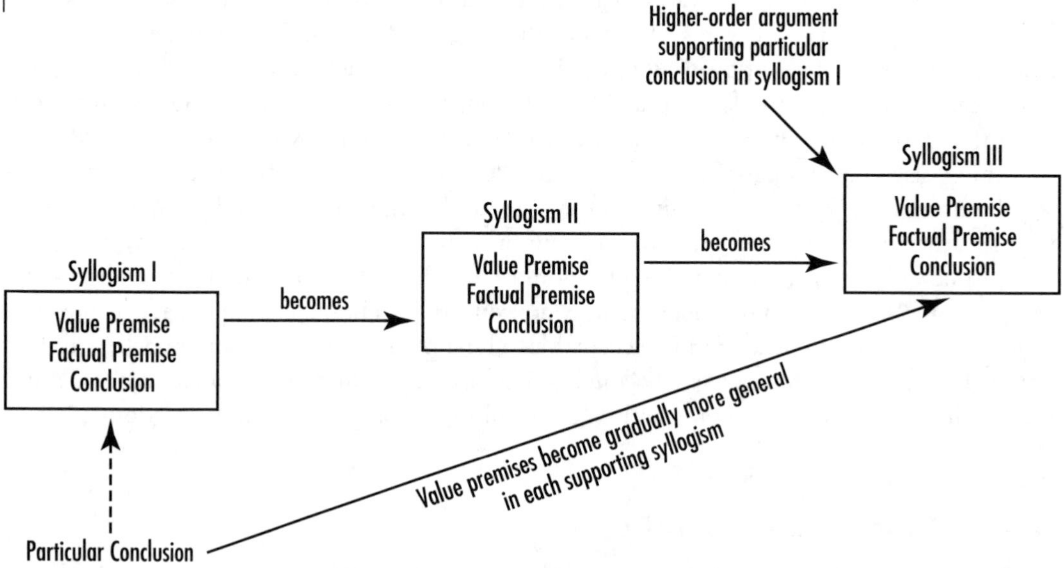

Source: Falikowski, *Mastering Human Relations,* p. 127.

of an argument, namely, the value premise, is acceptable, we should be able to derive it from a broader or so-called higher-order principle. See Figure 9.1. Also see Figure 9.2 for an example of a higher-order principle test that has been worked out. The conclusion in this case, i.e., that throwing rocks through windows is wrong, is ultimately justified by the higher-order value premise that "Violating individual rights is wrong."

The truth is great, but there's a time and place for everything.

Lori Villamil

PHILOSOPHERS AT WORK

Instructions: Evaluate the value premises/principles stated below using any one of the four tests of adequacy, i.e., the role-exchange, new cases, higher-order principle or consistency and universalizability test.

1. You should lie to others when it is to your advantage.
2. Stealing is always wrong.

3. Your should take shortcuts to school even if this involves trespassing on other people's property.
4. You should never use people solely as a means to get what you want out of life.
5. Visible ethnic and racial minorities should not be allowed into this country.
6. Everyone, but me, should fill out their income tax forms honestly.

Answer Key

1. unacceptable—fails universalizability test
2. unacceptable—fails new cases test
3. unacceptable—fails role-exchange test and universalizability test
4. acceptable—principle is consistent and universalizable, passes role-exchange test, etc.
5. unacceptable—fails role-exchange test
6. unacceptable—fails consistency and universalizability test

Figure 9.2 EXAMPLE USING HIGHER-ORDER PRINCIPLE TEST

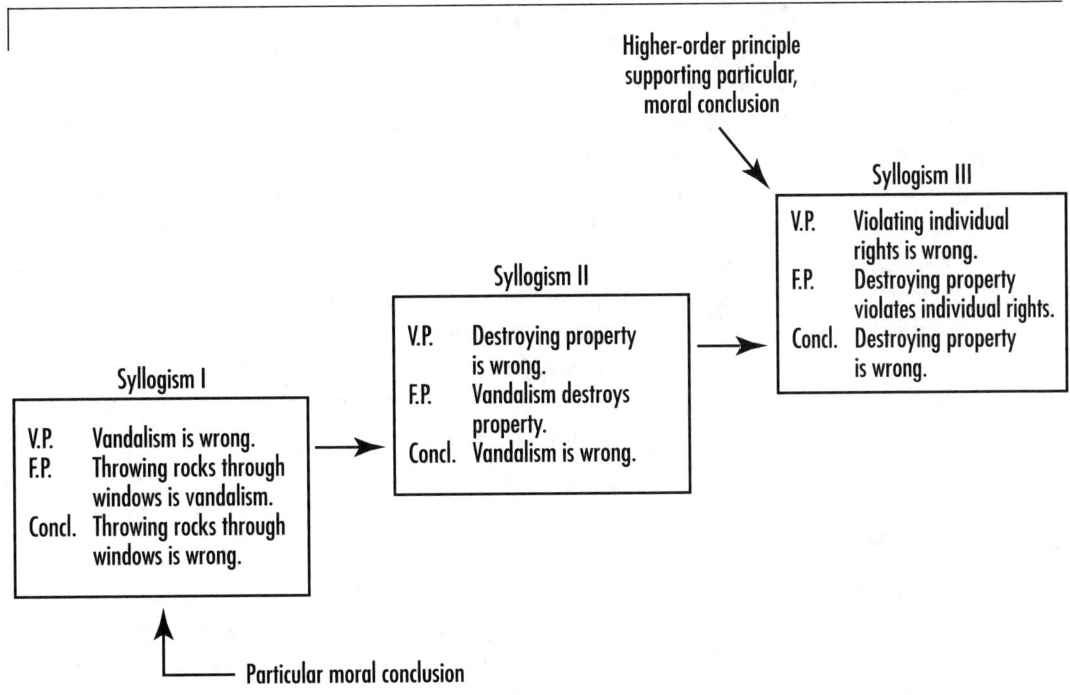

Source: Falikowski, *Mastering Human Relations*, p. 128.

Before we move on to the next section of this chapter, let us review what we have learned so far. First, we have clarified our understanding of logical validity by contrasting it with truth and soundness. Second, we have looked at ways and means of evaluating practical syllogisms. We have learned that bad reasoning results when:

1. Conclusions do not follow from preceding premises;
2. Minor/factual premises are false; and
3. Major/value premises are unacceptable.

Another thing we have learned in this chapter is how to appraise the acceptability of value premises by using four logical tests of adequacy. Thus, we now have a number of rational strategies we can use when evaluating arguments that are presented to us.

In this last section of Chapter Nine, we will try to enhance our powers of critical, logical analysis. We will look at some dishonest **rhetorical** devices that are often used to win debates and persuade people. To protect ourselves against the use of such devices, it is important to be able to recognize and label them. The next section is designed to help us do just that.

9.5 LOGICAL FALLACIES: IRRATIONAL WAYS TO ARGUE

People who fail to appreciate the benefits of argument often feel threatened when their viewpoints are challenged. If there has been a lot of ego investment in a particular viewpoint or a deep involvement of personal feelings, improper forms of reasoning called **logical fallacies** may be used to perform the emotional rescue of the threatened self. Fallacies are irrational. They are designed to persuade us emotionally and psychologically, not rationally (Johnson and Blair, 1983, p. 71). People who use them try to divert attention from the real issues and arguments under discussion to something more favorable to them. Fallacies can also be used as forms of intimidation. Defensive people worried about being wrong may respond aggressively toward others. Putting someone else on the defensive requires you to be less defensive about yourself. Essentially, fallacies work through diversion and attack. As instruments of persuasion and rhetoric, they are, unfortunately, sometimes very effective. As ways of correct thinking, however, they are always wrong. Logical fallacies are sometimes committed unconsciously and without malicious intent. Some people are simply unaware of their bad reasoning. Regardless of whether the "sleazy logic" is intentional or not, let us look at some common fallacies you will need to guard against in your own logical self-defense.

9.6 *Ad Hominem* Fallacy

When you disagree with someone, the proper response is to criticize your opponent's position. If, instead of debating the issues involved, you attack your opponent personally, you then commit the ***ad hominem*** **fallacy**. For example, a wasteful person who resents the inconvenience brought about by recycling might refuse to support ideas and arguments presented by Pollution Probe on the grounds that all environmentalists are "60s losers." Of course, the mer-

Figure 9.3 ***AD HOMINEM* FALLACY**

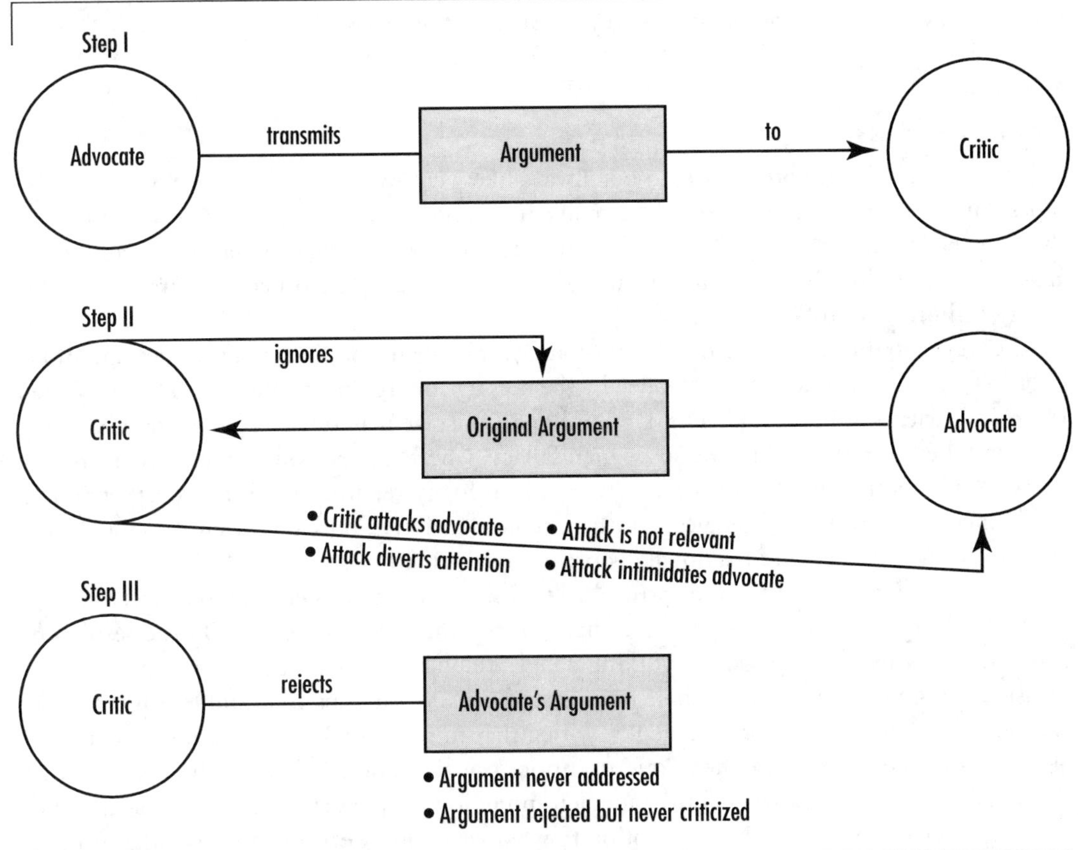

Source: Adapted from Falikowski, *Mastering Human Relations*, p. 131.

its of an argument should not be judged by what generation the person advocating it is from. Recycling is either good or bad, regardless of its advocates' birthdates. To better understand how *ad hominem* reasoning works, see Figure 9.3.

Despite the ill logic it contains, *ad hominem* reasoning is very common in everyday discussion and debate. This type of thinking process can be emotionally satisfying in so far as it belittles or puts down people with whom we disagree. We find it unsettling to be forced to concede that an individual we dislike has made a valid point. Also, if we are highly committed to the viewpoint that is being attacked by another, we may erroneously perceive such an attack as a personal assault. In reflex fashion, we may counterattack with an *ad hominem* verbal barrage against the perceived threat. When we do, we allow irrationality, hostility, and aggression to interfere with productive argument. Our own defensiveness becomes an offensive act targeted at others. Look for *ad hominem* attacks whenever people's personalities, characters, ethnic/racial backgrounds, underlying motives or special interests are criticized in response to messages perceived to be threatening. Also, do not allow yourself to be sidetracked when presenting your own viewpoints by defending yourself in response to others' *ad hominem* attacks on you. Stick to the issues!

9.6

Straw Man Fallacy

When we disagree with others, we do not always like what we hear. In response, we may misrepresent what others have said so we can make their arguments clearly unacceptable. We may then proceed to argue against the unsatisfying versions to reject the original, but unaddressed arguments. In doing this, we commit the **straw man fallacy**. The process of straw man reasoning is illustrated in Figure 9.4.

A caution might be in order here. Occasionally, it happens that recipients of messages honestly do not understand what was intended by the message or argument conveyed. They may then respond to what was never said. This kind of honest mistake may reflect a problem of listening or comprehension. It is unlike the straw man fallacy, where one person deliberately misrepresents the viewpoints of another. I guess we get into foggy territory when misrepresentations occur unconsciously in psychological efforts to reduce anxiety. Conscious or unconscious, however, straw man fallacies are irrational distortions of the truth.

Suppose that a new governor or provincial premier has just been elected to office. She supports tax increases for middle-income earners. In response, someone says "This doesn't surprise me! She's always been against working people belonging to unions and this is just another measure designed to undermine their interests. If we allow unions to crumble, then democracy in this country will be threatened!" Notice that in the critic's reply, democracy, unions and working people are brought to our attention, not the rationale behind the tax increases. Presumably, it is easier to argue for democracy and union people than it is to argue against unwanted tax increases. By diverting attention to what we do like or want and, from that vantage point, criticizing what we do not want (i.e., increased taxes), the original position supporting tax increases is rejected, though never properly addressed.

Because you can appreciate how annoying it is when others criticize what you never said, be sure to ask questions for clarification before criticizing others' arguments or viewpoints. Your criticisms are valuable only if they relate to what was actually intended and said. Conversely, before allowing others to criticize your arguments and viewpoints, you could ask others to repeat in their own terms what they think you have said and meant. If necessary, clarifications could be made. In the end, this extra step could reduce miscommunication and save time.

9.6

Circular Reasoning/Begging the Question

Have you ever been involved in an argument that seemed to go around in circles? If you have, perhaps someone in the argument was using **circular reasoning**, also known as the **fallacy of**

Figure 9.4 STRAW MAN FALLACY

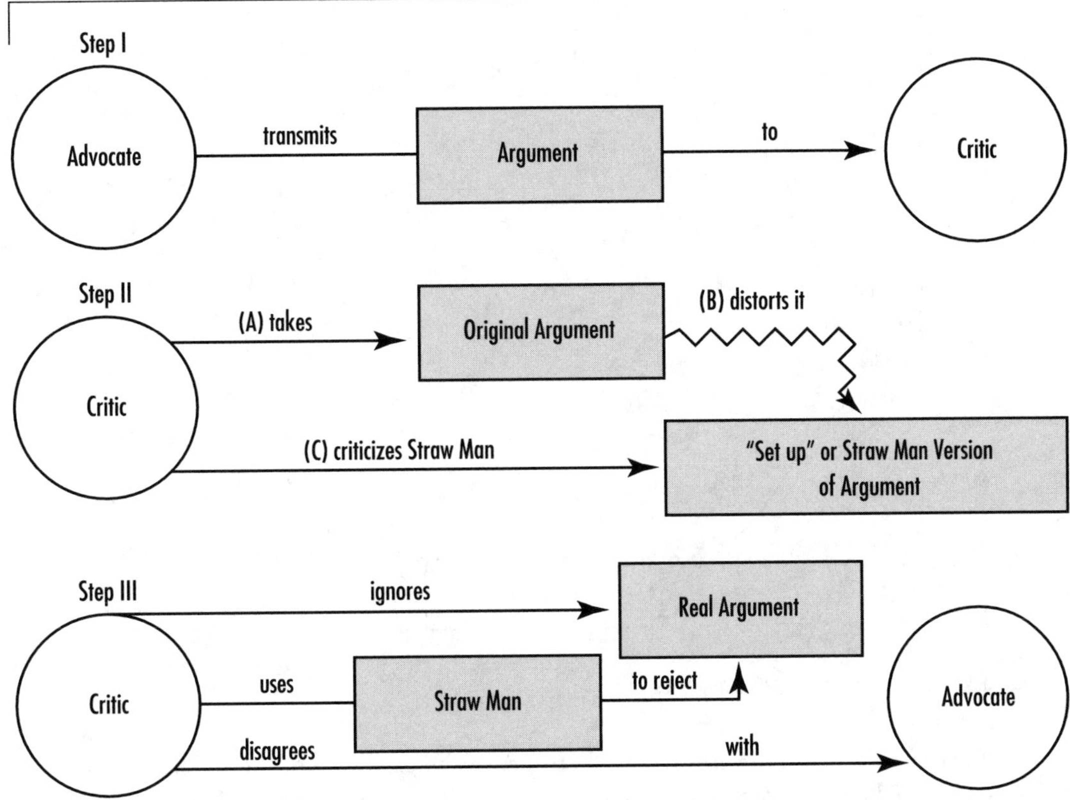

Source: Adapted from Falikowski, *Mastering Human Relations*, p. 132.

begging the question. In circular reasoning people use, as a premise of their argument, the conclusion they are trying to establish. In other words, people assume as true in the beginning what they intend to prove logically at the conclusion of their argument. When this is done, there is prejudgment (prejudice) on the issue being debated. The "logical" argument does not take you anywhere except back to what was assumed to be true at the outset. For this reason, begging the question is circular, taking us around and around. What we assume is what we set out to prove, and what we prove is what we originally assumed. Circular reasoning is, perhaps, most evident in religious discussions.

I.M. Agnostic:	How do you know God exists?
B. Lever:	Because it says so in the Bible.
I.M. Agnostic:	How do you know the Bible is telling you the truth?
B. Lever:	Because it is the inspired word of God.

Figure 9.5 CIRCULAR REASONING

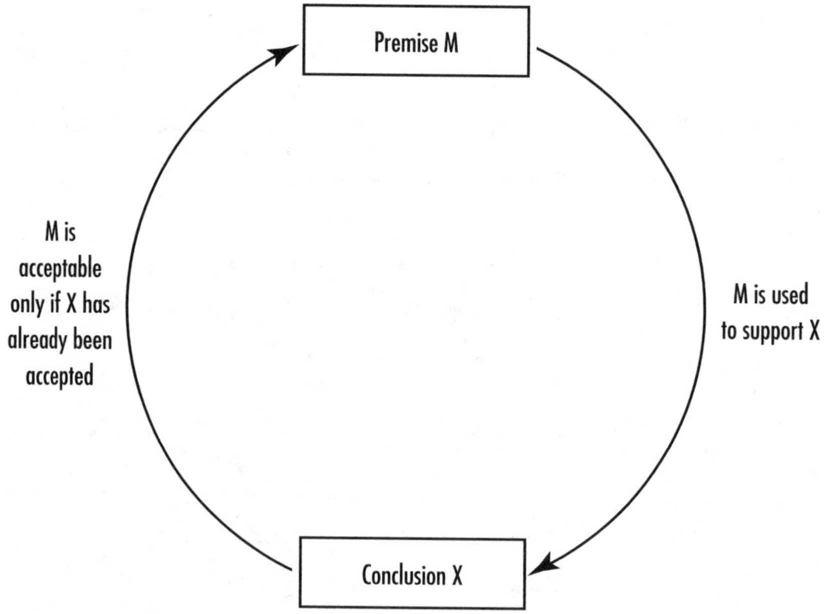

Source: Falikowski, *Mastering Human Relations,* p. 133.

In this example, B. Lever uses the Bible to prove the existence of God. The authority of the Bible is based on the premise that God inspired it. It is, therefore, assumed that God actually does exist (the point under debate). But, if B. Lever assumes to be true at the beginning what B. Lever is trying to prove in the end, nothing has, in fact, been proven and we have just gone around in a circle. I do not mean to suggest that rational proofs cannot be given for God's existence, only that circular arguments do not work. Look at Figure 9.5 to better appreciate the process of circular reasoning.

9.6
Two Wrongs Fallacy

Committing the **two wrongs fallacy** involves defending a particular wrong-doing by drawing attention to another instance of the same behavior that apparently went unchallenged and was, therefore, accepted by implication. For instance, I remember that back in my student days there were traditional initiation rituals for University of Toronto "frosh" (first-year students) that required minor acts of vandalism (e.g., painting a certain statue in Queen's Park). Confronted about the justifiability of such acts, a student (guess who?) responded by saying that frosh had been doing these acts for years. Apparently, for this poor misguided soul, the previous years' vandalism served as a justification for his wrong-doing.

Figure 9.6 TWO WRONGS FALLACY

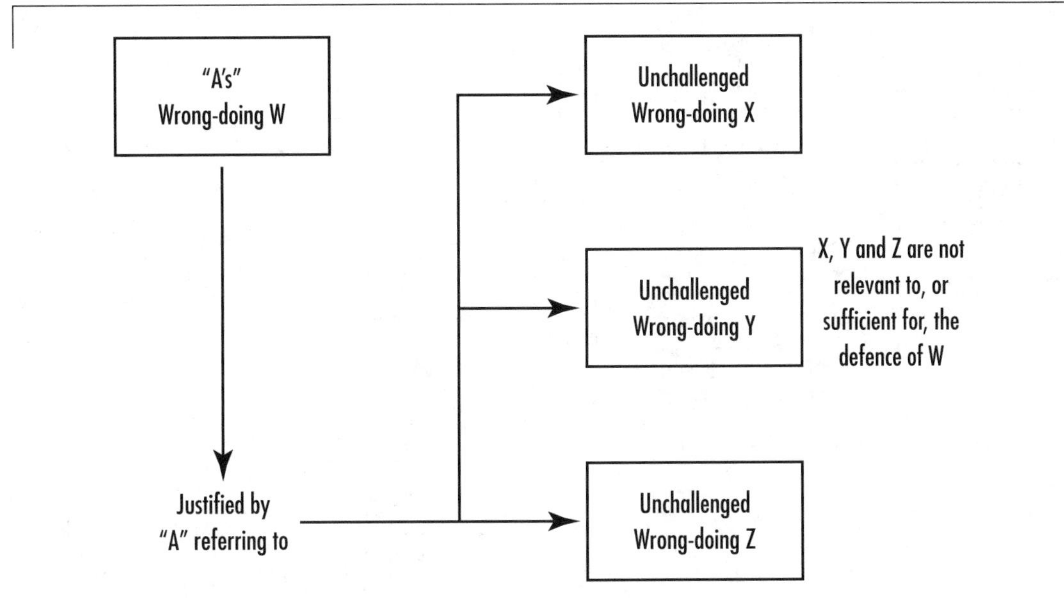

Source: Falikowski, *Mastering Human Relations*, p. 134.

Highway speeders also provide us with an example of two wrongs fallacious reasoning. When stopped for speeding, those charged often argue with the officers that they were just keeping up with traffic. In other words, they were doing nothing other than breaking the law, just like everybody else. As you may have learned from experience, most police officers will not accept this line of reasoning. The two wrongs fallacy is illustrated in Figure 9.6.

9.6

Slippery Slope Fallacy

People who commit the **slippery slope fallacy** display this form of ill logic when they object to something because they incorrectly assume that it will necessarily lead to other undesirable consequences. For example, you may object to smoking marijuana. You could reason that such behavior will lead to harder drug usage, addiction, and, eventually, to a life of crime. Because crime is unwanted, you conclude that smoking marijuana is therefore wrong.

Notice that in this hypothetical example, the major objection is to crime, the presumed eventual result of smoking marijuana. The conclusion drawn here, however, is not inevitable. After experimenting once, you may choose to avoid marijuana in the future. Or, you might decide to use it only very occasionally in a recreational way. Maybe, after smoking it, you could become a crusader leading the way against mood altering drugs. The point is that smoking marijuana is a separate and distinct act from harder drug use, addiction, and crime. Each must be considered

Figure 9.7 SLIPPERY SLOPE FALLACY

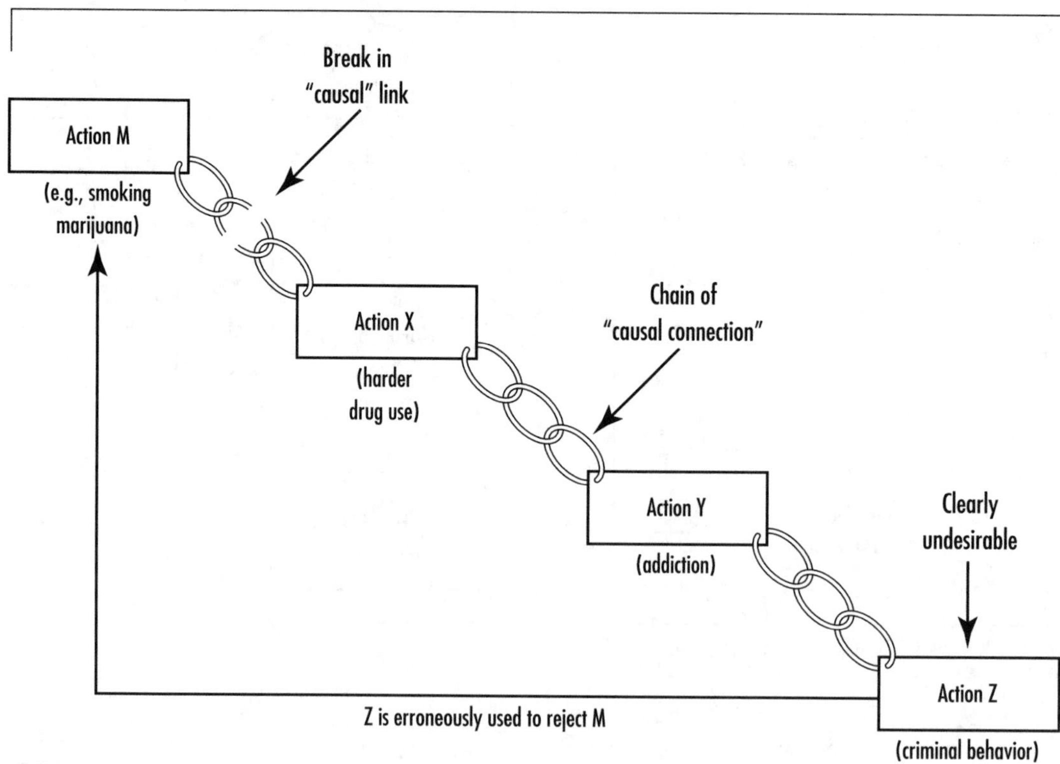

Source: Falikowski, *Mastering Human Relations,* p. 135.

independently and evaluated on its own terms. Although it may be that many criminals and addicts begin their lives of crime by smoking marijuana, not everybody who smokes marijuana becomes a criminal addict. Many law-abiding, nonaddicted people have experimented with marijuana; therefore, there is no necessary **causal connection** between marijuana and criminality. This means that there is no cause-and-effect relationship. One thing does not have to lead to the other. If you can find a break in the causal chain that, presumably, links two unrelated acts, you can uncover the presence of a slippery slope. See Figure 9.7.

9.6
Fallacy of Appealing to Authority

> ***Man is a credulous animal and tends to believe what he is told. Historically, philosophers . . . have taken great pains to point out that authority is at least as important a source of error as it is of knowledge.***
>
> *Joseph Brennan*

When people get into debates and disagreements, they frequently commit the **fallacy of appealing to authority** to justify their positions. See Figure 9.8 for a visual depiction of the fallacy of appealing to authority. Some appeals to authority are proper, others are not. Proper appeals can be made to support factual claims within larger arguments. If, in the previous example about marijuana, someone had wanted to condemn its use on medical grounds, scientific and empirical research data could have been presented to support claims about marijuana's adverse physical effects. As long as the data presented were based on the recognized contributions of medical researchers in the field and were accepted after peer review and evaluation, such data could have been justifiably used to support factual claims imbedded in the broader argument. Of course, recognized researchers do not always agree amongst themselves—a reason why scientific method cannot yield "absolute" proof. Even when citing scientific data, then, it is important to exercise some caution. To appreciate why, just ask what current scientific studies reveal about the effects of drinking coffee, for example. Some studies suggest caffeine is harmful, others disagree. In such cases, it is prudent to go with the weight of the evidence. Ask "What do most studies suggest?" or "Is there overwhelming evidence one way or another?" When the data are highly suggestive one way or another, references to them go beyond personal opinion to a recognized body of knowledge. Authoritative appeals can best be made in the hard sciences. Statements made in these disciplines can be verified in principle and hypotheses can be tested. There are clear public standards to test the validity of claims made.

When questions of value are at issue, it is much more difficult, and usually unjustifiable, to make authoritative appeals. Normative assumptions and principles of conduct (e.g., people should always behave in their own self-interest) cannot be proven true or false by empirical observation or by scientific experiment. Whether or not people actually behave in their own self-interest cannot tell us whether or not they should. Where matters of value are concerned, authoritative appeals cannot be made in rationally acceptable ways. This idea also applies where interpretation and personal preferences play a role or where the boundaries of subject matter are in dispute. Where experts have no empirical means or scientific procedures to settle disputes, authoritative appeals should be avoided. Such disputes must be settled by reason and argument. The next time you get into an argument, you should ask yourself what kind of claim is being made. Is the claim factual in nature? If so, where can you obtain legitimate support? If the claim is normative or value-related, how should you proceed to justify your position or to criticize that of another?

One improper appeal to authority involves the notion of popularity or democracy. In this case, a conclusion is supported by an appeal to numbers—if a majority of people supports something, then that something is necessarily good, right or praiseworthy. Of course, numbers guarantee nothing. Historically speaking, majorities have been proven wrong. The fact that a majority of people in the southern United States once favored slavery does not justify it. Reference to the will of the majority proves nothing. The moral status of slavery must be considered independently from its supporters. If 51 percent of the people in Lunenburg, Nova Scotia were in favor of cheating Revenue Canada on their income taxes, this fact alone would not make it right. The next time you think about trying to convince your parents, friends or spouse that you should be allowed to do something "just because everybody else says it is OK," reflect on the fallacy of appealing to authority. Could you give other reasons to support what you want to do?

Figure 9.8 FALLACY OF APPEALING TO AUTHORITY

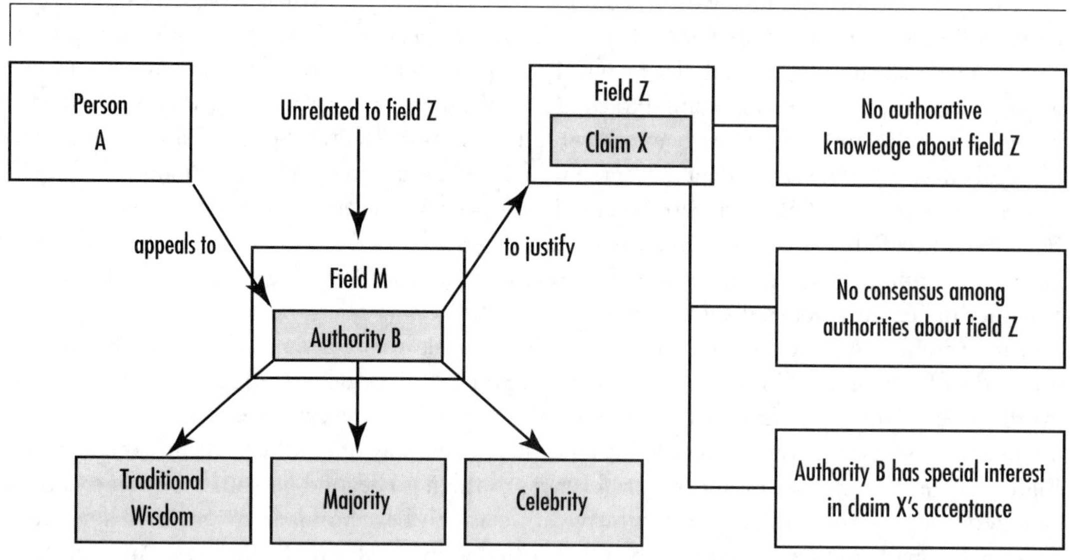

Source: Falikowski, *Mastering Human Relations,* p. 138.

Appeals to traditional wisdom are also fallacious. In this case, actions are justified by saying "This is the way it's always been done." Other actions are rejected by saying "We have never done things this way before." Actions that are justified by reference to past conventions (i.e., socially accepted ways of doing things), however, are not necessarily justified at all. For instance, suppose someone said "We should never have allowed a woman, especially Kim Campbell, to become prime minister of Canada because we have never had a woman occupy that office before." Obviously, a history of gender bias and discrimination cannot properly serve as a justification for continuing this practice. While tradition often gives us many valuable insights, it also presents its own moral problems. In itself, traditional wisdom is not unconditionally valid. Be careful, though, not to throw the traditional "baby" out with the "dirty bathwater." Tradition does have its legitimate place in human experience.

A final criticism of authoritative appeals is that authorities often disagree among themselves when matters of value are at issue. If authorities cannot reach a consensus, we cannot rely on authoritative judgments to settle disputes. Maybe you could look for an authority over authorities, but even this would be a problem. Your ultimate authority (e.g., God) may not be accepted by others (e.g., atheists). In a tolerant, democratic, multicultural society, it is usually, if not always, improper to use your chosen authority figure as a reference point for judgment when dealing with others. Commitments to your own beliefs should not violate the rights of others. The rules and regulations of your religious, political or military authorities, for example, may contain little rational moral force when applied to those who have different commitments. To put the danger of authoritative appeals into perspective, suppose someone's supreme authority were Luc Jouret, leader of the Solar Temple cult in Québec. You will recall that his cult took part in a mass murder-suicide in 1994, with incidents in both Canada and Switzerland. Nobody knows all the details of what happened, but let us speculate that Jouret ordered his followers to kill themselves. Would this action, in itself, justify their actions? Rational thinking requires that we say no. In fact, many philosophers (e.g., Immanuel Kant) have argued that suicide is inherently irrational and, therefore, unjustified. Trying to justify murder-suicide by reference to Jouret's authority would thus involve the use of fallacious reasoning.

9.6 Red Herring Fallacy

The **red herring fallacy** is another favorite form of ill logic used by rationally dishonest or unconsciously irrational individuals. The name of this fallacy comes from the sport of fox hunting. In this sport, hunters on horseback follow a pack of hounds tracking a fox's scent. To save the fox from being caught, dried and salted red herring is drawn across the fox's tracks ahead of the pack. The herring is then pulled in a direction away from that which the fox took. The dogs are diverted by the stronger and fresher scent of the herring. The fox is left alone.

In the red herring fallacy a controversial claim or position is defended by taking the offensive. This tactic involves setting up a new issue that has only a weak or tenuous connection with the original one. Because this original position is weak, the defender proceeds to argue for the new issue or position that is more supportable. In other words, attention is deflected from the original position to a new one, which is probably less open to question and debate. Below is an example of red herring reasoning. Notice what the patriotic bartender does when he perceives his country is under attack. He diverts attention from the Canadian's allegations of crime, violence, discrimination, and influence peddling to space technology, universities, and military power. The latter can more easily support his claim that "America is the greatest." The Canadian's critical comments make such a claim highly questionable.

Detroit Bartender:	The United States is the best country in the world.
Canadian Tourist:	You must be kidding. The United States is falling apart at the seams. Thousands of murders are committed every year. Women and minorities are discriminated against. Lobby groups have too much power in Washington. On top of this, fear of being victimized in street crimes keeps people from going outdoors in the evening. Face it, your nation is in decline.
Detroit Bartender:	What are you talking about? We are the greatest military power in the world. We have the best universities and the most advanced space technology. America is the greatest.

The red herring is illustrated in Figure 9.9.

Figure 9.9 RED HERRING FALLACY

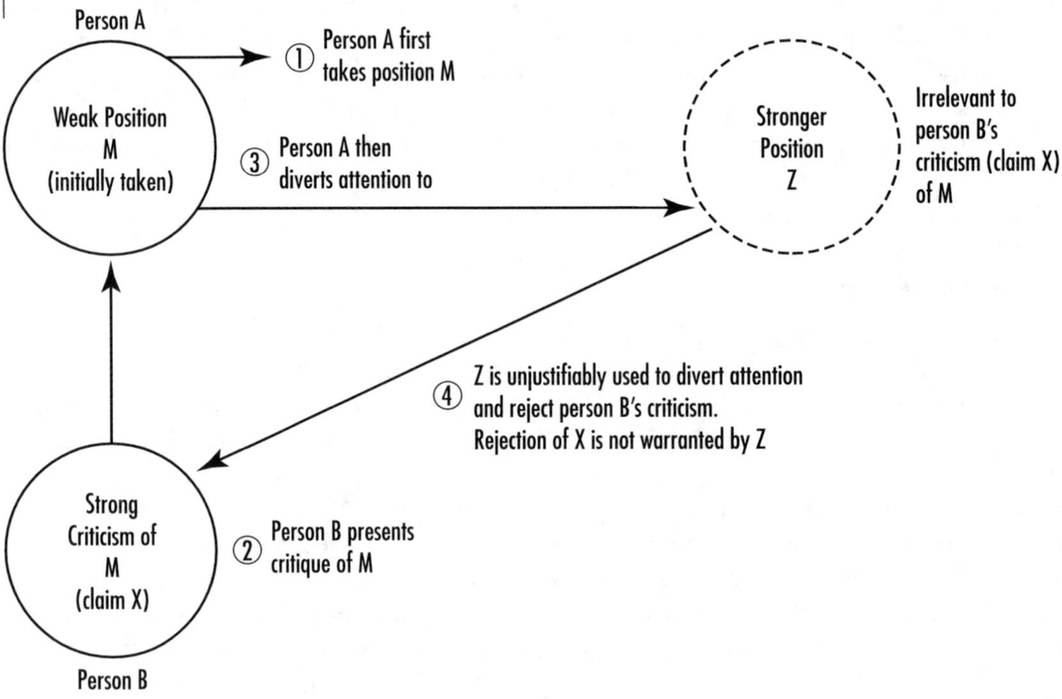

Person A

Weak Position M (initially taken)

① Person A first takes position M

③ Person A then diverts attention to

Stronger Position Z

Irrelevant to person B's criticism (claim X) of M

④ Z is unjustifiably used to divert attention and reject person B's criticism. Rejection of X is not warranted by Z

Strong Criticism of M (claim X)

② Person B presents critique of M

Person B

Source: Falikowski, *Mastering Human Relations*, p. 139.

9.6 Fallacy of Guilt by Association

This form of ill logic is generally used in adversarial situations in an attempt to discredit an opponent or that opponent's arguments. It draws attention to the opponent's alleged association with some group or an individual that has already been discredited. The attempt to discredit is not direct as in typical *ad hominem* arguments, but is indirect. The guilt of the discredited individual or group is transferred to the opponent.

Let us suppose that someone refuses to vote "socialist" in the next election. His reason is that the "Socialist Party almost sent England and France into bankruptcy." The unspoken claim is that, if elected here, they will bankrupt this country too. Apparently, for this voter, socialist mismanagement across the ocean is enough to convict socialists here of incompetence. They are found guilty prior to doing anything wrong. It is possible, in principle, that a socialist government could mismanage a country like Canada—some argue that the Liberal and Conservative Parties have been doing so for years! But, in any case, actions and policies of foreign socialist governments

Figure 9.10 FALLACY OF GUILT BY ASSOCIATION

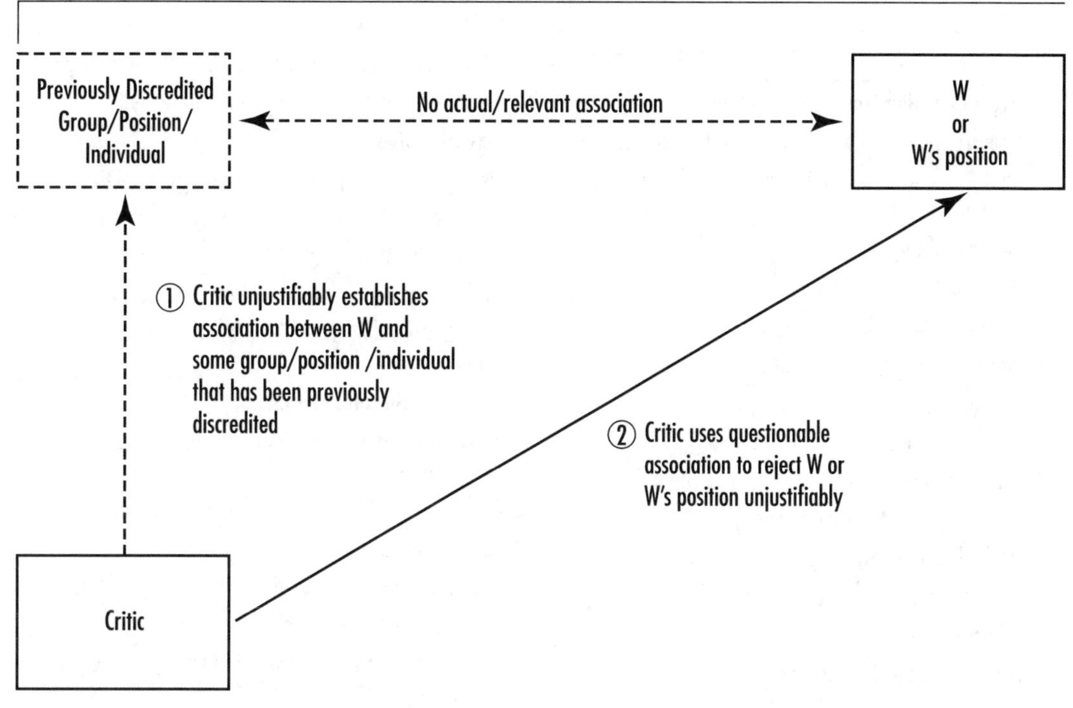

Source: Falikowski, *Mastering Human Relations,* p. 140.

alone cannot serve as an adequate basis of judgment on domestic socialism. Our socialism may be different in significant ways. Our socialists may have learned from the mistakes of their European counterparts. Perhaps contemporary North American socialism has evolved into something more akin to capitalism? There could be almost no political communication between the two socialist groups named. Who knows? Simply put, you cannot pin incompetence on Canadian socialists because of what foreign socialists have done. To do so is to commit the **fallacy of guilt by association**. Nonetheless, by using this diversionary tactic, fear can be created in the minds of unreflective voters and it may work as a means of persuasion. Creating fear is not very rational, but against people lacking the skills of logical self-defense, it often works. This fallacy is illustrated in Figure 9.10.

9.7

Finally, in conclusion to our discussion of logic and reasoning in Part Two, I invite you to review "Some Do's and Don'ts for Argument's Sake." I also invite you to do the reasoning self-diagnostic again (at the start of Part Two.) See if your scores have improved as a result of your logical studies.

Table 9.1 SOME DO'S AND DON'TS FOR ARGUMENT'S SAKE

DON'T	DO
Attack or intimidate	Adopt the proper attitude (i.e., Socratic humility)
Divert attention from the real issues	Remain rational and emotionally detached
Base arguments on emotional or psychological appeals	Stay objective
Build false or questionable claims into your argument	Listen to opposing viewpoints with openness
Use invalid logic	Analyze conflicting positions fairly and impartially
Use unjustifiable premises	Appraise factual claims
Make questionable assumptions	Evaluate major premises and assumptions
Confuse valid logic with truth	Examine the logical thinking behind particular conclusions
Take disagreements personally	Look for fallacious reasoning
Appeal to authorities unjustifiably	Appeal to higher-order values to justify your viewpoints
Attribute to others what they didn't say	Distinguish between opinions and arguments
Make illegitimate associations	Stick to the issues
Contradict yourself	Use proper processes of deductive and inductive logic
Change the subject when challenged	Base your positions on sound arguments
Be inconsistent	Avoid diversion and intimidation by fallacious reasoning
Use faulty causal reasoning	
Justify one wrong-doing with another	

Source: Adapted from Falikowski, *Mastering Human Relations*, p. 141.

PHILOSOPHERS AT WORK

Identify the Fallacy: This exercise will give you an opportunity to apply your knowledge and understanding of fallacious reasoning. Practice here will help you to develop your skills of logical self-defense. Being able to identify fallacious reasoning will protect you against illogical attacks and irrational attempts to manipulate your thinking. Recognizing fallacies will also help you to minimize them in your own reasoned arguments.

Instructions: Below are some examples of fallacious reasoning. Identify which fallacies are present by placing the appropriate letter next to the example. This exercise can be done individually or in groups. For classroom discussion purposes, be prepared to provide explanations for each identification.

a. *ad hominem* fallacy
b. straw man fallacy
c. circular reasoning/fallacy of begging the question
d. fallacy of two wrongs
e. slippery slope fallacy
f. fallacy of appealing to authority
g. red herring fallacy
h. fallacy of guilt by association

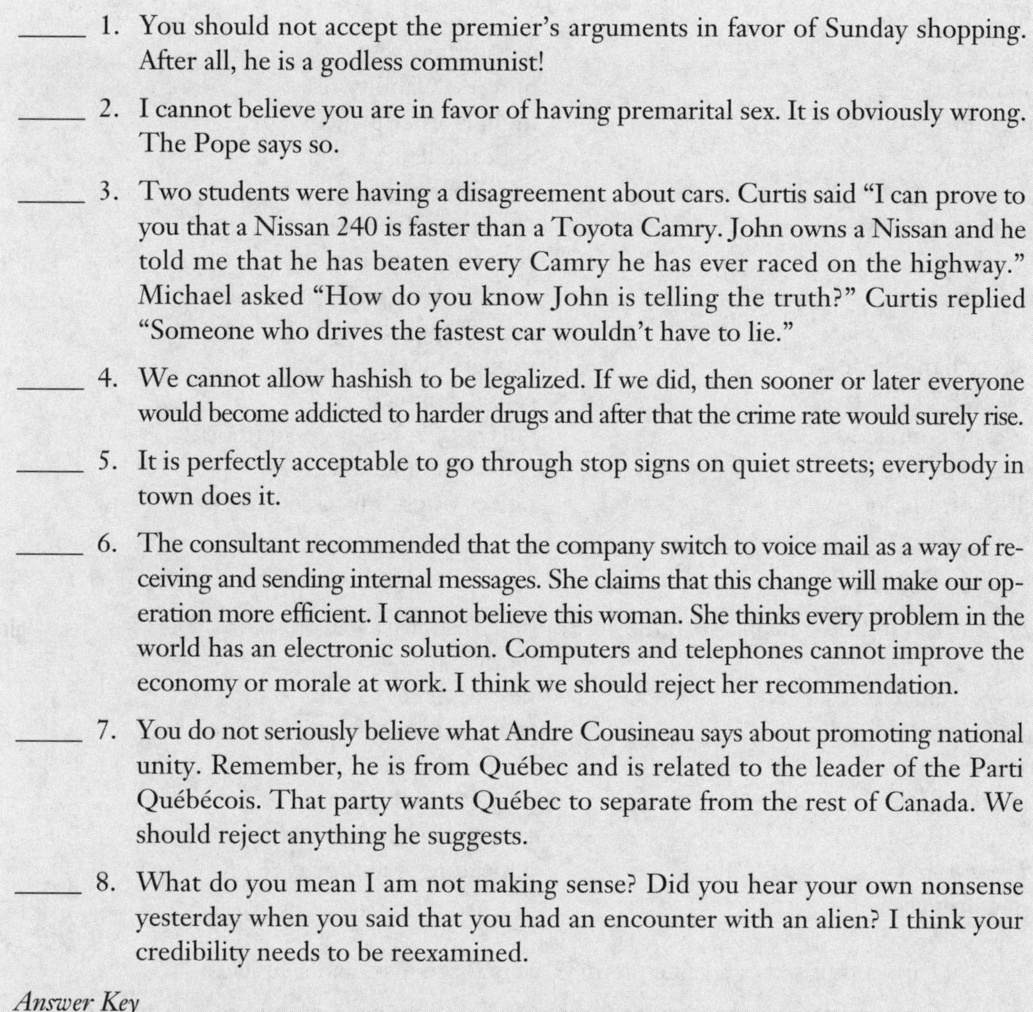

_____ 1. You should not accept the premier's arguments in favor of Sunday shopping. After all, he is a godless communist!

_____ 2. I cannot believe you are in favor of having premarital sex. It is obviously wrong. The Pope says so.

_____ 3. Two students were having a disagreement about cars. Curtis said "I can prove to you that a Nissan 240 is faster than a Toyota Camry. John owns a Nissan and he told me that he has beaten every Camry he has ever raced on the highway." Michael asked "How do you know John is telling the truth?" Curtis replied "Someone who drives the fastest car wouldn't have to lie."

_____ 4. We cannot allow hashish to be legalized. If we did, then sooner or later everyone would become addicted to harder drugs and after that the crime rate would surely rise.

_____ 5. It is perfectly acceptable to go through stop signs on quiet streets; everybody in town does it.

_____ 6. The consultant recommended that the company switch to voice mail as a way of receiving and sending internal messages. She claims that this change will make our operation more efficient. I cannot believe this woman. She thinks every problem in the world has an electronic solution. Computers and telephones cannot improve the economy or morale at work. I think we should reject her recommendation.

_____ 7. You do not seriously believe what Andre Cousineau says about promoting national unity. Remember, he is from Québec and is related to the leader of the Parti Québécois. That party wants Québec to separate from the rest of Canada. We should reject anything he suggests.

_____ 8. What do you mean I am not making sense? Did you hear your own nonsense yesterday when you said that you had an encounter with an alien? I think your credibility needs to be reexamined.

Answer Key
1. a; 2. f; 3. c; 4. e; 5. d; 6. b; 7. h; 8. g

MINDWORK MEDITATION

Think about the last time you "smelled a rat" in someone's argument. You sensed something was wrong, but just could not put your finger on it. Now that you know more about valid logic and fallacious reasoning, think back to that argument. What was the argument about? What claims or assumptions were included in it? Was the logic valid? Were the claims supported or verified? Would the value premises involved pass the tests of adequacy? Was the other party guilty of any logical fallacies? Take some time now to rationally reflect. Jot down your revelations in your philosophical journal.

Key Terms

validity
soundness
unsound
veracity
truth
practical syllogisms
factual premise
value premise
conclusion
role-exchange test
new cases test
logically consistent
universalizable
self-contradictory
consistency test
universalizability test
higher-order principle test
logical fallacies
ad hominem fallacy
straw man fallacy
circular reasoning
fallacy of begging the question
two wrongs fallacy
slippery slope fallacy
causal connection
fallacy of appealing to authority
red herring fallacy
fallacy of guilt by association

Progress Check 9.1

Instructions: Fill in the blanks with the appropriate responses listed below.

sound
role-exchange test
circular reasoning
straw man
logical fallacies
universalizability
ad hominem
value premise
irrational
new cases test
red herring
slippery slope
practical syllogisms
two wrongs fallacy
appealing to authority

1. _____ are comprised of a value premise, factual premise, and a conclusion.
2. _____ involve irrational thought processes intended to persuade, intimidate, and divert attention.
3. A valid argument with true premises and a necessary conclusion can be described as _____.
4. If the _____ of a valid practical syllogism is unacceptable, the conclusion that follows from it must be rejected.
5. When applying the _____ to a particular principle, one takes the position of the person or persons most disadvantaged by the application of the principle to see if it would be acceptable from that perspective.
6. A principle that is self-contradictory is _____ and unacceptable.
7. According to the _____ criterion, a principle must apply to everyone absolutely if it is to be considered moral.

8. According to the _____, if a principle is ethically acceptable in one set of circumstances, then it must be found to be acceptable in other similar sorts of circumstances.
9. If, during a debate, you attack your opponent and not your opponent's argument, then you commit the _____ fallacy.
10. If you assume at the outset of your argument that which you are trying to prove in the end, then you commit the fallacy of _____.
11. Justifying one wrong-doing by another wrong-doing is the definition of the _____ fallacy.
12. Justifying an ethical position by using majority opinion reflects the fallacy of _____.
13. If, instead of criticizing someone's actual argument, you attack a set-up version of it before rejecting your opponent's position, you commit the _____ fallacy.
14. If, when you are caught up in your own bad argument, you change it subtly and then try to advance your original position by defending a variation of it, you commit the _____ fallacy.
15. If one condemns an action by arguing that it will eventually lead to a series of other unwanted outcomes, which, in fact, is not necessarily the case, one commits the _____ fallacy.

Summary of Major Points

1. How are validity, truth, and soundness different?
   Validity refers to the form of an argument.
   Truth refers to factual premises and conclusions.
   Soundness refers to valid arguments having true premises leading to necessary and acceptable conclusions.
2. Must valid arguments be accepted?
   If a valid argument contains faulty premises, then it does not have to be accepted.
   If a valid argument contains acceptable premises and if the conclusion follows necessarily, then it is sound and therefore acceptable.
3. At what three levels can a practical syllogism be evaluated?
   (1) The level of conclusion: Does it follow from preceding premises?
   Is it true or highly probable?
   Is it justifiable?
   (2) The level of factual premise: Is it true or highly probable?
   Does it have empirical support?
   (3) The level of value premise: Does the value premise pass the four tests of adequacy?
4. What tests can be used to evaluate value premises?
   The tests are: the role-exchange test;
   the new cases test;
   the consistency and universalizability test; and
   the higher-order principle test.

5. What is a logical fallacy?
   A logical fallacy is: a rhetorical device;
   an irrational form of reasoning designed to persuade emotionally and psychologically, not rationally;
   used to divert attention and sometimes intimidate others; and
   used to win arguments.
6. What are some examples of logical fallacies?
   Examples are: *ad hominem*, straw man, circular reasoning/begging the question, two wrongs, slippery slope, appealing to authority, red herring, and guilt by association.

Source References and Related Readings

Cohen, Elliot D. *Making Value Judgements: Principles of Sound Reasoning*. Malabar, Fla.: Krieger Publishing Co., Inc., 1985.

Coombs, Jerrold, Leroi Daniels and Ian Wright. "Introduction to Value Reasoning" in *Prejudice: Teacher's Manual*. Value Reasoning Series. Toronto: The Ontario Institute for Studies in Education, 1978.

Falikowski, Anthony. *Mastering Human Relations*. Scarborough, Ont.: Prentice Hall Canada, 1996.

———. *Moral Philosophy: Theories, Skills, and Applications*. Upper Saddle River, N.J.: Prentice Hall, 1990.

Johnson, R.H. and J.A. Blair. *Logical Self-Defense*, 2nd edition. Toronto: McGraw-Hill Ryerson, 1983.

McDonald, Daniel. *The Language of Argument*, 4th edition. New York: Harper & Row Publishers, 1983.

Runkle, Gerald. *Good Thinking: An Introduction to Logic*, 2nd edition. New York: Holt, Rinehart & Winston, 1981.

Woodhouse, Mark. *A Preface to Philosophy*, 3rd edition. Belmont, Cal.: Wadsworth Publishing Co., 1984.

3

PART THREE

APPLYING ETHICS IN THE REAL WORLD

So far, on our travels into the moral domain, we have acquired a basic knowledge and understanding of three major ethical perspectives that have dominated western rational thought (i.e., Greek character-ethics, utilitarianism, and deontology). Also, we have learned to navigate our way through the dense fog of moral ambiguity by mastering some fundamental logical-analytical reasoning skills. With knowledge and skills at our disposal, we are now better prepared to put ethics into action, theory into practice and logic into service of philosophical critique and practical moral decision making. Although our journey has been a long and difficult one thus far, we are finally ready to apply ethics in the real world in a rational and informed way. In the following pages, we will look at a number of real-life problems and controversies arising out of the fields of business ethics, legal and societal ethics, biomedical ethics, sexual ethics, and global ethics. Our rational treatment of these issues will be facilitated by several different learning aids prepared especially for this section of the book.

Learning Aids for Part Three

Synopsis: A brief synopsis of each article is provided to help place the issues addressed into moral context. Each synopsis acts as a preview of what is to come.

Content Quiz: To make sure that you have understood and mastered the material within each reading, a "Content Quiz" is offered. The Content Quiz is essentially the same as the "Progress Check" with which you are already familiar. Rather than help you master theories and skills, as the Progress Checks were designed to do, the Content Quizzes are intended to help you verify your correct understanding of the readings comprising Part Three of the text. There is little point in agreeing or disagreeing with an author's point of view if you do not understand what was meant or if you misconstrue the intended purpose of the writer. If you fail to get most, or all, of the questions right, you can go over the reading again, ask your instructor for help or discuss the reading with fellow classmates to further your understanding.

Discussion Questions: As mentioned at the outset of this book, philosophy (i.e., philosophical ethics) is more a method of thinking than a body of knowledge. To facilitate the process of ethical argument and debate, discussion questions will be provided. They should stimulate thought and generate productive dialogue.

Argument Analysis Worksheet: A generic "Argument Analysis Worksheet" has been provided to facilitate thoughtful study and analysis of the arguments found in each of the readings. This analytical tool serves to fully integrate theories, skills, and applications. For practical purposes, you may wish to make enough copies of this worksheet for the actual number of readings you plan to cover in your course.

The Argument Analysis Worksheet can be used for writing critical papers or as a basis of classroom and tutorial discussion. Completion of the worksheet offers a structured and detailed format for analyzing ethical issues and moral arguments. The worksheet also helps to enhance understanding and appreciation of any author's position or thesis defense.

Instructors and students are at liberty, of course, to bypass the Argument Analysis Worksheet so discussions may be more spontaneous and open-ended. Informal discussions may be preferred. The worksheet simply provides one structured alternative you might find useful.

ARGUMENT ANALYSIS WORKSHEET

Reading: ______________________________

1. In general terms, what is the moral topic or issue addressed by this reading?

____

____

____

____

____

2. Specifically, what moral values, ideals or ethical principles are in conflict?

____

____

____

____

3. What position is taken by the author? What is the author's primary thesis?

____

____

____

____

4. List the major "factual claims" used by the author to defend the position taken.

   (a) ______________________________

   (b) ______________________________

   (c) ______________________________

5. How are the factual claims in the argument supported, if at all? What evidence is given? Are there any statistics, surveys, experiences, examples, empirical studies or processes of inductive logic used to justify the factual claims? Illustrate and explain. Is the support for the factual claims adequate? Why or why not?

____

____

____

____

____

____

____

6. Are the ethical principles, values or normative assumptions imbedded in the reading justifiable? Do they pass the tests of adequacy discussed in the book (e.g., role-exchange, new cases, higher-order principle, consistency, and universalizability)?

____

____

____

____

____

7. Is the logic valid? Are the arguments sound? Do the moral/ethical/logical conclusions follow from preceding premises?

____

____

____

____

8. Are any logical fallacies included in the argument? Do you find any diversionary tactics, emotional appeals or attempts to intimidate? If so, which ones (e.g., *ad hominem*, red herring)?

____

____

____

____

9. Is the moral position taken by the author adequately defended, given your earlier answers? What could strengthen the position? What is weakest about the position? Are you persuaded in the end by the author's arguments? Why or why not?

____

____

____

____

10. Finally, are the arguments presented more utilitarian, deontological or character-based? Does the writer stress results and consequences (utilitarianism), rights, duties and fairness (deontology) or matters of virtue, self-realization and personhood (Greek character-ethics)? Discuss.

____

____

____

____

CHAPTER TEN

10 BUSINESS ETHICS

PROFITS AND LIBERTY

John Hospers

Synopsis

In this article, John Hospers defends profits and profit making in a capitalist free-market economy. He begins by enumerating the advantages that profits and their allure bring to the market place. Hospers contends that profits and the prospect of increased wealth benefit not only the entrepreneur but also the consumer and worker.

Hospers considers criticisms of profit and profit making to be groundless and absurd. He contends that those criticizing profitmakers are ignorant of how a free-market economy really works. He also objects to the notion that wealth is somehow fixed or static and that the rich can become rich only by taking money or wealth from the poor. In short, Hospers' article represents an ethical justification for a profit-driven free-market economy.

"He's earning too much—take it away from him!" "A hundred thousand a year while some people in the world are hungry? Nobody ought to be allowed to earn that much!" Such remarks are made, and they have a "humanitarian" sound. Yet, as I shall try to show, they result from ignorance of the function of profits in an economy: and to the extent that the suggestion is followed, the result is poverty for everyone.

In a free economy—one in which wages, costs, and prices are left to the competitive market—profits have a very important function: they help to decide what products shall be made, of what kinds, and in what amounts. It is the hope of profits that leads people to make the products (or provide the services): if little or nothing can be made from producing them, or not enough to justify the risk of investing the capital, the product will not be made; but the more one hopes to make from it, the more people will bend over backwards to produce it. The hope of profits channels the factors of production, causing products to be made in whatever quantities the public demands. In a state-controlled economy, controlled by bureaucrats, nothing at all may be made of a certain product much in demand, because the ruling decision makers have decided simply not to make it; and at the same time, millions of other things that nobody wants may be produced again because of a bureaucratic decision. And the bureaucracy need not to respond to public demand. But in a free-enterprise economy, the producer who does not respond to public demand will soon find his warehouse full of unsalable products and his business bankrupt.

The hope of profits also makes for an enormous increase in the efficiency of production, for, other things being equal, the most efficient producer—the one who can cut out waste and motivate his workers to produce the most and best products—will earn the highest profits. And is there any reason why these profits should not be applauded? To the consumer, these profits mean that the industry producing the goods he wants is healthy and nicely functioning—one that can continue to deliver the goods, and probably for at least as low a price as its competitor, since otherwise more customers would have turned to the competitor. To the workers, profits of their employer mean that the employer is doing a good job for his customers—good enough so that they keep buying his product—and thus that they, the employees, are more secure in their jobs, and are more likely to receive higher wages in the future than are the employees of a company that is just barely making it. And as for the enterprisers, who can honestly say that they do not deserve the profits they received? First, they are risk-takers: they risked their capital to start the business, and had they lost no one would have helped them. Second, they spent not only their money (and borrowed money) on the enterprise, but, in most cases, years of their lives, involving planning, down to the last detail of production, the solution of intractable problems having to do with materials, supplies, and availability of trained help. Third, they anticipated the market, and did so more expertly than their competitors, for in order to make profits they had to have the right amount of merchandise at the right places for sale at the right time. Fourth, they provided the consumer a product or service (they could not *force* the consumer to buy from them; the consumer voluntarily elected to buy), in quantity—for a price, of course (after all his time and effort, should the enterpriser give it away, or sell it without receiving a return on it?), but nevertheless they provided it at a price which the consumer was willing to pay.

But the public, or a large segment of it, becomes envious and bitter, seeing that the man makes a profit. Perhaps the envious man has tried to start a business himself and lost it; or perhaps he just lost his job or can't pay some of his bills, and sees the employer living in a large luxurious house, in any case, he doesn't understand what side his bread is buttered on, for he doesn't realize that if the employer couldn't keep going, he himself would have no job. For whatever reason, he curses the employer because the man has a larger annual income than he does. Never mind that the employer took the risks, made the innumerable decisions (any one of which could have wrecked the business), and made *his* job possible in the first place: he, the employer, must be brought down to the worker's level. So he curses him, envies him, and votes for higher taxes for his employer, which, if passed, will mean that the employer won't expand his business and hire extra employees, and in fact may even have to cut it down some, even including his (the worker's) job. Officially, his line is that the employer's profits are ill-got. And yet when one examines it carefully the complaint is groundless and absurd.

Suppose that an enterprise can make a thousand dollars in profits by a certain amount of capital investment; let us call this amount of investment C. Suppose also there is a second enterprise, less efficiently run than the first, which can only make that same amount of profit by investing twice the capital—2C. People will then say that the first, the efficient, manager, is reaping an excessive profit. For on the same investment of capital he can make twice the profits as his sloppy competitor; and for this his profits are branded as "excessive." But this is absurd: the efficient producer who gets more profits has more money to convert into plant expansion, more reserve for research so that he can improve his product, more wherewithal to reduce consumer prices and still make a healthy profit, thus benefiting the consumer with lower costs. The consumer ought to be anxious to have the most efficient producer possible; for only in that way can he be sure of getting the best possible product at the lowest possible price. By producing efficiently, the producer can undercut his competitors and thus benefit the consumer, while at the same time earning larger profits by capturing a larger share of the market for himself. We should applaud, not condemn, efficient production.

Add to this the fact that our present insane tax laws penalize the producer for his profits, and thus penalize efficiency. "Taxing profits is tantamount to taxing success in best serving the public. . . . The smaller the input (of money) required for the production of an article becomes, the more of the scarce factors of production is left for the production of other articles. But the better an entrepreneur succeeds in this regard, the more he is vilified, and the more he is soaked by taxation. Increasing costs per unit of output, that is, waste, is praised as a virtue."[1]

> There would not be any profits but for the eagerness of the public to acquire the merchandise offered for sale by the successful entrepreneur. But the same people who scramble for these articles vilify the businessman and call his profit ill-got.
>
> One of the main functions of profits is to shift the control of capital to those who know how to employ it in the best possible way for the satisfaction of the public. The more profits a man earns, the greater his wealth consequently becomes, the more influential does he become in the conduct of business affairs. Profit and loss are the instruments by means of which the consumers pass the direction of production activities into the hands of those who are best fit to serve them. Whatever is undertaken to curtail or to confiscate profits, impairs this function. The result of such measures is to loosen the grip the consumers hold over the course of production. The economic machine becomes, from the point of view of the people, less efficient and less responsive.[2]

Many people are so envious of, and bitter against, the man who earns a large salary or makes large profits, that they are unable to stand back impartially and try to understand what the role of profit is in an economy, and how it tends to increase everyone's income, not merely that of the man who receives it.

The man who receives a salary of $100,000 a year from his company—why does he get it? If he rendered no service, or if the company gained $10,000 as a consequence of hiring him, they would never pay him the $100,000. If they did, their costs of production overhead would be that much higher and they would have to charge more for their product (thus causing consumers to buy another brand instead) or absorb the cost somewhere else. Even if the man saved them just $100,000 a year, it would be no gain to them—they would just break even with him. But if his services save them $1,000,000 a year, then paying him the $100,000 is well worth it—and they would gladly pay him more in order to keep him. People who begrudge him the salary should ask, "Am *I* ingenious enough to save the company over $100,000 a year, if it hired me?"

Now the man who does the employing: let us say that his business is successful and through the years he has become a millionaire. Special venom is reserved by the populace for such men, but this is entirely without justification. If he got a million a year as salary for some tax-supported office, or in graft from the taxpayers' money, then they would have a right to complain; for they would have to work that much harder to make up the difference. But if he gets a profit of a million a year *on the free market*, there is no cause for complaint. I may dislike the latest rock-and-roll singer who gets a million a year, but not one penny of his income comes out of my taxes; and on a free market I am in no way forced to buy (or listen to) his product. I can live in serene independence of his millions; I didn't pay a dime nonvoluntarily to put this money into his coffers. I may think the public foolish for buying nonnutritional cereals, thus making the company receive large profits, but this only prompts in me a reflection on the foolishness of much public taste: I do not have to buy the cereal nor contribute to the cereal company in any way. (In fact the shoe is on the other foot: the company, because of its large profits, pays extremely high taxes. Could it be that I pay less tax as a result?) Should I then support a campaign to force people by law *not* to buy the cereal, and thus decimate the company's profits? If I do this—and thus set a precedent against freedom of choice—the next year or the next decade, by the same token, by the same precedent I have set, someone may mount a successful campaign to force people by law not to buy whatever goods or service *I* produce. And if this happens, I shall deserve my fate, since I approved the principle of coercion in the first place. People should be free to make their own choices—which includes, of course, their own mistakes.

Instead of resenting it when individuals or companies make a million dollars, we should be happy. That million dollars means that there is a prosperous enterpriser who has created many jobs for people and bought equipment and so on (which in turn requires jobs to produce) to keep the product going. A million dollars made on the free market means that a great deal of money has filtered down to a very large number of people in the economy—and that a product is available at a competitive price, else the consumers would not have bought it in sufficient quantity to make our company its million. By contrast, a million dollars earned in government jobs means a million dollars milked from the taxpayer, which he could have spent in other ways.

> The future prosperity of everyone—including the needy—depends on *encouraging* persons to become millionaires; to build railroads, houses, and power plants; to develop television, plastics, and new uses for atomic power. The reason is simple: *No man in a free country can make a million dollars through the machinery of production without producing something that we common men want at prices we are willing to pay*. And no man will continue to produce something we want at a price we are willing to pay unless he has the *chance* to make a profit, to become rich—yes, even to become a millionaire.[3]

There is an old saying, "No one should have caviar until everyone has bread." This is, when one examines it, one of the most confused statements ever made, though it is easily mouthed and chanted and is useful for political campaigns. If the enterpriser were not permitted to have his caviar, he would have far less incentive (perhaps no incentive at all) to produce anything, with the result that in the end fewer people would have even bread. The correct slogan would be, "If no one were permitted to have caviar, finally not many people would have bread."

One of the prevailing impressions, which underlies many arguments in this area but seldom itself surfaces to the level of explicit argument, is that the riches of the rich are the cause of the poverty of the poor. The impression is one of a certain fixed quantity of wealth, and that if some persons have more, this must inevitably mean that others have less.

A little reflection is enough to refute this assertion. If there were only a fixed quantity of wealth, how is it that we have many hundreds of millionaires now, hundreds and even thousands of men with elaborate houses, cars, lands, and other possessions, whereas only a few kings and noblemen had anything like this in bygone ages? Where long ago only a comparative handful of people could live, at the borderline between existence and extinction, in a given area of land, today a thousand times that number live, and live so well that they need spend only 10 to 15 percent of their income on food and all the rest goes for other things, most of which were inconceivable to the population of centuries past.

What people do not comprehend is that wealth is not static, but *grows* as long as people are free to use their ingenuity to improve the quality of their life. Here are deposits of iron, lying in the ground century after century; they do no good to anyone as long as they are just lying there. Now someone devises an economical process for removing the iron from the ground; another devises a means for smelting it, and another for combining it with manganese and other metals to produce steel that can be used in buildings, railroad tracks, and countless other things. When all these factors of production are functioning and the steel is produced, the world's wealth has been increased. Consumers have something to use that they didn't have before, and workers have jobs that didn't exist before. Every party to the transaction is a gainer.

When ten men are adrift on a lifeboat and there is only a certain quantity of provisions, if one person takes more than his share it necessarily follows that others must have less. The example of the lifeboat, or something like it, seems to be the dominating image of those who think in this primitive way about wealth. They apparently believe that because some men are rich, others must therefore be poor, since the rich have taken it away from the poor. Now this *is* the case when a bandit takes away some of your possessions—he has more, and as a consequence you have less. Bandits do not create wealth, they only cause the same amount to change hands. The same happens when the tax-collector takes away by force some of what you have earned; the government too is not creative—it takes away from you to give to others. But the capitalist in a free society is *not* like that; he cannot force the money of you, the consumer, out of your hands; you pay him for a product or a service that did not exist, or did not exist as efficiently or in the same form, prior to his creative endeavor; his product (e.g., a car) or service (e.g., railroad transportation) is good enough in your eyes so that you voluntarily pay some of the money you have earned in exchange for it. The entrepreneur has brought something into being and offered it on the open market in exchange. He has created something new under the sun, which people may buy or not buy as they prefer.

No the world is not like a lifeboat. Wealth does increase, and it increases for all as a result of the efforts of a few creative men. The riches of the rich are not the cause of the poverty of the poor: the rich in a free enterprise society can become rich only (1) by hiring workers to produce something and (2) because these consumers on a free market choose to buy what the entrepreneur has offered. They are rich precisely *because* innumerable consumers have, through their purchases, voted for whatever product or service they have to offer. Not one penny of their income on the free market came from the taxed income of anyone else.

One would think that entrepreneurs were armed bandits robbing them by force, to hear the complainers talk, instead of the risk-takers who had the ideas, and, if things went right, benefited the public. But the fallacy persists; many well-meaning people, ignorant of how an economy functions, are trying their best to do them in. In a South American factory, agitated workers demanded a larger share of the profits, held meetings and finally burned down the factory. "That'll show the filthy profiteer!" they cried. And it is true that they had indeed done him in; his entire life's work and capital were burned to the ground in one night. But they too had lost: they were out of jobs—the jobs that the factory had provided no longer existed. Neither did the products that the factory had made, and consumers had that much less choice in deciding what to buy at the store.

Notes

1. Ludwig von Mises, *Planning for Freedom* (South Holland, IL: Libertarian Press, 1952), p. 121.
2. Ibid., pp. 122, 123.
3. Dean Russell, *Cliches of Socialism* (Irving-on-Hudson, NY: Foundation for Economic Education, 1970), p. 186.

Content Quiz 10.1

Instructions: Fill in the blanks with the appropriate responses listed below.

free-enterprise	success
filtered	state-controlled
poverty	riches
profits	lifeboat
static	caviar
risk-takers	choice

1. _____ help to determine what kinds of products will be made and in what amounts.
2. A _____ economy is, according to Hospers, less productive, efficient, and market-sensitive as compared with a _____ economy.
3. For Hospers, taxing profits is tantamount to taxing _____.

4. Instead of resenting prosperous millionaires, Hospers suggests that we applaud them because a million dollars made on the free market means that a lot of money has been _____ down to a very large number of people.
5. "No one should have _____ until everyone has bread" is described in the reading as one of the most confused statements ever made.
6. Hospers does not believe that the _____ of the rich are the cause of the _____ of the poor.
7. Wealth is not _____; it grows along with human ingenuity.
8. According to this reading, wealth is not like a _____ where, if one takes more than one's share of provisions, another must accept a lesser share.
9. Entrepreneurs are not bandits, but rather _____.
10. Supporting campaigns to force people by law to refrain from buying a certain product reduces profits and violates a person's freedom of _____.

Discussion Questions

1. Is there such a thing as a "just wage"? Can it be said that someone earns too much or too little? If so, what would be the basis of such a claim?
2. Are the products that consumers want always worth producing solely because of profit potential? Why?
3. Should the welfare and financial security of workers in our society rest solely on the employer's ability to earn a profit? Do employers have any responsibilities toward their workers? If so, what are they? If not, why not?
4. In a free-market economy, do some individuals start with an unfair advantage? Do profits always benefit the worker and consumer at large? Should average people consider themselves lucky that there are rich entrepreneurs? Explain.

BUSINESS ETHICS: PROFITS, UTILITIES, AND MORAL RIGHTS

Alan H. Goldman

Synopsis

In contrast to the previous article by John Hospers, who champions the capitalistic pursuit of profits, Alan H. Goldman is much more critical of it. In this reading, he examines the moral justifiability of the "profit maximization principle" in business. He puts forward the view that pursuing profits within legal limits is not always morally justifiable and that "moral rights" create boundaries or constraints within which profit making must occur if it is to be deemed acceptable. After addressing the issue of responsibilities to shareholders and delineating a number of utilitarian, consequentialist and efficiency-based arguments in favor of profit maximization, Goldman proceeds to offer his critique. He demonstrates that profit maximization is not always most efficient and that it does not always increase aggregate utility. Further, he argues that profit maximization for stockholders or even benefits for the majority of consumers cannot excuse violations of basic moral rights. So, while allowing for profit making, Goldman does not unconditionally endorse profit maximization.

I

Arguments in favor of the primacy of pursuit of profit generally begin by appealing to classic analyses of the role of profit in a purely competitive free-market system. In this situation, given fluid resources and labor, knowledge of prices and product quality, the pursuit of profit results in the most efficient collective use and development of economic resources. Businesspeople motivated by the prospect of profit, produce what has the greatest surplus of value to the public over cost. Public demand for a good or a service allows prices in that industry to rise. This attracts more producers to develop supplies or substitutes in order to satisfy that demand, until the marginal value of further production falls to that of other goods. At the same time goods or services are distributed to those whose demand, measured in terms of willingness to pay, is greatest. Thus pursuit of profit results in optimal allocation of resources, maximizing the value of economic output to society as a whole. Efficiency is achieved in satisfying demand at a given time, and increased productivity, through minimizing costs relative to output, is encouraged. This generates the economic progress necessary to social progress in satisfying needs and wants. Profits function in this system as incentives to investors or risk-takers and as rewards to firms that use economic resources more efficiently than others.

Thus, it is argued, pursuit of profit in a competitive situation best promotes aggregate social good. Profits measure the surplus of the value to society of goods produced over the value of resources taken from the social pool. If the primary social function of business is to achieve the most efficient allocation and use of resources for satisfying the wants of the public, then degree of profit measures degree of fulfillment of social responsibility.[1] When competition reduces costs, reduces prices relative to costs, and attracts resources to satisfy demand, the market gives the public what it wants most efficiently. Aggregate created wealth is maximized and distributed to those with greatest dollar demand. Pursuit of goals other than maximizing profits will hinder the economic enterprise vital to self-defined aggregate social welfare. Profits of course benefit stockholders and executives, but if pursuit of profit is at the same time pursuit of maximum value to the public, then managers should be wary of the call to sacrifice self-interest to other values.

This defense of placing profit first is thoroughly utilitarian: it provides maximum satisfaction of aggregate demand or wants. But it can also be argued that pursuit of profit in a free market honors rights of free producers and consumers. Fewer rights will be violated in this system than in alternative economies, since here goods will be produced and distributed through a series of voluntary transactions. Partners enter contractual relations only when they view the transactions as benefiting them. Selling an item for a profit extends alternatives to consumers rather than restricting freedoms or rights. In order to make a profit, a business must offer an alternative at least as attractive as others will offer to prospective buyers. Free agreements for mutual benefit will violate rights of neither party (assuming that no fraud is involved). But if the businessperson tries to place other values over the maximization of profit, he may in effect diminish alternatives and force consumers to pay for products or features of products they might not want or be willing to pay for given the choice. Thus aiming at profits in a free competitive market maximizes satisfaction of wants as well as the possibilities for free transactions. If maximizing alternatives in order to satisfy the demands of consumers maximizes the range of their free choices, then this free economic system appears to be justified in terms of freedom and satisfaction of rights as well as in terms of greatest utility.

The substitution of the values of the business manager for those of the public, expressed through demand as this creates opportunities for profit, appears to limit the choices of consumers and stockholders. Consider, first, arguments on the relative authority of managers and stockholders. As Milton Friedman points out, managers are employees of stockholders; they are entrusted with their money for the express purpose of earning a return on it. But if they sacrifice profits in order to aid what they perceive to be moral or social causes—for example, by contributing to charity or by exceeding legal requirements for safety or anti-pollution devices not demanded by consumers—then they are in effect taxing stockholders without authority to do so.[2] A business manager whose direct application of personally held moral principles makes a difference to a decision is spending the money of other persons, money that is not his own, in a way that these other persons would not choose to spend it. The organization then operates as an extra-governmental institution for selective taxation and public spending. But these functions are better left to the real government. Restraints on private actions to promote the public good should be generated through the political process, embodying principles of majority rule and proper checks and balances. Public officials can be controlled by the electorate and endowed with the resources to determine properly the effects of taxation and public spending upon the general welfare. Businesspeople lack the same restraints; they are not appointed on the basis of their ability to tax and spend for social welfare. The morally zealous manager assumes power without the accountability of the electoral process. He also is likely to lack the expertise to judge accurately the effects of his presumed moral sacrifice of profits.

Piecemeal decisions of individual managers cannot be based upon accurate prediction of cumulative effects on the economy or on consumer choice. Decisions that negatively affect profits will hurt stockholders, may hurt employees in terms of wages or jobs, may misallocate resources away from production with maximum public value, and may be cumulatively damaging to the economy. The point here is that the individual manager is not in a position, as the well advised government official presumably is, to assess these cumulative effects. Thus there are good reasons why corporate owners or stockholders do not trust executives to spend their money in accord with personal moral judgments, why they trust them only to maximize returns through most efficient allocation of resources. Other uses of corporate assets, which may be inconsistent with the values of those who own the assets, is a violation of that trust and exceeds the legitimate delegated authority of executives. Or so argues Friedman.

Consider next the argument that claims that managerial decisions which sacrifice prospective profits limit consumer choice. When managers seek to maximize profits by maximally satisfying consumer demand, they allow the public to impose its own values upon business through the market mechanism. When competition exists, consumers need not buy from firms considered to violate the public interest or legitimate moral constraints. Certainly they will not buy products from which they expect harm to exceed benefit to themselves. The market, as reflected in potential profits, appears to be a more sensitive mechanism for satisfying a diverse set of values and preferences than either imposition of managerial values and moral opinions or centralized political decision, even if democratically determined.[3] The reason is that the values of any sizeable minority, even if very small relative to the entire population, can create a potential profit for some astute businessperson. But these values may not match those independently held by business managers, and the minority may not be sizeable or well organized enough to affect centralized decisions of government. An argument for deviating from the profit motive therefore must be an argument for imposing the independent judgments of business managers upon the consuming public, for substituting the values of the former small minority for those of all the various segments of the majority.

Turning more specifically to moral constraints, if a significant segment of the population considers a given moral norm important, the market should operate to impose that norm upon business, or at least to make it worthwhile for some business to accept or operate within its constraints.[4] The public's own values are built into the market structure via consumer demand. But if business managers seek to substitute their own moral judgments for the operation of the market—say by adding to a new line of automobiles safety features for which there is no demand rather than more lush interiors for which there is a demand—they either coerce the public into paying for what it would not want given the choice, or else lose out to the competition that provides what the public does want. Once again the managers will have exceeded the authority delegated to them by the public to use resources efficiently to satisfy expressed wants, and that delegated by stockholders to compete for returns on their funds.

The case is totally different when moral commitment contributes to long-range profit by according with the public's values as expressed through the market or as imposed by law. Safety or antipollution devices required by law or for which the public is willing to pay, contribution to programs that improve the community environment and thereby improve employee morale or create effective public relations can all be justified in the name of long-run profit maximization. Here there is no limitation of public choice or taxation of stockholders. The businessperson stays within proper bounds as long as he accepts the public's values, as expressed through projected demand curves, rather than imposing his own. It is not a question of business managers having a license to be grossly immoral or harmful to consumers. Certainly no serious moral argument could support such license. It is a question only of whose opinion regarding satisfying wants and needs, realizing values, and honoring free choice should prevail—that of the business manager or that of the consuming public. The manager is under moral restraint to subordinate his opinion of what has maximum value to the opinion of the public as expressed through the market. But this restraint is equivalent to the demand to aim first at maximum long-range profits for his corporation. Harmful products or practices may increase short-term profits if they cut costs, but since they generate bad publicity, they are unlikely to be profitable in the long run. Given this moral constraint of the competitive market itself, the primary criterion for business decision must remain profitability, if business is to serve its vital social function rather than usurp that of government or individual free choice.

The argument on sacrificing profits by failing to set prices at maximal profit levels, say from the commendable desire not to contribute to inflation, is somewhat different from that on product features. In the case of prices, by failing to charge full value, the manager may fail to distribute his goods according to greatest demand, and, more importantly, he will encourage overconsumption in the present, create greater shortages of supplies in the future, and fail to encourage the development of more supplies or substitutes to meet real future demand. Thus, once again, well-intentioned sacrifices on the part of managers can have unintended and unfortunate economic effects, effects that derive from failure to conform to market forces.

In this set of arguments for the moral primacy of the profit principle in business, there is a final point suggested earlier that requires some expansion. A single firm or its managers that sacrifices profits to a moral norm is unlikely, in a competitive situation, to succeed in imposing the moral norm. Suppose, for example, that an executive in the automobile industry is convinced, and is objectively correct, that safety in cars is more important than glamour, comfort, or speed, but that cost-benefit market analysis clearly reveals that consumers are not (up to a certain degree—it is always a question of how much safety at what cost). The competition is ready to cater to the public's demand, even though consumer preference reflects only carelessness, ignorance, or failure to apply probabilities. If, under these circumstances, the executive strays too far from consumer preference or the pursuit of profit, he will not succeed in protecting the true public interest. First of all, it is always problematic to assume that interests of others vary from their preferences. In this case it might not be uncontroversially irrational for people to take risks by sacrificing some degree of safety for other values. But the thrust of the final consequentialist argument is independent of the validity of this assumption in particular cases. When consumers can buy from firms that give them what they freely choose to pay for, the firm that attempts to limit their choices by imposing its own values will simply lose out to the competition.

If opposed by consumer preference, a manager's personal moral norm may fail to take effect, and his attempt to impose it may well cause him to be replaced by the stockholders or cause his firm to become bankrupt. Then he will have sacrificed not only his own interest and that of his family without positive effect but also that of his employees and the segment of his community dependent on the position of his corporation. Actions that result in so much more harm than benefit are morally suspect even if well intentioned. The imposition of special norms, such as the pursuit of profit principle, that prevent such actions are then supported.

The converse of this argument also seems to follow. That is, the degree to which managers can afford to sacrifice profits to personal moral constraints indicates an unhealthy lack of competition in the industry in question. The luxury of abandoning the profit principle exists only for those who have somehow limited the entry of competitors who will aim to satisfy the public's values and demands.[5]

Thus, to the degree that competition for profits exists, the attempt by business managers to impose their own moral principles at the expense of profits is unlikely to succeed in affecting what the public buys, but is likely to produce unintended harm to those dependent on their firms. To the degree that managers can succeed in making stockholders and consumers pay for the moral scruples of their firms, they will have exceeded their legitimate delegated authority to give the public what it wants efficiently, and this will indicate an economic fault in their industry. Business should then aim to satisfy the moral demands of the public as these are imposed by law and reflected in long-range profit potential. But their authority to act directly on personal values in managerial decisions should be limited by the profit principle itself.

This completes the initial case for strong role-differentiation in business according to the primacy of profit principle. Subsequent sections will attempt to expose its weaknesses.

II

The arguments outlined above can be attacked initially by showing that profit maximization need not be efficient or maximize satisfaction of consumer wants. To the extent that maximum profits do not guarantee maximal aggregate utility to the public, the norm of profit maximization lacks even purely utilitarian justification. Counterarguments often begin by pointing out that the rider attached to the initial premise regarding market conditions is never perfectly satisfied in practice. Profit maximization is maximally efficient to the public only when conditions are purely competitive (when each firm is too small to influence prices in the industry single-handedly or to exclude other firms) and when consumers have perfect knowledge of product features, defects, prices, and alternative products. Lack of alternatives under more monopolistic conditions render business decisions inherently coercive in determining what the public must pay for features of products that may be more or less essential. Size generates power over consumers that must be countered by acceptance of moral restraints. To the degree that the market in a particular industry is noncompetitive, profits might be maximized by lowering quality while raising prices. Business managers in such industries must therefore recognize moral responsibility to the public as a reason for not doing so.

Second, as technological sophistication of products increases, public knowledge of their features decreases. To the degree that businesses can succeed in hiding from the public defects that would be costly to remedy, they can maximize profits at the expense of consumers. It is not always a matter of outright lying or fraud—few businesses would be expected to pay for publicizing every conceivable malfunction or accident involving their products. When relatively few consumers may be harmed by a defect, when consumption of the product is geographically widespread and knowledge of such harm is unlikely to influence consumption greatly, cost-benefit analysis might well call for ignoring the defect in order to maximize profit. If harm to the few is likely to be serious, then ignoring the defect is morally objectionable. In this case, the moral restraint necessary to protect the consuming public is not compatible with profit maximization.

Third, social costs or harm to the public does not always figure in producers' costs or in projected demand for products. Direct harm from products themselves might be expected to influence demand for them (although, as argued in the previous paragraph, not always enough to make it profitable to prevent it); but harm from a production process that does not attach to the product may not influence demand at all. Pollution and waste disposal fall into this category. If such harms are imposed upon neighborhoods in which production is located and not internalized as costs to producers, then production is not maximally efficient to the public. Resources will be overused in relation to net value when full costs are not figured in potential profits. Some restraint, then, on the part of business on moral grounds in the way of refraining from polluting the environment or imposing other neighborhood costs will be a move toward more efficiency to the public. It might nevertheless not be profit maximizing, since consumers far removed from the neighborhood of production will be unlikely to choose products on the normal basis of whether or not neighborhood costs are imposed by the producer. Again we see a gap between profit maximization and public utility, a gap that could be filled by direct acceptance of responsibility for avoiding harm to the public, even at the expense of profits.

Fourth, even creating maximum value in terms of satisfying net dollar demand when social costs are figured will not necessarily create maximum aggregate utility to the public. The reason is that dollar demand is as much a function of the existent distribution of wealth and income as it is a reflection of intensity of wants or needs for the goods in question. Distributing goods to those most willing to pay for them is not necessarily distributing them to those who want or need them most. Thus their distribution does not maximize aggregate utility or satisfaction, unless wealth is distributed equally or the effect of inequalities upon willingness to pay is negligible. For major necessities, unequal distribution will affect not only willingness, but ability to pay. If there is not enough decent housing or medical care to go around, for example, distributing them via a free market will not maximize satisfaction of want, need, or value—that is, it will not maximize aggregate utility. Those willing or able to pay most will not be those with greatest housing or medical needs. Rights aside, considerations of utility alone would not justify such a method of distribution. If prices are permitted to rise to what the market can bear, important needs and wants, indeed often those most vital and intensely felt, will go unsatisfied. There are many who cannot express their demands through the market. In areas of public decision making we certainly would not consider it fair to allocate votes according to wealth. Why should we think it fair to allow production and distribution of economic goods to be determined by a system of voting with dollars? Once more, moral restraint in setting prices on the part of producers of necessities, and, in the case of services, on the part of professionals, seems necessary not only to protect rights to necessities, but to maximize utilities by distributing goods to those who need them most or would benefit most from them.

Fifth, there is the problem of the relation of consumer preferences to true interest and needs. In section 1, I argued that opposing preferences expressed through the market to a different conception of interests is often as problematic and objectionable as unwarranted paternalism. But, as Galbraith has argued, when honoring preferences does not seem to lead to long-range satisfaction or happiness, they become suspect as being largely created by those who benefit from satisfying them.[6] The satisfaction of wants is utility-maximizing when the wants are given and represent disutilities when unsatisfied. But if the process in question includes creation of the wants themselves, and if their satisfaction results in greater wants or in other harmful side effects, then the whole process may be objectionable from a utilitarian point of view. As the ancient Greeks realized, contentment may be easier to achieve by eliminating superfluous desires than by creating and attempting to satisfy them.

Certainly for many businesses the goal of profit maximization requires the creation of demand as much as its satisfaction. Advertising and salesmanship are not merely informative. The fact that a certain set of desires is created by those who then attempt to satisfy them is not in itself grounds for condemning the desires or the process that creates them. Such cycles are as characteristic of desires for the most exalted aesthetic experience—appreciation of fine opera, for example—as they are of desires for electric gadgets or tobacco?[7] But this shows only that Galbraith's argument is incomplete, not that it is enthymemically unsound. When we have an independent criterion for wants worth fulfilling, then processes can be condemned which create those that fail to satisfy this criterion. One weak criterion that can be adopted from a want-regarding or utilitarian moral theory relates to whether satisfaction of the desires in question increases overall satisfaction in the long run, whether it contributes to a fulfilled or worthwhile life. Desires are irrational when their satisfaction is incompatible with more fundamental or long-range preferences, either because of harmful side effects or because of the creation of more unsatisfied desires. Alcoholism is an example of such irrational desire, the satisfaction of which is harmful overall. Processes that create and feed such desires are not utility-maximizing, since even the satisfaction of these desires lowers the subject's general level of utility. The pursuit of profit might well encourage the creation of such wants, especially desires for quickly consumable products. When this occurs, the appearance of efficiency masks a deeper utilitarian inefficiency. The profit motive contributes more to negative than positive utility, creating more unsatisfied than satisfied wants.

It has been argued also against Galbraith that most people are not so influenced by advertisement. They learn to be distrustful of claims made in ads and take them with a grain of salt. But while it is true that consumers become resistant to specific product claims of advertisers, it is not at all so clear that they can easily resist the total life style that bombards them constantly in subtle and not so subtle ways in ads for beer, cars, perfume, clothes, and whatever else can be conspicuously consumed.[8] The desire for this life style may in turn influence particular desires for products or features of products that are irrational and would not arise without this continuous programming. Consumers may desire flashy and fast automobiles more strongly than safe ones; but this may be only because safety cannot be conspicuously consumed or because it does not provide the kind of dashing sexual allure that car advertisers attempt to project onto their products. If this preference is suspect in itself, it certainly appears more so when we recognize its source. In some industries there is a natural lack of rational restraint on the part of consumers of which those out for maximum profits can take advantage, for example in the funeral or health-care industries. In others, consumers can be influenced to view certain products as symbols of a glamorous life style and desire them on those grounds. Furthermore, the encouragement of a life style of super consumption by numerous advertisers probably results in overproduction of consumable products and underutilization of resources for public goods that are not advertised, not conspicuously consumed, and less immediately enjoyed—for example clean air, water, and soil, quality schools, and so on. The congruence between free-market outcome and aggregate utility or social good is once more suspect.

Thus the pursuit of profit is efficient to the public only if it operates under certain moral constraints. It is not efficient or utility-maximizing if it results in elimination of competition and hence of alternatives for consumers, in deception regarding product defects, imposition of neighborhood social costs, the creation and exploitation of irrational desires, or the neglect of needs and wants to those unable to express demand from lack of wealth.[9] And it is likely to result in all of these if maximization of profits is accepted as the principal norm of business ethics. We have also countered the claim (suggested early in the first section) that immorality in business is never profit maximizing in the long run. Certain immoral practices of a business will hurt its profits, since they will outrage the public, make consumers wary of the products of that business, and reduce demand for those products. Other objectionable practices, such as dishonesty toward suppliers or total callousness toward employees, will be damaging to the production process. The market does impose some moral constraints. But other practices—such as retaining defects in products while hiding them from the public (which is sometimes possible), inadequately servicing products, bribing officials or wholesale buyers, polluting and dumping wastes, or creating desires for harmful products—might maximize profits while being inefficient to the consuming public.

Still other practices might be both profit maximizing and efficient in relation to consumers and yet morally questionable. This would be the case if a product was desired (or desired at low cost) by many and yet extremely harmful to relatively few. Nuclear power plants or glamorous, yet potentially dangerous, automobiles might be examples. In the former case, aggregate utility might be maximized through cheap production of electricity, given enough customers who benefit, but is it justified to allow considerations of aggregate utility to outweigh the shortened lives of a few plant workers or neighborhood residents? Another example in this category relates to work and working conditions. Total exploitation of workers, even if possible, might not be profit maximizing, since production suffers when employee morale is low. But, as Henry Ford discovered long ago, productivity does not vary always with the meaningfulness of work; in fact, in certain contexts it may vary inversely with the interest and possibility for self-realization in work. Nor is consumer demand linked to these variables in working conditions. Profit maximization and efficiency may sometimes call for reducing work to series of simple menial tasks. But the quality of a people's lives depends substantially upon the type of work they do and their interest in it. Thus we may ask on moral grounds whether gains in efficiency or aggregate utility (up to a certain point), as signaled by increased profit potential, justify reducing work to a menial and dehumanizing level. Numerous other examples in this category involving workers or neighborhoods of production could be produced: questions such as the firing of longtime employees, or the relocation of businesses, in which profit maximization and even aggregate social utility might not be morally decisive.

This last category of immorality that is potentially profit maximizing takes the argument to a new level. Prior paragraphs argued within a utilitarian moral framework: the point was to show how profit maximization may not be efficient in the deeper sense of utility maximization. But the cases just cited appeal to the notion of moral rights as opposed to aggregate utilities. For our purposes we may define a right as a moral claim to a good that overrides considerations of utility.[10] The fact that others might benefit more than I from my property does not justify transferring it to them against my wishes. In the first section, the proponent of profit maximization argues that pursuit of profit in a free competitive market results in maximum efficiency—that is, in optimal allocation of resources for satisfying aggregate demand at least overall cost—and also honors rights and preserves freedoms by extending opportunities for free transactions. One who makes this claim might also argue against some of the initial utilitarian arguments in this section by appealing to rights. The argument that unsatisfied wants and low utility from distribution by demand are results of unequal wealth would be countered by appeal to an individual's right to keep or spend what he or she earns and to be rewarded in relation to productivity, which is more nearly approximated in a profit-oriented free market than in other economies.

But appeal to a plausible full theory of rights undoubtedly favors counterarguments to the profit maximization principles. To the argument that business managers have no right to impose their moral opinions on the majority of consumers or upon stockholders, it can be replied that the majority has no right to maximal utility or the stockholders to maximal profits resulting from violation of the moral rights of even a small minority. Suppose the market reveals aggregate public preference for cheap electricity. Even if the majority of consumers are willing to take the risks involved in generating electricity by unsafe nuclear reactors, do they have a right to impose the risks and resulting severe harms on those who are unwilling to accept them? (The case is different if all are willing to take the risks and are equally exposed to them, or if those unwilling are able to avoid them without undue hardship.) The market reveals the preferences of consumers (sometimes based on ignorance or deception), as well as their willingness to pay for protection of rights of others. But whether rights ought to be honored does not depend upon the willingness of the majority to bear the sacrifices of honoring them. When buying goods, most consumers are not concerned with whether processes involved in their production impose severe harms or violate rights of others. But the effect of moral norms upon consumer demand is not a measure of the obligations they impose, nor even of their acknowledgment by individuals outside their roles as consumers. The business manager does not have the right to make decisions or retain products or processes that maim, poison, severely deprive, or contaminate even a few individuals unwilling to take such risks in the name of efficiency to the public or profits to stockholders. In general one cannot morally do for others what they would be morally unjustified in doing for themselves.

It is not sufficient that business internalize costs imposed upon the community or compensate victims harmed by their products or processes. This might be sufficient in cases like that of strip mining, where the costs of restoring land can be assigned to coal producers, but not when rights of persons against serious harm or risk are involved. The user of the asbestos-filled hair dryer or the driver of the Pinto that explodes or the infant deformed by chemical waste may not be willing to be harmed and then compensated. Rights are violated precisely when the harms imposed are so severe that we do not allow additions of lesser utilities to override. While rights cannot be overridden by aggregate utility, they can be and sometimes are overridden by other rights. Thus at certain stages of economic development, when scarcity is still the rule and the means for survival of many people depends upon further growth, expansion of gross output spurred by the profit motive may be a reasonable social goal. But in such a case, rights to survival and satisfaction of basic needs are at stake, not utility or efficiency.[11] At later stages of relative abundance, as in our society, whatever efficiency is generated by maximization of profits cannot excuse violations of moral rights in the process. The rights and freedoms exemplified in free-market exchange are only a small subclass of those potentially at stake in economic transactions and decisions.[12] If there are, in addition to rights to earn and spend money as one chooses, negative rights not to be severely harmed and positive rights to have basic needs fulfilled, then the latter will not be adequately protected by free-market exchange when businessmen place profits first.

The profit-maximization principle, then, does not appear to be morally justifiable, except within ordinary moral constraints of honoring rights. It is not a question of business managers imposing purely subjective opinions upon a majority who hold contrary opinions. When moral rights of the kind I have mentioned are violated, the harms imposed are severe. Such cases are relatively easy to identify. When the profit-principle blinder is removed from the eyes of business executives, when consumers outside their roles as consumers are asked, they do not try to justify the imposition of such harms in the name of profit or efficiency. Indeed it is plausible to suppose that neither the public nor the majority of businesspersons approve of the maximization of profit principle, not because they are confused about the operation of a free market or ignorant of its virtues, but because a theory of moral rights of the type I am discussing captures significant aspects of commonsense moral consciousness. Rights against being harmed and to satisfaction of basic needs are seen to override considerations of efficiency or utility. When this theory is taken into account, the position of business manager does not appear to be strongly role-differentiated: profits cannot be placed above moral rights that impose constraints in all areas of nonprofessional behavior as well.

Notes

1. Compare David Novick, "Cost-Benefit Analysis and Social Responsibility," *Social Issues in Business*, ed. F. Luthans and R. M. Hodgetts (New York, 1976), pp. 561–573.
2. See Milton Friedman, "The Social Responsibility of Business Is to Increase Its Profits," *Ethical Issues in Business*, ed. T. Donaldson and P. H. Werhane (Englewood Cliffs, NJ, 1979), pp. 191–197; see also his *Capitalism and Freedom* (Chicago, 1962), pp. 133–136.
3. Friedman, *Capitalism and Freedom*, p. 94.
4. Compare Joseph A. Pichler, "Capitalism in America," *Ethics, Free Enterprise, and Public Policy*, ed. R. T. De George and Joseph A. Pichler (New York, 1978), pp. 19–39.

5. See Charles F. Phillips, Jr., "What Is Wrong with Profit Maximization?" in *Issues in Business and Society*, ed. W. T. Greenwood (Boston, 1977), pp. 77–88.
6. See John Kenneth Galbraith, *The Affluent Society* (Boston, 1958), chap. 2.
7. For this reply to Galbraith, see F. A. von Hayek, "The Non Sequitur of the 'Dependence Effect,'" in *Ethical Theory and Business*, ed. Tom Beauchamp and Norman Bowie (Englewood Cliffs, NJ, 1979), pp. 508–512.
8. Compare John I. Coppett, "Consumerism from a Behavioral Perspective," in *Social Issues in Business*, pp. 444–454.
9. See also Thomas M. Garrett, *Business Ethics* (Englewood Cliffs, NJ, 1966), pp. 25, 144.
10. For expansion on this definition and defense of the claim that rights always override utilities, see Alan Goldman, "Rights, Utilities and Contracts," *Canadian Journal of Philosophy* 3 (sup. vol., 1977): 121–135.
11. Compare Robert Hay and Ed Gray, "Social Responsibilities of Business Managers," in *Social Issues in Business*, pp. 104–113.
12. See Peter Singer, "Rights and the Market," *Justice and Economic Distribution*, ed. John Arthur and W. H. Shaw (Englewood Cliffs, NJ, 1978), pp. 207–221; also Alan H. Goldman, "The Entitlement Theory of Distributive Justice," *The Journal of Philosophy* 73 (1976): 823–835.

Content Quiz 10.2

Instructions: Fill in the blanks with the appropriate responses listed below.

utilitarian	opinions
rights	distribution
efficient	responsibility
choice	competitive
constraints	unfortunate effects

1. Allowing the profit maximization principle to operate in the market place will, presumably, extend consumer _____.
2. The _____ of wealth in a society where inequities exist will not facilitate maximum aggregate utility through profit maximization in the market place.
3. We need moral restraint in setting prices not only to protect people's _____ to necessities but also to maximize utilities by distributing goods to those who need them most or would benefit most from them.
4. Many business managers believe that stockholders are their primary _____.
5. Well-intentioned managers who allow their personal moral opinions to influence business decisions may find that, as a product of their efforts, a number of _____ result.
6. Arguments that justify the application of the principle of profit maximization by referring to its efficient collective use and development of economic resources are _____.

7. According to Goldman, moral _____ involving rights override the profit maximization principle.
8. It could be argued that business managers should not impose their personal moral _____ in business-related matters.
9. Where profit maximization rules, some would argue the market place is most _____.
10. Goldman rejects the claim that profit maximization will always lead to the most _____ use of resources.

Discussion Questions

1. Is making a profit simply a matter of business, or, can it somehow relate to issues of morality? Explain.
2. What are some of the perceived disadvantages of allowing business managers to have their personal moral beliefs and values enter into decisions regarding profit maximization?
3. Can you find examples in the reading that show how profit maximization may not always be most efficient?
4. What objection can be raised to the claim that the public's moral norms will operate in the market place? What factors could diminish the moral influence of consumers upon producers and price setters?
5. How is society's distribution of wealth related to the ethical justifiability of profit maximization?
6. Does business simply satisfy consumer wants or does it create them? Are the wants that are satisfied or created always good and worth satisfying or creating? Explain.
7. What objections could be raised to the claim that satisfying the majority's wants justifies profit maximization?

ADVERTISING AND CORPORATE ETHICS

Vincent Barry

Synopsis

This reading by Vincent Barry deals with the morality of advertising. In it, Barry examines the ethical implications of using certain advertising tactics and methods of persuasion. He points out that moral conflicts frequently arise between advertising's informative and persuasive functions. He claims that corporations often use puffery and deception to increase sales at the expense of bona fide *consumer education about particular products and services being offered. According to Barry, by using morally questionable strategies, advertisers violate their obligation to provide clear, honest information and, as a result, create situations of potential harm to consumers.*

Most moral issues related to advertising exist because of a conflict between its informative and persuasive functions. On the one hand, advertising functions to provide consumers information about the goods and services available to them. On the other hand, it serves to persuade them to purchase one product rather than another. These two functions are not always compatible. In an attempt to persuade, advertisers often obfuscate, misrepresent, or even lie. Moral issues arise when, in an attempt to persuade, advertisers are ambiguous, conceal facts, exaggerate, or employ psychological appeals. . . .

Ambiguity. When ads are ambiguous, they can be deceiving. Suppose, for example, a government study found that Grit filter cigarettes were lower in tar and nicotine than their filter-tip competitors. As part of its advertising, Grit claims, "Government Supported Grit Filters." *Supported* here is ambiguous. It can not only mean that government research supports Grit's claim that it's lower in tar and nicotine than its competitors but also that the government endorses the use of Grit. The Continental Baking Company was charged with such ambiguity by the Federal Trade Commission (FTC). In advertising its Profile Bread, Continental implied that eating the bread would lead to weight loss. The fact was that Profile had about the same number of calories per ounce as other breads but each slice contained seven fewer calories only because it was sliced thinner than most breads. Continental issued a corrective advertisement.

In all aspects of advertising, much potential moral danger lies in the interpretation. The Profile ad is a good example. A large number of people interpreted that ad to mean that eating Profile Bread would lead to a weight loss.[1] Likewise, for years consumers have inferred from its advertisements that Listerine mouthwash effectively fought bacteria and sore throats. Not so; in 1978 the FTC ordered Listerine to run a multimillion-dollar disclaimer. In such cases, advertisers and manufacturers invariably deny intending the inference that consumers draw. But sometimes the ad is so ambiguous that a reasonable person couldn't infer anything else. Thus, when a cold tablet advertises, "At the first sign of a cold or flu—Coricidin," what is the consumer likely to think? The fact is that neither Coricidin nor any other cold remedy can cure the common cold. At best it can only provide temporary symptomatic relief. But a consumer is left to draw his or her own conclusion, and it's likely to be the wrong one.

A striking example of this "open-to-interpretation" aspect of ambiguity can be seen in the battle over a seemingly harmless topic—buying a tire. Uniroyal advises consumers to buy the numbers: use the numbers and letter molded into the sidewalls under a federally mandated tire-grading system to select the best tire value. Goodyear counters that the numbers are misleading and that the only reliable way to buy a tire is by brand name and dealer recommendations. (It is hardly any coincidence, of course, that Uniroyal has the highest tread-wear number on its first-line radials, those supplied to auto dealers; and Goodyear has the best-known brand, the biggest advertising budget, and the most stores and dealers.)

The dispute is long-standing. In the mid-sixties the government responded to concern about quality and safety by proposing a quality grading system. Producers fought tire grading for over ten years, but a 1979 court decision forced them to start using grade labels. Under the law, each manufacturer can grade its own tires, and the government randomly checks to see that the tires measure up to the ratings. Although grading began with the bias-ply tires, in 1980 tire makers also had to begin putting separate A, B, or C grade ratings on radials for traction and ability to withstand heat buildup from high-speed driving. In response, tire makers simply put on a number to indicate expected wear and left it at that.

But early in 1981 Uniroyal, which had rated its "Steeler" at 220 (indicating 66,000 miles of useful life[2]), started advertising that its Steelers were better than Goodyear's Custom Polysteel, which had been rated at 170 (51,000 miles), and other competing brands. As a result, Goodyear, Firestone Tire and Rubber, B. F. Goodrich, and General Tire were put in the ludicrous position of having to convince tire dealers and motorists that their grade ratings were really meaningless, and that no one should take them seriously.

Each of these companies insisted that the test results on which the ratings were based are so variable that they are not reliable. Goodyear, for example, said tests on its Polysteel tires ranged from 160 to 420, with a 13-inch size ranking the lowest. Goodyear therefore assigned a grade of 160 for 13-inch tires and 170 for 14- and 15-inch sizes to assure that all tires met the grade. Fair or not, Goodyear began running ads declaring that, in comparative tests, its Custom Polysteel Tires averaged 229 and 329 ratings in 14- and 15-inch sizes, higher than the 250 and 277 averaged for Uniroyal's Steelers. For its part, Uniroyal insisted that the records of the tests they had run showed that the Goodyear tires didn't test as well as the Steelers.

What, then, does a tire grade mean? What kind of information does it provide the consumer? You be the judge.

Aiding and abetting ambiguity in ads is the use of "weasel" words, words used to evade or retreat from a direct or forthright statement or position. Consider the weasel *help*. *Help* means "aid" or "assist" and nothing else. Yet, as one author has observed, "'help' is the one single word which, in all the annals of advertising, has done the most to say something that couldn't be said."[3] Because the word *help* is used to qualify, once it's used almost anything can be said after it. Thus, we're exposed to ads for products that "help us keep young," "help prevent cavities," "help keep our houses germ-free." Consider for a moment how many times a day you hear or read phrases like these: "helps stop," "helps prevent," "helps fight," "helps overcome," "helps you feel," "helps you look." And, of course, *help* is hardly the only weasel. "Like," "virtual" or "virtually," "can be," "up to" (as in "provides relief *up to* eight hours"), "as much as" (as in "saves *as much as* one gallon of gas"), and numerous other weasels function to say what can't be said.

That ads are open to interpretation doesn't exonerate advertisers from the obligation to provide clear information. Indeed, this fact intensifies the responsibility, because the danger of misleading through ambiguity increases as the ad is subject to interpretation. At stake is not only people's money but also their health, loyalties, and expectations. The potential harm a misleading ad can cause is great, not to mention its cavalier treatment of the truth. For these reasons ambiguity in ads is of serious moral concern.

A final word about this topic. As far back as 1944 the United States Supreme Court, speaking about the issue of truthful advertisement, proposed a standard whose spirit might still be used in evaluating ads. In insisting on the literal truthfulness of an ad, the Court recommended "a form of advertising clear enough so that, in the words of the prophet Isaiah, 'wayfaring men, though fools, shall not err therein.'"[4]

Concealed facts. When advertisers conceal facts, they suppress information which is unflattering to their products. Put another way, a fact is concealed when its availability would probably make the desire, purchase, or use of the product less likely than in its absence. The case of Pertussin is a case in point. Surely if consumers had known of the potentially fatal ingredients the vaporizer contained, they'd have been less likely to purchase the product than they apparently were. Concealed facts concern us in ethics not only because they can exploit by misleading as much as ambiguity can but also because they wantonly undermine truth telling.

Truth rarely seems foremost in the minds of advertisers. As Samm Sinclair Baker writes in *The Permissible Lie*: "Inside the agency the basic approach is hardly conducive to truth telling. The usual thinking in forming a campaign is first what can we say, true or not, that will sell the product best? The second consideration is, how can we say it effectively and get away with it so that (1) people who buy won't feel let down by too big a promise that doesn't come true, and (2) the ads will avoid quick and certain censure by the FTC."[5] In this observation we can see the businessperson's tendency to equate what's legal with what's moral, an attitude we previously alluded to. It's precisely this outlook that leads to advertising behavior of dubious morality.

One needn't look far to find examples of concealed facts in ads. You may recall the old Colgate-Palmolive ad for its Rapid Shave Cream. It showed Rapid Shave being used to shave "sandpaper": "Apply, soak, and off in a stroke." This was an impressive ad for any man who's ever scraped his way awake. Unfortunately, what Colgate concealed was that the sandpaper in the ad was actually Plexiglas and that actual sandpaper had to be soaked in Rapid Shave for about eighty minutes before it came off in a stroke.[6]

More recently Campbell vegetable soup ads showed pictures of a thick, rich brew calculated to whet even a gourmet's appetite. Supporting the soup were clear glass marbles deposited into the bowl to give the appearance of solidity.

Then there's the whole area of feminine deodorant sprays (FDS), one rife with concealed facts. Currently an industry in excess of $55 million, FDS ads not only fail to mention that such products in most cases are unnecessary but that they frequently produce unwanted side effects: itching, burning, blistering, and urinary infections. A Food and Drug Administration (FDA) "caution" now appears on these products.

If business has obligations to provide clear, accurate, and adequate information, we must wonder if it meets this charge when it hides facts relevant to the consumer's need and desire for or purchase of a product. Hiding facts raises serious moral concerns relative to truth telling and consumer exploitation. This exploitation takes the form of real injuries that can result to users of products and also of abridgments to consumers' personal freedom. When consumers are deprived of comprehensive knowledge about a product, their choices are constricted.

Exaggeration. Advertisers can mislead through exaggeration; that is, by making claims unsupported by evidence. For example, claims that a pain reliever provides "extra pain relief" or is "50% stronger than aspirin," that it "upsets the stomach less frequently," or that it's "superior to any other nonprescription painkiller on the market" contradict evidence which indicates that all analgesics are effective to the same degree.[7]

In recent years the FTC has been making numerous companies substantiate their claims, as in the Profile and Listerine cases. In the tire industry, the FTC has questioned Goodyear's claim that its Double-Eagle Polysteel Tires can be driven over ax blades without suffering damage. It has also asked Sears, Roebuck and Company to prove its claim that its steel-belted radial tires can give 60,000 to 101,000 miles of service. In the auto industry, the FTC has questioned Volkswagen's claim that its squareback sedan gets about 25 miles per gallon and that it gives drivers 200 gallons of gas more a year compared with the average domestic compact. In addition, the FTC has asked General Motors to verify its claim that its Vega's ground beams provide more side-impact collision protection than those of any other comparable compact. And it has questioned Chrysler's claim that its electronic system never needs tuning.[8]

Clearly the line between deliberate deception and what advertising mogul David Ogilvy has termed *puffery* is not always clear. By *puffery* Ogilvy means the use of "harmless" superlatives. Thus advertisers frequently boast of the merits of their products by using words such as *best*, *finest*, or *most*. In many instances the use of such puffery is indeed harmless, as in the claim that a soap is the "best loved in America." Other times, however, it's downright misleading, as in the Dial soap ad which claimed that Dial was "the most effective deodorant soap you can buy." When asked to substantiate that claim, Armour-Dial Company insisted that it was not claiming product superiority; all it meant was that Dial soap was *as effective as* any other soap.

Of moral importance in determining the line between puffery and deliberate deception would seem to be the advertiser's intention and the likely interpretation of the ad. Are the claims intended as no more than verbal posturing, or are they intended to sell through deceptive exaggeration? Are advertisers primarily interested in saying as much as they can without drawing legal sanction or in providing consumers with accurate information? But even when the intention is harmless, advertisers must consider how the ad is likely to be interpreted. What conclusion is the general consuming public likely to draw about the product? Is that conclusion contrary to likely performance? Without raising questions like these about their ads, advertisers and manufacturers run risks of warping truth and injuring consumers, two significant moral concerns.

Psychological appeals. A psychological appeal is one that aims to persuade exclusively by appealing to human emotions and emotional needs and not to reason. This is potentially the area of greatest moral concern in advertising. An automobile ad that presents the product in an elitist atmosphere peopled by members of the "in" set appeals to our need and desire for status. A life insurance ad that portrays a destitute family woefully struggling in the aftermath of a provider's death aims to persuade through pity and fear. Reliance on such devices, although not unethical *per se*, raises moral concerns because rarely do such ads fully deliver what they promise.

Ads that rely extensively on pitches to power, prestige, sex, masculinity, femininity, acceptance, approval, and the like aim to sell more than a product. They are peddling psychological satisfaction.

Psychological messages raise serious moral questions about inner privacy. Perhaps the best example is the increasingly explicit and pervasive use of sexual pitches in ads.

Scene:	An artist's skylit studio. A young man lies nude, the bedsheets in disarray. He awakens to find a tender note on his pillow. The phone rings and he gets up to answer it.
Woman's voice:	"You snore."
Artist (smiling):	"And you always steal the covers."

More cozy patter between the two. Then a husky-voiced announcer intones: "Paco Rabanne. A cologne for men. What is remembered is up to you."[9]

Although sex has always been used to sell products, it has never before been used as explicitly in advertising as it is today. And the sexual pitches are by no means confined to products like cologne. The California Avocado Commission supplements its "Love Food From California" recipe ads with a campaign featuring leggy actress Angie Dickinson, who is sprawled across two pages of some eighteen national magazines to promote the avocado's nutritional value. The copy line reads: "Would this body lie to you?" Similarly, Dannon Yogurt recently ran an ad featuring a bikini-clad beauty and the message: "More nonsense is written on dieting than any other subject—except possibly sex."

Some students of marketing claim that ads like these appeal to the subconscious mind of both marketer and consumer. Purdue University psychologist and marketing consultant Jacob Jacoby contends that marketers, like everyone else, carry around sexual symbols in their subconscious that, intentionally or not, they use in ads. A case in point: the widely circulated Newport cigarette "Alive with Pleasure" campaign. One campaign ad featured a woman riding the handlebars of a bicycle driven by a man. The main strut of the bike wheel stands vertically beneath her body. In Jacoby's view, such symbolism needs no interpretation.

Author Wilson Bryan Key, who has extensively researched the topic of subconscious marketing appeals, claims that many ads take a subliminal form. *Subliminal advertising is advertising that communicates at a level beneath our conscious awareness*, where some psychologists claim that the vast reservoir of human motivation primarily resides. Most marketing people would likely deny that such advertising occurs. Key disagrees. Indeed, he goes so far as to claim: "It is virtually impossible to pick up a newspaper or magazine, turn on a radio or television set, read a promotional pamphlet or the telephone book, or shop through a supermarket without having your subconscious purposely massaged by some monstrously clever artist, photographer, writer, or technician."[10]

Concern with the serious nature of psychological appeals is what the California Wine Institute seemed to have in mind when it adopted an advertising code of standards. The following restrictions are included:

- No wine ad shall present persons engaged in activities which appeal particularly to minors. Among those excluded: amateur or professional sports figures, celebrities, or cowboys; rock stars, race car drivers.
- No wine ad shall exploit the human form or "feature provocative or enticing poses or be demeaning to any individual."
- No wine ad shall portray wine in a setting where food is not presented.
- No wine ad shall portray wine in "quantities inappropriate to the situation."
- No wine ad shall portray wine as similar to another type of beverage or product such as milk, soda, or candy.

- No wine ad shall associate wine with personal performance, social attainment, achievement, wealth, or the attainment of adulthood.
- No wine ad shall show automobiles in a way that one could construe their conjunction.

As suggested, the code seems particularly sensitive to the subtle implications that wine ads often carry. In a more general sense it alerts us to the psychological nuances of ads. In adopting such a rigorous code of advertising ethics, the California Wine Institute recognizes the inextricable connection between *what* is communicated and *how* it is communicated. In other words, as media expert Marshall McLuhan always insisted, content cannot be distinguished from form, nor form from content. Sensitivity to this proposition would go far toward raising the moral recognition level in advertising and toward alerting businesspeople to the moral overtones of psychological appeals. . . .

Notes

1. See "Mea Culpa, Sort Of," *Newsweek*, September 27, 1971, p. 98.
2. A rating of 100 supposedly equals 30,000 miles of useful life.
3. Paul Stevens, "Weasel Words: God's Little Helpers," in *Language Awareness*, ed. Paul A. Eschhol, Alfred A. Rosa, Virginia P. Clark (New York: St. Martin's Press, 1974), p. 156.
4. "Charles of the Ritz District Corporation v. FTC, 143 F.2d 276 (2d Cir. 1944)," in David A. Aaken and George S. Day, *Consumerism: Search for the Consumer Interest* (New York: The Free Press, 1974), p. 140.
5. Samm Sinclair Baker, *The Permissible Lie* (New York: World Publishing Co., 1968), p. 16.
6. Ibid.
7. The editors of *Consumers Reports*, *The Medicine Show* (Mt. Vernon, N.Y.: Consumers Union, 1972), p. 14.
8. Fred Luthans and Richard M. Hodgetts, *Social Issues in Business* (New York: Macmillan, 1976), p. 353.
9. Gail Bronson, "Sexual Pitches in Ads Become More Explicit and Pervasive," *The Wall Street Journal*, November 18, 1980, p. 1.
10. Wilson Bryan Key, *Subliminal Seduction* (New York: New American Library, 1972), p. 11.

Content Quiz 10.3

Instructions: Fill in the blanks with the appropriate responses listed below.

weasel	psychological
exaggeration	subliminal
inner privacy	satisfaction
persuasive	ambiguous
puffery	facts

1. Moral considerations in advertising revolve around the conflict between informative and _____ functions.

2. Words in advertisements that can be understood in more than one way are _____.
3. _____ words can serve to aid and abet ambiguity in advertising by evading or retreating from direct and forthright statement.
4. According to Barry, by concealing _____, advertisers exploit consumers by misleading them and wantonly undermining truth telling.
5. By the use of _____, advertisers can make inflated claims unsupported by evidence.
6. According to advertising giant, David Ogilvy, words like "best," "finest," and "most" are examples of _____ that involve nothing more than the use of harmless superlatives.
7. Persuasive appeals that are not rational, but emotional, in nature can be described as _____.
8. The use of sexual pitches in ads could violate _____.
9. Advertising that is designed to appeal to us subconsciously is _____.
10. Ads that pitch things like power, prestige, and sex aim at selling more than the product; they peddle psychological _____.

Discussion Questions

1. What do you think the proper job of advertising should be?
2. What are some ethically questionable techniques used by advertisers to promote their products and services?
3. Apart from those discussed in the reading, can you think of any advertisements that could be criticized or condemned on ethical grounds? If so, which ones? What is "wrong" with them?
4. How do you think advertising executives would defend their actions? How would you respond to them?

IF YOU LIGHT UP ON SUNDAY, DON'T COME IN ON MONDAY

How companies are attempting to clamp down on the after-hours activities of employees

Zachary Schiller, Walecia Konrad and Stephanie Anderson Forest

Synopsis

This article from Business Week *deals with the ethical treatment of employees and new job applicants. It addresses workplace privacy issues like: "How much say should an employer have in an employee's life?" and "Does an employer have a right to discriminate against employees or potential employees on the basis of unhealthy lifestyle habits?" In the article, we are presented with numerous examples of how companies have either refused to hire people with high-risk lifestyles or charged them more for private health care coverage once employed. As we learn, opponents to lifestyle discrimination claim that employers have no right to tell employees how to run their private lives, as long as what employees do does not interfere with their effectiveness at work.*

Two years ago, Ford Meter Box in Wabash, Ind., decided it would no longer hire any smokers. Janice Bone was a payroll clerk for the small manufacturer. When a urine test uncovered nicotine traces in Bone's sample, Ford fired her. The incident helped privacy proponents pass an Indiana state law protecting employees who smoke away from work. But Bone, who has filed suit against Ford, has not gotten her job back.

Daniel C. Winn made nearly $9 an hour setting up machinery at Indianapolis' Best Lock Corp. He was fired after he testified in a relative's legal hearing that he drank socially from time to time: Best Lock forbids alcohol consumption by employees, even after work. Best also contested his right to receive unemployment benefits, claiming he was fired for cause. A state court ruled Winn eligible, but Best notes that the court didn't hold its "no-drinking" rule invalid.

Do you smoke? Drink? Eat more than you should? Your employer is getting very interested in your answer. It may cost you more in insurance coverage; there's even an off chance that it could cost you your job. As medical expenses whirl skyward, more companies have begun to see smokers, drinkers, and workers who engage in other "high-risk"—but legal—activities as a burden. Johnson & Johnson Health Management Inc. of New Brunswick, N.J., which sells wellness programs to companies, estimates that 15% to 25% of corporate health care costs stem from employees' "unhealthy lifestyle conditions." With health care costs rising a grim 9% each year, employers note, why shouldn't individual employees take responsibility for their behavior—especially since corporate health coverage is a perk in the first place?

The employers' concerns are justifiable. Still, they raise a range of questions about the employee's right to privacy away from the workplace. So far, only a handful of companies have taken the extreme stance of Ford Meter or Best Lock. But many others are instituting disincentives for staffers they deem high-risk—charging them more for health insurance, for example.

Existing civil rights laws don't generally protect against "lifestyle discrimination," because smokers and skydivers aren't named as protected classes. But since 1989, 20 states have passed laws banning discrimination against smokers, and a few give much broader protection (see "Smokers Have Rights"). The backers of such laws are tapping a wellspring of sentiment that employers have no business telling employees how to run their private lives, as long as what they do doesn't interfere with how they do their jobs. "When they start telling you you can't smoke on your own time, the next thing you know they'll tell you you can't have sex but once a week, and if you have sex twice a week you're fired," declares Oklahoma State Senator Carl Franklin, a backer of Oklahoma's smoker-protection law.

AFTER HOURS. Employers have always had concerns about some off-hours activities: moonlighting, politicking, fraternizing with competitors' employees. But the technological advances and social ills of the 1980s brought with them a host of workplace privacy issues. The result was a new generation of laws and court decisions spelling out how far an employer can go in certain areas. Congress has largely banned the use of polygraph testing. The U.S. Supreme Court has upheld a federal law that prohibits discrimination by federal contractors against persons with communicable diseases such as AIDS. Ten states have restricted drug testing.

Nevertheless, some companies continue to decide what's best for their workers. For example, Johnson Controls Inc., a Wisconsin auto-battery maker, had a policy that barred female employees of childbearing age from certain jobs—because the exposure to lead in those jobs might harm any fetus they might conceive. In March, the Supreme Court struck down that policy, ruling that an employer's assessment of risks should not be substituted for an individual's own judgment. And plenty of employers still try to enforce their own moral codes when it comes to the sensitive issue of sexual preferences (see "The Right to Privacy").

The privacy issue is touching more aspects of life after hours: everyday activities such as whether you use a seat belt, how much you exercise, and even what sports you like. Multi-Developers Inc., a 100-employee property-development and management company in Georgia, won't employ workers who engage in "hazardous activities and pursuits [including] such things as skydiving, riding motorcycles, piloting private aircraft, mountain climbing, motor vehicle racing, etc." The impetus for this policy was a very large injury claim the company recently paid. Without this step, Multi-Developers says, coverage for all its employees might have gotten too expensive.

DRINKERS, DAREDEVILS, AND SMOKERS BEWARE

- You may not be hired, might even be fired, and could end up paying a monthly penalty if your way of life offends the actuaries

LIFESTYLE POLICIES: WHAT'S ALLOWED AND WHAT'S NOT

Company	Policy	Started
Baker Hughes	$10 monthly surcharge on health insurance for smokers	1990
Exxon	Employees who have been through rehabilitation for substance abuse can't work in "safety-sensitive" jobs. Workers in these jobs must report any arrest for drug or alcohol offenses	1989
ICH	$15 a month off medical contributions for employees who haven't smoked for 90 days and meet a weight guideline	1991
Multi-Developers	Won't hire anyone engaging in what company views as high-risk activities; skydiving, piloting private aircraft, mountain climbing, motorcyling	1991
Texas Instruments	$10 monthly surcharge on health insurance for employees and dependents who smoke	1991
Turner Broadcasting	Won't hire smokers	1985
U-Haul International	Biweekly $5 charge for health insurance for employees who smoke, chew tobacco, or whose weight exceeds guidelines	1990

Data: BW Bureaus

SMOKE-BUSTERS. Already, many employers won't hire smokers. Since 1987, USG Corp., a Chicago building-materials maker, has banned smokers from the ranks of 1,200 workers in eight plants. Its concern: Smoking might lead to a higher incidence of lung disease among workers who work with mineral fiber used in making tile. Turner Broadcasting System Inc. won't hire smokers at all. "We think we have the right to employ the kind of person we want to have—and that's a nonsmoker," says William M. Shaw, vice-president for administration.

The city of North Miami requires job applicants to sign affidavits certifying they don't smoke, and haven't for a year. Arlene Kurtz, a candidate for a clerk-typist position, refused to sign and now is suing the city for violation of her right to privacy. Fumes Kurtz (a smoker): "How can they tell me what to do when I'm at lunch, or in my own home, or over the weekend?" To save on health costs, replies the city's attorney, Pedro P. Echarte: "As a taxpayer, I would like to see my money go into improved schools, roads, and parks, not smoking-related illnesses of government employees."

Cracking down on smokers is understandable, because the dangers of tobacco are so well-established. The fear, of course, is that once employers start questioning one type of employee behavior, the list of unsuitable habits will grow. "Why would an employer tell you to knock off smoking at home and not tell you to knock off the beer, if the beer is bad for you, too?" asks Lewis L. Maltby, director of the American Civil Liberties Union National Task Force on Civil Liberties in the Work Place. Muses Michael E. Miller, vice-president for administration at Monsanto Co. in St. Louis: "What about the guy who eats fried chicken 20 times a month? I can hear it all coming." In fact, it did come to Athens, Ga. The city government there used to give every job applicant a cholesterol test, eliminating candidates whose levels ranked in the highest 20%. Local protest scotched the policy.

It is mainly small businesses that so far are taking broad measures. But not even large employers can ignore the fact that certain habits and health conditions can prove expensive. A four-year study of Control Data Corp. employees found that people with hypertension spent 25% more days in the hospital than those with normal blood pressure and that medical claims of overweight people were 11% higher than those of people who weren't. Smokers who work for the state of Kansas spent 69% more time in the hospital than nonsmokers did last year and cost an average $1,137, vs. $854 for nonsmokers.

Many companies take a positive approach, in the shape of financial incentives that give employees who live right the chance to profit by it. Half of the 22,000 persons covered by Southern California Edison Co.'s medical plan have reduced their annual premium by $120 under the corporation's good-health rebate program. They qualify if their weight, cholesterol, and other statistics are within certain bounds. At Atco Properties & Management Inc., a small New York City real estate firm, CEO H. Dale Hemmerdinger pays employees for each pound they lose. And if they walk up the 16 flights of stairs to the office all year, they win a $500 bonus.

SIN SURCHARGE. But while some companies proffer a carrot, others favor the stick. In a recent Harris Poll for Metropolitan Life Insurance Co., 86% of 1,175 executives surveyed found it "acceptable" to charge higher premiums for unhealthy habits. Since the presence of smokers in a work force drives the group rate up, there is a growing interest in charging smokers more for their insurance—rather than spreading the cost equally among all employees. "Why should we continue to do that when all the medical evidence says smoking leads to health problems?" asks Miller of Monsanto, which is toying with a surcharge.

No reason at all, or so Texas Instruments Inc. figured. This July, spurred by an in-house study showing that smokers' health costs at TI were 50% higher than nonsmokers', the company began charging employees $10 a month for smoking outside work. The same sum is levied for up to two of the employees' dependents if they smoke, too.

The new charges have prompted no great outcry, perhaps because smokers recognize their puffing is so unpopular. Most of them are bothered, though, that the charge doesn't apply to other habits. "I think they should go and investigate all types of lifestyles that may increase risk to the company," says a TI programmer who pays $20 more each month because he and his wife smoke. "Someone who jumps out of airplanes for jollies or who races cars on weekends, that could cost the company, too."

Such disincentives will save plenty, enthusiasts say. Oil-field equipment maker Baker Hughes Inc. says its $10 surcharge on smokers has helped reduce the number of employees who call themselves smokers by 7% in the past year. (Baker Hughes and other companies generally rely on an honor system to identify smokers.) Its renewal rates for health coverage won't rise at all this year, compared with 20% increases for the last four years.

But as much as companies can associate unhealthy habits with higher costs, there's precious little data proving that they can significantly lower costs by inducing employees to change those habits. Although high blood cholesterol is associated with higher health risks and costs, notes Kenneth E. Warner, professor of public-health policy at the University of Michigan at Ann Arbor, "What happens when you lower that? We don't know yet."

SMOKERS HAVE RIGHTS—JUST ASK THE TOBACCO COMPANIES

Last spring, a Georgia State Senator introduced into committee a "smokers'-rights" bill outlawing discrimination against people who smoke off the job. In the ensuing week, the lieutenant governor's office got a flood of phone calls supporting the law. So many, in fact, that the phone system broke down.

A strong grass-roots response from the good folk of Georgia? Yes, to some extent. But these complaining constituents got a little help from Philip Morris Cos. When Georgia residents called a toll-free hotline, they heard a recorded message lambasting the lieutenant governor—who was against the bill—for interfering with smokers' rights.

Prairie Fire? The recording then encouraged callers to "stay on the line—we can connect you to his office right now, toll-free." Hence, the flood of calls. A Philip Morris spokesperson says: "We want to make it easier for consumers to voice their concerns."

The Georgia bill was ultimately withdrawn. But 20 other states have passed similar legislation. Antismoking and health groups warn, however, that these laws are not some "prairie wildfire among state legislators," as Walker P. Merryman, vice-president of the Tobacco Institute, describes them. Rather, they represent a campaign by the deep-pocketed tobacco companies to counter the antismoking movement. Replies Tobacco Institute spokesman Thomas Lauria: "These bills are put through by the ACLU and the AFL-CIO. The tobacco companies simply help smokers'-rights groups that have already formed."

Early this year, a bill that would prohibit companies from refusing to hire smokers or firing people who smoke was introduced in the state legislature of New Jersey. The tobacco industry hired lobbyists to get lawmakers to vote for the bill. Philip Morris also blanketed the state with support-the-bill letters. R.J. Reynolds Tobacco Co. joined in, using videotapes, sample petitions, and slide shows to help smokers start activist groups. Ultimately, the measure passed the legislature, and the governor allowed it to become law without his signature in July.

The tobacco companies also target big businesses opposed to smokers'-rights bills. Last year, the New York State Legislature passed a broadly worded law that would have prohibited companies from forbidding any legal activity off the job. IBM, Eastman Kodak Co., and other businesses wrote strong letters against the bill, arguing that it would let employees ignore corporate conflict-of-interest policies. Governor Mario M. Cuomo vetoed it.

Now, another version is about to be presented to Cuomo. This time, however, there is no outcry from IBM and Kodak. The reason: Tobacco companies are big buyers of IBM computers and materials for cigarette filters made by Kodak. Rather than risk their accounts, the companies have withdrawn from the debate, say state government officials and sources close to the companies. Neither Kodak nor IBM will comment on their change of heart, saying only they take no position on the bill.

Surveys show that employees are concerned about employers' legislating their lifestyles. Aware of this, says Joseph Marx of the American Cancer Society: "The tobacco companies are trying to elevate smoking to a civil right"—and taking care of business at the same time.

By Walecia Konrad in Atlanta

THE RIGHT TO PRIVACY: A $5.3 MILLION LESSON FOR SHELL?

In many ways, Jeffrey Collins was the very model of a company man—Shell Oil Co., that is. His father retired after 37 years with Shell. Collins spent his entire career there, rising after 19 years to become the No. 2 executive at its Triton Biosciences Inc. unit in Alameda, Calif. But he has spent the past five years suing Shell for wrongful discharge. In June, he won that suit, along with $5.3 million in damages.

Collins' life with Shell ended abruptly in November, 1985. He had used the office computer to prepare invitations for a nude party planned by his gay sex club. A secretary found one and showed it to company officials. They discharged Collins—wrongfully, a California state judge found. Blasting the company for "outrageous" behavior, Judge Jacqueline Taber held that Shell broke state laws by using information about Collins' personal life as the basis for firing him. "The evidence is clear and convincing that [he] was terminated for private homosexual conduct away from his employment . . . and not for unsatisfactory job performance," her decision said.

LIFESTYLE QUESTION. Shell, which denies the charges, plans to appeal. A Shell lawyer maintains that Collins was terminated "for preparing a sexually explicit memo" at the office, using company equipment, and "for leaving it where it could offend other employees." The company, which has since sold Triton, denies that it discriminates because of sexual orientation: In fact, it once fired a heterosexual employee for preparing and circulating sexually explicit documents in the office. "We do consider lifestyle characteristics a private matter," the spokesman says.

The Shell case is yet another unsettling reminder to employers of the growing controversy and litigation concerning privacy in the workplace. The Shell judgment "expands the rights of employees who are being discriminated against because of lifestyle. Employers must make employment decisions on job-related criteria," says Victor Schachter, a prominent employment lawyer in San Francisco who represents several national corporations. Employers certainly will notice the initial size of Collins' award—the largest award yet in a homosexual discrimination case, says Jury Verdict Research Inc.

Indeed, Taber's decision went far in denouncing Shell. Not only did she conclude that Collins' dismissal was "solely" because of his homosexuality but she criticized Shell's handling of the termination. To justify it, Taber held, managers in Alameda and Houston, the company's headquarters, inappropriately told a headhunter of his homosexuality. And she concluded that the termination was an "overreaction" to Collins' mistake: leaving the party memo in the office.

Paul F. Wotman, Collins' lawyer, says the Shell verdict "has sent a message throughout Corporate America that being gay isn't an acceptable reason for firing someone." Connecticut, Hawaii, Massachusetts, and Wisconsin—along with some 100 cities and counties—have passed laws protecting gays from bias in housing and employment. No federal law exists, though gay activists have been lobbying since the mid-1970s for a "sexual orientation" amendment to the Civil Rights Act of 1964.

For Collins, 47, redress comes not a minute too soon. Unable to find a job comparable to his $115,000 position at Triton, he now makes $25,000 a year at a San Francisco company that ships pets across the U.S. Still, Collins says hopefully, his court win "will offer a lot of encouragement to people who suffered what I did."

By Maria Shao in San Francisco, with Heidi Dawley in Houston

MORE CAUTION. Obesity also has been linked to higher incidence of major illnesses and chronic diseases. However, some medical evidence suggests that losing and regaining weight may be more hazardous than being overweight in the first place. In some states, obese individuals have brought—and won—weight-discrimination lawsuits. In 1985, Xerox Corp. had to offer a position, some back pay, and accumulated pension to Catherine McDermott, who was refused a job because of her weight. Xerox claimed that if she were hired, it would have to pay higher disability and life-insurance costs. That argument didn't persuade the court, which held that obesity was a handicap under state law.

Such rulings may become more common when the Americans with Disabilities Act takes effect in 1992. Although it doesn't protect lifestyle behavior per se, the act will force more caution in the use of preemployment medical exams. Employers will be able to reject only applicants who can't perform the job. Concern about medical costs won't be a reason for withdrawing a job offer.

These measures are not likely to solve the basic question of how much say an employer should have in an employee's life. Columbia University professor and privacy expert Alan F. Westin worries that if the trend toward lifestyle discrimination persists, employers will eventually hire from a narrow group, "those that are healthiest and cost us less." Eventually, we "could become a two-class society," Westin argues, with "one that is perceived as fit and healthy and the [unhealthy] rest who would be unemployed or marginally employed."

Even if things never get to that point, there's ample evidence that the conflict over workplace privacy is intensifying: As more states pass lifestyle discrimination laws, they provide grounds for legal suits over these issues. Until the verdicts are in, it will be tough both for employers and employees to draw the line between "what's good for business" and "minding your own business."

Content Quiz 10.4

Instructions: Fill in the blanks with the appropriate responses listed below.

right
sin surcharge
unhealthy lifestyle conditions
unsuitable habits
workplace privacy
lifestyle discrimination
financial incentives

1. _____ account for 15-25% of corporate health care costs, according to a New Jersey Management Consultant firm.
2. Some employers engage in _____, forcing employees with unhealthy habits to pay premiums (i.e., monthly penalties) on their privately funded health care plans.
3. Turner Broadcasting Inc. discriminates against smokers, claiming that they have the _____ to employ the kind of person they want to have.
4. Critics of discrimination against high-risk employees fear that the list of _____ to be used for purposes of discrimination will grow.
5. Some companies take a positive approach to lifestyle management, offering _____ to employees whose weight and cholesterol levels are within certain bounds.
6. Charging higher premiums for unhealthy habits is a form of _____.
7. According to Zachary Schiller, conflict over _____ is intensifying as more states pass lifestyle discrimination laws.

Discussion Questions

1. Do you think employers should have a right to determine what you do in your private life? Is what executives and other workers do on their own time their own private business no matter what? Why or why not?
2. Suppose you were an employer who had just invested a great deal of money in the training and development of one of your employees whose lifestyle choices became a constant source of illness and absenteeism and, therefore, additional medical costs and office inefficiencies. Under these circumstances, would you have the right to tell your employee what to do or what not to do? Would the employee have any duties or responsibilities to you the employer who provided him with his training and development, not to mention his weekly paycheck? Explain.
3. If an employer does not like smoking and drinking, is it not within his or her rights not to hire people exhibiting these "distasteful" habits? Can we say employers have a "duty" to hire people with undesirable lifestyles or that smokers and drinkers, for example, have a "right" to a job created by an independent businessperson? Why?
4. Should smokers, drinkers, and daredevils be defined as a minority group like women, gays, and blacks? Should they have the same rights? Why or why not?
5. Does the issue of employee privacy change at all if the employer is a public institution like a hospital, school or governmental agency? Can we make lifestyle demands on teachers and public servants that we cannot make on employees of private corporations? If so, why? If not, why not?

CHANGING UNETHICAL ORGANIZATIONAL BEHAVIOUR

Richard P. Nielsen

Synopsis

This reading deals with the subject of organizational ethics. It raises a two-part fundamental question that can be expressed in the following fashion: "Should we ever take action against unethical organizational behavior and, if so, what exactly should we do?" By making reference to Paul Tillich's book, The Courage to Be, Nielsen intimates that living a courageous life may sometimes require individuals to stand up and oppose unethical behavior. Also, adapting from Tillich's distinction between "Being as an Individual" and "Being as a Part of a Group," Nielsen discusses the various strategies one can use to put an end to unethical practices within organizations. He provides case study illustrations for each type of strategic approach and points out their limitations as well. In the end, he concludes that there are realistic ethical leadership and intervention action strategies. He states his preference for leadership strategies over intervention strategies, when it comes to ethical change management, but admits that the latter can sometimes be the more effective short- and medium-term approach.

"To be, or not to be: that is the question:
Whether 'tis nobler in the mind to suffer
The slings and arrows of outrageous fortune,
Or to take arms against a sea of troubles,
And by opposing end them?"

—WILLIAM SHAKESPEARE, *Hamlet*

What are the implications of Hamlet's question in the context of organizational ethics? What does it mean to be ethical in an organizational context? Should one suffer the slings and arrows of unethical organizational behavior? Should one try to take arms against unethical behaviors and by opposing, end them?

The consequences of addressing organizational ethics issues can be unpleasant. One can be punished or fired; one's career can suffer, or one can be disliked, considered an outsider. It may take courage to oppose unethical and lead ethical organizational behavior.

How can one address organizational ethics issues? Paul Tillich, in his book *The Courage to Be*, recognized, as Hamlet did, that dire consequences can result from standing up to and opposing unethical behavior. Tillich identified two approaches: *being* as an individual and *being* as a part of a group.[1]

In an organizational context, these two approaches can be interpreted as follows: (1) Being as an individual can mean intervening to end unethical organizational behaviors by working against others and the organizations performing the unethical behaviors; and (2) being as a part can mean leading an ethical organizational change by working with others and the organization. These approaches are not mutually exclusive; rather, depending on the individual, the organization, the relationships, and the situation, one or both of these approaches may be appropriate for addressing ethical issues.

Being as an Individual

According to Tillich, the courage to be as an individual is the courage to follow one's conscience and defy unethical and/or unreasonable authority. It can even mean staging a revolutionary attack on that authority. Such an act can entail great risk and require great courage. As Tillich explains, "The anxiety conquered in the courage to be . . . in the productive process is considerable, because the threat of being excluded from such a participation by unemployment or the loss of an economic basis is what, above all, fate means today . . . ."[2]

According to David Ewing, retired executive editor of the *Harvard Business Review*, this type of anxiety is not without foundation.

> "There is very little protection in industry for employees who object to carrying out immoral, unethical or illegal orders from their superiors. If the employee doesn't like what he or she is asked to do, the remedy is to pack up and leave. This remedy seems to presuppose an ideal economy, where there is another company down the street with openings for jobs just like the one the employee left."[3]

How can one *be* as an individual, intervening against unethical organizational behavior? Intervention strategies an individual can use to change unethical behavior include: (1) secretly blowing the whistle within the organization; (2) quietly blowing the whistle, informing a responsible higher-level manager; (3) secretly threatening the offender with blowing the whistle; (4) secretly threatening a responsible manager with blowing the whistle outside the organization; (5) publicly threatening a responsible manager with blowing the whistle; (6) sabotaging the implementation of the unethical behavior; (7) quietly refraining from implementing an unethical order or policy; (8) publicly blowing the whistle within the organization; (9) conscientiously objecting to an unethical policy or refusing to implement the policy; (10) indicating uncertainty about or refusing to support a cover-up in the event that the individual and/or organization gets caught; (11) secretly blowing the whistle outside the organization; or (12) publicly blowing the whistle outside the organization. Cases of each strategy are considered below.

Cases

1. *Secretly blowing the whistle within the organization.* A purchasing manager for General Electric secretly wrote a letter to an upper-level manager about his boss, who was soliciting and accepting bribes from subcontractors. The boss was investigated and eventually fired. He was also sentenced to six months' imprisonment for taking $100,000 in bribes, in exchange for which he granted favorable treatment on defense contracts.[4]

2. *Quietly blowing the whistle to a responsible higher-level manager.* When Evelyn Grant was first hired by the company with which she is now a personnel manager, her job included administering a battery of tests that, in part, determined which employees were promoted to supervisory positions. Grant explained:

> "There have been cases where people will do something wrong because they think they have no choice. Their boss tells them to do it, and so they do it, knowing it's wrong. They don't realize there are ways around the boss . . . . When I went over his [the chief psychologist's] data and analysis, I found errors in assumptions as well as actual errors of computation . . . . I had two choices: I could do nothing or I could report my findings to my supervisor. If I did nothing, the only persons probably hurt were the ones who 'failed' the test. To report my findings, on the other hand, could hurt several people, possibly myself."

She quietly spoke to her boss, who quietly arranged for a meeting to discuss the discrepancies with the chief psychologist. The chief psychologist did not show up for the meeting; however, the test battery was dropped.[5]

3. *Secretly threatening the offender with blowing the whistle.* A salesman for a Boston-area insurance company attended a weekly sales meeting during which the sales manager instructed the salespeople, both verbally and in writing, to use a sales technique that the salesman considered unethical. The salesman anonymously wrote the sales manager a letter threatening to send a copy of the unethical sales instructions to the Massachusetts insurance commission and the *Boston Globe* newspaper unless the sales manager retracted his instructions at the next sales meeting. The sales manager did retract the instructions. The salesman still works for the insurance company.[6]

4. *Secretly threatening a responsible manager with blowing the whistle outside the organization.* A recently hired manager with a San Francisco Real Estate Development Company found that the construction company his firm had contracted with was systematically not giving minorities opportunities to learn construction management. This new manager wrote an anonymous letter to a higher-level real estate manager threatening to blow the whistle to the press and local government about the contractor unless the company corrected the situation. The real estate manager intervened, and the contractor began to hire minorities for foremen-training positions.[7]

5. *Publicly threatening a responsible manager with blowing the whistle.* A woman in the business office of a large Boston-area university observed that one middle-level male manager was sexually harassing several women in the office. She tried to reason with the office manager to do something about the offensive behavior, but the manager would not do anything. She then told the manager and several other people in the office that if the manager did not do something about the behavior,

she would blow the whistle to the personnel office. The manager then told the offender that if he did not stop the harassment, the personnel office would be brought in. He did stop the behavior, but he and several other employees refused to talk to the woman who initiated the actions. She eventually left the university.[8]

6. *Sabotaging the implementation of the unethical behavior.* A program manager for a Boston-area local social welfare organization was told by her superior to replace a significant percentage of her clients who received disability benefits with refugee Soviet Jews. She wanted to help both the refugees and her current clients; however, she thought it was unethical to drop current clients, in part because she believed such an action could result in unnecessary deaths. Previously, a person who had lost benefits because of what the program manager considered unethical "bumping" had committed suicide: He had not wanted to force his family to sell their home in order to pay for the medical care he needed and qualify for poverty programs. After her attempts to reason with her boss failed, she instituted a paperwork chain with a partially funded federal agency that prevented her own agency from dropping clients for nine months, after which time they would be eligible for a different funding program. Her old clients received benefits and the new refugees also received benefits. In discussions with her boss, she blamed the federal agency for making it impossible to drop people quickly. Her boss, a political appointee who did not understand the system, also blamed the federal agency office.[9]

7. *Publicly blowing the whistle within the organization.* John W. Young, the chief of NASA's astronaut office, wrote a 12-page internal memorandum to 97 people after the Challenger explosion that killed seven crew members. The memo listed a large number of safety-related problems that Young said had endangered crews since October 1984. According to Young, "If the management system is not big enough to stop the space shuttle program whenever necessary to make flight safety corrections, it will not survive and neither will our three space shuttles or their flight crews." The memo was instrumental in the decision to broaden safety investigations throughout the total NASA system.[10]

8. *Quietly refraining from implementing an unethical order/policy.* Frank Ladwig was a top salesman and branch manager with a large computer company for more than 40 years. At times, he had trouble balancing his responsibilities. For instance, he was trained to sell solutions to customer problems, yet he had order and revenue quotas that sometimes made it difficult for him to concentrate on solving problems. He was responsible for signing and keeping important customers with annual revenues of between $250,000 and $500,000 and for aggressively and conscientiously representing new products that had required large R&D investments. He was required to sell the full line of products and services, and sometimes he had sales quotas for products that he believed were not a good match for the customer or appeared to perform marginally. Ladwig would quietly not sell those products, concentrating on selling the products he believed in. He would quietly explain the characteristics of the questionable products to his knowledgeable customers and get their reactions, rather than making an all-out sales effort. When he was asked by his sales manager why a certain product was not moving, he explained what the customers objected to and why. However,

Ladwig thought that a salesman or manager with an average or poor performance record would have a difficult time getting away with this type of solution to an ethical dilemma.[11]

9. *Conscientiously objecting to an unethical policy or refusing to implement it.* Francis O'Brien was a research director for the pharmaceutical company Searle & Co. O'Brien conscientiously objected to what he believed were exaggerated claims for the Searle Copper 7 intrauterine contraceptive. When reasoning with upper-level management failed, O'Brien wrote them the following:

> "Their continued use, in my opinion, is both misleading and a thinly disguised attempt to make claims which are not FDA approved . . . . Because of personal reasons I do not consent to have my name used in any press release or in connection with any press release. In addition, I will not participate in any press conferences."

O'Brien left the company ten years later. Currently, several lawsuits are pending against Searle, charging that its IUD caused infection and sterility.[12]

10. *Indicating uncertainty about or refusing to support a cover-up in the event that the individual and/or organization gets caught.* In the Boston office of Bear Stearns, four brokers informally work together as a group. One of the brokers had been successfully trading on insider information, and he invited the other three to do the same. One of the three told the others that such trading was not worth the risk of getting caught, and if an investigation ever occurred, he was not sure he would be able to participate in a cover-up. The other two brokers decided not to trade on the insider information, and the first broker stopped at least that type of insider trading.[13]

11. *Secretly blowing the whistle outside the corporation.* William Schwartzkopf of the Commonwealth Electric Company secretly and anonymously wrote a letter to the Justice Department alleging large-scale, long-time bid rigging among many of the largest U.S. electrical contractors. The secret letter accused the contractors of raising bids and conspiring to divide billions of dollars of contracts. Companies in the industry have already paid more than $20 million in fines to the government in part as a result of this letter, and they face millions of dollars more in losses when the victims sue.[14]

12. *Publicly blowing the whistle outside the organization.* A. [Ernest] Fitzgerald, a former high-level manager in the U.S. Air Force and Lockheed CEO, revealed to Congress and the press that the Air Force and Lockheed systematically practiced a strategy of underbidding in order to gain Air Force contracts for Lockheed, which then billed the Air Force and received payments for cost overruns on the contracts. Fitzgerald was fired for his trouble, but eventually received his job back. The underbidding/cost overruns, on at least the C-5/A cargo plane, were stopped.[15]

Limitations of Intervention

The intervention strategies described above can be very effective, but they also have some important limitations.

1. *The individual can be wrong about the organization's actions.* Lower-level employees commonly do not have as much or as good information about ethical situations and issues as higher-level managers. Similarly, they may not be as experienced as higher-level managers in dealing with specific ethical issues. The quality of experience and information an individual has can influence the quality of his or her ethical judgments. To the extent that this is true in any given situation, the use of intervention

may or may not be warranted. In Case [8], for example, if Frank Ladwig had had limited computer experience, he could have been wrong about some of the products he thought would not produce the promised results.

2. *Relationships can be damaged.* Suppose that instead of identifying with the individuals who want an organization to change its ethical behavior, we look at these situations from another perspective. How do we feel when we are forced to change our behavior? Further, how would we feel if we were forced by a subordinate to change, even though we thought that we had the position, quality of information, and/or quality of experience to make the correct decisions? Relationships would probably be, at the least, strained, particularly if we made an ethical decision and were nevertheless forced to change. If we are wrong, it may be that we do not recognize it at the time. If we know we are wrong, we still may not like being forced to change. However, it is possible that the individual forcing us to change may justify his or her behavior to us, and our relationship may actually be strengthened.

3. *The organization can be hurt unnecessarily.* If an individual is wrong in believing that the organization is unethical, the organization can be hurt unnecessarily by his or her actions. Even if the individual is right, the organization can still be unnecessarily hurt by intervention strategies.

4. *Intervention strategies can encourage "might makes right" climates.* If we want "wrong" people, who might be more powerful now or in the future than we are, to exercise self-restraint, then we may need to exercise self-restraint even when we are "right." A problem with using force is that the other side may use more powerful or effective force now or later. Many people have been punished for trying to act ethically both when they were right and when they were wrong. By using force, one may also contribute to the belief that the only way to get things done in a particular organization is through force. People who are wrong can and do use force, and win. Do we want to build an organization culture in which force plays an important role? Gandhi's response to "an eye for an eye" was that if we all followed that principle, eventually everyone would be blind.

Being as a Part

While the intervention strategies discussed above can be very effective, they can also be destructive. Therefore, it may be appropriate to consider the advantages of leading an ethical change effort (being as a part) as well as intervening against unethical behaviors (being as an individual).

Tillich maintains that the courage to be as a part is the courage to affirm one's own being through participation with others. He writes,

> "The self affirms itself as participant in the power of a group, of a movement. . . . Self-affirmation within a group includes the courage to accept guilt and its consequences as public guilt, whether one is oneself responsible or whether somebody else is. It is a problem of the group which has to be expiated for the sake of the group, and the methods of punishment and satisfaction . . . are accepted by the individual. . . . In every human community, there are outstanding members, the bearers of the traditions and leaders of the future. They must have sufficient distance in order to judge and to change. They must take responsibility and ask questions. This unavoidably produces individual doubt and personal guilt. Nevertheless, the predominant pattern is the courage to be a part in all members of the . . . group. . . . The difference between the genuine Stoic and the neocollectivist is that the latter is bound in the first place to the col-

lective and in the second place to the universe, while the Stoic was first of all related to the universal Logos and secondly to possible human groups. . . . The democratic-conformist type of the courage to be as a part was in an outspoken way tied up with the idea of progress. The courage to be as a part in the progress of the group to which one belongs. . . ."[16]

Leading Ethical Change

A good cross-cultural conceptualization of leadership is offered by Yoshino and Lifson: "The essence of leadership is the influential increment over and above mechanical compliance with routine directives of the organization."[17] This definition permits comparisons between and facilitates an understanding of different leadership styles through its use of a single variable: created incremental performance. Of course, different types of leadership may be more or less effective in different types of situations; yet, it is helpful to understand the "essence" of leadership in its many different cultural forms as the creation of incremental change beyond the routine.

For example, Yoshino and Lifson compare generalizations (actually overgeneralizations) about Japanese and American leadership styles:

> "In the United States, a leader is often thought of as one who blazes new trails, a virtuoso whose example inspires awe, respect, and emulation. If any individual characterizes this pattern, it is surely John Wayne, whose image reached epic proportions in his own lifetime as an embodiment of something uniquely American. A Japanese leader, rather than being an authority, is more of a communications channel, a mediator, a facilitator, and most of all, a symbol and embodiment of group unity. Consensus building is necessary in decision making, and this requires patience and an ability to use carefully cultivated relationships to get all to agree for the good of the unit. A John Wayne in this situation might succeed temporarily by virtue of charisma, but eventually the inability to build strong emotion-laden relationships and use these as a tool of motivation and consensus building would prove fatal."[18]

A charismatic "John Wayne type" leader can inspire and/or frighten people into diverting from the routine. A consensus-building, Japanese-style leader can get people to agree to divert from the routine. In both cases, the leader creates incremental behavior change beyond the routine. How does leadership (being as a part) in its various cultural forms differ from the various intervention (being as an individual) strategies and cases discussed above? Some case data may be revealing.

Cases

1. *Roger Boisjoly and the Challenger launch.*[19] In January 1985, after the postflight hardware inspection of Flight 52C, Roger Boisjoly strongly suspected that unusually low temperatures had compromised the performance effectiveness of the O-ring seals on two field joints. Such a performance compromise could cause an explosion. In March 1985, laboratory tests confirmed that low temperatures did negatively affect the ability of the O-rings to perform this sealing function. In June 1985, the postflight inspection of Flight 51B revealed serious erosion of both primary and backup seals that, had it continued, could have caused an explosion.

These events convinced Boisjoly that a serious and very dangerous problem existed with the O-rings. Instead of acting as an individual against his supervisors and the organization, for example, by blowing the whistle to the press, he tried to lead a change to stop the launching of flights with unsafe O-rings. He worked with his immediate supervisor, the director of engineering, and the organization in leading this change. He wrote a draft of a memo to Bob Lund, vice-president of engineering, which he first showed and discussed with his immediate supervisor to "maintain good relationships." Boisjoly and others developed potential win-win solutions, such as investigating remedies to fix the O-rings and refraining from launching flights at too-low temperatures. He effectively established a team to study the matter, and participated in a teleconference with 130 technical experts.

On the day before the Challenger launch, Boisjoly and other teams members were successful in leading company executives to reverse their tentative recommendation to launch because the overnight temperatures were predicted to be too low. The company recommendation was to launch only when temperatures were above 53 degrees. To this point, Boisjoly was very effective in leading a change toward what he and other engineering and management people believed was a safe and ethical decision.

However, according to testimony from Boisjoly and others to Congress, the top managers of Morton Thiokol, under pressure from NASA, reversed their earlier recommendation not to launch. The next day, Challenger was launched and exploded, causing the deaths of all the crew members. While Boisjoly was very effective in leading a change within his own organization, he was not able to counteract subsequent pressure from the customer, NASA.

2. *Dan Phillips and Genco, Inc.*[20] Dan Phillips was a paper products group division manager for Genco, whose upper-level management adopted a strategy whereby several mills, including the Elkhorn Mill, would either have to reduce costs or close down. Phillips was concerned that cost cutting at Elkhorn would prevent the mill from meeting government pollution-control requirements, and that closing the mill could seriously hurt the local community. If he reduced costs, he would not meet pollution-control requirements; if he did not reduce costs, the mill would close and the community would suffer.

Phillips did not secretly or publicly blow the whistle, nor did he sabotage, conscientiously object, quietly refrain from implementing the plan, or quit; however, he did lead a change in the organization's ethical behavior. He asked research and development people in his division to investigate how the plant could both become more cost efficient and create less pollution. He then asked operations people in his division to estimate how long it would take to put such a new plant design on line, and how much it would cost. He asked cost accounting and financial people within his division to estimate when such a new operation would achieve a breakeven payback. Once he found a plan that would work, he negotiated a win-win solution with upper-level management: in exchange for not closing the plant and increasing its investment in his division, the organization would over time benefit from lower costs and higher profitability. Phillips thus worked with others and the organization to lead an inquiry and adopt an alternative ethical and cost-effective plant.

3. *Lotus and Brazilian Software Importing.*[21] Lotus, a software manufacturer, found that in spite of restrictions on the importing of much of its software to Brazil, many people there were buying and using Lotus software. On further investigation, the company discovered that Brazilian businessmen, in alliance with a Brazilian general, were violating the law by buying Lotus software in Cambridge,

Massachusetts and bringing it into Brazil.

Instead of blowing the whistle on the illegal behavior, sabotaging it, or leaving Brazil, Lotus negotiated a solution: In exchange for the Brazilians' agreement to stop illegal importing, Lotus helped set them up as legitimate licensed manufacturers and distributors of Lotus products in Brazil. Instead of working against them and the Lotus salespeople supplying them, the Lotus managers worked with these people to develop an ethical, legal, and economically sound solution to the importing problem.

And in at least a limited sense, the importers may have been transformed into ethical managers and businesspeople. This case may remind you of the legendary "Old West," where government officials sometimes negotiated win-win solutions with "outlaw gunfighters," who agreed to become somewhat more ethical as appointed sheriffs. The gunfighters needed to make a living, and many were not interested in or qualified for such other professions as farming or shopkeeping. In some cases, ethical behavior may take place before ethical beliefs are assumed.

4. *Insurance company office/sales manager and discrimination.*[22] The sales-office manager of a very large Boston-area insurance company tried to hire female salespeople several times, but his boss refused to permit the hires. The manager could have acted against his boss and the organization by secretly threatening to blow the whistle or actually blowing the whistle, publicly or secretly. Instead, he decided to try to lead a change in the implicit hiring policy of the organization.

The manager asked his boss why he was not permitted to hire a woman. He learned that his boss did not believe women made good salespeople and had never worked with a female salesperson. He found that reasoning with his boss about the capabilities of women and the ethics and legality of refusing to hire women were ineffective.

He inquired within the company about whether being a woman could be an advantage in any insurance sales area. He negotiated with his boss a six-month experiment whereby he hired on a trial basis one woman to sell life insurance to married women who contributed large portions of their salaries to their home mortgages. The woman he hired was not only very successful in selling this type of life insurance, but became one of the office's top salespeople. After this experience, the boss reversed his policy of not hiring female salespeople.

Limitations to Leading Ethical Organizational Change

In the four cases described above, the individuals did not attack the organization or people within the organization, nor did they intervene against individuals and/or the organization to stop an unethical practice. Instead, they worked with people in the organization to build a more ethical organization. As a result of their leadership, the organizations used more ethical behaviors. The strategy of leading an organization toward more ethical behavior, however, does have some limitations. These are described below.

1. In some organizational situations, ethical win-win solutions or compromises may not be possible. For example, in 1975 a pharmaceutical company in Raritan, New Jersey decided to enter a new market with a new product.[23] Grace Pierce, who was then in charge of medical testing of new products, refused to test a new diarrhea drug product on infants and elderly consumers because it contained high levels of saccharin, which was feared by many at the time to be a carcinogen.

When Pierce was transferred, she resigned. The drug was tested on infant and elderly consumers. In this case, Pierce may have been faced with an either-or situation that left her little room to lead a change in organizational behavior.

Similarly, Errol Marshall, with Hydraulic Parts and Components, Inc.,[24] helped negotiate the sale of a subcontract to sell heavy equipment to the U.S. Navy while giving $70,000 in kickbacks to two materials managers of Brown & Root, Inc., the project's prime contractor. According to Marshall, the prime contractor "demanded the kickbacks. . . . It was cut and dried. We would not get the business otherwise." While Marshall was not charged with any crime, one of the upper-level Brown & Root managers, William Callan, was convicted in 1985 of extorting kickbacks, and another manager, Frank DiDomenico, pleaded guilty to extorting kickbacks from Hydraulic Parts & Components, Inc. Marshall has left the company. In this case, it seems that Marshall had no win-win alternative to paying the bribe. In some situations it may not be possible to lead a win-win ethical change.

2. Some people do not understand how leadership can be applied to situations that involve organizational-ethics issues. Also some people—particularly those in analytical or technical professions, which may not offer much opportunity for gaining leadership experience—may not know how to lead very well in any situation. Some people may be good leaders in the course of their normal work lives, but do not try to lead or do not lead very well when ethical issues are involved. Some people avoid discussing ethical, religious, and political issues at work.

For example, John Geary was a salesman for U.S. Steel when the company decided to enter a new market with what he and others considered an unsafe new product.[25] As a leading salesman for U.S. Steel, Geary normally was very good at leading the way toward changes that satisfied customer and organizational needs. A good salesman frequently needs to coordinate and spearhead modifications in operations, engineering, logistics, product design, financing, and billing/payment that are necessary for a company to maintain good customer relationships and sales. Apparently, however, he did not try to lead the organization in developing a win-win solution, such as soliciting current orders for a later delivery of a corrected product. He tried only reasoning against selling the unsafe product and protested its sale to several groups of upper-level engineers and managers. He noted that he believed the product had a failure rate of 3.6% and was therefore both unsafe and potentially damaging to U.S. Steel's longer-term strategy of entering higher technology/profit margin businesses. According to Geary, even though many upper-level managers, engineers, and salesmen understood and believed him, "the only desire of everyone associated with the project was to satisfy the instructions of Henry Wallace [the sales vice-president]. No one was about to buck this man for fear of his job."[26] The sales vice-president fired Geary, apparently because he continued to protest against sale of the product.

Similarly, William Schwartzkopf of Commonwealth Electric Co.[27] did not think he could either ethically reason against or lead an end to the large-scale, long-time bid rigging between his own company and many of the largest U.S. electrical contractors. Even though he was an attorney and had extensive experience in leading organizational changes, he did not try to lead his company toward an ethical solution. He waited until he retired from the company, then wrote a secret letter to the Justice Department accusing the contractors of raising bids and conspiring to divide billions of dollars of contracts among themselves.

Many people—both experienced and inexperienced in leadership—do not try to lead their companies toward developing solutions to ethical problems. Often, they do not understand that it is possible to lead such a change; therefore, they do not try to do so—even though, as the cases here show, many succeed when they do try.

3. Some organizational environments—in both consensus-building and authoritarian types of cultures—discourage leadership that is nonconforming. For example, as Robert E. Wood, former CEO of the giant international retailer Sears, Roebuck, has observed, "We stress the advantages of the free enterprise system, we complain about the totalitarian state, but in our individual organizations we have created more or less a totalitarian system in industry, particularly in large industry."[28] Similarly, Charles W. Summers, in a *Harvard Business Review* article, observes, "Corporate executives may argue that . . . they recognize and protect . . . against arbitrary termination through their own internal procedures. The simple fact is that most companies have not recognized and protected that right."[29]

David Ewing concludes that "It [the pressure to obey unethical and illegal orders] is probably most dangerous, however, as a low-level infection. When it slowly bleeds the individual conscience dry and metastasizes insidiously, it is most difficult to defend against. There are no spectacular firings or purges in the ranks. There are no epic blunders. Under constant and insistent pressure, employees simply give in and conform. They become good 'organization people.'"[30]

Similar pressure can exist in participative, consensus-building types of cultures. For example, as mentioned above, Yoshino and Lifson write, "A Japanese leader, rather than being an authority, is more of a communications channel, a mediator, a facilitator, and most of all, a symbol and embodiment of group unity. Consensus building is necessary to decision making, and this requires patience and an ability to use carefully cultivated relationships to get all to agree for the good of the unit."[31]

The importance of the group and the position of the group leaders as a symbol of the group are revealed in the very popular true story, "Tale of the Forty-Seven Ronin." The tale is about 47 warriors whose lord is unjustly killed. The Ronin spend years sacrificing everything, including their families, in order to kill the person responsible for their leader's death. Then all those who survive the assault killed themselves.

Just as authoritarian top-down organizational cultures can produce unethical behaviors, so can participative, consensus-building cultures. The Japanese novelist Shusaku Endo, in his *The Sea and Poison*, describes the true story of such a problem.[32] It concerns an experiment cooperatively performed by the Japanese Army, a medical hospital, and a consensus-building team of doctors on American prisoners of war. The purpose of the experiment was to determine scientifically how much blood people can lose before they die.

Endo describes the reasoning and feelings of one of the doctors as he looked back at this behavior:

"'At the time nothing could be done. . . . If I were caught in the same way, I might, I might just do the same thing again. . . . We feel that getting on good terms ourselves with the Western Command medical people, with whom Second [section] is so cosy, wouldn't be a bad idea at all. Therefore we feel there's no need to ill-temperedly refuse their friendly proposal and hurt their feelings. . . . Five doctors from Kando's section most likely will be glad to get the chance. . . . For me the pangs of conscience . . . were from childhood equivalent to the fear of disapproval in the eyes of others—fear of the punishment which society would bring to bear. . . . To put it quite bluntly, I am able to remain quite undisturbed in the face of someone else's terrible suffering and death. . . . I am not writing about these experiences as one driven to do so by his conscience . . . all these memories are distasteful to me. But looking upon them as distasteful and suffering because of them are two different matters. Then why do I bother writing? Because I'm strangely ill at ease. I, who fear only the eyes of others and the punishment of society, and whose fears disappear when I am secure from these, am now disturbed. . . . I have no conscience, I suppose. Not just me, though. None of them feel anything at all about what they did here.' The only emotion in his heart was a sense of having fallen as low as one can fall."[33]

What to Do and How to Be

In light of the discussion of the two approaches to addressing organizational ethics issues and their limitations, what should we do as individuals and members of organizations? To some extent that depends on the circumstances and our own abilities. If we know how to lead, if there's time for it, if the key people in authority are reasonable, and if a win-win solution is possible, one should probably try leading an organizational change.

If, on the other hand, one does not know how to lead, time is limited, the authority figures are unreasonable, a culture of strong conformity exists, and the situation is not likely to produce a win-win outcome, then the chances of success with a leadership approach are much lower. This may leave one with only the choice of using one of the intervention strategies discussed above. If an individual wishes to remain an effective member of the organization, then one of the more secretive strategies may be safer.

But what about the more common, middle range of problems? Here there is no easy prescription. The more win-win potential the situation has, the more time there is, the more leadership skills one has, and the more reasonable the authority figures and organizational cultures are, the more likely a leadership approach is to succeed. If the opposite conditions exist, then forcing change in the organization is the likely alternative.

To a large extent, the choice depends on an individual's courage. In my opinion, in all but the most extreme and unusual circumstances, one should first try to lead a change toward ethical behavior. If that does not succeed, then mustering the courage to act against others and the organization may be necessary. For example, the course of action that might have saved the Challenger crew was for Boisjoly or someone else to act against Morton Thiokol, its top managers, and NASA by blowing the whistle to the press.

If there is an implicitly characteristic American ontology, perhaps it is some version of William James' 1907 *Pragmatism*, which, for better or worse, sees through a lens of interactions the ontologies of being as an individual and being as a part. James explains our situation as follows:

"What we were discussing was the idea of a world growing not integrally but piecemeal by the contributions of its several parts. Take the hypothesis seriously and as a live one. Suppose that the world's author put the case to you before creation, saying: 'If I am going to make a world not certain to be saved, a world the perfection of which shall be conditional merely, the condition being that each several agent does its own 'level best.' I offer you the chance of taking part in such a world. Its safety, you see, is unwarranted. It is a real adventure, with real danger, yet it may win through. It is a social scheme of co-operative work genuinely to be done. Will you join the procession? Will you trust yourself and trust the other agents enough to face the risk? . . . Then it is perfectly possible to accept sincerely a drastic kind of a universe from which the element of 'seriousness' is not to be expelled. Who so does so is, it seems to me, a genuine pragmatist. He is willing to live on a scheme of uncertified possibilities which he trusts; willing to pay with his own person, if need be, for the realization of the ideals which he frames. What now actually are the other forces which he trusts to co-operate with him, in a universe of such a type? They are at least his fellow men, in the stage of being which our actual universe has reached."[34]

In conclusion, there are realistic ethics leadership and intervention action strategies. We can act effectively concerning organizational ethics issues. Depending upon the circumstances including our own courage, we can choose to act and be ethical both as individuals and as leaders. Being as a part and leading ethical change is the more constructive approach generally. However, being as an individual intervening against others and organizations can sometimes be the only short or medium term effective approach.

Acknowledgments

I would like to acknowledge and thank the following people for their help with ideas presented in this article: the members of the Works in Progress Seminar of Boston College particularly Dalmar Fisher, James Gips, John Neuhauser, William Torbert, and the late James Waters; Kenneth Boulding of the University of Colorado; Robert Greenleaf; and, Douglas Steere of Haverford College.

Notes

1. Paul Tillich, *The Courage to Be*. New Haven, CT: Yale University Press, 1950.
2. See Endnote 1, page 159.
3. David Ewing, *Freedom Inside the Organization*. New York: McGraw-Hill, 1977.
4. The person blowing the whistle in this case wishes to remain anonymous. See also Elizabeth Neuffer, "GE Managers Sentenced for Bribery," *The Boston Globe*, July 26, 1988, p. 67.
5. Barbara Ley Toffler, *Tough Choices: Managers Talk Ethics*. New York: John Wiley, 1986, pp. 153–169.
6. Richard P. Nielsen, What Can Managers Do About Unethical Management?" *Journal of Business Ethics*, 6, 1987, 153–161. See also Nielsen's "Limitations of Ethical Reasoning as an Action Strategy," *Journal of Business Ethics*, 7, 1988, pp. 725–733, and "Arendt's Action Philosophy and the Manager as Eichmann, Richard III, Faust or Institution Citizen," *California Management Review*, 26, 3, Spring 1984, pp. 191–201.
7. The person involved wishes to remain anonymous.
8. The person involved wishes to remain anonymous.

9. See Endnote 6.
10. R. Reinhold, "Astronauts Chief Says NASA Risked Life for Schedule," *The New York Times*, 36, 1986, p. 1.
11. Personal conversation and letter with Frank Ladwig, 1986. See also Frank Ladwig and Associates' *Advanced Consultative Selling for Professionals*. Stonington, CT.
12. W. G. Glaberson, "Did Searle Lose Its Eyes to a Health Hazard?" *Business Week*, October 14, 1985, pp. 120–122.
13. The person involved wishes to remain anonymous.
14. Andy Pasztor, "Electrical Contractors Reel Under Charges that They Rigged Bids," *The Wall Street Journal*, November 29, 1985, pp. 1, 14.
15. A. Ernest Fitzgerald, *The High Priests of Waste*. New York: McGraw-Hill, 1977.
16. See Endnote 1, pp. 89, 93.
17. M. Y. Yoshino and T. B. Lifson, *The Invisible Link: Japan's Saga Shosha and the Organization of Trade*. Cambridge, MA: MIT Press, 1986.
18. See Endnote 17, p. 178.
19. Roger Boisjoly, address given at Massachusetts Institute of Technology on January 7, 1987. Reprinted in *Books and Religion*, March/April 1987, 3–4, 12–13. See also Caroline Whitbeck, "Moral Responsibility and the Working Engineer," *Books and Religion*, March/April 1987, 3, 22–23.
20. Personal conversation with Ray Bauer, Harvard Business School, 1975. See also R. Ackerman and Ray Bauer, *Corporate Social Responsiveness*. Reston, VA: Reston Publishing, 1976.
21. The person involved wishes to remain anonymous.
22. The person involved wishes to remain anonymous.
23. David Ewing, *Do It My Way or You're Fired*. New York: John Wiley, 1983.
24. E. T. Pound, "Investigators Detect Pattern of Kickbacks for Defense Business," *The Wall Street Journal*, November 14, 1985, pp. 1, 25.
25. See Endnote 23. See also Geary vs. U.S. Steel Corporation, 319 A. 2d 174, Supreme Court of Pa.
26. See Endnote 23, p. 86.
27. See Endnote 14.
28. See Endnote 3, p. 21.
29. C. W. Summers, "Protecting All Employees Against Unjust Dismissal," *Harvard Business Review*, 58, 1980, pp. 132–139.
30. See Endnote 3, pp. 216–217.
31. See Endnote 17, p. 187.
32. Shusaku Endo, *The Sea and Poison*. New York: Taplinger Publishing Company, 1972. See also Y. Yasuda, *Old Tales of Japan*. Tokyo: Charles Tuttle Company, 1947.
33. See Endnote 32.
34. William James, *Pragmatism: A New Name for Some Old Ways of Thinking*. New York: Longmans, Green and Co., 1907, pp. 290, 297–298.

Content Quiz 10.5

Instructions: Fill in the blanks with the appropriate responses listed below.

leading
secretly threatening
consensus building
dire consequences
constructive
intervention strategies
courage to be
win-win
intervening
charismatic
limitations

1. _____ can result when people stand up to and oppose unethical behavior in organizations.
2. _____ and _____ are two approaches, derived from Paul Tillich's work, that can be used to deal with ethical improprieties.
3. _____ involves the will and strength to follow one's conscience and to defy unethical and/or unreasonable authority.
4. _____ a responsible manager with blowing the whistle outside the organization is an example of an intervention strategy.
5. Intervention strategies have their _____ as, for example, relationships can be damaged and organizations can be hurt unnecessarily.
6. "John Wayne" leadership is more _____ and inspirational.
7. Japanese-style management tends to based more on _____.
8. One limitation of the strategy of leading an organization toward more ethical behavior is that it may not always lead to ethical _____ solutions.
9. "Being as a Part" and leading ethical change is generally more _____ than intervening.
10. "Being as an Individual" is a concept adapted from Tillich and used by Nielsen to discuss _____.

Discussion Questions

1. Why do some people avoid addressing "ethical issues" when they arise within organizations?
2. What two basic approaches can be adopted when one tries to end unethical organizational behavior?
3. What are some specific examples of each basic approach to ending unethical organizational behavior?
4. What are the limitations of each basic approach?
5. Which approach to ending unethical organizational behavior do you prefer? Why?

11 CHAPTER ELEVEN

LEGAL AND SOCIETAL ETHICS

DEFENDING THE DEATH PENALTY

Walter Berns

Synopsis

In this reading, Walter Berns presents a defense of capital punishment. While recognizing that the death penalty has a long and sometimes disturbing history behind it, he points out that most philosophers have traditionally favored it. The problem today is that, for Berns, we have become morally ambivalent about punishing wrong-doing. He says we find it difficult to punish anyone in good conscience and without guilt. Rejecting what, in his mind, are feeble justifications for punishment, stemming from notions like rehabilitation and deterrence, Berns argues that the primary reason to punish criminals should be to "pay back." He believes that a moral community must exact retribution to preserve law and order. For Berns, once a criminal has committed a vile crime like murder, then that criminal has lost his or her human dignity and the basic rights that flow from it. By threatening potential criminals and punishing murderers with the death penalty, in effect we praise the law-abidingness of law-abiding citizens and calm the anger of law-abiding people who properly get upset about crime. According to Berns, anger thus serves to unite us with others and strengthen the bonds between us. The death penalty creates awe or respect for the law and, by satisfying our anger, thus proves to be a useful means of preserving and protecting the public order. The only legitimate objection to the death penalty that Berns accepts rests on the grounds of fairness and discriminatory practices regarding its application. Berns recognizes that if we administer capital punishment, we must be fair and nondiscriminatory, otherwise we are not justified in so punishing.

For Capital Punishment is, so far as I know, the first book-length defense of the death penalty written by someone other than a professional law-enforcement officer.[1] As its author, I expected to be denounced in the liberal press, and I was. The best I could have hoped for was that the book would not be reviewed in certain journals. Unfortunately, the *New York Review of Books* did review it,[2] in a manner of speaking (the reviewer suggested that its author ought to be psychoanalyzed). Surprisingly, the *New York Times*, at least in its daily edition, gave it a good review, one I could have written myself;[3] Garry Wills, on the other hand, devoted an entire column to the book, during the course of which he told several outright lies about me and the book.[4] Then when I appeared on a live television show in Washington debating the death penalty with a man who has devoted his entire professional life to the effort to abolish it, my wife, at home, began to receive threatening telephone calls, many of them saying that her husband was the only person who deserved to be executed (or, as one persistent caller put it, "to sizzle"); these calls continued until we were forced to change our telephone number, which is now unlisted.

I recite these events only to make the point that capital punishment is a subject that arouses the angriest of passions. I suspect that opponents of the death penalty also receive threatening telephone calls, but somehow I doubt that theirs could match mine in nastiness. To the opponents of the death penalty, nothing can be said in its favor, and anyone who tries is a scoundrel or a fool. "Hang-hards" (Arthur Koestler's term) might defend it, the Ayatollah Khomeini might defend it, and police officers might be forgiven for defending it, but no rational person can defend it. That was Garry Wills's opinion, and that appears to be the opinion of the liberal world in general.

In one respect, at least, I have no quarrel with my hostile critics. The history of capital punishment is surely one that should give everyone pause: too many fanatics, too much ruthlessness, and too many disgusting public spectacles. On the other hand, there is also a history of the argument concerning capital punishment, and that history reveals something that ought to give pause to its opponents and arouse some doubts regarding the opinion prevailing in today's intellectual circles. Long before the current debate, political philosophers addressed themselves to the question of justice and, therefore, of crime and punishment; none of them, with the qualified exception of Jeremy Bentham, opposed the death penalty.[5] Opposition to capital punishment is in fact a modern phenomenon, a product of modern sentiment and modern thought. Except to unreconstructed progressives—I mean persons who believe that every area of thought is characterized by progress—this fact is one that ought to cause us at least to hesitate before, so to speak, picking up the telephone.

Do we really know more about crime and punishment than did the ancients? Are we better qualified to speak on these subjects than Sir Thomas More? Are we more concerned with human rights than were the founders of the school of human rights—say, John Locke? Than the founders of the first country—our own—established specifically to secure these rights? In matters of morality are we the superiors of Kant? Are we more humane than Tocqueville? Than John Stuart Mill? Thomas Jefferson? George Washington? Abraham Lincoln?

Or, alternatively, have we become so morally ambivalent, and in some cases, so guilt ridden, that we cannot in good conscience punish anyone and certainly not to the extent of putting him to death? In this connection, it is relevant to point out that, contrary to the public statements of some modern churchmen, the Bible cannot be read to support the cause of abolition of capital punishment—not when its texts are read fairly.[6] Furthermore, it is not insignificant that in the past, when the souls of men and women were shaped by the Bible and the regimes that ruled in the

West were those that derived their principles from the Bible, death was a customary penalty. Some of these regimes were the most sanguinary known to history, which suggests that piety and harsh punishment go together.

I am not contending that there might not be moral objections to capital punishment (there certainly are when it cannot be imposed fairly, or in a nondiscriminatory fashion), but only that neither political philosophy nor the Bible lends support to these objections. The abolition movement stems, instead, from what can fairly be described as an amoral, and surely an antireligious, work: Cesare Beccaria's unusually influential *On Crimes and Punishments*, first published in 1764.[7] Beccaria, whose teacher was Thomas Hobbes, set out to accomplish more than a few changes in the criminal codes of Western European countries: His revisions required the establishment of the modern liberal state, a state from which the Church's influence would be excluded. Like Hobbes, Beccaria argued that there is no morality outside the positive law.[8] Here is the source of that moral ambivalence to which I referred and which has gradually come to characterize the so-called enlightened opinion respecting punishment; the public opinion lags behind somewhat. A Norwegian judge (quoted by the well-known criminologist Johannes Andenaes) remarked this when he said that "our grandfathers punished, and they did so with a clear conscience [and] we punish too, but we do it with a bad conscience."[9]

Why, indeed, do we punish criminals? Some of us try to ease our uneasy consciences by saying that the purpose of punishment is the rehabilitation of the criminal. But we ought to know by now that we cannot in fact rehabilitate criminals. An occasional criminal, yes, but not criminals as a class or in significant numbers. We cannot rehabilitate them any more successfully than our penitentiaries can cause them to repent, or to become penitent. One reason for this is that too many of us, and especially those of us in the rehabilitation business, are of the opinion that criminals are not wicked. Who are we to ask them to repent when, essentially, we think they have nothing to repent of? How can we in good conscience ask them to be rehabilitated when, in effect, we deny that there is a moral order to which they should be restored? We look upon the criminal as disturbed, yes; sick, perhaps; underprivileged, surely; but wicked, no. Karl Menninger, a leading criminal psychologist, accuses us in *The Crime of Punishment* of being criminals because we damn "some of our fellow citizens with the label 'criminal.'"[10] We who do this are, he says, the only criminals. The others are sick and deserve to be treated, not punished. The immorality of this position, whose premise is that no one is responsible for his acts, requires no elaboration.

Or we punish criminals in order to deter others from becoming criminals. Punishment for this purpose is utilitarian, and, like Beccaria, we can justify something if it is truly useful. But again, to inflict pain on one person merely to affect the behavior of others is surely immoral, as our criminology texts have not hesitated to tell us.

Perhaps we can be persuaded of the necessity to punish criminals in order to incapacitate them, thereby preventing them from committing their crimes among us (but not, of course, against their fellow prisoners). I must point out, however, that unless we concede, as I do, that even incarcerated criminals are no less worthy of our concern than are law-abiding persons, this policy is also immoral.

What we have not been able to do (although

there are signs here and there that this is changing[11]) is to admit that we punish, in part at least, to pay back the criminal for what he has done to us, not as individuals but as a moral community. We exact retribution, and we do not like to admit this. Retribution smacks of harshness and moral indignation, and our Hobbesian-Beccarian principles forbid the public expression of moral indignation. In the 1972 death penalty cases, Justice Marshall went so far as to say that the eighth amendment forbidding cruel and unusual punishment, forbids "punishment for the sake of retribution."[12] In the words of Marshall's closest colleague, Justice Brennan, to execute a person in order to exact retribution is to deprive him of his human dignity, and "even the vilest criminal [is] possessed of common human dignity."[13]

In the past, when men reflected seriously on the differences between human and other beings, human dignity was understood to consist of the capacity to be a moral being, a being capable of choosing between right and wrong and, with this freedom, capable of governing himself.[14] Unlike other animals, a human being was understood to be a responsible moral creature. The "vilest criminal" was not being deprived of his human dignity when he was punished, not even when he was punished by being put to death; he had lost his dignity when he freely chose to commit his vile crimes. Retribution means to pay back, or to give people what they deserve to get, and it implies that different people deserve to get different things. But if human dignity is the standard according to which we determine who deserves to get what, and if everyone, no matter what he does, possesses human dignity, as Brennan would have it, then no one deserves to be treated differently and, unless everyone deserves to be punished, no one deserves to be punished.

I agree that a world built on Brennan's idea of human dignity may not exact retribution. It has lost all confidence in its opinions of right and wrong, good and evil, righteous and wicked, deserving and undeserving, and human and inhuman. It is, as the most eloquent opponent of the death penalty put it—I refer to the late Albert Camus—a world without God. As he said so well in his brilliant novel, *L'Etranger*, this is a world of hypocrites affecting the language of justice and moral outrage. Of course it is entitled to execute no one; such a world may punish no one. And that, he said, is our world. He did not act as if he believed it—he was a very brave enemy of both Hitler and Stalin—but he did most emphatically say it.[15]

The issue of capital punishment can be said to turn on the kind of world we live in (or the world we want to live in); a moral world or a morally indifferent world.

Contrary to Justices Marshall and Brennan, we in the United States have always recognized the legitimacy of retribution. We have schedules of punishment in every criminal code according to which punishments are designed to fit the crime, and not simply to fit what social science tells us about deterrence and rehabilitation: the worse the crime, the more severe the punishment. Justice requires criminals (as well as the rest of us) to get what they (and we) deserve, and what criminals deserve depends on what they have done to us.

To pay back criminals is not only just but, as Andenaes allows us to see, useful as well. For years he has been speaking of what he calls "general prevention," by which he means the capacity of the criminal law to promise obedience to law, not by instilling fear of punishment (the way of deterrence), but by inculcating law-abiding habits. I think the criminal law has this capacity, although Andenaes has never been able to explain the mechanism by which it works. To do so requires me to adopt an old and by now familiar manner of speaking of the law.

The law, and especially the criminal law, works by praising as well as by blaming. It attaches blame to the act of murder, for example, by making it a crime and threatening to punish anyone convicted of having committed it. This function of the law is familiar to us. What is unfamiliar is the way in which the law, by punishing the guilty and thereby blaming them for deeds they commit, also praises those persons who do not commit those deeds. The mechanism involved here is the satisfaction of the law-abiding person's anger, the anger that person ought to feel at the sight of crime. This anger has to be controlled, of course, and we rightly condemn persons who, at the sight of crime, take it upon themselves to punish its perpetrators. But we ought not condemn the anger such persons feel; indeed, that anger is a condition of a decent community. When no one, whether out of indifference or out of cowardice, responds to a Kitty Genovese's screams and plaintive calls for help, we have reason really to be concerned. A *citizen* ought to be angry when witnessing a crime, and, of course, that anger takes the form of wanting to hurt the cause of the anger—for example, whoever it was who mugged and murdered Kitty Genovese. The law must control or calm that anger, and one way it can do that is by promising to punish the criminal. When it punishes the criminal it satisfies that anger, and by doing so, it rewards the law-abiding persons who feel it. This is one purpose of punishment: to reward the law-abiding by satisfying the anger that they feel, or ought to feel, at the sight of crime. It rewards, and by rewarding praises, and therefore teaches, law-abidingness.

Anger, Aristotle teaches us,[16] is the pain caused by him who is the object of anger. It is also the pleasure arising from the hope of revenge. It has to be controlled or tamed, but it is not in itself reprehensible; it can be selfish, but, contrary to Freud, it need not be selfish. In fact, it is one of the passions that reaches out to other persons—unlike greed, for example, which is purely selfish—and, in doing so, can serve to unite us with others, or strengthen the bonds that tie us to others. It can be an expression of our caring for others, and society needs people who care for each other, people who, as Aristotle puts it, share their pleasures and their pains, and do so for the sake of others. Anger, again unlike greed or jealousy, is a passion that can cause us to act for reasons having nothing to do with selfish or mean calculation; indeed, when tamed and educated, it can become a most generous passion, the passion that protects the community by demanding punishment for its enemies (and criminals are enemies). It is the stuff from which both heroes and law-abiding citizens are made; and when it is aroused for the right reasons (and it is the job of the law to define those reasons), it deserves to be rewarded.

Criminals are properly the object of anger, and the perpetrators of great crimes (James Earl Ray and Richard Speck, for example) are properly the objects of great anger. They have done more than inflict injury on isolated individuals (and this is especially evident in the case of Ray). They have violated the foundations of trust and friendship, the necessary elements of a moral community. A moral community, unlike a hive of bees or hill of ants, is one whose members (responsible moral creatures) are expected *freely* to obey the laws; and, unlike a tyranny, are *trusted* to obey the laws. The criminal has violated that trust, and in doing so, has injured not merely his immediate victim but also the community as such. It was for this reason that God said to the Jewish community, "Ye shall take no satisfaction [or ransom] for the life of a murderer, which is guilty of death: but he shall be surely put to death."[17] The criminal has called into question the very possibility of that community by suggesting that human beings cannot be trusted freely to respect the property, the person, and the dignity of those with whom they are associated. Crime is an offense against the public, which is why the public prosecutes it.

If, then, persons are not angry when someone else is robbed, raped, or murdered, the implication is that there is no moral community because these persons do not care for anyone other than themselves. When they are angry, that is a sign of their caring; and that anger, that caring, should be rewarded. We reward it when we satisfy it, and we satisfy it when we punish its objects, criminals.

So the question becomes, how do we pay back those who are the objects of great anger because they have committed terrible crimes against us? We can derive some instruction in this subject from the book of Genesis, where we find an account of the first murder and of the first disagreement as to the appropriate punishment of a murderer. Cain killed Abel, and, we are told, God forbade anyone to kill Cain in turn: Vengeance, said the Lord, is mine, and he exacted that vengeance by banishing Cain "from the presence of the Lord."[18] The appropriate punishment would appear to be death or banishment; in either case, the murderer is deprived of life in the community of moral persons. As Justice Frankfurter put it in a dissent in one of the expatriation cases, certain criminals are "unfit to remain in the communion of our citizens."[19]

To elaborate this point, in my book I discussed two famous literary works dealing with murders: Shakespeare's *Macbeth* and Camus' *L'Etranger* (variously translated as *The Stranger* or *The Outsider*).[20] I pointed out that in *Macbeth* the murderer was killed, and I argued that the dramatic necessity of that death derived from its moral necessity. That is how Shakespeare saw it.

As I indicated above, Camus' novel treats murder in an entirely different context. A moral community is not possible without anger and the moral indignation that accompanies it; and it is for this reason that in this novel Camus shows us a world without anger. He denies the legitimacy of it, and specifically of an anger that is aimed at the criminal. Such an anger, he says, is nothing but hypocrisy. The hero—or antihero—of this novel is a stranger or outsider not because he is a murderer, not because he refuses to cry at his mother's funeral, not because he shows and feels no remorse for having murdered (and murdered for no reason whatever); he is a stranger because, in his unwillingness to express what he does not feel—remorse, sadness, regret—he alone is not a hypocrite. The universe he says at the end of the novel, is "benignly indifferent" to how we live. Such a universe, or such a world, cannot justify the taking of a life—even the life of a murderer. Only a moral community may do that, and a moral community is impossible in our time; which means there is no basis for friendship or for the ties that bind us and make us responsible for each other and to each other. The only thing we share, Camus says in his essay on the death penalty, is our "solidarity against death," and an execution "unsets" that solidarity.[21]

Strangely, when some of the abolitionists speak of the death penalty as a denial of human dignity, this is what they mean. Abe Fortas, writing after he left the supreme court, said that the "essential value," the value that constitutes the "basis of our civilization," is the "pervasive, *unqualified* respect for life."[22] This is what passes for a moral argument for him (and I have no doubt that he speaks for many others). In contrast, Lincoln (who, incidentally, greatly admired Shakespeare's *Macbeth*[23]), who respected life and grieved when it was taken, authorized the execution of 267 men. His respect of life was not "unqualified." He believed, as did the founders of our country, that there were some things for which people should be expected to give up their lives. For example, as he said at Gettysburg, Americans should be expected to give up their lives in order that this nation "shall have a new birth of freedom."

There are vast differences between Camus, a man of deep perception and elegance of expression, and Fortas, but they shared a single vision of our world. Camus, however, gave it a label appropriate to the vision: a world without dignity, without morality, and indifferent to how we treat each other. There are statutes in this world forbidding crimes, but there is no basis in the order of things for those statutes. It is a world that may not rightly impose the sentence of death on anyone—or for that matter punish anyone in any manner—or ask any patriot to risk his or her life for it.

Shakespeare's dramatic poetry serves to remind us of another world, of the majesty of the moral order and of the terrible consequences of breaching it through the act of murder (the worst offense against that order). Capital punishment, like banishment in other times and places, serves a similar purpose: It reminds us, or can remind us, of the reign of the moral order, and enhances, or can enhance, its dignity. The law must not be understood to be merely statute that we enact or repeal at our pleasure and obey or disobey at our convenience, especially not the criminal law. Whenever law is regarded as *merely* statutory, by which I mean arbitrary or enacted out of no moral necessity or reflecting no law beyond itself, people will soon enough disobey it, and the clever ones will learn to do so with impunity. The purpose of the criminal law is not merely to control behavior—a tyrant can do that—but also to promote respect for that which should be respected, especially the lives, the moral integrity, and even the property of others. In a country whose principles forbid it to preach, the criminal law is one of the few available institutions through which it can make a moral statement and, thereby, hope to promote this respect. To be successful, what it says—and it makes this moral statement when it punishes—must be appropriate to the offense and, therefore, to what has been offended. If human life is to be held in awe, the law forbidding the taking of it must be held in awe; and the only way it can be made to be awful or awe-inspiring is to entitle it to inflict the penalty of death.

Death is the most awful punishment available to the law of our time and place. Banishment (even if it were still a legal punishment under the constitution[24]) is not dreaded, not in our time; in fact, to judge by some of the expatriated Vietnam war resisters I used to see in Toronto, it is not always regarded as punishment. And, despite the example of Gary Gilmore, the typical offender does not prefer death to imprisonment, even life imprisonment. In prison the offender still enjoys some of the pleasures available outside and some of the rights of citizens, and is not utterly outside the protection of the laws. Most of all, a prisoner has not been deprived of hope—hope of escape, of pardon, or of being able to do some of the things that can be done even by someone who has lost freedom of movement. A convicted murderer in prison (Ray) has retained more of life than has the victim (Martin Luther King). A maximum-security prison may be a brutal place, and the prospect of spending one's life there is surely dreadful, but the prospect of being executed is more dreadful. And for the worst of crimes, the punishment must be most dreadful and awful—not most painful (for the purpose of punishment is not simply to inflict pain on the guilty offender), but awful in the sense of "commanding profound respect or reverential fear."

Whether the United States, or any of them, should be permitted to carry out executions is a question that is not answered simply by what I have written here. The answer depends on our ability to restrict its use to the worst of our criminals and to impose it in a nondiscriminatory fashion. We do not yet know whether that can be done.

Notes

1. Walter Berns *For Capital Punishment: Crime and the Morality of the Death Penalty* (New York: Basic Books, 1979).
2. June 28, 1979, pp. 22–25.
3. July 16, 1979, III, p. 14.
4. Garry Wills, "Capital Punishment and a Non Sequitur," *Washington Star*, Apr. 16, 1979, A–11. Wills's column was actually devoted to an excerpt from the book which was published in *Harper's* (April 1979). My reply to Wills was published in the *Washington Star*, April 21, 1979, A–9.
5. See Berns, *For Capital Punishment*, pp. 21–22.
6. Ibid., pp. 11–18.
7. Cesare Beccaria, *On Crimes and Punishments*, trans. Henry Paolucci (Indianapolis: Bobbs-Merrill, Library of Liberal Arts, 1963).
8. Ibid., p. 41.
9. Johannes Andenaes, *Punishment and Deterrence*, with a foreword by Norval Morris (Ann Arbor, Mich.: University of Michigan Press, 1984), p. 133.
10. Karl Menninger, *The Crime of Punishment* (New York: Viking Press, 1969), p. 9. At the twenty-second National Institute on Crime and Delinquency, Menninger was given the Roscoe Pound Award for his outstanding work in "the field of criminal justice"; see *American Journal of Corrections*, July-August 1975, p. 32.
11. See, for example, Norval Morris, "The Future of Imprisonment: Toward a Punitive Philosophy," *Michigan Law Review*, May 1974, pp. 1161–1180; and Andrew von Hirsch, *Doing Justice: The Choice of Punishments*, Report of the Committee for the Study of Incarceration (New York: Hill & Wang, 1976).
12. *Furman v. Georgia*, 408 U.S. 238, 343–1244 (1972).
13. Ibid., pp. 272–273.
14. Pico Della Mirandola, *Oration on the Dignity of Man*, trans. A. Robert Caponigri (Chicago: Henry Regnery, Gateway Editions, 1956).

15. See comments below.
16. Aristotle, *Rhetoric* 1378bl–5.
17. Numbers 35:31.
18. Genesis 4:15–16.
19. *Trop v. Dulles*, 356 U.S. 86, 122 (1958). Dissenting opinion.
20. Camus was the most powerful and eloquent opponent of capital punishment. See Albert Camus, "Reflections on the Guillotine," in *Resistance, Rebellion and Death*, trans. Justin O'Brien (New York: Knopf, 1961).
21. Ibid., p. 222.
22. Abe Fortas, "The Case against Capital Punishment," *New York Times Magazine*, Jan. 23, 1977, p. 29. Italics added.
23. In a letter from Lincoln to James H. Hackett written on August 17, 1863, Lincoln says, "Some of Shakespeare's plays I have never read, whilst others I have gone over perhaps as frequently as any unprofessional reader. Among the latter are *Lea*, *Richard Third*, *Henry Eighth*, *Hamlet*, and especially *Macbeth*. I think nothing equals *Macbeth*. It is wonderful." *The Collected Works of Abraham Lincoln*, vol. 6, Roy P. Basler, Ed., (New Brunswick, NJ: Rutgers University Press, 1953), p. 393.
24. Banishment, insofar as it would be comprehended by expatriation, has been declared an unconstitutionally cruel and unusual punishment. *Affroyim v. Rusk*, 387 U.S. 253 (1967).

Content Quiz 11.1

Instructions: Fill in the blanks with the appropriate responses listed below.

awful	community
Cesare Beccaria	ambivalent
rehabilitation	Jeremy Bentham
retribution	deterrence
anger	dignity

1. The fear of punishment acts as a _____ to crime.
2. Many people have become hesitant and guilt-ridden about punishment because they have become morally _____.
3. *On Crimes and Punishments* was written by _____. It advocates the establishment of a modern liberal state.
4. One political philosopher opposed to the death penalty is _____.
5. Punishment, seen as giving a person what he or she deserves, is a form of _____.
6. _____ need not be selfish like jealousy or greed. It can serve to unite people and to consolidate bonds of trust.

7. The law must be made _____ in the sense that it must evoke reverential respect.
8. In order to assuage their guilt, some people regard punishment as a form of _____ for the criminal.
9. Indifference and cowardice in the face of crime undermines the bonds of _____.
10. Berns argues that criminals lose their _____ when they commit vile crimes.

Discussion Questions

1. Historically speaking, has capital punishment been generally accepted or rejected?
2. Why are people reluctant to punish?
3. What reasons can be given to justify punishment?
4. Does Berns believe that all people possess human dignity unconditionally?
5. Must punishment concern itself only with fear and deterrence? Does it have any positive function?
6. Is the emotion of anger wrong in itself? Are there situations wherein anger is desirable? How should it be dealt with?
7. What is meant by the concept of moral community?
8. In what sense should the law be awful, according to Berns?

THE FOLLY OF CAPITAL PUNISHMENT

Arthur Koestler

Synopsis

In this article, Arthur Koestler addresses himself to the "deterrence argument" frequently used to defend capital punishment. He recognizes that humanitarian arguments could be brought forward as a basis for objecting to capital punishment as a deterrent, but he chooses instead to reject deterrence on purely utilitarian grounds. He argues that capital punishment is not effective as a deterrent and that, consequently, the deterrence argument used in its favor should be rejected.

In building his argument, Koestler asks who, in fact, is deterred by capital punishment. After eliminating numerous types of murderers, he suggests that it is only the professional criminal class that remains to be deterred. As he quickly points out, however, murders are not usually committed by members of this class, but by amateurs. In his rejection of the deterrence argument, Koestler also presents statistical, historical and international evidence that calls into further question the notion that capital punishment dissuades people from committing murder. The facts repeatedly suggest that the absence of capital punishment, or its abolition, has no appreciable effect on murder and crime rates.

In the last part of the article, Koestler responds to possible objections to his statistically based arguments against capital punishment. Noting that defenders of capital punishment, who tend to ignore evidence contrary to their position, often say things like "statistics lie" or that "foreign experience" does not apply here, Koestler defends statistical analysis by pointing to the fact that governments, insurance companies, physicists, and engineers all base their daily business activities on them. Also, Koestler, underscores the fact that proper statistical analysis is designed to cancel out individual and national differences with the use of large and varied samples. Given that overwhelming statistical evidence shows that capital punishment does not, in fact, deter, Koestler expresses his amazement that advocates of capital punishment continue to use deterrence as an argument in support of it.

The arguments in defense of capital punishment have remained essentially the same since Lord Ellenborough's days. In the recent Parliamentary debates the Home Secretary, Major Lloyd George, again patiently trotted out the three customary reasons why the Government opposed abolition: that the death penalty carried a unique deterrent value; that no satisfactory alternative punishment could be designed; and that public opinion was in favor of it.

The second and third points will be discussed in later chapters. At present I am only concerned with the first and main argument. To give it a fair hearing, we must set all humanitarian considerations and charitable feelings aside, and examine the effectiveness of the gallows as a deterrent to potential murderers from a coldly practical, purely utilitarian point of view. This is, of course, a somewhat artificial view, for in reality "effectiveness" can never be the only consideration; even if it were proved that death preceded by torture, or on the wheel, were more effective, we would refuse to act accordingly. However, it will be seen that the theory of hanging as the best deterrent can be refuted on its own purely utilitarian grounds, without calling ethics and charity to aid.

A deterrent must logically refer to a "deterree," if the reader will forgive me for adding a verbal barbarity to the barbarous subject. So the first question is: who are the hypothetical deterrees, who will be prevented from committing murder by the threat of hanging, but not by the threat of long-term imprisonment? The fear of death is no doubt a powerful deterrent; but just how much more powerful is it than the fear of a life sentence?

The gallows obviously failed as a deterrent in all cases where a murder has actually been committed. It is certainly not a deterrent to murderers who commit suicide—and one-third of all murderers do. It is not a deterrent to the insane and mentally deranged; nor to those who have killed in a quarrel, in drunkenness, in a sudden surge of passion—and this type of murder amounts to 80 percent to 90 percent of all murders that are committed. It is not a deterrent to the type of person who commits murder because he desires to be hanged; and these cases are not infrequent. It is not a deterrent to the person who firmly believes in his own perfect method—by poison, acid bath, and so on—which, he thinks, will never be found out. Thus the range of hypothetical deterrees who can only be kept under control by the threat of death and nothing short of death, is narrowed down to the professional criminal class. But both the abolitionists and their opponents agree that "murder is not a crime of the criminal classes"; it is a crime of amateurs, not of professionals. None of the points I have mentioned so far is controversial; they are agreed on by both sides. . . .

Who, then, are the deterrees for whose sake this country must preserve capital punishment, as the only European democracy except Eire and France—which, from the judicial point of view, is not very enviable company? What type of criminal, to repeat the question in its precise form, can only be ruled by the threat of hanging, and nothing short of hanging? It is at this point that the issue between abolitionists and their opponents is really joined. The opponents' argument may be summed up as follows. As things stand, the professional criminal rarely commits murder; but if the threat of the gallows were abolished, he would take to murder, and the crime rate would go up.

This, of course, is an unproved assumption: a hypothesis whose truth could only be tested either (a) by experiment, or (b) by drawing on analogies from past experiences in Britain and abroad. The House of Commons in 1948 voted for the experiment. It said: let us suspend executions for five years, and see what happens. The House of Lords rejected it after it was informed by the Lord Chief Justice that the twenty Judges of the King's Bench were unanimous in opposing the measure. His main argument against the five-year suspension was that the experiment would be too dangerous; his second argument, that if the dangerous experiment were tried, abolition would come to stay. He used both arguments in the same speech. So much for the experimental method.

Now for the second method: by analogy or precedent. Perhaps the oddest thing about this whole controversy is that the Judges, who live on bread and precedent, never quote a precedent in support of their thesis that abolition leads to an increase in crime. After all, the burden of proof for this assumption lies on them; and since there is a gold mine of precedent at their disposal of what happened after the abolition of capital punishment for some two hundred and twenty different categories of crime, why do they never, never treat us to a single case? Why do we never hear: you want to repeal the capital statute for murder; look what happened after the repeal of statute 14 Geo. 2, c. 6, s. 1 (174) [sic] (burglary), 7 Will. 4 & 1 Vic., c. 89, s. 2 (arson), 9 Geo. 4, c. 31, s. 16 (rape), 8 Geo. 1, c. 22 (1921) (forgery)? Why is it that the reformers, these reckless destroyers of the bulwarks of tradition, always rely on history for support, whereas on this particular issue the keepers of tradition act as if the past did not exist?

Yet the present situation is fraught with precedents and echoes of the past. In the ten years 1940–49 the number of murders known to the Police in England and Wales amounted to 1,666 cases; the number of executions in the same period was 127. Expressed in annual averages, we have 170 murders but only 13 executions. That means that the law as it stands is only found applicable in practice in 7 percent of all cases; in Scotland even less: only 1 in 35, that is, under 3 percent of all murderers are actually executed. The law says that murder shall be punished by death; but in about 95 out of 100 cases the law cannot be applied for a variety of reasons which will be discussed in detail later on. And that again means, as in all cases in the past when such glaring discrepancies occurred, that the law has outlived its time and has become an anachronism.

There are, as we saw before, two methods of remedying such a situation. The first is to bring the law up to date; the second, to put the clock of history back. The latter solution was advocated by the Lord Chief Justice in his evidence before the Royal Commission of 1948, when he suggested that fewer people ought to be reprieved and that it was perfectly proper to hang a person who is certified insane, but is not insane according to the M'Naghten Rules of 1843. We have discussed in sufficient detail the disastrous results to which such attempts to put the clock back have led in the course of the eighteenth and early nineteenth centuries.

The opposite method was tried from approximately 1920 onward. The basic reason why it was tried was the same which underlies the present inquiry: the law had become outdated, and therefore largely inapplicable and ineffective. In November 1830, the Jurors of London presented their remarkable petition to the Commons. It ran:

> That in present state of the law, jurors feel extremely reluctant to convict where the penal consequences of the offense excite a conscientious horror in their minds, lest the rigorous performance of their duties as jurors should make them accessory to judicial murder. Hence, in Courts of Justice, a most necessary and painful struggle is occasioned by the conflict of the feelings of a just humanity with the sense of the obligation of an oath.

The deterrent of the gallows affected the jury more than the criminal; the juries went on strike, as it were. They made it a rule, when a theft of goods worth forty shillings was a capital offense, to assess the value of the goods at thirty-nine shillings; and when, in 1827, the capital offense was raised to five pounds, the juries raised their assessment to four pounds nineteen shillings. Present-day juries, as we shall see, bring in verdicts of "guilty, but insane" in cases where, according to medical evidence and the Judge's direction, the accused must be regarded as sane before the law. "It would be following strict precedent," says Mr. Gardiner in the *Law Quarterly*, "for the perversity of jurors to be the prelude to reform."

The perversity of the jurors reached such an extent that it led, in 1830, to the famous "Petition of Bankers from 214 cities and towns," urging Parliament to abolish the death penalty for forgery—not for any sentimental, humanitarian motives, but to protect themselves against the forgers to whom the gallows proved no deterrent. Here is the full text of the petition:

> That your petitioners, as bankers, are deeply interested in the protection of property, from forgery, and in the infliction of punishment on persons guilty of that crime.
>
> That your petitioners find, by experience, that the infliction of death, or even the possibility of the infliction of death, prevents the prosecution, conviction and punishment of the criminal and thus endangers the property which it is intended to protect.
>
> That your petitioners, therefore, earnestly pray that your honorable House will not withhold from them that protection to their property which they would derive from a more lenient law.

Few of the bankers may have read Beccaria or Jeremy Bentham, and few would probably have subscribed to their philosophy. Yet for reasons of hard-headed expediency, they subscribed to the theory of the "minimum effective penalty." It took Parliament another six years to abolish capital punishment for forgery. The usual warnings were uttered that this measure would lead to the "destruction of trade and commerce" and in Chief Justice Lord Manfield's opinion the answer to the predicament was that capital sentences for forgery ought always to be carried out. Yet when death for forgery was abolished, the number of commitments for that crime fell from 213 in the three years before repeal to 180 in the three subsequent years.

If the death penalty were a more effective deterrent than lesser penalties, then its abolition for a given category of crime should be followed by a noticeable increase in the volume of that crime, precisely as the hanging party says. But the fact tells a different story. After the great reform, the crime rate did not rise; it fell—as everybody except the oracles had expected. And yet the era of reform coincided with one of the most difficult periods in English social history. As if History herself had wanted to make the task of the abolitionists more difficult, the repeal of the death penalty for offenses against property during the 1830's was immediately followed by the "hungry forties." The great experiment of mitigating the rigor of the law could not have been carried out under more unfavorable circumstances. Yet halfway through the experiment, when the number of capital offenses had been reduced to fifteen, His Majesty's Commissioners on Criminal Law, 1836, summed up their report as follows:

> It has not, in effect, been found that the repeal of Capital Punishment with regard to any particular class of offenses has been attended with an increase of the offenders. On the contrary, the evidence and statements to be found in our appendix go far to demonstrate that . . . the absolute number of the offenders has diminished.

And at the conclusion of the most dangerous experiment in the history of English criminal law, Sir Joseph Pease was able to state in the House of Commons that "the continual mitigation of law and of sentences has been accomplished with property quite as secure, and human life quite a sacred."

"Deterrence" is an ugly and abstract word. It means, according to the *Oxford Dictionary*, "discouragement by fear." If the arguments in favor of the gallows as the supreme deterrent were true, then public executions would have the maximum discouraging effect on the criminal. Yet these public exhibitions, intended to prove that "crime does not pay," were known to be the occasion when pickpockets gathered their richest harvest among the crowd. A contemporary author explains why: "The thieves selected the moment when the strangled man was swinging above them as the happiest opportunity, because they knew that everybody's eyes were on that person and all were looking up."

Public executions not only failed to diminish the volume of crime; they often caused an immediate rise in their wake. The hanging of a criminal served, less as a warning, than as an incitement to imitate him. Fauntleroy confessed that the idea of committing forgery came to him while he watched a forger being hanged. A juryman, who found Dr. Dodd guilty of forgery, committed soon afterwards the same crime and was hanged from the same gallows. Cummings was hanged in Edinburgh in 1854 for sexual assault, which immediately led to a wave of similar assaults in the region. In 1855, Heywood was hanged in Liverpool for cutting the throat of a woman; three weeks later, Ferguson was arrested in the same town for the same crime. The list could be continued indefinitely. The evidence was so overwhelming that a Select Committee of the House of Lords was appointed in 1856; it recommended that public executions should be abolished because they did not deter from crime. The Lords would not believe it, and did nothing. Ten years later, the Royal Commission of 1866 inquired into the same question, and came to the same result as the Select Committee. One of the most striking pieces of evidence before the Commissioners was a statement by the prison chaplain in Bristol, the Reverend W. Roberts, that out of 167 persons awaiting execution in that prison, 164 had previously witnessed at least one execution. What would the British Medical Association say of the value of a patent medicine for the prevention of polio, if it were found in 167 polio cases that 164 had been treated with that medicine?

Two years after the Royal Commission's reports, Parliament decided that executions should henceforth be private. However, if watching with one's own eyes the agony of a person being strangled on the gallows does not deter, it seems logical to assume that an unseen execution in a more gentlemanly manner would deter even less. One may further argue that if the penalty of hanging does not frighten even a pickpocket, it would not frighten a potential murderer, who acts either in momentary passion, or for incomparably higher stakes. Yet these were not the conclusions reached by the lawgivers. They assumed that while watching an execution from a few yards' distance did not act as a deterrent, reading a Home Office communique about it did.

The results of the abolition of the death penalty for crimes against property provide a powerful argument for abolishing it altogether. But in itself, the argument is not conclusive. The fact that abolition of the death penalty did not increase the volume of cattle stealing strongly suggests, but does not prove, that abolition of the death penalty would not increase the volume of murder. That proof can only be initiated by analogy with other crimes; it must be completed by actual precedents for the crime of murder itself.

Fortunately, these precedents are available through the experience of the thirty-six states which have abolished capital punishment in the course of the last hundred years.

The evidence has been studied by criminologists and Departments of Justice all over the world, and summarized with previously unequalled thoroughness by the British Parliamentary Select Committee of 1929–30 and the Royal Commission on Capital Punishment of 1948–53. The report and evidence of the first fills some eight hundred closely printed pages; the report of the second, plus its Minutes of Evidence, nearly fourteen hundred pages of quarto and folio. The conclusion of the Select Committee is summed up as follows:

> Our prolonged examination of the situation in foreign countries has increasingly confirmed us in the assurance that capital punishment may be abolished in this country without endangering life or property, or impairing the security of society.

The conclusions of the Royal Commission were essentially the same, although more cautiously expressed. Their terms of reference prevented them from considering the question whether capital punishment should be abolished or not; they were only allowed to make recommendations concerning changes in the existing capital law. Moreover, their report was unanimous, whereas the Select Committee report of 1930, as the previous Royal Commission report of 1866, was a majority report. The Commission's final conclusion regarding the expected consequences of abolition (which they managed to smuggle in, though the terms of reference excluded this question) was formulated thus:

> There is no clear evidence of any lasting increase [in the murder rate following abolition] and there are many offenders on whom the deterrent effect is limited and may often be negligible. It is therefore important to view the question in a just perspective and not to base a penal policy in relation to murder on exaggerated estimates of the uniquely deterrent force of the death-penalty.

They reached this conclusion by taking two types of evidence into account: on the one hand, the crime statistics of foreign countries; on the other, the opinion of the British Police Force, the prison services, and the judges. It is to this second, or local evidence that the expression "exaggerated estimates" refers; and in their conclusions the Commissioners make some allowances for it. But in the text of their report, as distinct from their cautious "conclusions," they make their findings unmistakeably clear. They dismiss the police's and the judges' contention that abolition would entice burglars to wear firearms: "We received no evidence that the abolition of capital punishment in other countries had in fact led to the consequences apprehended by our witnesses in this country." Their opinion on the general effect of abolition on the crime rate in foreign countries is equally unambiguous. They analyzed the staggeringly extensive material which they had assembled under three headings:

(a) by comparing the homicide statistics of a given country before and after abolition of the death penalty;
(b) by comparing the homicide statistics of neighboring countries of a similar social structure, some of which have abolished the death-penalty and some not, over the same period of time;
(c) by analyzing the possible influence of the number of executions in a given country in a particular year on the homicide rate in the immediately following period.

Concerning (a), they state: "The general conclusion which we have reached is that there is no clear evidence in any of the figures we have examined that the abolition of capital punishment has led to an increase in the homicide rate, or that its reintroduction has led to a fall."

Concerning (b), their findings are mainly based on comparisons between the homicide curves in closely related states in the U.S.A.; and between New Zealand and the Australian states:

> If we take any of these groups we find that the fluctuations in the homicide rate of each of its component members exhibit a striking similarity. We agree with Professor Sellin that the only conclusion which can be drawn from the figures is that there is no clear evidence of any influence of the death-penalty on the homicide rates of these States, and that, "whether the death-penalty is used or not, and whether executions are frequent or not, both death-penalty States and abolition States show rates which suggest that these rates are conditioned by other factors than the death-penalty."

Concerning (c), they state: ". . . about the possible relation between the number of executions in particular years and the incidence of murder in succeeding years . . . we are satisfied that no such relationship can be established."

Once more the mountains labored and a mouse was born. The mountainous statistical survey of the Royal Commission of 1948 merely confirmed the findings of the Select Committee of 1930, which confirmed the findings of all abolitionist countries in the course of the last century for crimes against property: to wit, that abolition has not caused an increase in murder nor stopped the fall of the murder rate in any European country; and that in the non-European countries, the U.S.A., Australia, and New Zealand, the ups and downs of the murder rate show a striking similarity in states of similar social structure whether the death penalty is used or not.

The defenders of capital punishment are well aware that the statistical evidence is unanswerable. They do not contest it: they ignore it. When pressed in debate, they invariably fall back on one of two answers: (a) "statistics lie" or "do not prove anything"; (b) that the experience of foreign countries has no bearing on conditions in Britain. Let us examine both answers.

That "statistics don't prove anything" is, of course, nonsense; if it were true, all insurances [sic] companies, physicists, and engineers would have to go out of business, and the Chancellor of the Exchequer could never present a Budget. Statistics are indispensable in every human activity; and like every tool they can be put to careless and dishonest use. Statistics cannot prove or disprove that smoking "causes" lung cancer; it can prove that the average Englishman is taller than the average Italian. In the first example, the observational range is too small in relation to the number of causative factors involved. In the second example, the statistician merely states a fact which can be interpreted in various ways; by race, nourishment, climate, and so on.

In discussing the statistics of abolitionist Europe, we have to distinguish with great care between fact and interpretation. The facts are beyond dispute; throughout the twentieth century, abolition was in no European country followed by an increase in the murder rate, and was in nearly all countries followed by a decrease. These facts can be interpreted in the following manners:

(1) Abolition causes a fall in the murder rate.
(2) Abolition causes an increase in the murder rate, but this increase is too small to stop the general downward trend of the murder rate, which is due to different causes.
(3) Abolition does not perceptibly influence the murder rate one way or another.

All three interpretations are possible, although the examples of post-war Germany and post-war Italy . . . seem to contradict the second hypothesis; but that, of course, is not conclusive. It is at this point that the comparisons between similar states with different legislation come in. They prove that "both death-penalty states and abolition states show rates which suggest that they are conditioned by other factors than the death penalty. . . . The general picture is the same—a rise in the rates of the early twenties and a downward trend since then."

This eliminates interpretations (1) and (2) and leaves us with (3): that the death penalty cannot be proved to influence the murder rate one way or another.

Let us make the point clearer by a familiar example. If the medical profession wants to test the efficiency of a new serum there are, by and large, two methods of doing this. The first is to administer the serum to a number of patients and see how the results compare with the use of older medicines. The substitution of prison sentences in lieu of capital punishment was an experiment of this kind. It showed that it was followed nearly everywhere in Europe by a fall in the fever chart of crime. This in itself did not prove that the new treatment was the direct *cause* of the improvement, because perhaps the epidemic was on the wane anyway; but it did prove that the new treatment could at least not be sufficiently harmful to impede the fall on the fever chart, whatever the cause of that fall. The second method is used as a check on the first. The new serum is administered to patients in one hospital ward, and the rate of recovery is then compared to that in a second or "control" ward, where treatment is continued on the old lines. If the rate of recovery remains substantially the same in both wards, the British Medical Association will conclude that the new treatment is just as good or bad as the old one, as far as its deterrent effect on the disease goes. The choice will then be decided by other considerations. If the new treatment is less painful or repellent, then only the oldest fogeys of the profession will, just for the hell of it, stick to their ancient method.

To sum up: the experience of the civilized world proves as conclusively as the most rigorously sifted evidence can ever prove, that the gallows is no more effective than other nonlethal deterrents.

But statistics don't bleed; let us always remember the individual sample falling through the trap.

So much for the contention that "statistics don't prove anything." The second stock answer of the hang-hards runs: "Foreign experience doesn't prove anything, because foreigners are different." It was said in defense of death for shoplifting when all the rest of Europe had abandoned it; it is repeated today with the same unction. The grain of truth in it is that no nation is like any other nation; thus the example of, say, Switzerland *alone* would be of little value because Switzerland is a more "peaceful" country than England. But the whole point of the statistical approach is that, over a larger number of samples, individual differences cancel out, and the general trend common to all is revealed.

Now the evidence concerning abolition embraces thirty-six countries with vastly different populations, and in different periods of development; agricultural and industrial nations, old and new civilizations, countries rich and countries poor, Latin, Anglo-Saxon, and Germanic races, hot-tempered and placid people, countries which became abolitionist after a long period of peace and security, and others, like Germany and Italy, which have only just emerged from war, demoralized by defeat, brutalized by years of totalitarian terror. The convincingness of the proof rests precisely in the fact that, however different the countries and conditions, abolition was nowhere followed by an increase in the crime rate, or any other noticeable ill effect.

The general reader who is new to this controversy would naturally assume that the opponents of abolition have their own arguments, figures, and evidence on the same reasoned and factual level as the abolitionists, and that it would require a good deal of expert knowledge to decide which party is right. This is not the case. The defenders of capital punishment have produced no evidence of their own; nor contested the correctness of the documentary material assembled by Royal Commissions, Select Committees, etc.; nor even tried to put a different interpretation on it. They simply ignore it; as they ignore the experience gained from mitigations of the law in this country's own past. When challenged, they invariably and uniformly trot out the same answers: there is no alternative to capital punishment; statistics don't prove anything; other nations can afford to abolish hanging, but not Britain, because the criminal Englishman (or Welshman or Scotsman) is different from any other criminal in the world; for foreigners prison may be a sufficient deterrent, the English criminal needs the gallows.

Since the Select Committee's report, the Royal Commission has vastly extended the scope of the former's inquiry, and arrived at the same results. The answer of the hang-hards remained the same. It seems hardly believable that in a nation-wide controversy which has now been going on for some twenty-five years, one side should produce, with ant-like diligence, facts, figures, and historic precedent, mobilize the whole array of psychiatry and social science, borne out by impartial Royal Commissions—and the other side should content themselves with evasions, stonewalling, and the ever repeated nonsense about the unique and indispensable deterrent value of the death penalty. The legend about the hangman as the protector of society has been refuted and exposed to ridicule on every single past occasion, and yet it popped up again on the next.

This is perhaps the saddest aspect in this whole heart- and neck-breaking business. For it shows that an officially sponsored lie has a thousand lives and takes a thousand lives. It resembles one of the monster squids of deep-sea lore; it spurts ink into your face, while its tentacles strangle the victim in the interest of public welfare.

Content Quiz 11.2

Instructions: Fill in the blanks with the appropriate responses listed below.

anachronism	deterrence
burden of proof	utilitarian
precedent	public executions
capital punishment	fact
professional criminal class	deterree

1. Koestler's objection to using capital punishment as a deterrent is not based on moral principle, but rather on _____ considerations.
2. Judges and others in favor of capital punishment as a deterrent never quote _____ to support their claim that abolition of the death penalty leads to an increase in crime.
3. The _____ falls on those advocating capital punishment to show that it does, in fact, deter.
4. An outdated law is an _____.
5. _____ means "discouragement by fear."
6. _____ have failed to diminish the amount of crime.
7. The conclusion of the British Parliamentary Select Committee (1929–1930) was that _____ could be abolished without risking property and the security of society.
8. When discussing the statistics on capital punishment, it is important to distinguish between _____ and interpretation.
9. One who is deterred is a _____.
10. The _____ rarely commits murder.

Discussion Questions

1. What is Arthur Koestler's position on capital punishment?
2. What exactly is meant by deterrence? How is it different from retribution? Are retribution and deterrence necessarily related?
3. Given the evidence, would capital punishment be effective if it were more frequently and publicly administered? Why or why not?
4. What support, if any, can be mustered for using the death penalty as a deterrent?

IS PORNOGRAPHY BENEFICIAL?

G.L. Simons

Synopsis

In this article G.L. Simons argues against the censorship of pornography. He believes that this kind of censorship constitutes an indefensible restriction of human freedom. He maintains that imposing restrictions on individual liberty is justifiable only if what is being restricted clearly produces significant harm—a harm that far outweighs other positive consequences. In defense of his position, Simons cites U.S. and Danish studies which conclude that pornography cannot be linked to any significant negative consequences. The same studies suggest that pornography may even be beneficial in certain circumstances by (a) providing pleasure, (b) alleviating sexual frustration, (c) providing an outlet for lonely and deprived people to make sexual contact, and (d) by offering a "catharsis" that can neutralize aberrant sexual behavior. For Simons, if pornography produces enjoyment or pleasure, if this enjoyment is not to be condemned, and if there is no evidence to show serious countervailing harm, then the case for making pornography available is unassailable.

It is not sufficient, for the objectors' case, that they demonstrate that some harm has flowed from pornography. It would be extremely difficult to show that pornography had *never* had unfortunate consequences, but we should not make too much of this. Harm has flowed from religion, patriotism, alcohol and cigarettes without this fact impelling people to demand abolition. The harm, if established, has to be weighed against a variety of considerations before a decision can be reached as to the propriety of certain laws. Of the British Obscenity Laws the Arts Council Report comments[1] that "the harm would need to be both indisputable and very dire indeed before it could be judged to outweigh the evils and anomalies inherent in the Acts we have been asked to examine."

The onus therefore is upon the antipornographers to demonstrate not only that harm is caused by certain types of sexual material but that the harm is considerable: if the first is difficult the second is necessarily more so, and the attempts to date have not been impressive. It is even possible to argue that easily available pornography has a number of benefits. Many people will be familiar with the *catharsis* argument whereby pornography is said to cut down on delinquency by providing would-be criminals with substitute satisfactions. This is considered later but we mention it here to indicate that access to pornography may be socially beneficial in certain instances, and that where this is possible the requirement for antipornographers to *justify* their objections must be stressed.

The general conclusion[2] of the U.S. Commission was that no adequate proof had been provided that pornography was harmful to individual or society—"if a case is to be made out against 'pornography' [in 1970] it will have to be made on grounds other than demonstrated effects of a damaging personal or social nature. . . ."

The heresy (to some ears) that pornography is harmless is compounded by the even greater impiety that it may be beneficial. Some of us are managing to adjust to the notion that pornography is unlikely to bring down the world in moral ruin, but the idea that it may actually do good is altogether another thing. When we read of Professor Emeritus E. T. Rasmussen, a pioneer of psychological studies in Denmark, and a government adviser, saying that there is a possibility "that pornography can be beneficial," many of us are likely to have *mixed* reactions, to say the least. In fact this thesis can be argued in a number of ways.

The simplest approach is to remark that people enjoy it. This can be seen to be true whether we rely on personal testimony or the most respectable index of all in capitalist society—"preparedness to pay." The appeal that pornography has for many people is hardly in dispute, and in a more sober social climate that would be justification enough. Today we are not quite puritan enough to deny that *pleasure* has a worthwhile place in human life: not many of us object to our food being tasty or our clothes being attractive. It was not always like this. In sterner times it was *de rigueur* to prepare food without spices and to wear the plainest clothes. The cult of puritanism reached its apotheosis in the most fanatical asceticism, where it was fashionable for holy men to wander off into a convenient desert and neglect the body to the point of cultivating its lice as "pearls of God." In such a bizarre philosophy pleasure was not only condemned in its sexual manifestations but in all areas where the body could conceivably take satisfaction. These days we are able to countenance pleasure in most fields but in many instances still the case for *sexual* pleasure has to be argued.

Pleasure is not of course its own justification. If it clearly leads to serious malaise, early death, or the *dis*pleasure of others, then there is something to be said against it. But the serious consequences have to be demonstrated: it is not enough to condemn certain forms of pleasurable experience on the grounds of *possible* ill effect. With such an approach *any* human activity could be censured and freedom would have no place. In short, if something is pleasurable and its bad effects are small or nonexistent then it is to be encouraged: opposition to such a creed should be recognized as an unwholesome antipathy to human potential. Pleasure is a good except where it is harmful (and where the harmfulness is *significant*). . . .

That pornography is enjoyable to many people is the first of the arguments in its favor. In any other field this would be argument enough. It is certainly sufficient to justify many activities that have—unlike a taste for pornography—demonstrably harmful consequences. Only in a sexually neurotic society could a tool for heightening sexual enjoyment be regarded as reprehensible and such as to warrant suppression by law. The position is well summarized[3] in the *first* of the Arts Council's twelve reasons for advocating the repeal of the Obscenity Publications Acts:

> "It is not for the State to prohibit private citizens from choosing what they may or may not enjoy in literature or art unless there were incontrovertible evidence that the result would be injurious to society. There is no such evidence."

A further point is that availability of pornography may *aid*, rather than frustrate normal sexual development. Thus in 1966, for example, the New Jersey Committee for the Right to Read presented the findings of a survey conducted among nearly a thousand psychiatrists and psychologists of that state. Amongst the various personal statements included was the view that "sexually stimulating materials" might help particular people develop a normal sex drive.[4] In similar spirit, Dr. John Money writes[5] that pornography "may encourage normal sexual development and broadmindedness," a view that may not sound well to the antipornographers. And even in circumstances where possible dangers of pornography are pointed out conceivable good effects are sometimes acknowledged. In a paper issued[6] by The Danish Forensic Medicine Council it is pointed out that neurotic and sexually shy people may, by reading pornographic descriptions of normal sexual activity, be freed from some of their apprehension regarding sex and may thereby attain a freer and less frustrated attitude to the sexual side of life. . . .

One argument in favor of pornography is that it can serve as a substitute for actual sexual activity involving another person or other people. This argument has two parts, relating as it does to (1) people who fantasize over *socially acceptable* modes of sexual involvement, and (2) people who fantasize over types of sexual activity that would be regarded as illegal or at least immoral. The first type relates to lonely and deprived people who for one reason or another have been unable to form "normal" sexual contacts with other people; the second type are instances of the much quoted *catharsis* argument.

One writer notes[7] that pornography can serve as a substitute for both the knowledge of which some people have been deprived and the pleasure in sexual experience which they have not enjoyed. One can well imagine men and women too inhibited to secure sexual satisfaction with other adults and where explicit sexual material can alleviate some of their misery. It is facile to remark that such people should seek psychiatric assistance or even "make an effort": the factors that prevent the forming of effective sexual liaisons are just as likely to inhibit any efforts to seek medical or other assistance. Pornography provides *sex by proxy*, and in such usage it can have a clear justification.

It is also possible to imagine circumstances in which men and women—for reasons of illness, travel or bereavement—are unable to seek sexual satisfaction with spouse or other loved one. Pornography can help here too. Again it is easy to suggest that a person abstain from sexual experience, or, if having *permanently* lost a spouse, seek out another partner. Needless to say such advice is often quite impractical—and the alternative to pornography may be prostitution or adultery. Montagu notes that pornography can serve the same purpose as "dirty jokes," allowing a person to discharge harmlessly repressed and unsatisfied sexual desires.

In this spirit, Mercier (1970) is quoted by the U.S. Commission:

> ". . . it is in periods of sexual deprivation—to which the young and the old are far more subject than those in their prime—that males, at any rate, are likely to reap psychological benefit from pornography."

And also Kenneth Tynan (1970):

> "For men on long journeys, geographically cut off from wives and mistresses, pornography can act as a portable memory, a welcome shortcut to remembered bliss, relieving tension without involving disloyalty."

It is difficult to see how anyone could object to the use of pornography in such circumstances, other than on the grounds of a morbid antisexuality.

The *catharsis argument* has long been put forward to suggest that availability of pornography will neutralize "aberrant" sexual tendencies and so reduce the incidence of sex crime or clearly immoral behavior in related fields. (Before evidence is put forward for this thesis it is worth remarking that it should not be necessary to demonstrate a *reduction* in sex crime to justify repeal of the Obscenity Laws. It should be quite sufficient to show that an *increase* in crime will not ensue following repeal. We may even argue that a small increase may be tolerable if other benefits from easy access to pornography could be shown: but it is no part of the present argument to put this latter contention.)

Many psychiatrists and psychologists have favored the catharsis argument. Chesser, for instance, sees[8] pornography as a form of voyeurism in which—as with sado-masochistic material—the desire to hurt is satisfied passively. If this is so and the analogy can be extended we have only to look at the character of the voyeur—generally furtive and clandestine—to realize that we have little to fear from the pornography addict. Where consumers are preoccupied with fantasy there is little danger to the rest of us. Karpman (1959), quoted by the U.S. Commission, notes that people reading "salacious literature" are less likely to become sexual offenders than those who do not since the reading often neutralizes "aberrant sexual interests." Similarly the Kronhausens have argued that "these 'unholy' instruments" may be a safety valve for the sexual deviate and potential sex offender. And Cairns, Paul and Wishner (1962) have remarked that *obscene materials* provide a way of releasing strong sexual urges without doing harm to others.

It is easy to see the plausibility of this argument. The popularity of all forms of sexual literature—from the superficial, *sexless*, sentimentality of the popular women's magazine to the clearest "hard-core" porn—has demonstrated over the ages the perennial appetite that people have for fantasy. To an extent, a great extent with many single people and frustrated married ones, the fantasy constitutes an important part of the sex life. The experience may be vicarious and sterile but it self-evidently fills a need for many individuals. If literature, as a *symbol* of reality, can so involve human sensitivities it is highly likely that when the sensitivities are *distorted* for one reason or another the same sublimatory function can occur: the "perverted" or potentially criminal mentality can gain satisfaction, as does the lonely unfortunate, in *sex by proxy*. If we wanted to force the potential sex criminal on to the streets in search of a human victim perhaps we would do well to deny him his sublimatory substitutes: deny him fantasy and he will be forced to go after the real thing. . . .

The importance of this possibility should be fully faced. If a casual connection *does* exist between availability of pornographic material and a *reduction* in the amount of sex crime—and the evidence is wholly consistent with this possibility rather than its converse—then people who deliberately restrict pornography by supporting repressive legislation are prime architects of sexual offenses against the individual. The antipornographers would do well to note that their anxieties may be driving them into a position the exact opposite of the one they explicitly maintain—their commitment to reduce the amount of sexual delinquency in society.

The most that the antipornographers can argue is that at present the evidence is inconclusive. . . . But if the inconclusive character of the data is once admitted then the case for repressive legislation falls at once. For in a *free* society, or one supposedly aiming after freedom, social phenomena are, like individuals, innocent until proven guilty—and an activity will be permitted unless there is clear evidence of its harmful consequences. The point was well put—in the specific connection with pornography—by Bertrand Russell, talking[9] when he was well over 90 to Rupert Crawshay-Williams.

After noting how people beg the question of causation in instances such as the Moors murders (where the murders and the reading of de Sade *may* have a common cause), Russell ("Bertie") said that on the whole he disapproved of sadistic pornography being available. But when Crawshay-Williams put the catharsis view, that such material might provide a harmless release for individuals who otherwise may be dangerous, Russell said at once—"Oh, well, if that's true, then I don't see that there is anything against sadistic pornography. In fact it should be encouraged. . . ." When it was stressed that there was no preponderating evidence either way Russell argued that we should fall back on an overriding principle—"in this case the principle of free speech."

Thus in the absence of evidence of harm we should be permissive. Any other view is totalitarian. . . .

If human enjoyment *per se* is not to be condemned then it is not too rash to say that we *know* pornography does good. We can easily produce our witnesses to testify to experiencing pleasure. If in the face of this—and no other favorable argument—we are unable to demonstrate a countervailing harm, then the case for easy availability of pornography is unassailable. If, in such circumstances, we find some people unconvinced it is futile to seek out further empirical data. Once we commit ourselves to the notion that the evil nature of something is axiomatic we tacitly concede that evidence is largely irrelevant to our position. If pornography never fails to fill us with predictable loathing then statistics on crime, or measured statements by careful specialists, will not be useful: our reactions will stay the same. But in this event we would do well to reflect on what our emotions tell us of our own mentality. . . .

Notes

1. *The Obscenity Laws*, André Deutsch, 1969, p. 33.
2. *The Report of the Commission on Obscenity and Pornography*, part three, II, Bantam Books, 1970, p. 169.
3. *The Obscenity Laws*, André Deutsch, 1969, p. 35.
4. Quoted by Isadore Rubin, "What Should Parents Do about Pornography?" *Sex in the Adolescent Years*, Fontana, 1969, p. 202.
5. John Money, contribution to "Is Pornography Harmful to Young Children?" *Sex in the Childhood Years*, Fontana, 1971, pp. 181–185.
6. Paper from The Danish Forensic Medicine Council to The Danish Penal Code Council, published in The Penal Code Council Report on Penalty for Pornography, Report No. 435, Copenhagen, 1966, pp. 78–80, and as appendix to *The Obscenity Laws*, pp. 120–124.
7. Ashley Montagu, "Is Pornography Harmful to Young Children?" *Sex in the Childhood Years*, Fontana, 1971, p. 182.
8. Eustace Chesser, *The Human Aspects of Sexual Deviation*, Arrow Books, 1971, p. 39.
9. Rupert Crawshay-Williams, *Russell Remembered*, Oxford University Press, 1970, p. 144.

Further Readings

Berger, Fred R. *Freedom of Expression*. Belmont, CA: Wadsworth, 1980.
Clor, Harry M. *Obscenity and Public Morality*. Chicago: University of Chicago Press, 1965.
Dyal, Robert. "Is Pornography Good for You?" *Southwestern Journal of Philosophy*, 7 (Fall 1976): 95–118.
Simons, G. L. *Pornography without Prejudice*. London: Abelard-Schuman Ltd., 1972.

Content Quiz 11.3

Instructions: Fill in the blanks with the appropriate responses listed below.

sexual development	inconclusive
pleasure	consequences
catharsis	sex by proxy
causal connection	aberrant
onus	overriding principle

1. The _____ is upon antipornographers to demonstrate that pornography produces harm and that the harm is significant.
2. The evidence seems to suggest that there is a _____ between the availability of pornographic material and a reduction in the amount of sex crime.
3. In 1966, the New Jersey Committee for the Right to Read presented findings suggesting that pornography may in fact promote normal _____, not hinder it.
4. On the matter of sadistic pornography, Bertrand Russell argued that because there was no preponderance of evidence pointing to its condemnation, we should appeal to the _____ of free speech.
5. Those favoring pornography and the liberalization of pornography laws frequently present the _____ argument, which states that pornography allows for an emotional release or discharge of sexual tendencies, thereby reducing the chances of sex crime and other immoral behaviors.
6. Antipornographers claim that pornography produces harmful _____.
7. _____ is good and desirable except in cases where significant harm is the result.
8. For those unable to have relations because of illness, travel or bereavement, for example, pornography allows for _____.
9. Pornography may neutralize _____ sexual tendencies.
10. The evidence about the positive and negative consequences of pornography is _____.

Discussion Questions

1. When it comes to the pornography debate, how is it that the burden of proof rests on the shoulders of the antipornographers?

2. Arguments in favor of, and against, the availability of pornography refer heavily to alleged positive and negative consequences. Could the debate rest on other considerations? If so, what might they be?
3. What role does pleasure play in human life? Is it necessarily good or bad? How so?
4. By rejecting pleasure as a justification of pornography, does one necessarily buy into a "cult of puritanism" or "fanatical asceticism"?
5. Is it always desirable to help people develop a normal sex drive? If so, why? If not, why not?
6. How can pornography act as a catharsis? What benefits does pornography have as a catharsis?
7. Is it is acceptable to satisfy people's sexual appetites? Why?
8. What is the apparent causal connection between pornography and sex crimes?
9. Are there any good reasons for regarding pornography as inherently wrong? If so, what are those reasons?

PORNOGRAPHY AND RESPECT FOR WOMEN

Ann Garry

Synopsis

In this essay, Ann Garry provides us with a feminist perspective on pornography. She holds the view that current pornography is morally reprehensible because it "exemplifies and recommends behavior that violates the moral principle to respect persons." Garry's primary objection to pornography does not rest on its effects or consequences, but rather on the content itself, which, for her, recommends that we treat women as degraded sex objects to be manipulated and exploited.

In developing her argument, Garry explores the "respect" that men have had toward women in the past. She believes that it has traditionally been based on a double standard that makes some women a special class of inferior beings whose "respectfulness" hinges on one dimension of their lives, i.e., their sexuality; other women are considered "bad" and less deserving of respect, again, because of their sexuality. As Garry puts it, the respect men have shown in the past is not a "wholehearted respect for full-fledged human beings, but half-hearted respect for lesser beings, some of whom they feel a need to glorify and purify."

Also in this essay, Garry looks at what it means to be a sex object and how a sexual double standard connects sex objects to the concept of "harm" in a way that is difficult for many men to understand. She also points out that contemporary pornography is male-oriented and supportive of traditional sex roles. It is designed to turn a profit by appealing to male fantasies. Women's pleasure is seldom emphasized for its own sake.

Note that in part two of this article (not included here), Garry outlines a form of pornography that would be morally preferable because its content would be nonsexist and nondegrading. Acceptable pornography would sever the connections between sex and harm. It would treat men and women as equal sex partners. No one gender would control the circumstances or positions in which sex took place. There would also be no suggestion of male power play or conquest. Furthermore, the primary objective of sexual intercourse would not be male ejaculation. In acceptable pornography, characters would treat each other respectfully and with consideration. No attempts would be made to treat men and women with brutality or without thought.

The . . . argument I consider is that pornography is morally objectionable not because it leads people to show disrespect for women, but because pornography itself exemplifies and recommends behavior which violates the moral principle to respect persons. The content of pornography is what one objects to. It treats women as mere sex objects "to be exploited and manipulated" and degrades the role and status of women. In order to evaluate this argument I first clarify what it would mean for pornography itself to treat someone as a sex object in a degrading manner. I then deal with three issues which are central to the discussion of pornography and respect for women: how "losing respect" for a woman is connected with treating her as a sex object, what is wrong with treating someone as a sex object, and why it is worse to treat women rather than men as sex objects. I argue that today the content of pornography is sometimes in violation of the moral principle to respect persons. . . .

To many people, including [Susan] Brownmiller and some other feminists, it appears to be an obvious truth that pornography treats people, especially women, as sex objects in a degrading manner. And if we omit "in a degrading manner," it seems hard to disagree: how could pornography not treat people as sex objects?

First, is it permissible to talk about either the content of pornography or pornography itself degrading people or treating people as sex objects? It is not difficult to find examples of degrading content in which women are treated as sex objects. There are unnamed movies conveying the message that all women really want to be raped, so don't believe them when they struggle against you. By portraying women in this manner, the content of the movie degrades women. Degrading women is morally objectionable. Seeing the movie need not cause anyone to imitate the behavior shown. We can call the content degrading to women because of the character of the behavior and attitudes it recommends. The same kind of point can be made about films (books, or TV commercials) with other kinds of degrading, thus morally objectionable, content, for example, racist messages.

The next step in the argument is to infer that because the content or message of pornography is morally objectionable, we can call pornography itself morally objectionable. Support for this step can be found in an analogy. If a person takes every opportunity to recommend that men rape women, we would think not only that his recommendation is immoral but that he is immoral too. The objection to making the inference from that which is recommended to that which recommends in the case of pornography is that we ascribe such predicates as "immoral" differently to people than to objects such as films, books, and so on. A film which is the vehicle for an objectionable message is still an object independent of its message, its director, its producer, those who act in it, and those who respond to it. Hence one cannot make an unsupported inference from "the content of the film is morally objectionable" to "the film is morally objectionable." Because the central points in this paper do not depend on pornography itself (in addition to its content) being morally objectionable, I will not try to support this inference. The question about the relation of the content to the work itself, is of course, extremely interesting; but in part because I cannot decide which side of the argument is more persuasive, I will pass.[1] Certainly one appropriate way to evaluate pornography is in terms of the moral features of its content. If a pornographic film exemplifies and recommends attitudes or behavior which are morally objectionable, then its content is morally objectionable.

Let us turn to the first of the remaining three questions about respect and sex objects: what is the connection between losing respect for a woman and treating her as a sex object? Some people who have lived through the era in which women were taught to worry about men "losing respect" for them if they engaged in sex in inappropriate circumstances, find it troublesome or at least amusing that feminists, supposedly "liberated" women, are outraged at being treated as sex objects, either by pornography or in any other way. The apparent alignment between feminists and traditionally "proper" women need not surprise us when we look at it more closely.

The respect which men traditionally believed they had for women, hence which they could lose, is not a general respect for persons as autonomous beings, nor is it respect that is earned because of one's personal merits or achievements. It is respect that is an outgrowth of the "double standard." Women are to be respected because they are more pure, delicate, and fragile than men, have more refined sensibilities, and so on. Because some women clearly do not have these qualities, thus do not deserve respect, women must be divided into two groups—the good ones on the pedestal and the bad ones who have fallen from it. One's mother, grandmother, Sunday school teacher, and usually one's wife are "good" women. The appropriate behavior to express respect for good women would be, for example, not swearing or telling dirty jokes in front of them, giving them seats on buses, and other "chivalrous" acts. This sort of respect for good women is that which adolescent boys in back seats of cars used to "promise" not to lose. Note that men define, display, and lose this kind of respect. If women lose respect for women, it is not typically loss of respect for (other) women as a class, but loss of self-respect.

It has now become commonplace to acknowledge that although a place on the pedestal might have advantages over a place in the "gutter" beneath it, a place on the pedestal is not at all equal to the place occupied by other people, that is, men. "Respect" for those on the pedestal was not respect for whole, full-fledged people, but for a special class of inferior beings.

If someone makes two traditional assumptions—that (at least some) sex is dirty and that women fall into two classes, good and bad—it is easy to see how this person might think that pornography could lead people to lose respect for women or that pornography is itself disrespectful to women.[2] Pornography describes or shows women engaging in activities which are inappropriate for good women to engage in, or at least inappropriate for them to be seen by strangers engaging in. If one sees these women as symbolic representatives of all women, then all women fall from grace with these women. This fall is possible, I believe, because the "respect" men had for women was not genuine wholehearted respect for full-fledged human beings, but half-hearted respect for lesser beings some of whom they felt the need to glorify and purify.[3] It is easy to fall from a pedestal. Can we imagine 41% of men and 46% of women answering "yes" to the question, "Do movies showing men engaging in violent acts lead people to lose respect for men?"

Two interesting asymmetries appear. The first is that it is more difficult to lose respect for men as a class (men with power, typically Anglo men) than it is to lose respect for women or ethnic minorities as a class. Anglo men whose behavior warrants disrespect are more likely to be seen as exceptional cases than are women or minorities (whose "transgressions" may be far less serious.) Think of the following: women are temptresses; Blacks cheat the welfare system; Italians are gangsters; but the men of the Nixon administration are exceptions—Anglo men as a class did not lose respect because of Watergate and related scandals.

The second asymmetry concerns the active and passive roles of the sexes. Men are seen in the active role. If men lose respect for women because of something "evil" done by women (such as appearing in pornography) the fear is that men will then do harm to women, not that women will do harm to men. Whereas if women lose respect for male politicians because of Watergate the fear is still that male politicians will do harm, not that women will do harm to male politicians. This asymmetry might be a result of one way in which our society thinks of sex as bad—as harm men do to women (or to the person playing a female role, for example, in a homosexual rape). Robert Baker calls attention to this point in "'Pricks' and 'Chicks': A Plea for 'Persons.'"[4] Our slang words for sexual intercourse, "fuck," "screw," or older words such as "take" or "have" not only can mean harm but traditionally have taken a male subject and a female object. The active male screws, harms, the passive female. A "bad" woman only tempts men to hurt her further.

One can understand why one's proper grandmother would not want men to see pornography or lose respect for women. But feminists reject these "proper" assumptions: there are not good and bad classes of women and sex is not dirty (though many people believe it is). Why then are feminists angry at women's being treated as sex objects, and some feminists opposed to pornography?

The answer is that feminists as well as proper grandparents are concerned with respect. However, there are differences. A feminist's distinction between treating a woman as a full-fledged person and treating her as merely a sex object does not correspond to the good-bad woman distinction. In the latter distinction "good" and "bad" are properties applicable to groups of women. On the feminist view, all women really are full-fledged people, it is just that some are treated as sex objects and perhaps think of themselves as sex objects. A further difference is that although "bad" women correspond to those who have been thought to deserve to be treated as sex objects, good women have not corresponded to full-fledged people: only men have been full-fledged people. Given the feminist's distinction, she has no difficulty at all saying that pornography treats women as sex objects, not as full-fledged people. She can object morally to pornography or anything else treating women as sex objects.

One might wonder whether any objection to being treated as a sex object implies that the person objecting still believes, deep down, that sex is dirty. I don't think so. Several other possibilities emerge. First, even if I believe intellectually and emotionally that sex is healthy, I might object to being treated *only* as a sex object, in the same spirit that I would object to being treated only as a maker of chocolate chip cookies or as a tennis partner—only a few of my talents are being valued. Second, perhaps I feel that sex is healthy, but it is apparent to me that you think it is dirty; so I don't want you to treat me as a sex object. Third, being treated as any kind of object, not just a sex object, has an unappealing ring to it. I would rather be a partner (sexual or otherwise) than an object.

Fourth, and more plausible than the first three, is Robert Baker's view mentioned above. Both (i) our traditional double standard of sexual behavior for men and women and (ii) the linguistic evidence that we connect the concept of sex with the concept of harm, point to what is wrong with treating women as sex objects. As I said earlier, in their traditional uses, "fuck" and "screw" have taken a male subject, a female object, and have had at least two meanings: harm and have sexual intercourse with. (In addition, a prick is man who harms people ruthlessly; and a motherfucker is so low that he would do something very harmful to his own dear mother.)[5] Because in our culture we connect sex with harm that men do to women and think of the female role in sex as that of harmed object, we can see that to treat a woman as a sex object is automatically to treat her as less than fully human. To say this does not imply that no healthy sexual relationships exist; nor does it say anything about individual men's conscious intentions to degrade women by desiring them sexually (though no doubt some men have these intentions). It is merely to make a point about the concepts embodied in our language.

Psychoanalytic support for the connection between sex and harm comes from Robert J. Stoller. Stoller thinks that sexual excitement is linked with a wish to harm someone (and at least a whisper of hostility). The key process of sexual excitement can be seen as dehumanization (fetishization) in fantasy of the desired person. He speculates that this is true in some degree of everyone, men and women, with "normal" or "perverted" activities and fantasies.[6]

Thinking of sex objects as harmed objects enables us to explain some of the first three reasons why one wouldn't want to be treated as a sex object. (1) I may object to being treated only as a tennis partner, but being a tennis partner is not connected in our culture with being a harmed object. (2) I may not think that sex is dirty and that I would be a harmed object; I may not know what your view is; but what bothers me is that this is the view embodied in our language and culture.

Awareness of the connection between sex and harm helps us to explain other interesting points. Women are angry about being treated as sex objects in situations or roles in which they do not intend to be thought of in that manner, for example, serving on a committee or attending a discussion. It is not merely that a sexual role is inappropriate for the circumstances, it is thought to be a less fully human role than the one in which they intended to function.

Finally, the sex-harm connection makes it clear why it is worse to treat women as sex objects than to treat men as sex objects, and why some men have had difficulty understanding women's anger about the matter. It is more difficult for heterosexual men than for women to assume the role of "harmed object" in sex; for men have the concept of themselves as sexual agents, not as passive objects. This is also related to the point I made earlier about the difference in the solidity of respect for men and for women: respect for women is more fragile. Although there are exceptions, it is generally harder to degrade men sexually or nonsexually than to degrade women. Men and women have grown up with different patterns of self-respect and expectations about the extent to which they will be respected and the extent to which they deserve respect or degradation. The man who doesn't understand why women do not want to be treated as sex objects (because he'd sure like to be) would not think of himself as being harmed by that treatment: a woman might. Pornography, probably more than any other contemporary institution, succeeds in treating men as sex objects.

Having seen that the connection between sex and harm helps to explain both what is wrong with treating someone as a sex object and why it is worse to treat a woman in this way, I want to use the sex-harm connection to try to resolve a dispute about pornography and women. Recall Brownmiller's view that pornography is "the undiluted essence of antifemale propaganda" whose purpose is to degrade women.[7] Some people object to Brownmiller by saying that since pornography treats both men and women as sex objects for the purpose of arousing the viewer, it is not sexist, not antifemale, not designed to degrade women. It just happens that degrading women arouses some men. How can the dispute be resolved?

Suppose we were to rate the content of all pornography from most morally objectionable to least morally objectionable. Among the most objectionable would be the most degrading, for example, "snuff" films or movies which recommend that men rape women, molest children and puppies, and treat nonmasochists very sadistically. Next we would find a large number of cases, probably most pornography, which are not quite so blatantly offensive. In these cases it is relevant to appeal to the analysis of sex objects given above. As long as sex is connected with harm done to women, it will be very difficult not to see pornography as degrading to women. We can agree with Brownmiller's opponent that pornography treats men as sex objects, too, but maintain that this is only pseudo-equality: such treatment is still more degrading to women.

In addition, pornography often exemplifies the active-passive, harmer-harmed object roles in a very obvious way. Because pornography today is male oriented and supposed to make a profit, the content is designed to appeal to male fantasies. Judging from the content of the most popular legally available pornography, male fantasies still run along the lines of stereotypical sex roles and, if Stoller is right, include elements of hostility. In many cases the women's purpose is to cater to male desires, to service the man or men. Her own pleasure is rarely emphasized for its own sake; she is merely allowed a little heavy breathing, perhaps in order to show her dependence on the great male "lover" who produces her pleasure. In addition, women are clearly made into passive objects in still photographs showing only close-ups of their genitals. Even in movies which are marketed to appeal to heterosexual couples, such as "Behind the Green Door," the woman is passive and undemanding (and in this case kidnapped and hypnotized as well). Although there are many kinds of specialty magazines and films for different sexual tastes, very little in contemporary pornography goes against traditional sex roles. There is certainly no significant attempt to replace the harmer-harmed distinction with anything more positive and healthy. There are, of course, stag movies in which men are treated sadistically by women; but this is an attempt to turn the tables on degradation, not a positive improvement. . . .

Notes

1. In order to help one determine which position one feels inclined to take, consider the following statement: It is morally objectionable to write, make, sell, act in, use, and enjoy pornography; in addition, the content of pornography is immoral; however, pornography itself is not morally objectionable. If this seems extremely problematic, then one might well be satisfied with the claim that pornography is degrading because its content is.
2. The traditional meaning of "lose respect for women" was evidently the one assumed in the Abelson survey cited by the Presidential Commission. No explanation of its meaning is given in reporting the study. See H. Abelson et al., "National Survey of Public Attitudes toward and Experience with Erotic Materials," *Tech Report* 6, 1-137.
3. Many feminists point this out. One of the most accessible references is Shulamith Firestone, *The Dialectic of Sex: The Case for the Feminist Revolution* (New York: Morrow, 1970); see especially 128-132.
4. In Richard Wasserstrom, ed., *Today's Moral Problems* (New York: Macmillan, 1975), 152-172. See 167-171.
5. Baker, 168-169.
6. "Sexual Excitement," *Archives of General Psychiatry* 33 (August 1976): 899-909, especially 903. The extent to which Stoller sees men and women in different positions with respect to harm and hostility is not clear. He often treats men and women alike, but in *Perversion: The Erotic Form of Hatred* (New York: Pantheon Books, 1975), 89-91, he calls attention to differences between men and women, especially regarding their response to pornography, lack of understanding by men of women's sexuality, and so forth. Given that Stoller finds hostility to be an essential element in male-oriented pornography and given that women have not responded readily to it, one can think of possibilities for women's sexuality; their hostility might follow a different scenario; they might not be as hostile, and so on.
7. Susan Brownmiller, *Against Our Will: Men, Women and Rape* (New York: Simon and Schuster, 1975), 394.

Further Readings

Devlin, Patrick. *The Enforcement of Morals*. New York: Oxford University Press, 1965.

Holbrook, David (ed.). *The Case against Pornography*. New York: Library Press, 1973.

The Report of the Commission on Obscenity and Pornography. Washington, DC: Government Printing Office, 1970.

Content Quiz 11.4

Instructions: Fill in the blanks with the appropriate responses listed below.

morally objectionable	sex-harm
attitude	roles

respect for persons
sex objects
equal
degrading
inferior beings
spirit

1. According to Ann Garry, much of contemporary pornography violates the principle of _____.
2. Pornography views women undimensionally as _____.
3. Even a modified, ethically acceptable pornography must be appreciated by the audience in the proper _____.
4. To make pornography less sexist and morally objectionable, the _____ link must be broken.
5. When men place "good" women on a pedestal, they still treat them as _____ whose human value can be withdrawn at any time.
6. Feminists would prefer that men and women be _____ partners in pornographic scenarios.
7. Some pornography is exploitive and _____ in so far as it conveys the message that women really wish to be raped and hurt.
8. If a pornographic film exemplifies and recommends ethically offensive attitudes or behaviors, then its content must be considered _____.
9. Garry is cautious about giving wholehearted approval to any pornography viewed today because of the possibility that audience _____ may be inappropriate.
10. Along with treating men and women as equals in regard to functioning genitalia, acceptable pornography would display men and women in equally valued social _____.

Discussion Questions

1. How can the concept of "respect" (for persons) be understood? Traditionally, what kind of respect have men had for women?
2. Garry distinguishes between being treated as a sex object and being treated as a sex object in a degrading manner. What is the difference?
3. On what grounds does Garry object to contemporary pornography?
4. What reasons could women give for resenting being treated as sex objects?
7. How is sex related to harm in pornography?
8. Do you think there is such a thing as "acceptable pornography"?

[ABORIGINAL RIGHTS AND] LIBERALISM IN CULTURALLY PLURAL SOCIETIES

Will Kymlicka*

Synopsis

In this reading, Will Kymlicka draws our attention to the conflicts and tensions between individual and collective minority rights as they arise in the context of a pluralistic liberal society. Specifically, he uses the rights of aboriginal peoples in Canada and the United States as a focal point for explaining broader issues about the role of cultural membership in liberal theory. Kymlicka suggests that if we are to respect aboriginals as individuals, then we must also respect and recognize their culture at the same time, since for aboriginals, their sense of self and personal identity are inextricably bound up with the culture from which they come. As Kymlicka points out, liberalism is reluctant to give independent weight to cultural membership, demanding equal rights for all citizens. For Kymlicka, however, liberalism's emphasis on individualism and egalitarianism has the net effect of endangering some minority cultures like the native peoples of North America. Kymlicka thus takes the position that in culturally pluralistic societies, differential citizenship rights may be required to protect particular cultural communities from unwanted disintegration. Although the special status granted to aboriginal people might be regarded as an imperfect resolution to the conflict between the demands of individual citizenship and cultural membership, it is, for the time being, the most acceptable. As Kymlicka points out, supporters of aboriginal self-government might favor seeking some other moral theory besides liberalism on which to base their claims, one which recognizes the importance of cultural membership and the legitimacy of minority rights. Nonetheless, Kymlicka believes the attempt to reconcile minority rights and liberal equality is worth considering, even if it requires that we go back to the heart of liberal theory and start making changes there.

So far . . . I have not made any explicit distinction between two different kinds, or different aspects, of community. On the one hand, there is the political community, within which individuals exercise the rights and responsibilities entailed by the framework of liberal justice. People who reside within the same political community are fellow citizens. On the other hand, there is the cultural community, within which individuals form and revise their aims and ambitions. People within the same cultural community share a culture, a language and history which defines their cultural membership.

Now clearly these two may simply be aspects of the same community: those people who have the same citizenship may also have the same cultural membership. A political community may be coextensive with one cultural community, as is envisaged in the 'nation-state,' and this seems to be the situation implicitly assumed in most contemporary political theory. But the two forms of community may not coincide: the political community may contain two or more groups of people who have different cultures, speaking different languages, developing different cultural traditions. This is the situation in multinational, or culturally plural, states, and these form the vast majority of the world's states (Connor, 1972 pp. 319–21, van den Berghe, 1981 p. 62).

How should liberals respond to a situation of cultural plurality? Clearly the answer depends

---

**The following is excerpted from a book in which Will Kymlicka tries to find the appropriate value of community within a liberal framework.*

on the role cultural membership plays in liberal theory. But this is not a simple matter, and immediately raises a number of questions. What does it mean for people to 'belong' to a cultural community—to what extent are individuals' interests tied to, or their very sense of identity dependent on, a particular culture? And what follows from the fact that people belong to different cultures—do people have a legitimate interest in ensuring the continuation of their own culture, even if other cultures are available in the political community? If they do have such an interest, is it an interest which needs to be given independent recognition in a theory of justice?

These are all questions which arise most pressingly in a culturally plural state, but they go to the heart of the liberal conception of the relationship between self and community. And they give rise to an important political issue: the rights of minority cultures. In [what follows] I use the question of minority rights, and in particular the rights of the aboriginal population in Canada and the United States, as a focal point for exploring these questions about the role of cultural membership in liberal theory.

Aboriginal rights are a part of political life in North America, and perhaps they are the most familiar example of minority rights to the Anglo-American world. Yet they are very much at odds with some of our common self-perceptions. While the United States is often viewed as a 'melting-pot,' without permanently distinct minority cultures, this is clearly not true of the aboriginal population. There is a system of reservations for the American Indian population, within which the members of particular Indian communities have been able (to a greater or lesser degree) to protect their culture. But their ability to do so has rested on having, as a community, unusual rights and powers. The reservations form special political jurisdictions over which Indian communities have certain guaranteed powers, and within which non-Indian Americans have restricted mobility, property, and voting rights.

This scheme for the protection of a minority culture is often treated as an exception, an issue which arises prior to, or outside the bounds of, liberal theory. But it is far from unique in contemporary liberal democracies. It is similar to legislation which establishes special political and social rights for aboriginal peoples in Canada, New Zealand, and Australia as well. And these are similar to many of the special measures of political and cultural autonomy for minorities in the multicultural countries of Western Europe, such as Belgium and Switzerland. And if we look beyond Western liberal democracies to many African, or Eastern-bloc, countries, the story is very similar. On all continents, in countries of all ideological stripes, we find cultural minorities that have a distinct legal and political status. In these countries, individuals are incorporated into the state, not 'universally' (i.e. so that each individual citizen stands in the same direct relationship to the state), but 'consociationally' (i.e. through membership in one or other of the cultural communities). Under consociational modes of incorporation, the nature of people's rights, and the opportunities for exercising them, tend to vary with the particular cultural community into which they are incorporated. And the justification for these measures focuses on their role in allowing minority cultures to develop their distinct cultural life, an ability insufficiently protected by 'universal' modes of incorporation.

How should liberals respond to these kinds of measures for minority cultures? They may seem at first glance, to be inconsistent with liberal theories of justice, and that indeed is the common presumption. But, if so, that is a serious matter, for these measures have been important to the political legitimacy, and very stability, of many multicultural countries. Wars have been fought in order to gain or protect these measures. Removing them would have a profound effect on the political culture of these countries, and on the lives of the members of the minority cultures.

It's surprising, then, that liberal theorists haven't explicitly defended, or even discussed, this implication of their theories . . . .

Why is it commonly supposed that liberals must oppose special status for minority cultures? Liberal opposition is often explained in terms of an alleged conflict between individual and collective rights. This is exhibited in recent debates concerning the constitutional definition of the special status of the aboriginal peoples of Canada (i.e. Indian, Inuit, and Métis). This special status was recognized, but left undefined, in Section 35 of the 1982 Constitution Act. Greater specification of this status was to be reached through a series of annual constitutional conferences between government and aboriginal leaders. There was a general consensus that aboriginal peoples should be self-governing, in contrast to the paternalistic legislation under which reservation life had been regulated in detail for decades. But aboriginal leaders said that the principle of aboriginal self-government must include the recognition of certain collective rights, rights which need to be weighed alongside and balanced against more traditional individual rights. For example, self-government would include the ability of aboriginal communities to restrict the mobility, property, and voting rights of non-aboriginal people. Many government officials, on the other hand, demanded that aboriginal self-government operate in a way that leaves intact the structure of individual rights guaranteed elsewhere in the constitution. So the initial agreement soon gave way to disagreement over the relationship between individual and collective rights. (These differences have, so far, proven too great to overcome, and the constitutional rights of aboriginal peoples in Canada remain undefined.)

The accepted wisdom is that liberals must oppose any proposals for self-government which would limit individual rights in the name of collective rights. I think that is a mistake, one that has caused serious harm to the aboriginal population of North America, and to the members of minority cultures in other liberal democracies. This chapter will explore some of the reasons why liberals have opposed collective rights for minority cultures[1]. . . .

What explains the common liberal opposition to such minority rights? It's not difficult to seen why liberals have opposed them. Liberalism, as I've presented it, is characterized both by a certain kind of *individualism*—that is, individuals are viewed as the ultimate units of moral worth, as having moral standing as ends in themselves, as 'self-originating sources of valid claims' (Rawls 1980 p. 543); and by a certain kind of *egalitarianism*—that is, every individual has an equal moral status, and hence is to be treated as an equal by the government, with equal concern and respect (Dworkin 1983 p. 24; Rawls 1971 p. 511). Since individuals have ultimate moral status, and since each individual is to be respected as an equal by the government, liberals have demanded that each individual have equal rights and entitlements. Liberals have disagreed amongst themselves as to what these rights should be, because they have different views about what it is to treat people with equal concern and respect.

But most would accept that these rights should include rights to mobility, to personal property, and to political participation in one's community. The new Canadian Charter of Rights and Freedoms embodies these liberal principles, guaranteeing such rights to every citizen, regardless of race or sex, ethnicity or language, etc. (Asch pp. 86–7; Schwartz ch. 1).

There seems to be no room within the moral ontology of liberalism for the idea of collective rights. The community, unlike the individual, is not a 'self-originating source of valid claims.' Once individuals have been treated as equals, with the respect and concern owed them as moral beings, there is no further obligation to treat the communities to which they belong as equals. The community has no moral existence or claims of its own. It is not that community is unimportant to the liberal, but simply that it is important for what it contributes to the lives of individuals, and so cannot ultimately conflict with the claims of individuals. Individual and collective rights cannot compete for the same moral space, in liberal theory, since the value of the collective derives from its contribution to the value of individual lives.

The constitutional embodiment of these liberal principles, in Canada and elsewhere, has played an important role in many of liberalism's greatest achievements in fighting against unjust legislation. For example, in the *Brown v. Board of Education* case, ([1954] 347 US 483), the Fourteenth Amendment of the American Constitution, guaranteeing equal protection of the law to all its citizens, was used to strike down legislation that segregated blacks in the American South. The 'separate but equal' doctrine which had governed racial segregation in the United States for sixty years denied blacks the equal protection of the law. That case dealt solely with segregated school facilities, but it was a major impetus behind the removal of other segregationist legislation in the 1950s, the passage of the Civil Rights and Voting Rights Acts in the 1960s, and the development of mandatory busing, 'head start,' and affirmative action programs in the 1970s; which in turn were the catalyst for similar programs to benefit other groups—Hispanics, women, the handicapped, etc. Indeed, "its educative and moral impact in areas other than public education and, in fact, its whole thrust toward equality and opportunity for all men has been of immeasurable importance" (Kaplan p. 228). The 'thrust' of this movement was sufficiently powerful to shape nondiscrimination and equal protection legislation in countries around the world, and it provided the model for various international covenants on human rights (especially the Convention on the Elimination of All Forms of Racial Discrimination, adopted by the UN General Assembly in 1965). It also underlies the prominent philosophical accounts of liberal equality.

The history of these developments is one of the high points of Western liberalism in the twentieth century, for there is a powerful ideal of equality at work here in the political morality of the community—the idea that every citizen has a right to full and equal participation in the political, economic, and cultural life of the country, without regard to race, sex, religion, physical handicap—without regard to any of the classifications which have traditionally kept people separate and behind.

The logical conclusion of these liberal principles seems to be a 'colorblind' constitution—the removal of all legislation differentiating people in terms of race or ethnicity (except for temporary measures, like affirmative action, which are believed necessary to reach a colorblind society). Liberal equality requires the 'universal' mode of incorporating citizens into the state. And this indeed has often been the conclusion drawn by courts in Canada and the United States.

This movement exercised an enormous influence on Canadian Indian policy as well (Berger 1984 p. 94). The desirability of a colorblind constitution was the explicit motivation behind the 1969 proposals for reforming the Indian Act in Canada. In 1968 Pierre Trudeau was elected Prime Minister of Canada on a platform of social justice that was clearly influenced by the American political movements. Canada didn't have a policy of segregating blacks, but it did have something which looked very similar. As in the United States, the native Indian population was predominantly living on segregated reserves, and was subject to a complex array of legislation which treated Indians and non-Indians differentially. While every Indian had the right to live on the land of her band, there were restrictions on her ability to use the land, or dispose of her estate as she saw fit, and there was a total prohibition on any alienation of the land. The reservation system also placed restrictions on the mobility, residence, and voting rights of non-Indians in the Indian territory; and in the case of voting rights, the restriction remained even when the non-Indian married into the Indian community. There were, in other words, two kinds of Canadian citizenship, Indian and non-Indian, with different rights and duties, differential access to public services, and different opportunities for participating in the various institutions of Canadian government.

Dismantling this system was one of the top priorities of Trudeau's 'Just Society' policy, and early in 1969 the government released a White Paper on Indian Policy which recommended an end to the special constitutional status of Indians (DIAND 1969). The government proposed that the reservation system, which had protected Indian communities from assimilation, be dismantled. Indians would not, of course, be compelled to disperse and assimilate. They would be free to choose to associate with one another, and coordinate the way they used their resources in the market, so as to preserve their way of life. Freedom of association is one of the individual rights to be universally guaranteed in a colorblind constitution. But they would receive no legal or constitutional help in their efforts. Legislation discriminating against non-Indians in terms of property rights, mobility rights, or political rights would not be allowed.

From its very conception to the choice of language in the final draft, the policy reflected the powerful influence of the ideal of racial equality which was developing in the United States and the United Nations. Paraphrasing UN human rights instruments, the authors said that the policy rested "upon the fundamental right of Indian people to full and equal participation in the cultural, social, economic and political life in Canada," and this required that the legislative and constitutional bases of discrimination be removed (DIAND 1969 pp. 201–2). Echoing the *Brown* decision, the policy proposed that Indians no longer receive separate services from separate agencies, because "separate but equal services do not provide truly equal treatment" (DIAND 1969 p. 204). Echoing Justice Harlan's famous dictum that the American Constitution should be colorblind, the Canadian proposal said that "The ultimate aim of removing the specific references to Indians from the constitution may take some time, but it is a goal to be kept constantly in view" (DIAND 1969 p. 202). Perhaps it was the weight of all this normative authority that gave the authors such a sense of righteousness. It is, they said, 'self-evident' that the constitution should be colorblind, an "undeniable part of equality" that Indians should have equal access to common services; "There can be no argument. . . . It is right" (DIAND 1969 pp. 202–3).

It is worth emphasizing that the issue was not about temporary measures to help Indians overcome their disadvantaged position in the broader society. While not all liberals are prepared to allow even temporary measures which differentiate on the basis of race or ethnicity, the government proposal followed the more common view that measures such as affirmative action are acceptable. But they are acceptable precisely because they are viewed as appropriate or necessary means to the pursuit of the ideal of a colorblind constitution. Affirmative action of this sort appeals to the values embodied in that ideal, not to competing values. The issue posed by the special status of Canada's Indians, therefore, was not that of affirmative action, but "whether the granting of permanent political rights to a special class of citizens (rather than special rights on a temporary basis) is possible within an ideology that maintains the principle of equality of consideration" (Asch p. 76). And for the liberal architects of the 1969 proposal, the answer was that liberal equality was incompatible with the permanent assigning of collective rights to a minority culture.

The proposal was immediately applauded by the media, even by opposition parties, as a triumph for liberal justice. Indians, on the other hand, were furious, and after six months of bitter and occasionally violent Indian protest, the policy was withdrawn. In the words of one commentator, the policy was a response "to white liberal demands from the public, not to Indian demands" (Weaver 1981 p. 196). But liberals have only reluctantly retreated from that policy, despite the almost unanimous opposition it received from the Indians themselves. Liberals fear that any deviation from the strict principle of equal individual rights would be the first step down the road to apartheid, to a system where some individuals are viewed as first-class citizens and others only second-class, in virtue of their race or ethnic affiliations. These fears are strengthened when liberals see white South African leaders invoke minority rights in defense of their system of apartheid, and compare their system of tribal homelands to our system of Indian reservations and homelands (*International Herald* p. 2; *Toronto Star* p. B3). If we allow Indians to discriminate against non-Indians in the name of their collective rights, how can we criticize white South Africans for discriminating against blacks in the name of their collective rights?. . .

The crucial difference between blacks and the aboriginal peoples of North America is, of course, that the latter value their separation from the mainstream life and culture of North America. Separation is not always perceived as a 'badge of inferiority.' Indeed, it is sometimes forgotten that the American Supreme Court recognized this in the *Brown* desegregation case. The Court did not reject the 'separate but equal' doctrine on any universal grounds. The Court ruled that, in the particular circumstances of contemporary American white-black relations, segregation was perceived as a 'badge of inferiority.' The lower motivation of black children in their segregated schools was a crucial factor in their decision. But in Canada, segregation has always been viewed as a defense of a highly valued cultural heritage. It is forced *integration* that is perceived as a badge of inferiority by Indians, damaging their motivation. While there are no special problems about motivation on segregated reserve schools, the drop-out rate for Indians in integrated high schools was over 90 percent, and in most areas was 100 percent for postsecondary education (Cardinal 1977 p. 194; Gross p. 238).

Michael Gross distinguishes the case of blacks and Indians this way:

> Where blacks have been forcibly *excluded* (segregated) from white society by law, Indians—aboriginal peoples with their own cultures, languages, religions and territories—have been forcibly *included* (integrated) into that society by law. That is what the [Senate Subcommittee on Indian Education] meant by coercive assimilation—the practice of compelling, through submersion, an ethnic, cultural, and linguistic minority to shed its uniqueness and mingle with the rest of society (Gross p. 244).

Gross argues that the "integration of Indian children in white-dominated schools had the same negative educational and emotional effects which segregation was held to have on blacks in *Brown*" (Gross p. 245). Therefore, the 'underlying principle' which struck down legislated segregation of blacks (i.e. that racial classifications harmful to a racial minority are unconstitutional) would also strike down legislated integration of Indians (Gross p. 248).[2] Assimilation for the Indians, like segregation for the blacks, is a badge of inferiority which, in the words of the Senate Subcommittee, fails "to recognize the importance and validity of the Indian community" and which results in a "dismal record" of "negative self-image [and] low achievement" as the "classroom and the school [become] a kind of battleground where the Indian child attempts to protect his integrity and identify as an individual by defeating the purposes of the school" (Gross p. 242). Similar situations arise when Indians have to assimilate later in life, e.g. at work.

But to say that segregation is preferred by the Indians is not to say it is, or even could be, the natural result of the interplay of preferences in the market. On the contrary, the viability of Indian communities depends on coercively restricting the mobility, residence, and political rights of both Indians and non-Indians. It is this which raises the need for the minority rights that are decried by many liberals, rights that go beyond nondiscrimination and affirmative action.

These special needs are met, in Canada, by two different forms of aboriginal community arrangements (Asch, ch. 7). In the reservations of southern Canada, where the population is high and land scarce, the stability of Indian communities is made possible by denying non-Indians the right to purchase or reside on Indian lands (unless given special permission). In the north, however, they are creating political arrangements for the Indian and Inuit population which would have none of these restrictions. Under these arrangements, non-aboriginal people will be free to take jobs, buy land, and reside as long as they want; the inhospitability of the environment ensures that aboriginal people are not likely to be outnumbered by non-aboriginal permanent residents. However, northern Canada is rich in resources, and development projects will often bring in huge influxes of temporary resident workers. While very few, if any, of these workers are likely to remain in the north for more than seven years, so that the aboriginal people will continue to constitute the majority of permanent residents, at any one time non-aboriginal people may well form the majority. If non-aboriginal transient workers were allowed to vote, they would probably decide to use public money to provide amenities for themselves—movie theatres, dish antennas for television reception, even a Las Vegas-styled resort. Since many aboriginal people in the north are dependent on short-term work projects due to the seasonal nature of most economic activity in the area, such a policy could force them to move into localities dominated by whites, and to work and live in another culture, in a different language. Transient residents might also use their voting power to demand that public services and education be provided in their own language, at the expense of the provision of services and education in aboriginal languages.[3]

To guard against this, aboriginal leaders have proposed a three-to-ten-year residency requirement before one becomes eligible to vote for, or hold, public office, and a guaranteed 30 percent aboriginal representation in the regional government, with veto power over legislation affecting crucial aboriginal interests. If this scheme proved unable to protect aboriginal communities, they would have the power to impose even greater restrictions, most likely on immigration, and thereby move closer to the southern model, which avoids the necessity of restricting voting rights by simply denying non-aboriginal people a chance to gain residence. In other words, there is a continuum of possibilities, involving greater or lesser guarantees of power for aboriginal people, and greater or lesser restrictions on the mobility and political rights of non-aboriginal people (see Bartlett, and Lyon pp. 48–65, for some of the variants). Aboriginal groups have demanded the restrictions they believe to be necessary to protect their communities.

Historically, the evidence is that when the land on which aboriginal communities are based became desirable for white settlement and development, the only thing which prevented the undesired disintegration of the community was legally entrenched nonalienability of land. Indeed the most common way of breaking open stubbornly held Indian land for white settlement was to force the Indians to take individual title to alienable land, making the pressure on some individuals to sell almost unbearable, partly because Indians were financially deprived (and hence in need of money to meet the basic needs of the family), and also because they were culturally ill-equipped to understand the consequences of having (or selling) title to land (Sanders 1983*a* pp. 4–12; Kronowitz *et al.* pp. 530–1; MacMeekin p. 1239). Such measures to endow individual title are usually justified as giving Indians greater choice. The White Paper, for example, proclaimed that "full and true equality calls for Indian control and ownership of reserve land. . .[this] carries with it the free choice of use, retention, or of disposition" (DIAND 1969 p. 209). The Minister responsible for the policy said he was only trying to give Indians the same freedom to manage their own affairs as other Canadians (Bowles *et al.* p. 215). But Indians have as much free choice over the use of their land as the average renter has over her public-housing apartment. Indeed rather more, since the Indian bands are like cooperatively-managed apartment buildings. Moreover, unlike renters, Indians get a per capita share of the band's funds if they choose to leave the reservation. The reservation system can thus combine considerable freedom of individual choice over the use of one's resources with protection of the community from the disintegrating effects of the collective action problem that would result were the costs of maintaining the community borne individually. Whatever the motivation for the endowing of individual title, the effect has been to sacrifice the Indian community in order to protect the mobility rights of individual non-Indians.

But the reservation system causes a problem in the case of mixed marriages. Every member of an Indian band has the right to reside on the band reserve—not the right to buy land on the reserve, since that land can't be bought or sold, but the right to be allocated a plot of land to live on. If the band population grew at a natural rate from purely intraband marriages, there wouldn't be a problem. But when there are a substantial number of marriages to people from outside the band, if the majority of such mixed couples prefer to live on the reserve (as they do), then there will soon be a problem of overcrowding. Unless there is the possibility of expanding the land-base, some mechanism is needed to control the membership.

In the United States, they use a blood criterion. Only those with a certain proportion of Indian blood can be full members of the band, so non-Indian spouses never acquire membership, nor do the children if they have less than the required proportion. Nonmembers never acquire the right to participate in band government, and should the Indian spouse die, they have no right to residence and so can be evicted; while nonmember children must leave the reserve at the age of eighteen. In Canada, the obvious drawbacks of the blood criterion are replaced by a kinship system; everyone in a nuclear family has the same status. If one person in the family has membership, they all do, and so all have full noncontingent rights of residence and participation in band government. Clearly, however, not every mixed family can have membership—that would create overpopulation. If some non-Indians gain membership for themselves and their children by marrying an Indian, there must also be some Indians who give up membership for themselves and their children by marrying a non-Indian. In Canada, until recently it has been Indian women who lose status upon entering into a mixed marriage.

There is an obvious trade-off here—sexual equality for family integrity. There are other models for regulating membership (Sanders 1972 pp. 83–7; Manyfingers) some of which are more equitable. But all options have this in common; if the land-base is fixed and overpopulation threatens, some Indians will not legally be able to marry a non-Indian and have him or her move in and become a full and equal member of the community. Again, there is a continuum of possibilities involved: some proposals allow non-Indian spouses to vote but not to hold office, others allow nonmember spouses and children to remain after the death of the Indian spouse but not to vote, etc. (DIAND, 1982). In all cases there are restrictions on the marriage and voting rights of both Indians and non-Indians: these are viewed as the concomitants of the reservation system needed to protect Indian cultural communities.

There are also controversial measures concerning language rights. The Charter of Rights and Freedoms guarantees to all Canadian citizens the right to a public education in either of the two official languages (English or French), and to deal with all levels of government in either of these languages, where numbers permit. Aboriginal leaders have sought exemption from this. Allowing new residents in the community to receive education and public services in English would weaken the long-term viability of the community. Not only will new residents not have to fully integrate into the minority culture, the establishment of an anglophone infrastructure will attract new anglophone arrivals who may have no interest in even partial integration into the aboriginal community. This is a concern for French-Canadians in Quebec, who want to limit access to English-language schools for people moving into the province. On the other hand, parents will demand their right to a publicly funded education in English so that their children will not be at a disadvantage if they choose to enter the historically dominant and privileged social, political, and economic life in English Canada.

This is just a partial survey of some of the aspects of the aboriginal rights question in Canada. The arrangements are not uniform across the country, and they are all in a state of flux as a result of the unfinished constitutional negotiations. But we can at least get a sense of the basic issues raised for a liberal theory of justice. The common element in all these measures is that some of the recognized rights and liberties of liberal citizenship are limited, and unequally distributed, in order to preserve a minority culture. And we could tell similar stories about the goals and effects of minority rights schemes in other countries, notwithstanding their many variations.

As we've seen, many liberals treat these measures as obviously unjust, and as simple disguises for the perpetuation of ethnic or racial inequality. But once we recognize the differences between these measures and the segregation of blacks, judgments of fairness become more complex, and our intuitions concerning individual and collective measures may be divided.

What underlies this conflict of intuitions? At first glance, someone might suppose that the conflict is between 'respect for the individual' and 'respect for the group.' On this view, to endorse minority rights at the expense of individual rights would be to value the group over the individual. But there is another, and I believe more accurate, view of our intuitions. On this view, both sides of the dilemma concern respect for the individual. The problem is that there are two kinds of respect for individuals at stake here, both of which have intuitive force.

If we respect Indians as Indians, that is to say, as members of a distinct cultural community, then we must recognize the importance to them of their cultural heritage, and we must recognize the legitimacy of claims made by them for the protection of that culture. These claims deserve attention, even if they conflict with some of the requirements of the Charter of Rights. It may not seem right, for example, that aboriginal homelands in the north must be scrapped just because they require a few migrant workers to be temporarily disenfranchised at the local level. It doesn't seem fair for the Indian and Inuit population to be deprived of their cultural community just because a few whites wish to exercise their mobility rights fully throughout the country. If aboriginal peoples can preserve their cultural life by extending residency requirements for non-aboriginal people, or restricting the alienability of the land-base, doesn't that seem a fair and reasonable request? To give every Canadian equal citizenship rights without regard to race or ethnicity, given the vulnerability of aboriginal communities to the decisions of the non-aboriginal majority, does not seem to treat Indians and Inuit with equal respect. For it ignores a potentially devastating problem faced by aboriginal people, but not by English-Canadians—the loss of cultural membership. To insist that this problem be recognized and fairly dealt with hardly sounds like an insistence on racial or ethnic privilege.

Yet if we respect people as Canadians, that is to say as citizens of the common political community, then we must recognize the importance of being able to claim the rights of equal citizenship. Limitations on, and unequal distribution of, individual rights clearly impose burdens. One can readily understand the feeling of discrimination that occurs when an Indian woman is told she can't get a publicly funded education in English for her child (or when a white man is told that he can't vote in the community he resides in or contributes to).

There is, I think, a genuine conflict of institutions here, and it is a conflict between two different considerations involved in showing respect for persons. People are owed respect as citizens and as members of cultural communities. In many situations, the two are perfectly compatible, and in fact may coincide. But in culturally plural societies, differential citizenship rights may be needed to protect a cultural community from unwanted disintegration. If so, then the demands of citizenship and cultural membership pull in different directions. Both matter, and neither seems reducible to the other. (Indeed, when Charles Taylor wanted to illustrate the ultimate plurality of moral value, he chose precisely this conflict between equality for Indians *qua* members of a cultural community and equality for Indians *qua* citizens of the political community: C. Taylor 1988 p. 25.)

The special status of aboriginal people can be viewed as an acceptable, if imperfect, resolution of this conflict. Such conflicts are, in fact, endemic to the day-to-day politics of culturally plural societies, and various schemes of minority rights can be understood and evaluated in this light.

Liberalism, as commonly interpreted, doesn't recognize the legitimacy of one half of this dilemma. It gives no independent weight to our cultural membership, and hence demands equal rights of citizenship, regardless of the consequences for the existence of minority cultures. As Taylor has said: "The modern notion of equality will suffer no differences in the field of opportunity which individuals have before them. Before they choose, individuals must be interchangeable; or alternatively put, any differences must be chosen" (C. Taylor 1979 p. 132). This conception of equality gives no recognition to individuals' cultural membership, and if it operates in a culturally plural country, then it tends to produce a single culture for the whole of the political community, and the undesired assimilation of distinct minority cultural communities. The continued existence of such communities may require restrictions on choice and differentials in opportunity. If liberal equality requires equal citizenship rights, and equal access to a common 'field of opportunity,' then some minority cultures are endangered. And this, I believe, does not respond to our intuitions about the importance of our cultural membership.

If we are troubled by this failure of liberal theories to do justice to our institutions about the importance of cultural membership, two responses are possible. One response is to say that liberals have misinterpreted the role that cultural membership can or must play in their own theory. On this view, the correct interpretation of liberalism does not require universal incorporation or a colorblind constitution, and liberals should accept the possible legitimacy of minority rights. The other response is to accept that liberalism accords no role to cultural membership, and precludes minority rights, but then say that liberalism is incomplete, or perhaps entirely inapplicable to the case of minority rights at stake. On this view, we should seek some other moral theory or set of values which will recognize the importance of cultural membership and the legitimacy of minority rights.

Supporters of aboriginal self-government in Canada have tended to adopt this second approach, defending aboriginal rights *against* liberalism. Liberalism is said to be incomplete or inapplicable for a number of reasons: some claim that the aboriginal population has special rights because their ancestors were here first (Cardinal 1969; Dene Nation; Robinson and Quinney); others claim that Indians and Inuit are properly viewed as 'peoples' under international law, and so have the right of self-determination (Sanders 1983*a* pp. 21–5; Robinson and Quinney pp. 141–2; L.C. Green p. 346); some claim that aboriginal peoples have a different value system, emphasizing the community rather than the individual, and hence group rights rather than individual rights (Ponting and Gibbins 1986 p. 216; Little Bear, Boldt, and Long p. xvi; Svensson pp. 451–2); yet others suggest that aboriginal communities *themselves* have certain rights, because groups as well as individuals have legitimate moral claims (Boldt and Long 1985 pp. 343–5). These are all common ways of defending aboriginal rights against liberalism, by locating our intuitions in favor of them in some non-liberal theory of rights or values.[4]

However, I think that the first response—the attempt to reconcile minority rights and liberal equality—is worth considering, whether one's first commitment is to liberalism, or to minority rights . . . .

The current liberal hostility to minority rights is, I [shall] argue, misguided. However, it is not the result of any simple or obvious mistake, and identifying the problem requires looking deep into the liberal view of the self and community. And even if we recognize the problem there is no simple or obvious way to correct it within a liberal theory of justice. The issue for liberal theory is not as simple as Trudeau once suggested, in response to a question about his reasons for advancing and then withdrawing the 1969 proposal:

> We had perhaps the prejudices of small 'l' liberals and white men at that who thought that equality meant the same law for everybody, and that's why as a result of this we said 'well let's abolish the Indian Act and make Indians citizens of Canada like everyone else. And let's let Indians dispose of their lands just like every other Canadian. And let's make sure that Indians can get their rights, education, health and so on, from the governments like every other Canadian.' But we learned in the process we were a bit too abstract, we were not perhaps pragmatic enough or understanding enough. (Quoted in Weaver 1981 p. 185.)

I shall argue that the problem isn't just one of pragmatism or prejudice. The idea of collective rights for minority cultures doesn't just conflict with the prereflective habits or prejudices of liberals. It seems in direct conflict with some of the most fundamental liberal principles, even in their most theoretically sophisticated formulations. And so the search for a liberal defense of minority rights will take us back into the heart of liberal theory . . . .

Notes

1. One terminological point concerning the specific example of minority rights or special status that I am using: the issue of minority rights is raised in many countries by the presence of aboriginal peoples who have been conquered, colonized, or simply overrun by settlers from other countries and continents. The rights of Canada's aboriginal peoples are, therefore, representative of a major class of minority rights questions. However, the term 'aboriginal rights' is sometimes used in a more restricted sense, to refer solely to those rights which flow from original occupancy of the land. Hence some writers distinguish between the 'aboriginal rights' of aboriginal peoples (e.g. land claims) and their 'national rights,' 'minority rights,' or 'human rights' (e.g. to cultural freedom, self-determination, language rights, etc.)—e.g. Barsh and Henderson 1982 p. 96. But this restricted usage is uncommon, and I shall be using 'aboriginal rights' to refer to the rights of aboriginal peoples, not simply to those rights which aboriginal people have because they are the original occupants of the land.

   One of the most important aspects of minority rights claims concerns the ability of minority cultures to restrict the mobility or voting rights of nonmembers. In the context of Canada's aboriginal people, this is invariably phrased as a matter of whether aboriginal communities can restrict the rights of 'whites.' The historical basis for this usage is obvious, and it has become an unquestioned part of the political vocabulary of the debate over aboriginal rights. But it is important to note that 'whites' is not being used as a racial term—many people who are racially white have become members of aboriginal communities (by marriage or adoption), and Canadians who are not members of aboriginal communities have diverse racial ancestry (including aboriginal ancestry). The terms 'aboriginal' and 'white' refer to cultural membership, not race. 'White' has simply become a general label for those Canadians who are not members of aboriginal communities. Hence many of the aboriginal people who demand restrictions on the mobility of 'whites' have some white ancestry, and many of the people whose mobility is being restricted have some aboriginal (or black, or Asian, etc.) ancestry.
2. Similarly, the principles underlying the Supreme Court decisions which struck down legislation redrawing political boundaries so as to *exclude* blacks from political subdivisions (e.g. *Gomillion v. Lightfoot* [1960] 364 US 339) would seem to argue against legislation to *include* Indians in political subdivisions which are unrepresentative and therefore harmful to their interests (Gross p. 250).
3. This is precisely what happened to the Métis in Manitoba, and to the Hispanic population in the American Southwest, during the second half of the nineteenth century. These groups formed a majority in their respective regions, and had rights to public services and education in their own languages. But once their regions became incorporated into the larger Canadian and American federations, these groups became outnumbered by anglophone settlers, who quickly proceeded to take away those rights (see J. Weinstein pp. 46–7 on the Métis; Glazer 1975 p. 25 and 1983 p. 277 on the Spanish-speaking population of the Southwest). Aboriginal self-government proposals have been designed with these dangers and historical precedents in mind. (J. Weinstein p. 47; Purich p. 229).

4. I shall discuss the weakness of the last two arguments (about the different value systems of aboriginal peoples, and the moral standing of communities) [elsewhere]. I am unsure what to say about the first two, partly because they in fact have many variants, some of which contradict others. But I should say something about them, since they are important not only in Canada, but in the emerging international norms concerning aboriginal rights.

The fact of original occupancy is invoked to defend at least two different aboriginal claims. The first is 'aboriginal title' (i.e. ownership or usufructuary rights over land and natural resources), the second is sovereignty. I'll discuss sovereignty together with the self-determination argument, since they raise similar questions of international law.

The 'aboriginal title' claim, by itself, does not justify permanent special political status, unless it is further claimed that "the ownership of the land is the fundamental concept on which other rights, including the right to self-government, are based" (Sanders, 1983*b* pp. 328–9). This is in fact the argument amongst some aboriginal groups whose land-base is secure and legally recognized. However, the emphasis on aboriginal title raises a number of questions. Firstly, it is far from clear why it matters who first acquired a piece of land, unless one is inclined to a Nozick-like theory of justice. (Lyons; McDonald 1976) Aboriginal communities were, of course, unjustly deprived of much of their land when whites settled, and those injustices have lingering effects which warrant some form of compensation. But that is not yet a reason why the ultimate goal shouldn't be some form of equality of resources for all the citizens of the country, rather than any permanent special status. Secondly, if self-government is supposed to flow from aboriginal title, then there may not be any grounds to demand that the federal government fund aboriginal self-government (Lyon pp. 13–14). Finally, it won't justify either land or self-government for some aboriginal groups, who for various (and often historically arbitrary) reasons lack recognizable title (Robinson and Quinney pp. 51, 86; Opekokew).

The sovereignty claim says that because aboriginal nations were here first, and have not officially relinquished their sovereignty, therefore, as a matter of international law, domestic Canadian law does not apply to aboriginal communities. Any relationship between the federal government and the aboriginal communities must be concluded by what are essentially state-to-state treaties. On the self-determination view, aboriginal peoples are entitled to the same right to self-determination that previously colonized peoples claim under Article 1 of the International Covenant on Civil and Political Rights. The two views often go hand in hand (e.g. Robinson and Quinney), but they are distinct, since aboriginal communities could have sovereignty even if they are not 'peoples' under international law, or they could be 'peoples' even if they do not have sovereignty under international law.

However, neither claim has heretofore been explicitly recognized in international law. Aboriginal rights have instead been viewed as coming under Article 27 of the Covenant, dealing with minority rights (see e.g. United Nations 1983 pp. 94–104), which is roughly how I have been treating them. Most aboriginal leaders have been concerned to change that pattern (see e.g. Sanders 1983*b* pp. 21–5, Barsh 1983 pp. 91–5, 1986 pp. 376–7; Kronowitz *et al.* pp. 598–600; L.C. Green p. 346; Robinson and Quinney pp. 141–2), although some people have thought Article 27 sufficient (e.g. Svensson p. 438). Aboriginal advocates rightly point out that international rulings have been quite arbitrary in limiting the recognition of sovereignty or peoplehood to overseas colonies (the 'Blue Water Thesis'), while denying it to internal groups who share many of the same historical and social features (e.g., Barsh 1983 pp. 84–91).

But since advocates of self-determination and sovereignty views are not in fact seeking a sovereign state, it is not immediately clear what rests on the distinction between Article 1 and Article 27 rights. Article 27 has occasionally been interpreted as merely requiring nondiscrimination against minorities. But the recent Capotorti report on the international protection of minority rights decisively rejects that view, and insists that special measures for minority cultures are required for 'factual equality,' and that such measures are as important as nondiscrimination in 'defending fundamental human rights' (Capotorti pp. 40–1, 98–9). If the goal is not a sovereign state, then Article 27 may be as good as Article 1 in arguing for the right of minority cultures to freely develop and express their own culture. As Wirsing notes, recent changes in the interpretation of Article 27 go 'some distance towards closing the gap' between the expectations of minority cultures and the concessions of the international community (Wirsing 1980 p. 228). And while elimination of the 'Blue Water Thesis' in regard to the definition of 'peoples' would eliminate some arbitrariness, it would also essentially eliminate the category of 'minorities' (most groups which have sought special measures under Article 27 would constitute peoples, not minorities, according to the definitions offered by some aboriginal groups—e.g. the Mikmaq proposal quoted in Barsh 1983 p. 94).

One worry aboriginals have about Article 27, even on an expansive reading, concerns not the content of the rights it may accord to minorities, but the question of who *delegates* the rights. They are aware of the vulnerability created by the American system of aboriginal rights, in which self-government "is a gift, not a right . . . a question of policy and politics" (Kronowitz *et al.* pp. 533, 535; cf. Barsh 1983 p. 103). Some aboriginal leaders believe that claims to sovereignty are needed to avoid this vulnerability (see e.g. Robinson and Quinney p. 123). But others say that such claims heighten misunderstanding and prevent the negotiation of adequate guarantees. "The maximum height on the government side is generated by the word 'sovereignty'; and on the aboriginal side, by the word 'delegated.' Somewhere between the two lies an area of potential agreement" (M. Dunn p. 37).

Since Article 1 has not been applied to the aboriginal peoples of North America, and since Article 27 may still be too weak, some aboriginal groups have been pressing for the recognition of a specifically aboriginal category between those of 'peoples' and 'minorities,' in which self-determination is neither sovereign nor delegated (see Moore pp. 27–8; Kronowitz *et al.* pp. 612–20; Barsh 1986 pp. 376–8; Sanders 1983*b* pp. 28–9). The question of whether self-government is delegated or not is clearly important, but it is somewhat distinct from the questions I am addressing. If aboriginal rights to self-determination are not delegated, or indeed if aboriginal communities retain their legal sovereignty, then aboriginals should be able to reject the substantive provisions of a Canadian government proposal for self-government, should they view them as unjust. My question is the prior one of evaluating the justice of the provisions. And it may be that the same substantive provisions would be just whether aboriginal groups are viewed as peoples, or as minorities, or as their own third category. The different categories would affect not only the justice of their claims, but their domestic and international ability to negotiate for those just claims.

Even if aboriginal peoples have substantive claims which cannot be derived from Article 27, in virtue of aboriginal title or legal sovereignty, it is still important for liberals to determine what is owed minorities under that article. Even if aboriginal peoples have special rights beyond those owed them as a minority culture, liberals should ask what they (or other minorities) are owed just in virtue of plural cultural membership. In any event, it is doubtful whether all North American aboriginal groups could qualify as sovereign or self-determining peoples under international law. So a liberal defense of minority rights, if one can be found, would be a helpful argument for many aboriginal groups, and may be the only argument available for some of the groups.

References

Asch, M. (1984). *Home and Native Land: Aboriginal Rights and the Canadian Constitution*. Toronto: Methuen.

Barsh, R. (1983). 'Indigenous North American and Contemporary International Law.' *Oregon Law Review*. Vol. 62.

———. (1986). 'Indigenous Peoples: An Emerging Object of International Law.' *American Journal of International Law*. Vol. 80.

Barsh, R. and Henderson, J.Y. (1982). 'Aboriginal Rights, Treaty Rights, and Human Rights: Indian Tribes and Constitutional Renewal.' *Journal of Canadian Studies*. Vol. 17.

Barlett, R. (1986). *Subjugation, Self-Management and Self-Government of Aboriginal Lands and Resources in Canada*. Kingston, Ont.: Institute of Intergovernmental Relations.

Berger, T. (1984). 'Towards the Regime of Tolerance.' In *Political Thought in Canada: Contemporary Perspectives*. Ed. S. Brooks. Toronto: Irwin Publishing.

Boldt, M., and Long, J.A. (1985). 'Tribal Philosophies and the Canadian Charter of Rights and Freedoms.' In *The Quest for Justice: Aboriginal People and Aboriginal Rights*. Eds. Boldt, M., and Long, J.A. Toronto: University of Toronto Press.

Bowles, R., Hanley, J., Hodgins, B., and Rawlyk, G. (1972). *The Indian: Assimilation, Integration or Separation?* Scarborough, Ont.: Prentice-Hall.

Capotorti, F. (1979). *Study on the Rights of Persons Belonging to Ethnic, Religious and Linguistic Minorities*. UN Doc. E/CN 4/Sub. 2/384 Rev. 1.

Cardinal, H. (1969). *The Unjust Society*. Edmonton: Hurtig Publishers.

———. (1977). *The Rebirth of Canada's Indians*. Edmonton: Hurtig Publishers.

Connor, W. (1972). 'Nation-Building or Nation-Destroying?' *World Politics*, Vol. 24.

Dene Nation (1977). 'A Proposal to the Government and People of Canada.' In *Dene Nation: The Colony Within*. Ed. M. Watkins. Toronto: University of Toronto Press.

DIAND (Department of Indian Affairs and Northern Development). (1969). 'A Statement of the Government of Canada on Indian Policy.' In Bowles *et al.* (1972).

———. (1982). 'The Elimination of Sex Discrimination from the Indian Act.' R32-59/1982. Ottawa.

Dunn, M. (1986). *Access to Survival: A Perspective on Aboriginal Self-Government for the Constituency of the Native Council of Canada*. Kingston, Ont.: Institute of Intergovernmental Relations.

Dworkin, R. (1983). 'In Defence of Equality.' *Social Philosophy and Policy*, Vol. 1.

Glazer, N. (1975). *Affirmative Discrimination: Ethnic Inequality and Public Policy*. New York: Basic Books.

———. (1983). *Ethnic Dilemmas: 1964–1982*. Cambridge, Mass.: Harvard University Press.

Green, L.C. (1983). 'Aboriginal Peoples, International Law and the Canadian Charter of Rights and Freedoms.' *Canadian Bar Review*, Vol. 61.

Gross, M. (1973). 'Indian Control for Quality Indian Education.' *North Dakota Law Review*, Vol. 49.

International Herald Tribune (1985). 'Botha Rejects Plea From Within Party to End Home School Segregation.' 3 Oct.

Kaplan, J. (1964). 'Comment on "The Decade of School Desegregation".' *Columbia Law Review*, Vol. 64.

Kronowitz, R., Lichtman, J., McSloy, S., and Olsen, M. (1987). 'Toward Consent and Cooperation: Reconsidering the Political Status of Indian Nations.' *Harvard Civil Rights—Civil Liberties Review*, Vol. 22.

Little Bear, L., Boldt, M., and Long, J. (1984). *Pathways to Self-Determination: Canadian Indians and the Canadian State*. Toronto: University of Toronto Press.

Lyon, N. (1984). *Aboriginal Self-Government: Rights of Citizenship and Access to Government Services*. Kingston, Ont.: Institute of Intergovernmental Relations.

Lyons, D. (1981). 'The New Indian Claims and Original Rights to Land.' In *Reading Nozick: Essays on Anarchy, State and Utopia*. Ed. J. Paul. Totowa, NJ: Rowman and Littlefield.

McDonald, M. (1976). 'Aboriginal Rights.' In *Contemporary Issues in Political Philosophy*. Eds. W. Shea and J. King-Farlow. New York: Science History Publications.

MacMeekin, D. (1969). 'Red, White and *Gray*: Equal Protection and the American Indian.' *Stanford Law Review*, Vol. 21.

Manyfingers, M. (1986). 'Determination of Indian Band Membership: An Examination of Political Will.' *Canadian Journal of Native Studies*, Vol. 6.

Moore, K. (1984). *The Will to Survive: Native People and the Constitution*. Val d'Or, Que.: Hyperborea Publishings.

Opekokew, D. (1987). *The Political and Legal Inequalities Among Aboriginal Peoples in Canada*. Kingston, Ont.: Institute of Intergovernmental Affairs.

Ponting, J., and Gibbins, R. (1986). 'An Assessment of the Probable Impact of Aboriginal Self-Government in Canada.' In *The Politics of Gender, Ethnicity, and Language in Canada*. Eds. A. Cairns and C. Williams. Toronto: University of Toronto Press.

Rawls, J. (1971). *A Theory of Justice*. London: Oxford University Press.

———. (1980). 'Kantian Constructivism in Moral Theory.' *Journal of Philosophy*. Vol. 77.

Robinson, E., and Quinney, H. (1985). *The Infested Blanket: Canada's Constitution—Genocide of Indian Nations*. Winnipeg: Queenston House.

Sanders, D. (1972). 'The Bill of Rights and Indian Status.' *University of British Columbia Law Review*. Vol. 7.

———. (1983*a*). 'The Re-Emergence of Indigenous Questions in International Law.' *Canadian Human Rights Yearbook 1983*. Toronto: Carswell.

———. (1983*b*). 'The Rights of the Aboriginal Peoples of Canada.' *Canadian Bar Review*. Vol. 61.

Schwartz, B. (1986). *First Principles, Second Thoughts: Aboriginal Peoples, Constitutional Reform and Canadian Statecraft*. Montreal: The Institute for Research on Public Policy.

Svensson, F. (1979). 'Liberal Democracy and Group Rights: The Legacy of Individualism and Its Impact on American Indian Tribes.' *Political Studies*. Vol. 27.

Taylor, C. (1979). *Hegel and Modern Society*. Cambridge: Cambridge University Press.

———. (1988). *Justice After Virtue*. Legal Theory Workshop Series, Faculty of Law, University of Toronto. WS 1987–88 no. 3.

Toronto Star (1986). 'Botha's Warning.' 28 Sept.

United Nations Human Rights Committee. (1983). *Considerations of Reports Submitted by States Parties under Article 40 of the Covenant: Canada*. CCPR/C/1/Add. 62.

van de Berghe, P. (1981). *The Ethnic Phenomenon*. New York: Elsevier.

Weaver, S. (1981). *Making Canadian Indian Policy*. Toronto: University of Toronto Press.

Weinstein, J. (1986). *Aboriginal Self-Determination off a Land Base*. Kingston, Ont.: Institute of Intergovernmental Relations.

Wirsig, R. (1980). 'Cultural Minorities: Is the World Ready to Protect Them?' *Canadian Review of Studies in Nationalism*. Vol. 7.

Content Quiz 11.5

Instructions: Fill in the blanks with the appropriate responses listed below.

status	differential citizenship rights
aboriginal	collective
egalitarianism	affirmative action
moral existence	political
cultural	badge of inferiority
forced integration	moral worth

1. A _____ community is one in which individuals exercise their rights and responsibilities entailed by a framework of liberal justice.
2. A _____ community is one in which individuals share a culture, language, and history defining their group membership.
3. One way of preserving the cultural autonomy for minorities in multicultural nations has been to give them distinct legal and political _____.
4. Advocates of liberalism sometimes object to granting special status to particular groups because of an alleged conflict between individual and _____ rights.

5. _____ leaders in North America argue that their community's self-government must include the legal recognition of certain collective rights.
6. According to liberalism, individuals are viewed as ultimate units of _____.
7. The liberal idea that every individual has equal moral status and, hence, is to be treated as an equal by the government is called _____.
8. According to liberal justice, the community has no _____ or claims of its own.
9. _____ is one temporary policy accepted by some liberals to achieve a colorblind society.
10. For the aboriginal peoples, separation from mainstream North American life and culture is not always perceived as a _____.
11. _____ is something that has been used to ensure liberal equality for Blacks in the United States, but is regarded by North American aboriginals as something undesirable, a form of coercive assimilation.
12. In culturally plural societies _____ may be required to protect a cultural community from unwanted disintegration.

Discussion Questions

1. What is the difference between a political community and a cultural community?
2. How does the notion of "group rights" or "community rights" pose a problem when viewed from the standpoint of the traditional liberal theory of justice?
3. On what grounds, if any, can we justify giving special legal and political status to minority groups within a pluralistic society?
4. Are liberal notions of individualism and egalitarianism conducive or detrimental to protecting the rights of aboriginal peoples? Why?
5. How do "integration" and "separation" work in opposite ways for Blacks and for Native Peoples of North America?
6. What are some examples of how the rights and liberties of individuals have been limited and unequally distributed to preserve a minority culture?

A TREATISE ON THE RIGHTS OF THE ABORIGINAL PEOPLES OF THE CONTINENT OF NORTH AMERICA

Fred Plain

Synopsis

In this reading, Fred Plain argues that the aboriginal peoples of North America generally, and the Nishnawbe-Aski in particular, have a right to self-government including the right to determine their future and their chosen goals. Although the white man's society has often found it difficult to define exactly what is meant by aboriginal rights, Plain offers us a clear definition, including all that it entails. In fleshing out his definition and justification of aboriginal rights, he explains terms such as "aborigine," "civilization," "independence," and "nationhood." He rejects federal efforts to reduce aboriginal rights questions to a series of legal issues to be disputed in a white man's court. He argues that the European settlers to the continent had no right to trample the existing native system of law and that, ultimately, rights to self-determination originate with the Creator and, hence, are non-negotiable.

I want to deal in this paper with our understanding of the meaning of "aboriginal rights." First of all, I want to quote from a paper produced by the Union of Ontario Indians in 1970. I was president of the union at that time, and I authorized the following statement, which was presented to a special committee dealing with the constitution of Canada.

> As Indian people we will always see our special status and our legal right as flowing from the original sovereignty of our nations. The colonial legal system to a large degree denied that sovereignty, but they never denied the existence of rights based on the aboriginal possession of tribal territories. It was the unauthorized violation of these rights that led to the unrest which prompted the Royal Proclamation of 1763.
>
> That document, the first written constitutional document for British North America, recognized the existence of Indians' territorial rights, and established legal procedures for the surrender of these rights. The lands which today comprise Ontario were Indian lands. In the words of the Proclamation, they had not been ceded to or purchased by the colonial power. The procedures established by the Royal Proclamation for ceding Indian lands remain in force today. The last treaty signed under these procedures was in 1956, the Soto adhesion to Treaty #6.
>
> Areas remain today in Ontario for which no valid treaty or surrender exists. Therefore, the procedures of the Royal Proclamation are still of practical consequence even in Ontario. Section 91.24 of the British North American Act of 1867 gave jurisdiction over Indians and lands reserved for the Indians to the Federal Government. This was not enacted as seems popularly believed out of a paternalistic concern for Native peoples.
>
> It was enacted to make clear the power of the Federal Government to engage in colonial expansion in the West. The phrase "land reserved for Indians" included lands not ceded by treaty as of 1867, which for Ontario comprised by far the greater part of the present territory of this Province. If the Indians and their lands had not been crucial to the opening of the West, it would have been more logical to place Indians under Provincial jurisdictions as somewhat different terms of Indian policy developed in each colony of 1867.
>
> Following the surrender of the Hudson's Bay Company Charter in 1869/70, the Governor General, exercising prerogative power in compliance with the procedures established by the Royal Proclamation, began

negotiating a series of treaties with the Indian nations in Ontario and the Northwest. The treaties were constitutional documents. They were seen by both sides as establishing basic patterns of interrelationship for the future. They were based on the idea of mutual consent and the understanding that the Indians had legal rights in their patrimony. To violate these documents is to compromise the integrity of the Canadian legal system. The Migratory Birds Convention Act, and the decisions in Regina vs. Sekina in 1964, and in Regina vs. George in 1966, and Daniels vs. White and the Queen in 1968, to Indian people represent violations of basic legal commitments.

The basic rights of the Indian peoples are of constitutional significance. Yet, these rights have not been uniformly safeguarded under the present constitutional structure. This should change.

What Are Aboriginal Rights?

In white society there has always been confusion as to what actually is meant by the term "aboriginal rights." In 1970, for example, Prime Minister Pierre Trudeau was reported to have said that the concept of aboriginal rights is so complicated as to be unworkable. But to us, the Nishnawbe-Aski, the concept is basic, simple, and unambiguous. Our definition of aboriginal rights can be summed up in one phrase: "the right of independence through self-government." When we say that our right to self-government, our right to self-determination, our right to nationhood must be recognized in any new Canadian constitution, we are defining aboriginal rights. This is the goal of the Nishnawbe-Aski as outlined in the Declaration of Nishnawbe-Aski of 1977.

Aboriginal rights defined in this way include the right to develop our own life-style and our own economy, and to protect and encourage the practice of our sacred traditions as we know them. We, the Nishnawbe-Aski, have the inherent right to determine what our future will be. We shall determine the destiny of our land. We want to see the continued development of our people under their own governing systems. Aboriginal rights were a mere concept of Prime Minister Trudeau's mind, but to my people they are a reality. We have the inherent right to develop and grow under our own system, and our own system will flow from our own people, who will develop our own constitution. Our Indian constitutions have every right to be recognized in any new Canadian constitution. This is the true meaning of aboriginal rights.

What Is an Aborigine?

The aborigines are the indigenous inhabitants of a country. For instance, the people that we know as the Indian nations of North and South America are the aborigines of these two continents. They were the first people to live in this part of the world.

Because we were the first people to live here we have a claim to certain rights. These rights include human rights—that is, the basic right to life claimed by all people. However, when we talk about aboriginal rights, we are also talking about the inherent right to self-determination that applies to all aborigines.

What Is Civilization?

To understand aboriginal rights we must understand the meaning of civilization. Civilization is the accumulation of the traditions and culture of a people: their ability to express themselves in a variety of ways—in dance, music, art, law, religion, the telling of stories, the writing of books, and so on. The aboriginal people of North and South America constituted a number of different civilizations.

Aboriginal rights guarantee each indigenous nation the right to develop its own traditions and culture—its own civilization. Each aboriginal nation has the inherent right to seek happiness and a comfortable way of living, and to develop itself at its own pace. This was the right of each aboriginal nation from its beginning, and it exists today. Each nation exercised aboriginal rights within its own lands and boundaries and under its own sovereignty.

To recognize that the aboriginal people were a civilization long before the white man came to North America is to acknowledge that as an aboriginal people we exercised our aboriginal right to govern ourselves. Conversely, to acknowledge that we have aboriginal rights is to recognize that these rights flow from our long-standing civilization.

Aboriginal and European Attitudes Toward the Land

Nishnawbe-Aski means "the people and the land." Our links with the earth are sacred links that no man can ever sever. We are one with the earth, and the earth is one with us. The Nishnawbe-Aski Declaration states that we have the right to govern and control our own people in our own land, and the right to remedy our own situations. The efforts that are made to meet our needs must come from our own people.

As nations of people we made laws to govern ourselves. Among the laws that we made were laws governing our use of the land and its resources. But our attitude toward the land and its use was and still is very different from the European attitude. We aboriginal people believe that no individual or group owns the land, that the land was given to us collectively by the Creator to use, not to own, and that we have a sacred obligation to protect the land and use its resources wisely. For the Europeans, the idea that land can be owned by a person or persons and exploited for profit is basic to the system. The European political and legal systems have been developed to reflect this concept of the land.

Many European and Canadian laws have to do with regulating private property in one form or another and with governing relations among people with respect to private property. The sovereign government has created laws to govern the distribution of the scarce resource of property. The most basic form of property, other than one's own body, is land.

The idea that land can be bought and sold, or that you can exercise some rights but not others in the land, is absolutely foreign to the Nishnawbe-Aski way of thinking. Yet this is the basis for all legislation that has been enacted since the coming of the Europeans to North America.

Legislation Affecting Aboriginal Rights

The Royal Proclamation of 1763 was passed in the British Parliament because of the struggles between Indians and Europeans over the land. This document recognized the existence of Indians' territorial rights and established the legal procedures for the giving up of those rights.

The Constitution Act, 1867, established Canada as a nation. The act sets out the division of power between the provinces and the federal government. Section 91(24) of the act gives jurisdiction over Indians and lands reserved for Indians to the federal government.

The act was intended to make clear the power of the federal government to engage in colonial expansion in the west. This was done because we Indians and our lands were crucial to the opening of the west, and the federal government wanted to be able to control us and our land in order to consolidate its power over the country.

After the Royal Proclamation, and until as recently as 1956, treaties were signed between the government and the Indian nations. These treaties were seen by both sides as establishing basic patterns of future interrelationships. They were based on the idea of mutual consent and on the understanding that Indians had legal rights in and control of the land.

The treaties were a recognition by colonial law that we Indian people had sovereignty in our land. In fact, there was a widespread acknowledgment that the aboriginal occupants of the land had certain legal claims because of their historical sovereignty over the land. The English legal system developed a theory that those claims were limited in certain ways, but the aboriginal tribes had the legal right to possess their tribal territories. Under the English legal system if the lands passed into non-Indian hands, then the Indian claims had to be extinguished by a formal treaty and by some form of compensation.

The treaties were negotiated sometimes before white settlement, sometimes after. The effect of the treaties was to extinguish many aboriginal rights; to preserve some residual rights, such as hunting, fishing, and trapping; and to create some new rights, such as schooling, medical care, and annuity payments.

While the treaties have not been totally in our favor, the law has never denied that the aboriginal tribes have legal rights to possess their tribal territories.

What Does It Mean to Be a Nation?

Our aboriginal right allows us to determine our future as the Nishnawbe-Aski Nation. What does it mean to be a nation? In 1977, an international conference on discrimination against indigenous populations of the Americas put forward a declaration of principles aimed at gaining recognition for indigenous or aboriginal peoples as nations under international law. The criteria for recognition as a nation are: that the people have a permanent population; that they have a defined territory; that they have a government; that they have the ability to enter into relations with other states. We can assure Canada and the international community that using these criteria we can define ourselves as a nation. We have a population that is permanent; we have always existed and we are not going to die out or fade into oblivion. We have a defined territory stretching from James Bay and Hudson Bay west to the Manitoba boundary; from Hudson Bay and James Bay southward to the height of land known as the Arctic watershed and east to the borders of Quebec. We have a democratic government given to us by the Creator. The Royal Proclamation of 1763 refers to our sovereignty, and the government of Canada approaches us as a nation to enter into a treaty with them. We continue to have the right to enter into relations with other states.

Under these criteria, the Nishnawbe-Aski have a solid basis for claiming our aboriginal right to determine what our future will be and to determine how we are going to attain our goals.

Do the Indian People Have a System of Government?

When the white man first came to America, there were systems of government in operation in this new land. The democratic system employed by the great Six Nations Confederacy was studied by the Europeans, and was picked up and incorporated into their governing systems. Democracy was already flourishing in

North America before the white man came. The right to govern one's people, the right to govern one's destiny, the right to determine the paths that a nation will follow to reach its objectives must be recognized as sovereign and aboriginal rights.

We had a government. The government has been dormant because of the influx of federal law, particularly the Indian Act and its administrators, the Department of Indian Affairs. Our government has remained hidden in the hearts of our people, but it has never died. Our government will come forth under the careful guidance and leadership of the Nishnawbe-Aski Commission. We will be prepared to put the constitution of the Nishnawbe-Aski on paper, if that is what is required. Our government is a reality.

We must draw out from our people what they want to see developed in their community with regard to their own governing structure. Only then can we begin to educate our people in the traditional ways of living, traditional Indian government, and the traditional right to determine our future.

What Does It Mean to Be Independent?

When the Nishnawbe-Aski made their declaration in 1977, they stressed that their objective was to see the full development of cultural, economic, spiritual, and political independence. We think that we have to come to grips with the fact that cultural independence and economic independence cannot be divorced. One cannot exist without the other.

At the time the white man came here, our educational system was complete. The educational system and the political development of the various Indian nations in Canada determined the life-style of the particular tribe in whatever area of America they lived in. For instance, the economy of the Ojibway and the Cree living in this part of North America was based on the presence of animal, fish, bird, and plant life destined to give sustenance to the people. Hunting, fishing and trapping, and gathering were not separate issues to be dealt with at a political level by certain components of the government; they were part of the socioeconomic system of our people, and they are included in the overall definition of aboriginal rights. Before the white man came, all Indian nations were independent and exercised their aboriginal rights within their own lands.

The Nishnawbe-Aski and the Constitution

We did not question the statement of Prime Minister Pierre Trudeau that the people of this country have a right to their own constitution. We support the principle of patriation; Canadians have a right to determine the instrument by which government is going to make laws that apply to them.

When the constitutional negotiations became an issue, we told the British parliamentarians that we were not fighting the patriation of the constitution to Canada. We felt that the Canadian people had a right to their own constitution, but we also believed that the Nishnawbe-Aski Nation, which existed before the Europeans came to North America, have a right to their own constitution, and that they must not be deprived of the right to make their own laws and determine their own destiny through their own governing system. Because the Canadian government was unwilling to recognize our right to our own constitution, we challenged the patriation of the British North America Act.

We, the aboriginal people, must clearly spell

out the true aboriginal rights that must be recognized in any Canadian constitution. These rights are nonnegotiable. But we must take a united stand, or we will find it difficult to persuade Canada's first ministers to heed our claims.

What the Canadian Government Wants from the Aboriginal People

We are in the heat of a tremendous battle, a battle that is focused on jurisdiction. The premiers of the provinces and the prime minister are trying to reduce the aboriginal rights question to a series of legal issues that they can contest or disregard. At the same time, they attempt to placate the Indian people by saying, "We will look after you; we will improve your conditions; we will accommodate your needs." But ultimately they will try to consolidate their jurisdiction over our land and our resources. The first ministers have only one goal in mind in the constitutional negotiations: they hope to gain complete control over all Indian lands and resources. This is what the constitutional process is all about.

The Canadian Government's Attitude to Aboriginal Rights

The Honourable Jean Chrétien had these words to say about aboriginal and treaty rights: "We will honor our lawful obligations to the aboriginal people." Precisely what did he mean? He meant that Canada has obligations to native people only if such obligations will stand the test of the law. If the law decrees that certain obligations must be met, and if those obligations are defined in such a manner that the government can accept the definition, then they will be honored. But what does the term "law" mean? Law, in the modern liberal state, is the creation of an autonomous and general legal system composed of: private parties; a legitimate legal sovereignty and its administrative agencies (the governor-in-council or Parliament, or the government of Canada, and its cabinet and various departments); and the independent judiciary.

When the explorers from the European nations came to America, they found a land with people and law. The Europeans had no right to come and trample that system of laws underfoot and impose a new legal system in North America. But this fact is not readily going to be recognized and acknowledged by the people who in the first instance denied the existence of the aboriginal system of law. They will fight any attempt to bring truth to bear.

Let us go back to the quotation from the Nishnawbe-Aski declaration. In the minds of our people who hunt, trap, and fish the forests, lakes, and rivers of Nishnawbe-Aski land, there is a clear concept of what our land tenure is. However, according to the government of Canada, which makes the laws, aboriginal rights are to be determined by a court interpretation. As far as the courts are concerned aboriginal rights are conceptual rights only; that is to say, they are a concept that exists only in the mind until drafted into some kind of law that makes sense in a legal system. The government makes the law dealing with aboriginal rights and the government appoints judges who interpret the law dealing with aboriginal rights. If the government of Canada has its way, the white man's law and the white man's courts will determine how the concept of land tenure is defined in practice.

Who Will Decide What Our Aboriginal Rights Are?

Court cases have never solved the riddle of aboriginal rights. The *Baker Lake* case is a prime instance of what happens when the dominant governing society, through its enacted laws and its judicial system, decides what constitutes aboriginal rights. In the *Baker Lake* case, the court said that the Inuit do have aboriginal rights because they have been here from time immemorial. Because of that one basic fact, the court recognized that aboriginal rights do exist. However, the Supreme Court of Canada took it upon itself to define what the aboriginal right is not. The judgment states that the aboriginal right is not a proprietary right. In other words, the right of the aboriginal people does not relate to the land, and therefore the land is open to those exploiters who want to extract the gas and the oil, destroy the environment, and then move out. The indigenous population is then left with evil consequences that greatly outweigh any potential benefits that might come to them from the resource exploitation.

In the communities of the Nishnawbe-Aski Nation, our fishermen, our trappers, our hunters, our schoolchildren, and our women who maintain our homes understand what our aboriginal rights are. Aboriginal rights are a riddle only to those who do not want to hear or face the truth, who do not want their taking of the land interfered with by the aboriginal owners of this continent.

The aboriginal people have a clear concept of land tenure in their minds; therefore our chiefs, our elders, our people, our children, should define our aboriginal rights—not the federal government, the provinces, or the Canadian courts. It is we who must protect our aboriginal right to self-determination as a nation and our right to develop and use the resources of the land free of interference and intimidation. We have an obligation to preserve the rights granted to us by the Creator. We have that right now. We have always had that right. We are determined to have that right in the future. We don't have to beg the prime minister of Canada and the provincial premiers to recognize that we have certain basic human and aboriginal rights.

Conclusion

I close this paper with a prayer. Great Grandfather, our hearts and our minds are joined together. We rejoice to know that our right to live and enjoy the beauty of this great land was given to us, not by any foreign government, but by yourself. Great Grandfather, you gave us the land and its resources; you made us one with the birds, the animal life, the fish life; you made us one with nature itself. This is our aboriginal right. It is a right that no government can interpret for us.

Because you gave it to us, no man has a right to take it away from us. Many times, our hearts have been made heavy when we have seen the devastation of our land by those who seek only to mine it for its wealth and then leave it. Our hearts have been made heavy because other powers have come in and made laws that have restricted our free movement of spirit. Yet you have put it in our hearts this day to stand upon our feet once again, and boldly claim that our aboriginal right is forever.

Breathe upon us with your spirit of life, and give us greater determination to press for this right to be fully restored to us and recognized by all people. Great Grandfather, be with us in all of our deliberations, for without your leadership and guidance we are weak and helpless. Cause the sound of the drum to be loud and clear to our hearts and minds in this crucial hour.

Content Quiz 11.6

Instructions: Fill in the blanks with the appropriate responses listed below.

aboriginal rights	Royal Proclamation of 1763
Nishnawbe-Aski Declaration	civilization
european attitude	treaties
nation	court interpretation
British North America Act of 1867	aborigines

1. The _____ was the first written constitutional document for British North America that recognized the existence of Indian territorial rights.
2. According to Fred Plain, the _____ gave jurisdiction over Indians and Indian land reserves to the federal government, not out of paternalistic concern, but for colonial expansion in the west.
3. A simple definition of _____ is "the right of independence through self-government."
4. _____ are the indigenous inhabitants of a country.
5. To appreciate the meaning and implications of aboriginal rights, we must understand what is meant by _____.
6. The _____ states that this Indian nation has the right to govern and control its own people in its own land.
7. Contrary to the _____, aboriginal people do not believe in the idea that land can be "owned" by individuals or groups and exploited for profit.
8. _____ signed as recently as 1956 acknowledged, in effect, that aboriginal occupants of land have certain legal claims because of historical sovereignty over it.
9. A(n) _____ is constituted by a people who have a permanent population, a defined territory, a government, and an ability to enter into relations with other states.
10. In this paper, Fred Plain makes it clear that he is not willing to subject aboriginal rights to a white man's _____.

Discussion Questions

1. How does the author of this reading define "aboriginal rights"? What do they include?
2. How are aboriginal and European settlers' attitudes toward the land different?
3. Why are North American aboriginals, especially those in Canadian provinces, reluctant to fight for their rights in the legal courts of the country?
4. If and when Indian land claims conflict with provincial or federal ones, whose rights should prevail? Why?

CHAPTER TWELVE

12 BIOMEDICAL ETHICS

A FEMINIST VIEW OF ABORTION

Jean MacRae

Synopsis

Jean MacRae's article presents a pro-abortion argument from a feminist's perspective. The article begins by trying to explode several myths about the premature termination of pregnancies. Specifically, MacRae contends that abortion is not some kind of rare or necessarily traumatic experience; neither is it some kind of unnatural renunciation of motherhood. In her article MacRae defends abortion by describing unwanted pregnancy as a form of physical violence against women. She points to society's sexist attitudes and double standards that foist the responsibility of birth control flatly on women, who, because of social pressure, are often forced into having intercourse as a way of ensuring marriage—something women have been conditioned to believe is highly important.

As part of her pro-abortion stance, MacRae also rejects biological arguments that give the fetus independent status from the mother. For her, the fetus is parasitic upon the mother as evidenced by the drain and strain pregnancy often causes. The "humanness" of the fetus is also called into question by MacRae. She refers to the work of some theologians who characterize distinctively human life as expressing language, values, imagination, creativity, and so on—things not exhibited by the developing fetus.

When biological and theological arguments, both in favor and against abortion, are put aside, the ultimate question, for MacRae, involves the problem of what kind of sacrifice is excessive to demand of one person for the welfare of another. In her estimation, compulsory pregnancy is too much of a sacrifice, placing more importance on a potential life than on a real, existing one. Absolutizing the value of the life of the fetus results in the manipulation of the bodily and mental integrity of women and, hence, their dehumanization.

Finally, MacRae underscores human values besides those pertaining to physical life alone. She maintains that abortion is, in fact, an affirmation of values (of those negatively impacted). She holds that men will have to learn that unwanted pregnancies bring other values into play, more important than those pertaining to the nascent fetus. Through aborting unwanted fetuses, women affirm the value of their own personhood as more multidimensional than simply bearers of children.

Before describing women's experience of unwanted pregnancy as I have observed it in my counselling work, an analysis of some of the mythology which has grown up around abortion might be helpful. A taboo topic in our society until relatively recently, abortion was thought to be anathema, a dark, unusual happening. It has also been a long-held belief that any woman who undergoes abortion will suffer trauma and deep-seated guilt for years after, presumably because what she has done is inherently wrong and unnatural. Abortion is murder and the renunciation of maternity. Undoubtedly there has been some truth to this assertion, as a result of the dutiful internalization on the part of women of this very construction. It must also be taken into account that in a society in which abortion is proscribed by law, women must go underground to terminate pregnancies. As a result, many women may well be traumatized by abortion, but it is the clandestine and anxiety-ridden task of obtaining the abortion rather than the event itself that induces trauma and guilt. The same might be said of the procedure of obtaining a legal so-called "therapeutic" abortion involving a demonstration of mental instability or illness. It is inevitable that many women come out of such an experience thinking of themselves as mentally unstable or sick by virtue of having wanted an abortion.

With the advent of more liberal laws on abortion in some European countries, abortion has been experienced in a more neutral environment, and the psychological and moral sequelae of abortion have been researched. Several studies conducted in Europe have exploded the myth of guilt and traumatic reaction to abortion. A study done by Dr. Martin Ekblad in Sweden of 479 women interviewed at least twenty-two to thirty months after abortion showed that 75% had no self-reproach, 14% had mild self-reproach and 11% reported serious self-reproach. Many of these women had suffered deep anxiety prior to the abortion; in a "normal" group only 6% suffered from serious self-reproach. Other studies have corroborated these results or show that an even smaller percentage of women suffer from guilt or trauma following hospital abortion.[1] This is not to say that decisions about abortion are easy. Unwanted pregnancy and abortion are usually difficult and unhappy experiences and the decision to abort is made with serious consideration. This research material only calls into question the assertion that abortion is morally and naturally wrong as evidenced by the inevitable guilt reaction of most women who choose it.

In addition to myth-breaking research, cross-cultural studies have raised doubts about the "nature" of abortion. Lawrence Lader gives several examples of societies in which abortion is considered a matter of course:

> The Mataco, for example, a South American Indian tribe supposedly abort the first fetus to make subsequent child-bearing easier. Among American Indians the Crow and the Assiniboni favor abortion in cases of desertion. In New Britain, it is considered essential for a pregnancy in the first year of marriage.[2]

Abortion has been widely practiced not only in societies where it is accepted, but also in countries where it is illegal. In spite of the illegality of abortion, it is estimated that there are more abortions than live births every year in

France. If, as John Noonan entitled an article on the subject, the anti-abortion position has been "an Almost Absolute Value in History," it must also be remembered that not only was he talking about the history of Western Christian, male-dominated society alone, but also that in the unofficial history of women everywhere abortion has been universally and frequently experienced.

What is the experience of women with unwanted pregnancies? First, we must take seriously the fact that they are aware that their bodies are transformed against their wills. For all, this means a new bodily feeling and eventually a new shape. For many, it means nausea, dizziness, and inability to work and be normally active. For some, it means illness, exacerbation of other medical problems, and perhaps even threat of death. Experienced as a result of choice, pregnancy, like sex, can be a happy event or at least one happily taken on in the desire of children. Unwanted pregnancy is experienced as a form of physical violence. It has been observed that oppressed groups suffer from unequal access to goods and services and also from physical violence and intimidation. Kate Millet observes that an example of such physical violence in the case of women is the death of a number of women each year as a result of illegal abortion.[3] She might well add the incidence of unwanted pregnancy.

Any discussion of unwanted pregnancy is incomplete without an investigation of how such pregnancies occur. Some ethicists have been puzzled at the meaning of the phrase "compulsory pregnancy." They argue that women know very well that they're risking pregnancy when they engage in sexual intercourse and that they are free to practice contraception or refuse sexual intercourse. Hence any pregnancy that accrues was freely risked, if not chosen, and there is no such thing as a compulsory pregnancy. Such a view is not surprisingly naive but also overlooks the technological inadequacy of birth control and the affects of sexism in connection with the use of birth control and psychological pressures on women.

The fact that we have no "ideal" method of birth control has often been forgotten. Harriet Pilpel has noted that if all married women used the IUD (which not all women can accommodate) there would be from 350,000 to 700,000 unwanted pregnancies every year.[4] Added to the unequal distribution of contraceptive information and devices among different age and class groups of women, such facts demonstrate that contraception is not an adequate solution at this time. Not only has technology and the social system been inadequate, but the sexist structure of our society has set the stage for numbers of unwanted pregnancies. With regard to birth control, Pam Lowry, coordinator of Pregnancy Counselling Service, has pointed out that traditional female taboos have discouraged women from using contraceptives which entail touching their own genitals (foam and diaphragm) and have kept them away from doctors who give pelvic examinations. The double standard, still a reality in our society, and the lack of sex education, militate against women, who are primarily responsible for contraception, given the extant methods, consciously taking responsibility for birth control. To do this would mean consciously admitting they were going to enter into a sexual relationship. Rather, they will subconsciously wait to be "swept off their feet." Furthermore, both partners could take responsibility for seeing that birth control is used, but often the responsibility is foisted only on the woman. In a society in which women's social status and security are largely dependent on their associations with males, our idea of rape may be extended to include not only forced physical assault, but intercourse forced by social and psychological pressures. Many women who are about to become engaged conceive unwanted pregnancies in an effort to insure marriage, which they were conditioned to regard as of paramount importance. When this desperate act fails or promises to endanger a young relationship, the pregnancy is finally approached more realistically.

What of the woman's relationship to the fetus? With the development of embryology and fetology, we have learned that the genetic code determining individual biological identity is set at conception and that rapid growth of the fetus gives it a recognizable form very early in pregnancy. In addition, the circulatory and other physiological systems of the fetus are independent, and the placenta and umbilical connection are outgrowths of the fetus, not the mother. Ramsay says "The blastocyst now devotes some of its foreordained cellular powers to throwing out a lifeline by which it can be attached to the life of the mother."[5] Although Ramsay admits that the placenta takes from the mother what it needs, he concludes that ". . . the navel, which is supposed to be an external mark of the dependence of everyone since Adam and Eve, is actually a sign of independent and entitatively distinct activity of the germinating cells."[6]

Much of the biological argument against abortion is presented in this way. It seems probable that there is often a selective process in presenting biological data, and that in the material of Ramsay's, the parasitic character of the relationship of mother and fetus is obscured by fetus-oriented biology. No matter how true it is that the fetus' system is independent, it cannot be overlooked that the nourishment for its growth comes from the mother's nutritive resources. Rachel Conrad Wahlberg states in her article "The Woman and the Fetus 'One Flesh,'" "There is a cannibalistic element here; the fetus actually feeds on the mother's body. . . . The parasitical aspect is reflected in the fact that a mother's health can be dragged down during pregnancy if she is not getting the proper nourishment."[7] What of the mother's experience of the fetus? Whether the fetus is an independent organism, it is inside the body of the mother and is constituted of her nourishment. Experientially it is one flesh with the mother.

Women who abort do not perceive themselves as murderers. Nor is this perception an incidental or purely subjective reaction on the part of an aberrant few acting in their own interests. Those who consider the fetus to be inviolable base its humanity on its biological nature. In contrast, however, some theologians have considered other dimensions more centrally constitutive of life as human. Gordon Kaufman has pointed out:

> If anyone were to ask us in a context not so loaded with emotion and misconception what characterizes human life as distinct from other forms of life? We would be likely to suggest that such features as the use of language, concern for value, ideals, morality, religiousness, a power of imagination and creativity which makes possible production of magnificent works of art, the capacity to decide and act and the like.[8]

In addition to these general characteristics of humanity, Professor Kaufman discusses those which are reflected in the religious category "ensouled," a term often applied to the fetus in traditional theological anti-abortion arguments.

> God's gift of the "soul" . . . is not the special implantation of a distinct substance at conception; it is rather the evoking of selfhood and responsibility and the capacities for love and trust, through the loving care of parents in the first years of life.[9]

The "abortion is murder" assertion may seem so extreme that we need not concern ourselves with it, but it is just this definition that forms the basis of anti-abortion legislation, according to which the state protects the life of the fetus, and therefore it does have to be dealt with. The fact that the overwhelming majority of women who freely choose abortion do not experience themselves as murderers, and the fact that abortion is not an aberrant or strange, but a frequent and culturally universal experience, forces us to question the validity of a material description of abortion. We must ask whether the well-being of the more actual than potential human life of the mother is not in fact more important than the physical existence of the more potential than actual fetus. Perhaps no bell tolls for the fetus because the reality of the fetus is significantly different than that of a more actualized human being.

Another important observation can be made. The question of abortion has to do with the *unique* struggle between two living beings. It is only in the case of unwanted pregnancy that the *body* and the whole well-being of a person is controlled by another human being. This observation helps us cut through the "wedge arguments" such as: if the fetus does not possess human characteristics such as language, neither does the one-month-old child—will infanticide be next? It is only in the case of the fetus that only one person can take responsibility for its nurture, the biological mother. The state or society can intervene in the case of the unwanted child, but must force a woman to endure an unwanted bodily and social identity in the case of the fetus. In the last analysis, we are not dealing with the problem of the nature of the fetus, but with the problem of what kind of sacrifice is excessive to demand of one person for the welfare of another being. Women are simply saying, in their demand for access to abortion, that compulsory pregnancy is too much. The humanization of the fetus cannot take place at the cost of the dehumanization of another human being. This is especially true given the nature of the parent-child relationship and the effects of maternal deprivation of unwanted children on the children themselves.

The refusal to treat the values of women with unwanted pregnancies seriously has been part of our history of not taking women seriously in general, but it has also resulted from a tradition of regarding the value of human physical life as absolute. Keeping in mind theories of just war and other situations in which killing has been justified, it seems that the fetus has been a symbol used to bolster up this tradition. Several Christian ethicists, however, have criticized this tradition, which is the absolutization of a finite value. Joseph Fletcher has called it a kind of vitalism and even Barth, in his discussion of abortion, has questioned whether God's will might not indicate the termination of pregnancy in some cases. In fact, as James Gustafson has pointed out, both Christian theology and human experience point to the fact that human life is many-valued, and the value of human life is not absolute. A belief in a transcendent God leaves us with no concrete guidelines for the solution of moral problems:

> Insofar as the transcendent God is the One beyond many (H. R. Niebuhr) or the unspeakable ground of being (Tillich) he is particulary devoid of meaningful content, and thus man is left almost no substantial theological resources

> in the determination of the values and purposes which ought to govern his participation in the created order including his use of physical life.[10]

Even if we can attribute some character to God in our theological affirmations, they are nonconcrete. We may say God is just, or God is love, but have no more of a guideline as to what love might dictate in a concrete situation. "Although God is loving and wills that men shall be loving, love is not *prima facie* consistent with the preservation of human life under all circumstances."[11] It is impossible to erect a rigid valuational structure, and it is untenable to establish any one value as absolute. We can't rest on the security of the absolute value of physical life, but may find ourselves acting arbitrarily and without meaning if we cannot give expression to the other legitimate values which motivate our action.

Gustafson observes that ". . . men have learned that circumstances of human experience often require them to alter things they professed to be of absolute value."[12] In the case of abortion, men will have to learn from women that unwanted pregnancy brings other values into play which are of relatively greater importance than the physical life of the nascent fetus.

What values does the movement for the liberation of women and the new self-understanding of women bring to the discussion of abortion? While the traditional moral arguments against abortion have focused their thinking on the nature of the life of the fetus, the women I have encountered seeking abortion have focused their thinking on the social and emotional problems involved. They consider the desirability of making or prolonging a bad marriage, interrupting their education or work, having more children than they feel they can cope with, traumatizing or burdening their parents, or suffering rejection and the stigma of extramarital pregnancy. Some of these concerns center around the welfare of other persons involved.

The demand for abortion-law repeal has undeniably come about in a time when women are beginning to break away from concepts of themselves as both virgins and mothers. Sexual freedom unmatched by an adequate response from the society in terms of sex education and availability of contraceptive devices has led to many unwanted pregnancies. Unwanted pregnancy is less and less something to which women unquestioningly surrender themselves. In seeking abortion, they are not negating the value of human life but are affirming other values of their own lives and the lives of significant others who would be adversely affected by their pregnancy and the birth of an unwanted child. They are affirming the value of their own personhood as more multidimensional than childbearer. It is not simply a matter of convenience on the part of women, but a matter of taking into their own hands the definition of their selves. It is not only women but also families, friends, and society which stand to benefit from the contribution of mature, responsible persons, who as such have an active and creative capacity to give to others rather than simply a passive and nonpersonal surrender of their bodies and "maternal instincts." If an absolutizing affirmation of the value of the life of the fetus results in the manipulation of the bodily and mental integrity of women, the value of life as a whole is neglected and many individuals are done a serious wrong.

A balanced construction of our concept of abortion would be one which would not manipulate women into seeing themselves as guilty or as passive servants of procreation. Valerie Goldstein's analysis of the danger for women at this point in history of masculine theology which emphasizes the virtues of selflessness is applicable to the abortion problem.[13] The pressure of theological and secular anti-abortion arguments on women to be selfless and regard their own welfare as secondary to that of a barely beginning life which will become determinative of their identity, reinforces women in their sins of failing to become whole selves and failure to establish their own understanding of the reality they experience. If women can resist these pressures, abortion will be reconceptualized and renamed.

This process is as important as changing legislation on abortion. Many see abortion as a temporary problem with the hope that better methods and distribution of birth-control devices will make the need for abortion obsolete. In the meantime, they argue that abortion laws should remain restrictive as an affirmation of the value of life will stand society in good stead in the long run of dealing with the larger issues of life and death. Whether pro or con the repeal of abortion laws, I think every sensitive person hopes the need for abortion will diminish. Obviously it is not the ultimate answer to unwanted pregnancy. However, it is unlikely that technical advances in birth control or sex education will in themselves solve the problem. For women the issue of abortion must be a larger issue in that the concern with the right to control one's bodily existence must be expanded to comprehend a more basic sense of autonomy on the part of women. The right to abortion is more than a necessary stop-gap. While relatively safe, any medical procedure should be avoided if possible. But more important, unwanted pregnancy is by definition a situation in which women find themselves against their better judgment. With the exception of rape and contraceptive failure, unwanted pregnancy is the result of a lack of intentionality and self-love (caring) in women. In saying this, I do not intend to "blame the victim" as I think is clear from the above, but to point out that a thorough-going sense of autonomy and self-esteem in women will be one of the most significant ways in which abortion will be eliminated. Only when women are raised to care enough for themselves to deal with their relations to men, their futures, and their personhood, will they be able to avoid self-destructive situations such as unwanted pregnancy. While the drive for autonomy which is embodied in the women's liberation movement seems to propound an ethic which is individualistic to the point of selfishness, I feel the real importance of an authentic sense of self is that one gives to others best from a position of strength rather than of weakness.

Postscript: July, 1982

In the ten years that have passed since this article was written, the struggle to establish and maintain the right to choose abortion has become an integral part of gaining that ability to be autonomous, referred to in the last paragraph, that will eventually lessen the need for abortion. In the early 1970s, feminists were beginning to fathom the power of men in patriarchal society to trap women in roles that serve men's interests. Since then, an understanding of the range of that power has unfolded as we have learned more about the pervasiveness of sexual harassment in the workplace, the frequency of rape and incest, and the extent and severity of wife-beating. Not only has the last decade not brought major improvements in contraception, but the safety of the most widely used methods has been called into question.

In light of these developments, I would no

longer speak of "women's sins of failing to become whole selves" or unwanted pregnancy as the result of a "lack of intentionality and self-caring in women." My hope for the possibility of such individual control over women's destinies was informed by the central role of consciousness-raising in the early women's movement. While still affirming the power of women to take control of their own lives, I now believe that this must happen in the context of concerted action to win and protect women's rights. Many abortion-rights groups have expanded their concerns to include working against sterilization abuse, another abridgment of reproductive freedom. These struggles in themselves will be part of the process of transforming society. Only in a society that recognizes women's basic right to self-determination in formal ways such as equal rights and access to abortion for all women, rich and poor, will women and men, girls and boys, be able to respect women's and girls' rights not to risk unwanted pregnancy as well as to terminate it.

Notes

1. Lawrence Lader, *Abortion* (Indianapolis: The Bobbs-Merrill Company, Inc., 1966), pp. 21–22.
2. Ibid., p. 22.
3. Kate Millet, *Sexual Politics* (New York: Avon, 1969), p. 44.
4. Harriet Pilpel, "The Right to Abortion," *Atlantic Monthly*, June 1969.
5. Paul Ramsay, "Points in Deciding about Abortion," in *The Morality of Abortion*, John T. Noonan Jr., Ed. (Cambridge, MA: Harvard University Press, 1970), p. 70.
6. Ibid., p. 72.
7. Rachel Conrad Wahlberg, "The Woman and the Fetus 'One Flesh'," *The Christian Century*, Sept. 8, 1971, p. 1046.
8. Gordon Kaufman, "An Unexamined Question," *The Unauthorized Version*, Harvard Divinity School, Vol. II, no. 6, 1971, p. 2.
9. Ibid.
10. James Gustafson, "God's Transcendence and the Value of Human Life," *Christian Ethics and the Community* (Philadelphia: Pilgrim Press Book, 1971), p. 143.
11. Ibid., p. 146.
12. Ibid., p. 142.
13. Valerie Saiving Goldstein, "The Human Situation: A Feminine Point of View," pp. 10–12.

Content Quiz 12.1

Instructions: Fill in the blanks with the appropriate responses listed below.

motherhood	absolute
rape	trauma
parasitic	physical violence
self-reproach	Mataco
selfless	autonomy

1. Forcing women to endure unwanted pregnancies is a form of _____.
2. Masculine theology and sexist secular anti-abortion arguments demand that women be _____ and place their own welfare below that of the developing fetus.
3. In so far as the fetus depends on the mother for survival and growth, it is _____.
4. In a society where women's social status and security largely depend on associations with males, intercourse forced by social and psychological pressures may be regarded as a form of _____.
5. Some see abortion as a renunciation of _____.
6. European studies indicate that far less _____ results from abortion than is usually thought.
7. Pro-abortionists like MacRae reject the idea that the value of physical life is _____ and that it overrides other psychological and social values.
8. One "myth" MacRae attempts to explode is the one about abortion necessarily resulting in emotional or psychological _____.
9. Abortion can be regarded not as a rejection of life but an affirmation of women's _____.
10. The _____ abort the first fetus to make later child-bearing easier.

Discussion Questions

1. What "myths" surround the abortion issue?
2. How is unwanted pregnancy related to physical violence?
3. Is it possible to be in favor of abortion from a religious perspective? Explain.
4. In what way are the mother and fetus involved in a struggle?
5. What role does sexism play in the abortion debate?

THE UNBORN CHILD IN CIVIL AND CRIMINAL LAW

Ian Gentles

Synopsis

This essay draws attention to the contradiction between civil and criminal law on the issue of abortion. Court cases are cited that indicate that the unborn child has the legally recognized right to inherit property, the right to sue for injuries while in the womb, and the right to be protected from abuse or neglect by the mother. The point is also stressed, however, that under existing laws the unborn child has no right not to be killed by the mother through intentional and premature termination of pregnancy, better known as abortion. Because the right to life is indispensable for the exercise of these other rights and because it is not protected or guaranteed vis-à-vis *the mother, who can kill the fetus with impunity, Gentles concludes that current civil and criminal laws pertaining to the unborn child are contradictory. By law, a mother may not abuse her unborn child, though she may kill it at will.*

Gentles begins with a brief review of the status of the unborn child in the legal traditions of western civilization. After providing historical examples of how the rights of the unborn have been recognized and upheld throughout the centuries, he draws attention to the liberalization of abortion laws in North America and this continuing trend throughout the rest of the world. The movement toward eliminating hindrances against abortion is regarded as a striking contrast to the growing recognition of the civil rights of the unborn child as evidenced by numerous court decisions which are cited and described.

Gentles maintains that the contradiction at the root of our legal system must be removed. Two options are possible. The civil rights of the unborn child must be eliminated or the fundamental right of the unborn not to be killed must be upheld and protected. A single, consistent moral position must be taken by society through the law.

The "argument from pluralism," which is discussed, demands that abortion be accepted and removed from legal consideration on the grounds that one has no right to impose one's own personal moral views on others, especially not in a tolerant, liberal democratic society. Gentles rejects this argument on several counts. Gentles also rejects the "pragmatic argument" in favor of abortion. It is based on the assumption that women who are prevented from legally procuring an abortion will obtain one by illegal means. Gentles argues that because a law is frequently broken that does not justify the abolition of the law. If it did, then laws prohibiting theft and tax evasion would have to be likewise eliminated. Besides, according to Gentles, studies show that only a small fraction of women who are denied legal abortions actually resort to illegal means of obtaining them, though threats are often made.

Finally, Gentles concludes his article by advocating legislation to provide solid protection for the unborn child. He favors abortion only in those cases when pregnancy threatens the physical life of the mother. Adopting this position is to accept the duty to protect innocent human life. For Gentles, this is a duty any civilized society should accept.

There exists today a grotesque contradiction at the heart of our legal system as it touches the unborn child. On the one hand, the unborn child enjoys the right to inherit property; she* can sue for injuries inflicted while in the womb; and she has the right to be protected from abuse or neglect by her mother. On the other hand, she no longer enjoys that right which is the indispensable precondition of the exercise of all her other rights—the right not to be killed. How has this contradiction come about? Is there any way it can be resolved?

To begin answering these questions we shall review briefly the status of the unborn child in the legal traditions of Western civilization. An interesting fact is that from the earliest times, protection of the unborn has never been a merely Judeo-Christian idiosyncrasy. Many centuries before Christ, the Sumerians, the Assyrians, and the Hittites protected prenatal human life in their legal codes.[1] The oath framed for physicians by the Greek doctor Hippocrates in the fourth century B.C. was well-known for its pledge "not to give a deadly drug to anyone if asked for it, nor to suggest it. Similarly, I will not give to a woman an abortifacient pessary. In purity and holiness I will guard my life and my art." The authorities on the English common law, from Bracton in the thirteenth century through Coke in the seventeenth century to Blackstone in the eighteenth, all treated abortion as a crime.[2] Blackstone summed up the law's position in the second half of the eighteenth century in the following words:

> Life is the immediate gift of God, a right inherent by nature in every individual; and it begins in contemplation of law as soon as an infant is able to stir in the mother's womb. For if a woman is quick with the child, and by a potion or otherwise killeth it in her womb; or if any one beat her, whereby the child dieth in her body and she is delivered of a dead child, this, though not murder, was by the ancient law homicide or manslaughter. But the modern law doth not look upon this offense in quite so atrocious a light, but merely as heinous misdemeanor.[3]

There is a vivid illustration of the law's concern for the unborn child in the Salem witch trials. In the summer of 1692 six people were found guilty of witchcraft and promptly sentenced to death. On August 19 of that year all but one—a certain Elizabeth Proctor—were hanged. Taking refuge in a custom honored by the common law, good-wife Proctor pleaded pregnancy. Her execution was accordingly stayed until such time as her child should have been born, on the ground, as the historian of these events has put it, "that the child she was carrying was an innocent person." Happily, even after her child was born, the sentence against Elizabeth Proctor was allowed to lapse and she lived out her natural life.[4]

With their primitive medical knowledge, the jurists of the premodern period did not believe that it was possible to speak of an abortion before the time of quickening (i.e., the time when the mother feels the child move in her womb). Since human life did not evidently come into existence before quickening, there could not be a law against destroying it before that time. However, this anomaly was abruptly eliminated in 1803, when a law was passed making abortion a felony at any time during pregnancy.[5] This law was inherited by Canada and remained unaltered until 1969. In that year the law was amended to make an abortion permissible in cases when a three-member hospital abortion committee deemed that continuation of the pregnancy would endanger the life or health of the mother. Four years later, the United States Supreme Court swept away all criminal legislation against abortion in that country in the historical decision in *Roe v. Wade* (January 22, 1973).

The trend throughout the world in the past fifteen years toward eliminating legal hindrances against abortion is in striking contrast to the growing recognition of the civil rights of the unborn child. As recently as the end of the last century, Chief Justice Holmes in the United States had declared that the unborn child had no rights in a court of law, since he was merely a part of his mother, and not, legally speaking, a person.

This statement disregarded the fact that the unborn child's right to inherit had already been established in English common law as early as 1798, at which time it was declared that whenever it would be for his benefit, the child in the womb "shall be considered as absolutely born."[6] The first Canadian case to overturn the prevalent view expressed by Holmes was *In Re Charlton Estate* (1919). A certain Charlton had left a sum of money to be divided among "all the living children" of his brother. A child who was born three and half months after Charlton died subsequently sued for a share of the estate, asserting that he was living at the time of his uncle's death. The Manitoba Court of King's Bench upheld the suit on the ground that a gift to "all living children" included the child who was in his mother's womb ("*en ventre sa mère*") at the time.[7]

The same principle was upheld in another case the following year. A certain Mrs. Giddings successfully sued the Canadian

Northern Railway for negligence in the death of her husband, a locomotive fireman. In addition to the damages she won for herself, the court also awarded her child $6,000, even though he was unborn at the time of his father's death. The fact that he was unborn was judged to be "immaterial so long as the action is for the benefit of the child."[8]

These two cases influenced many other decisions, with the result that the unborn child's right to inherit and own property is now clearly recognized.

The much more difficult question of the unborn child's right to compensation for injuries suffered in the womb has also been decisively settled in this century in the child's favor. The Supreme Court of Canada seems to have set the standard for the rest of the English-speaking world by its momentous decision in the case of *Montreal Tramways v. Léveillé* (1933).[9] The court recognized that in 1933, "the great weight of judicial opinion in the common-law courts denies the right of a child when born to maintain an action for prenatal injuries." Nevertheless, it boldly reversed judicial precedent by declaring that a child who suffers injury while in its mother's womb as the result of a wrongful act or default of another has the right, after birth, to maintain an action for damages for its prenatal injury. Judge Lamont justified the rejection of precedent in this case on the basis of the following principle:

> If a child after birth has no right of action for prenatal injuries, we have a wrong inflicted for which there is no remedy. . . . If a right of action be denied to the child it will be compelled, without any fault on its part, to go through life carrying the seal of another's fault and bearing a very heavy burden of infirmity and inconvenience without any compensation therefor.

The principle laid down by Judge Lamont was confirmed in 1972 in *Duval et al. v. Séguin et al.*[10] The child of Thérèse Duval was permanently handicapped both physically and mentally, as a direct result of a car accident which occurred while she was *en ventre sa mère*. In deciding in favor of the child, the judge quoted Lord Atkin's dictum: "The rule that you are to love your neighbor becomes, in law, you must not injure your neighbor." Although the unborn child was to be regarded as the "neighbor" of the negligent driver, the judge declined to state whether the child was a person in law, or at which stage she became a person.

In the case of *Watt v. Rama* in the Supreme Court of Victoria in the same year, there was no such reluctance to recognize the unborn child as a legal person.[11] The plaintiff, Sylvia Watt, had suffered brain damage and epilepsy as a result of a car accident involving her mother when the mother was two months pregnant. The defense argued that a two-month-old fetus was merely part of her mother and therefore not entitled to legal protection. The judge rejected the plea, observing that there was no essential difference between a newborn child and a child not yet born.

> As its property, real or personal, is protected, so should its physical substance be similarly protected by deeming it to be a person in being and imposing a duty of care on any other person not to commit any act of carelessness which as a reasonable man he should anticipate would injure the physical substance of the unborn child.

The judge concluded by affirming that, for the purpose of protecting her interests, Sylvia Watt was deemed to be a person at the time of the collision—two months after conception—and was thus entitled to compensation for the injuries she had suffered at that time.

The progress of the civil law in recognizing the personhood of the unborn child is trenchantly summarized by William L. Prosser, the dean of American tort law. Before 1946, he points out, most American authorities were agreed that the child could not sue for prenatal injuries. However, the situation was transformed so rapidly in the next quarter of a century that "it is now apparently literally true that there is no authority left still supporting the older rule." Furthermore, "all writers who have discussed the problem have joined in condemning the old rule, in maintaining that *the unborn child in the path of an automobile is as much a person in the street as the mother*, and in urging that recovery should be allowed upon proper proof" (emphasis added).[12]

One problem has not yet been resolved: whether the child has to be born alive in order for a suit to be entered on her behalf. Prosser believes that the trend is in the direction of holding that the child does not have to be born alive.[13] This would seem to be a logical conclusion, since it is hard to see why one should be less liable for destroying a child's life than for merely causing her to be injured. Indeed, a large number of recent cases in American courts have ruled not only that the unborn child is a person, but that an action for the wrongful death of an unborn child is maintainable even when she is stillborn.[14]

In North America, then, it is clear that no one has the right to kill the unborn child, or injure her, or deprive her of her property. No one, that is, except her mother. And after the decision in *Roe v. Wade*, the mother has, in the United States, the unrestricted right to take the child's life. Moreover, given the abortion-on-demand situation that prevails in most large Canadian cities, the mother has practically the same right in this country. This has created a profound conflict between the civil and the criminal law. Take the hypothetical example of a woman who is pregnant with her first child at the time of her husband's death. In his will he has divided his estate between his wife and all his living children. The law has established that the child in the womb can rightfully inherit a share of his father's estate. Canadian criminal law, as it is interpreted in many parts of the country, also permits the woman to destroy her child at will, right up to the moment before it is born. Legally speaking therefore, the woman would be at liberty to have an abortion in order to keep all of her husband's estate to herself.

We can think of another instance where the interest of the unborn child may clash with those of the mother and father. Since 1963, thanks to the work of the New Zealand fetologist Dr. Albert Liley, it has been possible to make life-saving transfusions of blood to fetuses that have developed acute anemia in the womb. In one such instance where a blood transfusion had been diagnosed as medically necessary to save the unborn child's life, the mother refused the transfusion for religious reasons. Nonetheless, the New Jersey Supreme Court ordered the transfusion to be administered, stating that

> We are satisfied that the unborn child is entitled to the law's protection and that an appropriate order should be made to insure such transfusions to the mother in the event that they are necessary in the opinion of the physician in charge at the time.[15]

In 1981 the first reported successful out-of-the-womb surgery was carried out on a five-month-old unborn baby. Performed in San Francisco, the critical thirty-minute operation now points the way to the correction of a whole series of birth defects in the future.[16] The irony of this particular medical breakthrough is that, during the half hour she spends outside the womb during the operation, the child enjoys the status of a legal person, with her life fully protected. Once back in the womb, however, she resumes the status of a nonperson, having, in effect, re-entered a free-fire zone where she could be killed with impunity.

The contradiction between the unborn child's status under the civil law and her status under the criminal law has led to schizophrenic behavior in the courts. In 1972, for example, an Ottawa woman was approved for a legal abortion by a hospital therapeutic-abortion committee, but her husband objected to the abortion, was able to have himself recognized as the guardian of the unborn child, and secured a temporary injunction against the abortion. Before his application for a permanent injunction could be heard, he and his wife were reconciled and she abandoned her attempts to abort the child.[17]

In 1981, the boyfriend of a girl in Thunder Bay who had been pressured into having an abortion by her parents won an injunction against the abortion on behalf of himself and the unborn child. This injunction, the first to be granted involving an unmarried couple, confirmed that an unborn child can, in effect, act as co-plaintiff to defend her own life.[18] More interesting still was the decision of a Halifax Family Court judge not only to stop an abortion at the request of the woman's estranged husband, but to appoint a private citizen, unrelated to the family, as the unborn child's legal guardian. While the court may have exceeded its jurisdiction, it seems to have established the first instance where a child in the womb has had a guardian appointed on her behalf.[19]

To compound the confusion further, two recent cases, one Canadian, one British, have recognized the personhood of the unborn child in criminal suits. The British judge ruled that a Belfast child wounded by a bullet fired into her mother's abdomen was a legal person, with the right to sue for damages for criminal injury, and awarded her $8,800.[20] In the Canadian case, which involved a charge of criminal negligence, a British Columbia judge ruled that a fetus in the process of birth is a person under the Criminal Code. The baby in question was stillborn, allegedly because of the criminal negligence of the midwife in attendance. The defense lawyer had argued that there could be no charge of criminal negligence, since the fetus was not a person. Prior to the judge's decision, a child was not, in fact, considered to be a person under the Criminal Code until she had emerged in a living state from the body of her mother.[21]

So far, we can see that the unborn child's rights have been won *vis-à-vis* the outside world. It could be maintained that there is nothing inconsistent or irrational in allowing the child's mother to kill her through abortion, while at the same time denying to everyone else the right to injure her or deprive her of her property. The mother, after all, is the only one who has to surrender her body for the nine months of possible discomfort, embarrassment, or even physical hazard that a pregnancy can entail. Her relationship with her unborn child is clearly unique, and qualitatively different from anyone else's relationship with the child. Given that her body is being occupied by a fetus who may not be welcome in her eyes, should the mother not at least have the right to dispose of it as she pleases?

Just recently, this argument, which is condensed in the popular phrase "a woman's right to control her own body," has had to face an unexpected and awkward challenge. Since about 1970, in Canada and elsewhere, there has been much concern about child abuse, together with a determination to reduce its prevalence. In addition, there is now a much sharper awareness of how crucial are the nine months before birth in shaping the individual's whole future physical and psychological well-being. Many proponents of child welfare therefore urge that protection against abuse should extend into the prenatal period, and that mothers should be accountable for the welfare of their unborn children. Furthermore, they should, like anyone else, be liable for prosecution if they are guilty through negligence or abuse, of causing injury to their unborn child.

In 1981, the Ontario Family Court in Kenora recognized a fetus as "a child in need of protection" under the terms of the Child Welfare Act because of the physical abuse she suffered through her mother's excessive consumption of alcohol and the mother's failure to obtain proper treatment. The implication was clear that the fetus is protected from abuse by her mother during the full nine months of pregnancy, starting from conception. In fact, it was noted that fetal damage from alcohol is most likely to occur during the first three months of pregnancy.[22]

The Supreme Court of British Columbia came to a similar conclusion in 1982, in the case of a heroin-addicted mother whose newborn baby suffered violent symptoms of withdrawal and possible long-term damage to her health. After about seven weeks, when the baby was taken off opium, she

> demonstrated the effects of withdrawal with the following severe physical symptoms: Incessant, inconsolable crying, vomiting, inability to sleep, twitching, reluctance to feed, poor sucking performance, irritability, resistance to being held, explosive diarrhea, profuse sweating, jittery limbs, barking cough, physical tension and squirming. The diarrhea was of special concern, because if not corrected the resultant water loss could lead to shock and death. In addition the baby developed severe anemia which continues to be a danger.

At four months of age the baby was still withdrawing from addiction, according to the attending physician.

> . . . The infant goes through the same withdrawal syndrome as an adult and experiences extreme spasms in the stomach, excruciating pain, and vomiting.

Moreover, the baby required very careful attention to her nutrition, since drug-addicted babies need twice the calories of a normal child for brain and organ growth.

In light of this harrowing description of the consequences of the mother's heroin addiction, the court ruled that the fetus whose mother is drug-addicted is "a child in need of protection," and that such a child "is born *having been abused*" (emphasis added). There was therefore no need to wait until the mother abused the child after birth before requiring that she submit to involuntary supervision.[23]

The Ontario and British Columbia decisions find support in David M. Steinberg's *Family Law in Family Courts*, where it is stated that a child in the womb may be considered a child in order to secure protection from abuse by her mother.[24]

So a mother may not neglect or abuse her unborn child. But she may still legally kill her. Aware of the pressing need to remedy this state of affairs, the director of the Canadian Law Reform Commission advocates that the unborn child's rights already established by judicial decision should be enshrined in a statute. According to Edward Keyserlingk, "there should be no contest at all between a mother's desire to smoke or consume drugs excessively and the unborn's right to be legally protected against the serious risk of resulting disability." The provision of adequate nutrition, adequate prenatal checkups, the avoidance of excessive smoking, drinking, or drug-taking should be made into a legal obligation involving potential liability for parents, doctors, and others. ". . . The law must conclude more coherently and explicitly than it has to date that the unborn has its own juridical [legal] personality and rights."[25] Yet he goes on to say that the unborn's rights would end when the mother decides to have an abortion.

Does this make sense? Would *you* rather have the right to "adequate prenatal checkups" than the right not to be killed through abortion? The stark absurdity of this position grows out of the irreducible reality that all the rights the unborn has won in the course of this century depend, as their indispensable precondition, on the right to live. Since I possess the right to inherit, to own property, and not to be injured, neglected or abused before I am born, then logically I must also possess the right to life, since without it none of my other rights can be exercised.[26]

This terrible contradiction at the heart of our legal system cannot endure. Either we shall have to eliminate the civil rights that have been so painfully won for the unborn child, or we shall have to recognize her most fundamental right, the right not to be killed, even by her parents. We cannot have it both ways. Moreover, whatever we do, a morality will have been imposed. To think that the neutral, liberal, and value-free policy is to remove abortion from the law is to be misled. To accept the argument from pluralism is to turn a blind eye to the silent victim of every abortion—the child in the womb. It would be hardly less logical to advocate removing murder from the criminal code on the ground that, in a pluralistic society, we do not have any right to impose our moral views upon those who wish to murder.

The argument from pluralism also ignores the fact that societies that do eliminate abortion from their legal codes do not thereby give people a free choice in the matter. Instead, an "abortion climate" takes over, and overwhelming pressure is exerted on women to resort to abortion as the way out of any distressful or inconvenient pregnancy. This pressure is exerted by husbands, boyfriends, parents, peers, social workers, doctors, and governments. Governments find abortion an easy way of avoiding hard social problems like the shortage of reasonably priced family housing.

There is yet another defect in the argument from pluralism. It is said that, since there is disagreement about whether the fetus is a human being, we should allow those who believe that abortion is morally permissible to act on their beliefs. Some people certainly *wish* that there were disagreement about the humanity of the fetus. Virtually all medical authorities, however, agree that the life of the human individual begins at the moment of conception.[27] But even if there were disagreement, would it not be both prudent and humane to give the fetus the benefit of the doubt, to accept its humanity and therefore its right to legal protection? What would we say if people were arguing that blacks instead of fetuses were not human, and that people should have the right to kill them? This, after all, is the position that some people took in the United States of America just more than a century ago. Would we not argue that blacks should have the benefit of the doubt and be included within the human family, with appropriate legal protection? Is not the best rule of thumb to frame our definition of who is human broadly enough to avoid excluding particular classes of people who may happen to be out of public favor at a given moment?

At this point some people will raise a pragmatic argument. It is all very well to talk of protecting the unborn child, they say, but women have always had abortions, and they always will. No law can stop them. The only question is whether they should have abortions that are legal and safe, or should be condemned to seek back-alley "butchers," criminal abortionists who endanger their life and health.

This argument has a particle of truth to it, but only a particle. There are some women in every society and in every age who will seek abortions no matter what the law says. But the number is far smaller than is usually alleged by advocates of legalized abortion.[28] But there is little doubt that a strong law protecting the unborn child, especially if it is combined with life-promoting social policies, will reduce the incidence of abortion. This conclusion is borne out by studies, conducted in several countries, of women who were refused legal abortions. In every study it was found that only a small proportion of the women resorted to criminal abortions, although many of them had threatened to do so. Even more surprising, it was discovered in a Danish study that four-fifths of the women later said they were satisfied to have borne their children. Moreover, a Czech study revealed that these children fared just as well as children whose mothers had not tried to abort them.[29] No law is ever completely effective, but laws do have an educative function. They express the commonly accepted standards of behavior of a society, and many people consciously model their behavior according to what the law informs them is acceptable. The fact that a law is frequently broken is no reason in itself for doing away with that law. The laws against child abuse, theft, tax evasion, and assault are broken far more often than the laws against abortion. But they are still useful, both because they express our public moral standards, and because they undoubtedly prevent an even greater incidence of the offenses they prohibit.

If the argument of this essay is correct, the most enlightened social policy would be to legislate solid protection of the unborn child. Such protection means that abortion would only be permissible when continuation of the pregnancy would result in the death of the mother. To adhere to this position is not to adopt a censorious moralism. It is simply to recognize that the protection of innocent human life is the most basic duty of any civilized community. Our community will be neither healthy nor civilized so long as we fail in that duty.

Notes

* I have referred to the unborn child as "she" and "her" throughout this essay, as a reminder that at least half the victims of abortion are female.

1. James B. Pritchard, *Ancient Near Eastern Texts Relating to the Old Testament*, 2nd ed. (Princeton: 1955), pp. 175 181, 184 ff., 190.
2. Dennis J. Horan, et al., "The Legal Case for the Unborn Child," in T. W. Hilgers and D. J. Horan, eds., *Abortion and Social Justice* (New York: 1972), pp. 122–24.
3. *Blackstone's Commentaries*, 15th ed., vol. I, p. 129.
4. Edward Synan, "Law and the Sin of the Mothers," in E. A. Synan and E. J. Kremer, eds., *Death Before Birth: Canadian Essays on Abortion* (Toronto, 1974), pp. 146f.

5. Proclaimed by George III in 1803.
6. *Thellusson v. Woodford* (1798–9), *English Reports*, vol. 3, p. 163.
7. *Western Weekly Reports* (1919), vol. I, p. 134.
8. *Giddings v. Canadian Northern Railway Company*, *Dominion Law Reports* (1920), vol. 53.
9. *Supreme Court Reports* (1933), p. 456.
10. *Ontario Reports* (1972), vol. II.
11. *Victoria Reports* (Australia), 1972, p. 353.
12. William L. Prosser, *Handbook of the Law of Torts*, 4th ed. (St. Paul, 1974), pp. 335–6. The other eminent authority on tort law, the Australian, John G. Fleming, agrees that courts in Britain and the Commonwealth are now willing to entertain suits for prenatal injuries. *The Law of Torts*, 5th ed. (Sydney, 1977), p. 159.
13. Prosser, p. 338. Fleming, on the other hand, holds that the child must still be born alive in order to be a plaintiff (p. 161).
14. Horan et al., art. cit., p. 113 and references cited in n. 35.
15. Ibid., p. 115.
16. *Globe and Mail*, 16 November 1981.
17. Ibid., 28 January 1972.
18. Ibid., 6 February 1981.
19. Ibid., 25 September 1979.
20. Ibid., 3 November 1979.
21. Ibid., 8 November 1979.
22. *Re Children's Aid Society of Kenora and Janis L.*, 14 September 1981. Ontario Provincial Court of the District of Kenora. (Not reported.) See the judgment of Madam Justice Proudfoot in this chapter.
23. *Re In the matter of judicial review of a decision of Judge P. d'A. Collings respecting female infant born Dec. 11th, 1981.* Supreme Court of British Columbia, 13 April 1982.
24. Carswell, 1981, vol. 1, 2nd ed., p. 112.
25. *Globe and Mail*, 2 April 1982.
26. E.-H. W. Kluge, "The Right to Life of Potential Persons," *Dalhousie Law Journal*, vol. 3, 1977, pp. 846–7.
27. See for example, a standard textbook, Leslie B. Arey, *Developmental Anatomy*, revised 7th edition (Philadelphia, 1974), p. 55.
28. See the *Report of the Committee on the Operation of the Abortion Law* [The Badgley Report] (Ottawa, 1977), pp. 71–2, and C. B. Goodhart, "On the Incidence of Illegal Abortion," *Population Studies*, vol. xxvii (1973), pp. 207–33.
29. Cf. Hans Forssman and Inga Thuwe, "One Hundred and Twenty Children Born after Application for Therapeutic Abortion Refused," *Acta Psychiatrica Scandinavica*, 42 (1966), 71–74; Henrik Hoffmeyer, "Medical Aspects of the Danish Legislation on Abortion," in David T. Smith, ed., *Abortion and the Law* (Cleveland, 1967), p. 201; V. Schuller and E. Stupkova, "The Unwanted Child in the Family," *International Mental Health Research Newsletter*, 14/3 (Fall, 1972), 7f.

Content Quiz 12.2

Instructions: Fill in the blanks with the appropriate responses listed below.

censorious moralism	pragmatic
pluralism	quickening
contradiction	indispensable precondition
abortifacient pessary	*Roe v. Wade*
Montreal Tramways v. Léveillé	unique relationship

1. While pro-abortionists would generally oppose that those other than the mother decide whether or not a pregnancy can or should be terminated, they believe the mother should have the right to choose whether or not a pregnancy will be continued because of her _____ to the fetus.
2. The Greek doctor, Hippocrates, pledged never to give women a(n) _____ as a way of preventing pregnancy and childbirth.
3. The right to life is a(n)_____ for the exercise of the rights to inherit property and to be protected from injury and abuse.
4. The _____ argument assumes that women will obtain illegal abortions from backstreet butchers if they are prevented from procuring them by legal means.
5. The _____ decision in the United States swept abortion away from all criminal legislation.
6. Jurists in the premodern period believed that _____ marked the point at which human life begins.
7. The argument from _____ states that in liberal democratic society, individual women should have the right of personal choice in private matters of abortion and that, in a spirit of tolerance and freedom, no one else should have the right to impose his or her own will upon the mother.
8. The case of _____ reversed judicial precedent by deciding that a child still in the womb who suffers injury as a result of a wrongful act has the right, after birth, to sue for damages.
9. According to Ian Gentles, there exists a(n) _____ between current civil and criminal laws as they relate to matters of abortion.
10. Gentles does not believe his anti-abortion position reflects a(n) _____, but rather a recognition that we all have a basic duty to protect innocent human life.

Discussion Questions

1. Are matters of abortion and protection of the unborn unique to North American society in the twentieth century? Explain and illustrate.
2. What is meant by "quickening"? What historical significance does it have for the abortion issue?
3. Does the unborn child possess any legal rights? Provide evidence.

4. What argument can be given to support the notion that the mother should have the right to dispose of the fetus as she deems fit?
5. How can the contradiction regarding abortion in civil and criminal law be resolved?
6. What is the argument from pluralism and why is it rejected?
7. What is the pragmatic argument and why is it rejected?
8. What does Gentles recommend on the abortion issue?

ACTIVE AND PASSIVE EUTHANASIA

James Rachels

Synopsis

The traditional distinction between active and passive euthanasia requires critical analysis. The conventional doctrine is that there is such an important moral difference between the two that, although the latter is sometimes permissible, the former is always forbidden. This doctrine may be challenged for several reasons. First of all, active euthanasia is in many cases more humane than passive euthanasia. Secondly, the conventional doctrine leads to decisions concerning life and death on irrelevant grounds. Thirdly, the doctrine rests on a distinction between killing and letting die that itself has no moral importance. Fourthly, the most common arguments in favor of the doctrine are invalid. I [James Rachels] therefore suggest that the American Medical Association policy statement that endorses this doctrine is unsound.

The distinction between active and passive euthanasia is thought to be crucial for medical ethics. The idea is that it is permissible, at least in some cases, to withhold treatment and allow a patient to die, but it is never permissible to take any direct action designed to kill the patient. This doctrine seems to be accepted by most doctors, and it is endorsed in a statement adopted by the House of Delegates of the American Medical Association on December 4, 1973:

> The intentional termination of the life of one human being by another—mercy killing—is contrary to that for which the medical profession stands and is contrary to the policy of the American Medical Association.
>
> The cessation of the employment of extraordinary means to prolong the life of the body when there is irrefutable evidence that biological death is imminent is the decision of the patient and/or his immediate family. The advice and judgment of the physician should be freely available to the patient and/or his immediate family.

However, a strong case can be made against this doctrine. In what follows I will set out some of the relevant arguments, and urge doctors to reconsider their views on this matter.

To begin with a familiar type of situation, a patient who is dying of incurable cancer of the throat is in terrible pain, which can no longer be satisfactorily alleviated. He is certain to die within a few days, even if present treatment is continued, but he does not want to go on living for those days since the pain is unbearable. So he asks the doctor for an end to it, and his family joins in the request.

Suppose the doctor agrees to withhold treatment, as the conventional doctrine says he may. The justification for his doing so is that the patient is in terrible agony, and since he is going to die anyway, it would be wrong to prolong his suffering needlessly. But now notice this. If one simply withholds treatment, it may take the patient longer to die, and so he may suffer more than he would if more direct action were taken and a lethal injection given. This fact provides strong reason for thinking that, once the initial decision not to prolong his agony has been made, active euthanasia is actually preferable to passive euthanasia, rather than the reverse. To say otherwise is to endorse the option that leads to more suffering rather than less, and is contrary to the humanitarian impulse that prompts the decision not to prolong his life in the first place.

Part of my point is that the process of being "allowed to die" can be relatively slow and painful, whereas being given a lethal injection is relatively quick and painless. Let me give a different sort of example. In the United States about one in 600 babies is born with Down's syndrome. Most of these babies are otherwise healthy—that is, with only the usual pediatric care, they will proceed to an otherwise normal infancy. Some, however, are born with congenital defects such as intestinal obstructions that require operations if they are to live. Sometimes, the parents and the doctor will decide not to operate, and let the infant die. Anthony Shaw describes what happens then:

> When surgery is denied [the doctor] must try to keep the infant from suffering while natural forces sap the baby's life away. As a surgeon whose natural inclination is to use the scalpel to fight off death, standing by and watching a salvageable baby die is the most emotionally exhausting experience I know. It is easy at a conference, in a theoretical discussion to decide that such infants should be allowed to die. It is altogether different to stand by in the nursery and watch as dehydration and infection wither a tiny being over hours and days. This is a terrible ordeal for me and the hospital staff—much more so than for the parents who never set foot in the nursery.[1]

I can understand why some people are opposed to all euthanasia, and insist that such infants must be allowed to live. I think I can also understand why other people favor destroying these babies quickly and painlessly. Buy why should anyone favor letting "dehydration and infection wither a tiny being over hours and days"? The doctrine that says that a baby may be allowed to dehydrate and wither, but may not be given an injection that would end its life without suffering, seems so patently cruel as to require no further refutation. The strong language is not intended to offend, but only to put the point in the clearest possible way.

My second argument is that the conventional doctrine leads to decisions concerning life and death made on irrelevant grounds.

Consider again the case of the infants with Down's syndrome who need operations for congenital defects unrelated to the syndrome to live. Sometimes, there is no operation, and the baby dies, but when there is no such defect, the baby lives on. Now, an operation such as that to remove an intestinal obstruction is not prohibitively difficult. The reason why such operations are not performed in these cases is, clearly, that the child has Down's syndrome and the parents and the doctor judge that because of that fact it is better for the child to die.

But notice that this situation is absurd, no matter what view one takes of the lives and potentials of such babies. If the life of such an infant is worth preserving what does it matter if it needs a simple operation? Or, if one thinks it better that such a baby should not live on, what difference does it make that it happens to have an unobstructed intestinal tract? In either case, the matter of life and death is being decided on irrelevant grounds. It is the Down's syndrome, and not the intestines, that is the issue. The matter should be decided, if at all, on that basis, and not be allowed to depend on the essentially irrelevant question of whether the intestinal tract is blocked.

What makes this situation possible, of course, is the idea that when there is an intestinal blockage, one can "let the baby die," but when there is no such defect there is nothing that can be done, for one must not "kill" it. The fact that this idea leads to such results as deciding life or death on irrelevant grounds is another good reason why the doctrine would be rejected.

One reason why so many people think that there is an important moral difference between active and passive euthanasia is that they think killing someone is morally worse than letting someone die. But is it? Is killing, in itself, worse than letting die? To investigate this issue, two cases may be considered that are exactly alike except that one involves killing whereas the other involves letting someone die. Then, it can be asked whether this difference makes any difference to the moral assessments. It is important that the cases be exactly alike, except for this one difference, since otherwise one cannot be confident that it is this difference and not some other than accounts for any variation in the assessments of the two cases. So, let us consider this pair of cases:

In the first, Smith stands to gain a large inheritance if anything should happen to his six-year-old cousin. One evening while the child is taking his bath, Smith sneaks into the bathroom and drowns the child, and then arranges things so that it will look like an accident.

In the second, Jones also stands to gain if anything should happen to his six-year-old cousin. Like Smith, Jones sneaks in planning to drown the child in his bath. However, just as he enters the bathroom Jones sees the child slip and hit his head, and fall face down in the water. Jones is delighted; he stands by, ready to push the child's head back under if it is necessary, but it is not necessary. With only a little thrashing about, the child drowns all by himself, "accidentally," as Jones watches and does nothing.

Now Smith killed the child, whereas Jones "merely" let the child die. That is the only difference between them. Did either man behave better, from a moral point of view? If the difference between killing and letting die were in itself a morally important matter, one should say that Jones's behavior was less reprehensible than Smith's. But does one really want to say that? I think not. In the first place, both men acted from the same motive, personal gain, and both had exactly the same end in view when they acted. It may be inferred from Smith's conduct that he is a bad man, although that judgment may be withdrawn or modified if certain further facts are learned about him—for example, that he is mentally deranged. But would not the very same thing be inferred about Jones from his conduct? And would not the same further considerations also be relevant to any modification of this judgment? Moreover, suppose Jones pleaded, in his own defense, "After all, I didn't do anything except just stand there and watch the child drown. I didn't kill him; I only let him die." Again, if letting die were in itself less bad than killing, this defense should have at least some weight. But it does not. Such a "defense" can only be regarded as a grotesque perversion of moral reasoning. Morally speaking, it is no defense at all.

Now, it may be pointed out, quite properly, that the cases of euthanasia with which doctors are concerned are not like this at all. They do not involve personal gain or the destruction of normal healthy children. Doctors are concerned only with cases in which the patient's life is of no further use to him, or in which the patient's life has become or will soon become a terrible burden. However, the point is the same in these cases: the bare difference between killing and letting die does not, in itself, make a moral difference. If a doctor lets a patient die, for humane reasons, he is in the same moral position as if he had given the patient a lethal injection for humane reasons. If his decision is wrong—if, for example, the patient's illness was in fact curable—the decision would be equally regrettable no matter which method was used to carry it out. And if the doctor's decision was the right one, the method used is not in itself important.

The AMA policy statement isolates the crucial issue very well; the crucial issue is "the intentional termination of the life of one human being by another." But after identifying this issue, and forbidding "mercy killing," the statement goes on to deny that the cessation of treatment is the intentional termination of a life. This is where the mistake comes in, for what is the cessation of treatment, in these circumstances, if it is not "the intentional termination of the life of one human being by another"? Of course it is exactly that, and if it were not, there would be no point to it.

Many people will find this judgment hard to accept. One reason I think, is that it is very easy to conflate the question of whether killing is, in itself, worse than letting die, with the very different question of whether most actual cases of killing are more reprehensible than most actual cases of letting die. Most actual cases of killing are clearly terrible (think, for example, of all the murders reported in the newspapers), and one hears of such cases every day. On the other hand, one hardly ever hears of a case of letting die, except for the actions of doctors who are motivated by humanitarian reasons. So one learns to think of killing in a much worse light than of letting die. But this does not mean that there is something about killing that makes it in itself worse than letting die, for it is not the bare difference between killing and letting die that makes the difference in these cases. Rather, the other factors—the murderer's motive of personal gain, for example, contrasted with the doctor's humanitarian motivation—account for different reactions to the different cases.

I have argued that killing is not in itself any worse than letting die; if my contention is right, it follows that active euthanasia is not any worse than passive euthanasia. What arguments can be given on the other side? The most common, I believe, is the following:

> The important difference between active and passive euthanasia is that, in passive euthanasia, the doctor does not do anything to bring about the patient's death. The doctor does nothing, and the patient dies of whatever ills already afflict him. In active euthanasia, however, the doctor does something to bring about the patient's death: he kills him. The doctor who gives the patient with cancer a lethal injection has himself caused his patient's death; whereas if he merely ceases treatment, the cancer is the cause of death.

A number of points need to be made here. The first is that it is not exactly correct to say that in passive euthanasia the doctor does nothing, for he does one thing that is very important: he lets the patient die. "Letting someone die" is certainly different, in some respects, from other types of action—mainly in that it is a kind of action that one may perform by way of not performing certain other actions. For example, one may let a patient die by way of not giving medication, just as one may insult someone by way of not shaking his hand. But for any purpose of moral assessment, it is a type of action nonetheless. The decision to let a patient die is subject to moral appraisal in the same way that a decision to kill him would be subject to moral appraisal: it may be assessed as wise or unwise, compassionate or sadistic, right or wrong. If a doctor deliberately let a patient die who was suffering from a routinely curable illness, the doctor would certainly be to blame if he had needlessly killed the patient. Charges against him would be appropriate. If so, it would be no defense at all for him to insist that he didn't "do anything." He would have done something very serious indeed, for he let his patient die.

Fixing the cause of death may be very important from a legal point of view, for it may determine whether criminal charges are brought against the doctor. But I do not think that this notion can be used to show a moral difference between active and passive euthanasia. The reason why it is considered bad to be the cause of someone's death is that death is regarded as a great evil—and so it is. However, if it has been decided that euthanasia—even passive euthanasia—is desirable in a given case, it has also been decided that in this instance death is no greater an evil than the patient's continued existence. And if this is true, the usual reason for not wanting to be the cause of someone's death simply does not apply.

Finally, doctors may think that all of this is only of academic interest—the sort of thing that philosophers may worry about but that has no practical bearing on their own work. After all, doctors must be concerned about the legal consequences of what they do, and active euthanasia is clearly forbidden by the law. But even so, doctors should also be concerned with the fact that the law is forcing upon them a moral doctrine that may be indefensible, and has a considerable effect on their practices. Of course, most doctors are not now in the position of being coerced in this matter, for they do not regard themselves as merely going along with what the law requires. Rather, in statements such as the AMA policy statement that I have quoted they are endorsing this doctrine as a central point of medical ethics. In that statement, active euthanasia is condemned not merely as illegal but as "contrary to that for which the medical profession stands," whereas passive euthanasia is approved. However, the preceding considerations suggest that there is really no moral difference between the two, considered in themselves (there may be important moral differences in some cases in their *consequences*, but, as I pointed out, these differences may make active euthanasia, and not passive euthanasia, the morally preferable option). So, whereas doctors may have to discriminate between active and passive euthanasia to satisfy the law, they should not do any more than that. In particular, they should not give the distinction any added authority and weight by writing it into official statements of medical ethics.

Note

1. Anthony Shaw, "Doctor, Do We Have a Choice?" *The New York Times Magazine*, 30 January 1972, 54.

Content Quiz 12.3

Instructions: Fill in the blanks with the appropriate responses listed below.

mercy killing	defense
irrelevant grounds	morally permissible
conditioned	active
passive	humanitarian
action	morally relevant differences

1. _____ euthanasia involves the doctor taking direct action to kill the patient.
2. _____ euthanasia involves the doctor withholding treatment and letting the patient die.
3. The deliberate taking of a patient's life for "humanitarian" reasons of relieving suffering is sometimes called _____.
4. Once an initial decision has been made not to prolong a patient's agony, letting the patient die may be less _____ than quickly and painlessly killing the person.
5. For Rachels, the distinction between active and passive euthanasia often leads to decisions concerning life and death made on _____.
6. In some cases, simply standing by and letting someone die is not really a(n) _____, but a grotesque perversion of moral reasoning.
7. For Rachels, there are no _____ between active and passive euthanasia since both involve "the intentional termination of the life of one human being by another", simply using different means.
8. People are generally opposed to killing because they have learned or been _____ to think about it in negative terms. Killing is usually reported in the context of murder, not in context of humanitarian service.
9. On the issue of euthanasia, Rachels argues that "letting die" or "doing nothing" is, in fact, a form of _____ requiring justification and acceptance of responsibility.
10. For Rachels, just because the law permits passive euthanasia and prohibits active euthanasia does not necessarily make the distinction between them reasonable or the acceptance of the former more _____ or justifiable. The law itself is not beyond moral appraisal.

Discussion Questions

1. What is the official position of the American Medical Association on euthanasia?
2. What is the difference between active and passive euthanasia? Does Rachels believe the difference is morally relevant? Why?
3. How can it be said that "mercy killing" is the humanitarian thing to do?
4. On what grounds could one be in favor of passive euthanasia but be opposed to active euthanasia? Would you accept these grounds? Why?

THE DUTCH WAY OF DEATH

Doctors and nurses in the Netherlands can practice euthanasia if they stick to certain guidelines. Yet many patients receive lethal injections without giving their consent

Rachel Nowak

Synopsis

In this article, Rachel Nowak provides a descriptive account of the moral problem of euthanasia as it is currently practiced in the Netherlands. She, herself, does not take a position. Nowak points out that while technically illegal, euthanasia has become an accepted part of Dutch health care policy. Citing the Remmelink report—a government sponsored survey—Nowak informs us that involuntary euthanasia of sick and elderly people is commonplace in the Netherlands and that patients often opt for it, not to avoid unnecessary physical suffering but to avoid becoming a nuisance. As we learn, these findings raise fears that euthanasia is impossible to regulate. They lead some to conclude that voluntary euthanasia should never be permitted because it will, inevitably, lead to involuntary euthanasia. One politician believes that through proper legislation and education on euthanasia, its abuses can be stamped out. A medical ethicist argues that it is impossible to regulate and control euthanasia because the matter is essentially a private transaction between doctor and patient. It is claimed that the slippery slope from voluntary to involuntary euthanasia is not theoretical but real, as evidenced in Holland. The article ends by suggesting that fears surrounding euthanasia may, in the end, be lost among concerns about patient autonomy and growing health care costs for aging populations. What does seem to be inevitable is that the issue of euthanasia is here to stay.

When a patient requests euthanasia, Jans Borleffs feels "honored" to oblige. "It's very personal," he says, "not a kick, not a feeling of power." But like most doctors who enter the moral maze of euthanasia, Borleffs is also awed by his responsibilities. "How is it possible that I am the one who can decide about life and death, when to terminate a life?" Borleffs has helped two people to die and has promised to help others. All are terminally ill with AIDS. All want their suffering to end before the illness finally claims their lives.

Although technically illegal in the Netherlands, over the past decade euthanasia has become an accepted part of Dutch health policy. While elsewhere doctors and philosophers remain locked in debate over the ethics of helping the dying to die, Dutch doctors have grasped the nettle. Each year they respond to requests for euthanasia from some 2700 terminally ill patients. Most ask their doctors to inject them with a fatal dose of drugs; some ask to be given drugs so that they can take their own lives. A further 22 500 Dutch patients per year receive "passive" euthanasia, where a doctor shortens a life either by withdrawing treatment or deciding not to start it.

In some hospitals, doctors routinely approach patients who are terminally ill, offering to inject them with lethal doses of barbiturates and curare when and if their suffering becomes too great. As long as physicians follow a set of guidelines on euthanasia, issued in 1987 by the Royal Dutch Medical Association, they will not be prosecuted.

1: The means to the end

Drugs given for euthanasia should induce a deep, irreversible coma within 30 minutes and kill within hours. They should not induce hallucinations or convulsions, and any risk of vomiting should be countered by giving the patient additional drugs.

This is the advice contained in a document on euthanasia written for doctors by the Royal Dutch Association for Advancement of Pharmacy.

Twenty years ago, before euthanasia became an accepted part of Dutch health care policy, a patient who requested euthanasia risked a less dignified demise. Then, physicians desperate to put patents out of their suffering, but with little knowledge of the best drugs for the job, resorted to inducing hypoglycaemic comas with overdoses of insulin, injecting heart-stimulating drugs in an attempt to induce fatal heart attacks, or even suffocating their patients with pillows.

Now, the method of choice is an intravenous injection of a barbiturate to induce coma, followed by the injection of a muscle relaxant to paralyze the respiratory system.

Very occasionally Dutch doctors use suppositories containing barbiturates. The RDAAP document, however, points to a potential drawback: as death approaches, the body cools, and this slows release of the drugs from the suppository. If, after administering 15 suppositories (at the rate of three per hour), the patient is still alive, the physician must be prepared to terminate life with a muscle relaxant, says the document.

Borleffs, who works at the Teaching Hospital in Utrecht, represents the acceptable face of this experiment with euthanasia: a humane doctor, striving to alleviate suffering while giving his patients the autonomy to determine the time and place of their own deaths. But Dutch euthanasia has its sinister side, too. A government survey published last September—dubbed the Remmelink report in honor of the attorney-general of the Dutch Supreme Court who chaired the commission—reveals that involuntary euthanasia of sick and elderly people is commonplace in the Netherlands, and that when patients do opt for euthanasia, it is frequently out of fear of being a nuisance rather than to avoid unnecessary physical suffering.

The details are alarming. At least a third of the 5000 or so Dutch patients who each year receive lethal doses of drugs from their doctors do not give their unequivocal consent. About 400 of these patients never even raise the issue of euthanasia with their doctors. Moreover, of those who willingly opt for euthanasia, only about 5 percent do so solely because of unbearable pain. A much higher proportion, about a third, do so partly for fear of becoming dependent on others. Additionally, Dutch doctors kill about 1300 terminally ill patients each year by upping their dose of painkillers. In these cases, says the Remmelink report, the doctors acknowledge that their intention is to shorten the lives of the patients, not to alleviate pain.

These revelations strike a blow at the two central canons of the worldwide euthanasia lobby: that euthanasia should be used only as a means to end pointless physical suffering, and that the patient alone should make the decision. Now, some medical ethicists are saying that the Remmelink report proves that euthanasia is impossible to regulate, and that voluntary euthanasia should never be permitted because once sanctioned it leads inexorably to involuntary euthanasia.

Unnatural causes

The Dutch parliament will be grappling with these issues later this year when it votes on whether to legalize euthanasia and strengthen the existing guidelines. These currently stipulate that: the patient must explicitly and repeatedly request euthanasia; the patient must be subject to unbearable and intractable suffering; the physician must get a second opinion from another doctor before resorting to euthanasia; that the death be reported as due to euthanasia and not natural causes. In reality, one in five Dutch physicians fails to consult with a colleague, while some frequently pass off deaths caused by lethal injections as being from natural causes.

However, neither these nor any of the other charges contained in the Remmelink report have succeeded in galvanizing world medical opinion against euthanasia. "The abuses do not weaken the argument for voluntary euthanasia," says William Collins, a psychologist based at Cornell University in New York who studies euthanasia in the US. "Instead, they argue for closer supervision of physicians, and penalties for those who step outside the boundaries."

Legalization, together with educational programs on euthanasia for patients and physicians would help to stamp out its abuse in the Netherlands, argues Jacob Kohnstamm, a Dutch MP. At present, he says, patients and physicians are reluctant to discuss euthanasia because, although increasingly practiced, it still carries the stigma of a crime. And that makes it difficult to obtain unequivocal consent.

The Remmelink investigation bears this out. In more than half of the 1000 or so cases of unrequested euthanasia, the physicians said that the patients had at least alluded to euthanasia. Even though the criterion of repeated requests had not been met, the physicians believed they had acted according to their patients' wishes.

A slippery slope?

Opponents of euthanasia remain unconvinced. Daniel Callahan, director of the Hastings Center, a medical ethics think-tank in Briarcliff Manor, New York, believes that because euthanasia is an essentially private transaction between doctor and patient, it is impossible to regulate and should simply be prohibited. "The slippery-slope argument against euthanasia has always been that once you start on voluntary euthanasia, you are likely to gravitate towards involuntary euthanasia," he says. "In Holland, this is no longer theoretical. It is actually happening."

Callahan blames the drift towards involuntary euthanasia on the fact that doctors become inured to death. "Euthanasia starts in the hands of a few very cautious, responsible people," he says, "but when it becomes a mass phenomenon, don't count on the same high standards." In the Netherlands, standards may have fallen already.

Few of those involved in the debate doubt that the Remmelink report provides an accurate account of the overall incidence of euthanasia and euthanasia malpractice in the Netherlands. Where it has failed, say its detractors, is in depicting the gravity of the abuse. Carlos Gomez, a doctor at the University of Virginia Hospital in Charlottesville, Virginia, believes this can only be achieved by examining individual case histories of euthanasia. His doctoral thesis, researched in the Netherlands, details 26 such cases. While the majority of the patients appeared to meet the criteria for euthanasia, says Gomez, in at least four cases they did not.

In one case, a doctor injected a lethal dose of potassium chloride into someone who had been severely injured in a car accident and looked unlikely to recover. The doctor wanted to spare the family the emotional suffering, says Gomez. The same fate awaited a person who had suffered a stroke and looked unlikely to make a swift recovery. The third case involved a 78-year-old woman in a nursing home who had suffered several bouts of pneumonia. "It was unclear what her wishes were, but clear what the doctors wanted," says Gomez. But the most flagrant abuse of euthanasia was the killing of a two-day-old child with Down's syndrome—a child who would probably have lived for 40 or 50 years.

Such blatant disregard for the regulations is not limited to one incident. A Dutch physician told me of a similar abuse. One night the doctor discovered that his five-month-old son had stopped breathing. He was suffering from sleep apnoea, a condition thought to be responsible for many cot deaths. The doctor was able to revive his son, but not before the child had suffered severe brain damage. He subsequently arranged for a colleague to kill his son.

In the Netherlands, the central argument used to support euthanasia is the right of patients to determine when and how they die. Nonetheless, many Dutch physicians concede (often with an unnerving air of indifference) that involuntary euthanasia occurs. "In Holland, you feel that something else is going on behind the argument for patient's autonomy," says Gomez. "Some physicians think that certain patients are better off dead than alive and they are willing to make that decision."

Moral killing

Some Dutch physicians readily acknowledge that this is the case. One such person is Cor Spreeuwenberg, a general practitioner, committed Christian and veteran of nine cases of euthanasia. If a patient is suffering unbearably but unable to consent to euthanasia, he says, a physician will have to decide whether it is better to allow the fruitless suffering to continue, or to end that person's life. "Sometimes killing the person will be the morally correct thing to do," he argues.

Kohnstamm weighs in with the example of a patient dying of throat cancer. "[Physicians] say it is one of the most horrible deaths you can imagine. At a certain point you can't breath. It takes four to eight hours to die, fighting for every breath. The doctor can do two things: put the patient in an isolated room where nobody can hear or see his [or her] suffering and come back in 10 hours when the patient is dead; or decide to kill the patient."

The battle lines are thus drawn. Those in Kohnstamm's camp argue that voluntary euthanasia for a patient who is dying in agony—perhaps even involuntary euthanasia if he or she is too delirious to make a request—can be justified on grounds of compassion. Others, such as Callahan, categorically reject euthanasia either with or without consent. The need for compassion, they argue, does not outweigh the risk of people feeling coerced into opting for euthanasia.

That risk is likely to be all the greater when people die at home, as most do in the Netherlands, surrounded by the relatives who are "burdened" with looking after them. The problem of coercion looms larger still in the US, where patients without health insurance must pay for their own health care or rely on relatives to do so. For an American family, euthanasia for grandad may mean the difference between whether or not a younger member of the family can go to college, or whether the old station wagon can be traded in for a new one.

Of course, it is impossible to predict what effect, if any, the Netherlands' experiment with euthanasia will ultimately have on policymakers. The abuse exposed by the Remmelink report may scare some. But equally its message may eventually be lost amid the growing cries for patient autonomy and the burgeoning costs of caring for aging populations. Perhaps the only certainty is that, legal or not, euthanasia is here to stay. As one Dutch doctor puts it: "Everywhere doctors are terminating lives. The only difference in Holland is that here we talk about it."

2: THE DEBATE GATHERS PACE IN AUSTRALIA

Doctors and nurses in the Australian state of Victoria have admitted in separate surveys that they have hastened the death of terminally ill patients. This is contrary to state law in Victoria which allows passive euthanasia—the withdrawal of medical treatment such as a life-support system—but not active euthanasia.

A majority of both doctors and nurses in Victoria favor a change in the law along the lines of the Dutch guidelines. But, according to a survey of nurses published earlier this year, nurses are more strongly in favor of changing the law in this way than doctors—75 percent of nurses surveyed, compared with 60 percent for doctors. The doctors' survey was published in 1988.

According to Peter Singer and Helga Kushe, the researchers from Monash University who conducted both surveys, this suggests that nurses have a closer relationship than doctors with the terminally ill, and a better understanding of their plight.

A minority of nurses are prepared to take treatment into their own hands. Sixteen nurses, or 5 percent of the respondents, said that they had complied with a patient's request to directly end his or her life without consulting a doctor. Another 37 nurses admitted performing passive euthanasia without the knowledge of a doctor. Rodney Syme, of the Voluntary Euthanasia Society, said these nurses were risking prosecution. The survey of nurses has caused controversy in Australia. Ann Monkivitch, a registered nurse, claimed in a letter to *The Age*, Victoria's main daily newspaper, that the questionnaire made no allowances for responses that would indicate opposition to euthanasia.

"The phrasing of the questions made the desired result inevitable," she said.

Both Singer and Kushe, from the Center for Human Bioethics at Monash, have publicly supported euthanasia, but they vehemently deny any bias in the survey. Nurses were able to voice their opposition by ticking "no" in relevant boxes, they say.

Calls to change, or at least clarify, the law have been made since publication of the nurses survey. Active euthanasia is practiced secretly in Australia, according to Singer. "In Australia we have a *de facto* practice of completely uncontrolled euthanasia," he says. Doctors and nurses widely believe that in theory they could be charged with murder.

Belinda Morleson from the Australian Nursing Federation said that health professionals were put in an untenable position because of the discrepancy between law and accepted practice. David Lanham, a law professor at the University of Melbourne, has urged a public inquiry into the law.

According to his interpretation of the law, it is possible for doctors, with a patient's consent, to administer drugs that will relieve pain but also shorten life. Singer says that if this view is correct, it is not widely appreciated by doctors.

But some doctors believe that the law should be kept well away from medical practice. "Legislation has nothing to offer the intimacy of the doctor-patient relationship which is potentially a very powerful mechanism for resolution of suffering," one doctor wrote in the survey.

Another doctor wrote: "I am opposed to the Dutch measures and similar laws here because this is an area best left to the doctor to act as he thinks best—outside of legal constraints—as occurs right now."

The nurses and doctors were asked almost identical questions. The survey of 869 doctors revealed that 107 doctors, or 29 percent of doctors asked by a patient to hasten death, had complied with the request. Of those who did not comply, 65 percent said that illegality was the reason. Two-thirds of nurses thought it was proper to assist a doctor based on the practice in the Netherlands.

The doctors were divided on the question of whether or not they would practice active voluntary euthanasia if it were legal: 41 percent said no; 40 percent said yes, and the rest did not answer.

Ian Anderson

Content Quiz 12.4

Instructions: Fill in the blanks with the appropriate responses listed below.

lethal doses of barbiturates
nuisance
stigma
killing the person
dead
abuses
coerce
involuntary euthanasia
autonomy
passive euthanasia

1. Thousands of Dutch patients receive _____ every year as doctors either withdraw treatment or decide not to start it.
2. One method of euthanizing is to inject _____.
3. Euthanasia can contribute to patients' _____ by allowing them to alleviate their suffering and to determine the time and place of their own deaths.
4. In Holland, people sometimes opt for euthanasia not to relieve unbearable suffering, but frequently out of fear of becoming a _____.
5. Some medical ethicists believe the Remmelink report proves that voluntary euthanasia is impossible to regulate and that once allowed, it will necessarily lead to _____.
6. Patients and physicians are reluctant to discuss euthanasia because it still carries the _____ of a crime.
7. Some people believe that if euthanasia is legalized, then _____ are inevitable.
8. According to some Dutch physicians in favor of euthanasia, _____ is the morally correct thing to do if it terminates fruitless suffering.
9. Daniel Callahan, director of the Hastings Center, fears that legalizing euthanasia will _____ some patients into opting for it, because they see themselves as a "burden" on their families or on the health care system.

10. Some doctors believe that certain patients are better off _____ than alive and those doctors are willing to make that decision.

Discussion Questions

1. What is the difference between voluntary and involuntary euthanasia?
2. If "putting a sick animal to sleep" is the humane thing to do, is the same true in the case of sick persons? Why or why not?
3. What is the "slippery slope" argument as it involves euthanasia? Is a fallacy involved here? Explain.
4. If you were believed to be terminally ill and unconscious, would you want to give your doctor the right to end your life? Why or why not?

CHAPTER THIRTEEN

13 SEXUAL ETHICS

THE JUSTIFICATION OF SEX WITHOUT LOVE

Albert Ellis

Synopsis

In the first part of this article, Albert Ellis presents and defends the thesis that sexual relations based on love are desirable but not necessary. He prefers sex to be love-based (affectional), but he holds the position that nonaffectional sex (sex without love) is also acceptable. After presenting seven supporting arguments, he summarizes his position by stating that we should accept our biosocial tendencies and stop blaming ourselves for drives and desires that are a normal expression of our humanness. If we insist that love is a pre-requisite to acceptable sex, then we unnecessarily condemn millions of people to self-blame and atonement.

In the second part of his article, Ellis acknowledges and critically responds to several objections to his position. Contrary to critics of nonaffectional sex, Ellis argues that people engaging in it will not necessarily miss out on the greater enjoyment of affectional sex. He also argues that there is no greater pleasure in love-based sex in the future, if one sacrifices sex without love now; further, he does not agree that if both forms of sex are allowed, then nonaffectional sex will drive out love-based sex. Ellis is interested in promoting happiness in people's lives and believes that both loving and nonloving sex can contribute significantly to their pleasure and life satisfaction.

A scientific colleague of mine, who holds a professorial post in the department of sociology and anthropology at one of our leading universities, recently asked me about my stand on the question of human beings having sex relations without love. Although I have taken something of a position on this issue in my book, *The American Sexual Tragedy*, I have never quite considered the problem in sufficient detail. So here goes.

In general, I feel that affectional, as against nonaffectional, sex relations are *desirable* but not *necessary*. It is usually desirable that an association between coitus and affection exist—particularly in marriage, because it is often difficult for two individuals to keep finely tuned to each other over a period of years, and if there is not a good deal of love between them, one may tend to feel sexually imposed upon by the other.

The fact, however, that the coexistence of sex and love may be desirable does not, to my mind, make it necessary. My reasons for this view are several:

1. Many individuals—including, even, many married couples—*do* find great satisfaction in having sex relations without love. I do not consider it fair to label these individuals as criminal just because they may be in the minority.

Moreover, even if they are in the minority (as may well *not* be the case), I am sure that they number literally millions of men and women. If so, they constitute a sizable subgroup of humans whose rights to sex satisfaction should be fully acknowledged and protected.

2. Even if we consider the supposed majority of individuals who find greater satisfaction in sex-love than in sex-sans-love relations, it is doubtful if all or most of them do so for *all* their lives. During much of their existence, especially their younger years, these people tend to find sex-without-love quite satisfying, and even to prefer it to affectional sex.

When they become older, and their sex drives tend to wane, they may well emphasize coitus with rather than without affection. But why should we condemn them *while* they still prefer sex to sex-love affairs?

3. Many individuals, especially females in our culture, who say that they only enjoy sex when it is accompanied by affection are actually being unthinkingly conformist and unconsciously hypocritical. If they were able to contemplate themselves objectively, and had the courage of their inner convictions, they would find sex without love eminently gratifying.

This is not to say that they would *only* enjoy nonaffectional coitus, nor that they would always find it *more* satisfying than affectional sex. But, in the depths of their psyche and soma, they would deem sex without love pleasurable *too*.

And why should they not? And why should we, by our puritanical know-nothingness, force these individuals to drive a considerable portion of their sex feelings and potential satisfactions underground?

If, in other words, we view sexuoamative relations as desirable rather than necessary, we sanction the innermost thoughts and drive of many of our fellowmen and fellowwomen to have sex *and* sex-love relations. If we take the opposing view, we hardly destroy these innermost thoughts and drives, but frequently tend to intensify them while denying them open and honest outlet. This, as Freud . . . pointed out, is one of the main (though by no means the only) source of rampant neurosis.

4. I firmly believe that sex is a biological, as well as a social, drive, and that in its biological phases it is essentially nonaffectional. If this is so, then we can expect that, however we try to civilize the sex drives—and civilize them to *some* degree we certainly must—there will always be an underlying tendency for them to escape from our society-inculcated shackles and to be still partly felt in the raw.

When so felt, when our biological sex urges lead us to desire and enjoy sex without (as well as with) love, I do not see why we should make their experiencers feel needlessly guilty.

5. Many individuals—many millions in our society, I am afraid—have little or no capacity for affection or love. The majority of these individuals, perhaps, are emotionally disturbed, and should preferably be helped to increase their affectional propensities. But a large

number are not particularly disturbed, and instead are neurologically or cerebrally deficient.

Mentally deficient persons, for example, as well as many dull normals (who, together, include several million citizens of our nation) are notoriously shallow in their feelings, and probably intrinsically so. Since these kinds of individuals—like the neurotic and the organically deficient—are for the most part, in our day and age, *not* going to be properly treated and *not* going to overcome their deficiencies, and since most of them definitely *do* have sex desires, I again see no point in making them guilty when they have nonloving sex relations.

Surely these unfortunate individuals are sufficiently handicapped by their disturbances or impairments without our adding to their woes by anathematizing them when they manage to achieve some nonamative sexual release.

6. Under some circumstances—though these, I admit, may be rare—some people find more satisfaction in nonloving coitus even though, under other circumstances, these *same* people may find more satisfaction in sex-love affairs. Thus, the man who *normally* enjoys being with his girlfriend because he loves as well as is sexually attracted to her, may occasionally find immense satisfaction in being with another girl with whom he has distinctly nonloving relations.

Granting that this may be (or is it?) unusual, I do not see why it should be condemnable.

7. If many people get along excellently and most cooperatively with business partners, employees, professors, laboratory associates, acquaintances, and even spouses for whom they have little or no love or affection, but with whom they have certain specific things in common, I do not see why there cannot be individuals who get along excellently and most cooperatively with sex mates with whom they may have little else in common.

I personally can easily see the tragic plight of a man who spends much time with a girl with whom he has nothing in common but sex: since I believe that life is too short to be well consumed in relatively one-track or intellectually low-level pursuits. I would also think it rather unrewarding for a girl to spend much time with a male with whom she had mutually satisfying sex, friendship, and cultural interest but no love involvement. This is because I would like to see people, in their 70-odd years of life, have maximum rather than minimum satisfactions with individuals of the other sex with whom they spend considerable time.

I can easily see, however, even the most intelligent and highly cultured individuals spending a *little* time with members of the other sex with whom they have common sex and cultural but no real love interests. And I feel that, for the time expended in this manner, their lives may be immeasurably enriched.

Moreover, when I encounter friends or psychotherapy clients who become enamored and spend considerable time and effort thinking about and being with a member of the other sex with whom they are largely sexually obsessed, and for whom they have little or no love, I mainly view these sexual infatuations as one of the penalties of their being human. For humans are the kind of animals who are easily disposed to this type of behavior . . . .

I believe that one of the distinct inconveniences or tragedies of human sexuality is that it endows us, and perhaps particularly the males among us, with a propensity to become exceptionally involved and infatuated with members of the other sex whom, had we no sex urges, we would hardly notice. That is too bad; and it might well be a better world if it were otherwise. But it is *not* otherwise, and I think it is silly and pernicious for us to condemn ourselves because we are the way that we are in this respect.

We had better *accept* our biosocial tendencies, or our fallible humanity—instead of constantly blaming ourselves and futilely trying to change certain of its relatively harmless, though still somewhat tragic, aspects.

For reasons such as these, I feel that although it is usually—if not always—*desirable* for human beings to have sex relations with those they love rather than with those they do not love, it is by no means *necessary* that they do so. When we teach that it *is* necessary, we only needlessly condemn millions of our citizens to self-blame and atonement.

The position which I take—that there are several good reasons why affectional, as against nonaffectional, sex relations are desirable but not necessary—can be assailed on several counts. I shall now consider some of the objections to this position to see if they cannot be effectively answered.

It may be said that an individual who has nonloving instead of loving sex relations is not necessarily wicked but that he is self-defeating because, while going for immediate gratification, he will miss out on even greater enjoyments. But this would only be true if such an individual (whom we shall assume, for the sake of discussion, *would* get greater enjoyment from affectional sex relations than from nonaffectional ones) were *usually* or *always* having nonaffectionate coitus. If he were *occasionally* or *sometimes* having love with sex, and the rest of the time having sex without love, he would be missing out on very little, if any, enjoyment.

Under these circumstances, in fact, he would normally get *more* pleasure from *sometimes* having sex without love. For the fact remains, and must not be realistically ignored, that in our present-day society sex without love is *much more frequently* available than sex with love.

Consequently, to ignore nonaffectional coitus when affectional coitus is not available would, from the standpoint of enlightened self-interest, be sheer folly. In relation both to immediate *and* greater enjoyment, the individual would thereby be losing out.

The claim can be made of course that if an individual sacrifices sex without love *now* he will experience more pleasure by having sex with love in the future. This is an interesting claim; but I find no empirical evidence to sustain it. In fact, on theoretical grounds it seems most unlikely that it will be sustained. It is akin to the claim that if an individual starves himself for several days in a row he will greatly enjoy eating a meal at the end of a week or a month. I am sure he will—provided that he is then not too sick or debilitated to enjoy anything! But, even assuming that such an individual derives enormous satisfaction from his one meal a week or a month, is his *total* satisfaction greater than it would have been had he enjoyed three good meals a day for that same period of time? I doubt it.

It may be held that if both sex with and without love are permitted in any society, the nonaffectional sex will drive out affectional sex, somewhat in accordance with Gresham's laws of currency. On the contrary, however, there is much reason to believe that just because an individual has sex relations, for quite a period, on a nonaffectional basis, he will be more than eager to replace it, eventually, with sex with love.

From my clinical experience, I have often found that males who most want to settle down to having a single mistress or wife are those who have tried numerous lighter affairs and found them wanting. The view that sex without love eradicates the need for affectional sex relationships is somewhat akin to the ignorance is bliss theory. For it virtually says that if people never experienced sex with love they would never realize how good it was and therefore would never strive for it.

Or else the proponents of this theory seem to be saying that sex without love is so greatly satisfying, and sex with love so intrinsically difficult and disadvantageous to attain, that given the choice between the two, most people would pick the former. If this is so, then by all means let them pick the former—with which, in terms of their greater and total happiness, they would presumably be better off.

I doubt, however, that this hypothesis *is* factually sustainable. From clinical experience, again, I can say that individuals who are capable of sex with love usually seek and find it; while those who remain nonaffectional in their sex affairs generally are not particularly capable of sex with love and need psychotherapeutic help before they can become thus capable.

Although, as a therapist, I frequently work with individuals who are only able to achieve nonaffectional sex affairs and, through helping them eliminate their irrational fears and blockings, make it possible for them to achieve sex-love relationships, I still would doubt that *all* persons who take no great pleasure in sex with love are emotionally deficient. Some quite effective individuals—such as Immanuel Kant, for instance—seem to be so wholeheartedly dedicated to *things* or *ideas* that they rarely or never become amatively involved with people.

As long as such individuals have vital, creative interests and are intensely absorbed or involved with *something*, I would hesitate to diagnose them as being necessarily neurotic merely because they do not ordinarily become intensely absorbed with *people*. *Some* of these nonlovers of human beings are, of course, emotionally disturbed. But *all*? I wonder.

Disturbed or not, I see no reason why individuals who are dedicated to things or ideas should not have, in many or most instances, perfectly normal sex drives. And, if they do, I fail to see why they should not consummate their sex urges in nonaffectional ways in order to have more time and energy for their nonamative pursuits.

Content Quiz 13.1

Instructions: Fill in the blanks with the appropriate responses listed below.

affection	guilty
unthinkingly conformist	necessary
biosocial tendencies	biological
clinical experience	ideas
nonaffectional sex	sex without love

1. Albert Ellis believes that affectional sex relations are desirable, but not _____.
2. Many individuals in society have no capacity for _____.
3. Sex is a _____ drive.
4. People who claim that sex is enjoyable only when accompanied by affection are being _____.
5. We should not feel _____ when our sex urges lead us to desire and enjoy coitus without love.

6. Rather than continually blaming ourselves and trying to change, we should accept our _____.
7. According to Ellis, it is wrong to believe that _____, if permitted, will eventually drive out affectional sex.
8. _____ informs Ellis that those who desire stable loving relationships have frequently had lighter affairs and found them lacking in many important respects.
9. People dedicated to _____ have normal sex drives usually and should not be prevented from satisfying their biosocial needs.
10. Younger people often find _____ quite satisfying.

Discussion Questions

1. To what kind of "necessity" is Ellis making reference when he argues that affectional sex is desirable but not necessary.
2. What seems to be the moral and philosophical basis of Ellis' argument that nonaffectional sex is acceptable in many cases?
3. Is Ellis guilty of committing the "is-ought" fallacy? Explain.
4. What response do you have to Ellis' claim that, "We had better accept our biosocial tendencies, or our fallible humanity—instead of constantly blaming ourselves and futilely trying to change certain of its relatively harmless, though still somewhat tragic, aspects."?
5. Does Ellis adequately take into account the rights and feelings of those with whom one has nonaffectional sex? Do they matter? Does moral responsibility enter into the situation of nonaffectional sex? If so, how? If not, why not?

CHRISTIAN SEXUAL ETHICS

Lewis B. Smedes

Synopsis

In his essay, Lewis Smedes addresses the issue of sexual morality. More specifically, he examines the acceptability of sexual intercourse outside of marriage from four moral perspectives: (1) the morality of caution, (2) the morality of concern, (3) the morality of personal relationships, and (4) the morality of law. After a consideration and appraisal of these various moral perspectives, Smedes endorses the morality of law which, in effect, reflects Christian New Testament thinking. In his estimation, the other moralities either trivialize the ethical dimensions of sexual intercourse or they make decision making contingent on questionable factors such as circumstances and uncertain personal insights—things that do not allow for clear-cut moral judgments. For Smedes, sexual intercourse is a life-uniting act that should have life-uniting intent. In his view, when two individuals have sex without a life-long commitment to each other, they break the moral law.

1. The Morality of Caution

Any reasonable single person trying to make a rational decision about his sexual activity will "count the cost." The first thing they may ask is: "Am I likely to get hurt?" Sexual intercourse has some risk along with certain possible rewards for unmarried people, and the cautious person will weigh the risks. The question of "getting hurt" has two parts: (1) how seriously can I get hurt, and (2) how great is the risk of getting hurt? If the odds are not good and the possible hurt pretty serious, the cautious person may decide to wait until marriage, when the risk will be mostly eliminated.

The hurts that sexual intercourse could cause unmarried people are obvious enough. Getting pregnant, even in a permissive society, is a painful experience for an unmarried woman. Once pregnant, she has no way of escaping a painful decision: she can abort the fetus, she can give the baby up for adoption, or she can rear the child herself. Or, of course, she can get married—but this may not be an option for her. The route of abortion has been paved by liberalized laws. But no matter how easy it may be to get, and no matter what her intellectual view of abortion may be, she is likely to find out afterwards that it is a devastating experience for herself, especially if she is sensitive to the value of human life. Adoption is another route. Every child given up for adoption may be God's gift to some adoptive parents. This is a compensation. But giving up children nourished to birth inside their own bodies is something few young women can do without deep pain. Keeping the baby and rearing it may be easier than it used to be. Many communities no longer lash the unwed mother with their silent judgment: this may be only because the community does not care, but it still makes life easier for the mother. But rearing the baby alone is still heavy with problems for the unmarried mother in the most tolerant society. Some may have a chance at marriage; but marriage forced on two people is an invitation to pain. In short, pregnancy can cause considerable hurt.

While pregnancy still hurts, the risk of it is not threatening to many unmarried people. However, any notion that the risk has been eliminated is careless thinking. The contraceptive pill has cut the chances, but it has not removed the possibility. Unwanted children, both in marriage and out of it, testify that no birth control device known up to this point is fail-proof. And, of course, there is the risk of that accidental time when precautions were neglected. As a matter of fact, the majority of young people having intercourse for the first time do not use any preventive means at all. Many young women refuse to take precautions because they do not want to think of themselves as planning for intercourse; it must happen only as they are swept into it in a romantic frenzy. Still, all things considered, the risk of pregnancy may have become small enough so that the cautious person may decide it is worth taking.

The threat of disease is a real one, especially for the promiscuous person. Antibiotics, once heralded as a sure cure, have stimulated virus strains more potent than ever. And venereal disease is currently in a virtual epidemic stage. Still, for prudent and selective people the odds seem comfortably against infection.

The risk of threatening an eventual marriage by premarital sex is hard to calculate. A deeply disappointing sexual experience before marriage could, one supposes, condition a person against happy sex in marriage. But, of course, unmarried people considering intercourse do not plan on having a bad experience. Guilt feelings about a premarital experience can inhibit one's freedom of self-giving in marriage sex: for example, a woman's inability to experience orgasm in marriage is sometimes traceable to guilt about premarital sex. And promiscuity before marriage could possibly make extra-marital sex easier to fall into should marriage sex be unrewarding. But all these threats depend too much on how individual people feel; they are not useful as blanket judgments. The question of threat to marriage has to be answered in terms of the individuals involved.

Jane, who believes religiously that sexual intercourse before marriage is a sin, runs a fairly strong chance of making marriage harder for herself by premarital intercourse, especially if she has sex with someone besides the man she marries. But Joan, who was reared in a moral no man's land, may not risk marriage happiness at all by having premarital sex, though she may risk it for much deeper reasons. All in all, the argument that sexual intercourse by unmarried people threatens their future marriage is a flimsy one; too much depends on the moral attitudes of the persons involved. This implies, of course, that one does not have to be one hundred percent moral to have a happy marriage, though it may help.

The morality of caution leaves us with no clear-cut decision. Christian morality cannot support a blanket veto of sexual intercourse for unmarried people on this basis. It all depends on how the risks are calculated in each person's situation. The morality of caution will lead prudent people to ask with whom, why, and when they are having intercourse. But it is not enough to tell them that they ought not do it. Following the morality of caution alone, sexual morality comes down to this: if you are reasonably sure you won't get hurt, go ahead.

The point to notice is that the morality of caution is concerned only with possible hurt to the person involved. It does not bother with questions about the kind of act sexual intercourse is; it does not ask whether unmarried people are morally qualified for it on the basis of either their relationship or the nature of the act. I do not suppose that many people, in their best moments, will decide on the basis of caution alone. But wherever it is snipped away from the other considerations, it works on the assumption that sexual intercourse as such has no more *moral* significance than a gentle kiss.

2. The Morality of Concern

Here we move beyond caution to a personal concern about the risk of causing hurt to others. The morality of caution asks: am I likely to get hurt? The morality of concern asks: am I likely to hurt someone else? The calculations of both moralities are roughly the same. The difference is that here concern is directed toward the other person. The crucial questions here will be how far one's concern reaches and how sensitive one is to the kinds of hurt he could cause. It may be that the concerned person will interpret the risks differently than the merely cautious person will.

For instance, a girl may be willing to take the risk of pregnancy as far as she is concerned. But if she considers the hurt that pregnancy may involve for the unwanted child, she may weigh the odds quite differently: the risk of pregnancy will be the same, but the possible hurt to others may count against having intercourse more heavily than if its pleasure is matched only against possible hurt to herself. If she gets pregnant, the girl may decide to abort or give the child up for adoption. The fetus has no choice. Here she is dealing with a potential person's right to exist. If she gives the child up for adoption, she is determining that the child will not be reared by its natural parents. And if she decides to keep the child, she may be forcing a situation of permanent disadvantage on another human being. This may sound as though only the woman is making the decision; but the same considerations must go into the thinking of her partner. By his act he may be risking severe disadvantages for another human being—or at least a potential human being—and giving that human being no choice in the matter. The unmarried couple may be able to opt for the risk; but the unwanted offspring is not given a chance to weigh the odds.

But again, the risk may seem small enough to take for the sophisticated person. And for some couples there is always a backup emergency plan—marriage. But here again the element of concern is brought in: are the people involved reasonably sure that they won't hurt each other by getting married? The person with concern will ask the question and seek advice in answering it: but only he or she can give the answer for himself.

No person who makes decisions out of concern for others will run much risk of infecting another person with venereal disease. And a person who is truly concerned will be least likely to be a threat: he would not likely be a person who goes in for casual bed-hopping. The risk is not great for two people who are serious about sexual intercourse as an expression of deeply involved affection because the probability of promiscuity is not great. At any rate, the morality of concern would tell a person to be very careful, but it would probably not tell him to abstain from sexual intercourse entirely.

Personal concern looks a lot deeper than the risk of getting someone pregnant or spreading a disease. A concerned person will wonder how sexual intercourse will affect his partner as a whole person, because each person's sexual experiences are a major theme in the symphony he is creating with his life. No one can take sex out at night and put it away until he wants to play with it again. What we do with sex shapes what we are; it is woven into the plot of a drama we are writing about ourselves. The person with whom we have sexual relations cannot let his sexual passions dance on stage, take a curtain call, and go back to some backstage corner to let the rest of the play go on. So a concerned person will ask how a sexual experience can fit into the total life—the whole future—of that other person. Where will it fit in his memories? How will it be digested in his conscience? What will it do to his attitude toward himself? How will it help create the symphony that he can make of his life? The morality of concern reaches out into the tender tissues of the other person's whole life; and it refuses to endorse any act that will stunt that person's movement into a creative, self-esteeming, and freely conscious life.

However, it also goes beyond the other person. It asks about the people around them—their friends, their families, and their community. A single, discreet, and very secret affair may not bring down the moral walls of Jericho. But a Christian person of concern will think beyond his own affair: he must universalize his action and ask what the effects would be if unmarried people generally followed his example.

Much depends, naturally, on the kind of sex he is thinking about. If he is thinking about casual sex, on the assumption that all two people need for good sex is to like each other, we have one set of problems. If he is thinking about sleeping only with the person he is planning to marry, we have another. If he is thinking of casual sex, he will have to ask about the burdens on society created by a considerable number of unwanted children, a formidable increase in venereal disease, and a general devaluation of sexual intercourse as an expression of committed love. But if he is thinking only of sex between two responsible people who are profoundly in love—though not legally married—the question is limited to what the effect on public morals would be if everyone in *his* position felt free to have sexual intercourse. He might respond by saying that if it *were* moral [for] him, it would be moral for others. Thus public morality would not be damaged if everyone did it; habits and customs might change, and moral *opinions* would change, but morality itself would be unscathed. And he would be right—on this basis.

Concern for the other person and his community sets the question within the perimeter of Christian love. It comes within the single blanket law that all of our decisions are to be made in responsible love. In the terms of this morality, sexual intercourse is morally neutral, and the question of its rightness or wrongness is answered only in relation to its consequences for other people. If the risk of harmful consequences is small enough, single people are free to go ahead. The morality of concern forces people to judge according to circumstances; for example, the answer to the question whether two mature retirees should refrain from sexual intercourse may be very different from that concerning two youngsters on a sexual high. Acting only out of loving concern, one puts aside the possibility that there may be something special about sexual intercourse that disqualifies everyone but married persons. It demands only that each person weigh the risks carefully and then make a responsible decision for his particular case.

3. The Morality of Personal Relationships

Two things set off the morality of personal relationships from the first two: first, its focus is on how intercourse will affect the *relationship* between the two persons; second, its concern is more positive. The clinching question is whether sexual intercourse will strengthen and deepen the relationship. If it can be a creative factor in the relationship, it is good—provided, of course, neither person gets hurt individually. Behind this way of deciding the right and wrong of intercourse lies a whole new understanding of human beings as persons-in-relationship. The view is that the individual comes into his own in relationship: the "I" is a truly human "I" only as it exists in an "I-You" relationship. The tender spot in human morality, then, is always at the point of personal contact with another. And this is why the effect sexual intercourse has on the relationship is the pivotal question.

The relationship can be creatively supported only when two people have regard for each other as ends to be served rather than as means to be used. When two people use each other in sexual intercourse, they hurt the relationship and corrupt the sexual act. They twist the relationship into a functional association. One has a functional relationship with a person whenever he concentrates on getting a service from him. What one wants from a plumber is to have his leaky faucet fixed, what he wants from a dentist is to have his toothache cured; what one may want from a sexual partner is to have his ego served or his sex drive satiated. In these cases one is after a functional association. But what someone wants in a personal relationship is to let the other person thrive as a person, to give him the regard and respect he merits as a friend, and to be privileged to grow into a relationship in which they will both desire no more from each other than mutual concern and enjoyment. In short, he wants the other person to be something along *with* him rather than merely to do something *for* him.

Now in most cases, two people in love treat each other in both functional and personal ways. There is constant tension between expecting one's friend to deliver the pleasures of friendship and respecting him only for what he is. In sexual love, the functional side often *tends* to shove the personal side into the background. The sex drive is so intense that it becomes a temptation to manipulate and even exploit the other person. To the extent that the functional is predominant in our sex lives, we treat the other person as a means and thus dehumanize him. When this happens sexual intercourse is immoral, not because it is sexual intercourse between two unmarried people but because it distorts and destroys a personal relationship.

Sexual intercourse can deepen and enrich a personal relationship only when it takes place within the reality of a personal relationship. This means that the preliminary questions two unmarried people must ask each other are: Do we already have a genuinely personal relationship that can be deepened and enriched? Do we have deep personal regard for each other? Do we treat each other now in integrity? Do we say no to any temptation to use each other? Did we accept each other as friends before sexual intercourse entered our heads? The possibility that sexual intercourse might be good for them travels with the answers to these preliminary considerations. Then they have to ask the clinching question: will sexual intercourse deepen and enrich or will it threaten and distort our relationship?

But how can they possibly know what it will do? First of all, each person has to examine himself. He or she will have to probe his/her own feelings and ask personal questions about them: Is he being exploitative? Is he pressing the other person to do something he/she may not want to do? Is he minimizing the other person's freedom and dignity? But these questions are about negative factors that could hurt the relationship. How does he know that sexual intercourse will actually strengthen the relationship? This exposes the Achilles' heel of the morality of personal relationships.

Furthermore, how can this standard be applied? How can two unmarried people know ahead of time whether sexual intercourse will enrich their relationship? They could probably try it and find out. But that would summarily throw the moral question out of court. And perhaps this is the only way out for the morality of personal relationships. At best, the decision has to be made on very uncertain personal insights: the people involved can only guess beforehand what will happen to their relationship after they have got out of bed. They can probe their readiness with all honesty and still not know for sure how they will feel toward each other afterward.

If we were talking about two people's date for dinner or a concert, almost any risk might be worth taking. But sexual intercourse opens trap doors to the inner cells of our conscience, and legions of little angels (or demons) can fly out to haunt us. There is such abandon, such explosive self-giving, such personal exposure that few people can feel the same toward each other afterward. And if one thinks he is ready, he cannot be sure the other person is. The problem is not just that one of the two will feel sour toward the other; the problem is that one of the partners may unleash feelings of need for the other that he/she had no inkling existed. He/she may thus be catapulted into a commitment that the other is not ready to take. And so the relationship can be injured by one person's making demands on it that the other is not ready for. And the person who is least committed is likely to withdraw inwardly from a relationship that demands more than he can give.

If we could somehow segregate people according to maturity, and if only people over fifty used the morality of personal relationships, we might have a workable standard. If in addition to this, the decision were made with moral assistance from a community of friends and family, it might be a usable norm. And if the decision were made in the cool of the day, it would at least be manageable. But unmarried people moving toward sexual intercourse include many people whose experience in durable and creative relationships is almost nil. A decision concerning sex is often made alone in the passions of the night, when every untested lust may seem like the promptings of pure love. Perhaps there is a moral elite who could responsibility use a moral guideline with as many loose ends as this one; but there is no way of knowing for sure who they are.

So we are back where we started. Each of the three moralities for sexual intercourse focuses on factors outside of the act itself. None of them assumes that sexual intercourse has a built-in factor that in itself would disqualify unmarried people for it. But Christian morality has traditionally believed that there is such a factor. For it has maintained that, even if nobody gets hurt and even if a personal relationship could be enriched by it, it is wrong for all but married people. It has taught that there is more to sexual intercourse than meets the eye—or excites the genitals. Sexual intercourse takes place within a context of what persons really are, how they are expected to fulfill their lives in sexual love, and how they are to live together in a community that is bigger than their private relationships. We now go on to ask about this special ingredient of sexual intercourse, for it stands behind the traditional Christian negative to unmarried people.

4. The Morality of Law

New Testament morality on this point is a morality of law. Some things were morally indifferent; Paul insisted on this. For some things there was no law except the law of love; and love flourished in freedom. But when people, as in Corinth, applied Christian freedom to sex, Paul put up fences. One of the fences was marriage. He made no distinctions between casual sex, sex between engaged couples, or sex between mature widowed people. The no was unqualified. The question is: Why?

Before getting into Paul's sexual morality, we must concede that the Old Testament gives him shaky support. Female virginity had a high premium; but male virginity was not all that important. And female virginity was demanded not so much for virginity's sake as for social reasons: the family line had to be guarded at all cost. And the male in particular had a right to be absolutely certain that his children were his own. The society had no place in it for the unmarried woman, no place except the brothel. So the rules said that if a woman had sexual intercourse before marriage, then tried to fake virginity with her bridegroom and was exposed by failure to produce a bloodied sheet, she would be executed forthwith (Deut. 22:13–21). However, this was probably not likely to happen. If a man slept with a virgin who was not betrothed, he was obligated to pay a dowry to her father and marry her (Deut. 22:28, 29). And the prospects for an unmarried girl who had lost her virginity were so bad that no woman was likely to keep quiet about the affair. She would at least tell her father, who, threatened with loss of dowry, would put the fear of God into a reneging sex partner. A man was in real trouble, however, if he slept with a virgin betrothed to another man; he was in trouble with her fiancé and with her father, for it was especially their rights that he had abused. He would be stoned to death; and if their act was discovered in the city, the woman would also be stoned—on the assumption that she failed to cry for help (Deut. 22:23–27). But if a man slept with a prostitute, nothing was said because nothing was lost. Casual sex between young people, however, was probably nonexistent. Once a boy slept with a girl, he was expected to marry her; and the girl was not likely to be noble about it and let him off the hook.

The Old Testament as a whole did not read the seventh commandment as a no to sexual intercourse between unmarried people. The morality of sexual intercourse did not rest with the character of the act as much as with its possible consequences. What was wrong was for a man's rights to be violated. Unmarried sex violated the command against stealing as clearly as it did the command against adultery.

The New Testament looks at the question from a very different standpoint. It has a blanket word for sexual immorality: *porneia*, translated as fornication in the older versions and as immorality in the newer. Fornication includes more than sexual intercourse between people who are not married. It does refer to breaking one's oath of fidelity to a husband or wife (Matt. 5:32; 19:9); but it could include a lot of other practices, like homosexual relations. And Paul makes clear that it also means sexual intercourse for unmarried people. In I Cor. 7 he concedes that to be both unmarried and a virgin is, under the circumstances, the best life. But "because of the temptation to immorality, each man should have his own wife and each woman her own husband" (I Cor. 7:2). Better to marry, he said, than to be ravished with unfulfilled desires. So he must have meant that "immorality" included sexual intercourse outside marriage. And if unmarried sexual intercourse was wrong, it was a serious wrong; it ought not even be talked about (Eph. 5:3). God's will is that we abstain from fornication, not giving way to "the passion of lust like heathen who do not know God" (I Thess. 4:6). Fornication is sin; intercourse by unmarried people is fornication; therefore, intercourse by unmarried people is sin.

We must now ask the crucial question about Paul's blanket rule. What is there about sexual intercourse that makes it morally improper for unmarried people? Surely not every instance of coitus by unmarried people is simply a surrender to lust "like the heathen." And if it is not in lust, and it hurts no one, why is it wrong? Did Paul assume that it would always be in lust or would always be harmful? And if some unmarried people's sex was not lustful, would it then be morally proper? Divine law, though often expressed in negative rules, is rooted in a positive insight. The law against adultery, for example, reflects a positive view of marriage and fidelity. And this view of marriage rests on an insight that God created men and women to live out their closest personal relationship in a permanent, exclusive union. We may suppose that behind Paul's vigorous attack on fornication is a positive view of sexual intercourse.

Sexual intercourse involves two people in a life-union; it is a life-uniting act. This is the insight that explains Paul's fervent comment on a member of Christ's body sleeping with a prostitute (I Cor. 6:12-20): "Do you not know that he who joins himself to a prostitute *becomes one body* with her?" (v. 16—italics mine). Of course, Paul is horrified that a prostitute is involved: a Christian man is a moral clown in a brothel. But the character of the woman involved is not his basic point. Paul would just as likely have said: "Do you not know that he who joins himself to the prim housewife next door becomes one body with her?" And the incongruity would have been the same. Paul bases his remark on the statement in Genesis 2 that "the two shall become one." And he sees sexual intercourse as an act that signifies and seeks the intrinsic unity—the unbreakable, total, personal unity that we call marriage.

It does not matter what the two people have in mind. The whore sells her body with an unwritten understanding that nothing personal will be involved in the deal. She sells the service of a quick genital massage—nothing more. The buyer gets his sexual needs satisfied without having anything personally difficult to deal with afterward. He pays his dues, and they are done with each other. But none of this affects Paul's point. The *reality* of the act, unfelt and unnoticed by them, is this: it unites them—body and soul—to each other. It unites them in that strange, impossible to pinpoint sense of "one flesh." There is no such thing as casual sex, no matter how casual people are about it. The Christian assaults reality in his night out at the brothel. He uses a woman and puts her back in a closet where she can be forgotten; but the reality is that he has put away a person with whom he has done something that was meant to inseparably join them. This is what is at stake for Paul in the question of sexual intercourse between unmarried people.

And now we can see clearly why Paul thought sexual intercourse by unmarried people was wrong. It is wrong because it violates the inner reality of the act; it is wrong because unmarried people thereby engage in a life-uniting act without a life-uniting intent. Whenever two people copulate without a commitment to life-union, they commit fornication.

Thus Paul's reason for saying no to sexual intercourse for the unmarried goes a crucial step beyond all the common practical reasons. We can suppose that Paul would appreciate anyone's reluctance to risk getting hurt; we can be sure he would see a Christian impulse in a person's concern for the other person; and we may assume that he would endorse the notion that sexual intercourse ought to promote the personal relationship between the two partners. But his absolute no to sexual intercourse for unmarried people is rooted in his conviction that it is a contradiction of reality. Intercourse signs and seals—and maybe even delivers—a life-union; and life-union means marriage.

Content Quiz 13.2

Instructions: Fill in the blanks with the appropriate responses listed below.

the morality of concern	New Testament
the morality of caution	morally neutral
the morality of law	ends
the morality of personal relationships	functional association
casual sex	life-uniting

1. _____ involves a type of cost-benefit analysis of hurt with respect to oneself.
2. _____ considers sexual intercourse outside of marriage as contrary to nature.
3. _____ differs from the morality of caution in so far as attention is directed toward the hurt likely to be caused to the other person.
4. _____ underscores the importance of establishing and maintaining an emotional bond between sex partners.
5. The morality of law is most closely related to the moral views expressed in the _____.
6. According to Smedes, there is no such thing as _____, only people who engage in intercourse lightly.
7. Smedes argues that if the acceptability of sexual intercourse is made contingent on circumstances and consequences, then intercourse outside of marriage becomes _____.
8. The morality of personal relationships dictates that other people should be regarded as _____ to be served, not as means to be used.
9. In situations where people mutually and openly use each other in sexual intercourse (i.e., prostitution), their relationship is transformed into a(n) _____.
10. From the perspective of Christian morality of law, intercourse is a(n) _____ act.

Discussion Questions

1. What normative moral theory would be most closely related to the morality of caution (utilitarianism, deontology, virtue-ethics)? Why?
2. How is the morality of caution different from the morality of concern? Could it be argued that the latter is more adequate than the former? Explain.
3. What is Smedes' worry about making the justifiability of sexual intercourse relative to circumstances and its consequences for other people?
4. Why does Smedes consider the morality of personal relationships inadequate?
5. Smedes uses the views of Saint Paul to explain what it is about sexual intercourse that makes it improper outside of marriage. What are those views? Do you agree or disagree? Why?

GAY BASICS: SOME QUESTIONS, FACTS, AND VALUES

Richard D. Mohr

Synopsis

As its title suggests, this article addresses some basic questions, facts, and values pertaining to gays (homosexuals) and gay experience. It is comprised of seven parts. In Part One, Mohr begins by asking "Who are gays anyway?"; citing research that a significant percentage of people have had homosexual experiences, he points out that gays come from all walks of life. In Part Two, Mohr suggests that ignorance about gays has led to unfortunate stereotyping that, indirectly, has had the negative effect of reinforcing traditional gender roles and maintaining a false sheen of absolute innocence for the nuclear family. In Part Three, Mohr discusses the widespread discrimination against gays and the violence directed toward them. In Part Four, he objects to the notion that the mistreatment of gays is acceptable because they are "immoral" anyway. We learn that historical and anthropological evidence has shown that opinion about gays has not always been universally negative, that the Bible does not clearly and unequivocally condemn it, and that even if it did, the separation of church and state would not permit systematic discrimination against gays on religious grounds. In Part Five, Mohr takes up the argument that homosexuality is "unnatural." After looking at different senses of "natural," he concludes that body parts like the mouth can have more than one "natural function" (e.g., eating, talking, love-making) and that procreation is not the only use of human genitalia. In Part Six, Mohr reminds us that to hold a person accountable for something over which the person has no control is a major form of prejudice. Arguing that gays do not "choose" homosexuality as a lifestyle, but "discover" it as a reality about themselves, they should not be held morally blameworthy nor condemned for who they find themselves to be. Finally, in Part Seven, Mohr challenges the idea that civilization would be threatened if gays were socially accepted. He supports his claims that cities would not crumble and families would not self-destruct by citing U.S. examples of states and cities where homosexual acts have been decriminalized and where statutes have already been passed to protect gays.

I. Who Are Gays Anyway?

A recent Gallup poll found that only one in five Americans reports having a gay or lesbian acquaintance.[1] This finding is extraordinary given the number of practicing homosexuals in America. Alfred Kinsey's 1948 study of the sex lives of 12,000 white males shocked the nation: 37 percent had at least one homosexual experience to orgasm in their adult lives; an additional 13 percent had homosexual fantasies to orgasm; 4 percent were exclusively homosexual in their practices; another 5 percent had virtually no heterosexual experience and nearly 20 percent had at least as many homosexual as heterosexual experiences.[2]

Two out of five men one passes on the street have had orgasmic sex with men. Every second family in the country has a member who is essentially homosexual and many more people regularly have homosexual experiences. Who are homosexuals? They are your friends, your minister, your teacher, your bank teller, your doctor, your mail carrier, your office-mate, your roommate, your congressional representative, your sibling, parent, and spouse. They are everywhere, virtually all ordinary, virtually all unknown.

Several important consequences follow. First, the country is profoundly ignorant of the actual experience of gay people. Second, social attitudes and practices that are harmful to gays have a much greater overall harmful impact on society than is usually realized. Third, most gay people live in hiding—in the closet—making the "coming out" experience the central fixture of gay consciousness and invisibility the chief characteristic of the gay community.

II. Ignorance, Stereotype, and Morality

Ignorance about gays, however, has not stopped people from having strong opinions about them. The void which ignorance leaves has been filled with stereotypes. Society holds chiefly two groups of anti-gay stereotypes; the two are an oddly contradictory lot. One set of stereotypes revolves around alleged mistakes in an individual's gender identity: lesbians are women that want to be, or at least look and act like, men—bull dykes, diesel dykes; while gay men are those who want to be, or at least look and act like, women—queens, fairies, limp-wrists, nellies. These stereotypes of mismatched genders provide the materials through which gays and lesbians become the butts of ethniclike jokes. These stereotypes and jokes, though derisive, basically view gays and lesbians as ridiculous.

Another set of stereotypes revolves around gays as a pervasive, sinister, conspiratorial threat. The core stereotype here is the gay person as child molester, and more generally as sex-crazed maniac. These stereotypes carry with them fears of the very destruction of family and civilization itself. . . .

[A]nti-gay stereotypes surrounding gender identification are chiefly means of reinforcing still powerful gender roles in society. If, as this stereotype presumes and condemns, one is free to choose one's social roles independently of gender, many guiding social divisions, both domestic and commercial, might be threatened. The socially gender-linked distinctions between breadwinner and homemaker, boss and secretary, doctor and nurse, protector and protected would blur. The accusations "dyke" and "fag" exist in significant part to keep women in their place and to prevent men from breaking ranks and ceding away theirs.

The stereotypes of gays as child molesters, sex-crazed maniacs, and civilization destroyers function to displace (socially irresolvable) problems from their actual source to a foreign (and so, it is thought, manageable) one. Thus the stereotype of child molester functions to give the family unit a sheen of absolute innocence. It keeps the unit from being examined too closely for incest, child abuse, wife-battering, and the terrorism of constant threats. The stereotype teaches that the problems of the family are not internal to it, but external.[3]

One can see these cultural forces at work in society's and the media's treatment of current reports of violence, especially domestic violence. When a mother kills her child or a father rapes his daughter—regular Section B fare even in major urban papers—this is never taken by reporters, columnists, or pundits as evidence that there is something wrong with heterosexuality or with traditional families. These issues are not even raised. But when a homosexual child molestation is reported it is taken as confirming evidence of the way homosexuals are. One never hears of heterosexual murders, but one regularly hears of "homosexual" ones. Compare the social treatment of Richard Speck's sexually motivated mass murder of Chicago nurses with that of John Wayne Gacy's murders of Chicago youths. Gacy was in the culture's mind taken as symbolic of gay men in general. To prevent the possibility that The Family was viewed as anything but an innocent victim in this affair, the mainstream press knowingly failed to mention that most of Gacy's adolescent victims were homeless hustlers. That knowledge would be too much for the six o'clock news and for cherished beliefs. . . .

III. Are Gays Discriminated Against? Does it Matter?

Partly because lots of people suppose they don't know any gay people and partly through willful ignorance of its own workings, society at large is unaware of the many ways in which gays are subject to discrimination in consequence of widespread fear and hatred. Contributing to this social ignorance of discrimination is the difficulty for gay people, as an invisible minority, even to complain of discrimination. For if one is gay, to register a complaint would suddenly target one as a stigmatized person, and so in the absence of any protections against discrimination, would simply invite additional discrimination. . . .

[G]ays are subject to violence and harassment based simply on their perceived status rather than because of any actions they have performed. A recent extensive study by the National Gay Task Force found that over 90 percent of gays and lesbians had been victimized in some form on the basis of their sexual orientation.[4] Greater than one in five gay men and nearly one in ten lesbians had been punched, hit, or kicked; a quarter of all gays had had objects thrown at them; a third had been chased; a third had been sexually harassed; and 14 percent had been spit on—all just for being perceived as gay.

The most extreme form of anti-gay violence is "queerbashing"—where groups of young men target a person who they suppose is a gay man and beat and kick him unconscious and sometimes to death amid a torrent of taunts and slurs. Such seemingly random but in reality socially encouraged violence has the same origin and function as lynchings of blacks—to keep a whole stigmatized group in line. As with lynchings of the recent past, the police and courts have routinely averted their eyes, giving their implicit approval to the practice.

Few such cases with gay victims reach the courts. Those that do are marked by inequitable procedures and results. Frequently judges will describe "queerbashers" as "just all-American boys." Recently a District of Columbia judge handed suspended sentences to queerbashers whose victim had been stalked, beaten, stripped at knife point, slashed, kicked, threatened with castration, and pissed on, because the judge thought the bashers were good boys at heart—after all, they went to a religious prep school.[5]

Police and juries will simply discount testimony from gays; they typically construe assaults on and murders of gays as "justified" self-defense—the killer need only claim his act was a panicked response to a sexual overture. Alternatively, when guilt seems patent, juries will accept highly implausible "diminished capacity" defenses, as in the case of Dan White's 1978 assassination of openly gay San Francisco city councilman Harvey Milk: Hostess Twinkies made him do it. . . .[6]

Gays are subject to widespread discrimination in employment—the very means by which one puts bread on one's table and one of the chief means by which individuals identify themselves to themselves and achieve personal dignity. Governments are leading offenders here. They do a lot of discriminating themselves, require that others do it (e.g., government contractors), and set precedents favoring discrimination in the private sector. The federal government explicitly discriminates against gays in the armed forces, the CIA, FBI, National Security Agency, and the state department. The federal government refuses to give security clearances to gays and so forces the country's considerable private sector military and aerospace contractors to fire known gay employees. State and local governments regularly fire gay teachers, policemen, firemen, social workers, and anyone who has contact with the public. Further, through licensing laws states officially bar gays from a vast array of occupations and professions—everything from doctors, lawyers, accountants, and nurses to hairdressers, morticians, and used car dealers. The American Civil Liberties Union's handbook *The Rights of Gay People* lists 307 such prohibited occupations.[7]

Gays are subject to discrimination in a wide

variety of other ways, including private-sector employment, public accommodations, housing, immigration and naturalization, insurance of all types, custody and adoption, and zoning regulations that bar "singles" or "nonrelated" couples. All of these discriminations affect central components of a meaningful life; some even reach to the means by which life itself is sustained. In half the states, where gay sex is illegal, the central role of sex to meaningful life is officially denied to gays. . . .

IV. But Aren't They Immoral?

Many people think society's treatment of gays is justified because they think gays are extremely immoral. To evaluate this claim, different senses of "moral" must be distinguished. Sometimes by "morality" is meant the overall beliefs affecting behavior in the society—its mores, norms, and customs. On this understanding, gays certainly are not moral: lots of people hate them and social customs are designed to register widespread disapproval of gays. The problem here is that this sense of morality is merely a *descriptive* one. On this understanding *every* society has a morality—even Nazi society, which had racism and mob rule as central features of its "morality," understood in this sense. What is needed in order to use the notion of morality to praise or condemn behavior is a sense of morality that is *prescriptive* or *normative*—a sense of morality whereby, for instance, the descriptive morality of the Nazis is found wanting. . . .

Furthermore, recent historical and anthropological research has shown that opinion about gays has been by no means universally negative. Historically, it has varied widely even within the larger part of the Christian era and even within the church itself.[8] There are even societies—current ones—where homosexuality is not only tolerated but a universal compulsory part of social maturation.[9] . . .

If popular opinion and custom are not enough to ground moral condemnation of homosexuality, perhaps religion can. . . .

One of the more remarkable discoveries of recent gay research is that the Bible may not be as univocal in its condemnation of homosexuality as has been usually believed.[10] Christ never mentions homosexuality. Recent interpreters of the Old Testament have pointed out that the story of Lot at Sodom is probably intended to condemn inhospitality rather than homosexuality. Further, some of the Old Testament condemnations of homosexuality seem simply to be ways of tarring those of the Israelites' opponents who happened to accept homosexual practices when the Israelites themselves did not. If so, the condemnation is merely a quirk of history and rhetoric rather than a moral precept.

What does seem clear is that those who regularly cite the Bible to condemn an activity like homosexuality do so by reading it selectively. Do ministers who cite what they take to be condemnations of homosexuality in Leviticus maintain in their lives all the hygienic and dietary laws of Leviticus? If they cite the story of Lot at Sodom to condemn homosexuality, do they also cite the story of Lot in the cave to praise incestuous rape? It seems then not that the Bible is being used to ground condemnations of homosexuality as much as society's dislike of homosexuality is being used to interpret the Bible.[11]

Even if a consistent portrait of condemnation could be gleaned from the Bible, what social significance should it be given? One of the guiding principles of society, enshrined in the Constitution as a check against the government, is that decisions affecting social policy are not made on religious grounds. If the real ground of the alleged immorality invoked by governments to discriminate against gays is religious (as it has explicitly been even in some recent court cases involving teachers and guardians), then one of the major commitments of our nation is violated.

V. But Aren't They Unnatural?

. . . Though the accusation of unnaturalness looks whimsical, in actual ordinary discourse when applied to homosexuality, it is usually delivered with venom aforethought. It carries a high emotional charge, usually expressing disgust and evincing queasiness. Probably it is nothing but an emotional charge. For people get equally disgusted and queasy at all sort of things that are perfectly natural—to be expected in nature apart from artifice—and that could hardly be fit subjects for moral condemnation. Two typical examples in current American culture are some people's responses to mothers' suckling in public and to women who do not shave body hair. When people have strong emotional reactions, as they do in these cases, without being able to give good reasons for them, we think of them not as operating morally, but rather as being obsessed and manic. So the feelings of disgust that some people have to gays will hardly ground a charge of immorality. People fling the term "unnatural" against gays in the same breath and with the same force as when they call gays "sick" and "gross." When they do this, they give every appearance of being neurotically fearful and incapable of reasoned discourse.

When "nature" is taken in *technical* rather than ordinary usages, it looks like the notion also will not ground a charge of homosexual immorality. When unnatural means "by artifice" or "made by humans," it need only be pointed out that virtually everything that is good about life is unnatural in this sense, that the chief feature that distinguishes people from other animals is their very ability to make over the world to meet their needs and desires, and that their well-being depends upon these departures from nature. On this understanding of human nature and the natural, homosexuality is perfectly unobjectionable.

Another technical sense of natural is that something is natural and so, good, if it fulfills some function in nature. Homosexuality on this view is unnatural because it allegedly violates the function of genitals, which is to produce babies. One problem with this view is that lots of bodily parts have lots of functions and just because some one activity can be fulfilled by only one organ (say, the mouth for eating) this activity does not condemn other functions of the organ to immorality (say, the mouth for talking, licking stamps, blowing bubbles, or having sex). So the possible use of the genitals to produce children does not, without more, condemn the use of the genitals for other purposes, say, achieving ecstasy and intimacy. . . .

Further, ordinary moral attitudes about childbearing will not provide the needed supplement which in conjunction with the natural function view of bodily parts would produce a positive obligation to use the genitals for procreation. Society's attitude toward a childless couple is that of pity not censure—even if the couple could have children. . . . The couple who discovers they cannot have children are viewed not as having thereby had a debt canceled, but rather as having to forgo some of the richness of life, just as a quadriplegic is viewed not as absolved from some moral obligation to hop, skip, jump, but as missing some of the richness of life.

Consistency requires then that, at most, gays who do not or cannot have children are to be pitied rather than condemned. What *is* immoral is the willful preventing of people from achieving the richness of life. Immorality in this regard lies with those social customs, regulations, and statutes that prevent lesbians and gay men from establishing blood or adoptive families, not with gays themselves . . . .

If one looks to people . . . for a model—and looks hard enough—one finds amazing variety, including homosexuality as a social ideal (upper-class fifth-century Athens) and even as socially mandatory (Melanesia today). When one looks to people, one is simply unable to strip away the layers of social custom, history, and taboo in order to see what's really there to any degree more specific than that people are the creatures that make over their world and are capable of abstract thought. That this is so should raise doubts that neutral principles are to be found in human nature that will condemn homosexuality.

On the other hand, if one looks to nature apart from people for models, the possibilities are staggering. There are fish that change gender over their lifetimes: should we "follow nature" and be operative transsexuals? Orangutans, genetically our next of kin, live completely solitary lives without social organization of any kind: ought we to "follow nature" and be hermits? There are many species where only two members per generation reproduce: should we be bees? The search in nature for people's purpose, far from finding sure models for action, is likely to leave one morally rudderless.

VI. But Aren't Gays Willfully the Way They Are?

It is generally conceded that if sexual orientation is something over which an individual—for whatever reason—has virtually no control, then discrimination against gays is especially deplorable, as it is against racial and ethnic classes, because it holds people accountable without regard for anything they themselves have done. And to hold a person accountable for that over which the person has no control is a central form of prejudice.

Attempts to answer the question whether or not sexual orientation is something that is reasonably thought to be within one's own control usually appeal simply to various claims of the biological or "mental" sciences. But the ensuing debate over genes, hormones, twins, early childhood development, and the like, is as unnecessary as it is currently inconclusive.[12] All that is needed to answer the question is to look at the actual experience of gays in current society and it becomes fairly clear that sexual orientation is not likely a matter of choice. For coming to have a homosexual identity simply does not have the same sort of structure that decision making has.

On the one hand, the "choice" of the gender of a sexual partner does not seem to express a trivial desire that might be as easily well fulfilled by a simple substitution of the desired object. Picking the gender of a sex partner is decidedly dissimilar, that is, to such activities as picking a flavor of ice cream. If an ice-cream parlor is out of one's flavor, one simply picks another. And if people were persecuted, threatened with jail terms, shattered careers, loss of family and housing, and the like, for eating, say, rocky road ice cream, no one would ever eat it; everyone would pick another easily available flavor. That gay people abide in being gay even in the face of persecution shows that being gay is not a matter of easy choice.

On the other hand, even if establishing a sexual orientation is not like making a relatively trivial choice, perhaps it is nevertheless relevantly like making the central and serious life choices by which individuals try to establish themselves as being of some type. Again, if one examines gay experience, this seems not to be the case. For one never sees anyone setting out to become a homosexual, in the way one does see people setting out to become doctors, lawyers, and bricklayers. One does not find "gays-to-be" picking some end—"At some point in the future, I want to become a homosexual"—and then setting about planning and acquiring the ways and means to that end, in the way one does see people deciding that they want to become lawyers, and then sees them plan what courses to take and what sort of temperaments, habits, and skills to develop in order to become lawyers. Typically gays-to-be simply find themselves having homosexual encounters and yet at least initially resisting quite strongly the identification of being homosexual. . . . Only with time, luck, and great personal effort, but sometimes never, does the person gradually come to accept her or his orientation, to view it as a given material condition of life, coming as materials do with certain capacities and limitations. The person begins to act in accordance with his or her orientation and its capacities, seeing its actualization as a requisite for an integrated personality and as a central component of personal well-being. As a result, the experience of coming out to oneself has for gays the basic structure of a discovery, not the structure of a choice. . . .

VII. How Would Society at Large Be Changed if Gays Were Socially Accepted?

Suggestions to change social policy with regard to gays are invariably met with claims that to do so would invite the destruction of civilization itself: after all, isn't that what did Rome in? Actually Rome's decay paralleled not the flourishing of homosexuality but its repression under the later Christianized emperors.[13] Predictions of American civilization's imminent demise have been as premature as they have been frequent. Civilization has shown itself rather resilient here, in large part because of the country's traditional commitments to a respect for privacy, to individual liberties, and especially to people minding their own business. . . .

Half the states have decriminalized homosexual acts. Can you guess which of the following states still have sodomy laws: Wisconsin, Minnesota; New Mexico, Arizona; Vermont, New Hampshire; Nebraska, Kansas. One from each pair does and one does not have sodomy laws. And yet one would be hard pressed to point out any substantial difference between the members of each pair. (If you're interested, it is the second of each pair with them.) Empirical studies have shown that there is no increase in other crimes in states that have decriminalized.[14] Further, sodomy laws are virtually never enforced. They remain on the books not to "protect society" but to insult gays, and for that reason need to be removed.

Neither has the passage of legislation barring discrimination against gays ushered in the end of civilization. Some 50 counties and municipalities, including some of the country's largest cities (like Los Angeles and Boston), have passed such statutes and among the states and colonies Wisconsin and the District of Columbia have model protective codes. Again, no more brimstone has fallen in these places than elsewhere. Staunchly antigay cities, like Miami and Houston, have not been spared the AIDS crisis.

Berkeley, California, has even passed domestic partner legislation giving gay couples the same rights to city benefits as married couples, and yet Berkeley has not become more weird than it already was.

Seemingly hysterical predictions that the American family would collapse if such reforms would pass proved false, just as the same dire predictions that the availability of divorce would lessen the ideal and desirability of marriage proved completely unfounded. Indeed if current discriminations, which drive gays into hiding and into anonymous relations, were lifted, far from seeing gays raze American families, one would see gays forming them.

Virtually all gays express a desire to have a permanent lover. Many would like to raise or foster children—perhaps those alarming numbers of gay kids who have been beaten up and thrown out of their "families" for being gay. But currently society makes gay coupling very difficult. A life of hiding is a pressure-cooker existence not easily shared with another. Members of non-gay couples are here asked to imagine what it would take to erase every trace of their own sexual orientation for even just a week. . . .

Finally . . ., in extending to gays the rights and benefits it has reserved for its dominant culture, America would confirm its deeply held vision of itself as a morally progressing nation, a nation itself advancing and serving as a beacon for others—especially with regard to human rights. The words with which our national pledge ends—"with liberty and justice for all"—are not a description of the present but a call for the future. Ours is a nation given to a prophetic political rhetoric which acknowledges that morality is not arbitrary and that justice is not merely the expression of the current collective will. It is this vision that led the black civil rights movement to its successes. Those congressmen who opposed that movement and its centerpiece, the 1964 Civil Rights Act, on obscurantist grounds, but who lived long enough and were noble enough, came in time to express their heartfelt regret and shame at what they had done. It is to be hoped and someday to be expected that those who now grasp at anything to oppose the extension of that which is best about America to gays will one day feel the same.

Notes

1. "Public Fears—And Sympathies," *Newsweek*, August 12, 1985, p. 23.
2. Alfred C. Kinsey, *Sexual Behavior in the Human Male* (Philadelphia: Saunders, 1948), pp. 650–51. On the somewhat lower incidences of lesbianism, see Alfred C. Kinsey, *Sexual Behavior in the Human Female* (Philadelphia: Saunders, 1953), pp. 472–475.
3. For studies showing that gay men are no more likely—indeed, are less likely—than heterosexuals to be child molesters and that the largest groups of sexual abusers of children and the people most persistent in their molestation of children are the children's fathers or stepfathers or mother's boyfriends, see Vincent De Francis, *Protecting the Child Victim of Sex Crimes Committed by Adults* (Denver: The American Humane Association, 1969), pp. vii, 38, 69–70; A. Nicholas Groth, "Adult Sexual Orientation and Attraction to Underage Persons," *Archives of Sexual Behavior* 7 (1978): 175–181; Mary J. Spencer, "Sexual Abuse of Boys," *Pediatrics* 78, no. 1 (July 1986): 133–138.
4. See National Gay Task Force, *Anti-Gay/Lesbian Victimization* (New York: NGTF, 1984).

5. "2 St. John's Students Given Probation in Assault on Gay," *The Washington Post*, May 15, 1984, p. 1.
6. See Randy Shilts, *The Mayor of Castro Street: The Life and Times of Harvey Milk* (New York: St. Martin's, 1982), pp. 308–325.
7. E. Carrington Boggan, *The Rights of Gay People: The Basic ACLU Guide to a Gay Person's Rights* (New York: Avon, 1975), pp. 211–235.
8. John Boswell, *Christianity, Social Tolerance and Homosexuality: Gay People in Western Europe from the Beginning of the Christian Era to the Fourteenth Century* (Chicago: University of Chicago Press, 1980).
9. See Gilbert Herdt, *Guardians of the Flute: Idioms of Masculinity* (New York: McGraw-Hill, 1981), pp. 232–239, 284–288; and see generally Gilbert Herdt, ed., *Ritualized Homosexuality in Melanesia* (Berkeley: University of California Press, 1984). For another eye-opener, see Walter L. Williams, *The Spirit and the Flesh: Sexual Diversity in American Indian Culture* (Boston: Beacon, 1986).
10. See especially Boswell, *Christianity*, ch. 4.
11. For Old Testament condemnations of homosexual acts, see Leviticus 18:22, 21:3. For hygienic and dietary codes, see, for example, Leviticus 15:19–27 (on the uncleanliness of women) and Leviticus 11:1–47 (on not eating rabbits, pigs, bats, finless water creatures, legless creeping creatures, etc.). For Lot at Sodom, see Genesis 19:1–25. For Lot in the cave, see Genesis 19:30–38.
12. The preponderance of the scientific evidence supports the view that homosexuality is either genetically determined or a permanent result of early childhood development. See the Kinsey Institute's study by Alan Bell, Martin Weinberg, and Sue Hammersmith, *Sexual Preference: Its Development in Men and Women* (Bloomington: Indiana University Press, 1981); Frederick Whitam and Robin Mathy, *Male Homosexuality in Four Societies* (New York: Praeger, 1986), ch. 7.
13. See Boswell, *Christianity*, ch. 3.
14. See Gilbert Geis, "Reported Consequences of Decriminalization of Consensual Adult Homosexuality in Seven American States," *Journal of Homosexuality* 1, no. 4 (1976): 419–426; Ken Sinclair and Michael Ross, "Consequences of Decriminalization of Homosexuality: A Study of Two Australian States," *Journal of Homosexuality* 12, no. 1 (1985): 119–127.

Content Quiz 13.3

Instructions: Fill in the blanks with the appropriate responses listed below.

queerbashing
universally negative
discovery
procreation
gay stereotypes
discrimination
hysterical predictions
social attitudes and practices
selectively
church and state

1. _____ that are harmful to gays have a much greater overall harmful impact on society than is generally realized, because of the numbers of practicing homosexuals in America.
2. _____ deflect attention from traditional gender-role identifications and the problems inherent in the nuclear family.
3. _____ takes place when groups of people gang up on a person they suppose is gay and beat and kick that person unconscious and sometimes to death, amid a torrent of taunts and slurs.
4. Gays are subject to widespread _____ in employment, especially in government, but also in the private sector.
5. Historical and anthropological research reveals that attitudes and opinions toward the gay population have by no means been _____.
6. The Bible cannot be used to condemn and prohibit homosexuality by law or statute, certainly not in a country that separates _____.
7. _____ is not the only "natural function" of human genitalia.
8. Homosexuality is not a rational choice, but a _____ about oneself and one's sexual orientation.
9. The claim that legalizing homosexuality and barring discrimination against gays will destroy the conventional institutions of family and marriage is based on _____.
10. Those who cite the Bible to condemn homosexuality do so by reading it _____.

Discussion Questions

1. Do the statistics cited by Mohr convince you that homosexuality and homosexual experiences are as widespread and common as he alleges? Why or why not?
2. How do people often stereotype gays? What do these stereotypes serve to do indirectly?
3. How are gays treated generally in North American society?
4. What could gays say in response to the claim that they deserve what they get because of their own sexual immorality?
5. How could a gay defend against the charge that homosexuality is unnatural?
6. Should gays not accept the negative consequences of choosing a homosexual lifestyle?
7. Is it true that the basic traditional institutions of society (e.g., the family) are threatened if we promote gays and gay rights? Why?

A CASE AGAINST HOMOSEXUALITY

Paul Cameron

Synopsis

In this article, Paul Cameron presents a case against homosexuality. He claims that past social policies that have discriminated in favor of heterosexuality and against homosexuality are required to maintain the social good. Cameron makes no apologies for discrimination as such. For societies to function properly, discriminatory judgments and decisions must be made constantly he says. The question thus becomes one of justification. Is the discrimination called for? And, how much is necessary? Cameron's point is that homosexuals should, quite properly, be discriminated against and that reasoned opinion can be offered in support of such action.

Because homosexuals are the ones who wish to make social changes, Cameron places the burden of proof on them to show that homosexuality is not socially disruptive, something he claims they have yet failed to do. He seems disinclined to accommodate homosexuals claiming that, because of a variety of factors discussed, odds are already tilted in favor of children developing homosexual preferences in the first place, unless they are taught and encouraged otherwise. For Cameron, sexuality is something learned and it is in society's interest to promote roles and traits that contribute to social cohesion and betterment. For Cameron, pro-social elements are most clearly developed in a context of heterosexuality and heterosexual relationships. By contrast, in ways illustrated by Cameron, homosexuality does not promote effort and durability in social relationships, nor does it further delay of gratification, all necessary features of a successfully functioning social system. Beyond this, homosexuality presents obstacles to personal happiness because it does little to foster trust and long-term caring relationships.

In some segments of the mass media, the homosexuality issue takes on the appearance of a struggle between orange juice peddlers and bathhouse owners. At a different level individual rights vs. the interests of society provide the conflict. Some argue that adult homosexuals ought to be allowed to do what they want behind closed doors. Others, often seeing the issue in terms of rights, honesty, and overpopulation, seek to grant homosexuality equal status with heterosexuality. The school system of San Francisco, apparently resonating with the latter tack, is offering a course including "homosexual life-styles." Liberals attempt to shame as unenlightened all who oppose complete equality as vigorously as conservative Bible-thumpers threaten wrath from above.

No known human society has ever granted equal status to homo- and heterosexuality. What information do those who desire social equivalence for these two sexual orientations possess that assures them that this new venture in human social organization is called for at this time? Have the cultures of the past practiced discrimination against homosexuality out of a mere prejudice, or was there substance to their bias? At the risk of seeming rather out of step with the academic community, no new information has surfaced that would lead me to discount the social policies of the past. On the contrary, the policies of the past in regard to homosexuality appear generally wise, and considerable discrimination against homosexuality and for heterosexuality, marriage and parenthood appears needful for the social good.

Discrimination

Discrimination is something all humans, and all human communities do. Individually we discriminate for certain things and against others, e.g., movies over T.V. Collectively we discriminate for and against selected: 1) acts (pleasantries, sharing vs. murder, robbery) 2) traits (generous, kind vs. whiny, hostile) and 3) life-styles (independent, productive vs. gambling, indolent). Prejudice is unwarranted discrimination. The issue is not whether discrimination should exist—for human society to exist, it must. The issues are always: 1) is discrimination called for? and 2) how much is necessary? Reasonable people can and do disagree on what ought to be discriminated for and against, to what degree, and even if discrimination is prejudicial rather than called for. But reasoned opinion *can* hold that homosexuality and homosexuals ought to be discriminated against. . . .

The Case Against Homosexuality/Wisdom of the Ages

No contemporary society accords homosexuality equivalent status with heterosexuality. No known society has accorded equivalent status in the past (Karlen, 1971). No current or ancient religion of any consequence has failed to teach discrimination against homosexuality. The Judeo-Christian tradition is no exception to this rule. The Old Testament made homosexuality a capital offense, and while the New Testament writers failed to invoke capital punishment for any offense, they did manage to consign homosexuals to eternal hell for the practice. Church fathers and traditions have stayed in line with this position until recently. To the degree that tradition and agreed-upon social policy ought to carry weight in our thinking about issues, the weight of tradition is preponderately on the side of discrimination. . . .

While one cannot carry the "wisdom of the ages" argument too far—just because all peoples up to a certain point in time believed something does not necessarily mean that it was so—yet it appears more than a little injudicious to cast it aside as merely "quaint." Probably no issue has occupied man's collective attentions more than successful living together. That such unanimity of opinion and practice should exist must give one pause. Certainly such congruence "puts the ball in the changer's court." As in so many spheres of human endeavor, when we know that we can get on in a particular way, the burden of proof that we can get on as well or better by following a different custom falls upon those seeking the change. . . .

To date, those seeking change have not been flush with scientific evidence that homosexuality is not socially disruptive. On the contrary, the arguments that have been advanced have been little more than "people ought not to be discriminated against; homosexuals are people; ergo homosexuals ought not to be discriminated against" shouted larger and louder. No one to my knowledge has ever claimed that homosexuals were not people, and one would have to be a dunce to believe that being a person qualifies one, *ipso facto*, for nondiscrimination. Aside from this argument repeated in endless variations and *ad nauseam*, the evidence is simply not there. . . .

Homosociality Coupled With Increasing Self-Centeredness Could Lead to Widespread Homosexuality

. . . Jimmy Carter said: "I don't see homosexuality as a threat to the family" *(Washington Post*, June 19, 1977). His sentiments probably echo those of the educated class of our society. They trust that "only deviants" are really into homosexuality anyway, and, more importantly, that "mother nature" will come through in the last analysis. Biology, they assume, has a great deal to do with sexuality and sexual attraction, and millions of years of heterosexuality has firmly engraved itself on the genetic code.

Such thinking betrays a lack of appreciation of the enormous component of learning that goes into human sexuality. The point that anthropology has made over the past hundred years is the *tremendous diversity of human social organization*. . . . While the onset of the events of puberty vary relatively little from one society to another, the onset of copulation varies over a full quarter of the life-span—from 5 or 6 years of age to mid-20s. . . . Many mammals practice sex for only a few days or weeks in the year, but man varies from untrammeled lust to studied virginity. While I have enumerated my reasons more fully elsewhere (Cameron, 1977), I believe that the most reasonable construal of the evidence to date suggests that *human sexuality is totally learned*. . . .

Because human sexuality is totally learned, humans must be pointed in the "right" direction, and taught how and with whom to perform. And there's the rub. Homosexuality and heterosexuality do not start off on the same footing. *Au contraire*, one gets a number of important boosts in the scheme of things. In our society the development process is decidedly *tilted toward the adoption of homosexuality*!

Part of the homosexual tilt is the extreme homosociality of children starting around the age of 5. As everyone is aware, boys want to play with boys and girls with girls, and they do so with a vengeance. It's quite reasonable, on their part. First, boys' and girls' bodies are different and they are aware that their bodies-to-be will differ still more. In part because of this the games, sports and skills they practice differ. As if in anticipation of the differing roles they will have, their interests and proclivities differ. Even if they try, few girls can do as well as most boys at "boy things" and few boys can do as well as girls at "girl things." They almost inhabit different worlds. Not surprisingly for members of two different "races," poles apart psychologically, socially, and physically, they "stick to their own kind." . . .

There are three other components that contribute to the homosexual tilt. First, on the average in our society, males are considerably more taken with sex than females are. In my 1975 survey of 818 persons on the east coast of the U.S., respondents were asked to rate the degree of pleasure they obtained from 22 activities including "being with one's family," "listening to music," "being out in nature," "housework," and "sexual activity." Between the late teens through middle age, sexual activity topped the male list as the "most pleasurable activity." It did manage to rank as high as fifth place for young adult women (aged 18 to 25), but, overall for the female life span, was outscored by almost everything including "housework" (which, incidentally, ranked dead last among males). . . .

How well suited are "hot" males to "cool" females? Not very. One of (if not the) most common problems in marital counseling is sexual incompatibility. *Females pay sex as the price of love/companionship and males pay love for sex.* While this is rather too aphoristic to capture all that goes on in the male-female struggle, there is a great deal of truth to it. Even among homosexuals, the males probably out sex lesbians by a factor of 5 to 1 (see Tripp's sympathetic treatment for elaboration on this theme). Where is a male most apt to find his counterpart, among maledom or femaledom? If he wants hot, dripping sex, what better place to find it than with another of similar bent? If she wants tender companionship, which sex is most apt to provide the partner? The answers are obvious.

The second part of the homosexual tilt derives from the fact that [the] *homosexual encounter offers better sex*, on the average, *than heterosexual sex*. If pleasure is what you are after, who better to fulfill you than a partner who has a body and predilections like yours? One of the things that both the male homosexual and lesbian societies advertise is that "they satisfy" . . . From a sexual standpoint, a female can offer a little extra orifice as compensation for her: ignorance, timidity, desire for companionship first, etc. Further, sex between members of a sex assures that there will be no pregnancy problems further on down the line.

Another developmental boost for homosexuality comes from the self-servingness/egocentricity of the young. Humans are born with, at best, rudimentary consciousness. Then, over time and experience, they learn to differentiate themselves from the environment. From about the age of 5 or 6 onward for the next decade or so for life, they are engrossed in themselves, in the service of themselves, their pleasures, their interests, their ways. Reciprocity of interaction is rendered begrudgingly, certainly far from spontaneously. My research, involving the interviewing of over 8,000 respondents from the U.S. and five other nations, in which we asked persons to tell us: 1) whose interests they had just been thinking about serving—their own or another's or others' and 2) whether they had just been thinking about themselves, things, or other people, indicated that younger persons more frequently reported themselves in a self-serving attitude and thinking about themselves than adults did. In the U.S., adults of both sexes typically reported themselves in an other-serving attitude. But U.S. males "switched" from self-servingness to other-servingness around age 26 while for females the switch occurred in the middle teens. If one is after self-fulfillment, pleasure for self, which sexual orientation "fits" better? Homosexuality, obviously. One can have his homosociality and sex too. One can comfortably neglect the painful transformation from self-interest to other-interest. Me and mine to the fore.

Which kind of sexuality is the more compelling? The one that can say "come, sex my way and I will show you a life of complexity. Of children and responsibility. Of getting on with 'that other kind.' I will offer you poorer sex initially, and, who knows, perhaps you will just have to satisfy yourself with poorer sex permanently. But you will be able to 'glimpse immortality in your children' (Plato)." Or "come, sex my way and I will give it to you straight and hot. Pleasures of the best quality, almost on demand, with persons with whom you already share a great deal, and I will enable you to share more. It will not be difficult, in fact, it will be fun. You will not have to change or adapt your personality style or your egocentric orientation. You'll fit right in immediately. None of this hemming and hawing—you'll get what you want when you want it. Motto? Pleasure—now. The future? Who knows, but the present is going to be a dilly." Which kind of sexuality is the more compelling? Does anyone doubt which way most youth would turn if equivalent social status attended homosexuality and heterosexuality? . . .

A Cluster of Undesirable Traits is Disproportionately Associated With Homosexuality

Though some may shriek that "my personality traits are my business," let us acknowledge that some traits are society's business. A person's traits can lead to actions which affect the collectivity. Megalomania often proves socially disruptive, and sometimes, as in the case of Hitler, leads to incredible human destruction. It is obviously in society's interest to encourage those social roles and traits that tend to social cohesion and betterment. Similarly, it is in the social interest to discourage those that tend to produce disruption and harm. . . .

It would be as silly to contend that each of the following traits is associated with each homosexual as to argue that none of these appear in heterosexuals (or even worse, that the obverse of these traits always accompanies heterosexuality). However, for social policy formulation, it is enough to demonstrate disproportionate "loading" of undesirable traits within a given subgroup or subculture to justify social discrimination.

The Egocentric/Supercilious/Narcissistic/Self-Oriented/Hostile Complex

This cluster of traits appears to "go together" with homosexuality. . . . A person who, in part, seeks more of himself in his lover, is more apt to remain in the egocentric/self-centered orientation of youth. Such a person is more apt to gravitate toward those kinds of professions in which he can be a "star" and be noticed. . . .

The "star" lives for gratification of self. *My* way is his motto. . . . The star need not accommodate himself to the needs of others to the same degree as most folk. If a current love is "not working out" he can be discarded and a more suitable one found. . . .

Superciliousness—an attitude of aloof, hostile disdain—is also consonant with the egocentric person. If you will not realize his marvelous qualities and pay homage, he still has you one down. After all he treated you with contempt *first*. Even if you become hostile, his preceded yours. . . .

The greatest component of the childish "I want it my way" associated with homosexuality stems, in part, from the greater ease connected with homosexual attachments. Developmentally, both hetero- and homosexuals want things "their way." But the kinds of accommodations and adjustments necessary for successful heterosexuality assure participants that it won't be all their way. Just because so much of the time things don't work out perfectly in the face of such effort helps wean one from the coddled security of childhood. Parents and the rest of society work to "make the world nice" for children. Every childhood painting is worthy of note, as is every musical note. But adulthood is strewn with disappointments. Heterosexuality is a "maturing" sexual orientation. . . .

It appears to me that homosexuality leads to a shallower commitment to society and its betterment. Such shallowness comes about both because of a lack of children and the ease of sexual gratification. The *effort* involved in being heterosexual, the *effort* expended in being a parent—these are denied the homosexual. As he *has* less responsibility and commitment, so he *is* or becomes less responsible and committed. It is difficult to develop personality characteristics that fail to resonate with one's environment. While we are not totally creatures of our environment, it is far easier to "swim with the tide."

It is difficult to find anything like "hard" scientific evidence to substantiate the notion that homosexuals are on the average, less responsible/trustworthy than heterosexuals. The Weinberg and Williams sample of homosexuals was asked a question that bears upon the issue. Do you agree or disagree with the statement "most people can be trusted"? To a degree, since a person cannot know "most people" it appears reasonable to assume that he might project his own personality onto "most people" and/or assume that those people with whom he comes in contact are like "most people." While 77% of a reasonably representative sample of the U.S. population chose "agree," only 47% of the homosexuals ticked the same response. Because of the ambiguity of such items, I would not make too much of the difference. But it could suggest that homosexuals are less trustworthy.

Homosexuality is Associated With Personal Lethality

One of the more troubling traits associated with homosexuality is personal lethality. Extending back in time to classical Greece, a lethal theme shines through. In Greece, if historical sources are to be believed, companies of homosexual warriors were assembled because it was believed that they made better killers. The same pattern appears to be repeated in history. . . .

In our society the childless are more apt to suicide and childless couples are more apt to be involved in homicide. Further, both suicide and homicide accompany divorce and separation disproportionately frequently. Social cohesion needs to be developed and maintained for optimum personal and social health. . . .

Heterosexuality Provides the Most Desirable Model of Love

Myths are created not only by storytellers but by people living within the myths. Almost all (95% or so) heterosexuals get married, and 75%-80% stay married to their original partner till death. To be sure, there are marriage "hogs" within the heterosexual camp who play serial monogamy and assure that a third of all marriages end in divorce. Further, about half of all married men and about a third of all married women admit to one or more infidelities over the duration of their marriage (probably the greater bulk of the "cheaters" come from the serial monogamy camp). While heterosexuality's colors are far from simon pure, the relationship heterosexuality spawns is among, if not *the*, most enduring of human bonds. . . .

Homosexuality offers no comparison in durability. While "slam, bam, thank you ma'am" occurs in heterosexuality, few heterosexuals could more than fantasize about what occurs in homosexual bathhouses or tearooms. As Weinberg and Williams note, the homosexual community typically features "sex for sex's sake." Their survey in which two thirds of their respondents chose to respond "no" to whether they had limited their ". . . sexual relationships primarily to (another)" is telling. Names and banter are typically neglected in bathhouses. . . .

When people are merely "getting their jollies," and fantasizing perfection while doing so, reduced communication is an asset. If you discover that your beautiful lover holds political views antithetical to your own, how can you really enjoy him/her? The "less known the better" is fantasy sex. Communicating, mutually knowledgeable people often have to "work it out" before attempts at sex can even occur. But while typically short on durability, some homosexual relationships are more lasting. The quality of even these is often questionably desirable. Part of the problem lies in the lack of commitment that follows lower effort in the homosexual pairing. Tripp, for instance, opines that part ". . . of the reason many homosexual relationships do not survive the first serious quarrel is that one or both partners simply find it much easier to remarket themselves than work out conflicts (p. 155)." In heterosexuality, no matter how similar the participants, there is always a considerable gap between them. To stay together takes great effort, and the expenditure of this effort prompts both personal and social commitment to the partner. . . .

Because the heterosexual partners are so dissimilar, accommodation and adjustment are their key strategies. Because mutually satisfying heterosexual sexing takes so long and so much effort, both participants have to "hang in there" long after "sane people" would have toddled off in frustration. *We become the way we act. The heterosexual relationship places a premium on "getting on" and thus provides a model to smooth countless other human interactions.* The homosexual model is a considerably less satisfactory one upon which to build a civilization. Note Tripp again (p. 167): ". . . the problems encountered in balancing heterosexual and homosexual relationships are strikingly different. The heterosexual blend tends to be rich in stimulating contrasts and short on support—so much so that popular marriage counseling literature incessantly hammers home the advice that couples should develop common interests and dissolve their conflicts by increasing their 'communication.' By comparison, homosexual relationships are overclose, fatigue-prone, and are often adjusted to such narrow, trigger-sensitive tolerances that a mere whisper of disrapport can jolt the partners into making repairs, or into conflict." . . .

Our social system also features large components of delay of gratification. The heterosexual "carrot" is hard to get and requires a lot of input before successful outcome is achieved. The homosexual model is too immediate and influences people to expect instant results. . . .

In short, heterosexuality is effortful, durable, and demands delay of gratification. While any human relationship takes effort, homosexuality pales in comparison to heterosexuality on each count. . . .

From the prudent standpoint, homosexuality is an obstacle in the pursuit of happiness. . . .

Does homosexuality make being happy more difficult? In the Weinberg and Williams study, homosexuals were asked to respond "yes" or "no" to the statement "no one cares what happens to you." While a general population sample had chosen "yes" 23% of the time, 34% of homosexuals chose "yes." . . . Homosexuality, with its emphasis upon self-gratification, does little to generate others who care about you. . . . *In the long run*, heterosexuality has a lot more to offer as a life-style than homosexuality. . . .

Summary

In sum, there are a number of reasons why homosexuality is best treated as a deviant sexual mode. I do not believe that homosexuality ought to be placed on an even-keel with heterosexuality. Further, homosexuals ought not, in my opinion, to be permitted to openly ply their sexual orientation and retain influential positions in the social system. Thus teachers, or pastors who "come out," ought, in my opinion, to lose their claim to the roles they occupy.

References

Allport, G. W. *The Person in Psychology*. NY: Beacon, 1961.
Atkins, J. *Sex in Literature*. NY: Grove Press, 1970.
Bergler, E. *Homosexuality: Disease or Way of Life?* NY: Macmillan, 1956.
Bieber, I. *Homosexuality: A Psychoanalytic Study*. NY: Basic Books, 1962.
Cameron, P. "Immolations to the Juggernaut," *Linacre Quarterly*, 1977, 44, 64–74.
Cameron, P. *The Life-Cycle: Perspectives and Commentary*. NY: General Health, 1977.
Cameron, P. & Oeschger, D. "Homosexuality in the Mass Media as Indexed by Magazine Literature over the Past Half Century in the U.S." Paper presented at Eastern Psychological Association Convention, New York, April 4, 1975.
Davis, N. & Graubert J. *Heterosexual*. NY: Vantage Press, 1975.
Freud, S. "Three Contributions to Sexual Theory," *Nervous and Mental Disease Monograph Series*, 1925, 7.
Gubrium, J. F. "Being Single in Old Age," *International Journal of Aging and Human Development*, 1975, 6, 29–41.
Hunt, M. *Sexual Behavior in the 1970s*. Chicago: Playboy Press, 1974.
Karlen, A. *Sexuality and Homosexuality*. NY: Norton, 1971.
Kastenbaum, R. J. & Costa, P. T. "Psychological Perspectives on Death," *Annual Review of Psychology*, 1977, 28, 225–49.
Maugham, S. *El Greco*. NY: Doubleday, 1950.
Sears, R. R. "Sources of Life Satisfactions of the Terman Gifted Man," *American Psychologist*, 1977, 32, 119–128.
Tripp, C. A. *The Homosexual Matrix*. NY: McGraw-Hill, 1975.
Weinberg, M. S. & Williams, C. J. *Male Homosexuals: Their Problems and Adaptations*. NY: Oxford University Press, 1974.

Content Quiz 13.4

Instructions: Fill in the blanks with the appropriate responses listed below.

burden of evidence
egocentric self-servingness
homosexuals
superciliousness
human sexuality
homosexuality
shallower commitment
prejudice
heterosexuality
social cohesion

1. Although discriminating is something all societies do, _____ is unwarranted discrimination.
2. The weight of traditional society and religion is clearly on the side of discriminating against _____.
3. On the debate concerning the acceptability of homosexuality, the _____ is on homosexuals to prove that homosexual practices are not socially disruptive or harmful to society.

4. Cameron believes that _____ is totally learned.
5. In our society, the developmental process is decidedly tilted toward the adoption of _____ as a sexual preference.
6. The _____ of the young can make homosexual sex more appealing than heterosexual encounters.
7. It is better for society to encourage the development of those traits that tend to _____.
8. The egocentric/self-centered orientation more often found in homosexuals is related to their _____ or attitude of aloof hostile disdain.
9. Homosexuality leads to a(n) _____ to society and its betterment.
10. _____ spawns the most enduring of human bonds.

Discussion Questions

1. Is discrimination something we can and should try to rid ourselves of in society? Why?
2. Is past treatment of homosexuals any justifiable basis for current and future treatment of them? Why or why not?
3. Must any special care be taken to steer children toward the development of heterosexual lifestyles? Why?
4. According to Cameron, what socially destructive traits does homosexuality promote?
5. Do you believe that heterosexuality is more conducive than homosexuality to the betterment of society? What arguments could you make?

CHAPTER FOURTEEN

14 GLOBAL ETHICS

LIVING ON A LIFEBOAT

Garrett Hardin

Synopsis

The subject of Garrett Hardin's article is human survival as viewed from the vantage point of world population and food supply. Hardin uses the metaphor of "living on a lifeboat" to help us appreciate the current global situation and prospects for the future. He says that each rich nation amounts to a lifeboat full of comparatively wealthy people. The poor nations of the world are in other more crowded lifeboats. Because of the crowding situation in the latter case, some of the poor continuously fall out of their lifeboats and are forced to swim, hoping to be admitted to a rich lifeboat. This situation captures the dilemma of lifeboat ethics: What should the rich people or rich nations of the world do? Should wealthier countries rescue the hungry of the world or not?

After briefly considering several possible actions that could be taken to help the poor, Hardin examines the issue of hunger in light of reproduction, commonly shared resources, world food banks, something he calls the "ratchet effect," and the green revolution. First, he argues that rich nations may be able to help poorer nations, or temporarily bail them out of their predicament, but because poorer nations reproduce at higher rates than richer nations, sharing becomes suicidal in the end. In time, it will become impossible for richer nations to sustain poorer ones, as well as themselves. Second, if rich nations choose to live by a sharing ethic, what will result is a "tragedy of the commons." The idealism of humanitarian aid does not allow for errors in the system. If we treat world (food) resources like a commonly shared pasture, there will be those who fail to restrain themselves, taking more than they need; others will fail to fulfill their responsibilities to look after the commons, doing damage and depleting resources in the process. Although the sharing ethic reflects noble sounding Christian-Marxist ideals, mutual ruin in the commons is inevitable, for Hardin, because it does not allow for error and human imperfection.

Hardin is also skeptical of world food banks. Under the guise of humanitarian aid, there is a major tax grab, Hardin claims, that serves the economic interests of food producers, farm equipment manufacturers, and shippers. In addition, international food "debts" are often excused, stretching the metaphor of "bank" beyond reasonable limits. Regarding the international food bank as little more than a disguised one-way transfer of wealth from richer countries to poorer ones, Hardin argues that it creates a "ratchet effect," one which does not end famine or food shortage emergencies, but simply escalates them. Finally, Hardin questions the ultimate value of the green revolution's "miracle wheats and rices" being developed to improve agriculture in hungry nations. Even if food needs are satisfied for populations that are out of control, we still contribute to the depletion of resources like forests, clean air and water, and unspoiled natural beauty. Hardin ends by pointing to the irony that past well-intentioned efforts to help poorer countries have, in the end, created bad results, ones from which people have had to shield their tender consciences.

Susanne Langer[1] has shown that it is probably impossible to approach an unsolved problem save through the door of metaphor. Later, attempting to meet the demands of rigor, we may achieve some success in cleansing theory of metaphor, though our success is limited if we are unable to avoid using common language, which is shot through and through with fossil metaphors. (I count no less than five in the preceding two sentences.)

Since metaphorical thinking is inescapable it is pointless merely to weep about our human limitations. We must learn to live with them, to understand them, and to control them. "All of us," said George Eliot in Middlemarch, "get our thoughts entangled in metaphors, and act fatally on the strength of them." To avoid unconscious suicide we are well advised to pit one metaphor against another. From the interplay of competitive metaphors, thoroughly developed, we may come closer to metaphor-free solutions to our problems.

No generation has viewed the problem of the survival of the human species as seriously as we have. Inevitably, we have entered this world of concern through the door of metaphor. Environmentalists have emphasized the image of the earth as a spaceship—Spaceship Earth. Kenneth Boulding[2] is the principal architect of this metaphor. It is time, he says, that we replace the wasteful "cowboy economy" of the past with the frugal "spaceship economy" required for continued survival in the limited world we now see ours to be. The metaphor is notably useful in justifying pollution control measures.

Unfortunately, the image of a spaceship is also used to promote measures that are suicidal. One of these is a generous immigration policy, which is only a particular instance of a class of policies that are in error because they lead to the tragedy of the commons.[3] These suicidal policies are attractive because they mesh with what we unthinkingly take to be the ideals of "the best people." What is missing in the idealistic view is an insistence that rights and responsibilities must go together. The "generous" attitude of all too many people results in asserting inalienable rights while ignoring or denying matching responsibilities.

For the metaphor of a spaceship to be correct the aggregate of people on board would have to be under unitary sovereign control.[4] A true ship always has a captain. It is conceivable that a ship could be run by a committee. But it could not possibly survive if its course were determined by bickering tribes that claimed rights without responsibilities.

What about Spaceship Earth? It certainly has no captain, and no executive committee.

The United Nations is a toothless tiger, because the signatories of its charter wanted it that way. The spaceship metaphor is used only to justify spaceship demands on common resources without acknowledging corresponding spaceship responsibilities.

An understandable fear of decisive action leads people to embrace "incrementalism"—moving toward reform by tiny stages. As we shall see, this strategy is counterproductive in the area discussed here if it means accepting rights before responsibilities. Where human survival is at stake, the acceptance of responsibilities is a precondition to the acceptance of rights, if the two cannot be introduced simultaneously.

Lifeboat Ethics

Before taking up certain substantive issues let us look at an alternative metaphor, that of a lifeboat. In developing some relevant examples the following numerical values are assumed. Approximately two-thirds of the world is desperately poor, and only one-third is comparatively rich. The people in poor countries have an average per capita GNP (Gross National Product) of about $200 per year; the rich, of about $3,000. (For the United States it is nearly $5,000 per year.) Metaphorically, each rich nation amounts to a lifeboat full of comparatively rich people. The poor of the world are in other, much more crowded lifeboats. Continuously, so to speak, the poor fall out of their lifeboats and swim for a while in the water outside, hoping to be admitted to a rich lifeboat, or in some other way to benefit from the "goodies" on board. What should the passengers on a rich lifeboat do? This is the central problem of "the ethics of a lifeboat."

First we must acknowledge that each lifeboat is effectively limited in capacity. The land of every nation has a limited carrying capacity. The exact limit is a matter of argument, but the energy crunch is convincing more people every day that we have already exceeded the carrying capacity of the land. We have been living on "capital"—stored petroleum and coal—and soon we must live on income alone.

Let us look at only one lifeboat—ours. The ethical problem is the same for all, and is as follows. Here we sit, say 50 people in a lifeboat. To be generous, let us assume our boat has a capacity of 10 more, making 60. (This, however, is to violate the engineering principle of the "safety factor." A new plant disease or a bad change in the weather may decimate our population if we don't preserve some excess capacity as a safety factor.)

The 50 of us in the lifeboat see 100 others swimming in the water outside, asking for admission to the boat, or for handouts. How shall we respond to their calls? There are several possibilities.

One. We may be tempted to try to live by the Christian ideal of being "our brother's keeper," or by the Marxian ideal[5] of "from each according to his abilities, to each according to his needs." Since the needs of all are the same, we take all the needy into our boat, making a total of 150 in a boat with a capacity of 60. The boat is swamped, and everyone drowns. Complete justice, complete catastrophe.

Two. Since the boat has an unused excess capacity of 10, we admit just 10 more to it. This has the disadvantage of getting rid of the safety factor, for which action we will sooner or later pay dearly. Moreover, *which* 10 do we let in? "First come, first served?" The best 10? The neediest 10? How do we *discriminate*? And what do we say to the 90 who are excluded?

Three. Admit no more to the boat and preserve the small safety factor. Survival of the people in the lifeboat is then possible (though we shall have to be on our guard against boarding parties).

The last solution is abhorrent to many people. It is unjust, they say. Let us grant that it is.

"I feel guilty about my good luck," say some. The reply to this is simple: *Get out and yield your place to others*. Such a selfless action might satisfy the conscience of those who are addicted to guilt but it would not change the ethics of the lifeboat. The needy person to whom a guilt-addict yields his place will not himself feel guilty about his sudden good luck. (If he did he would not climb aboard.) The net result of conscience-stricken people relinquishing their unjustly held positions is the elimination of their kind of conscience from the lifeboat. The lifeboat, as it were, purifies itself of guilt. The ethics of the lifeboat persist, unchanged by such momentary aberrations.

This then is the basic metaphor within which we must work out our solutions. Let us enrich the image step by step with substantive additions from the real world.

Reproduction

The harsh characteristics of lifeboat ethics are heightened by reproduction, particularly by reproductive differences. The people inside the lifeboats of the wealthy nations are doubling in numbers every 87 years; those outside are doubling every 35 years, on the average. And the relative difference in prosperity is becoming greater.

Let us, for a while, think primarily of the U.S. lifeboat. As of 1973 the United States had a population of 210 million people, who were increasing by 0.8% per year, that is, doubling in number every 87 years.

Although the citizens of rich nations are outnumbered two to one by the poor, let us imagine an equal number of poor people outside our lifeboat—a mere 210 million poor people reproducing at a quite different rate. If we imagine these to be the combined populations of Colombia, Venezuela, Ecuador, Morocco, Thailand, Pakistan, and the Philippines, the average rate of increase of the people "outside" is 3.3% per year. The doubling time of this population is 21 years.

Suppose that all these countries, and the United States, agreed to live by the Marxian ideal, "to each according to his needs," the ideal of most Christians as well. Needs, of course, are determined by population size, which is affected by reproduction. Every nation regards its rate of reproduction as a sovereign right. If our lifeboat were big enough in the beginning it might be possible to live *for a while* by Christian-Marxian ideals. *Might*.

Initially, in the model given, the ratio of non-Americans to Americans would be one to one. But consider what the ratio would be 87 years later. By this time Americans would have doubled to a population of 420 million. The other group (doubling every 21 years) would now have swollen to 3,540 million. Each American would have more than eight people to share with. How could the lifeboat possibly keep afloat?

All this involves extrapolation of current trends into the future, and is consequently suspect. Trends may change. Granted: but the change will not necessarily be favorable. If—as seems likely—the rate of population increase falls faster in the ethnic group presently inside the lifeboat than it does among those now outside, the future will turn out to be even worse than mathematics predicts, and sharing will be even more suicidal.

Ruin in the Commons

The fundamental error of the sharing ethics is that it leads to the tragedy of the commons. Under a system of private property the men (or group of men) who own property recognize their responsibility to care for it, for if they don't they will eventually suffer. A farmer, for instance, if he is intelligent, will allow no more cattle in a pasture than its carrying capacity justifies. If he overloads the pasture, weeds take over, erosion sets in, and the owner loses in the long run.

But if a pasture is run as a commons open to all, the right of each to use it is not matched by an operational responsibility to take care of it. It is no use asking independent herdsmen in a commons to act responsibly, for they dare not. The considerate herdsman who refrains from overloading the commons suffers more than a selfish one who says his needs are greater. (As Leo Durocher says, "Nice guys finish last.") Christian-Marxian idealism is counterproductive. That it *sounds* nice is no excuse. With distribution systems, as with individual morality, good intentions are no substitute for good performance.

A social system is stable only if it is insensitive to errors. To the Christian-Marxian idealist a selfish person is a sort of "error." Prosperity in the system of the commons cannot survive errors. If *everyone* would only restrain himself, all would be well; but it takes *only one less than everyone* to ruin a system of voluntary restraint. In a crowded world of less than perfect human beings—and we will never know any other—mutual ruin is inevitable in the commons. This is the core of the tragedy of the commons.

One of the major tasks of education today is to create such an awareness of the dangers of the commons that people will be able to recognize its many varieties, however disguised. There is pollution of the air and water because these media are treated as commons. Further growth of population and growth in the per capita conversion of natural resources into pollutants require that the system of the commons be modified or abandoned in the disposal of "externalities."

The fish populations of the oceans are exploited as commons, and ruin lies ahead. No technological invention can prevent this fate: in fact, all improvements in the art of fishing merely hasten the day of complete ruin. Only the replacement of the system of the commons with a responsible system can save oceanic fisheries.

The management of western rangelands, though nominally rational, is in fact (under the steady pressure of cattle ranchers) often merely a government-sanctioned system of the commons, drifting toward ultimate ruin for both the rangelands and the residual enterprisers.

World Food Banks

In the international arena we have recently heard a proposal to create a new commons, namely an international depository of food reserves to which nations will contribute according to their abilities, and from which nations may draw according to their needs. Nobel laureate Norman Borlaug has lent the prestige of his name to this proposal.

A world food bank appeals powerfully to our humanitarian impulses. We remember John Donne's celebrated line, "Any man's death diminishes me." But before we rush out to see for whom the bell tolls let us recognize where the greatest political push for international granaries comes from, lest we be disillusioned later. Our experience with Public Law 480 clearly reveals the answer. This was the law that moved billions of dollars worth of U.S. grain to food-short, population-long countries during the past two decades. When P.L. 480 first came into being, a headline in the business magazine *Forbes*[6] revealed the power behind it: "Feeding the World's Hungry Millions: How it will mean billions for U.S. business."

And indeed it did. In the years 1960 to 1970 a total of $7.9 billion was spent on the "Food for Peace" program, as P.L. 480 was called. During the years 1948 to 1970 an additional $49.9 billion were extracted from American tax-payers to pay for other economic aid programs, some of which went for food and food-producing machinery. (This figure does *not* include military aid.) That P.L. 480 was a give-away program was concealed. Recipient countries went through the motions of paying for P.L. 480 food—with IOU's. In December 1973 the charade was brought to an end as far as India was concerned when the United States "forgave" India's $3.2 billion debt.[7] Public announcement of the debt was delayed for two months: one wonders why.

"Famine—1975!"[8] is one of the few publications that points out the commercial roots of this humanitarian attempt. Though all U.S. taxpayers lost by P.L. 480, special interest groups gained handsomely. Farmers benefited because they were not asked to contribute the grain—it was bought from them by the taxpayers. Besides the direct benefit there was the indirect effect of increasing demand and thus raising prices of farm products generally. The manufacturers of farm machinery, fertilizers, and pesticides benefited by the farmers' extra efforts to grow more food. Grain elevators profited from storing the grain for varying lengths of time. Railroads made money hauling it to port, and shipping lines by carrying it overseas. Moreover, once the machinery for P.L. 480 was established an immense bureaucracy had a vested interest in its continuance regardless of its merits.

Very little was ever heard of these selfish interests when P.L. 480 was defended in public. The emphasis was always on its humanitarian effects. The combination of multiple and relatively silent selfish interest with highly vocal humanitarian apologists constitutes a powerful lobby for extracting money from taxpayers. Foreign aid has become a habit that can apparently survive in the absence of any known justification. A news commentator in a weekly magazine,[9] after exhaustively going over all the conventional arguments for foreign aid—self-interest, social justice, political advantage, and charity—and concluding that none of the known arguments really held water, concluded: So the search continues for some logically compelling reasons for giving aid. . . ." In other words, *Act now, Justify later*—if ever. (Apparently a quarter of a century is too short a time to find the justification for expending several billion dollars yearly.)

The search for a rational justification can be short-circuited by interjecting the word "emergency." Borlaug uses this word. We need to look sharply at it. What is an "emergency"? It is surely something like an accident, which is correctly defined as *an event that is certain to happen, though with a low frequency*.[10] A well-run organization prepares for everything that is certain, including accidents and emergencies. It budgets for them. It saves for them. It expects them—and mature decision makers do not waste time complaining about accidents when they occur.

What happens if some organizations budget for emergencies and others do not? If each organization is solely responsible for its own well-being, poorly managed ones will suffer. But they should be able to learn from experience. They have a chance to mend their ways and learn to budget for infrequent but certain emergencies. The weather, for instance, always varies and periodic crop failures are certain. A wise and competent government saves out of the production of the good years in anticipation of bad years that are sure to come. This is not a new idea. The Bible tells us that Joseph taught this policy to Pharaoh in Egypt more than 2,000 years ago. Yet it is literally true that the vast majority of the governments of the world today have no such policy. They lack either the wisdom or the competence, or both. Far more difficult than the transfer of wealth from one country to another is the transfer of wisdom between sovereign powers or between generations.

"But it isn't their fault! How can we blame the poor people who are caught in an emergency? Why must we punish them?" The concepts of blame and punishment are irrelevant. The question is, what are the operational consequences of establishing a world food bank? If it is open to every country every time a need develops, slovenly rulers will not be motivated to take Joseph's advice. Why should they? Others will bail them out whenever they are in trouble.

Some countries will make deposits in the world food bank and others will withdraw from it: there will be almost no overlap. Calling such a depository-transfer unit a "bank" is stretching the metaphor of *bank* beyond its elastic limits. The proposers, of course, never call attention to the metaphorical nature of the word they use.

The Ratchet Effect

An "international food bank" is really, then, not a true bank but a disguised one-way transfer device for moving wealth from rich countries to poor. In the absence of such a bank, in a world inhabited by individually responsible sovereign nations, the population of each nation would repeatedly go through a cycle of the sort shown in Figure 1. P_2 is greater than P_1, either in absolute numbers or because a deterioration of the food supply has removed the safety factor and produced a dangerously low ratio of resources to population. P_2 may be said to represent a state of overpopulation, which becomes obvious upon the appearance of an "accident," e.g., a crop failure. If the "emergency" is not met by outside help, the population drops back to the "normal" level—the "carrying capacity" of the environment—or even below. In the absence of population control by a sovereign, sooner or later the population grows to P_2 again and the cycle repeats. The long-term population curve[11] is an irregularly fluctuating one, equilibrating more or less about the carrying capacity.

A demographic cycle of this sort obviously involves great suffering in the restrictive phase, but such a cycle is normal to any independent country with inadequate population control. The third century theologian Tertullian[12] expressed what must have been the recognition of many wise men when he wrote: "The scourges of pestilence, famine, wars, and earthquakes have come to be regarded as a blessing to overcrowded nations, since they serve to prune away the luxuriant growth of the human race."

Only under a strong and farsighted sovereign—which theoretically could be the people themselves, democratically organized—can a population equilibrate at some set point below the carrying capacity, thus avoiding the pains normally caused by periodic and unavoidable disasters. For this happy state to be achieved it is necessary that those in power be able to contemplate with equanimity the "waste" of surplus food in times of bountiful harvests. It is essential that those in power resist the temptation to convert extra food into extra babies. On the public relations level it is necessary that the phrase "surplus food" be replaced by "safety factor."

But wise sovereigns seem not to exist in the poor world today. The most anguishing problems are created by poor countries that are governed by rulers insufficiently wise and powerful. If such countries can draw on a world food bank in times of "emergency," the population *cycle* of Figure [14.1] will be replaced by the population *escalator* of Figure [14.2]. The input of food from a food bank acts as the pawl of a ratchet, preventing the population from retracing its steps to a lower level. Reproduction pushes the population upward, inputs from the world bank prevent its moving downward. Population size escalates, as does the absolute magnitude of "accidents" and "emergencies." The process is brought to an end only by the total collapse of the whole system, producing a catastrophe of scarcely imaginable proportions.

Such are the implications of the well-meant sharing of food in a world of irresponsible reproduction.

I think we need a new word for systems like this. The adjective "melioristic" is applied to systems that produce continual improvement; the English word is derived from the Latin *meliorare*, to become or make better. Parallel with this it would be useful to bring in the word *pejoristic* (from the Latin *pejorare*, to become or make worse). This word can be applied to those systems which, by their very nature, can be relied upon to make matters worse. A world food bank coupled with sovereign state irresponsibility in reproduction is an example of a pejoristic system.

This pejoristic system creates an unacknowledged commons. People have more motivation to draw from than to add to the common store. The license to make such withdrawals diminishes whatever motivation poor

Figure [14.1] THE POPULATION CYCLE OF A NATION

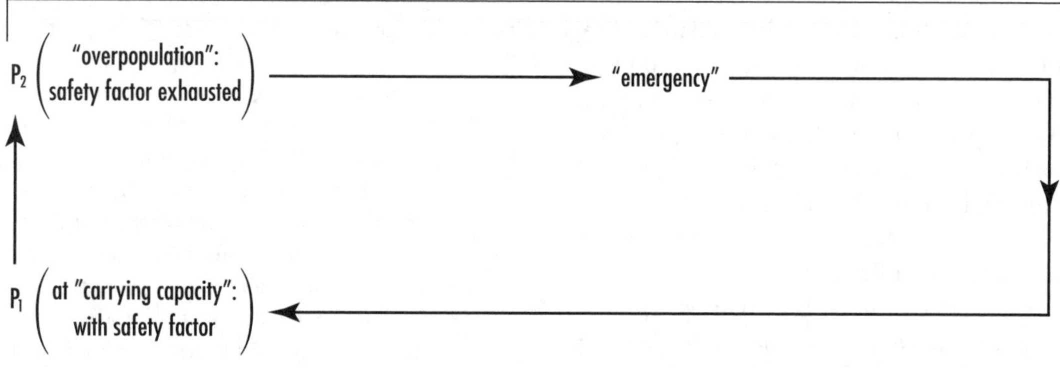

The population cycle of a nation that has no effective, conscious population control, and which receives no aid from the outside. P_2 is greater than P_1.

Figure [14.2] THE POPULATION ESCALATOR

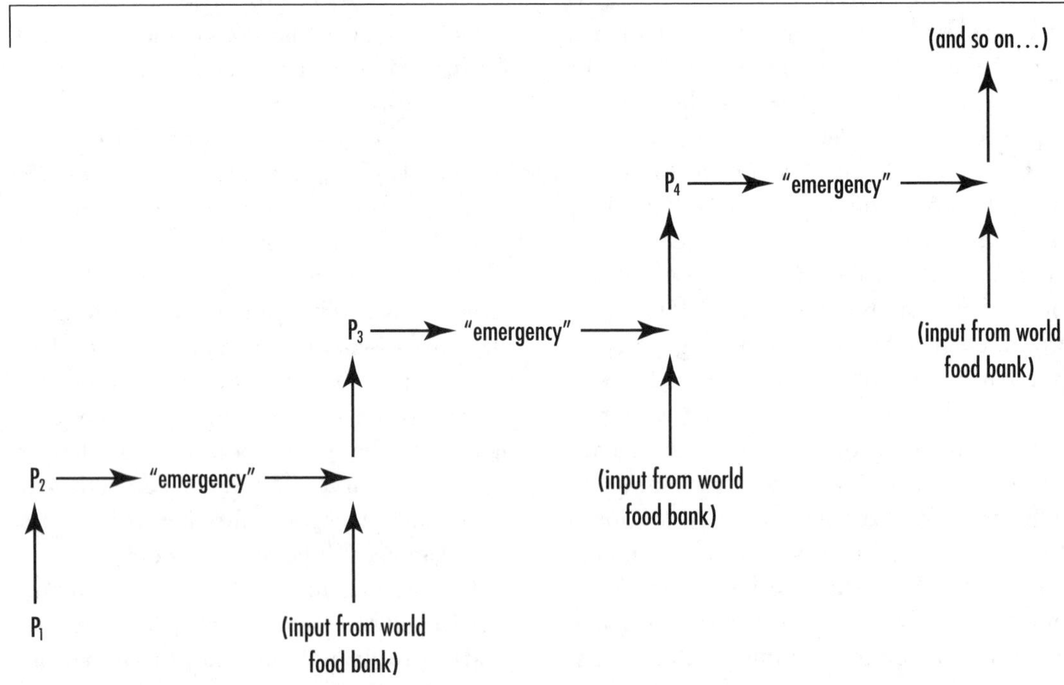

Note that input from a world food bank acts like the pawl of a ratchet, preventing the normal population cycle shown in Figure [14.1] from being completed. P_{n+1} is greater than P_n, and the absolute magnitude of the "emergencies" escalates. Ultimately the entire system crashes. The crash is not shown and few can imagine it.

countries might otherwise have to control their populations. Under the guidance of this ratchet, wealth can be steadily moved in one direction only, from the slowly-breeding rich to the rapidly-breeding poor, the process finally coming to a halt only when all countries are equally and miserably poor.

All this is terribly obvious once we are acutely aware of the pervasiveness and danger of the commons. But many people still lack this awareness and the euphoria of the "benign demographic transition"[13] interferes with the realistic appraisal of pejoristic mechanisms. As concerns public policy, the deductions drawn from the benign demographic transition are these:

1. If the per capita GNP rises the birth rate will fall; hence, the rate of population increase will fall, ultimately producing ZPG (Zero Population Growth).
2. The long-term trend all over the world (including the poor countries) is of a rising per capita GNP (for which no limit is seen).
3. Therefore, all political interference in population matters is unnecessary; all we need to do is foster economic "development"—*note the metaphor*—and population problems will solve themselves.

Those who believe in the benign demographic transition dismiss the pejoristic mechanism of Figure [14.2] in the belief that each input of food from the world outside fosters development within a poor country thus resulting in a drop in the rate of population increase. Foreign aid has proceeded on this assumption for more than two decades. Unfortunately it has produced no indubitable instance of the asserted effect. It has, however, produced a library of excuses. The air is filled with plaintive calls for more massive foreign aid appropriations so that the hypothetical melioristic process can get started.

The doctrine of demographic *laissez-faire* implicit in the hypothesis of the benign demographic transition is immensely attractive. Unfortunately there is more evidence against the melioristic system than there is for it.[14] On the historical side there are many counterexamples. The rise in per capita GNP in France and Ireland during the past century has been accompanied by a rise in population growth. In the 20 years following the Second World War the same positive correlation was noted almost everywhere in the world. Never in world history before 1950 did the worldwide population growth reach 1% per annum. Now the average population growth is over 2% and shows no signs of slackening.

On the theoretical side, the denial of the pejoristic scheme of Figure [14.2] probably springs from the hidden acceptance of the "cowboy economy" that Boulding castigated. Those who recognize the limitations of a spaceship, if they are unable to achieve population control at a safe and comfortable level, accept the necessity of the corrective feedback of the population cycle shown in Figure [14.1]. No one who knew in his bones that he was living on a true spaceship would countenance political support of the population escalator shown in Figure [14.2].

Eco-Destruction Via the Green Revolution

The demoralizing effect of charity on the recipient has long been known. "Give a man a fish and he will eat for a day: teach him how to fish and he will eat for the rest of his days." So runs an ancient Chinese proverb. Acting on this advice the Rockefeller and Ford Foundations have financed a multipronged program for improving agriculture in the hungry nations. The result, known as the "Green Revolution," has been quite remarkable. "Miracle wheat" and "miracle rice" are splendid technological achievements in the realm of plant genetics.

Whether or not the Green Revolution can increase food production is doubtful,[15] but in any event not particularly important. What is missing in this great and well-meaning humanitarian effort is a firm grasp of fundamentals. Considering the importance of the Rockefeller Foundation in this effort it is ironic that the late Alan Gregg, a much-respected vice-president of the Foundation, strongly expressed his doubts of the wisdom of all attempts to increase food production some two decades ago. (This was before Borlaug's work—supported by Rockefeller—had resulted in the development of "miracle wheat") Gregg[16] likened the growth and spreading of humanity over the surface of the earth to the metastasis of cancer in the human body, wryly remarking that "Cancerous growths demand food; but, as far as I know, they have never been cured by getting it."

"Man does not live by bread alone"—the scriptural statement has a rich meaning even in the material realm. Every human being born constitutes a draft on all aspects of the environment—food, air, water, unspoiled scenery, occasional and optional solitude, beaches, contact with wild animals, fishing, hunting—the list is long and incompletely known. Food can, perhaps, be significantly increased: but what about forests, and solitude? If we satisfy the need for food in a growing population we necessarily decrease the supply of other goods, and thereby increase the difficulty of equitably allocating scarce goods.[17]

The present population of India is 600 million, and it is increasing by 15 million per year. The environmental load of this population is already great. The forests of India are only a small fraction of what they were three centuries ago. Soil erosion, floods, and the psychological costs of crowding are serious. Every one of the net 15 million lives added each year stresses the Indian environment more severely. *Every life saved this year in a poor country diminishes the quality of life for subsequent generations.*

Observant critics have shown how much harm we wealthy nations have already done to poor nations through our well-intentioned but misguided attempts to help them.[18] Particularly reprehensible is our failure to carry out postaudits of these attempts.[19] Thus have we shielded our tender consciences from knowledge of the harm we have done. Must we Americans continue to fail to monitor the consequences of our external "do-gooding"? If, for instance, we thoughtlessly make it possible for the present 600 million Indians to swell to 1,200 millions by the year 2001—as their present growth rate promises—will posterity in India thank *us* for facilitating an even greater destruction of *their* environment? Are good intentions ever a sufficient excuse for bad consequences?

Notes

Footnotes have been renumbered—Ed.

1. Susanne Langer, *Philosophy in a New Key* (Cambridge, Mass., 1942).
2. Kenneth Boulding, "The Economics of the Coming Spaceship Earth," in H. Jarett, ed., *Environmental Quality in a Growing Economy* (Baltimore, Md., 1966).
3. Garrett Hardin, "The Tragedy of the Commons," *Science* 162 (1968), 1243–1248.
4. W. Ophuls, "The Scarcity Society," *Harpers* 248 (1974), 47–52.
5. Karl Marx, "Critique of the Gotha Program," in R. C. Tucker, ed., *The Marx-Engels Reader* (New York, 1972), 388.
6. See W. C. Paddock, "How Green is the Green Revolution?" *BioScience* 20 (1970) 897–902.
7. *The Wall Street Journal*, 19 February 1974.
8. W. C. Paddock and P. Paddock, *Famine 1975!* (Boston, 1967).
9. K. Lansner, "Should Foreign Aid Begin at Home?" *Newsweek*, 11 February 1974, 32.
10. Hardin, *Exploring New Ethics for Survival: The Voyage of the Spaceship* Beagle (New York, 1972), 81–82.
11. Hardin, in *Biology: Its Principles and Implications*, 2nd ed. (San Francisco, 1966), chap. 9.
12. Hardin, *Population, Evolution, and Birth Control* (San Francisco, 1969), 18.
13. Hardin, *Stalking the Wild Taboo* (Los Altos, CA, 1973), chap. 23.
14. K. Davis, "Population," *Scientific American* 209, no. 3 (1963), 62–71.

15. M. Harris, "How Green the Revolution," *Natural History* 81, no. 3 (1972), 28–30; W. C. Paddock, "How Green is the Green Revolution?"; H. G. Wilkes, "The Green Revolution," *Environment* 14, no. 8, 32–39.
16. A. Gregg, "A Medical Aspect of the Population Problem," *Science* 121 (1955), 681–682.
17. Hardin, "The Economics of Wilderness," *Natural History* 78, no. 6 (1969), 20–27, and "Preserving Quality on Spaceship Earth," in J. B. Trefethen, ed., *Transactions of the Thirty-Seventh North American Wildlife and Natural Resources Conference* (Washington, D.C., 1972).
18. W. Paddock and E. Paddock, *We Don't Know How* (Ames, IA, 1973).
19. M. T. Farvar and J. P. Milton, *The Careless Technology* (Garden City, NY, 1972).

References

Aiken, William, and Hugh LaFollette. *World Hunger and Moral Obligation*. Englewood Cliffs, NJ: Prentice Hall, 1977.

Eberstadt, Nick. "Myths of the Food Crises," in *The New York Review of Books*, 19 February 1976. Reprinted in James Rachels, ed., *Moral Problems*, 3rd ed. New York: Harper & Row, 1979, pp. 292–312.

Hardin, Garrett. *Stalking the Wild Taboo*. Los Altos, CA: William Kauffman, 1978.

Lucas, George R., and Thomas W. Ogletree, eds. *Lifeboat Ethics: The Moral Dilemma of World Hunger*. New York: Harper & Row, 1976.

Content Quiz 14.1

Instructions: Fill in the blanks with the appropriate responses listed below.

metaphor
tragedy of the commons
Christianity
pejoristic system
ecodestruction
transfer device
errors
misguided
Marxism
ratchet effect

1. Garrett Hardin believes that foreign aid food donations are well-intentioned, but _____ efforts.
2. Producing enough food to feed all of the peoples of the world could reduce or eliminate starvation, but it does not prevent the _____ that results from very high population concentrations existing in relatively small geographic areas.
3. The _____ of a lifeboat is used to portray the human problem of survival as it relates to population and food supply.
4. "From each according to his abilities, to each according to his needs" is a basic principle of _____.
5. The prescription that we "be our brother's keeper" reflects a basic principle of _____.

6. The ethics of sharing is fundamentally wrong because it leads to the _____.
7. The concept of an international food bank is not intended to be a real bank, but a disguised one-way _____ for moving wealth from rich countries to poor countries.
8. A world food bank coupled with a country's irresponsibility in human reproduction does not improve anything because such a combination is an example of a _____.
9. When rich nations come to the rescue of starving nations, which, in turn, reproduce in such great numbers to again give rise to an emergency food shortage situation requiring further assistance, a _____ is created.
10. The problem with Christian-Marxist principles is that they cannot properly handle _____ in the social system, namely selfish people.

Discussion Questions

1. How is living on the planet earth like living on a lifeboat? Do you accept this metaphor? Why? Can you think of any others?
2. How do Christianity and Marxism enter into Hardin's discussion of lifeboat ethics? Is he in favor of Christian-Marxist ideals? Comment.
3. What assumptions does Hardin make about people? How are these assumptions relevant to his concept of the "tragedy of the commons"? Do you think his assumptions are acceptable? Why?
4. Who, according to Hardin, are the real beneficiaries of world food aid? Explain.
5. Why are interventions by international food banks ultimately destined to failure?
6. What are the ecological ramifications of having adequately fed but overpopulated countries?

KILLING AND STARVING TO DEATH

James Rachels

Synopsis

The problem of world hunger and the responsibility to do something about it are dealt with in this essay. James Rachels criticizes the philosophical claim that our "positive duty" to give aid to the hungry is weaker than our "negative duty" not to harm them. He presents and defends what he calls the "equivalence thesis." This thesis states that our duty not to let hungry people die is as strong as our duty not to kill them. Moral intuitions that letting hungry people die is not as bad as killing them are, according to Rachels, based on prereflective beliefs about right and wrong, which, in view of more careful rational analysis, must be rejected. Allowing people to die is, in fact, a type of action that is much closer to killing them than we normally assume. That those who are dying of starvation are often great distances away and many in number, and that others could help, or are in a better position to help, makes no moral difference for Rachels. He explains why by expanding upon his equivalency thesis and by responding to critics who, in the past, have argued that killing is worse than letting die. In the closing section of his article, Rachels suggests that it is, ultimately, human selfishness that leads us to view killing as worse than letting die and that it is to our advantage to hold this view. To recognize the moral equivalency between killing and letting die would require lifestyle adjustments that most affluent people simply would not accept.

Although we do not know exactly how many people die each year of malnutrition or related health problems, the number is very high, in the millions.[1] By giving money to support famine relief efforts, each of us could save at least some of them. By not giving, we let them die.

Some philosophers have argued that letting people die is not as bad as killing them, because in general our "positive duty" to give aid is weaker than our "negative duty" not to do harm.[2] I maintain the opposite: letting die is just as bad as killing.[3] At first this may seem wildly implausible. When reminded that people are dying of starvation while we spend money on trivial things, we may feel a bit guilty, but certainly we do not feel like murderers. Philippa Foot writes:

> Most of us allow people to die of starvation in India and Africa, and there is surely something wrong with us that we do; it would be nonsense, however, to pretend that it is only in law that we make a distinction between allowing people in the underdeveloped countries to die of starvation and sending them poisoned food. There is worked into our moral system a distinction between what we owe people in the form of aid and what we owe them in the way of noninterference.[4]

No doubt this would be correct if it were intended only as a description of what most people believe. Whether this feature of "our moral system" is rationally defensible is, however, another matter. I shall argue that we are wrong to take comfort in the fact that we "only" let these people die, because our duty not to let them die is equally as strong as our duty not to kill them, which, of course, is very strong indeed.

Obviously, this Equivalence Thesis is not morally neutral, as philosophical claims about ethics often are. It is a radical idea which, if true, would mean that some of our "intuitions" (our prereflective beliefs about what is right and wrong in particular cases) are mistaken and must be rejected. Neither is the view I oppose morally neutral. The idea that killing is worse than letting die is a relatively conservative thesis which would allow those same intuitions to be preserved. However, the Equivalence Thesis should not be dismissed merely because it does not conform to all our prereflective intuitions. Rather than being perceptions of the truth, our "intuitions" might sometimes signify nothing more than our prejudices or selfishness or cultural conditioning. Philosophers often admit that, in theory at least, some intuitions might be unreliable—but usually this possibility is not taken seriously, and conformity to prereflective intuition is used uncritically as a test of the acceptability of moral theory. In what follows I shall argue that many of our intuitions concerning killing and letting die *are* mistaken, and should not be trusted.

I

We think that killing is worse than letting die, not because we overestimate how bad it is to kill, but because we underestimate how bad it is to let die. The following chain of reasoning is intended to show that letting people in foreign countries die of starvation is very much worse than we commonly assume.

Suppose there were a starving child in the

room where you are now—hollow eyed, belly bloated, and so on—and you have a sandwich at your elbow that you don't need. Of course you would be horrified; you would stop reading and give her the sandwich, or better, take her to a hospital. And you would not think this an act of supererogation: you would not expect any special praise for it, and you would expect criticism if you did not do it. Imagine what you would think of someone who simply ignored the child and continued reading, allowing her to die of starvation. Let us call the person who would do this Jack Palance, after the very nice man who plays such vile characters in the movies. Jack Palance indifferently watches the starving child die; he cannot be bothered even to hand her the sandwich. There is ample reason for judging him very harshly; without putting too fine a point on it, he shows himself to be a moral monster.

When we allow people in far-away countries to die of starvation, we may think, as Mrs. Foot puts it, that "there is surely something wrong with us." But we most emphatically do not consider ourselves moral monsters. We think this, in spite of the striking similarity between Jack Palance's behavior and our own. He could easily save the child; he does not; and the child dies. We could easily save some of those starving people; we do not; and they die. If we are not monsters, there must be some important difference between him and us. But what is it?

One obvious difference between Jack Palance's position and ours is that the person he lets die is in the same room with him, while the people we let die are mostly far away. Yet the spatial location of the dying people hardly seems a relevant consideration.[5] It is absurd to suppose that being located at a certain map coordinate entitles one to treatment which one would not merit if situated at a different longitude or latitude. Of course, if a dying person's location meant that we *could not* help, that would excuse us. But, since there are efficient famine relief agencies willing to carry our aid to the far-away countries, this excuse is not available. It would be almost as easy for us to send these agencies the price of the sandwich as for Palance to hand the sandwich to the child.

The location of the starving people does make a difference, psychologically, in how we feel. If there were a starving child in the same room with us, we could not avoid realizing, in a vivid and disturbing way, how it is suffering and that it is about to die. Faced with this realization our consciences probably would not allow us to ignore the child. But if the dying are far away, it is easy to think of them only abstractly, or to put them out of our thoughts altogether. This might explain why our conduct would be different if we were in Jack Palance's position even though, from a moral point of view, the location of the dying is not relevant.

There are other differences between Jack Palance and us, which may seem important, having to do with the sheer numbers of people, both affluent and starving, that surround us. In our fictitious example Jack Palance is one person, confronted by the need of one other person. This makes his position relatively simple. In the real world our position is more complicated, in two ways: first, in that there are millions of people who need feeding, and none of us has the resources to care for all of them; and second, in that for any starving person we *could* help there are millions of other affluent people who could help as easily as we.

On the first point, not much needs to be said. We may feel, in a vague sort of way, that we are not monsters because no one of us could possibly save *all* the starving people—there are just too many of them, and none of us has the resources. This is fair enough, but all that follows is that, individually, none of us is responsible for saving everyone. We may still be responsible for saving someone, or as many as we can. This is so obvious that it hardly bears mentioning; yet it is easy to lose sight of, and philosophers have actually lost sight of it. In his article "Saving Life and Taking Life,"[6] Richard Trammell says that one morally important difference between killing and letting die is "dischargeability." By this he means that, while each of us can discharge completely a duty not to kill anyone, no one among us can discharge completely a duty to save everyone who needs it. Again, fair enough; but all that follows is that, since we are only bound to save those we can, the class of people that we have an obligation to save is much smaller than the class of people we have an obligation not to kill. It does *not* follow that our duty with respect to those we can save is any less stringent. Suppose Jack Palance were to say: "I needn't give this starving child the sandwich because, after all, I can't save everyone in the world who needs it." If this excuse will not work for him, neither will it work for us with respect to the children we could save in India or Africa.

The second point about numbers was that, for any starving person we *could* help, there are millions of other affluent people who could help as easily as we. Some are in an even better position to help since they are richer. But by and large these people are doing nothing. This also helps to explain why we do not feel especially guilty for letting people starve. How guilty we feel about something depends, to some extent, on how we compare with those around us. If we were surrounded by people who regularly sacrificed to feed the starving, and we did not, we would probably feel ashamed. But because our neighbors do not do any better than we, we are not so ashamed.

But again, this does not imply that we should not feel more guilty or ashamed than we do. A psychological explanation of our feelings is not a moral justification of our conduct. Suppose Jack Palance were only one of twenty people who watched the child die; would that decrease his guilt? Curiously, I think many people assume it would. Many people seem to feel that if twenty people do nothing to prevent a tragedy, each of them is only one-twentieth as guilty as he would have been if he had watched the tragedy alone. It is as though there is only a fixed amount of guilt which divides. I suggest, rather, that guilt multiplies, so that each passive viewer is fully guilty, if he could have prevented the tragedy but did not. Jack Palance watching the girl die alone would be a moral monster; but if he calls in a group of his friends to watch with him, he does not diminish his guilt by dividing it among them. Instead, they are all moral monsters. Once the point is made explicit, it seems obvious.

The fact that most other affluent people do nothing to relieve hunger may very well have implications for one's own obligations. But the implication may be that one's own obligations *increase* rather than decrease. Suppose Palance and a friend were faced with two starving children, so that, if each did his "fair share," Palance would only have to feed one of them. But the friend will do nothing. Because he is well-off, Palance could feed both of them. Should he not? What if he fed one and then watched the other die, announcing that he has done *his* duty and that the one who died was his friend's responsibility? This shows the fallacy of supposing that one's duty is only to do one's fair share, where this is determined by what would be sufficient *if* everyone else did likewise.

To summarize: Jack Palance, who refuses to hand a sandwich to a starving child, is a moral monster. But we feel intuitively that we are not so monstrous, even though we also let starving children die when we could feed them almost as easily. If this intuition is correct, there must be some important difference between him and us. But when we examine the most obvious differences between his conduct and ours—the location of the dying, the differences in numbers—we find no real basis for judging ourselves less harshly than we judge him. Perhaps there are some other grounds on which we might distinguish our moral position, with respect to actual starving people, from Jack Palance's position with respect to the child in my story. But I cannot think of what they might be. Therefore, I conclude that if he is a monster, then so are we—or at least, so are we after our rationalizations and thoughtlessness have been exposed.

This last qualification is important. We judge people, at least in part, according to whether they can be expected to realize how well or how badly they behave. We judge Palance harshly because the consequences of his indifference are so immediately apparent. By contrast, it requires an unusual effort for us to realize the consequences of our indifference. It is normal behavior for people in the affluent countries not to give to famine relief, or if they do give, to give very little. Decent people may go along with this normal behavior pattern unthinkingly, without realizing, or without comprehending in a clear way, just what this means for the starving. Thus, even though those decent people may act monstrously, we do not judge them monsters. There is a curious sense, then, in which moral reflection can transform decent people into indecent ones: for if a person thinks things through, and realizes that he is, morally speaking, in Jack Palance's position, his continued indifference is more blameworthy than before.

The preceding is not intended to prove that letting people die of starvation is as bad as killing them. But it does provide strong evidence that letting die is much worse than we normally assume, and so that letting die is much *closer* to killing than we normally assume. These reflections also go some way towards showing just how fragile and unreliable our intuitions are in this area. They suggest that, if we want to discover the truth, we are better off looking at arguments that do not rely on unexamined intuitions.

II

Before arguing that the Equivalence Thesis is true, let me explain more precisely what I mean by it. I take it to be a claim about what does, nor does not, count as a morally good reason in support of a value judgment: the bare fact that one act is an act of killing, while another act is an act of "merely" letting someone die, is not a morally good reason in support of the judgment that the former is worse than the latter. Of course there may be *other* differences between such acts that are morally significant. For example, the family of an irreversibly comatose hospital patient may want their loved one to be allowed to die, but not killed. Perhaps the reason for their preference is religious. So we have at least one reason to let the patient die rather than to kill him—the reason is that the family prefers it that way. This does not mean, however, that the distinction between killing and letting die *itself* is important. What is important is respecting the family's wishes. (It is often right to respect people's wishes even if we think those wishes are based on false beliefs.) In another sort of case, a patient with a painful terminal illness may want to be killed rather than allowed to die because a slow, lingering death would be agonizing. Here we have a reason to kill and not let die, but once again the reason is not that one course is intrinsically preferable to the other. The reason is, rather, that the latter course would lead to more suffering.

It should be clear, then, that I will *not* be arguing that every act of letting die is equally as bad as every act of killing. There are lots of reasons why a particular act of killing may be morally worse than a particular act of letting die, or vice versa. If a healthy person is murdered, from a malicious motive, while a person in irreversible coma is allowed to die upon a calm judgment that maintaining him alive is pointless, certainly this killing is very much worse than this letting die. Similarly, if an ill person who could be saved is maliciously allowed to die, while a terminal patient is killed, upon his request, as an act of kindness, we have good reason to judge the letting die worse than the killing. All that I want to argue is that, whatever reasons there may be for judging one act worse than another, the simple fact that one is killing, whereas the other is only letting die, is not among them.

The first stage of the argument is concerned with some formal relations between moral judgments and the reasons that support them. I take it to be a point of logic that moral judgments are true only if good reasons support them; for example, if there is no good reason why you ought to do some action, it cannot be true that you ought to do it. Moreover, when there is a choice to be made from among several possible actions, the preferable alternative is the one that is backed by the strongest reasons.

But when are the reasons for or against one act stronger than those for or against another act? A complete answer would have to include some normative theory explaining why some reasons are intrinsically weightier than others. Suppose you are in a situation in which you can save someone's life only by lying: the normative theory would explain why "Doing *A* would save someone's life" is a stronger reason in favor of doing *A* than "Doing *B* would be telling the truth" is in favor of doing *B*.

However, there are also some purely formal principles that operate here. The simplest and least controversial such principle is this:

> (1) If there are the *same* reasons for or against *A* as for or against *B*, then the reasons in favor of *A* are neither stronger nor weaker than the reasons in favor of *B*; and so *A* and *B* are morally equivalent—neither is preferable to the other.

Now, suppose we ask why killing is morally objectionable. When someone is killed, there may of course be harmful effects for people other than the victim himself. Those who loved him may grieve, and those who were depending on him in one way or another may be caused hardship because, being dead, he will be unable to perform as expected. However, we cannot explain the wrongness of killing purely, or even mainly, in terms of the bad effects for the survivors. The primary reason why killing is wrong is that something very bad is done to the victim himself: he ends up dead; he no longer has a good—his life—which he possessed before. But notice that exactly the same can be said about letting someone die. The primary reason why it is morally objectionable to let someone die, when we could save him, is that he ends up dead; he no longer has a good—his life—which he possessed before. Secondary reasons again have to do with harmful effects on those who survive. Thus, the explanation of why killing is bad mentions features of killing that are also features of letting die, and vice versa. Since there are no comparably general reasons in favor of either, this suggests that:

> (2) There are the same reasons for and against letting die as for and against killing.

And if this is true, we get the conclusion:

> (3) Therefore, killing and letting die are morally equivalent—neither is preferable to the other.

The central idea of this argument is that there is no morally relevant difference between killing and letting die, that is, no difference which may be cited to show that one is worse than the other. The argument therefore contains a premise—(2)—that is supported only inductively. The fact that the explanation of why killing is wrong applies equally well to letting die, and vice versa, provides strong evidence that the inductive generalization is true. Nevertheless, no matter how carefully we analyze the matter, it will always be possible that there is some subtle, morally relevant difference between the two that we have overlooked. In fact, philosophers who believe that killing is worse than letting die have sometimes tried to identify such differences. I believe that these attempts have failed; here are three examples:

1. The first is one that I have already mentioned. Trammell urges that there is an important difference in the "dischargeability" of duties not to kill and not to let die. We can completely discharge a duty not to kill anyone; but we cannot completely discharge a duty to save everyone who needs aid. This is obviously correct, but it does not show that the Equivalence Thesis is false, for two reasons. In the first place, the difference in dischargeability only shows that the class of people we have a duty to save is smaller than the class of people we have a duty not to kill. It does not show that our duty with respect to those we *can* save is any less stringent. In the second place, if we *cannot* save someone, and that person dies, then we do not let him die. It is not right to say that I let Josef Stalin die, for example, since there is no way I could have saved him. So if I cannot save everyone, then neither can I let everyone die.

2. It has also been urged that, in killing someone, we are *doing* something—namely, killing him—whereas, in letting someone die, we are not doing anything. In letting people die of starvation, for example, we only *fail* to do certain things, such as sending food. The difference is between action and inaction; and somehow, this is supposed to make a moral difference.[7]

There are also two difficulties with this suggestion. First, it is misleading to say, without further ado, that in letting someone die we do nothing. For there is one very important thing that we do: we let someone die. "Letting someone die" is different, in some ways, from other sorts of actions, mainly in that it is an action we perform *by way of* not performing other actions. We may let someone die by way of not feeding him, just as we may insult someone by way of not shaking his hand. (If it is said, "I didn't do anything; I simply refrained from taking his hand when he offered it," it may be replied "You did do one thing—you insulted him.") The distinction between action and inaction is relative to a specification of *what* actions are or are not done. In insulting someone, we may *not* smile, speak, shake hands, and so on—but we *do* insult or snub the person. And in letting someone die, the following may be among the things that are not done: we do not feed the person, we do not give medication, and so on. But the following is among the things that are done: we let him die.

Second, even if letting die were only a case of inaction, why should any moral conclusion follow from *that* fact? It may seem that a significant conclusion follows if we assume that we are not responsible for inactions. However, there is no general correlation between the action-inaction distinction and any sort of moral assessment. We ought to do some things, and we ought to not do others, and we can certainly be morally blameworthy for not doing things as well as for doing them—Jack Palance was blameworthy for not feeding the child. (In many circumstances we are even legally liable for not doing things: tax fraud may involve only "inaction"—failing to report certain things to the Department of Internal Revenue—but what of it?) Moreover, failing to act can be subject to all the other kinds of moral assessment. Not doing something may, depending on the circumstances, be right, wrong, obligatory, wise, foolish, compassionate, sadistic, and so on. Since there is no general correlation between the action-inaction distinction and *any* of these matters, it is hard to see how anything could be made out of this distinction in the present context.

3. My final example is from Trammell again. He argues that "optionality" is a morally relevant difference between killing and letting die. The point here is that if we fail to save someone, we leave open the option for someone else to save him; whereas if we kill, the victim is dead and that is that. This point, I think, has little significance. For one thing, while "optionality" may mark a difference between killing and *failing to save*, it does not mark a comparable difference between killing and *letting die*. If *X* fails to save *Y*, it does not follow that *Y* dies; someone else may come along and save him. But if *X* lets *Y* die, it does follow that *Y* dies; *Y* is dead and that is that.[8] When Palance watches the child die, he does not merely fail to save the child; he lets her die. And when we fail to send food to the starving, and they die, we let them die—we do not merely fail to save them.

The importance of "optionality" in any particular case depends on the actual chances of someone else's saving the person we do not save. Perhaps it is not so bad not to save someone if we know that someone else *will* save him. (Although even here, we do not behave as we ought; for we ought not simply to leave what needs doing to others.) And perhaps it even gets us off the hook a little if there is the *strong chance* that someone else will step in. But in the case of the world's starving, we know very well that no person or group of persons is going to come along tomorrow and save all of them. We know that there are at least some people who will *not* be saved, if we do not save them. So, as an excuse for not giving aid to the starving, the "optionality" argument is clearly in bad faith. To say of those people, after they are dead, that someone else *might* have saved them, in the very weak sense in which that will be true, does not excuse us at all. The others who might have saved them, but did not, are as guilty as we, but that does not diminish our guilt—as I have already remarked, guilt in these cases multiplies, not divides.

III

I need now to say a few more things about the counterintuitive nature of the Equivalence Thesis.

The fact that this view has radical implications for conduct has been cited as a reason for rejecting it. Trammell complains that "Denial of the distinction between negative and positive duties leads straight to an ethic so strenuous that it might give pause even to a philosophical John the Baptist."[9] Suppose John is about to buy a phonograph record, purely for his enjoyment, when he is reminded that with this five dollars a starving person could be fed. On the view I am defending, he ought to give the money to feed the hungry person. This may not seem exceptional until we notice that the reasoning is reiterable. Having given the first five dollars, John is not free to use another five to buy the record. For the poor are always with him: there is always *another* starving person to be fed, and then another, and then another. "The problem," Trammell says, "is that, even though fulfillment of one particular act of aid involves only minimal effort, it sets a precedent for millions of such efforts."[10] So we reach the bizarre conclusion that it is almost always immoral to buy phonograph records! And the same goes for fancy clothes, cars, toys, and so on.

This sort of *reductio* argument is of course familiar in philosophy. Such arguments may be divided into three categories. The strongest sort shows that a theory entails a contradiction, and, since contradictions cannot be tolerated, the theory must be modified or rejected. Such arguments, when valid, are of course devastating. Second, an argument may show that a theory has a consequence which, while not inconsistent, is nevertheless demonstrably false—that is, an independent proof can be given that the offensive consequence is unacceptable. Arguments of this second type, while not quite so impressive as the first, can still be irresistible. The third type of *reductio* is markedly weaker than the others. Here, it is merely urged that some consequence of a theory is counterintuitive. The supposedly embarrassing consequence is perfectly consistent, and there is no proof that it is false; the complaint is only that it goes against our unreflective, pretheoretical beliefs. Now sometimes even this weak sort of argument can be effective, especially when we have not much confidence in the theory, or when our confidence in the pretheoretical belief is unaffected by the reasoning which supports the theory. However, it may happen that *the same reasoning which leads one to accept a theory also persuades one that the pretheoretical beliefs were wrong*. (If this did not happen, philosophy would always be in the service of what we already think; it could never challenge and change our beliefs, and would be, in an important sense, useless.) The present case, it seems to me, is an instance of this type. The same reasoning which leads to the view that we are as wicked as Jack Palance, and that killing is no worse than letting die, also persuades (me, at least) that the prereflective belief in the rightness of our affluent life-style is mistaken.[11]

So, I want to say about all this what H. P. Grice once said at a conference when someone objected that his theory of meaning had an unacceptable implication. Referring to the supposedly embarrassing consequence, Grice said, "See here, that's not an *objection* to my theory—*that's* my theory!"[12] Grice not only accepted the implication, he claimed it as an integral part of what he wanted to say. Similarly, the realization that we are morally wrong to spend money on inessentials, when that money could go to feed the starving, is an integral part of the view I am defending. It is not an embarrassing consequence of the view; it is (part of) the view itself.

There is another way in which the counterintuitive nature of the Equivalence Thesis may be brought out. It follows from that thesis that if the *only* difference between a pair of acts is that one is killing, while the other is letting die, those actions are equally good or bad—neither is preferable to the other. Defenders of the distinction between positive and negative duties have pointed out that in such cases our intuitions often tell us just the opposite: killing seems obviously worse. Here is an example produced by Daniel Dinello:

> Jones and Smith are in a hospital. Jones cannot live longer than two hours unless he gets a heart transplant. Smith, who has had one kidney removed, is dying of an infection in the other kidney. If he does not get a kidney transplant, he will die in about four hours. When Jones dies, his one good kidney can be transplanted to Smith, or Smith could be killed and his heart transplanted to Jones . . . it seems clear that it would, in fact, be wrong to kill Smith and save Jones rather than letting Jones die and saving Smith.[13]

And another from Trammell:

> If someone threatened to steal $1000 from a person if he did not take a gun and shoot a stranger between the eyes, it would be very wrong for him to kill the stranger to save his $1000. But if someone asked from that person $1000 to save a stranger, it would seem that his obligation to grant this request would not be as great as his obligation to refuse the first demand—even if he has good reason for believing that without his $1000 the stranger would certainly die. . . . In this particular example, it seems plausible to say that a person has a greater obligation to refrain from killing someone, even though the effort required of him ($1000) and his motivation toward the stranger be assumed identical in both cases.[14]

The conclusion we are invited to draw from these examples is that, contrary to what I have been arguing, the bare difference between killing and letting die *must be* morally significant.

Now Dinello's example is badly flawed, since the choice before the doctor is not a choice between killing and letting die at all. If the doctor kills Smith in order to transplant his heart to Jones, he will have killed Smith. But if he waits until Jones dies, and then transfers the kidney to Smith, he will *not* have "let Jones die." The reason is connected with the fact that not every case of not saving someone is a case of letting him die. (Josef Stalin died, and I did not save him, but I did not let Stalin die.) Dinello himself points out that, in order for it to be true that *X* lets *Y* die, *X* must be "in a position" to save *Y*, but not do so.[15] (I was never in a position to save Stalin.) Now the doctor is in a position to save Jones only if there is heart available for transplantation. But no such heart is available—Smith's heart, for example, is not available since Smith is still using it. Therefore, since the doctor is not in a position to save Jones, he does not let Jones die.[16]

Trammell's position is not quite so easy to dismiss. Initially, I share the intuition that it would be worse to kill someone to prevent $1000 from being stolen than to refuse to pay $1000 to save someone. Yet on reflection I have not much confidence in this feeling. What is at stake in this situation described is the person's $1000 and the stranger's life. But we end up with the *same* combination of lives and money, no matter which option the person chooses: if he shoots the stranger, the stranger dies and he keeps his $1000; and if he refuses to pay to save the stranger, the stranger dies and he keeps his $1000. It makes no difference, either to the person's interests or to the stranger's interests, which option is chosen; why, then, do we have the curious intuition that there is a big difference here?

I conceded at the outset that most of us believe that in letting people die we are not behaving as badly as if we were to kill them. I think I have given good reasons for concluding that this belief is false. Yet giving reasons is often not enough, even in philosophy. For if an intuition is strong enough, we may continue to rely on it and assume that *something* is wrong with the arguments opposing it, even though we are not sure exactly what is wrong. It is a familiar remark: "*X* is more certain than any argument that might be given against it." So in addition to the arguments, we need some account of why people have the allegedly mistaken intuition and why it is so persistent. Why do people believe so firmly that killing is so much worse than letting die, both in fictitious cases such as Trammell's, and in the famine relief cases in the real world? In some ways the explanation of this is best left to the psychologists; the distinctly philosophical job is accomplished when the intuition is shown to be false. However, I shall hazard a hypothesis, since it shows how our intuitions can be explained without assuming that they are perceptions of the truth.

Human beings are to some degree altruistic, but they are also to a great degree selfish, and their attitudes on matters of conduct are determined by what is in their own interests, and what is in the interests of the few other people they especially care about. In terms of both the costs and the benefits, it is to their own advantage for people in the affluent countries to regard killing as worse than letting die. First, the *costs* of never killing anyone are not great; we can live very well without ever killing. But the cost of not allowing people to die, when we could save them, would be very great. For any one of us to take seriously a duty to save the starving would require that we give up our affluent life-styles; money could no longer be spent on luxuries while others starve. On the other side, we have much more to *gain* from a strict prohibition on killing than from a like prohibition on letting die. Since we are not in danger of starving, we will not suffer if people do not regard feeding the hungry as so important; but we would be threatened if people did not regard killing as very, very bad. So, both the costs and the benefits encourage us, selfishly, to view killing as worse than letting die. It is to our own advantage to believe this, and so we do.

Notes

1. For an account of the difficulties of getting reliable information in this area, see Nick Eberstadt, "Myths of the Food Crisis," *New York Review of Books*, 19 February 1976, 32–37.
2. Richard L. Trammell, "Saving Life and Taking Life," *Journal of Philosophy* 72 (1975), 131–137, is the best defense of this view of which I am aware.
3. This article is a companion to an earlier one, "Active and Passive Euthanasia," *New England Journal of Medicine* 202 (9 January 1975), 78–80 [reprinted in the present volume, 1–6], in which I discuss the (mis)use of the killing/letting die distinction in medical contexts. But nothing in this article depends on the earlier one.
4. Philippa Foot, "The Problem of Abortion and the Doctrine of the Double Effect," *Oxford Review* no. 5 (1967); reprinted in James Rachels, ed., *Moral Problems*, 2nd ed. (New York, 1975), 66.

5. On this point, and more generally on the whole subject of our duty to contribute for famine relief, see Peter Singer, "Famine, Affluence, and Morality," *Philosophy & Public Affairs* 1 (Spring 1972), 232.
6. Trammell, 133.
7. This argument is suggested by Paul Ramsey in *The Patient as Person* (New Haven, Conn., 1970), 151.
8. This difference between failing to save and letting die was pointed out by David Sanford in a very helpful paper, "On Killing and Letting Die," read at the Western Division meeting of the American Philosophical Association, in New Orleans, on 30 April 1976.
9. Trammell, 133.
10. Ibid., 134.
11. There is also some independent evidence that this prereflective belief is mistaken; see Singer, "Famine, Affluence, and Morality."
12. Grice made this remark several years ago at Oberlin. I do not remember the surrounding details of the discussion, but the remark seems to me an important one which applies to lots of "objections" to various theories. The most famous objections to act-utilitarianism, for example, are little more than descriptions of the theory, with the question-begging addendum, "Because it says *that*, it can't be right."
13. Daniel Dinello, "On Killing and Letting Die," *Analysis* 31, no. 3 (January 1971), 83, 86.
14. Trammell, 131.
15. Dinello, 85.
16. There is another way to meet Dinello's counterexample. A surprisingly strong case can be made that it would *not* be any worse to kill Smith than to "let Jones die." I have in mind adapting John Harris's argument in "The Survival Lottery," *Philosophy* 50 (1975), 81–87.

Further Readings

Aiken, William, and Hugh LaFollette. *World Hunger and Moral Obligation*. Englewood Cliffs, NJ: Prentice Hall, Inc., 1977.

Hardin, Garrett. *Stalking the Wild Taboo*. Los Altos, CA: William Kauffman, 1978.

Singer, Peter. "Famine, Affluence, and Morality." In *Moral Problems*, ed. James Rachels. New York: Harper & Row, 1979, 263–278.

Content Quiz 14.2

Instructions: Fill in the blanks with the appropriate responses listed below.

psychological explanation	lifestyles
good reason	bad faith
discharge	intuitions

optionality
counterintuitive
distinction
positive-negative

1. _____ are prereflective beliefs about what is right and wrong.
2. A(n) _____ of how we feel does not constitute an ethical justification for our conduct.
3. The _____ between action and inaction does not lead to any necessary moral assessment about what is or is not done.
4. If there is no _____ for performing some action, then it is not true that one ought to do it.
5. The fact that we cannot completely _____ a duty to save everyone needing aid does not mean that our duty to save those we can is any less stringent.
6. For Richard Trammell, _____ makes letting die less bad or wrong than killing, since others may choose to save the starving, even if we do not.
7. Arguments that lead to _____ conclusions are not always wrong or inadequate. The intuitions involved may be based on false assumptions.
8. Daniel Dinello accepts the _____ distinction among duties.
9. Serious attention to our responsibility to feed the starving of the world would require that we abandon our affluent _____.
10. When we rationalize our lack of action to save the hungry by pointing to others who could but do not help, we are guilty of _____, according to Rachels.

Discussion Questions

1. Are "killing" and "letting die" essentially different or are they equivalent to one another? Why?
2. What are some of the reasons why we, in affluent countries, feel so apathetic and unconcerned about the starving millions in developing nations? Are we justified in feeling this way? Why or why not?
3. Because others who are more affluent do not help, are we, as individuals, any more or any less responsible for feeding the starving? Explain.
4. Is it unrealistic to suggest that we have a duty to save all the starving in the world? If so, are we absolved of any and all responsibility to feed the hungry? Explain.
5. Are all wrong-doings by "omission" less morally objectionable than wrong-doings by "commission"? Justify.
6. Is it wrong to buy compact discs, cars, toys, and fancy clothes when so many others in the world lack basic necessities? What moral assessment can be made of our affluent society?

IN DEFENSE OF WAR

William Earle

Synopsis

William Earle's basic aim in this article is to show that the principle of pacifism is "practically absurd and morally deplorable." He supports his position by exposing and criticizing the underlying presuppositions of pacifism as well as by tracing the harmful consequences of it. Pacifism is described at the outset as principled opposition to war. From the idealistic perspective of pacifism, war is thought to be inherently evil and peace inherently good. To Earle's disapproval, much fuel has been fed to the pacifist's fire by television and by people whom he describes as retired baby doctors, neurotic poets and novelists, psychoanalysts, ministers and confused philosophers. For him, all of such people claim some kind of "special insight" qualifying them to speak for suffering humanity. The net result is the elimination of careful political thought and the emergence of preposterous slogans supported by elevated passions, demonstrations, and the exchange of insults. Since pacifists see no possible justification for war, they regard it as aberrant behavior for which there must be a cause and, presumably, a solution or cure of some description. For Earle, the justification of war is, in fact, its cause; hence, proponents of war do not need treatment, therapy, reconditioning or character education.

In the second part of the article, Earle goes on to spell out his justification for war. In certain circumstances, he regards war as the rational and morally proper course of action, something that allows people to live a life of dignity and honor. The opposition of war in these circumstances is both irrational and ethically deplorable. Further, given that all of the world's goods cannot be shared by everyone equally and that a ground for conflict is, therefore, inevitably created, he favors defending a nation's material self-interests, showing how they are inextricably linked with its ideals. For him, material factors make the achievement of social ideals possible. To fight for the former is to achieve the latter. According to Earle, fighting for our material self-interests is not a form of selfishness; it is a way for people to protect themselves and their families, as well as their friends and compatriots. It is a way of upholding a nation's values, including its laws, customs, institutions, and way of life generally. Life is all about inequalities and differences; this is the essence of history and, what he calls, the "individuated free choices of nations." For a nation to protect and, if necessary, fight for what belongs to it is justifiable in Earle's estimation.

In Part Three of the article, Earle addresses a number of objections to war. He rejects protests expressed by miscellaneous groups, random interests and the media reports of contrary opinions of ordinary individuals. He also rejects condemnations of war presented from the fighting soldier's perspective, as described by novelists for example. It is the proper responsibility of elected government representatives to make policy about war. Only they can, rationally and dispassionately, make decisions in a truly informed fashion.

Earle also rejects "psychologizing efforts" to assess policy through judgments of character and the assumed motives of the initiators of national policy. For him, wars are neither justified nor unjustified by the private motives of leaders; instead, government policies should be measured by their probable costs and effects.

A final objection in Part Three deals with the "sufferings of the people." Admitting that war is horrible and that it causes great pain, Earle maintains that we must, nonetheless, overcome our emotions in the face of suffering if we would live life honorably, with excellence and dignity. As he puts it, "There is no moral obligation to live at all costs and under any conditions; there is no moral obligation to live at all; there is a moral obligation to live honorably if one lives at all." In some circumstances, men may have to defend unto death what they take to be more valuable than mere existence itself. For Earle, to do this is an act of courage; to refuse to do this behind a veil of idealism or alleged humanitarianism is tantamount to cowardice.

Finally, in Part Four, Earle admits that victory in war does not always fall to the just. Yet, even in defeat, a nation can preserve its morale or self-respect which defines its humanity. For Earle, a life lived in dishonor and disgrace is not a life worth living; hence, the justification for war.

A philosophical consideration of political affairs has the disadvantage of being incapable, in and of itself, of implying any specific practical action or policy. It would, then, seem useless except for the accompanying reflection that specific policy undertaken without any attention to principles, is mindless; and mindless action can have no expectation either of practical effect or of intellectual defense. No doubt the relation of principles to action is complex indeed; but at least it can be said that practical principles without reference to possible action are vacuous, and action which can not be clarified by principle is aimless commotion. Principled action offers us then the best that can be hoped for. That, however, is the work not of philosophy but of statesmanship, a faculty which is as theoretically clear as it need be but also skilled by experience in reading the existing political scene. Accordingly my present remarks aim only at some principles involved in the understanding of war, focusing on those which seem conspicuously absent in contemporary discussion, and not at defending any specific judgments about the current war. Examples of incoherent principles will be drawn from present discussions; but any other war might have served equally well. No judgment about the present war can be derived from these remarks on principles; and if most of the false principles are quoted from the antiwar side, it is only because that side has been more vocal.

The villain of the present essay is *pacifism*, by which I mean a principled opposition to all war. Since it is a principled opposition, any appropriate opposition to pacifism must itself be a matter of principles. That pacifism is a principle and not a specific opposition to this war is sufficiently indicated by the suffix "ism," as well as by the arguments it mounts to make its principle plausible: it is war itself which is evil, and peace itself good under no matter what terms. Pacifism thinks it is sufficient to declare these ideals to win all hearts and minds; and if to some these pacifist principles seem impractical or indeed immoral, that can only be because the unconverted are hard of heart, slow of comprehension, or the world itself not yet ready for such a glory. That pacifism itself is practically absurd and morally deplorable is the chief burden of these present remarks. The argument will be by way of excavating the presuppositions and tracing the consequences of pacifism, and exhibiting them to the reader for his free choice. That pacifism itself is evil does *not*, needless to say, imply that the *persons* who hold that view are evil; a radical distinction between the character of persons and the character of their articulated views is the very basis of this or any other civilized discussion. If human beings could not be decent while their views are absurd, then all of us would fall into the abyss.

In any event, the first casualty of the present war seems to have been philosophy itself. The transition was easy: from an opposition to the war on whatever ground, a portion of the public mind rose to what it thought was the proper principle of that opposition: pacifism, the sentiment that war was itself evil. And its arguments proceeded down from that height. Flattering itself for its "idealism," it could only survey the home reality it had left with high indignation: *we were killing!* Children were trotted forth on TV to ask: why must men kill one another? Can we not all love one another, the child asks, having immediately forgotten his fight with his brother off-screen. Having been illuminated by the purity and innocence of children, the new pacifist can but flagellate himself in public remorse. Not merely must this war be stopped at once, but all war and forever; we must recompense our enemies for the damage wrought upon them; we must ask their forgiveness, for are they not really our friends and our friends our enemies? and as the confusion multiplies and moral passion inflames itself, nothing appears as too severe a punishment for ourselves; impeachment of our leaders and finally the impeachment of ourselves and our history seem too gentle. These public outbursts of moral self-hatred are, of course, not unknown in history; let Savonarola stand for them all. Today the uproar is orchestrated by retired baby-doctors, neurotic poets and novelists, psychoanalysts, ministers and confused philosophers, each of whom, armed with the authority of his special "insight," seeks to speak for suffering humanity. The message to be read through the tear-stained faces is the same: we must stop killing! Regardless of how one reads the present war, what is *said* publicly for or most usually against it, presents something like the eclipse of political thought. And with the eclipse of thought, we are left with some of the most preposterous slogans ever to find utterance. When supported by high passion, parades and demonstrations, insults in loud voices, we find ourselves once again in the theater of the absurd.

Why War?

Why indeed, asks the child? Why can not everyone love one another? Settle all disputes "rationally," so that all men could live as brothers, already having forgotten the first brothers, Cain and Abel? Thrashing around for "explanations" of the horrid fact that men can indeed be hostile to one another, the sloganeer with a smattering of pop-culture finds some answers ready to hand. War has a biological origin; it arises from an excess of testosterone in the male; maybe there is a biological solution, something like castration? That Indira Gandhi and Golda Meir have conducted their wars very successfully, is already forgotten. Or maybe they are men in disguise? Or the impulse to fight arises from some distorted family history, a son conditioned by a father who in turn was conditioned by his father to conceive war as particularly masculine, an expression of *machismo*; but that could be remedied by "treatment." Perhaps drugs, suggested a recent president of the American Psychological Society. Or perhaps war arises from selfishness, a moral flaw which could be remedied by a turn of the heart, that hoped for by a Quaker who during World War II looked Hitler straight in the eye and said: Thou art an evil man! If there is a warlike "instinct," maybe it could be diverted into harmless games like chess or the Olympics. And then maybe there is no such instinct? Animals like the gazelle or lamb may be found which are not particularly aggressive; why not take them for our ideal? Or, if not an animal "instinct," then surely it is generated by the capitalist society, which as everyone knows, fosters aggression, competition, acquisitiveness, imperialism. But then even the most casual glance sees that communist societies are even more imperialist and aggressive than the capitalist. And does not the stock market fall with each new bombing? Or, finally, it is all caused by presidents, who wish to be mentioned in the history books, or be reelected by the Veterans of Foreign Wars. The presidency should, accordingly, be abolished; policy should be turned over to the people. But which people? Those people who have been treated, have had a change of heart, who take flowers and gentle animals for their ideal, in a word, the saving remnant who through their dictatorship, will save the world from every war except that against themselves.

The generating assumption of this system of explanations is of course that there can be no *moral justification* for war at all. It is simply an evil; and since man is "naturally good," one must look for a "cause" of his distorted conduct. If war were morally justifiable, then that justification would remove any occasion for looking for pathological explanations. If one does not seek for "causes" for a man doing good works other than the goodness of the work itself, neither need one seek biological, psychological, cultural, sociopolitical causes for a justifiable war. The justification *is* the cause in this case.

And so then the question, why war? would be answered if any moral justification for it were forthcoming. A "justifiable war"? Is that not a contradiction in terms, or is it the pacifist who represents a living contradiction in terms?

This first answer to the question, why war, assumes at the start that it *is* evil, assumes that men are or could be "naturally good," meaning "peaceful," but since in point of fact they are not, the "explanation" is to be found in an artificial distortion of their passionate nature. The elimination of war will result from a correction of that passionate nature, through treatment whether physiological, psychological, social or rhetorical. In a word, either their bodies or their characters must be changed by whatever treatment promises success. The lion will lie down with the lamb, indeed will be indistinguishable from him. He will abandon pride, greed, egotism, the desire to display power, to intimidate, to coerce; he will at the end of history at last be good. But, of course, absolutely *all* men must be good; for if even a few are left who do *not* so envisage the good, our "good" men will be, of course, good-for-nothing, and their peace will be the peace determined by the wicked. Unwilling to fight for their lives or ideals, they are suppressed and at that point the whole of human history recommences as if there had been no interlude, or at best an interlude within common sense. The lamb who lies down with the lion may indeed be good for the lion when his appetites return; and if he is good in any other sense, it could only be on a mystic plane not exactly pertinent to the practical moral plane of existence. It is not surprising then that advocates in the church of the kingdom of heaven, do indeed place it in heaven, but never advocate it as political policy. After all, by definition, heaven has already expelled or refused admittance to the wicked, hence is hardly faced with problems commensurate with ours on earth. What does a lion *eat* in heaven? Men, needless to say, are not animals *simpliciter*, but rational or spirited animals; but neither reasons nor spirit so long as they remain living can *contradict* animal needs.

That rational animals engage in hostilities unto death has always seemed a scandal to those philosophers who neglect existence. If one stamp of moralist finds both the cause and solution to war in some alteration in body or character, many philosophers of abstractions find both the cause and solution to war in *thought* to be corrected by right reasoning. If rational men still fight, and if war is irrational, then there must be a rational solution to it. The medium of reason is the word, so we can expect this stamp of pacifist to praise the verbal solution to hostilities: the treaty. Would it not be reasonable to prevent or terminate hostilities by calculation, agreements, and solemnly pledged words? It is easy to forgive philosophers and the educated in general for their touching confidence in the power of words; they exercise a magical power in and over the mind; but perhaps that is their proper place. However, it is an outrageous neglect to fancy that they have any power except that over the mind, mind moreover which itself has the *obligation* to superintend the very existential conditions of its own life. Who then is surprised when he reads that in the last 350 years, something like 85 percent of the treaties signed in the Western world have been broken? But the treaty theory of peace can then congratulate itself on the fact that now a culprit can be identified, declared to be an aggressor, and, while the aggressor is condemned by the "enlightened goodwill of mankind," he nevertheless proceeds to enjoy his dinner, and later may be celebrated as a benefactor of mankind; he will certainly not hesitate to sign new treaties. Our question is what to do: wring one's hands over men's irrationality or rethink the meaning of war? In all of this, one can easily agree that treaties exercise some slight restraining power over the more rapacious inclinations; but would it not be criminal neglect to entrust the security of one's country to treaties? And in fact, does any responsible leader ever do it? No doubt, the lambs, since they have nothing better to work with.

And eventually, as the final rational "solution" to the problem of war, there is the idea of a single superstate, whether an enlargement of one of those now extant, such as the USA, Russia or China—or conceived as a super United Nations. This convulsive, "final solution" to the war problem particularly appeals to those who have little "negative capability" as Keats put it, little tolerance for the uncertain, for risk, for in fact the most fundamental characteristics of free human life. When put in the form of a super United Nations, it almost looks harmless. But it can more properly be put in uglier terms; if it were indeed to be a Super State, it could be nothing short of a Super Totalitarianism. The historical totalitarianisms we have all witnessed would be as nothing compared with this monstrosity; and, as has often been remarked, they grew in precisely the same spiritual soil, a certain inability to face risk, death, war or confusion, in a word, the existential conditions of a free life with dignity. Everything must be put *in order*! And if the World is not now in order and never has been, then the order will be imposed, imposed in fact by the very Force which once seemed so odious. A new order of the World; but now *its* dissidents become World-enemies and where are they to flee? Do they have a right to life itself? Are they not enemies of the World? In this abstract fantasia, the first thing lost sight of is a small annoying matter, a point of logic: any Order is also only itself a *specific* order. Law and Order, of course, are only universal abstractions, whose proper medium of existence is the word. In existence itself, it is always this or that order, that is, *somebody's* order; and then there is always a somebody else, who believes honestly in another order, one perhaps more favorable to himself or his ideal. Again the eternal hostilities break out, now however with a difference: hostilities between nations have not been eliminated, but only redubbed: each is now a *civil* war within the World State. Perhaps the candid observer will be excused if he fails to perceive the difference, except in the new savagery now morally permitted. And as for the individual? He has been forgotten for a long time in his prison or madhouse. He must be given therapy.

Many serious persons, of course, are sensitive to these paradoxes, and yet finally in desperation cling to the solution of a world state or world dictatorship as the only preventative of world destruction through nuclear holocaust. It is one thing to be willing to give one's own life for one's nation, but it is qualitatively different to destroy the habitable parts of the globe for "nothing but" freedom and dignity. For our present discussion, we shall assume that some such thing is possible now or in the not-too-distant future. The possibility raises questions, obviously, of an ultimate order. But I do not think it unambiguously true that some such possible world catastrophe compels assent to world totalitarianism. In any event, for the moment, it might seem that here, at last, pacifism becomes sanity; and that any acceptance of world destruction is the very essence of evil and immorality. I shall revert to this question at the end and touch upon it now only to complete this first part surveying various sentiments which find war, as such and in principle, intolerable with the ensuing effort to formulate a solution or eliminate the cause.

II. The Justification of War

The attitudes so far considered begin, as we have seen, by assuming war to be unjustifiable; *if* it is unjustifiable, then its cause must be found, in biological, psychological, social or moral distortions of an inherently peace-loving human nature; the cure is always some form of therapy. Or those who conduct war must have reasoned badly or given up the hope that rational discussion with its eventual treaty would be effective. Wars are "irrational," no philosophical justification of any is possible; thought will find the rational "solution." But on the other hand, if war is justifiable, then the search for its causes in either distortions of the passionate nature of man, or in errors or failures of reason, is downright foolish. The justification removes the premise of the search for causes and cures. The justification of war as a form of moral and rational excellence may seem scandalous to the pacifist, and yet it is that scandal I should like to defend. And as for talk about the greater or lesser of two evils, I shall try to avoid this ambiguous, slippery and ultimately meaningless effort to calculate the incalculable. The justification of war aims at showing both its morality and its rationality; if therefore there are occasions when a moral and rational man must fight, then a proscription of war in principle must be itself irrational and ethically deplorable.

In a word, the justification of war is existence; to will to exist is to affirm war as its means and condition. But perhaps the term "existence" puts the matter too abstractly. In the present context, and in its most abstract sense, existence is a synonym for life, and nonexistence for death. Wars then are justified as means taken to assure life and death. And yet little has been said; the life and death of what? Bare life measured by the beating of the heart, is hardly life at all; it would be prized only as the supporter and condition of a life *worth living*. Obviously men have always thought it justifiable to fight not merely to preserve their physical being, but also for those additional things which make that life worth living, fertile lands, access to the sea, minerals, a government of their choice, laws and customs and religions, and finally peace itself. Existence then is hardly bare survival but an existence in the service of all those concrete values which illuminate and glorify existence. They too must exist; it is almost by definition that values, in and of their intrinsic meaning, *demand existence*. Justice would misunderstand itself if it were content to remain abstract and merely ideal.

So much might easily be granted until another reflection arises, that perhaps the goods of existence could be shared by all men. This utopian notion is much beloved of *philosophers* or *art critics* who look upon the diversities of thought and cultural style as so many advantages and opportunities for spiritual growth. And indeed they are; but then those values are not exactly what war is about. If the library can house every book in peaceful coexistence, or if the museum can calmly exhibit the styles of the world, why must men themselves fight? Could the world not be like an international congress of philosophy or perhaps a quieter meeting of UNESCO: would this not be the civilized thing? Would it not be better if nations conducted themselves according to the model of a genteel conversation, where views are advanced and withdrawn without anger, and where men say "excuse me for interrupting"?

But elementary reflection is sufficient to dispel these dreams. Existence or life individuates itself; when it can speak it says "I," and what it possesses, "mine." Nothing is changed logically in this respect when the I becomes a We, and mine, Ours. That I am not you, or we are not they, is the ineluctable ground of war; individuation is essential to existence. That which is not individuated does not exist, but subsists as a universal or abstract meaning. Consequently the meaning of a book or cultural artifact can be shared by all; but the existent book or existent painting can not, and could supply a ground for conflict. No wonder philosophers or scientists or critics, accustomed to living in the domain of abstractions and ideal meanings which are not, like quantities of matter, diminished progressively by each man who partakes of them, find something scandalous and primitive about war or anything else appropriate in the domain of existence and life. Nothing is easier than for the spirit to neglect the conditions of its own existence, or indeed be outraged by them.

I have used the term "existential" intentionally in spite of its abstractness to avoid at all costs what might seem to be its more common equivalent, "material." Some sentimental pacifists think it sufficient to prove that a nation has gone to war for "material" interests to conclude, with cheers from their audience, that such a war is *immoral*. That idealism should find itself opposed to "matter," or its equivalent, life and existence, would certainly not have surprised the Buddha or Nietzsche, both of whom accurately perceived that the only surcease of war and public sorrow is in nothingness, Nirvana or eternity. And, as President Truman remarked, those who can not stand the heat should get out of the kitchen.

But of course, what the sentimental pacifist wants is nothing so radical as the genuine alternative of a Buddha; he wants an *existent* heaven, perpetual peace-on-earth, a mishmash which has never been or never will be seen, violating as it does patent ontological differences subsisting between existence and the abstract. The exposure of this error is not difficult. At what precise point do material interests become ideal? Is the health of a nation "material" or "ideal"? But its health depends, of course, upon its wealth; is the pursuit of that wealth ideal or materialistic and crass? Is the culture of a nation an ideal or material value? and is its culture dependent or not upon the wealth available for education and leisure? Is the wealth devoted to such tasks materialistic or idealistic? Money versus human life! All these false contrasts need not be multiplied to perceive the vacuity of any argument against war based upon "idealistic" as opposed to "materialistic" principles.

Functioning according to the same false logic is another simplistic contrast, also beloved of pacifists: that thought to exist between egoism and altruism. The high-minded rhetoric poured out against "selfishness" is laughable indeed when not taken seriously. Is it "selfish" for me to protect my own life, or those of my family, friends, or compatriots? And, moreover, not merely our physical existence, but our human life with its wealth, customs, laws, institutions, languages, religions, our autonomy? Or to protect the "material," i.e., economic conditions which support all these values? To affirm any form of life at all is at the same time to affirm the means to it; what *could* be more confused than to will our life and also to will the life opposed to it? The ultimate pacifist who would do nothing even to protect his own life for fear of killing another, is simply a case of self-hatred; but both nature and logic combine to guarantee that this particular illness never becomes widespread. Has or could there ever be a defense for the idea that everyone else's life is preferable to my own, particularly when adopted in turn by everyone else? To be bound together in friendship is certainly preferable to being torn apart by hostility; but is it not clear that neither the friendship of all nor the hostility of all is possible; the line to be drawn which assures the provisional existence of any state is to be drawn by practical statesmanship judging in its time for its time, and not by abstract, would-be idealistic principles, which by hoping to be valid for all times are pertinent to none.

Excursus on Equality. No doubt it will have been noted that war here has *not* been justified as a means of securing justice or equality. It has been justified as a means necessary to any nation to secure or preserve its own social good, and as such, is held to be eminently reasonable and honorable. However, the social life of a nation is not itself to be further judged by means of abstract categories such as justice or equality. Hasty thought frequently identifies justice with equality, particularly since justice is elusive and protean in its applications, whereas the notion of equality, being mathematical and abstract, is within the grasp of all. I either do or do not have as much as another; if I do not, am I not wronged? Can not anyone see this? and indeed they can, but what can not be so immediately seen is whether such inequality is also *ipso facto* unjust.

These confusions pour into those discussions which, for example, would justify any war at all against the United States; since we have more than anyone else, we could never have a right to defend that more. To have more is to be guilty before the abstract bar of Equality. But this last gasp of the French Revolution, amplified by Marxist bellows, blows against certain existential realities. Those realities are simply that the earth itself is differentiated by rivers, climates, flora and fauna, mountains, valleys and plains. Not all can live everywhere nor is this an injustice to them. And, to belabor the obvious, men are not equal, having very different temperaments, tastes, ideals, and histories. Not merely are men not equal, they are not unequal either, the category of "equality" being quantitative whereas a man or a nation is not a quantity of anything, but rather an individual or communal person aiming at a definite form of excellent life. Since nations and men are always already in a differentiated possession of the goods of the world, differentiated forms of excellence, differentiated histories and memories, the desire to equalize all is equivalent to the desire to obliterate history as well as the individuated free choices of nations and men. Computerized thought might delight in such simplicities, but is there any a priori reason why a truly just mind must accept it?

If I have not used the notion of justice in any abstract form to justify war, again, it is for the simple reason that it leads nowhere. Wars are fought *over* differing notions of justice; does any party to war ever think itself unjust? Justice in the abstract therefore is useless for purposes of condemnation or justification. Victory in war equally does not decide what is abstractly just, but which form of justice will prevail.

III. Objections to War

1. *What the "people" think of war.* I shall use this title for a slippery mass of appeals increasingly popular in the mass media. Reporters, seemingly getting the "objective" facts, can always ask some fleeing peasants: "do you want war?" Of course, the bewildered peasant replies that he only wishes to live in peace, that war has destroyed his family, his rice fields, that it is caused by "government," that he could live equally well under any regime, that in fact he does not know the enemy, or does, having relatives among them, etc., all of which is pathetic as much for the sufferings of the peasant as for the mindlessness of the reporter who imagines himself to be presenting an ultimate argument based upon "humanity."

Television, since it can not picture any thought about war, is confined to showing what can be shown: the dismembered, burned, legless, eyeless, as if to say: this is what war really is. And when the dead or wounded are little children, women, or old men, the very heart recoils; the argument is decisive. But not yet: the soldiers must be asked; have they not seen it first hand, fought it with their lives, seen their comrades fall before their very eyes? Any number can be rounded up to swear they haven't the faintest idea what all the killing is about, that it must be immoral or absurd, probably conducted by munition makers or politicians seeking reelection, in a word by all that "establishment" in which they never had much participation even during peace. Their own virtue is to be resigned or, if they "think," to wearing peace symbols.

As for the ideal component in war, the honor and courage of the soldier, that too is immediately debunked. "There's nothing heroic about war" says the soldier who may just yesterday have risked his life to save a comrade. War is nothing but living in the mud and rain, with poor food, disease, fatigue, danger and boredom; is that heroic? His reticence about "heroism" is admirable; but we need not believe what he says. Since heroism is doing one's duty or going beyond it under extreme conditions, it is difficult to see how the difficulties diminish the accomplishment; without those difficulties, genuine heroism would be nothing but parade-ground heroics. But let us look in more detail at these arguments of the people.

The "People": who are they? They are either citizens of their country or not; if not, they have no political right to complaint. If so, then their government is indeed theirs, and they have every political duty to observe its decisions or try to alter them legally. In any event, the people are all the people, not merely the peasants, and they are in their collective capacity *already* represented by their government, whose decisions they must respect as made by their legal representatives. If the people are in no way represented by their government, then the question shifts itself away from war to that of forming a representative government. In any event, war and peace are decisions which obviously fall to the national government and not to miscellaneous groups, random interests, or *ad hoc* political rallies. Nor, least of all, to the private opinions of reporters interviewing a few people, usually those with the least opportunity to consider and weigh what is at stake. To suggest opinion polls or referenda on these questions every month or so, simply offers us the idea of another form of government altogether, an unheard-of-populism which in effect negates representative government altogether and substitutes for it the ever-shifting voice of the street. And since that in turn clearly reflects the overwhelming influence of propaganda, immediate "democracy" of this order shifts the decision from government to the directors and voice of "news" media. It is hardly surprising that this prospect delights the media, but it is surprising that so many otherwise sensible citizens wish to shift their allegiance from their own duly elected representatives to the directors of news media whom they have not elected and for the most part hardly know, all the while imagining that this offers them an opportunity themselves to direct the course of events.

The truth is, unwelcome as it may be, that the "people," ordinary housewives, factory workers, farmers, etc., as fine as they may be personally, are in no position whatsoever to consider the wisdom of that very politics upon which their own lives depend. It is, naturally, for this reason that very few nations at all, and none of any importance, are run on any such scheme. It is precisely the responsibility of representatives of the people to occupy themselves with such questions, inform themselves and circumspectly weigh the possibilities. The limits of experience and political habits of thought which more or less make the ordinary private citizen private, at the same time warn us against encouraging any immediate or undue influence of his opinions on matters of state. What the people think is simply the repetition of slogans derived either from campaigning politicians or their favorite newspaper. For some researchers, the popular mind is a pool of infinite wisdom and goodness; the truth is it is nothing but an ephemeral reflection of popular songs, sandwich-board slogans, newspaper headlines and clichés. For the popular mind "thought" is what can be written on a placard or shouted at a rally; for the reflective, thought is precisely what eludes this form of expression. Who has the wind to shout a *qualified* thought?

Nothing could be more dangerous than the enthusiasms of the people. Mad joy at the beginning of hostilities; and rage when the bodies are brought in, the expenses reckoned up. But of course this is precisely what is to be expected from the people, suggestible, flighty, and unused to either foresight or circumspection. As for the shallow notion that the people want only peace, that all peoples love one another as brothers, and that war therefore is imposed upon them from above—could one find any stretch of history or any segment of the world where these notions are significantly illustrated? The natural brotherhood of man? The natural goodness of the people? Indeed! One could far better argue that there is nothing whatsoever "natural" in man; the natural is exactly what man *decides*.

When we substitute for the people, the common soldier, all the same applies. Their experience is always tempting to novelists, looking for the "reality" of war. The reality in question, it should be remembered, is the one they are best equipped to express with vividness: the day-to-day life in the foxhole, or in the pouring rain, the mudholes, the terror, sickness, ambiguities of fighting life. It is easy for novelists to enter into the mind of the G.I. who is presented as seeing only what lies before his eyes: a dead friend. *That* is the reality of war; meanwhile at headquarters, the colonels are arrogant, incompetent, not really suffering but instead well provided with booze and whores, no doubt profiteering from the PX, and in cahoots with the government, known to be corrupt. No doubt all this is true enough from time to time, and no doubt anyone at all can sympathize with the sentiments involved. And no doubt at all, the same structure can easily be found in any civil society that ever was in peace time as well. The question however concerns the exact pertinence of such considerations, to the justification or lack of it for any given war. Since wars are not fought in the first place to make common soldiers comfortable, nor to make generals live the same lives as privates, nor to remove corruption in the armies involved, the only pertinence of such observations when true would be to improve the army, not to stop the war. And that a platoon leader does not know the whole strategy from his experience, that a general can not perform his legitimate functions in the same state of exhaustion as the G.I., nor carry his maps and codes into the foxholes, nor subject himself to the same risks as the ordinary soldier, is all obvious but no doubt at times escapes the full approval of the G.I. which is why the G.I. is not a general.

Related, is the curious popular objection that war is immoral because the soldier does not know his enemy *personally*. A German soldier of World War I in *All Quiet on the Western Front* receives a shock when after killing a Frenchman, he realizes he never knew him personally. However he would have received a greater shock upon recovering his wits when he realized that if he *had* known him personally and acted out of personal rage, his act would be radically transformed in meaning. From being a soldier doing his *duty*, he would be transformed into a *murderer*. But no doubt this distinction is too fine for those who love to talk of war as "mass murder," oblivious to all distinctions between on the one hand the legitimate duties of the police and soldiers, and on the other punishable murder. This essential distinction is obliterated in that higher pacifistic fog where all "taking of human life" is immoral. There could hardly be anything more obscurantist than the desire to obliterate all distinctions of roles and offices of men into that warm, personal, brotherly unity of "the personal." Generals receive criticism for not taking a "personal" interest in each of their troops; I, for one, would demote any who did. If some such thing is the philosophy of the best seller, it is easy to predict that of the worst seller: the wise general and the stupid G.I. In all of this, it would hardly take a Nietzsche to perceive the influence of that old, popular motive, the resentment of authority. In the present instance it feeds pacifism.

Popular thought loves to "psych" its political leaders. In this, has it not been aided and abetted by the rise of psychological novels where the plot sinks into insignificance and the psychological analysis of motives occupies the stage, usually a popular version of Freud. Psychologizing has, undoubtedly, a limited relevance to political decision; national policies are at the same time policies of leaders, whose characters and temperaments are significant factors in their actions and reactions. Roosevelt and Churchill both considered the personalities of Hitler and Stalin in this fashion, and if their judgments left something to be desired, at least the pertinence of the question is undeniable; political personality is unquestionably a factor in objective policy. Which items in announced policy are sticking points, and which negotiable? Which remarks made to the inner constituency and which to the outer world? Generals also try to sense the temperament of their opponents, as one factor in the whole.

On the other hand, what could be more ludicrous than the popular effort to assess policy through a judgment of the character and assumed private motives of the initiators of that policy? Antiwar finds nothing but reprehensible private motives at the root of the matter; prowar finds nothing but heroic strength; reflection finds both irrelevant. Wars are neither justifiable nor unjustifiable in terms of the private motives of the leaders; wars are not personal acts of rage and revenge, but as von Clausewitz showed, an extension of policy by other means. Policies are measured by their probable costs and effects, and not by the motives of the agents.

The weighing of policy properly belongs in the hands of those responsible and thoughtful men who are experienced in such matters. It is not in any conspicuous sense the experience of pastors in their morality, poets with their sensitivity, the young with their "idealism," psychoanalysts with their probings of emotions, or news reporters with their "scoops."

The distressing thing about popular psychologizing is its confidence; it *knows* the black heart inside the political leader, and is certain that anything more complex or even favorable is "naive." All of which reflects the failure of both psychology and the psychological novel to make their point; should not popular wisdom at least be sensitive to the difficulties and ambiguities of searching out the motives of the human heart? If I can only seldom if ever be confident I know my own motives, how can I be so sure I know those of others?

I conclude that the "people" must take their chances in war, do not represent a pool of persons separate from the organized body of citizens with a government, and that their perception, judgment and analysis of public policy is sound only by accident. Public policy is beyond the scope of private people; since it is, the common people revert to something they imagine themselves to be expert in, the psychological motives of leaders; but alas, even that is beyond their or anyone else's proper grasp. At which point we have nothing to do but return to where we should never have left, the objective consideration of policy by those competent to consider it.

2. *The Sufferings of the People.* A final set of criticisms against war again purports to rest upon humanitarian or idealistic grounds: its argument is the simple exhibition of death, injuries, disease, poverty, destruction, the ravaging of both countryside and cities. Television makes it as vivid as possible, and the color photographs in *Life* magazine are almost enough to sicken the heart of the

bravest and to shake the firmest judgment. Indeed this is their overt intention, and it is not long before they end up on pacifist posters as ultimate arguments. But of course arguments they are not, at best facts to be considered; but then who hasn't already considered them? Is there anyone who imagines war to be anything but killing? The decision to fight is the decision to kill; such a decision, needless to say, is never easy although it may frequently be justified. *If justified*, what service is performed by such direct appeals to vital instinct and sentiment? At best they would enfeeble our powers of judgment, never too strong, so that we would choose the unjustifiable rather than the wise course.

These images thought to be decisive, are in reality nothing but kicks below the belt and from behind; reasonable moral judgment can never be a simple reaction to our emotions and sentiments; the emotions and sentiments themselves are more than enough for that; but it is the role of policy and judgment to judge *over* these forces. The job is no doubt the most difficult man faces; it is hardly made easier by the daily flood of images of suffering in the media.

The image in itself is no argument against anything. It would be easy indeed by vivid color photographs, accompanied by recordings of screaming, wailing and crying, to sicken anyone of the very project of living. Surgical operations would never be undertaken, women would be afraid to give birth to children; images of the old, sick and senile would convince us that life itself is folly; and some such thing is the conclusion of transcendental ascetics. But then such an ethic, by intention, is not pertinent to public policy, necessarily committed to not merely life, but the good life.

The humanitarian argument drawn from ruins and suffering, aims at a higher idealism; but with a suddenness which would have delighted Hegel, turns into its opposite, a crass materialism. If human life is justifiable in terms of its excellence, where is the idealism in locating that excellence in a clinging to cities and fields? Or finally, in clinging to mere life itself as our highest value? The founder of Western philosophy, Socrates, disdained to use arguments resting upon such sympathies in his own defense, and did *not* bring his wife and children to court to plead for him. Nor did he conjure up imaginative pictures of his own suffering. No doubt, this is old-fashioned. . . .

Since one dies anyway, the sole question would seem to be *how* one dies, with honor or not. There is no moral obligation to live at all costs and under any conditions; there is no moral obligation to live at all; there is a moral obligation to live honorably if one lives at all. What that obligation dictates under specific historical concrete circumstances clearly can not be decided for all and in general; but it can dictate that under some circumstances, some men must find their honor in defending unto death what they take to be more valuable than sheer existence, namely a human life dedicated to excellence and dignity. Human lives whose chief moral defense is that they have kept themselves alive, have at the same stroke lost *all* moral defense. Such is the age-old paradox of life.

Traditionally, the man who chose life and personal safety under any conditions was regarded as a coward, and his condition that of a slave. Do we now have new reasons for reversing this decision? Which is not to say that some have not tried; what other judgment could be pronounced upon the current rash of movies and novels all celebrating the *antihero* as a new form of excellence; sometimes it is even thought to be "authentic" or "existential"! What is it but mediocrity and cowardice? It follows that some are authentic cowards, but need we admire them? A footnote to the present confusion is the argument that war "brutalizes" the troops. The brutalization is rarely spelled out although hovering around the attack is the suspicion that troops are brutalized in their coarse speech, their terms of contempt for the enemy, their failure personally to consider the "justice" of every order, to bring their superiors before the bar of their own private conscience, their fondness for booze and camp followers above lectures and the opera. Well! But if brutalization means a willingness to kill the enemy, I for one fail to perceive the fault; that's what they are there for in the first place, and who is closer to the brute, a man afraid to kill the enemy, or one who will kill and die to preserve the freedom and dignity of himself and his compatriots?

There will always be occasions when human freedom and dignity are threatened; there will always be occasions then for a justifiable war, and the pacifistic argument fails. To attack the very idea of war is to attack something fundamental to the preservation of any honorable life, and to offer under the flag of idealism or humanitarianism, the very substance of cowardice. Having already denounced Soviet injustice, what could be a worse capitulation than Bertrand Russell's slogan: "Better Red than dead"?

IV. What War Decides

Needless to say, victory does not always fall to the just. And if not, then victory is no measure of the justice of the cause, a truth commonly recognized by the respect accorded to the defeated. For while they were indeed defeated with regard to the immediate occasion of the dispute, they were not defeated, if they fought well, with regard to something far more important, that infinite self-respect which defines their humanity. The morale of a nation, that is, its self-respect, is certainly tested by the war, and is that factor which nullifies the old Chinese warlord "solution" to the problem of war, much beloved of computer thinkers. Why not, the argument goes, have the leaders meet on a neutral ground, calculate their resources, and decide victory without bloodshed, as the story says the warlords did. Is this not the essence of "rationality"? If the idea seems preposterous is it not because there remains one *incalculable* factor, the morale of the troops and the nations behind them? No doubt, this factor was negligible when the troops in question were mercenaries without any morale whatsoever except that for their pay or "professional" reputation. And no doubt one can easily find battles when the odds are so unequal as to render armed resistance suicidal. But even such "suicidal" resistances *win something*, namely, the enacted courage unto death of the men fighting them; to think nothing of this or to regard it as pure folly is itself a judgment proceeding out of little but crass materialism. To offer it as a rational *idealism* is a betrayal of everything noble in the defeated. A man is not necessarily ignoble because he was defeated; but he is if there is nothing he will fight for except his own skin.

Courage then, about which little is said today without an accompanying smirk, is a virtue whose analysis quickly carries us into transcendental realms. It looks like madness or vanity or an "ego-trip" to those who imagine the issues of life settled, and settled into the values of biology, economics, or fundamentally *pleasure*. But courage puts all those values into question, discloses that as always, men today put to themselves a goal and destiny which has no common measure with mere life, mere well-being, or mere comfort. These things may properly be fought over, but they are not *in themselves* the full story of what is involved. That full story can never be told, but at very least it must include what here is called the transcendental, the domain of freedom and dignity which is never compromised by mere death, poverty, or defeat; but most certainly is compromised by a certain deafness to its claims. Wars are not fought to prove courage, but they do prove it all the same.

Further Readings

Narveson, Jan. "Violence and War." In *Matters of Life and Death*, ed. Tom Regan. New York: Random House, 1980, pp. 109–147.

Walzer, Michael. *Just and Unjust Wars*. New York: Basic Books, 1977.

Wasserstrom, Richard (ed.). *War and Morality*. Belmont, CA: Wadsworth, 1970.

Content Quiz 14.3

Instructions: Fill in the blanks with the appropriate responses listed below.

moral justification	altruism
rational	material
totalitarianism	pacifism
existence	pathological causes
biological origin	individuation
private motives	emotions and sentiments
dignity and excellence	cowardice

1. The principle that war is inherently evil and, therefore, unjustified is known as _____.
2. _____ means more than survival; it entails dignity and all those things for which life is worth living.
3. Pacifists believe that no _____ can be given for war.
4. Those who believe that war is irrational and symptomatic of disordered conduct have looked for the _____ of war.
5. The only form of life worth living is one with _____.
6. Analyzing the _____ of generals and politicians has little or nothing to do with the justification of the war process.
7. Reference to testosterone levels in those who engage in armed conflict points to the possibility of a(n) _____ to war.
8. Human existence entails a process of _____ whereby we begin to appreciate our uniqueness and separateness from others.
9. The false dichotomy between the _____ and the ideal serves as a basis for the pacifists' antiwar arguments.

10. The principle of _____ is inconsistent because not everyone can regard others' lives as more important than their own.
11. Under the guise of humanitarianism, those who refuse to fight for life's dignity and autonomy are hiding their own _____.
12. Horrific television images of war are irrelevant to discussions of its acceptability, for _____ play no role in the justification of the war process.
13. There is no _____ solution to war.
14. The idea of a super United Nations to govern the world's affairs and to safeguard its peace will, in the end, lead to a dangerous form of _____.

Discussion Questions

1. What is pacifism? What assumptions do pacifists make about human nature? Do you think they are correct? Why or why not?
2. Is Earle's description of antiwar advocates neutral and objective? Is he simply making a statement of fact or is he building something into his description? Comment.
3. What are Earle's reasons for rejecting the pathological causes of war? Do you agree with them? Can you see any problems in his rejections? If so, explain.
4. Why does Earle consider rational solutions to conflict to be ineffective and inappropriate?
5. How is Earle's justification of war tied to "existence"? Explain.
6. Is there anything wrong about a country going to war to protect its material interests? Why or why not?
7. What are Earle's views on abstract concepts like equality and justice?
8. Does Earle respect "popular" objections to war? Why or why not?
9. How does Earle understand the relationship between the government and the ordinary voting citizen? Do you agree with his assessment of their respective responsibilities?
10. How could it be irrational and morally deplorable not to go to war?

NUCLEAR ILLUSION AND INDIVIDUAL OBLIGATIONS

Trudy Govier*

Synopsis

Trudy Govier begins her article by introducing the danger of nuclear war as the most pressing problem of our time. She places this problem in a philosophical context by pointing out that discussions of moral values and political structures are absurd if they ignore the nuclear threat. A nuclear holocaust would quickly bring to an end most, if not all, human values and problems. Govier urges that philosophers address the nuclear war threat because their silence may implicitly convey the message that they condone the nuclear status

An earlier version of this paper was presented at the annual meeting of the Society for Women in Philosophy, London, Ontario, October 1982.

quo. Silence, Govier believes, is what allowed the world to move from a position in 1945 where there were only 3 nuclear weapons to a point today where we find 50 000 of them. She contends that as teachers of ethics, applied ethics and political philosophy, philosophers occupy a special role in ending the dangerous silence. Apart from the inherent perils of nuclear proliferation, Govier contends we should also increase our awareness of nuclear issues because the arms race is a powerful force behind the economics, technologies, ideologies, and scientific research programs of our day. If we choose to ignore the military developments associated with nuclear arms, we risk developing a distorted and inaccurate view of social reality.

To justify her claim that the nuclear arms race should be made a central issue for philosophers, Govier considers it from the vantage point of occupational ethics, nation states, life's meaning, the problem of self-deception, and individual responsibility. Because all of these things have been matters of philosophical concern in the past and because the nuclear arms race is pertinent to all of them, Govier concludes that nuclear proliferation is a proper subject for philosophical analysis and debate. Rather than place "our hope in the political and military leaders whose sanity and responsibility we have trusted beyond all evidence," we should as teachers and students of moral philosophy "play our own small part in changing the situation [on nuclear proliferation], and should now be convinced that we have a special obligation to do so."

If we ask why philosophers as such should contribute to public understanding of nuclear problems, answers are readily forthcoming. Fundamentally, the danger of nuclear war is the most pressing problem of our time. If there is a global nuclear war most (if not all) of the other human problems will entirely disappear. Any which remain will appear in a radically different context. Global nuclear war would, in all likelihood, end human social life as we know it. It could end the human race altogether and might even result in the death of virtually all mammalian life on the planet.[1] A discussion of moral values and political structures which ignores this pervasive threat is in a sense absurd, for the threat could eliminate all those things we value. And it is a real one. There is a genuine persistent risk of nuclear war and virtually all adult citizens are at some level aware of the risk. To "apply" ethics to such problems as abortion, sexism, and capital punishment and ignore the nuclear arms race is to suggest that these less cosmic problems are more real and pressing than the problem of global peace or war. It may also suggest to students and the public at large that philosophers who have studied moral theory, competing ideologies, and principles of probability and strategy, condone the nuclear status quo.

Secondly, if we do not discuss the nuclear arms race and related dangers, we contribute to the suppression of thought about the issue which has been such a dominate feature of the nuclear age. Public silence through much of the period between 1945 and the present has enabled the superpowers to move from a position where there were three nuclear weapons in 1945 to one where there are more than 50,000 today. Now, that silence is ending; awareness is increasing. And philosophers, especially in their role as educators, can play their part in ending the silence.

An additional point is that the nuclear arms race and the enormous accumulations of conventional arms weapons are important forces behind the economies, technologies, ideologies, and scientific research programs of our time. These military developments (said by some to occupy forty percent of the scientists and engineers on the earth) contribute to the world political and social scene in many ways. By ignoring them, we risk an analysis of social reality which is seriously distorted and inaccurate.

Obviously the reason for philosophers as people to become knowledgeable about nuclear problems is that their very survival is at stake. But the reason for philosophers as philosophers to do this is that they have special opportunities to educate people on the topic, and they have special obligations to do so, especially insofar as they teach ethics, applied ethics, and political philosophy.

To show that issues pertaining to nuclear arms are related to other matters which are already recognized to be legitimate topics of philosophical study, we go on to mention some specific topic areas.

Occupational Ethics: Defense Production

In the American Catholic bishops' pastoral letter on nuclear weapons, a very conditional endorsement of (strict?) nuclear deterrence is given. Maintaining a nuclear arsenal for deterrence is allowed to be morally acceptable for some period of time provided that all efforts are made to eliminate reliance on this arsenal for national defense. The bishops conclude that the traditional just war theory could not justify the use of nuclear weapons, for just war theory requires a strict distinction between combatants and civilians in war. The distinction cannot hold up when nuclear weapons are used. Their conclusion, then, is that it could never be morally acceptable to detonate nuclear weapons against targets in populated areas. Nuclear weapons can never be used.

Given this conclusion, some bishops (notably Archbishop Hunthausen of Seattle) went much further, developing the following argument: If it is not right to use nuclear weapons, then it is not right to threaten to use them. If it is not right to threaten to use them, then it is not right to possess them; possession itself might be said to constitute some kind of implicit threat or implicit intention to use. If it is not right to possess nuclear weapons, then it is not right to manufacture them. On this analysis those participating in the design, manufacture or testing of nuclear weapons are participating in immoral activities, and have an obligation to change their occupation. Hunthausen's view went further than that of the majority of bishops; many disagreed with him as to the soundness of the inference "if doing X is wrong, then threatening to do X is wrong." The argument raises some important and fascinating problems which should certainly be discussed by philosophers interested in occupational ethics.[2]

Nation States

In *The Fate of the Earth*, Jonathan Schell argues that the only way to eliminate the risk of nuclear war is to eliminate nation states. He says that the knowledge of nuclear weaponry is now a permanent feature of the human condition, and given this, any war will retain the potential for becoming a nuclear war. Thus nuclear weapons make *all* war obsolete as a means of resolving disputes. Yet, Schell claims, the ability to wage war in pursuit of its interests and in its own self-defense is an intrinsic feature of the sovereign nation state. For nuclear security to be possible, national sovereignty must go.[3]

There are many issues central to the appraisal of this argument. Among them are conceptual issues as to how we understand the nation state and national sovereignty. Also involved are evaluative issues. What is the value of nation states, as such? If they possess real cultural and social/psychological value, is the preservation of this value worth some attendant risks? Could it be worth the risk of global nuclear war? Of limited nuclear wars? Schell's instinct—shared by the present author—is to think that the nation state is a comparatively transient historical entity which does not possess a value worth preserving at jeopardy to the very survival of mankind as a whole. The question is arguable, however; if the risk of nuclear war is believed to be very small and the value of nation states very large, a different judgment would likely be made. A number of reviewers reacted with great hostility to Schell's conclusion that the world—the international order, in particular—would have to be "reinvented" in order to eliminate the risk of nuclear war. Suggestions of the necessity of some kind of world government struck them as utopian at best; Orwellian at worst. Yet the issues raised clearly bear thinking about, and should be central topics in political philosophy.

Future Generations

Philosophers have discussed the question of what kind of moral status people who do not yet exist, but will or may exist, should have. How should they count in our moral decision making, when we come to weigh the consequences of our actions? Equally with existing people? Or not at all, since they are not real at the time that a decision is made? Neither answer seems quite right, and compromise positions tend not to work very well.[4] Philosophers have also discussed reproductive morality: whether the interests of a prospective child should be taken into account when he or she is still nonexistent and an agent is deciding whether or not to produce him or her.

These topics are important and difficult to resolve, but the questions raised avoid yet another question. Will there be any future generations of humans? It is not certain that even a global nuclear war would end the era of human beings on the planet earth, but there is a very good chance that it would. There are indications that a large number of nuclear detonations would destroy the earth's protective ozone layer. If this were to happen, human and animal life could be entirely destroyed. Part of the problem about the moral status of future generations, then, is whether we have any obligation to work to ensure that they *can* persist on our globe. If there is such an obligation, it is rather different from others which have been discussed in the context of the moral status of future people. These have fallen into two categories: obligations to take into account the interests of people who will (or likely will) exist; and obligations pertaining to reproductive decision making. Obligations to ensure that some future people can exist on this globe would be another subject.

Would the annihilation of the human species be a tragedy? If so, to whom? If it were a tragedy would this be so only because those who were already alive wanted to live longer and (in some cases) suffered greatly in dying.[5] Or would there be a less person-related tragedy: the death of the species as a whole? To the last question most of us would probably give an instinctive affirmative answer. But we might not know just why. Such an answer is not easily made coherent with the individualistic ontology of such common moral theories as utilitarianism and contractarianism. Ecologically minded philosophers have reflected on whether and why it would be a bad thing for such species as the whale and the whooping crane to become extinct. The same questions can, alas, be extended to our own species.

The Meaning of Life

Discussions of the meaning of life have largely ignored the constant possibility that human life on this planet could simply end. The real possibility of a nuclear catastrophe at any time can cast a dark shadow of meaningless over all mundane activities which have a future orientation. For many, that simply means all mundane activities. (It need not, if one interprets and values activities in terms of their internal actions rather than in terms of their goals and results, but such an attitude is not common in western culture.) The prospect of the extinction of our social world is more radically disruptive psychologically than the prospect of our own individual death. Individual death is inevitable; social or (worse yet) species death is not. Individual death permits the survival of descendants and of valued projects; social or species death does not. All future-oriented meaning is in jeopardy when the very survival of our social world is at risk. Psychiatrist Robert Lifton has long argued that the pervasive and unspoken threat of nuclear disaster has been profoundly damaging to the psyche of post-war generations.[6] He believes that it is responsible for hedonistic and self-interested attitudes, for irresponsibility to the biosphere, and for the low birth rate in many industrialized countries.

Lifton's claims would be extremely difficult to verify. Yet there is a basic sense in which the nuclear threat does undermine the meaningfulness of many human activities and forces into new relief old questions about the very meaning of life itself. Many philosophers are still willing to acknowledge that reflection on the meaning of life is a fundamentally philosophical task. If this is so, then a central part of this task is to acknowledge the nuclear threat and try to make sense of it. For the time being, this is a fact about our world, and one which we cannot will away.

Self-Deception

Intricate articles have been written trying to make logical and psychological sense of self-deception. Traditionally, philosophers argued that self-deception was morally wrong, for all people in all circumstances. Recently some have revised this stance, contending that self-deception can be excusable or even admirable in some circumstances.[7] The nature of nuclear arms and the risks and nature of nuclear war are topics on which we may well have society-wide self-deception. The psychological need to repress information and to highlight any optimistic prospects is very great. For several decades between the early nineteen sixties and the present time, the arms race accelerated, billions were spent, accidents occurred, nuclear threats were made, and scarcely anyone thought much about it. Looking back, this hardly seems possible. Was this a case of society-wide self-deception? Does that idea make sense? What are the social, political, and linguistic strategies which a society employs in order to deceive itself? If we decide that societies have in fact deceived themselves about the role of nuclear weapons and the threat of nuclear war, this may make us want to re-examine the recent more charitable view of self-deception which allows that it can sometimes be a good thing. Public illusions and ignorance about the nature and role of nuclear weaponry have been a necessary condition of the perpetuation of the dangerous nuclear arms race.

Individual Responsibility in the Face of a Global Threat

Many people believe that no ordinary individual has a chance to make any difference to the unfolding of global events. If this is so, then individuals would have no obligation to try to affect the course of such events. They would not be morally responsible, either, when things go wrong. The traditional principle of "ought implies can" will give us these comfortable conclusions, provided of course that it is true that an individual cannot make a difference. In an obvious sense whether this principle is true will depend on which individual you are. Mohatma Gandhi, Bertrand Russell, Albert Einstein, and (more recently) Helen Caldicott and Rosalie Berthell *have* made some difference. But then we do not all have their special abilities and opportunities.

A more general point is that whether an individual can make a difference to the prospects of nuclear peace or nuclear war depends on how many other individuals are trying to make a difference. To say that a single person cannot make a difference may be true. But to say that a very large number of single persons cannot is obviously false. An energetic peace movement of 50,000,000 people within the United States could certainly do a very great deal to reduce the risk of nuclear war. A peace movement of 1,000,000 dedicated people in that country would have some chance of doing this, as would a movement of 100,000 dedicated people in Canada or another allied country.[8] Three or four hundred people would have a very limited chance of having any influence, unless they were in positions of special power and importance. In general, the impact of one person's actions will depend on how other people act. He or she will be impotent alone, but powerful as one of a number.

What we are able to do will depend, then, on what others do. Following on the "ought implies can" principle, it appears that what we are obliged to do will depend on what others do. How are we obligated to act when we do not know what others will do?

At this point we have reached an impasse familiar in moral philosophy. The problem is a dramatic version of that which arises whenever an agent questions an obligation to act at possible personal cost in a moral community which can offer no guarantee that all or most of its members will abide by moral rules. Though interest may be foregone to no avail unless a sufficient number of others abide by the rules, this does not appear to be an excuse for ignoring the obligation. At least, from the moral point of view it is not commonly taken to be an excuse. Plato, Hobbes, Gauthier and many others have wrestled with this problem, trying to show how a commitment to moral principles can be made rational in the sense of being in an agent's ultimate self-interest.

In a beautifully expressed essay entitled "Secular Faith," Annette Baier approached the problem differently. She made no attempt to justify moral action on the basis of reason alone: whether it be reason understood as enlightened pursuit of self-interest, or on some other model. Rather she argued that an individual's commitment to a project whose success requires the actions of a number of other individuals requires, in the end, *faith* in other people.

Baier wrote:

> If everyone insisted on knowing in advance that any sacrifice of independent advantage which they personally make, in joining or supporting a moral order, will be made up for by the return they will get from membership in that moral order, that moral order could never be created, nor, if miraculously brought about, sustained.[9]

For social life to continue we need to have a secular faith—the faith that enough other people will have the moral concern to make our own moral commitments practically significant.

It is such faith in other people that is needed in order to vindicate the individual sacrifices of time and valued projects which will be necessary for individuals to work to reduce the risk of nuclear war. The work is bound to go slowly and the task will be accomplished (if at all) only in many small stages. A large part of this work consists in seeking very basic changes in public attitudes toward nuclear weapons and their historical and present role. The illusion that these weapons have kept us safe, serve only to deter, and are being well-managed by people who know what they are doing has made the nuclear arms race possible. This illusion must be eliminated, and this is no easy task. No one person can do this alone; yet all are obliged to do their part.

Baier does not discuss the problem of global war but she makes a number of remarks which seem very appropriate to it.

> . . . the alternative, giving up on that crucial part of the moral enterprise which secures cooperation, must eventually lead to an outcome disastrous to all—although those with a taste for gun-running may make a good profit before doomsday dawns.

A morally serious person has no alternative to trying in such contexts though he has no guarantee that a sufficient number of others will make the effort. Although his action *can* succeed only if a substantial number of other people act in similar ways, he *ought* to undertake the action in any event. It is faith in other people which bridges the gap. It replaces the faith in God which played an analogous role for earlier generations. Instead of believing in a god who will reward the virtuous and punish the wicked (thus making morally good actions which turn out to be futile on earth "pay off" for the individual in heaven), we are to believe in the capacity of other people for those virtuous actions which we ourselves undertake, so that our own moral commitments may lead to the desired goals right here on this earth. We do not *know* that enough other people will abide by the moral code for this goal to be realized. No deductive or inductive argument can prove this either, given the nature of the problem. Our faith in other people is not rational in the sense of being warranted by proof or evidence. Yet it is rational in the broader sense of serving an overall purpose: it is the foundation of the social and moral order.

If secular faith is, as Baier argued, the necessary foundation for much moral action, then there is no special basis for denying the responsibility of individuals for the global nuclear situation. Although we cannot, as individuals, control what happens, collectively people do have an impact. And this collective capacity is a sufficient basis for individual commitment. Any single action taken by an individual toward the goal of reducing risks of nuclear war is likely to appear solitary and futile, the means seeming grotesquely disproportionate to the end. The action needs to be set in a context where many other people act in similar and related ways. In this context, it appears in a framework where people are working to do something they can do: stop the nuclear arms race and reduce the risks of nuclear war.

We need hope and a will to believe to remain within the moral order. So far as nuclear peace or war is concerned, we have had both. But they have been sadly misused. We have placed our hope in the political and military leaders whose sanity and responsibility we have trusted beyond all evidence. And we have willfully ignored the risks of nuclear disaster, while failing to place our confidence and trust in the moral capacities of our fellow human beings. Those of us who are students and teachers of moral philosophy can play our own small part in changing this situation, and should now be convinced that we have a special obligation to do so.*

April, 1983.

Notes

1. The grisly details are amply described in Schell's *The Fate of the Earth*. Precise predictions are obviously not possible, due to possible variations in numbers of weapons used, reliability of weapons, performance of weapons over a North-South route, weather conditions, and pertinent gaps in scientific knowledge.
2. For some discussion of the bishops' debate, see R. G. Hoyt. "The Bishops and the Bomb," *Christianity and Crisis*, August 9, 1982: Michael Novak, "Nuclear Morality." *America*, 147 (1982): 5–8; J. A. O'Hare, "One Man's Primer on Nuclear Morality," *America*, 147 (1982): 9–12; Francis X. Winters. "Catholic Debate and Division on Deterrence." *America*, 147 (1982): 127–131. Also relevant is Walter Wink. "Faith and Nuclear Paralysis." *Christian Century*, 99 (1982): 234–237.
3. Schell, *The Fate of the Earth*, part 3. This part of the book has been strongly criticized.
4. This comment applies to my own paper. "What Should We Do about Future People?" *American Philosophical Quarterly*, 16 (1979): 105–113. An indication as to just how complex these problems have become may be gleaned from Derek Parfit. "Future Generations: Further Problems." *Philosophy and Public Affairs*, 11 (1982): 113–172.
5. Schell dwells on these questions in a manner quite metaphysical in Part II of his book. They have also been addressed by John Leslie in "Why Not Let Life Become Extinct?", a paper presented at the Canadian Philosophical Association meetings in Montreal, June 1980. See also John Leslie, *Value and Existence* (Totowa, NJ: Rowman and Littlefield 1979).
6. See R. J. Lifton and Richard Falk. *Indefensible Weapons* (Toronto: CBC Publications 1982). Lifton's discussion of psychological effects of nuclear weapons comprises Part I of this work.
7. This view has been defended by Bela Szabados in "Self-Deception," *Canadian Journal of Philosophy*, 4 (1974): 41–49.
8. Moral perspectives on nuclear issues, and potential for political action to alter the status quo, vary considerably depending upon whether one is a citizen within a superpower or a citizen within an allied country. The difference in perspective is often blurred by uses of "we" which fail to make clear whether the point of view taken is that of the U.S., of Canada, or of any country within the NATO alliance.
9. Annette Baier. "Secular Faith." *Canadian Journal of Philosophy*, 10 (1980): 131–148.

Further Readings

Cohen, Avner, and Steven Lee (eds.). *Nuclear Weapons and the Future of Humanity*. Totowa, NJ: Rowman and Allenheld, 1984.

Kavka, Gregory. "Nuclear Deterrence: Some Moral Perplexities." In *The Security Gamble: Deterrence Dilemmas in the Nuclear Age*, ed. Douglas MacLean. Totowa, NJ: Rowman and Allenheld, 1984.

Hardin, Russell. "Unilateral versus Mutual Disarmament." *Philosophy and Public Affairs* 12(3) (1983): 255.

Lackey, Douglas. "Ethics and Nuclear Deterrence." In *Moral Problems: A Collection of Philosophical Essays*, 3rd ed., ed. James Rachels. New York: Harper & Row, 1979, pp. 426–442.

Content Quiz 14.4

Instructions: Fill in the blanks with the appropriate responses listed below.

public silence	conditional endorsement
responsibility	self-deception
absurd	nation states
threat	awareness
secular faith	distorted

1. It is not correct to say that individuals have no personal _____ to do anything about the nuclear arms race.
2. Philosophical discussions of moral values and political structures that ignore the nuclear threat are in some respects _____.
3. _____ for the last 40 years or so has greatly contributed to the proliferation of nuclear arms.
4. _____ are, according to Jonathan Schell, merely transient historical entities.
5. _____ is a means for coping with the horrors associated with nuclear holocaust.
6. In the American Catholic bishops' pastoral letter, a(n) _____ of nuclear deterrence is given.
7. According to Archbishop Hunthausen, if doing X is wrong, then making a _____ to do X is also wrong.
8. Acting responsibly as an individual hinges partly on a _____ that leads us to believe that others will act morally and that the moral concern of others will make our own moral commitments practically significant.
9. Philosophers have a special obligation to increase the public _____ of nuclear issues and to point out the moral implications of nuclear war.
10. Any interpretation of social reality that ignores the role and influence of nuclear arms is seriously inaccurate and _____.

Discussion Questions

1. Why is the nuclear arms issue so important? Can we not just live our lives normally without worrying about it? Why?
2. What is the religious (i.e., Catholic) perspective on nuclear arms?
3. In the context of the nuclear arms debate, are nation-states good or bad? Explain.
4. Should we worry about future generations and what the world be like in, say, the year 2050? What reasons can you give?
5. How is the meaning of life tied up with the nuclear arms issue?
6. As individuals, should we bother about getting involved in the nuclear arms issue? Why?
7. What role can philosophers play in the nuclear arms debate?

APPENDIX ONE

1

SO WHAT IS THE ANSWER?

PROGRESS CHECK 1.1

1. Academy 2. *Republic* 3. harmonious balance 4. teleology 5. soul 6. physical 7. self-assertion 8. reason 9. ignorance 10. guardian 11. tyrannical 12. oligarchic 13. timarchic 14. auxiliaries 15. forms

PROGRESS CHECK 2.1

1. Alexander the Great 2. Plato 3. teleologist 4. self-realization 5. entelechy 6. *eudaimonia* 7. intrinsic 8. means 9. successful 10. secondary 11. self-sufficient 12. hedonist 13. rational 14. cattle 15. insecure 16. complete 17. contemplative 18. divine 19. luck 20. intellectual 21. habit 22. deficiency 23. moderation 24. sake 25. modesty

PROGRESS CHECK 3.1

1. nature 2. Jeremy Bentham 3. spirit of scientific objectivity 4. consequences 5. principle of utility 6. utility 7. psychological egoist 8. ethical egoist 9. is-ought 10. sanction 11. political 12. retributivist 13. private ethics 14. inefficacious 15. retroactive legislation 16. hedonic calculus 17. intensity 18. fecundity 19. extent 20. intrinsically

PROGRESS CHECK 4.1

1. principle of utility 2. quality 3. intellect 4. sense of dignity 5. inferior type 6. infirmity of character 7. egoistic 8. disutility 9. incommensurable 10. entitlements 11. selfishness, mental cultivation 12. democracy

PROGRESS CHECK 5.1

1. deontological 2. moral certainty 3. structure of reason 4. good will 5. conditionally 6. duty 7. prudential 8. nonmoral 9. immoral 10. inclination 11. motive 12. duties to oneself 13. maxim 14. categorical imperative 15. formalist 16. objects 17. impartial 18. prescriptive 19. hypothetical 20. autonomy of the will

PROGRESS CHECK 6.1

1. utilitarianism 2. social contract theory 3. justice 4. inviolate 5. society 6. identity of interests 7. ideal observer 8. original position 9. veil of ignorance 10. mutually disinterested 11. principle of equal liberty 12. deontological ethics 13. difference principle 14. maximin principle 15. reciprocity

PROGRESS CHECK 7.1

1. empirical study 2. prescribe 3. metaethical 4. justify 5. ultimate foundations 6. factual claims, normative claims 7. nonmoral 8. prudential 9. mandatory 10. opinions 11. arguments 12. beliefs 13. social value 14. attitude adjustments 15. rational disinterestedness

PROGRESS CHECK 8.1

1. interpersonal 2. form 3. *Modus Ponens* 4. consequent 5. affirms 6. denies 7. invalid 8. hypothetical 9. disjunct 10. value 11. judgment 12. probable 13. inductive generalization 14. worse 15. analogical

PROGRESS CHECK 9.1

1. practical syllogisms 2. logical fallacies 3. sound 4. value premise 5. role-exchange test 6. irrational 7. universalizability 8. new cases test 9. *ad hominem* 10. circular reasoning 11. two wrongs fallacy 12. appealing to authority 13. straw man 14. red herring 15. slippery slope

CONTENT QUIZ 10.1

1. profits 2. state-controlled, free-enterprise 3. success 4. filtered 5. caviar 6. riches, poverty 7. static 8. lifeboat 9. risk-takers 10. choice

CONTENT QUIZ 10.2

1. choice 2. distribution 3. rights 4. responsibility 5. unfortunate effects 6. utilitarian 7. constraints 8. opinions 9. competitive 10. efficient

CONTENT QUIZ 10.3

1. persuasive 2. ambiguous 3. weasel 4. facts 5. exaggeration 6. puffery 7. psychological 8. inner privacy 9. subliminal 10. satisfaction

CONTENT QUIZ 10.4

1. unhealthy lifestyle conditions 2. lifestyle discrimination 3. right 4. unsuitable habits 5. financial incentives 6. sin surcharge 7. workplace privacy

CONTENT QUIZ 10.5

1. dire consequences 2. intervening, leading 3. courage to be 4. secretly threatening 5. limitations 6. charismatic 7. consensus building 8. win-win 9. constructive 10. intervention strategies

CONTENT QUIZ 11.1

1. deterrence 2. ambivalent 3. Cesare Beccaria 4. Jeremy Bentham 5. retribution 6. anger 7. awful 8. rehabilitation 9. community 10. dignity

CONTENT QUIZ 11.2

1. utilitarian 2. precedent 3. burden of proof 4. anachronism 5. deterrence 6. public executions 7. capital punishment 8. fact 9. deteree 10. professional criminal class

CONTENT QUIZ 11.3

1. onus 2. causal connection 3. sexual development 4. overriding principle 5. catharsis 6. consequences 7. pleasure 8. sex by proxy 9. aberrant 10. inconclusive

CONTENT QUIZ 11.4

1. respect for persons 2. sex objects 3. spirit 4. sex-harm 5. inferior beings 6. equal 7. degrading 8. morally objectionable 9. attitude 10. roles

CONTENT QUIZ 11.5

1. political 2. cultural 3. status 4. collective 5. aboriginal 6. moral worth 7. egalitarianism 8. moral existence 9. affirmative action 10. badge of inferiority 11. forced integration 12. differential citizenship rights

CONTENT QUIZ 11.6

1. Royal Proclamation of 1763 2. British North America Act of 1867 3. aboriginal rights 4. aborigines 5. civilization 6. Nishnawbe-Aski Declaration 7. european attitude 8. treaties 9. nation 10. court interpretation

CONTENT QUIZ 12.1

1. physical violence 2. selfless 3. parasitic 4. rape 5. motherhood 6. self-reproach 7. absolute 8. trauma 9. autonomy 10. Mataco

CONTENT QUIZ 12.2

1. unique relationship 2. abortifacient pessary 3. indispensable precondition 4. pragmatic 5. *Roe v. Wade* 6. quickening 7. pluralism 8. *Montreal Tramways v. Léveillé* 9. contradiction 10. censorious moralism

CONTENT QUIZ 12.3

1. active 2. passive 3. mercy killing 4. humanitarian 5. irrelevant grounds 6. defense 7. morally relevant differences 8. conditioned 9. action 10. morally permissible

CONTENT QUIZ 12.4

1. passive euthanasia 2. lethal doses of barbituates 3. autonomy 4. nuisance 5. involuntary euthanasia 6. stigma 7. abuses 8. killing the person 9. coerce 10. dead

CONTENT QUIZ 13.1

1. necessary 2. affection 3. biological 4. unthinkingly conformist 5. guilty 6. biosocial tendencies 7. nonaffectional sex 8. clinical experience 9. ideas 10. sex without love

CONTENT QUIZ 13.2

1. the morality of caution 2. the morality of law 3. the morality of concern 4. the morality of personal relationships 5. New Testament 6. casual sex 7. morally neutral 8. ends 9. functional association 10. life-uniting

CONTENT QUIZ 13.3

1. social attitudes and practices 2. gay stereotypes 3. queerbashing 4. discrimination 5. universally negative 6. church and state 7. procreation 8. discovery 9. hysterical predictions 10. selectively

CONTENT QUIZ 13.4

1. prejudice 2. homosexuals 3. burden of evidence 4. human sexuality 5. homosexuality 6. egocentric self-servingness 7. social cohesion 8. superciliousness 9. shallower commitment 10. heterosexuality

CONTENT QUIZ 14.1

1. misguided 2. ecodestruction 3. metaphor 4. Marxism 5. Christianity 6. tragedy of the commons 7. transfer device 8. pejoristic system 9. ratchet effect 10. errors

CONTENT QUIZ 14.2

1. intuitions 2. psychological explanation 3. distinction 4. good reason 5. discharge 6. optionality 7. counterintuitive 8. positive-negative 9. lifestyles 10. bad faith

CONTENT QUIZ 14.3

1. pacifism 2. existence 3. moral justification 4. pathological causes 5. dignity and excellence 6. private motives 7. biological origin 8. individuation 9. material 10. altruism 11. cowardice 12. emotions and sentiments 13. rational 14. totalitarianism

CONTENT QUIZ 14.4

1. responsibility 2. absurd 3. public silence 4. nation states 5. self-deception 6. conditional endorsement 7. threat 8. secular faith 9. awareness 10. distorted

APPENDIX TWO

HOW TO WRITE A MORAL POSITION PAPER

2

One of the hardest tasks facing you as a philosophical beginner is the writing of your first ethics paper. With this in mind, we will go through the process of structuring and organizing a "thesis defense." A thesis defense requires that you take a stand or position on some controversial moral issue. Let us go through the steps.

STEP ONE: PICK A "NORMATIVE ISSUE" OR TOPIC HAVING MORAL-ETHICAL IMPLICATIONS

When writing a "thesis defense" or "moral position paper," what you must first do is to pick an appropriate topic. What you *do not* want to do is to select a subject that may be better suited to psychology, sociology or anthropology, something philosophical beginners occasionally do. To ensure that your topic suits the course, be certain that it concerns matters of value and/or ethical principle. In your paper, you should say that something is good or bad, right or wrong, better or worse, praiseworthy or blameworthy. If your paper is about an action or policy decision, for instance, then you should state that it should or should not be done or that we ought or ought not do whatever is involved. By doing this, you will pick a normative issue or value-related topic for your paper. Again, what you *do not* want to do is to pick an empirical topic—one that can be settled by scientific investigation or statistical analysis. Functional explanations, matters of cause and effect, as well as those pertaining to correlations between variables, are best dealt with by empirical researchers (see Chapter Seven). Below are some sample topics and questions that are appropriate and inappropriate to the development of an ethical thesis.

Inappropriate Topics and Questions for a Moral Position Paper

1. The effects of child abuse on adult development
2. The effects of caffeine on memory

3. The relationship between income and family size
4. The correlation between intelligence and academic performance
5. Does watching violence on TV relieve stress?
6. How is personality related to birth order?
7. When will the world come to an end?
8. What is the function of morality in social organization?
9. How does moral conscience develop?
10. Why do some people choose to act immorally?

Appropriate Topics and Questions for a Moral Position Paper

1. Corporate Responsibility
   Is a company's right to earn a profit absolute?
   Is a company's sole responsibility to the shareholder?
   What obligations do corporations have toward society in general?
2. Pornography
   Should pornography be legal and easily available to the public?
   Should minors have access to pornography?
   Should pornographic material be banned on the Internet?
3. Capital Punishment
   Should convicted murderers be executed?
   Do convicted murderers lose their right to life?
   If all life is sacred, should murderers suffer capital punishment?

STEP TWO: MAKE SURE YOUR NORMATIVE ISSUE IS RELATED TO DISTINCTIVELY MORAL VALUES, NOT MERELY TO NONMORAL ONES

In Part Two of *Moral Philosophy for Modern Life*, a distinction was made between moral and nonmoral values. Although it is sometimes difficult to distinguish between the two, let us say, for our purposes, that moral values are those that affect human interests in important ways (see Chapter 7). They tend to be tied to things like virtue, rights, justice, fairness, liberty, equality, utility, and duty. Some regard moral duties to be so important that they are binding on, or prescriptive for, all of us. By contrast, nonmoral values entail optional duties. They depend on our personal tastes, preferences, wants and desires or catering to those of others. Nonmoral values are often related to prudential matters; that is, they pertain to what is good for us personally. They are not about what is dutiful and binding for all.

Examples of Nonmoral Value Statements

1. M & Ms are better than Smarties.
2. It is better to invest in stocks than to save your money in a bank.
3. Country music is terrible.
4. You should not buy an unreliable car.
5. Your choice in wallpaper was wrong.
6. It was good of you to share that useful information.

Examples of Moral Value Statements

1. We have an obligation to feed the world's hungry.
2. War is sometimes justifiable.
3. Affirmative action policies should be eliminated.
4. Criminals should not be punished, but rehabilitated.
5. Abortion is always wrong.
6. All people are created equal.

STEP THREE: STATE YOUR THESIS OR MORAL POSITION

Once you have selected your topic and identified the moral values involved, what you need to do is to express a position either positive or negative, for or against. Let us say, for instance, that you have decided to write a paper on biomedical ethics as it relates to the use of aborted fetal tissue in scientific research. Having picked your topic, you must eventually take a stand on the issue. Be careful, however, not to prejudge the issue before careful reflection, analysis, and evaluation. You do not want to decide in advance what you plan to justify in the end. This would be a form of "begging the question" (see Chapter Nine). For practical purposes, nonetheless, you should state a tentative position up front articulating arguments both for and against to see which are strongest and weakest. For our intentions, I am going to assume that you have picked a topic, that you have already conducted preliminary examination of the arguments on both sides of the issue and that you have decided where you stand. In other words, you have a moral position and are now prepared to formulate arguments in defense of your thesis. You are also prepared to criticize those arguments against the position you are taking.

STEP FOUR: PREPARE FORMAL ARGUMENTS ON BOTH SIDES OF THE ISSUE

In writing your thesis defense, it is not enough simply to pick an issue and argue one side of it. This, obviously, would make your argument "one-sided" and less persuasive than it could otherwise be. What you must do is produce arguments on both sides of the issue and demonstrate why those on the other or opposing side are inadequate, unjustifiable or unacceptable. From my own personal experience, I have found it helpful to ask two basic questions when forming syllogistic arguments. They are (1) Why? and (2) So what?

By asking the "why" question, you can uncover those facts or empirical variables relevant to your argument. Suppose the issue is smoking in public places and that your thesis is: "Smoking in public places should be prohibited"; you could then ask, "Why?" In response, you might claim that smoking in public places endangers the health of others. You could have some research evidence to support this empirical claim. Philosophically and ethically, however, the question would still remain, "So what?" What is it that you are suggesting that makes this empirical claim about smoking's harmful effects ethically relevant? The answer to the "So what?" question is the following: "That which endangers the health of others should be prohibited." By answering the "So what?" question, what you have formulated, in effect, is the value premise that gives your factual claim moral relevance, because together they lead to the conclusion that: "Smoking in public places should be prohibited." See how this argument can be expressed as a practical syllogism.

Value Premise:	That which endangers the health of others (a) should be prohibited (b).
Factual Premise:	Smoking in public places (c) endangers the health of others (a).
Value Conclusion:	Therefore, smoking in public places (c) should be prohibited (b).

Formal Structure:	A is B	
	C is A	(valid syllogism)
	Therefore, C is B	

In the example above, note that by asking the "why" question first, we initially arrived at our factual premise—actually the middle part of the syllogism. The second "So what" question gave us the value premise. Once we had the first two parts or statements in place, we could arrive at our conclusion and check for the validity of our argument by exposing its formal structure. This process of question asking can be used to produce practical syllogisms on both sides of the issue. Like before, we could ask ourselves what reasons could be given for opposing our thesis. If someone were opposed to banning smoking in public places, the question would arise, "Why?" Once an answer to this question was provided, then we could ask, "So what?" Again, our two answers could be pieced together to form a valid syllogism, only, in this case, in opposition to our thesis.

STEP FIVE: CRITICIZE OPPOSING ARGUMENTS

In defense of your moral thesis, it is not enough simply to offer arguments on both sides of the issue. To convince others that your stand is correct, you must show why opposing arguments are unjustified, inadequate or unacceptable. Given the skills you mastered in Part Two of *Moral Philosophy for Modern Life*, you can evaluate opposing arguments in the following fashion:

a. First, look at the conclusions of the opposing arguments. Do they follow from preceding premises? If not, then the arguments are invalid and may be rejected.
b. Second, are the factual claims in the opposing arguments acceptable? Are they based on

sufficient evidence, appropriate statistical analysis or acceptable inductive conclusions? If the factual claims imbedded in opposing arguments are unacceptable, then, again, the arguments can be rejected.

c. Third, do the value premises in the opposing arguments hold up under rational scrutiny? Do they pass the tests of adequacy (i.e., new cases, role exchange, higher-order principle, consistency and universalizability—see Chapter Nine)? If the value premise of a particular syllogism is not defensible, then the conclusion deriving from it can be rejected.

d. Fourth, look for informal fallacies (see Chapter Nine). Are any diversionary or intimidation tactics used? If so, then the counter-arguments based on them are weakened and, likely, need not be accepted.

STEP SIX: BE SURE THAT ALL OF *YOUR* SUPPORTING ARGUMENTS HOLD UP UNDER RATIONAL SCRUTINY AND CRITICAL EVALUATION

As the saying goes, "What's good for the goose is good for the gander." Be sure that your own conclusions follow from preceding premises and that you have adequate support for your factual claims. Be sure, as well, that your value premises are justifiable and that you have not included any informal fallacies (i.e., sleazy logic) on your side of the issue. Depending on how you have put together your arguments, some fine tuning may be required.

OTHER HELPFUL HINTS

The process of writing a thesis defense, as described above, can be simplified into structural elements. You might find it helpful to conceptualize its structure in the following fashion.

Topic Introduction and Thesis Statement

Supporting Arguments	**Opposing Arguments**
	Criticisms of Opposing Arguments

A paper containing this structural organization would begin with an introduction to the moral topic to be discussed. Then, its position or thesis would be stated, explained, and clarified in a few sentences. After this, the strongest arguments in favor of the thesis could be given, followed by arguments against. The paper would conclude, in this case, with criticisms of opposing arguments.

Alternatively, what you could do is

a. introduce the moral topic

b. state your position

ARGUMENT ASSEMBLY CHART

THESIS: Smoking in Public Places Should Be Prohibited

SUPPORTING ARGUMENTS			OPPOSING ARGUMENTS		
Value Premise	**Factual Premise**	**Conclusion**	**Value Premise**	**Factual Premise**	**Conclusion**
Argument 1 That which endangers the health of others should be prohibited.	Smoking in public places endangers the health of others.	Therefore, smoking in public places should be prohibited.	*Objection 1* That which interferes with everyday business practices should not be enforced	Public smoking regulations interfere with everyday business practices.	Therefore, public smoking regulations should not be enforced.
Argument 2 That which increases health care costs should be discouraged.	Smoking in public places increases health care costs.	Smoking in public places should be discouraged.	*Objection 2* Limiting individual choice is wrong.	Public smoking regulations limit individual choice.	Public smoking regulations are wrong.
Argument 3 Violating the rights of others is wrong.	Smoking in public places violates the rights of others.	Smoking in public places is wrong.			

Criticisms of Opposing Arguments

Opposing Argument 1

a. Logic and Conclusion: *Acceptable.*

b. Factual Premise: *Correct.*

c. Value Premise: *Unacceptable.* Fails new-cases test (e.g., regulations governing industrial wastes and car emissions interfere with business and profit maximization, yet we are in favor of them).

d. Fallacies: *None.*

Opposing Argument 2

a. Logic and Conclusion: *Acceptable.*

b. Factual Premise: *Acceptable.*

c. Value Premise: *Unacceptable.* Individual choice is acceptable only insofar as other's rights are not violated.

d. Fallacies: *None.*

Source: Falikowski, *Moral Philosophy: Theories, Skills, and Applications*, p. 335.

Adapted from the Association of Values Education and Research, *Value Reasoning Series*, the University of British Columbia, 1978–1981.

c. describe opposing arguments
d. criticize and reject those opposing arguments, and
e. finish up with your strongest "arguments for"

Either format is a matter of personal preference. If you are taking an unpopular position, however, the second alternative may be preferable. If you fairly and accurately state the opposing position and then give good reasons for rejecting it, greater openness to your own position can be created.

On page 450 is a sample "Argument Assembly Chart" containing all of the structural elements of a thesis defense. Specific arguments included in the chart are expressed in a kind of shorthand as practical syllogisms. An actual paper based on this chart would require that syllogisms be expanded and explained in proper written form. Fleshed out, each syllogism could comprise about one page of your paper, as could your introduction and explanation of your thesis. From the chart included here, I could imagine developing a five-to eight-page paper. I mention this because length often seems to be a concern among students I have taught. They frequently worry that they will not write enough. Let me assure you that if you follow the "recipe" here, you will write more than enough in most cases. In fact, I predict you will surprise yourself with how much you actually have to say. Good Luck!

3 APPENDIX THREE

PHILOSOPHER'S TOOL KIT

For those of you who plan to continue on your moral journey, I have provided a "tool kit" of information and resources which should come in handy. The Philosopher's Tool Kit includes the following:

- a bibliography of ethical readings containing perspectives other than those western rational ones covered in this book (e.g., existential, religious, and feminist);
- information on centers, institutes, and associations dealing with ethical research and practical ethical applications;
- websites of ethical interest including research networks, chat groups, directories, and listings of ethics scholars;
- titles of journals in the field of ethics; and
- philosophical software information.

BIBLIOGRAPHY OF ALTERNATIVE ETHICAL PERSPECTIVES

Existentialist Ethics

Barnes, Hazel E. *An Existentialist Ethics*. New York: Alfred A. Knopf, 1967.
Barrett, William. *Irrational Man*. New York: Doubleday, 1958.
Kaufmann, Walter. *Existentialism from Dostoevsky to Sartre*. London, 1957.
Nietzsche, Friedrich. *On the Genealogy of Morals*. Translated by Walter Kaufmann. New York: Random House, 1967.
Patka, Frederick. *Existentialist Thinkers and Thought*. New York: Philosophical Library, 1962.

Religious Ethics

Buddha. *The Teachings of Buddha*. Tokyo: Bukkyo Duedo Kyokai, 1976.

Chuang-Tzu: The Inner Chapters. Translated by A.C. Graham. London: George Allen & Unwin, 1981.

Confucius: The Analects. Translated by D.C. Lau. Hong Kong: Chinese University Press, 1983.

DeBenetittis, Suzanne. *Teaching Faith and Morals*. Minneapolis: Winston Press, 1981.

Gustafson, James. *Christ and the Moral Life*. Chicago: The University of Chicago Press, 1968.

Jaspers, Karl. *Socrates, Buddha, Confucius, Jesus: The Paradigmatic Individuals*. New York: Harcourt Brace Jovanovich.

Nigosian, S.A. *World Faiths*. New York: St. Martin's Press, 1994.

Peck, M. Scott. *The Road Less Traveled: A New Psychology of Love, Traditional Values and Spiritual Growth*. New York: Touchstone Books, 1978.

Feminist Ethics

Gilligan, Carol. *In A Different Voice*. Cambridge: Harvard University Press, 1982.

Jagger, Allison. *Feminist Politics and Human Nature*. Totowa: Rowman and Allanheld.

Shogan, Debra. *A Reader in Feminist Ethics*. Toronto: Canadian Scholar's Press, 1993.

ACADEMIC RESEARCH INSTITUTES INVOLVED IN ETHICAL INQUIRY

1. The Centre for Applied Ethics, The University of British Columbia
   Aim: to bring moral philosophy into the public domain by advancing research in applied ethics; to support courses with a significant ethical component; to act as a community resource; to give opportunities for academics, practitioners and others to engage in systematic and rational reflection on significant moral issues of the day

Website: www.ethics.ubc.ca/

2. Kennedy Institute of Ethics, Georgetown University
   - a teaching and research center established to offer moral and ethical perspectives on major policy issues

Website: http://guweb.georgetown.edu/kennedy/

3. Center for Biomedical Ethics, Case Western Reserve University
   Mission: to improve public and professional understanding of the ethical issues involved in health science research, health care delivery, and health policy development through teaching, conducting research, and stimulating community dialogue

Website: www.cwru.edu/cwru/Dept/Med/bioethics/bioethics. html

4. Dartmouth Ethics Institute
   - conducts research and teaching about ethical issues encountered in all professional areas, including law, medicine, education, management, and scientific research

Website: www.dartmouth.edu/artsci/ethics-inst/

5. Center for Human Values, Princeton University
   Aim: to support ethical inquiry into many disciplines; to foster far ranging examination of the ethical meaning of various human activities;
   - emphasizes ethical aspects of such disciplines as philosophy, religion, politics, the arts, literature, science, and engineering

Website: www.princeton.edu/~uchv/

6. The University of Alberta Bioethics Centre
   Aim: to increase awareness of bioethical issues in patient care; to examine ethics issues of hospital and health care administration; to develop community outreach information workshops and to undertake interdisciplinary research in bioethics

Website: http://gpu.srv.ualberta.ca/~ethics/bethics.htm

7. The Center for Bioethics, University of Pennsylvania
   Aim: to advance scholarly and public understanding of ethical, legal, social, and public policy issues in health care

Website: www.med.upenn.edu/~bioethic/center/

8. Westminster Institute for Ethics and Human Values
   University of Western Ontario
   London, Ontario, Canada
   N6A 3K7
   (519) 679-2111

9. MacLean Center for Clinical Medical Ethics, University of Chicago
   - consists of an interdisciplinary group of professionals who study and teach about practical ethical concerns confronting patients and health professionals

Website: http://ccme-mac4.bsd.uchicago.edu/ccme.html

10. Centre for Practical Ethics
    York University
    4700 Keele St.
    North York (Toronto), Ontario
    Canada, M3J 1P3

Website: www.yorku.ca/mclaughlin/ethics/ethics.htm

11. University of Toronto Joint Centre for Bioethics
    - a partnership among the University of Toronto, the Clarke Institute of Psychiatry, The Hospital for Sick Children, Mount Sinai Hospital, Sunnybrook Health Science Centre, and The Toronto Hospital
    - offers bioethics education and clinical ethics on a foundation of interdisciplinary research

- aims to foster interdisciplinary research and scholarship
- links graduate education to research
- addresses ethical issues encountered in the Centre and seeks to improve policies and practices

Website: www.utoronto.ca/jcb/

12. Centre for Bioethics, Clinical Research Institute of Montreal
    Aim: to raise the level of professional and public discourse on value conflicts in the contemporary practice of medicine
    - to clarify the goals and balance the priorities of biomedical research

    110 Ave des Pins,
    Montreal, Quebec
    Canada, H2W 1R7
    (514) 987-5500

Website: www.ircm.umontreal.ca/ext/ircm/sites/internes/bioeth/index-an.htm

RESEARCH NETWORKS AND CLEARING HOUSES

1. The Canadian Business and Professional Ethics Network
   Head: Colin Boyd, University of Saskatchewan
   - links Canadian researchers in many disciplines of business and professional business
   - members post e-mail to each other individually or to the whole membership list to relate news, opinions, letters, bibliographies, reading lists or want ads, in addition to regular scholarly or business discussions

E-Mail Address: Boyd@sask.usask.ca

2. CAERNETS (Canadian Applied Ethics Research Nets)
   - created by University of British Columbia, Centre for Applied Ethics
   - umbrella structure comprising six independent electronic networks
     - accounting ethics network (ACCNET)
     - Canadian Bioethics Network
     - Canadian Business and Professional Ethics Network
     - Cross-Cultural Health Care Ethics Network
     - Reseau Quebecois Des Ethiciennes et Ethiciens
     - Sustainable Development Ethics Network
   - provides unique, cost-effective and innovative infrastructure for Canadian applied ethics research and its dissemination
   - offers researchers easy access to timely information, services and innovative research tools
   - a valuable link with other researchers
   - helps in development of research tools, e.g., electronic data-bases and electronic journals

Website: www.ethics.ubc.ca/caernets/

PHILOSOPHY DOCUMENTATION CENTER

- nonprofit organization located at Bowling Green University
- serves the needs of the international philosophical community by providing accurate information, high quality products, and professional services
- reputation for excellence in publication and worldwide distribution of philosophy reference works, including directories, bibliographies, scholarly journals, and instructional software for philosophers

Website: www.bgsu.edu/pdc/

SOFTWARE

- the "Logicworks" software package can be obtained through the Philosophy Documentation Center
- this package complements instruction in introductory logic classes and may come in handy in the context of moral reasoning

PHILOSOPHY RESOURCES ON THE INTERNET

1. Philosophy in Cyberspace
    - annotated guide to a vast range of electronic information available on the internet to the philosophical community
    - helps to locate philosophical resources, assists research or study, faxes journal articles, locates resources relating to various branches of philosophy or others interested in your area of philosophy

Website: http://www-personal.monash.edu.au/~dey/phil/

ETHICS JOURNALS

Business Ethics Quarterly

- publishes scholarly articles from a wide variety of disciplines that focus on the general subject of the application of ethics to the international business community

Ethics

- an international journal of social, political, and legal philosophy
- the oldest, and one of the finest, ethics journals
- includes extensive book reviews and notices

Hastings Center Reports

- concerned primarily with issues in biomedical ethics

Journal of Ethics: An International Philosophical Review

- contains articles, commentaries, and reviews on mainstream topics and works in ethics and public affairs, including work on ethical theory, political liberalism, communitarianism, libertarianism, Marxism, moral responsibility, punishment, rights, ethics and language, ethics and metaphysics, African-American philosophy, international terrorism, etc.

Journal of Social Philosophy

- contains articles on the cutting edge of social controversies

Journal of Value Inquiry

- considers issues of aesthetic values as well as moral ones
- an excellent source of articles on a wide range of moral issues

Public Affairs Quarterly

- contains articles on the ethical dimensions of public policy issues

ASSOCIATIONS AND ORGANIZATIONS INVOLVED WITH ETHICS

1. American Philosophical Association
   University of Delaware
   Newark, Delaware, 19716
   Phone: (302) 831-1112
2. Association for Practical and Professional Ethics
   410 North Park Ave.
   Bloomington, Indiana, 47405
   (812) 855-6450
   Fax: (812) 855-3315

   E-Mail: appe@indiana.edu

3. Canadian Philosophical Association
   University of Windsor
   Windsor, Ontario, Canada
   N9P 3B4
   (519) 253-4232

4. Centre for Ethics and Corporate Policy
   Toronto Dominion Centre
   Commercial Union Tower
   Suite 204, P.O. Box 175
   Toronto, Ontario, M5K 1H6
   (416) 366-2643
5. American Association of Bioethics
   - promotes the exchange of ideas among bioethics scholars, clinicians, and policy makers
   - enhances the clinical activities of bioethicists
   - encourages discussion and research in the field of bioethics

Website: www.geog.utah.edu/~aab/

GLOSSARY

A priori: That which is not derived from experience, nor dependent upon it (e.g., *a priori* truths may be seen as necessary, certain and universally true, independent of all experience; nothing in experience can prove them false).

Altruistic utilitarianism: An ethical philosophy stressing the greatest happiness for the greatest number. It may require self-sacrifice and doing things for the sake of others.

Argument: A series of related statements (premises) leading to a conclusion.

Consequentialism: A type of ethical theory that determines the rightness or wrongness of any action on the basis of its consequences.

Consequentialist: One who evaluates the morality of an action by its consequences or results.

Contingencies: Conditional, varied or changing possibilities of what could happen.

Deontological ethics: An ethical perspective emphasizing the importance of doing your duty and adhering to rules and principles of right conduct.

Disinterestedness: A state that is free from personal interest or one not influenced by private advantage and selfish motivations.

Disutility: The opposite of utility; causing or increasing disadvantage, pain, misery, dissatisfaction and suffering.

Doctrine of teleology: The theory that everything in the universe has a proper function to perform within a harmonious hierarchy of purposes.

Doctrine of the mean: Applied to life, it implies choosing the mean point between excess and deficiency. This mean point is determined relative to particular individuals, not by some purely mathematical calculation.

Eudaimonia: The happiness achieved through well-living and well-acting; it is tied to the concept of successful living.

Elucidations: Explanations to remove obscurity and to clarify.

Empirical study: An investigation of any phenomenon using experience, experiment and/or sensory observation for verification.

Entelechy: An inner urge within each living thing to become its unique self, e.g., an acorn's urge to become an oak.

Ethical egoism: A moral position maintaining that it is right and good to pursue pleasure and that this is what we ought to do even if we choose not to.

Factual statement: A claim or assertion that is true or false in principle.

Functional explanation of morality: According to Plato, the morally good life is based on the proper inner workings of the soul.

Happiness: The ultimate end of life or purpose for which things are done.

Hedonic calculus: Jeremy Bentham's method of calculating or measuring the painful and pleasurable consequences of particular actions; it is used to arrive at morally correct decisions.

Hedonist: Someone who sees the chief good as the pursuit of pleasure.

Higher faculties: The elevated mental, spiritual, and emotional capacities that add to human dignity.

Higher pleasures: Satisfactions related to the intellect, to our feelings and imagination, and to our sense of dignity.

Ideal observer: One who can see a situation from all perspectives and without bias.

Infirmity of character: A weakness in moral personality that leads people to opt for lower and inferior pleasures.

Inviolability: A quality that makes irreverent treatment of any person wrong; actions that injure, harm or hurt others may also infringe upon people's inviolability.

Is-ought fallacy: Arguing that something should be the case simply because it is.

Just society (Plato): A society in which different classes of people live and function harmoniously together under the enlightened guidance of the guardians or philosopher kings.

Logical fallacy: A rhetorical device used to win arguments through diversion, emotional appeal and/or intimidation.

Logical form: The structure of an argument.

Lower pleasures: Satisfactions derived from physical and bodily pleasures.

Maxim: The rule of conduct implicit in any voluntary action.

Metaethics: A nonnormative, philosophical approach to ethics and the study of its foundations.

Nonmoral value judgments: Normative statements not related to morality.

Nonnormative: Not value-laden, but factual, logical, empirical or verifiable by experience or sensory observation.

Normative: Value-laden or relating to values and value judgments.

Practical reason: Reason in its application to morality.

Premise: A previous statement from which another is inferred.

Principle of utility: A general rule of conduct requiring us to maximize pleasure and minimize pain in situations where actions impact on human interests.

Prudence: The state or act of proceeding with caution or in the interests of oneself.

Psychological egoism: A behavioural theory stating that it is human nature to seek pleasure and to avoid pain.

Realm of forms: A realm beyond sensory experience knowable only by reason; permanent and immutable (unchanging); more real than perceived objects.

Retributivist: One who seeks retribution (punishment) for a wrong-doing and regards it as a proper response to mischievous acts; one who seeks payment in pain to reestablish the balance of justice.

Rhetorical: Designed to persuade or impress; artificial eloquence or flashy oratory.

Sanction: A source of pleasure and pain giving binding force to any law or rule of conduct; related also to reward and punishment.

Self-realization ethic: For Aristotle, a morality of self-fulfillment wherein the potential for moral conduct is actualized through the development of appropriate habits.

Society: A self-sufficient association of individuals who cooperate for mutual advantage under rules designed to promote the welfare of all.

Soul: A notion used by Plato to explain the main motives or impulses to action within any person; comprised of appetite, spirit, and reason; something akin to psyche, self or personality structure.

Tacit agreements: Understandings among people that are not spoken or explicitly stated; they are implied but are not expressed in words.

The categorical imperative: Immanuel Kant's supreme and unconditional principle of morality that serves as the basis for all other derivative moral commands.

The good life: A life of the intellect and rational activity in accordance with virtue.

Utilitarianism: A moral theory based on the principle of utility; it holds that good actions are those producing pleasure or happiness and minimizing pain or suffering.

Valid reasoning: An acceptable form of rational argument leading to a necessary conclusion.

Veil of ignorance: An imaginary veil that, theoretically, prevents people from knowing anything about themselves.

Veracity: Truthfulness or honesty; the accuracy of a statement.

INDEX

CREDITS

Page 5: Hagar cartoon, "What Have You Got That's Good?" Copyright © 1994 New York, NY: King Features Syndicate. Reprinted with special permission of King Features Syndicate. • Page 216: Hospers, John. "Profits and Liberty" in *Libertarianism*. York, PA: Nash Publishing, 1971. • Page 222: Goldman, Alan. "Business Ethics: Profits, Utilities, and Moral Rights." Copyright © 1980 by Princeton University Press. Reprinted by permission of Princeton University Press. • Page 234: Barry, Vincent. "Advertising and Corporate Ethics" in *Moral Issues in Business*, 2nd edition © 1979, 1983 Belmont, CA: Wadsworth Publishing Inc. • Page 241: Reprinted from August 26, 1991 issue of Business Week by special permission, copyright © 1991 by The McGraw-Hill Companies, Inc. • Page 249: Nielsen, Richard. "Changing Unethical Organizational Behavior" in *The Academy of Management Executive*. Briarcliff Manor, NY: The Academy of Management, May 1989: 123-30. • Page 264: Berns, Walter. "Defending the Death Penalty" in *Crime & Delinquency*. Thousand Oaks, CA: Sage Publications, Oct. 1980: 503. Reprinted by permission of Sage Publications Inc. • Page 273: Reprinted by permission of Sterling Lord Literistic, Inc. Copyright © 1957 by Koestler, Arthur. • Page 283: Simons, G. L. "Is Pornography Beneficial?" in *Pornography Without Prejudice*. Abelard-Schuman Ltd., 1972. • Page 289: Garry, Ann. "Pornography and Respect for Woman" in *Social Theory and Practice*, Vol. 4, No. 4, Spring 1978: 395-421. • Page 297: © Will Kymlicka 1989. Reprinted from *Liberalism, Community, and Culture* by Will Kymlicka (1989) by permission of Oxford University Press. • Page 316: Plain, Fred. "A Treatise on the Rights of The Aboriginal Peoples of The Continent of North America" in *The Quest for Justice* by Menno Boldt. Toronto: University of Toronto Press Inc., 1985. Reprinted by permission of University of Toronto Press Incorporated. • Page 324: MacRae, Jean. "A Feminist View of Abortion." Cambridge, MA: Harvard University Press. • Page 332: © Ian Gentles c/o Glendon College. "The Unborn Child in Civil and Criminal Law." • Page 343: Rachels, James. "Active and Passive Euthanasia" in *The New England Journal of Medicine*, vol. 292. Waltham, MA: Massachusetts Medical Society, 1975: 78-80. Copyright 1975 Massachusetts Medical Society. All rights reserved. • Page 349: Nowak, Rachel. "The Dutch Way of Death" in *New Scientist*, June 20, 1992: 28-30. • Page 356: Ellis, Albert. "The Justification of Sex Without Love" in *Sex and Guilt*. Secaucus, NJ: Lyle Stuart, 1958: 66-75. • Page 361: Smedes, Lewis. "Christian Sexual Ethics" in *Sex for Christians*. Grand Rapids, Michigan: Wm. B. Eerdmans Publishing Co., 1978: 115-130. • Page 370: Mohr, Richard. "Gay Basics: Some Questions, Facts, and Values" in *The Right Thing to Do* by James Rachels. New York, NY: Random House, 1989. • Page 381: Cameron, Paul. "A Case Against Homosexuality" in *Human Life Review*, vol. 4, 1978: 195-202. • Page 390: Hardin, Garrett, "Living on a Lifeboat" in *BioScience*, vol. 24, Oct. 1974: 561-568 © 1974 American Institute of Biological Sciences. • Page 402: Rachels, James. "Killing and Starving to Death" in *Philosophy*. New York, NY: Cambridge University Press, 1979: 54. © The Royal Institute of Philosophy 1979. • Page 415: Copyright © 1973, THE MONIST, La Salle, Illinois 61301. Reprinted by permission. • Page 430: Govier, Trudy. "Nuclear Illusion and Individual Obligations" in *Canadian Journal of Philosophy*, vol. 13, 1983: 483-492. • Page 450: "Argument Assembly Chart" in *Moral Philosophy: Theories, Skills, and Applications* by Anthony F. Falikowski. Englewood Cliffs, NJ: Prentice-Hall, Inc., 1990: 335.